A History of Greece

D1611224

Blackwell History of the Ancient World

This series provides a new narrative history of the ancient world, from the beginnings of civilization in the ancient Near East and Egypt to the fall of Constantinople. Written by experts in their fields, the books in the series offer authoritative accessible surveys for students and general readers alike.

Published

A History of the Hellenistic World
R. Malcolm Errington

A History of the Ancient Near East, second edition
Marc Van De Mieroop

A History of the Classical Greek World, second edition
P. J. Rhodes

A History of the Later Roman Empire, AD 284–621
Stephen Mitchell

A History of Byzantium, second edition
Timothy E. Gregory

A History of Ancient Egypt
Marc Van De Mieroop

A History of the Archaic Greek World, second edition
Jonathan M. Hall

A History of Greece, 1300 to 30 BC
Victor Parker

In Preparation

A History of the Roman Republic
John Rich

A History of the Roman Empire
Michael Peachin

A History of Babylon, 2200 BC – 75 AD
Paul-Alain Beaulieu

A History of the Achaemenid Persian Empire
Maria Brosius

A History of the Ancient Near East, third edition
Marc Van De Mieroop

A History of Greece

1300 to 30 BC

Victor Parker

WILEY Blackwell

Louise He
508202 6109

This edition first published 2014
© 2014 Victor Parker

Registered Office
John Wiley & Sons, Ltd, The Atrium, Southern Gate, Chichester, West Sussex, PO19 8SQ, UK

Editorial Offices
350 Main Street, Malden, MA 02148-5020, USA
9600 Garsington Road, Oxford, OX4 2DQ, UK
The Atrium, Southern Gate, Chichester, West Sussex, PO19 8SQ, UK

For details of our global editorial offices, for customer services, and for information about how to apply for permission to reuse the copyright material in this book please see our website at www.wiley .com/wiley-blackwell.

The right of Victor Parker to be identified as the author of this work has been asserted in accordance with the UK Copyright, Designs and Patents Act 1988.

All rights reserved. No part of this publication may be reproduced, stored in a retrieval system, or transmitted, in any form or by any means, electronic, mechanical, photocopying, recording or otherwise, except as permitted by the UK Copyright, Designs and Patents Act 1988, without the prior permission of the publisher.

Wiley also publishes its books in a variety of electronic formats. Some content that appears in print may not be available in electronic books.

Designations used by companies to distinguish their products are often claimed as trademarks. All brand names and product names used in this book are trade names, service marks, trademarks or registered trademarks of their respective owners. The publisher is not associated with any product or vendor mentioned in this book.

Limit of Liability/Disclaimer of Warranty: While the publisher and author have used their best efforts in preparing this book, they make no representations or warranties with respect to the accuracy or completeness of the contents of this book and specifically disclaim any implied warranties of merchantability or fitness for a particular purpose. It is sold on the understanding that the publisher is not engaged in rendering professional services and neither the publisher nor the author shall be liable for damages arising herefrom. If professional advice or other expert assistance is required, the services of a competent professional should be sought.

Library of Congress Cataloging-in-Publication Data

Parker, Victor, 1966–
   A history of Greece : 1300 to 30 BC / Victor Parker.
      pages cm
   Includes bibliographical references and index.
   ISBN 978-1-4051-9034-3 (cloth) – ISBN 978-1-4051-9033-6 (pbk.)   1. Greece–History–To 146 B.C.   2. Greece–History–146 B.C.–323 A.D.   I. Title.
   DF214.P35 2014
   938–dc23

                                                            2013028385

A catalogue record for this book is available from the British Library.

Cover image: 19th century watercolor painting of Greek trireme, by Rafael Monleon. Museo Naval / Ministerio de Marina, Madrid. Photo © Album / Oronoz / AKG
Cover design by Richard Boxhall Design Associates

Set in 10.5/12.5 pt Plantin Std by Toppan Best-set Premedia Limited

1   2014

Katherinae Adshead
Mentori Collegae Amicae
librum auctor DDD.

Contents

Figures

Tables

Boxes

Abbreviations and Reference Conventions

Authors' names are written out in full at their first appearance, thereafter generally in abbreviated form. The names of authors in the series *BNJ*, however, are written out in full throughout. As a general rule, only book and chapter are given in a reference unless a conveniently accessible translation indicates the division of chapters into paragraphs as well. In a reference an author's name in square brackets indicates that the work in question is traditionally, albeit falsely, attributed to that author. In a sentence in such a situation, the putative author's name stands within inverted commas. The author has indicated pseudonymity in these ways only when such pseudonymity is transparent or generally acknowledged.

General

cf.	*confer*, "compare"
e.g.	*exempli gratia*, "for example"
Fr.	Fragment (*pl.* Frr.)
i.e.	*id est*, "that is to say"
l.c.	*loco citato*, "in the place (just) cited" (*pl.* ll.cc.)
n.b.	*nota bene*, "note well"
Nr.	number (*pl.* Nrr.)
sqq.	*sequentes*, "and the following"
s.v.	*sub voce*, "under that word" (*pl.* ss.vv.)
T.	*Testimonium*

Collections of Sources and Reference Works:

ANET	Pritchard, J.B. (1969) *Ancient Near Eastern Texts relating to the Old Testament*. Princeton
ATL	Meritt, B.D., *et al.* (1939–1953) *The Athenian Tribute Lists*. Cambridge, MA

Austin	Austin, M.M. (1981) *The Hellenistic World from Alexander to the Roman Conquest.* Cambridge
BNJ	*Brill's New Jacoby*
Breasted	Breasted, J.H. (1906) *Ancient Records of Egypt.* Chicago
Burstein	Burstein, St. M. (1985) *The Hellenistic Age from the Battle of Ipsos to the Death of Kleopatra VII.* New York
CAH	*Cambridge Ancient History*
Cat. Gk. Coins	*A Catalogue of the Greek Coins in the British Museum* (individual volumes are not numbered, but bear an identifying subtitle)
Coldstream	Coldstream, J.N. (1977) *Geometric Greece.* London
Fornara	Fornara, C.W. (1977) *From Archaic Times to the End of the Peloponnesian War.* Baltimore
FGrHist	Jacoby, F. (1923–1959) *Die Fragmente der Griechischen Historiker.* Berlin, Leiden
GHI	Meiggs, R., and D.M. Lewis. (1988) *A Selection of Greek Historical Inscriptions to the End of the Fifth Century B.C.* Oxford
Gschnitzer	Gschnitzer, F. (1978) *Ein neuer spartanischer Staatsvertrag.* Meisenheim am Glan
Harding	Harding, Ph. (1985) *From the End of the Peloponnesian War to the Battle of Ipsus.* New York
IG	*Inscriptiones Graecae*
IvonMagnesia	Kern, O. (1900) *Die Inschriften von Magnesia am Maeander.* Berlin
IvonMilet	Herrmann, P. (1997–2006) *Die Inschriften von Milet.* Berlin
IvonPergamon	Fränkel, M. (1890–1895) *Die Inschriften von Pergamon.* Berlin.
Kent	Kent, R.G. (1953) *Old Persian: Grammar, Texts, Lexicon.* New Haven
OGIS	*Orientis Graeci Inscriptiones Selectae*
Pap.Eleph.	Rubensohn, O. (1867) *Elephantine-Papyri.* Berlin
Parker–Dubberstein	Parker, R.A., and W.H. Dubberstein. (1956) *Babylonian Chronology. 626 B.C. – A.D. 75.* Providence
POxy	(1898–) *The Oxyrhynchus Papyri.* London
RC	Welles, C.B. (1934) *Royal Correspondence in the Hellenistic Period.* London
RE	*Realencyclopädie der classischen Altertumswissenschaft.*
SEG	*Supplementum Epigraphicum Graecum*
Sherk	Sherk, R.K. (1984) *Rome and the Greek East to the Death of Augustus.* New York
Snell	Snell, B. (1971–2004) *Tragicorum Graecorum Fragmenta.* Göttingen

Sokolowski	Sokolowski, F. (1962) *Lois sacrées des cités grecques. Supplément*. Paris
Sommer	Sommer, F. (1932) *Die Ahhijava-Urkunden*. Munich
SVA	Schmitt, H.H. (1969–) *Die Staatsverträge der Altertums*. Munich
Tod	Tod, M.N. (1950–1951) *A Selection of Greek Historical Inscriptions*. Oxford

Aes.	Aeschylus	
	Pers. *Persae* (Men of Persia)	
Amm.Marc.	Ammianus Marcellinus	
And.	Andocides	
Aesch.	Aeschines	
App.	Appian	
	Bell.Civ.	*Bellum Civile* (Civil War)
	Lib.	*Libyan Wars*
	Mac.	*Macedonian Wars*
	Mith.	*Mithridatic Wars*
	Samn.	*Samnite Wars*
	Syr.	*Syrian Wars*
Arg.	*Argumentum* (a summary, composed in antiquity, of an ancient work; an *argumentum* is usually printed before the work itself)	
Arist.	Aristotle	
	Ath.Pol.	*Athenaion Politeia* (Constitution of the Athenians)
	Pol.	*Politics*
Aristoph.	Aristophanes	
	Ach.	*Acharnians*
Arr.	Arrian	
	Anab.	*Anabasis*
	Ind.	*Indica*
Asclep.	Asclepiodotus	
Ath.Pol	see Arist.	
Athen.	Athenaeus	
Behistun	see Kent (under "Collections of Sources")	
Caes.	C. Julius Caesar	
	Bell.Alex.	*Bellum Alexandrinum* (Alexandrian War)
	Civ.	*Civil War*
Cass.	Cassius Dio	
Cic.	Cicero	
	Ad Att.	*Letters to Atticus*
	De fin.	*De finibus bonorum et malorum* (On the ends of good and evil)
	De leg.	*De legibus* (On laws)

	De reg. Alex.	*De rege Alexandrino* (On the Alexandrian king)
	Leg.Agr.	*De lege agraria* (On the agrarian law)
	Tusc.	*Tusculan Disputations*
Curt.	Q. Curtius Rufus	
De uir. ill.	*De uiris illustribus* (On illustrious men)	
Dem.	Demosthenes	
Din.	Dinarchus	
Diod.	Diodorus	
Diog.Laert.	Diogenes Laertius	
Dion.Hal.	Dionysius of Halicarnassus	
	Rom.Ant.	*Roman Antiquities*
	Lys.	*Lysias*
Eur.	Euripides	
	Andr.	*Andromache*
Euseb.	Eusebius	
Front.	Frontinus	
	Strat.	*Strategemata*
Gell.	Aulus Gellius	
Hdt.	Herodotus	
Hell. Oxy.	*Hellenica Oxyrhynchia*	
Hyp.	Hypereides	
	Dem.	*Against Demosthenes*
Il.	*Iliad*	
Isoc.	Isocrates	
Jer.	Jeremiah	
Jos.	Josephus	
	Ant.	*Antiquities of the Jews*
	War	*Jewish War*
Just.	Justin	
Liv.	Livy	
	Per.	*Periocha*
Lk.	Luke	
Lyc.	Lycurgus	
	Leoc.	*Against Leocrates*
Lys.	Lysias	
Macc.	Maccabees	
Mk.	Mark	
Nep.	Nepos	
	Timoth.	*Timotheus*
Od.	*Odyssey*	
Paus.	Pausanias	
Pind.	Pindar	
	Nem.	*Nemean Odes*
	Pyth.	*Pythian Odes*

Plat.	Plato	
	Ax.	*Axiochus*
	Rep.	*Republic*
Plin.	Pliny the Elder	
	NH	*Natural History*
Plut.	Plutarch	
	Ages.	*Agesilaus*
	Alex.	*Alexander*
	Ant.	*Mark Antony*
	Arat.	*Aratus*
	Caes.	*Julius Caesar*
	Cim.	*Cimon*
	Cleom.	*Cleomenes*
	Dem.	*Demosthenes*
	Demetr.	*Demetrius*
	Eum.	*Eumenes*
	Flam.	*Flamininus*
	Lyc.	*Lycurgus*
	Lys.	*Lysander*
	Nic.	*Nicias*
	Paul.	*Aemilius Paulus*
	Pel.	*Pelopidas*
	Per.	*Pericles*
	Phil.	*Philopoemen*
	Phoc.	*Phocion*
	Pyrrh.	*Pyrrhus*
	Sol.	*Solon*
	Sul.	*Sulla*
	Them.	*Themistocles*
	Tib.	*Tiberius Gracchus*
	Tim.	*Timoleon*
Pol.	Polybius	
Poly.	Polyaenus	
Sal.	Sallust	
	H.R.	*Historiarum Reliquiae*
	Jug.	*Jugurthine War*
Sam.	Samuel	
Schol.	Scholium, Scholiast (a scholium is an ancient note in the margin of a manuscript of an ancient work; a scholiast is its author)	
Soph.	Sophocles	
	OC	*Oedipus at Colonus*
Strab.	Strabo	
Suet.	Suetonius	
	Aug.	*Augustus*
	Caes.	*Julius Caesar*

Suid.	Suidas	
Tac.	Tacitus	
	Ann.	*Annals*
Theoc.	Theocritus	
Thuc.	Thucydides	
Trog.	Trogus	
	Prol.	*Prologues* (printed at the back of the edition of Justin)
Xen.	Xenophon	
	Anab.	*Anabasis*
	Const.Lac.	*Constitution of the Lacedaemonians*
	Hell.	*Hellenica*
	Mem.	*Memorabilia*
	Oec.	*Oeconomicus*
Vit.	*Vita* (an ancient biography; for an ancient author, a *uita*, if it exists, is usually printed in an edition of the author's work)	
Zon.	Zonaras	

Preface

This book attempts to present in readable format the basic political history of the Greeks from about 1300 BC, when their earliest written records (the Linear B texts) begin, down to the death of the last Hellenistic monarch, Cleopatra VII of Egypt, in 30 BC. It is primarily addressed to university students in a course on Greek History or in an historically structured course on Greek Civilization. All the same, I have tried to keep in mind students who, although in another course, may need to familiarize themselves with some aspect of Greek history – those who in a course on Roman History wish to read about the situation in Greece before the Romans destroyed Corinth in the Achaian War in 146 BC; or those who in a course on philosophy wish to know something about Dionysius II of Syracuse whom Plato attempted to turn into a "philosopher-king"; or those who in a course on Greek Literature require the basic story of the Peloponnesian War because the comic playwright Aristophanes constantly alludes to it.

After all, no course touching ancient Greece, no matter how tightly it may focus on literary, cultural, social, artistic, or philosophical material, can dispense with the basic historical framework – dates must be given, historical events mentioned, and important literary and philosophical personages as well as works of art placed into a context of contemporary historical events which therefore continually intrude into such discussions. It is accordingly those "contemporary historical events" which this book wishes to present in accessible form across a period of some thirteen centuries.

To do so between two covers has presented challenges and made difficult decisions inescapable, in particular in regard to what has been omitted – and I am only too aware that I will not have pleased everyone at every point. Yet coverage of thirteen centuries has allowed comparisons which may, I hope, partially compensate for the many omissions. In a discussion of the "Ahhiyawa Question" in the chapter on the Bronze Age the reader can be referred to the situation of Rhodes around 300 BC. The historical development of the Seleucid Kingdom in the third and second centuries BC can be viewed with the history of the Persian Empire in the fifth and fourth in the background.

By the same token, the long view of matters has affected the presentation at various points. The prominence of leagues in the third and second centuries meant that these states could not be edited out of the chapters on the preceding centuries for then they would have appeared out of nowhere in chapter 21 or so. As a consequence, classical Greece is no longer a world exclusively of city-states, which must accordingly share the stage with the *ethne*, the tribe- or league-states right from the start. In chapter 4, then, the *polis* and the *ethnos* are accordingly described as two forms of state without the traditional favoring of the *polis* as "the" Greek state. Covering the rise of the Hellenistic kings in the fourth and third centuries meant that the Greeks' political development does not culminate with fifth-century Athenian democracy – their political development instead ebbs and flows from the Mycenaean monarchs to the oligarchs and democrats of the fifth and fourth centuries to the aforementioned Hellenistic kings in the third and second. Moreover, the political structure of the *ethne* receives its due alongside of Athenian democracy, and no attempt is made to prefer democracy over oligarchy. Taking the long view over thirteen centuries alters how one presents a specific period within that expansive timeframe.

The way, however, in which the nature of the evidence changes over the long span of time covered by this book has mandated a degree of unevenness from chapter to chapter. Where the evidence allows more to be said (for example, concerning the Peloponnesian War owing to Thucydides' extensive treatment – chapters 13 and 14), I have not shrunk from doing so. The narrative of the Hellenistic period, on the other hand, often resembles an outline because the evidence (Appian, Justin, and Trogus' prologues) simply allows for no more.

I have, however, accepted such unevenness as a necessary evil since a major goal in the writing of this book has been to keep students in constant touch with the chief narrative sources for Greek history. The Greek historiographical tradition is, among other things, a fine matter in its own right, and to give it pride of place in a book on Greek history should not require a defense. I have continually provided the references to it; I have attempted to give brief introductions to its main practitioners; I have paid it respect and deference. The desire to remain close to it has, unfortunately, severely constrained this textbook's ability to discuss economic, cultural, social, and intellectual history – omissions, as indicated above, had to be made, and this consideration has dictated some of them.

All the same, efforts have been made to include some of this material as it became relevant to the political history: for example, see Box 24.4 for economic history; Box 13.3 for social history; Box 23.1 for cultural history; Box 17.2 for intellectual history. In no case could the treatment be systematic, however. No book can do everything, and the hope was to do one thing in satisfactory fashion as opposed to many things badly. Discussing social history well, for example, would have required detailed treatment of a different set of sources and would therefore have entailed the ejection of far too much of the material on the ancient historians who were always to stand front and center in this textbook. Moreover, for many areas of Greek civilization – literature, philosophy, art, religion – good handbooks which cover the ground far more thoroughly than I can in one book are readily available, and entering into a hopeless competition with them had little point.

Largely refraining from such a competition has, however, allowed me to dedicate more space to the chief historical sources and, beyond introducing them to students, to let the latter see, in outline at least, how the reconstruction of historical events is attempted. Textbooks far too often assert as incontestable fact what has merely been accepted as probable after argument, combination, and conjecture. A great deal of work stands behind, for example, a table of dates; and many dates, far from being certain, are matters of dispute – the student is entitled to know this. One must, moreover, read ancient historians alertly and even with skepticism, and I try to offer guides to doing this. Most importantly, ancient historians can and do contradict one another, and the student is entitled to know about this too – modern scholars can reconstruct historical events in different ways. In the Further Reading at the end of each chapter I have listed works of modern scholarship which often enough disagree with what I have stated, and if students take this disagreement as the starting point for their own reflections, then my work will have been well done indeed.

Next, in Herodotean fashion I have striven to allow each city or league to have its story when that is known. Greece is more than Athens and Sparta. The Phocians are among the obscurest of the Greeks, yet their day does come in the mid-fourth century, and they have a right to have their accomplishments mentioned (chapter 18). Inevitably the book includes much discussion of Athens and Sparta since there is much more evidence about those two cities, but the Boeotians, the Corinthians, and the Argives receive some space too. Moreover, I have attempted a reasonably full treatment of the history of the western Greeks. Besides chapter 5 on colonization, the West is dealt with in sections in chapters 10 and 14 as well as two additional complete chapters (17 and 22).

The inclusion of the Hellenistic period (chapters 20 to 25), which is absent from many Greek history textbooks, has actually allowed a partial remedy to one of the book's omissions. Women do not figure prominently in the political history of the classical period, but the Hellenistic queens – Arsinoë, Cleopatra Thea, Cleopatra VII of Egypt to name just a few – are a different story entirely. These talented women quickly emerge as canny diplomats, influential power-brokers, and eventually as rulers in their own right. They deserve to be taken seriously, and I have attempted to provide a serious treatment.

The inclusion of the Hellenistic world at the end as well as the Mycenaean Age at the beginning will allow instructors, I hope, to maneuver among various starting and stopping points. Such points are to a degree arbitrary and occasionally determined by factors outside of an instructor's control (for example, an administratively imposed switch from semesters to trimesters or historical inertia within a department). Sometimes, however, instructors will vary the chronological and geographical parameters of a course merely to keep it from going stale – start with the Mycenaeans and end just before Alexander; start with the Persian Wars and go down to the destruction of Corinth in 146 BC; include Sicily and end a little earlier. All are legitimate. The chapters on the Hellenistic period are written such that one could assign just the sections relevant to Macedonia and Greece if wishing to end with the Roman destruction of Corinth in 146 BC.

I have also tried to bear in mind that an instructor might wish to make a course in Greek History work together with another course in the same department. I have written chapter 2 with emphasis on the Linear B tablets instead of the archaeological remains in part because the archaeological material is covered in easily accessible format in many books, whereas the Linear B material is for the most part confined to specialist works which are anything but accessible. In addition, since most courses on the Aegean Bronze Age are archaeological in inspiration, and rightly so, the instructor of a course on Greek History which starts with the Bronze Age may legitimately not wish to compete with them. However, covering the Linear B material may usefully complement them. The hope, then, is that this textbook will allow the instructor to make the course on Greek History work hand-in-hand with an archaeological one.

Likewise, an instructor wishing to coordinate a course on Greek History with one on Roman History could use the relevant sections in chapters 22 to 25, in all of which I have striven to avoid intruding on the territory of the Roman historian to whose wisdom I happily defer for a full discussion of, for example, the nature of Roman imperialism. Chapter 22, on Sicily and southern Italy from the late fourth to the mid-third century restricts itself to the side of the story not told in the Roman history textbook and makes no attempt at discussing, for example, the Samnite Wars or the First Punic War in any detail. The aim, again, is to complement another course, not to compete with it. Moreover, a concerted effort is made in the final chapters to show how the states in the Near East with which the Romans contended in the late second and first centuries – Bithynia, Pontus, Cappadocia, Armenia, Judea – had arisen. The story of Mithridates the Great of Pontus is told from the Hellenistic point of view with Mithridates firmly placed in his Hellenistic context – that is to say, not seen as a random Barbarian opponent of Rome. Others will have to judge to what degree I have been successful.

For many reasons this has not been an easy book to write. The latter stage in particular was complicated by the earthquakes which struck Christchurch in September of 2010 and February of 2011 and which forced the library of the University of Canterbury to close for several months on several occasions. I owe a great debt of thanks to Dr. Wolfgang Blösel (Düsseldorf and Essen) and Dr. Luke Fenwick (Oxford) who looked up references when all else failed. I also thank Dr. Frank Röpke (Heidelberg) for help with Egyptological matters. Several colleagues, especially Dr. Gary Morrison, generously shared their private holdings. Working without access to a library is an experience which I am not eager to repeat.

Finally, throughout the writing of this book, from start to finish, my two young sons, Timothy and Nicholas, have stood and played (loudly) in the background. In addition, their sister Josephine joined us in 2011. Because of them I became a familiar of the late hours in the evening and of the early hours in the morning. My wife endured my work on this book with a fortitude which has bordered on the heroic.

But it is now completed. My colleagues Prof. Graham Zanker and Dr. Morrison continually offered encouragement and advice and deserve express thanks for this. My chief and abiding collegial debt, however, is recorded elsewhere. Finally, I sincerely thank the editorial staff at Wiley-Blackwell, especially the phenomenally patient Deirdre Ilkson, for putting up with me and all my fussiness and for finding extremely polite ways of pointing out that this or that extended exposition was becoming difficult to comprehend and were better consigned to the rubbish bin.

Dabam in Aede Christi a.d. XI Kal. Feb. A.D. MMXIII.

Introduction

The guiding principle of this textbook is that students should not as a matter of course be asked to take statements on faith. Even a textbook aimed at undergraduates should always make the evidence available – the student may then check it and concur with the author's use, or, just possibly, reject the author's opinion and advance another. For reasons of space, exhaustive cataloging of the evidence was rarely possible, but the author hopes that in most cases sufficient evidence has been cited so that no assertion hangs in the air. When more than one reference is given, as a general rule the more important one is listed first – this is especially true when there are two parallel narratives (e.g., Xenophon and Diodorus from 411 to 362 BC), both of which need to be consulted. The useful abbreviation "cf." – *confer*, "compare" – often serves to direct the student to a source which is at odds with the one followed in the text. Occasionally, for reasons of space a reference is given, but the accompanying argument suppressed in the hope that the instructor can supply it readily enough if necessary. Where something is not attested directly, the author has indicated this together with the nature of the argument used to establish the conclusion – the reader, of course, is free to disagree.

For the standard literary authors, many translations exist, and most will serve the student's purpose most of the time. But even here the student may when it becomes necessary require assistance from the instructor with technically precise translation – the philologically inclined translator all too often fails to observe historically significant technicalities (for example, at Thuc. I 139,1 it is "embassies went back and forth" instead of, for example, the Penguin translation's "they sent another embassy"; at Thuc. I 100,1 it is "also after these events (i.e., the fighting at Carystus)" instead of the Penguin translation's "next"). In the case of inscriptions, papyri, and other less easily accessible texts, reference has been made, whenever possible, to existing collections of translations, preferably those with good notes. The editors and authors of the volumes from the series *Translated Documents of Greece and Rome* have rendered the student a service of incalculable value. All the same they could not translate every useful text, so the student, if the matter is important, may simply have to ask the instructor for assistance – many sources have never been translated, and some, such as Suidas, probably never will be.

One of the most important reference tools for the historian is Felix Jacoby's monumental collection of the fragmentary Greek historians, *Die Fragmente der Griechischen Historiker* or *FGrHist*. Since the texts in this collection are steadily being translated and made available on-line under the title *Brill's New Jacoby*, the references to it are simply given in the hope that all those fragments either are or soon will be fully available in translation. Each historian receives a number, and then the surviving *testimonia* (statements about the historian) and fragments (direct quotations from or paraphrases of the historian's work) are numbered as well. For the most part the numeration has remained the same across both editions so an older book's reference to *FGrHist* 70, T. 24 or Fr. 129 will correspond exactly to *BNJ* 70, T. 24 or Fr. 129. In *Brill's New Jacoby* there is commentary on each *testimonium* and fragment.

It is one thing for the student to have access to the evidence; it is another to interpret it. Every category of ancient evidence and indeed every ancient historian such as Herodotus or Xenophon presents the modern historian with certain problems. A full discussion of all of these is an impracticality in a textbook of this size. All the same, some narrative sources are more fundamental than others for the simple reason that long sections of any account of Greek history are based primarily on them – e.g., the Persian Wars and their prehistory (chapters 9 and 10) on Herodotus. For the major prose authors – Herodotus, Thucydides, Diodorus, Xenophon, Arrian, and Polybius – a basic guide to some of the payoffs and pitfalls is provided in the relevant chapters; a few more such guides have very selectively been included (e.g., Plutarch).

The nonliterary evidence (inscriptions, papyri, coins, etc.) presents special problems. Where practicable, basic remarks on the interpretation of such evidence (e.g., Box 2.1 on the Linear B tablets) have been included, but for the most part the student will here have to rely on the notes in standard collections as well as on the guidance of instructors. Finally, a certain amount of "extra-canonical" material is used in this textbook. Some of this (e.g., I and II Maccabees) should not give the classicist much pause, but others (e.g., an Akkadian letter of Suppiluliumas II or the Old Persian inscriptions) may. In these cases the author has striven to be as clear and as accurate as possible within the limitations imposed by the need to conserve space.

Next, scholarship on ancient Greece is not static. A textbook written in 1900 will have different "facts" from one written in 2000. For example, the descriptions of the battles of Cyzicus (410), Notium (406), Arginussae (406), and Aegospotami (405) in this textbook differ starkly from those in older ones. In 1900, the Lacedaemonians did not offer terms of peace to the Athenians after the Battle of Cyzicus; now they do. New evidence emerges; overlooked evidence is finally seen; once disparaged evidence is re-evaluated; and old opinions are abandoned and new interpretations advanced – rightly or wrongly. Some issues will probably always remain controversial. Every scholar, moreover, has some views which the scholarly community as a whole does not (yet?) share. The present author is no exception; but wherever his opinion differs starkly from that of his colleagues, he has noted it – and he has tried to present the reasoning and the evidence behind his view. Each reader is free to disagree.

At the end of each chapter, a basic and highly selective bibliography for further reading is given. Emphasis is placed on fundamental or newer discussions, and the following warning always applies: the newer works are not necessarily better and often presuppose an understanding of the older ones anyway. These bibliographies are mostly geared to the student's need for finding out more about a specific topic and are meant as a starting point only. Reasons of space precluded exhaustive listing of every work consulted by the author (however much guilt the author feels at this, long lists of highly specialized articles would not have served any real purpose). Items in the Further Reading may present different opinions from the ones advanced in this book – such is the nature of scholarship; and the author hopes that students will be encouraged by such disagreement to consider issues independently and to form their own conclusions.

At the end of each chapter there also stand some questions for review. These are meant solely as aids to students wishing to note down the salient points of a given chapter. The question for further study, on the other hand, invites the student to think critically about an aspect of the chapter – occasionally even to argue against the opinion which the author has advanced.

The book opens with a chapter on the geography of Greece and contains at the end a glossary and several tables of rulers. The chapter on geography need not serve as much more than a resource to which students may be referred as it becomes necessary; and students may well use it in this way on their own when a book on their reading list mentions the "Hypocnemidian Locrians" or the "Thessalian Perioeci." Some courses in Greek History will, however, include a lecture on the geographical setting of Greek history, and the author hopes that this chapter will prove itself suitable to that purpose also.

The glossary is designed to be a quick reference for basic information. For reasons of space it could not be encyclopedic in scope. All terms included in the glossary stand in boldface upon their first appearance in the text. I have included in the glossary every author mentioned in the text; in the case of the fragmentary historians, the glossary entry also contains the *BNJ* number. For other fragmentary authors, when students might be supposed to have problems in finding a translation, they are directed to one (usually the Loeb as the most readily available) if one exists. Toponyms, on the other hand, I have as a rule excluded from the glossary, though I have bent the rule when I thought that students might need to know more about the place than what they might ascertain from a map.

Particularly in the Hellenistic Age, the number of rulers whom one has to keep track of becomes little short of overwhelming, especially since names such as Ptolemy and Antiochus were repeatedly reused. For this reason a number of tables of rulers have been included at the back of the book as well; I have also added tables for the kings of Sparta and of Persia.

Here, at the end, a few remarks on the transliteration of Greek works and on the use of typefaces may be in order. As a general rule, where a standard English form of a proper name exists, I have retained it – Athens, Crete, Corsica, and Carthage instead of Athenai, Kreta, Kurno, and Karchedon. I have certainly not invented forms such as "Korsika." Otherwise I have applied the traditional Latin system for the proper names – Herodotus, Thucydides, Aeschylus instead of Herodotos, Thoukudides, Aiskhulos – with a few mostly traditional deviations such as Solon instead of Solo or Peisistratus instead of Pisistratus. The very few additional departures – for example, Knosos with one medial "s" – will, I hope, be forgiven me. Complete consistency is unobtainable in any case. Where, however, a Greek term is required in the text, I do transliterate directly and print it in italics (e.g., *Neodamodeis*). Since such Greek terms inevitably stand in the glossary, on their first appearance they are both boldface and italic (e.g., ***Neodamodeis***).

Rereading the book has made the author painfully aware of everything which he has left out. He would have dearly loved to include additional historiographical sections (for example, on Timaeus of Tauromenium or the Old Oligarch), more material on Greek law (especially the Law Code of Gortyn), more material on treaties and interstate relations, much more demography and far more institutional history especially of neglected corners of the Greek world (the Cyrenaean and Cyprian kings; the constitution of the Boeotian League; various oligarchies). There was limited space to give over to military developments, and coverage of one aspect (the Greek heavily armed infantryman or the Macedonian infantryman) meant neglect of another (the light-armed infantryman in the fourth century or the Macedonian cavalry respectively) as well as of naval developments almost completely. The decision to discuss Rhodes and Athens as surviving city-states in the Hellenistic world meant that Heracleia Pontica (as well as its chronicle's compiler, Memnon) would not be discussed.

Still, the author hopes that the truly important matters have received sufficient shrift; and that much of the traditional cultural material from ancient history to which, say, a modern film or novel might without hesitation refer (e.g., Leonidas' 300 Spartiates at Thermopylae, Alexander's horse that was afraid of his shadow, the Colossus of Rhodes) has at least been mentioned somewhere along the way.

Table 0.1 Major periods in Greek history

Conventional Name	Dates	Major Events
Late Bronze Age (Late Helladic, Late Minoan, Mycenaean)	circa 1500–1200 BC	Large Greek kingdoms at Pylos, Knosos, Thebes, and Mycene; Linear B script in use
Dark Age	circa 1200–800	The Mycenaean kingdoms are destroyed; steep decline in population and material culture; various migrations take place (e.g.: the Dorians enter Greece; Aeolians, Ionians, and Dorians settle the Aegean coast of Asia Minor)
Archaic Period	circa 800–480	The population grows again and material culture recovers; colonies founded in the West and elsewhere; wars for land in Greece; tyrants rule in many cities
Classical Period	480–323	Persian invasion repelled; Athenian empire rises and is destroyed in Peloponnesian War; Athens, Sparta, and Boeotia wage near continual warfare against each other until Macedonia conquers Greece; Alexander the Great conquers Persia
Hellenistic Period	323–30	Empire of Alexander breaks apart into three main kingdoms; Greece dominated by Achaian and Aetolian Leagues; rise of Rome ends Hellenistic states' independence; last independent Hellenistic monarch, Cleopatra VII, commits suicide in 30 BC

1

The Geography of Greece

Introduction

All history takes place within a geographical setting. It is not merely a matter of needing to know where places are in order to follow an historical narrative, but also one of understanding why over time certain recognizable patterns emerge and why the people who settle in a given region tend to develop in one way instead of in another. After general sections on the topography, climate, and use of the land overall, this chapter will present a tour of the Greek world to show how the specific geography of the major regions helped shape their historical development. The aim is to explain some of the "givens" in Greek history: why the Thessalians had the best horses and consequently the first cavalry in Greece; why the Greek cities on the coast of Asia Minor had more to do with mainland Greece than with the regions to the east; why most sea traffic from west to east passed over the Isthmus instead of around the Peloponnese, such that Sparta lay off the beaten track while Corinth on the Isthmus grew prosperous; and so on. The chapter serves both as an introduction to the narrative that follows, with references ahead to the relevant chapters, and also as a resource for consultation when appropriate.

General Topography

Greece lies at the base of the Balkan Peninsula in southern Europe. It juts out into the Mediterranean Sea between the Adriatic on its west and the Aegean on its east. Greece is a mountainous land, and the mountain ranges as a general

geography

A History of Greece: 1300 to 30 BC, First Edition. Victor Parker.
© 2014 Victor Parker. Published 2014 by John Wiley & Sons, Ltd.

rule run from northwest to southeast. They become progressively lower farther to the south and eventually dip below sea level. Their highest peaks, however, often still rise above sea level to form islands. Thus, the same geological formation which makes up Magnesia drops below sea level south of Cape Sepias before it again rises above the sea in the form of the island of Euboea. South of Carystus it drops again, but its highest peaks farther south appear as the islands of Andros and Tenos.

During unsettled times, the mountain ranges can direct the flow of migrations (see chap. 3) through the land: such migrations have tended to follow the ranges' northwest–southeast orientation southwards until reaching either a west–east pass (at which point the migrating peoples could turn left and proceed farther in an easterly direction) or an inlet of the sea (which the migrating peoples could then cross on makeshift boats). In settled times, the mountains can help divide the country into sections for human habitation, sections which can be identical with communities' territories: this is especially true for cities in mountain valleys (e.g., Tegea and Mantinea in Arcadia) or on small coastal plains (e.g., Troezen or Epidaurus in the Argolis). The mountainous nature of the country also means that fertile plains are few; but where such plains do exist, they tend to be intensely cultivated. The mountains also mark the coastline which, owing to the ruggedness and unevenness of the land, has thousands of inlets and gulfs. The largest of these is the Gulf of Corinth which, together with the Saronic Gulf, almost divides Greece in two; the land to the south of these two gulfs, the Peloponnese, is connected only by a narrow isthmus to the rest of Greece (see Figure 1.1). That isthmus – always known simply as "the Isthmus" – had importance both for land and sea traffic. All land travel between the Peloponnese and the rest of Greece had to pass across it. At the same time, it proved easier and quicker in antiquity for those transporting goods from west to east by sea to unload the goods at the Isthmus, to haul them across, and then to reload them on the other side (see also Box 1.1). The Isthmus, then, functioned as an important connecting point for sea travel as well.

Given the mountainous nature of the land, which tended to impede travel overland, much travel was in fact by sea; and the sea usually helped unite rather than divide Greece. This was especially true for the Aegean Sea. Islands dot the sea such that when sailing from mainland Greece to Asia Minor one never loses sight of land – from any one island the next is always visible. In effect, the islands function as stations on a road across the water.

As one moves farther east across the Aegean, one eventually reaches the mainland of Asia Minor. In this region Greeks settled in the eleventh to tenth centuries BC. (see chap. 3). They came from the West, moving across the water island by island. For this reason their settlements in Asia Minor tended to look westwards to the sea rather than farther inland. When the Persians in the early fifth century again took possession of those Greek cities which had risen up in the **Ionian Revolt** (see chap. 9), the Persians sent their fleet along the coast from city to city because the cities were far more easily accessible by sea than by land. Miletus, in the **classical** period the most important Greek settlement

Figure 1.1   Satellite image of the Isthmus. Source: Image Science and Analysis
Laboratory, NASA-Johnson Space Center. "The Gateway to Astronaut Photography of
Earth." <http://eol.jsc.nasa.gov/scripts/sseop/QuickView.pl?directory=ESC&ID=ISS023-E
-5385>01/10/2013 10:52:32

on the mainland in Asia Minor, provides a spectacular example of this orientation towards the sea. Although the city is technically on the mainland, mountains to the south make it almost inaccessible by land (see Figure 1.2). The
simplest way to travel from Miletus into the interior of Asia Minor was actually
to embark on a ship, to sail across an inlet of the sea, and then to disembark
in the plain of the Meander River. From here one could easily journey overland
into the interior.

Greeks reached the northern coast of the Aegean by sea as well – though a
little later this time, as late as the eighth century; and while expansion into the
interior here did take place (especially on account of the silver and gold mines
of Pangaeum), the same more or less held true here as for the settlements in Asia
Minor – they looked towards mainland Greece with which they were connected
by the Aegean Sea. In every respect the Aegean united Greeks; and the region
around the Aegean always formed the core territory of Greek civilization.

Another basic fact about Greece requires a brief comment at the end of this
section. Greece lies close to where the Eurasian and African tectonic plates
meet, and there is much seismic activity. Earthquakes and tsunamis are common
and occasionally devastating. Portions of the land, moreover, are of volcanic
origin – the island of Thera, with its active volcano which during the **Bronze**

Aegean

many
Earthqu-
akes &
tsunamis

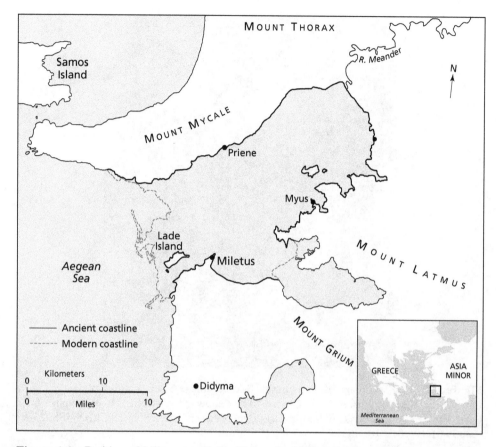

Figure 1.2   Position of Miletus on Gulf of Meander River in ancient times

Age (around the middle of the second millennium BC) erupted cataclysmically, is only the best known.

Climate

Greece is a <u>hot, thirsty land</u>. Most rivers are dry through the summer as evaporation proceeds more quickly than springs or rainfall can replenish the water. The rainy season begins in the late autumn, around November. With the rains, torrents rush down ravines and the dry beds of rivers are filled again.

The mountain ranges divide Greece up into countless "compartments," each with its own <u>microclimate</u> determined by whether the mountains shield it from rain or trap rain in it; by whether it is exposed or closed to breezes off the Aegean; and by whether it is protected from or open to storms. Despite the overall aridity of much of the land, pockets (such as the plain near the head of the Argolic Gulf) are moisture-laden or even swampy (for example, the land at the head of the Messenian Gulf). In such regions even water-intensive crops,

[margin note:] microclimates
cuz division
by mountains

Box 1.1   *Mt. Athos and Other Coastlines Exposed to the Aegean*

The prevailing weather patterns in the Aegean – in particular harsh storms from the east especially during the winter – combine with the geology of mainland Greece to create an unusual feature of its eastern coastline. The storms erode the land until they reach the hard bedrock of the mountains. The resulting coastline consists of steep, rugged cliffs with few harbors or safe anchorages. Wherever a mountain is directly exposed to the storms – Mt. Athos (see Figure 1.3), Magnesia, the island of Euboea, Cape Malea – such a coastline arises. But any body of water behind the exposed mountain – for example, the strait between Euboea and the mainland – remains calm with a gentle coastline replete with harbors on both sides. Thus, ships sailing northward from Attica kept to the west of Euboea. In the south, Cape Malea (see Figure 1.4) proved so prone to storms and so dangerous for mariners that circumnavigation of the Peloponnese rarely took place (major naval expeditions were the one exception). Hence, traffic west from the Aegean passed over the Isthmus and through the Gulf of Corinth.

Figure 1.3   The exposed eastern side of Mt. Athos. Source: Gabriel, http://commons.wikimedia.org/wiki/File:Mount_Athos_by_cod_gabriel_20.jpg (accessed 10th January 2013). CC BY 2.0

(Continued)

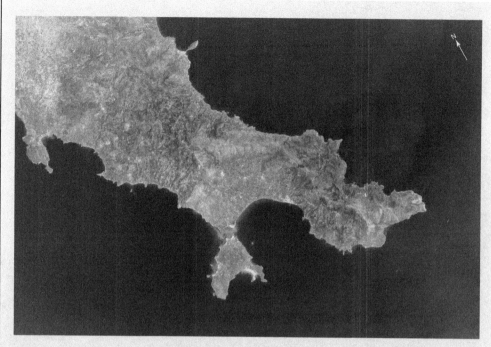

Figure 1.4   Satellite image of Cape Malea. Source: Image Science and Analysis Laboratory, NASA-Johnson Space Center. "The Gateway to Astronaut Photography of Earth." <http://eol.jsc.nasa.gov/scripts/sseop/QuickView.pl?directory=ESC&ID=ISS015-E-9024>01/10/2013 12:17:06

Flax & orange & lemon common, & barley; no wheat

such as flax in Messenia, can be planted; orange and lemon groves today cover the plain of Argos near the sea. The general paucity of water, however, means that the staple grain in Greece tends to be the less nutritious barley that grows in lower-quality soil and requires less water; only in a few regions, like the plain of Eleusis, can the more nutritious wheat be planted.

Towards the south the temperature, even during the winter, remains fairly warm. In the north, however, the winters can be bitterly cold. The severity of the winter can also vary a great deal according to altitude, with the lower regions having considerably warmer weather. Although one can make some generalizations, where climate is concerned, every region in Greece is unique.

The Use of the Land

agriculture & war cycles

The climate and the topography work together to affect how humans use the land. First, crops are planted during the winter – only then is there sufficient water –, and the harvest takes place in the early spring. This agricultural cycle, incidentally, dictated the military season in antiquity: over the winter men stayed home and farmed; only after they had gathered in the harvest could they go out to war. Summer, then, was the time for warfare. The storms which brought the rain also made the winter unsafe for sailing so naval campaigns were confined to the summer as well.

Second, because mountains make a large percentage of the land unusable for humans, the remaining land was intensely worked to best effect. First-rate land tended to be reserved for staple grains, while the second-rate land was planted with trees and used for grazing animals. Herdsmen drove flocks of sheep into mountain valleys and onto meadows too remote for other uses, and goats could find something to eat even on the rockiest patches of ground. Place names such as Aegospotami, "Goat's Creek" – i.e., only a goat could find something to eat there – provide evidence for the way in which the Greeks exploited goats to make even the least fruitful soil yield something useful.

The harsh struggle to win as much as possible from the land characterizes human settlement in Greece, especially in those periods when the population was growing rapidly. When the land could not yield enough staple crops, what it could produce was converted into food through trade. Megara, for example, had precious little good land after it lost the plain of Eleusis to Athens in the early sixth century (see chap. 5), but sheep could still be kept on the poorer land remaining. The Megarians could work the wool and sell it in Athens and throughout the Athenian Empire, at least until the Athenians banned this in the 430s (see chap. 12). The comic playwright **Aristophanes** (*Acharnians*, 519–535) actually states that the Megarians started to starve on account of this ban, and even if he was exaggerating for effect, it still shows how the people in a given area could use even second-rate land intensely to produce a commodity for export and thus secure their survival.

States likewise could come under pressure either to conquer additional arable land from neighbors (for example, the "land wars" of the **Archaic** period – see chap. 5) or to take new land in their territories under cultivation. This could be done by deforestation, but that is backbreaking labor and hence not lightly undertaken. One could also, however, cultivate marginal land which had hitherto served only for grazing. In the fourth century both the Phocians and the Western Locrians appear to have done precisely this. In both cases it led to so-called **Sacred Wars** since the land in question was dedicated to the god Apollo (see chap. 18). This example illustrates just how the pressure to gain land by whatever means could immediately drive historical developments.

Main Regions of Greece

Geologically, the Peloponnese is dominated by a large central massif, which several mountain ranges combine to produce. This central area – Arcadia – is rugged and isolated. When the Mycenaean kingdoms (see chap. 2) which dominated Greece in the thirteenth century fell circa 1200 (see chap. 3), some of the refugees from these kingdoms retreated into this intensely mountainous region. Agriculture was possible only in the valleys, and here settlements sprang up and eventually grew into cities of reasonable size. Nonetheless, Arcadia remained poor and backward: it was a region people tried to leave; no one ever much wanted to go to it. Like many impoverished mountainous regions throughout history it commonly provided surrounding regions with a steady stream of mercenaries – young men with little to do at home, young men whose only hope of escaping lay in taking pay in someone else's army (see, for example, chap. 18 for mass hiring of mercenaries).

To the south of Arcadia two mountain ranges, Taÿgetos and Parnon, run roughly northwest to southeast. A narrow valley separates them towards the north, but farther southwards the valley gradually widens until it becomes a sizable plain. This is the region known as Laconia; and the plain here is exceptionally fertile and well-watered: the Eurotas is one of the few rivers in Greece which carries water all the year round (see Figure 1.5). Here lay the city of Sparta, the predominant military power in Greece during the **classical** period. In the very earliest period Mt. Taÿgetos and Mt. Parnon delimited the territory of Sparta; but already in the seventh and sixth centuries BC the Spartans – or,

Figure 1.5   Eurotas River. Source: Aeleftherios, http://commons.wikimedia.org/wiki/File:Eurotas.JPG (accessed 10 January 2013)

to give them their proper name: Lacedaemonians – broke through these geographically dictated boundaries and conquered the regions lying west of Mt. Taÿgetos and east of Mt. Parnon. The two mountains extend out into the Mediterranean far beyond the point at which the Laconian Plain, built up by the sediment brought down by the Eurotas, ceases and form narrow, rocky fingers that frame the Laconian Gulf.

The fertility of the Laconian Plain notwithstanding, the Lacedaemonians eventually crossed Mt. Taÿgetos to conquer Messenia in the seventh century (see chap. 6). The fertile Messenian Plain, lying about the upper Pamisus River, was one of the first targets of the Lacedaemonian lust for land. Overlooking the plain stands Mt. Ithome, a vast natural fortress in which rebels against the Lacedaemonians would, in the fifth century, withstand a ten years' siege (see chap. 12). To the south of the Messenian Plain a squat peninsula, not nearly so long or so rugged as Taÿgetos, lies opposite, enclosing the Messenian Gulf. To the west and northwest of the Messenian Plain lies a smooth, gently curving coastline formed by rains which bring sediment down from the mountains at almost exactly the same rate at which erosion caused by the sea operates. The area towards the south about the Bay of Navarino has resisted this process of smoothing owing to tough rock formations.

In classical and later times the appellation "Messenia" applied to these three regions – upland plain, western coast, and southern peninsula. Over the centuries, however, the regions did not always form a political unity: they were united in the Kingdom of **Pylos** in the thirteenth century BC (see chap. 2); in the late eighth century BC the coastal regions in the West and the southern peninsula were politically independent of the Messenian Plain; from about 600 BC onwards all three regions were united politically with the Laconian Plain under Lacedaemonian control (see chap. 6); and after 370 BC they were united in an independent Messenian state (see chap. 16) until this state became part of the Achaian League in the course of the third century BC (see chap. 23).

Moving northward from Messenia, one crosses the River Neda to come to the border region of Triphylia – literally "three tribes' land" – which had received its name from three tribes that had long since disappeared by classical times. Eventually, the Arcadians to the west and the Eleans to the north laid claim to this region.

Continuing north, one comes to Elis, literally just "valley," the prominent and highly fertile valley of the Peneus River, and the original focal point of the Eleans' settlement. Although the Eleans never played a prominent role in Greek history, they did eventually have on their territory one of the most important Panhellenic sanctuaries, Olympia. The festival held here in honor of the god Zeus of Olympus over the course of many decades acquired significance far beyond Elis: already in the eighth century people from Messenia to the south were attending the festival; shortly thereafter people from other regions in the Peloponnese began to come; and by the late sixth people from all over Greece.

Eastwards from Elis one comes to a narrow strip of coastline between the waters of the Gulf of Corinth to the north and the mountains of Arcadia to the south. For most of the classical period this region, Achaia, consisted of poor fishing villages. In the third century BC, however, it would form the nucleus of the most powerful state in Greece, the Achaian League (see chap. 23 and 24). That **league** or **ethnos** (see Box 4.1) was an old structure, dating to the time of settlement by the Achaians; and initially it consisted of twelve cities which annually sent representatives to a centrally located communal sanctuary.

The regions discussed so far have been either impoverished (Arcadia, Achaia) or for various reasons off the beaten track (Elis, except for the Olympic festival; Arcadia; Laconia; Messenia). This last has mostly to do with the prevailing route for sea travel (see Box 1.1) which kept ships from going around the Peloponnese. Although Sparta had a harbor at Gythium, it had little practical use. Good harbors lay on the peninsula to the south of the Messenian Plain, but, again, little traffic came that way. The way in which the coast along the west of the Peloponnese had been formed meant that it had few harbors (Pylos on the Bay of Navarino is the chief exception); and marshes dominate much of the coast of the northwestern Peloponnese in Elis with little land suitable for a port (Cyllene is the chief exception).

However, as one proceeds eastwards from Achaia one finally comes to the well-connected region of the northeastern Peloponnese. Here lay the powerful cities of Corinth (which dominated the Isthmus at its southern and narrower end) and Argos which lay on the Argolic Gulf which led directly to the Aegean. Corinth controlled the land-route between the Peloponnese and the rest of Greece as well as the sea-route from the Saronic to the Corinthian Gulf.

Argos, meanwhile, lay at the head of an alluvial plain, remarkable for its fertility. This plain originally hosted any number of independent cities such as Nauplia and Asine, but eventually fell under Argive control. Eastwards of Argos lay the so-called Argolic Peninsula, the "thumb" of the three-fingered Peloponnesian hand. Some cities lay along the coast: Hermione, **Tiryns**, and Epidaurus (the site of the best-preserved Greek theater – see Figure 1.6). The Argolic Peninsula enclosed the Argolic Gulf on the northeast and protected it against Aegean storms from the east. The Gulf provided easy access to the Aegean.

Southwards of Argos lay the regions of the Thyreatis and the Cynuria which tapered off to the south in a narrow strip of habitable land between Mt. Parnon to the west and the Aegean to the east. Mt. Parnon separated these two regions from the Laconian Plain, though there were several passes which connected them with it. Those passes across Mt. Parnon formed Sparta's primary connection with the rest of Greece. In the mid-sixth century BC Sparta wrested control of the Thyreatis and Cynuria from Argos (see chap. 6) and for the first time gained access to the Aegean port of Prasiae, afterwards the main harbor for Sparta's navy. Argos, thereafter, was restricted to the plain at the head of the Argolic Gulf.

Argos had, however, not always dominated that region. In the plain, towards the east, lies the citadel of Tiryns on a low hill. In the thirteenth century BC. Tiryns dominated much of the plain although it may have shared dominance with the even more impressive fortress of **Mycene** high up in the mountains

Figure 1.6   The theater of Epidaurus (fourth century BC). The theater was a typical architectural feature of a Greek city. Source: Olecorre, http://commons.wikimedia.org/wiki/File :Theatre_of_Epidaurus_OLC.jpg (accessed 10 January 2013) CC BY-SA 3.0, 2.5, 2.0, 1.0

overlooking the plain to the North. These two citadels may in fact have belonged to one single kingdom during the so-called **Mycenaean** period (roughly the fourteenth and thirteenth centuries BC). However, both Mycene and Tiryns were destroyed around 1200 BC and in course of time political dominance passed to Argos.

Leaving the Peloponnese by way of the Isthmus one comes first to Megara (the "halls"), perched precariously on the northern half of the Isthmus and sandwiched between two powerful neighbors, Corinth and Athens. North of Megara one enters central Greece, dominated on the mainland by Athens to the east and Boeotia to the west. The large island of Euboea which runs parallel with the Attic and Boeotian coastline to the north also belongs to central Greece. Athens, by Greek standards, was of enormous size. It gained control of the plain of Eleusis in the west in the course of the early sixth century BC (see chap. 5). In addition to this rich, grain-producing region, Athens possessed substantial tracts of land which, although they were marginal in terms of grain production, could support olive plantations. Athens' chief export throughout the archaic and classical periods was always olive oil. Finally, in the southeastern quarter of the Attic peninsula lay rich silver mines at Laureium, mines which in the fifth century BC would provide the initial outlay for the construction of Athens' navy (see chap. 10).

Box 1.2   *The Size of Greek States*

The way in which the mountains divide Greece up into small valleys and small coastal plains has tended to make Greek states comparatively small in size. Even in those periods when larger states developed they are dwarfed by contemporary states in the Near East. Thus the **Hittite kingdom** during the Bronze Age in Asia Minor was far larger than any Mycenaean kingdom such as Pylos, **Thebes**, or **Knosos** in Greece; likewise the Achaian and Aetolian Leagues were minuscule next to the **Seleucid** and **Ptolemaic** kingdoms in the **Hellenistic** Age. For most of the archaic and classical periods, however, states in Greece were considerably smaller than, say, the Kingdom of Knosos or the Achaian League of the second century BC.

A hypothetical walking tour of the Argolic Peninsula may help to give a concrete idea of the size of a Greek state in the classical period (fifth to fourth centuries BC). If one began an overland journey on foot – granted one would need a certain amount of vigor as the terrain is rugged and mountainous – at the tip of the Argolic Peninsula in Hermione; and if one carefully planned one's route, one might in the course of a vigorous two days' hike cross the territories of no fewer than five fully independent states: from Hermione to Troezen (on the Saronic Gulf on a narrow coastal plain just south of Methana, a rough peninsula of volcanic origin) to Argos to Epidaurus (on another coastal plain farther to the northwest) and on to Phleius to the west just south of Corinth. In fact, if one planned the trek in the year 480, one could manage to visit the territories of two additional states, Mycene and Tiryns, which for a few years in the early fifth century were independent of Argos (which shortly thereafter reconquered them). Two days' vigorous walking could lead one, then, through seven states.

For most of the classical period the vast majority of states were so small that one could walk the length and breadth of them in less than a day. This holds true not just for the islands of the Aegean, but also for the mountain valleys in Arcadia and the small plains along the coast. There were, of course, exceptions: Sparta and Athens were comparatively large as were some of the league or **tribe** states such as Thessaly.

To the north of Athens lies the island of Euboea, the largest island in the Aegean. The island's eastern coast – raw, steep, and devoid of harbors – meets the Aegean storms head on, but the channel between the island and the mainland is sheltered and accordingly calm. All north–south navigation follows the course of the channel which has a wasp's-waist at the mid-point, the Euripus, where a stone's throw separates mainland from island (see Figure 1.7).

The Euripus was not just a major sea-route, but also a major land-route since all traffic between the mainland and Euboea went through this spot. Because of its propinquity to the mainland, Euboea's history is closely bound up with the history of its neighbors, Athens and Boeotia. In the thirteenth century BC

Figure 1.7 The Euripus today (spanned by a retractable bridge). Source: Georgios Pazios, http://commons.wikimedia.org/wiki/File:Evripos_moving_bridge_1.JPG (accessed 10 January 2012)

the Kingdom of Thebes in Boeotia controlled at least central and southern Euboea (see chap. 2); through much of the fifth and fourth centuries BC Athens controlled Euboea (see chaps. 11, 16. and 18). In the intervening period Euboea had been home to several independent states, the most important of which were Chalcis and Eretria, on the island's western side, close to the Euripus, at opposite ends of the Lelantine Plain – the most fertile area on Euboea. Chalcis and Eretria exhausted themselves in the so-called **Lelantine War** over this plain in the late eighth and early seventh centuries (see chap. 5).

Northwest of Attica and across the Euripus from Euboea lies Boeotia. Since Boeotia borders both the Aegean and the Corinthian Gulf, some trade moved overland across it between the two bodies of water – though never so much as across the narrower Isthmus. Dominating Boeotia politically, in all periods, was the city of Thebes. Already in the thirteenth century BC a Mycenaean kingdom was based there. For most of the archaic and classical periods Boeotia was, like Achaia, a league- or tribe-state, albeit one with a large, powerful city, Thebes, at its center. Theban predominance, however, drove other cities to attempt to leave this league; Plataea, for example, in southeastern Boeotia, until its destruction in 427 BC (see chap. 13), constantly sought support from Athens against Thebes.

Figure 1.8 The temple of Apollo at Delphi, with the theater in the foreground and the Pleistos Valley in the background. Source: Adam Carr, http://commons.wikimedia.org/wiki/File:Ac.delphi1.jpg (accessed 10 January 2013) CC BY-SA 3.0

Phocis & Locris

West of Boeotia one comes to Phocis and Locris. Phocis, another tribe-state, would have been very much on the periphery of the Greek world had it not *Delphi* been for the Temple of Apollo at **Delphi** (see Figure 1.8), the most important sanctuary in the Greek world and site of a much-frequented oracle.

Apart from Delphi, however, Phocis was an impoverished backwater of little relevance until 356 BC when the **Phocian War** broke out (see chap. 18). Locris was also of little importance, though its fragmentation requires some explanation. On either side of the Phocians lay the two chief groups of Locrians, the Ozolian or Western Locrians and the Opuntian or Eastern Locrians. These last are also called the Hypocnemidian Locrians, that is, the "Locrians at the foot of Cape Cnemis." The Opuntian Locrians were physically divided into two territories by Cape Cnemis which itself remained under Phocian control. Both Opuntian and Ozolian Locris were tribe-states with close ancestral ties while existing independently of one another. In Ozolian Locris lay the strategically important port of Naupactus, just east of the wasp's-waist of the Gulf of Corinth, between Rhium and Antirrhium. In 456 BC the Athenians appropriated Naupactus and held it for half a century (see chap. 12).

Figure 1.9   Satellite image of the Aegean Sea and surrounding land. Source: NASA, http://en.wikipedia.org/wiki/File:Aegeansea.jpg (accessed 10 January 2013)

Aetolia

West of Phocis and Locris one comes to Aetolia, another league. Aetolia very much lay on the periphery of the Greek world during the classical period; its inhabitants were considered semi-barbarous at best. In the third century BC, however, the Aetolian League would become the largest and most powerful state in Greece north of the Peloponnese (see chap. 21). West and northwest of Aetolia one comes to regions and peoples (e.g., the Acarnanians) not quite Greek, even if they did slowly become **Hellenized** during the classical period. Farther to the west, along the Adriatic Sea, however, there were a number of colonies founded in the eighth and seventh centuries by Corinth: Leucas, Anactorium, Ambracia, and, on an island off the coast, Corcyra.

North of Phocis and Locris, the pass of Thermopylae led to Thessaly, the chief state of northern Greece. Thessaly possessed the one large plain in Greece, the only place where the rearing of horses was practicable on a large scale. In the rest of Greece horses functioned chiefly as a status symbol since only the wealthy could afford to keep them, and the standard beast of burden remained the donkey. In Thessaly, however, the first true cavalry in Greece arose, and Thessalian breeds were much sought after when other states in Greece developed cavalries of their own. Thessaly was another tribe-state, traditionally under

Thessaly

horses – status symbol, while donkey

the leadership of an elective king called a **tagos.** Thessaly proper was limited to the plain, but by classical times the Thessalians had conquered a number of peoples living in the mountains about Thessaly, the so-called Thessalian **Perio-eci** ("dwellers-about"): clockwise from the southeast, the Phthiotic Achaians, the Perrhaebians, and the Magnesians. In the mountains to the north of the Thessalian plain, incidentally, lay Mt. Olympus, the home of the gods in Greek mythology.

A few words now, before leaving Thessaly, on the pass at Thermopylae. This long, narrow pass was the only good route from central Greece into Thessaly. As such it had both economic and military significance. With regard to the latter characteristic, those who held the pass attempted to keep it closed (e.g., during the Persian Wars when Greek troops vainly endeavored to prevent the Persians from entering central Greece – see chap. 10, and Figure 10.4), but with regard to the former and far more important characteristic, people strove to keep it open. To this end there grew up about the pass an association, the **Pylaean Amphictiony**, based at the sanctuary of Demeter of Anthela, which lay within the pass itself near the hot springs from which the pass got its name. ("Thermo-Pylae" means "Hot Gates," "gate" here being used, as often in Greek, in the sense of "pass.") The association consisted of those who dwelt on either side of the pass – "amphi-ctiones" in Greek just means "those who live on either side (i.e., of a natural landmark)" – and was dedicated in the first instance to the maintenance of the pass. In course of time this association took on other responsibilities (for example, the maintenance of the sanctuary at Delphi – see chap. 18) and various political functions.

To the north of Thessaly lies Macedonia, which, owing to its importance for the history of Greece from the mid-fourth century onwards (see chap. 18), may usefully be discussed here – quite apart from the much-vexed question of whether or not the Macedonians were Greeks. The heartland of Macedonia, the Emathia or "Lower Macedonia," lay in the plain between the River Axius to the northeast and the mountains of northern Thessaly to the south. Only in the fourth century did the Macedonians begin to expand eastwards of the Axius into Thrace. The coastal strip to the east of the Emathia was either marshy or held by Greek colonies such as Pydna and Methone, so in the early period the Macedonians lacked access to the Aegean. To the west of the plain lay mountain ranges which boxed highland regions such as Lyncestis and Orestis off from one another. These regions, collectively called "Upper Macedonia," stood under the control of the stronger Macedonian kings, but tended to become independent under the weaker ones. Even in the time of Philip II, the father of Alexander the Great, these highland areas were still imperfectly integrated into Macedonia as a whole.

During the eleventh and tenth centuries BC, Greeks migrated across the Aegean Sea to settle the islands in it as well as the western coast of Asia Minor. This migration will be discussed at greater length in Chapter 3, so here only the major regions affected need to be mentioned: Doris (southwestern Asia Minor), Ionia (the central portion of the western coast of Asia Minor), and Aeolis (the coastal region north of Ionia).

Box 1.3   *The Names of Peoples and Regions in Greece*

The relationship between the name of a region and the name of the people living there may reveal much. In Greece a region often receives its name from the people who live in it. Specifically, the name of the people is primary, and the name of the region is derived from the name of the people by the addition of a suffix. Here a few examples with the suffix "-ia":

Name of individual	*Name of region*
Magnes	Magnes-ia
Arcas (stem: Arcad-)	Arcad-ia
Boeotos (stem: Boeot-)	Boeot-ia

Next, two examples with the suffix "-id-" (which here appears as "-is"):

Name of individual	*Name of region*
Phoceus (stem: Phoc-)	Phoc-is
Locros (stem: Locr-)	Locr-is

On many occasions it is known that in this case – i.e., when the land received its name from the people – the people did not originally dwell in that land. That is to say, the people existed as an entity before their entrance into that land; and when they took possession of that land, they named it after themselves. This is most clearly the case along the coast of Asia Minor (to which no Greeks were native). The three main Greek-settled regions were called Aeolis, Ionia, and Doris. In each case the name conforms to the pattern just discussed:

Name of individual	*Name of region*
Aeoleus (stem: Aeol-)	Aeol-is
Ion	Ion-ia
Dorieus (stem: Dori-)	Dori-(i)s

The major island group within the Aegean are the so-called Cyclades, or "Circling Isles," in the center. Their name comes from their being imagined to circle about the small island of Delos, an important religious center. Off the southern coast of Asia Minor lie the Dodecanese ("Twelve Isles") or southern Sporades. This group is usually considered to belong to the Doris. A number of large islands lie off the coast of Asia Minor (from south to north): Rhodes, Cos (these two belong to the Dodecanese), Samos, Chios (these two are usually considered part of Ionia), and Lesbos (usually considered part of the Aeolis).

Most of these islands in the classical period were independent states; the largest ones (Lesbos and Rhodes) actually supported several independent states.

The Greeks penetrated at a surprisingly late date into the regions around the northern Aegean (see chap. 5). Here, both on the islands as well as on the mainland, dwelled non-Greek peoples. Greeks from Euboea settled the large, three-fingered peninsula of the Chalcidice, probably in the eighth century BC. As for the islands, Parians from the Cyclades settled the large island of Thasos in the mid-seventh century BC; the Athenians conquered Lemnos and Imbros from non-Greek inhabitants in the late sixth century; and not until the 470s did the Athenians drive the non-Greek Dolopians from the northern Sporades, in particular Scyros.

Two more islands remain to be mentioned. At the southern end of the Aegean lies the large, elongated island of Crete. Although out of the mainstream of Greek development for most of the period discussed in the book, it hosted an extremely important Greek kingdom during the thirteenth century BC (see chap. 2). Finally, far beyond the confines of the Aegean, in the northeastern corner of the Mediterranean, lies the island of Cyprus, opposite Cilicia and Phoenicia. Greek traders had been visiting Cyprus from time immemorial and had begun at some point to settle there. Large-scale settlement need not, however, have begun until the eleventh century BC. The Greeks who settled on Cyprus were closely related to those who settled in Arcadia in the central Peloponnese: the two groups spoke closely related dialects despite their geographical isolation from one another. The Greeks were not the only inhabitants of Cyprus, incidentally: Phoenicians settled large parts of it in the tenth century BC; and besides Greeks and Phoenicians there dwelled on the island another people which antedated both of them, the so-called **Eteocyprians**. The Greek cities on Cyprus, because of their distance from the rest of Greece, tended to have a distinct political and cultural development; but no one ever denied their Greekness or wished to exclude them from the wider Greek world.

FURTHER READING

The best atlas for the ancient Greco-Roman world is:
Talbert, R.J.A. (2000) *The Barrington Atlas of the Greek and Roman World*. Princeton. (The supplementary volumes contain valuable discussions and specific bibliography.)

Also useful is:
Talbert, R.J.A. (1985) *Atlas of Classical History*. London.

The standard survey of the geography of mainland Greece is in German:
Philippson, A., and E. Kirsten. (1950–1959) *Die griechischen Landschaften*. Frankfurt.

For the western coast of Asia Minor, see:
Philippson, A. (1910–1915) *Reisen und Forschungen im westlichen Kleinasien*. Gotha.

Much of the detailed geographical information about the ancient Greek world comes from two ancient sources, the *Description of Greece* by Pausanias and the *Geography* by Strabo. Both works are available in translation in the Loeb series, the former in a Penguin translation as well. On Strabo's *Geography*, see now D. Dueck (2010) "The Geographical Narrative of Strabo of Amasia," in: K. Raaflaub and R.J.A. Talbert (eds.), *Geography and Ethnography: Perceptions of the World in Pre-modern Societies*, 236–251. Maldon, MA.

Part I

Bronze and "Dark Age":
circa 1300–800 BC

2

The Mycenaean Age

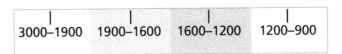

3000–1900	1900–1600	1600–1200	1200–900

Conventional Chronological Divisions of the Bronze Age in the Aegean

circa 3000–1900   **Early Bronze Age**
    in mainland Greece: Early Helladic
    on Crete: Early Minoan

circa 1900–1600   **Middle Bronze Age**
    in mainland Greece: Middle Helladic
    on Crete: Middle Minoan
    (Linear A in use on Crete)

circa 1600–1200   **Late Bronze Age**
    in mainland Greece: Late Helladic or Mycenaean
    on Crete: Late Minoan
    (Linear B in use on Crete and in mainland Greece)

Each period is conventionally subdivided into three phases: Early Helladic I, Early Helladic II, etc. The Late Bronze Age in mainland Greece is often subdivided as Early Mycenaean, Middle Mycenaean, and Late Mycenaean. N.b. that these terms, in the first instance, refer solely to phases in the production of pottery.

A History of Greece: 1300 to 30 BC, First Edition. Victor Parker.
© 2014 Victor Parker. Published 2014 by John Wiley & Sons, Ltd.

Prehistory

Human occupation of Greece began long before the earliest historically useful records. The best-known prehistoric people in Greece were the **Minoans** who lived on Crete in the Early and Middle Bronze Age. They are conventionally named after a mythological king of the island, **Minos**. The most spectacular archaeological site on the island is Knosos, excavated by Sir Arthur Evans. The Minoans left behind impressive palaces (see Figure 2.6 below), artwork of surpassing beauty (see Figure 2.1), and records in two hitherto undeciphered scripts known as **Cretan Hieroglyphic** and **Linear A** (see Figure 2.5 below).

The Minoans traded with **Egypt,** and a handful of Egyptian texts mention them under the name "Keftiu" (e.g., ANET, p. 242); and one text even speaks of a "King" of Crete (ANET, p. 248). If this sole text is accurate, then the island was apparently united under the rule of a single king. Minoan finds from throughout the Aegean region show that they were active as traders, and later Greek legends speak of a Minoan **thalassocracy** in the Aegean. Unfortunately, the Minoans' own texts, Cretan Hieroglyphic and Linear A, cannot yet be read and, aside from the few Egyptian references, the Minoans are known from archaeological finds only. As a result, the Minoans remain tantalizingly enigmatic despite their obvious importance.

On mainland Greece to the northwest of Crete lived other Bronze Age peoples also known almost exclusively from the physical remains they left behind. One

Figure 2.1   Bull Leaper Fresco from Knosos. How exactly Minoan acrobats leaped over bulls and what purpose the activity served remain unknown. Source: George Groutas, http://commons.wikimedia.org/wiki/File:Bull_leaping,_fresco_from_the_Great_Palace_at_Knossos ,_Crete,_Heraklion_Archaeological_Museum.jpg(accessed 10 January 2013) CC BY 2.0

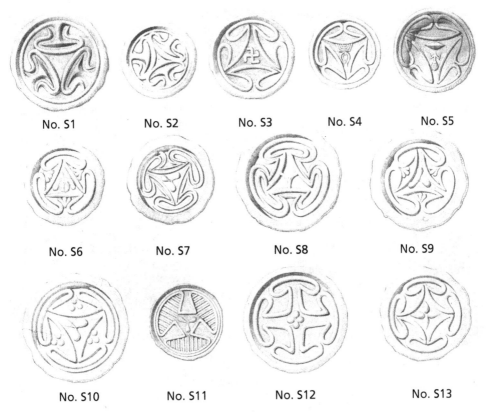

No. S1   No. S2   No. S3   No. S4   No. S5

No. S6   No. S7   No. S8   No. S9

No. S10   No. S11   No. S12   No. S13

Figure 2.2 Early Helladic sealings from Lerna. Source: American School of Classical Studies at Athens

people – conventionally called the **Early Helladics** after the archaeological period from which its remains come – is best known for its spectacular seals which seem to approach writing in their complexity (see Figure 2.2).

Another people, which inhabited the entire Aegean area, left behind a series of toponyms ending in *-nthus or -nda*; in Greece one finds toponyms such as Amarynthus or Olynthus; in Asia Minor one finds toponyms such as Alinda or Labraunda. The suffix *-nthus* is not Greek, and toponyms with it suggest the presence of an earlier, non-Greek people in the same way in which in the United States names such as Tuscaloosa, Coosa, or Talapoosa bear witness to the occupants of the land before European settlement. It is still unknown with which archaeologically attested culture these names in *-nthus* should be connected. All the same, occasional loan-words in Greek have the same suffix, and these words, which evidently come from the language of the people who left behind the toponyms in *-nthus*, do reveal a bit about this people's culture: the word *asaminthus* "bathtub" suggests that they washed themselves in tubs, and *minthus* "mint" suggests that they used the mint plant as a spice.

Figure 2.3   The "Lion Gate" at the entrance to the citadel of Mycene. Source: Andreas Trepte, http://commons.wikimedia.org/wiki/File:Lions-Gate-Mycenae.jpg (accessed 10 January 2013) CC BY-SA 2.5

All of these peoples belong, strictly speaking, not to history but to prehistory. It was also in prehistorical times that the ancestors of the Greeks arrived in the land which would eventually be named after them – the so-called "Coming of the Greeks." When exactly this took place and under what circumstances are still unanswerable questions. The Greeks of the Bronze Age are conventionally known as **Mycenaeans** after the important archaeological site of **Mycene** (see Figure 2.3), which in modern times was first excavated by Heinrich Schliemann, better known as the excavator of **Troy** in Asia Minor.

Mycene in later Greek myth was the residence of a mythological king called **Agamemnon** who in the **epic** poem the *Iliad* led the Greeks in a war against Troy. The best known remains from Mycene, such as the so-called Mask of Agamemnon (see Figure 2.4), come from the **Shaft Graves** here in the archaeological phase Middle Helladic III and Late Helladic I (Early Mycenaean), roughly the seventeenth century BC.

The Mycenaeans' material culture owed much to the Minoans', including the art of writing, for the Mycenaeans left behind documents in a script called

Figure 2.4   The Mask of Agamemnon. Source: Rosemania, http://commons.wikimedia
.org/wiki/File:MaskOfAgamemnon.jpg (accessed 10 January 2013) CC BY 3.0

Linear B (see Figure 2.5), which is derived from the older Minoan script,
Linear A.

Certain matters nonetheless distinguish Mycenaean culture from Minoan.
The most prominent architectural manifestation of the distinction is the presence in Mycenaean palaces of a ***megaron*** or central hall (see Figure 2.7), a
feature lacking in Minoan ones (see Figure 2.6).

At some point before the thirteenth century – when exactly is debated –
Mycenaeans from the mainland established on Crete a Mycenaean kingdom
that included the central and western parts of the island (see below). The
Minoans who remained under Mycenaean rule slowly became Hellenized, that
is, they assimilated to Greek culture.

Even if they did lose control of the bulk of the island, some Minoans may
still have held onto the eastern portion of Crete, and it is from the town of
Praesus in the east that a few so-called **Eteocretan** inscriptions of classical date
are known. These inscriptions are written in a non-Greek language which,
unfortunately, no one has succeeded in reading. This language might be the
classical descendant of that written on the Linear A tablets in the Bronze Age.

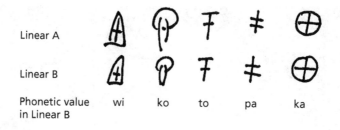

	wi	ko	to	pa	ka
Linear A					
Linear B					
Phonetic value in Linear B	wi	ko	to	pa	ka

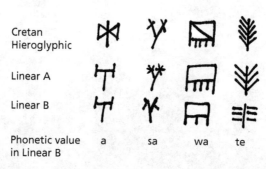

	a	sa	wa	te
Cretan Hieroglyphic				
Linear A				
Linear B				
Phonetic value in Linear B	a	sa	wa	te

Figure 2.5 The Linear B script is derived from the older Linear A script, and many signs are substantially the same in both (as the table at the top shows). A few signs of Linear A and B resemble signs of the so-called Cretan Hieroglyphic script (see table at the bottom). The phonetic values for the signs are, strictly speaking, known for Linear B only.

Linear B – read but not completely

The Linear B tablets, however, can be read, and these texts, chiefly from Pylos and Knosos, have significantly informed modern understanding of Mycenaean society. In 1953 an amateur linguist, Michael Ventris, published his decipherment of this **syllabary** with a collaborator, John Chadwick. The language on the Linear B tablets turned out to be Greek, but because it was a highly archaic form of Greek and because of the difficulties inherent in the system of writing, much about the tablets initially remained obscure. As late as two decades after the decipherment, Russell Meiggs in a then standard textbook could write of Linear B that the "decipherment is still so incomplete that the most interesting questions cannot yet be answered with any certainty" and add that "a wider measure of agreement among philologists is needed before historians can feel confidence" in reconstructing Mycenaean society. The philologists have fortunately made the progress which Meiggs desired; and historians may now feel confident in discussing the Mycenaeans of the thirteenth century, the period from which almost all surviving texts come. It is, then, in this period, thanks to their texts, that the Greeks emerge from prehistory into the full light of history.

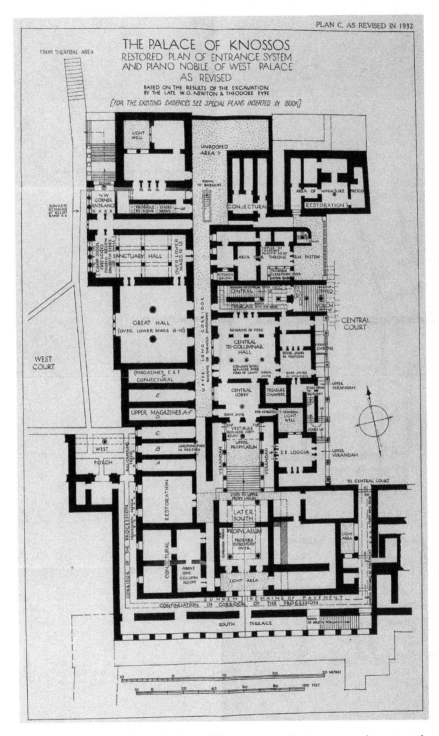

Figure 2.6 Plan of the Minoan Palace of Knosos; note the large central court at the right on the plan. Plan C from Sir Arthur Evans, *The Palace of Minos*, vol. IV.1 (London: Macmillan, 1935). Heidelberg University Library

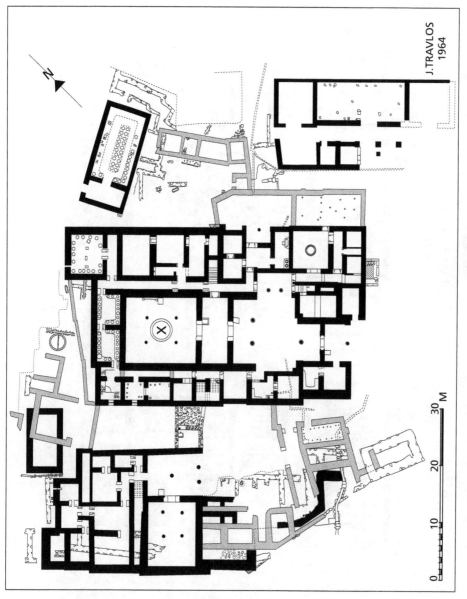

Figure 2.7 Plan of the Mycenaean Palace of Pylos; note the central hall, the "megaron" here labeled "X".
Source: Blegen, Carl. W. & Marion Rawson, eds. 1966. *The Palace of Nestor at Pylos in Western Messenia: Vol. 1. The Buildings and Their Contents.* Princeton Univ. Press. Part 2, Figure 417. Original measured and drawn by J. Travlos, 1964

The Linear B Texts

The Linear B tablets were a state bureaucracy's working documents and not intended as permanent historical archives. They contain frequent references to months, for example, but never refer to years by date. They do, however, occasionally speak of "this year" or "last year." In other words, the tablets record administrative acts during one single calendar year. These references to "last year" imply that the scribes kept other, more permanent, records (on, say, papyrus, leather, or wood) where one might look up the requisite information from "last year." The clay tablets, since they were temporary records documenting matters in progress during a single year only, were apparently discarded at the end of that year. Ironically, when the palaces burned to the ground, the permanent records were all destroyed, but the temporary records on clay tablets were baked rock hard and preserved for all time.

Because of their nature as temporary records, the Linear B tablets often disappoint the historian. Most are simple lists of goods or people associated in some way with the bureaucracy. Moreover, since the tablets refer to matters from one single year, they yield little direct information about preceding years.

Box 2.1   *Interpreting Linear B Texts*

Crucial to interpreting Linear B tablets is the concept of the "series." A tablet is rarely a stand-alone text. Instead, several tablets are usually related to each other, and only when the tablets are read as part of the series to which they belong can they be fully understood. For example, the tablet An 657 begins with the statement "Thus the watchers are keeping guard over the coastline." There follows information about the stationing of the soldiers of two small military details (called *orkhai* or "commands") at various points along the coast. The tablet An 657 provides the "heading" for four additional tablets (An 519, 654, 656, and 661) which each give such details for two more *Orkhai*. If An 657 had been lost, it would be impossible to determine that the *Orkhai* on the four other tablets were involved in a coastal watch. But when An 657 is placed in front of the other four, they too become intelligible.

The concept of the "series" also explains the method of citing Linear B texts. Before the texts could be read, the tablets were simply numbered according to the order in which they were inventoried during the excavation. Scholars later sorted the tablets by subject matter into large groups denoted by a capital letter (e.g., "M" for lists of agricultural commodities). These large groups were then subdivided into smaller ones, each of which was denoted by a lower-case letter after the capital. Each two-letter code is specific to an archive. Thus the tablet Ma 330 is the 330th tablet inventoried at Pylos; and it is a list of six agricultural commodities (like the other seventeen Ma-texts).

The two largest archives (from Pylos and Knosos) date mainly from the year in which the palaces were destroyed (around the turn of the thirteenth to twelfth centuries BC) and therefore from the very end of the states that compiled them. Thus the tablets directly illuminate only one point in time right at the end of the Mycenaean states' long history. All the same, the tablets still provide a surprising amount of information about these states and their development during the Late Bronze Age.

The Mycenaean States

First, the tablets reveal that there was no one "Mycenaean" state, but several of them governed by kings. On the basis of the identifiable toponyms mentioned in the tablets from the archive found at Pylos, the rough extent of the Kingdom of Pylos (conventionally named after the site of the palace) can be gauged. It covered most of the southwestern Peloponnese and extended as far north as Pisa in Elis. The toponyms on the tablets from the archive at Knosos show that the so-called Kingdom of Knosos controlled at least the central and western portions of the island of Crete. No toponym from the east of the island appears on those tablets, so the east may have lain beyond that kingdom's control. The tablets from the Kingdom of **Thebes** mention places in southern Boeotia and, surprisingly, central and southern Euboea. The situation in the Argolis is unclear since archives have been found both at Mycene (see Figure 2.3 above) and at **Tiryns** (see Figure 2.8). Both were important Bronze Age sites with heavily fortified citadels, and it is possible that a kingdom was centered on each. However, because Mycene and Tiryns lie so close to one another, some scholars have held it improbable that they should have belonged to two separate kingdoms. The evidence from the tablets is inconclusive so far. These four (or five) kingdoms are just the ones that are known; others surely existed, and many gaps remain in the political map of Mycenaean Greece.

Because of the number and specific nature of the Linear B tablets found at Pylos, this kingdom is the best known. It consisted of two provinces, the products of an administrative reform some time before the date of the tablets. The evidence for this reform comes from the two provinces' names: "Province West of Goat's Rock" and, to the east, "Province Beyond Goat's Rock" (Ng 319 and 322). "Goat's Rock" was a landmark that served as a boundary between the provinces. The eastern province that lay "beyond Goat's Rock" cannot have received that name except from the perspective of bureaucrats to the west of the landmark who were carrying out an artificial division of the kingdom for their convenience and imposing names that made sense from their point of view.

The two provinces were themselves divided into districts, nine in the western province (Cn 608) and seven in the "province beyond the rock" (Jn 829). One district, called *Helos* ("Marshland"), in the Yonder Province occasionally appears in the tablets as two subdistricts (Ma 330 and 335). A possible reason for this is that, in another administrative reform, two initially smallish districts were

Figure 2.8   The ruins of the citadel of Tiryns today. Note the solidity of the so-called Cyclopean walls which turned two low hills into a nearly impregnable fortification. Source: Nick Stenning, http://commons.wikimedia.org/wiki/File:Tiryns_-_Cyclopean_masonry. jpg?uselang=en-gb (accessed 14 January 2013) CC BY-SA 2.0

combined into one larger one or an overly large district was split into two new ones. If this reform had taken place in the very recent past, some parts of the bureaucracy might still have been using the old divisions in their records instead of the new. This could imply that the central bureaucracy of Pylos periodically reorganized the administrative units of the kingdom.

The Political Administration of Pylos

At the head of that central bureaucracy stood the king, or **wanax** ("lord"). While the title is known from the Homeric epics, where it usually refers to gods, the true position of the *wanax* emerges most strongly from the archaeological evidence – someone had to sit on the throne in the great hall or *megaron* in a Mycenaean palace such as Pylos (see Figure 2.6 above). The palace evidently served as the residence of the *wanax*. From the tablets we learn a little more about the role and position of the *wanax*. He appointed at least one official at the provincial level (Ta 711; On 300); and it is possible that he appointed all provincial and district officials.

The second-highest official at Pylos was the **lawagetas**. His title means "leader of the army." Both the *wanax* and the *lawagetas* held a plot of land called a **temenos** in one district (Er 312), and probably an additional one in every other district across the kingdom. The *temenos* of the *wanax* was three times the size of that of the *lawagetas*. This proportion, along with the *wanax*'s palace, gives some idea of the high position of the *wanax* within the kingdom.

Various minor functionaries at the local level (the village shepherd, cowherd, swineherd, and beekeeper: e.g., Ea 270, 481, 782) also received a plot of land from the **damos** – the formal term for the administrative unit beneath the district, most likely the "village" or "township" (Ea 824). These functionaries presumably received land from the *damos* in compensation for their services to it. For example, the village beekeeper provided the villagers with honey, for which the *damos* provided him with some land.

Another noteworthy official in the kingdom, the **gwasileus**, seems to have stood outside of the hierarchy running from the king down to the district officials. *Gwasileus* in later Greek became **basileus** – the most common later Greek word for "king." The *gwasileus* in the Kingdom of Pylos was a low-level functionary and clearly not the king; but he did sometimes function as the leader of a particular group (Jn 431, 601, and 845), and he could be reasonably wealthy (Jo 438). Moreover, the position of the *gwasileus* was probably hereditary (Jn 431) whereas it is likely that the *wanax* appointed all provincial and district officials. It is possible, therefore, that the *gwasileus* was a local official who had been retained from a previous era, even as the central administration began imposing its own order on the kingdom.

Land Tenure at Pylos

Land tenure was important for the administration of Pylos since all who rendered services to the kingdom or to a community within it received a plot of land in compensation. The various E-series list numerous plots of land and illuminate the system of land tenure. The term for a plot was **ktoina**, which etymologically meant "settled or worked plot" (i.e., under cultivation) as opposed to unworked land (not planted, but used for grazing). Oddly, however, the plots listed in the tablets are divided into two sorts, called **ktoinai ktimenai** (literally, "worked worked-plots") and **ktoinai kekhesmenai** (effectively "unworked worked-plots"). This distinction is strange because both types of plot are clearly being worked. A likely explanation is that the names of the two types of plot reflect distinct stages in the development of land tenure. Originally, the *ktoinai* comprised all land under cultivation at the time. Eventually, when the etymological meaning of *ktoina* had been forgotten and the word meant simply "plot," previously unworked land was also divided up into plots in a second stage of development. Now each of the two sorts of plot needed its own name – hence *ktoinai ktimenai* and *ktoinai kekhesmenai*. In a third stage, after the "unworked plots" themselves had come under cultivation, the system had two distinct categories of worked plot with no difference in size or use.

The division of grazing land into plots (the *ktoinai kekhesmenai*) and then the taking of these plots under cultivation together imply a growing population. Additionally, archaeological evidence for the settlement of this area shows that it was more heavily settled in the late Mycenaean period than at any other time before the modern era. By the end of the thirteenth century BC the population had grown dramatically, and its increasing demands on the land affected the system of land tenure as more and more land came under cultivation.

From this long process there had emerged two distinct categories of worked plot. The distinction had legal and social significance, for the holders of *ktoinai ktimenai* were very few, while the holders of *ktoinai kekhesmenai* were numerous. Moreover, a number of texts make clear that the *damos* retained ownership of *ktoinai kekhesmenai*. By implication, then, the holders of *ktoinai ktimenai* owned their land privately. So, in a given *damos* only a select few actually owned land, but they tended to own a great deal of it. The majority of landholders, however, only leased their plots, either directly from the *damos* or from the owner of a *ktoina ktimena* or, through a sublease, from the holder of a *ktoina kekhesmena*. Subletting, incidentally, was common.

The system of land tenure was, moreover, legally sophisticated. There were different types of leases, and occasionally disputes arose over the nature of a landholder's tenancy. Here is one interesting entry in a cadaster, in which such a dispute, unresolved at time of writing, was recorded:

Ep 704, lines 5–6:
"(Woman's name), a priestess, holds and solemnly affirms that she holds an e-to-ni-jo-*lease on behalf of a deity, but the* damos *says that she holds an* onaton-*lease on a* ktoina kekhesmena, *of such a size: 1 ⁹/₁₀ units."*

While the actual size of the Mycenaean unit of area is unknown, the two types of lease – *e-to-ni-jo* and *onaton* – surely differed somehow. For example, an *e-to-ni-jo*-lease might have accorded its holder greater rights in the use of the land or certain legal privileges.

The Mycenaean Army

The use of land to compensate those who rendered services to the state extended to the military as well, for example in the levies for the crews of ships in Pylos. In one case, approximately 600 men from places along the coast were being recruited to serve as rowers (An 610; cf. An 724). Most are referred to as **ktitai**, and a smaller number as **metaktitai**. A *ktitas* was probably the holder of a *ktoina ktimena*. A *metaktitas* had a dependent relationship to a *ktitas*, and was not the owner of a *ktoina ktimena*. Two closely related texts, unfortunately still imperfectly understood, provide the following formulae:

Aq 218, line 1: *"How they are obligated to put out to sea . . ."*
Aq 64, line 12: *"How they hold* ktoinai *. . ."*
Aq 218, line 9: *"How those without* ktoinai *. . ."*

Here the concept of the "series" is crucial (see Box 2.1). Both texts, Aq 64 and Aq 218, belong together; "how they do or do not hold *ktoinai*" has something to do with "how they are obligated to put out to sea." Although many problems remain with the interpretation of these two tablets, it appears that the owners of *ktoinai* (i.e., *ktoinai ktimenai* since ownership of the *ktoinai kekhesmenai* remained in the hands of the *damos*) bore some sort of an obligation to serve in the fleet.

Such obligations presumably extended to the rest of the military at Pylos as well. For example, a man named Cretheus held a certain plot specifically "on account of the horse" (Ea 59). Another tablet shows that this same Cretheus held the lease on the *ktoina kekhesmena* of the "Wagonwright of the *Lawagetas*" (Ea 809). That is, the wagonwright had received land from the *damos* (in compensation for his services to the *lawagetas*) and had then leased the land to Cretheus.

The elite arm of the Mycenaean military was the chariotry. Many tablets record large numbers of chariots and equipment for chariots (the Sa series from Pylos; the Sc, Sd, Se, and Sf series from Knosos). Chariots also appear frequently in visual depictions in the archaeological material (see Figure 2.9). The

Figure 2.9   Mycenaean chariot from stele from Shaft Graves at Mycene. Source: Photo © The Art Archive / DeA Picture Library / G. Nimatallah

wagonwright of the *lawagetas* probably was responsible for building and maintaining chariots and, predictably, he received land as compensation. Holding the land in turn obligated him to produce chariots. Cretheus in turn held a plot of land as compensation for his service, the maintenance of a horse. Holding the land, however, obligated him to keep the horse and to serve as a charioteer whenever called upon. If this is the way the *Wanax* of Pylos recruited for the chariotry as well as for the fleet, then in all likelihood he levied his infantry in a similar way.

Social Stratification in Pylos

The system of land tenure gives additional insight into the stratification of society in the Kingdom of Pylos. At the apex of the social pyramid stood the small number of landholders who owned the *ktoinai ktimenai* and whose estates tended to be very large. Perhaps these worthies of the realm participated in some of the leisure activities depicted in Mycenaean art, such as these hunting scenes on ceremonial swords (see Figure 2.10) from the Shaft Graves at Mycene,

Figure 2.10   Hunting scenes on a ceremonial sword from the Shaft Graves. Source: from Tomb IV, Grave Circle A, Mycenae Athens, National Archaeological Museum. Photo DEA / G. DAGLI ORTI. akg-images/De Agostini Picture Library

even if their actual hunts involved animals more prosaic than lions which were not native to Greece.

The next social group was the large number of those who did not own land, but instead leased it, either from the *damos* or from the holder of a *ktoina ktimena*. These lease-holders enjoyed a fair degree of prosperity as a sort of "middle class." Beneath them was the remainder of the free population in Pylos, who did not hold land either by deed or by lease.

At the bottom of the social pyramid were the so-called slaves. The Mycenaeans knew the classical Greek distinction between **eleutheros** and **do(h)elos**, "free" and "slave" (or more neutrally, "unfree"). However, in Mycenaean society the terms "free" and "unfree" in the first instance denoted legal status. For the Unfree in Pylos, somewhat surprisingly, were often prosperous landholders. According to Ep 212, line 9: "Idomeneia, a *do(h)ela* (the feminine to *do(h)elos*) of a deity, holds an *onaton*-lease on a *ktoina kekhesmena* from the *damos*." Numerous *do(h)eloi* of gods held such leases in Pylos. Occasionally, a *do(h)elos* belonging to a person (admittedly in all attested cases to a priest[ess]) also held a lease. Significantly, however, no *do(h)elos* ever owned land; in Pylos only the Free could actually own. The Unfree, however, could acquire leases and, economically at least, enter the "middle class."

Slavery in Pylos

The presence of *do(h)eloi* of gods in Mycenaean society suggests that, like contemporary temples in the Near East, Mycenaean temples also controlled estates which needed tending. Even in classical Greece a temple usually had land attached which might be worked or used for grazing (see Box 9.1). Slaves could have filled the role of managing and working temple lands, and some *do(h)eloi* who competently managed a temple estate could have achieved enough wealth and social status in that role to acquire a lease on land where they could work independently. Such *do(h)eloi*, however, were clearly the exception.

While some *do(h)eloi* obtained a degree of social mobility, one remarkable Pylian text, An 607, illustrates how unfree-status was inherited. In this text unfree women are listed with their parentage, and some have an unfree mother but a free father or vice versa. In each case the status of the woman in question goes according to the status of her unfree parent. Thus, the children of unions between Free and Unfree were themselves always unfree.

The Mycenaeans recognized (as did the classical Greeks) various gradations of Unfreedom, probably with differing legal rights. Because texts commonly note someone's status as a "*do(h)elos* of a deity" one should assume that such a *do(h)elos* had a different legal status from someone who was a *do(h)elos* of another human being. On An 607 in the case of one *do(h)ela* it is actually noted that her father was a *do(h)elos*, but her mother a *do(h)ela* of a goddess. It is unclear if *do(h)elai* of such mixed parentage had a specific legal status on that ground.

Box 2.2 *A Pylian Slaving Raid*

Not all Pylian slaves were native to Pylos. Groups of women and children, almost certainly slaves who carried out work for the kingdom, are registered in the Aa, Ab, and Ad series. In the tablets, the women are commonly referred to by adjectives derived from place-names. With comparable groups of female slaves in Knosos these adjectives in all clear cases are derived from place-names which lie within the kingdom. In Pylos, however, some of these adjectives are derived from place-names outside of the kingdom.

For example, there are women called *Lamniai* (from Lemnos), *Milatiai* (from Miletus), and *Knidiai* (from Cnidus), after places which lie along the western coast of Asia Minor. It is unlikely that Pylian administrators purchased these women in a slave market such as existed on the island of Delos in classical times, since, if this were the case, the women ought not all to have come from the same geographical region and similar groups of foreign-born slaves should have existed in Mycenaean kingdoms other than Pylos. In all likelihood, then, these women were captured in a plundering raid. Since these women were being kept at Pylos together with their children, the majority of the women must have been of approximately the same age; and therefore must have fallen victim to the raiders at about the same time.

It seems, then, that at some point within the last generation of the kingdom, the Pylians carried out a great raid along the coast of western Anatolia and captured groups of women and children to work as slaves. Interestingly the Homeric epics, in particular the *Iliad*, tell the story of a great expedition from the Greek mainland against a king in western Anatolia, Priam of Troy. The Pylian slave-raid may provide part of the historical context before which this (highly fictionalized) story arose.

Mycenaean Religion

Even before the decipherment of the tablets, scholars had deduced that most classical Greek gods had Mycenaean antecedents. Religious continuity from Mycenaean to classical times can be seen in sanctuaries and temples to the major classical Greek gods, which, according to the archaeological evidence, had remained in use from Mycenaean times. The Linear B tablets not only confirmed this, but also refined the details.

The major gods of classical Greece that were worshipped in Mycenaean Greece included Zeus, Hera, Poseidon, Hermes, Artemis, Ares, Athena, and Dionysus. Apollo is missing. Although no classical sanctuary of Dionysus dates to Mycenaean times, his place in the Mycenaean pantheon is confirmed by a tablet discovered in Khania, a town in northwestern Crete known as Cydonia both in Mycenaean and in classical times:

Gq 5
To the Temple of Zeus: To Zeus, honey, one vase
To Dionysus, honey . . .

This tablet also shows that a Mycenaean god, like his classical counterparts, might also receive sacrifices in a temple dedicated to another god to whom he stood in some sort of relationship. Here Dionysus receives sacrifices in a temple of Zeus.

heroes vs gods In general, Mycenaean religion was the same as classical Greek religion, including the distinction between **heroes and gods,** one of the most characteristic features of classical Greek religion. Heroes were immortals who received offerings, but were not considered gods in the strict sense. Similarly, in Pylos offerings were made to a unique figure known as the "Triple-Hero" (Tn 316). Both classical and Mycenaean Greeks also named their months after festivals for gods, such as *Diwjojo Menos,* the "Month of the Festival of Zeus" at Knosos (Fp 5). The only significant difference between Mycenaean and classical Greek religion lies in the presence of some gods in the Mycenaean period whose worship had ceased by classical times, for example, *Posideija,* a female counterpart to Poseidon (Tn 316).

Inevitably, much about Mycenaean religion remains unknown. Various possibly religious figurines are attested in the archaeological record – called "Psi" and "Phi" figurines (see Figure 2.11) for their rough resemblance to those

Figure 2.11   Mycenaean Psi and Phi figurines, circa 1400–1300 BC (terracotta). Source: Private Collection / Photo © Heini Schneebeli / The Bridgeman Art Library

---

Box 2.3   *Tn 316 – Human Sacrifice in Pylos?*

As discussed, the inhabitants of Pylos gave sacrifices and offerings to their gods. It is possible, however, that Mycenaean Greeks also practiced human sacrifice. This view is based on the tablet Tn 316. If this text should refer to the sacrifice of human beings, it would be among the most sensational found at Pylos. In the following excerpt from Tn316 (reverse, lines 8–10) the subject of the sentence is not entirely clear, but is possibly the *Wanax* of Pylos:

> "he performs a rite in the temple of Zeus and both bears gifts and leads po-re-na: to Zeus: 1 gold vase, 1 man; to Hera: 1 gold vase, 1 woman; to Drimius, the son of Zeus: 1 gold vase"

The words translated as "bears" and "leads" are functionally related, but with a key difference: "bears" is used for things which are carried in the arms and "leads" for things which can move by themselves (e.g., people or animals). The exact translation of the word *po-re-na* is difficult, but the context makes its general meaning clear. What are brought to the gods are vases (which one carries in one's arms) and what are led to the gods are human beings (who can walk on their own). The word *po-re-na*, therefore, refers to human beings who are given to gods. Is this human sacrifice? Possibly, but another conclusion is perhaps more likely. The gods in Pylos commonly owned slaves, so when Tn 316 speaks of gods who receive human beings, the gods may well be receiving human beings as slaves – the *do(h)eloi theoio*, "slaves of a deity."

---

letters in the Greek alphabet –, but which deities or heroes they might represent is unclear.

The Mycenaean Kingdoms in Historical Perspective

[handwritten: Mycenaean kingdoms were quite prosperous]

The Mycenaean kingdoms had enjoyed a long period of peace and stability with steady economic growth prior to their downfall. The Kingdom of Pylos in particular could look back on a long history during which the central administration carried out various reorganizations of the kingdom's territory, brought large tracts of grazing land under cultivation to meet the demands of a growing population, and presided over a period of prosperity during which more and more people (including some from the lowest ranks of society) rose to positions in which they could lease land and farm it independently. The Mycenaean kingdoms, moreover and despite occasional assertions to the contrary, were not particularly warlike. Although the *Wanax* of Pylos could call on a highly organized

[handwritten: not very warlike]

military, the tablets reveal just one warlike act in the last generation of the kingdom, a slaving raid in Anatolia.

The overall picture that emerges from the tablets is not so much one of warfare as one of bureaucracy. At Knosos the bureaucrats kept track of bulls by name: *Stomargos* ("Whitmouth"), *Podargos* ("Whitfoot"), and *Woinokworsos* ("Purple-Rump") (Ch 898, 899, and 897 respectively). Palace bureaucrats at both Pylos and Knosos requisitioned and distributed large amounts of natural produce, thus probably controlling a significant portion of the each kingdom's economic activity. Nevertheless, the Mycenaean states' high population must have produced and consumed far more in a given year than is recorded in the tablets. Either a great deal of economic activity was documented in the palace's lost permanent records or a significant portion of the kingdom's economy fell outside of the palace's purview.

From the Mycenaeans to the Later Greeks

The position of the Mycenaean kingdoms within the larger context of Greek history raises a much-vexed question. Did the Mycenaean kingdoms stand at the beginning of a long and continuous line of historical development stretching from the Bronze Age past the classical age into the Hellenistic world and beyond? Or were the Mycenaean kingdoms a dead end, with the slate wiped clean at their destruction, circa 1200 BC, so that the later Greeks had to start afresh?

Certainly, as has been discussed in this chapter, there is clear evidence of continuity between the Mycenaean and the later periods, for example, in the realm of religion, language, and even literature (see chap. 4). The more closely the Linear B texts are examined, the more continuity emerges. For example, the Mycenaean *temenos*, the plot of land held by the *wanax* and the *lawagetas*, and the Homeric *temenos*, which a king or another benefactor of the community may hold (*Iliad*, VI 194), are clearly the same institution. Similarly, some Linear B texts (e.g., Jn 829) mention a functionary with the title of *klawiphoros* ("key-bearer[ess]"). In one case (Ep 704) the functionary's name is known: *Karpathia* (i.e., she is female). In classical Greece the functionary who held the keys to the treasury in a sanctuary, the *kleidophoros* or *kleidouchos* ("key-bearer[ess]"), was usually female. There is continuity, then, even in so small a detail as the gender of a minor functionary.

Although the disruption caused by the kingdoms' downfall circa 1200 BC must have been severe, the people who had lived there before the catastrophe remained in the land. They rebuilt using the physical and cultural materials which they had inherited. What they built owed a great deal to their forebears, even if it inevitably differed somewhat from what had gone before. Nevertheless, the line between the Mycenaeans and the later Greeks, their descendants, was essentially unbroken.

Box 2.4 *The Ahhiyawa Question – Is the Place Ahhiyawa in the Hittite Texts a Mycenaean State?*

During the Mycenaean period in Greece, the Kingdom of the **Hittites** flourished in central Asia Minor. When, in the late fourteenth and thirteenth centuries BC, the Hittite kings Mursilis II, Muwatallis II, and Hattusilis III sought to gain control over the lands of western Asia Minor, they came into contact with another land which they called **Ahhiyawa**. It lay somewhere to the west of Asia Minor in the Aegean region as a fragmentary passage in the so-called Ten-Year Annals of Mursilis II shows.

According to this text, Mursilis II in his third year defeated the King of Arzawa which lay, roughly, on the territory of classical Lydia. After the battle Mursilis II marched into Arzawa's capital, Apasa (=Ephesus) and "he (Uhha-LÚ-is, the King of Arzawa) fled before me and went over the sea to an island and stayed there . . . Now Uhha-LÚ-is died there in the sea, but his sons separated . . . a son of Uhha-LÚ-is . . . came out of the sea and went to the King of the Land of Ahhiyawa . . . I (Mursilis II) sent . . . by ship" (Götze 1933: 50–66).

The island in question, since the King of Arzawa fled from Ephesus, could easily have been Samos or Chios. From western Asia Minor one gets to Ahhiyawa by sea only; this suggests that Ahhiyawa lay either on another Aegean island such as Rhodes or one of the Cyclades or even further to the west on mainland Greece. Ahhiyawa closely resembles, even if it is phonologically not demonstrably identical to, a Greek toponym which in a contemporary Linear B inscription (C 914) is written as *Akhaiwija* (=the classical Achaia). In that text from Knosos, goods are being sent to *Akhaiwija*, so *Akhaiwija* probably lay outside of the Kingdom of Knosos.

The story of the conflicts between Ahhiyawa and the Hittites provides additional clues as to Ahhiyawa's location. An Ahhiyawan raider, Piyamaradus (known from the Tawagalawas Letter: Sommer 1932: 2–18), attacked Lazpa (Lesbos) according to the Manappa-Tarhundas Letter, so Lesbos is ruled out as Ahhiyawa. Correspondence between the King of Ahhiyawa and the King of the Hittites (Sommer 1932: 268–270) mentions conflicts about islands in the northeastern Aegean, where Ahhiyawa held interests, but evidently did not lie. The Tawagalawas Letter shows that in western Anatolia Ahhiyawa held an outpost called Millawanda (probably Miletus), which the Hittite King Hattusilis III eventually captured. Since the Pylians carried out a raid on Miletus (see Box 2.2), Pylos presumably was not Ahhiyawa. Wherever Ahhiyawa lay, it need not have been large in size. The conflicts of Athens and Rhodes with the Persian Empire and Antigonus Monophthalmus' kingdom respectively in the classical and Hellenistic periods respectively show how even a comparatively small state in the Aegean could with a good fleet challenge a land-based empire in Asia Minor (see chap. 12 and Box 23.3). Finally, the conflict between Ahhiyawa and an Asiatic power suggests, as does the Pylian slaving raid (Box 2.2), a genuinely historical background to the (heavily fictionalized) story of the **Trojan War** in the *Iliad*.

QUESTIONS FOR REVIEW

1   What was the political organization of the Kingdom of Pylos?
2   How was land used to make the administration as well as the military of the Kingdom of Pylos function?
3   What developments can be traced in the system of land tenure in the Kingdom of Pylos? What does this say about the growth and organization of the kingdom?
4   What do the Mycenaeans have in common with the later Greeks?
5   What sorts of events may have provided an historical context for the (fictional) story of the Trojan War?

QUESTION FOR FURTHER STUDY

Mycenaean bureaucrats seem to have spent an inordinate amount of their time in keeping pedantically detailed lists of agricultural commodities, domesticated animals, armaments, plots of land and so on. Why? What did such bureaucracy achieve? What advantages did it confer on these states?

FURTHER READING

On Mycenaean Greece in general:
Chadwick, J. (1976) *The Mycenaean World.* Cambridge. (Based on the Linear B texts.)
Taylour, W. (1983) *The Mycenaeans* (2nd edn.). London. (Based on the archaeological evidence.)

On Bronze Age archaeology in Greece in general:
Dickinson, O.T.P.K. (1994) *The Aegean Bronze Age.* Cambridge.
Vermeule, E.D.T. (1972) *Greece in the Bronze Age* (2nd edn.). Chicago.

On the Linear B tablets in general:
Ventris, M. and J. Chadwick. (1973) *Documents in Mycenaean Greek* (2nd edn.). Cambridge.

The progress of Mycenology is best seen through the colloquia which have met periodically since the decipherment; the most recent to be published is:
Deger-Jalkotzy, S., *et al.* (1999) *Floreant Studia Mycenaea* (=Acts of the 10th International Mycenological Colloquium). Vienna.

For those interested in the story of the decipherment:
Chadwick, J. (1967) *The Decipherment of Linear B.* London.
Chadwick, J. (1999) "Linear B: Past, present, and future." In: S. Deger-Jalkotzy, *et al.*, *Floreant Studia Mycenaea*, 29–34. (An important addendum to Chadwick's book on the decipherment.)

The best introduction to the Linear B script is:
Chadwick, J. (1987) *Linear B and Related Scripts*. London.

The vast majority of the tablets themselves are available in the following standard editions:
Bennett, E.L. (1973–1976) *The Pylos Tablets Transcribed*. Vols. I–II. Rome.
Chadwick, J., *et al.* (1986–1998) *Corpus of Mycenaean Inscriptions from Knossos*. Vols. I–IV. Cambridge.
Melena, J. (1991) *Tithemy. The Tablets and Nodules in Linear B from Tiryns, Thebes, and Mycene*. Salamanca.

The standard dictionary for Mycenaean Greek:
Aura Jorro, F. (1985–1993) *Diccionario Micénico*. Vols. I–II. Madrid.

A few specialized studies relevant to the issues covered in this chapter (very selective):
Carlier, P. (1995) "*Qa-si-re-u* et *qa-si-re-wi-ja.*" In: R. Laffineur and W.-D. Niemeier (eds.), *Politeia. Society and State in the Aegean Bronze Age*, 355–366. Liège.
Gschnitzer, F. (1981) *Griechische Sozialgeschichte*, 10–26. Wiesbaden. (On the Mycenaean period.)
Gschnitzer, F. (1999) "Zum Heerwesen der mykenischen Königreiche." In: S. Deger-Jalkotzy, *et al.*, *Floreant Studia Mycenaea*, 257–264.
Parker, V. (1999) "Die Aktivitäten der Mykenäer in der Ostägäis im Lichte der Linear B Tafeln." In: S. Deger-Jalkotzy, *et al.*, *Floreant Studia Mycenaea*, 495–502.
Parker, V . (2007) "From Mycenaean to Classical Times: Continuity or Discontinuity?" *Prudentia* 39: 1–26.

On the Ahhiyawa Question:–
A general treatment of the so-called Ahhiyawa Question in English:
Bryce, T. (2005) *The Kingdom of the Hittites*, 392–404. Oxford.
On the Hittite texts referred to in Box 2.4:
Götze, A. (1933) *Die Annalen des Mursilis. Mitteilungen der Vorderasiatisch-Aegyptischen Gesellschaft* 38.
Houwink ten Cate, P.H.J. (1983) "Sidelights on the Ahhiyawa Question from Hittite Vassal and Royal Correspondence," *Jaarbericht Ex Oriente Lux* 28: 33–79.
Sommer, F. (1932) *Die Ahhijava-Urkunden*. Munich.

3

The End of the Bronze Age and the Great Migrations

1600–1200	1200–900	900–750

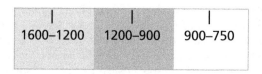

circa 1200	Sea Peoples; Mycenaean kingdoms fall
11th (?) and 10th centuries	Dorians enter Greece
11th and 10th centuries	Greeks settle eastern coast of Asia Minor

The Downfall of the Mycenaean Kingdoms

Around the turn of the thirteenth to the twelfth centuries BC, the palaces at Pylos and Knosos burned to the ground. The citadels at Mycene and Tiryns in the Argolis were also destroyed, and the same pattern of destruction is found elsewhere across Mycenaean Greece. Along with these palaces and citadels, the Mycenaean kingdoms, too, fell. So much is not in dispute. What remains in dispute is the cause of all this destruction. The archaeological evidence is limited to proving that the destruction occurred as well as how widespread it was: in most cases it is very difficult to tell the difference between destruction wrought by human agency and that wrought by an earthquake.

Earthquakes occur with distressing frequency in Greece (see chap. 1), and it is theoretically possible that a series of devastating earthquakes destroyed the

A History of Greece: 1300 to 30 BC, First Edition. Victor Parker.
© 2014 Victor Parker. Published 2014 by John Wiley & Sons, Ltd.

Mycenaean citadels and caused so much damage that the various states, unable
to cope with the refugees, the chaos, and the social upheaval, simply collapsed.
On the other hand, unless all the earthquakes in all those places occurred
simultaneously, one ought to find some trace of this posited social upheaval in
the texts of the yet unaffected kingdoms. If, for example, earthquakes on the
Peloponnese had already caused sufficient destruction and social upheaval to
destroy several states on the Peloponnese, but Pylos still stood untouched, then
one might expect to catch some glimpses of the situation in Pylos' archives.
Instead one sees bureaucrats calmly recording deeds and leases to property and
the dispositions for troops assigned to a watch along the coast. Now one might
suggest that Pylos was the first of the states to be destroyed by a severe earthquake; but in no kingdom does the archive give the impression of a world col-
lapsing just beyond the borders.

Surveying the Linear B archives also helps to dispose of another theory which
scholars have sometimes raised, whether in complete or partial explanation of
the Mycenaean kingdoms' destruction. This is the Aegean–Anatolian drought.
In the envisioned scenario the drought is so severe that the kingdoms have great
difficulty in feeding their burgeoning populations. The kings resort to warfare
with each other in an increasingly desperate attempt to acquire foodstuffs and,
effectively, destroy themselves as well as their kingdoms. Yet once again the
archives, from their respective kingdoms' final year, provide no evidence of any
such endemic, internecine warfare. Quite the contrary, one large-scale slaving
raid within the last generation of the Pylian kingdom is the only genuine act of
war attested in the evidence, however indirectly. Moreover, as far as the drought
itself is concerned, the flax harvest in Pylos was proceeding smoothly (Na-series).
Flax is a water-intensive crop; and the presence of such a crop strongly suggests
that there was no drought in Pylos during the kingdom's last year.

Another theory posits that internal instability within the kingdoms themselves led to their collapse. Yet if there is anything that the Linear B tablets show
us, it is placid stability. In any case the archaeological evidence demonstrates
that the destruction was not limited to the Mycenaean kingdoms – the Hittite
capital Hattusa was destroyed around this time and the Hittite kingdom disappeared; cities in Syria, in Palestine, and on Cyprus were also destroyed. It is
asking a lot to expect internal instability or social upheaval in every single place.
Internally, in any case, all seems in order in the Mycenaean kingdoms (as it
does in the Hittite kingdom – very little, if indeed anything at all, in the Hittite
texts suggests that the kingdom was on the verge of collapse circa 1200 BC).

If internally nothing was wrong with the Mycenaean (or Hittite) kingdoms,
was there an external threat? An Egyptian text from the eighth year of the
reign of Ramses III (1188 BC) suggests there may have been. According to
Ramses III invaders from the north attacked various lands in the eastern
Mediterranean:

No land could stand before their arms. From Hatti [i.e., the Hittite kingdom in
central Anatolia], *Kode* [i.e., roughly Cilicia], *Carchemish* [an inland town on the

Euphrates], *Arzawa* [a land in western Anatolia], *and Alashiya* [Cyprus] *on, being cut off at (one time). A camp (was set up) in one place in Amor* [Syria]. *They desolated its people and its land was like that which has never come into being. They were coming forward toward Egypt, while the flame was prepared before them.* (ANET, p. 262)

attack evidence

Ramses III's account finds independent corroboration in several essential respects. First, the archaeological evidence shows that all the places which Ramses III claims were devastated actually were devastated. Second, the attack on the island of Cyprus implies that the marauders were sea-borne; and this too is independently confirmed (see Boxes 3.1 and 3.2 for the evidence from contemporary letters from Cyprus, **Ugarit**, and the Hittite kingdom, all of which speak of sea-borne invaders in the eastern Mediterranean). In addition one of the reliefs which accompany Ramses III's inscription depict some of the invaders in ships (see Figure 3.1).

These so-called **Sea Peoples**, to give them their conventional name, were very real then; and not just Ramses III, but other rulers in the eastern Mediterranean, viewed them as highly dangerous. Where, however, did these Sea Peoples come from? If one plots on a map the places which Ramses III

Figure 3.1   Relief from Medinet Habu showing sea-borne invaders attacking Egypt.
Source: photo © Erich Lessing / akg-images

Box 3.1 *The Shikalaeans*

Ramses III mentions several peoples who attempted to invade Egypt. The name of one of them is written in the Egyptian consonantal script (so-called hieroglyphs) as *tkr*. The *t* represents the sound "ch" as in "church." The Egyptian script does not write vowels consistently or reliably, but fortunately in this case the vowels are known, thanks to a remarkable Akkadian-language text discovered in Ugarit, a Phoenician city-state which at the time was a (sub)vassal of the Hittites:

> *Thus (speaks) My Sun, the Great King* [i.e., the Hittite king, Suppiluliumas II]: *Speak to the City Prefect! The King (who's with you), your Lord, is young. He knows nothing. But I, My Sun, have given him an assignment with regard to (the man) Lunadusu, whom the Shikalaeans captured, (the ones) that dwell on ships. Now, Nisahili – (he's been) with me –, the groom, I've sent to you. You, however, shall send me Lunadushu, whom the Shikalaeans captured. I will interrogate him concerning the matter with (the Land) Shikalaea.* (M. Dietrich and O. Leretz [1979], *Ugaritforschungen* X, p. 55)

The author of the letter is Suppiluliumas II, the king of the Hittites; "My Sun" is an honorific title roughly equivalent to "My Majesty" or the like. "Speak to the City Prefect!" corresponds roughly to a modern salutation at the start of a letter; literally it is a command to the clay tablet to deliver the message inscribed on it to the addressee. The letter, incidentally, shows how little confidence Suppiluliumas II reposed in this particular vassal king – actually a vassal directly of the King of Cyprus who was himself a vassal of the Hittite king.

Suppiluliumas II thinks that Lunadushu, whom the Shikalaeans had captured, but who has since gone free, has information on these people. For this reason he wishes to question Lunadushu. As soon as the text was published, it was immediately seen that the "Shikalaeans" were identical with the *tkr* of Ramses III's text. There is no way to write the sound "ch" in Akkadian cuneiform, so the Hittite scribes took the nearest equivalent, the sound "sh." Finally, the Egyptian script does not distinguish between the sounds "r" and "l" – the "r" in *tkr* can represent either sound.

Now Suppiluliumas describes the Shikalaeans as living "on ships" – i.e., as seaborne. Moreover, their capture of Lunadushu shows that they were raiders of some sort; and Suppiluliumas' desire to have Lunadushu sent to him for debriefing in the Hittite capital shows how seriously Suppiluliumas was taking the threat which the Shikalaeans posed.

The Shikalaeans later settled in the town of Dor, just south of Mt. Carmel on the Palestinian coast. An Egyptian official, Wen-Amun, whom Ramses XII had sent on a mission to Phoenicia in the eleventh century BC, traveled through Dor and mentioned them in his later report to the Pharaoh (Breasted, Vol. IV, Nr. 565).

mentions (even if he himself does not put them in order), then one sees a path which begins in the west with Arzawa, moves eastwards till Carchemish in Syria, and then southwards to the borders of Egypt. One could extrapolate backwards from this trajectory and posit that the Sea Peoples came from some place farther to the west of Arzawa.

Next there is the evidence from the names of the individual Sea Peoples. Ramses III goes on to name five invading peoples, three of whom can convincingly be identified: the **Philistines** who eventually settled in the southwestern corner of Palestine (which the Greeks later named after them); the **Shikalaeans** who settled in the town of Dor just south of Mt. Carmel on the Palestinian Coast (see Box 3.1); and the **Dananaeans** who settled in Adana in what later became Cilicia. The name of the Philistines alone can be analysed. In Greek they are called *Palaistinoi*. This is a so-called ethnicon or noun derived from a place-name – like "New Yorkers" from the place called "New York." In Greek *Palaistinoi* means (and can only mean) "the people from the place called *Palaist-*." Such a town (Palaiste) lies in Illyria, on the Adriatic Sea to the northwest of Greece. If the *Palaistinoi* were to get by sea from Illyria to Palestine, then they must have passed by the Aegean. The other Sea Peoples may have had different points of origin from that of the *Palaistinoi* – it commonly happened that peoples on the move like this joined up with others also on the move at the same time (e.g., the Cimbri and the Teutones in the second century BC.)

Third, according to five texts from the Linear B archive at Pylos (An 519, 654, 656, 657, and 661 – on this "series," see Box 2.1), the Pylian kingdom in its final year assigned military units to watch its coastline – as though the kingdom viewed a sea-borne attack as a possibility. Fourth, according to several passages in the Old Testament (e.g., Amos IX 7 and Jer. XLVII 4), the Philistines, before they arrived in Palestine, had dwelt on Crete, an island home to another Mycenaean kingdom destroyed around 1200 BC. That is to say, evidence places the Philistines at the scene of the crime, as it were. Additionally, according to Ramses III, the Philistines aided in the destruction of one state in the eastern Aegean (Arzawa) as well as in that of Cyprus before attacking Egypt and settling in Palestine. So in nearby regions they engaged in the very same activity of which they stand accused on Crete and in mainland Greece.

The evidence supporting the theory that the Sea Peoples caused the destruction of the Mycenaean kingdoms may be circumstantial, but cumulatively is not easily refutable. So, in brief, around 1200 BC violent sea-borne raiders, some of whom came from Illyria, caused the destruction of many states and cities in the northeastern Mediterranean; and they also destroyed the Mycenaean kingdoms.

The Arrival of New Peoples after the Catastrophe

These sea-borne invaders did not settle in Greece. As so often happens when peoples like this are on the move, they burned, pillaged, and left. They did settle

Box 3.2 *The Alasiya-Correspondence*

More about the disturbances caused by sea-borne raiders in the eastern Mediterranean emerges from a series of letters between Ugarit and Cyprus circa 1200 BC. The letters more or less speak for themselves and can be quoted with minimal commentary; a few polite, but essentially immaterial phrases have here been omitted:

Ras Shamra L 1 (Letter of the King of Cyprus to his vassal the King of Ugarit)
Thus (speaks) the King: Speak to Hammurabi, the King of Ugarit! . . . Concerns what you wrote: "They have seen enemy ships on the seas." Well, if they really have seen ships, then you should arm yourself as best you can. Now your own troops and ships – where are they? Are they not with you? Some enemy or other will be attacking you from the west. Surround your cities with walls! Bring troops and chariots within them! Wait on the enemy! In this way you will be as strong as possible.

(N.b. that the King of Cyprus quotes from an earlier letter from the King of Ugarit to him; note also that they are speaking of sea-borne invaders.)

Ras Shamra 20.238 (Letter of the King of Ugarit to his overlord the King of Cyprus)
To the King of Cyprus, my father, speak! Thus (speaks) the King of Ugarit, your son: . . . My father, enemy ships have now come. The enemy have burnt my cities with fire and done terrible things in the land. Doesn't my father know that all of my master's, my father's, troops (i.e., the King of Ugarit is politely avoiding saying "my troops"), are in the land of Hatti (i.e., the Hittite kingdom)? And that all my ships are in the land of Lycia? They have not yet come back. Thus, ~~defenseless~~ *the land here lies (bare). May my father know of this thing. Just now (it has been) seven enemy ships which came. They've done terrible things to us! From now on, when enemy ships appear, would you tell me about it, so that I will be informed?*

(N.b. that a vassal always addresses his overlord as "my father" – this is a polite address, not an acknowledgment of paternity. Note again the emphasis on sea-borne invaders, their raids, as well as the Hittite king's transfer of Ugarit's fleet to the Lycian coast.)

Ras Shamra 20.18 (Letter of an official on Cyprus to the King of Ugarit)
Thus (speaks) Eshuwara, the Commandant of Cyprus: Speak to the King of Ugarit! . . . Concerns the matter of how the enemy did unto those citizens of your land as well as to your ships the following: they carried out a surprise attack

(Continued)

against those citizens of your land. But do not complain to me! And now the 20 ships, which the enemy have not carried into the mountains, are not taking up positions. Instead, they have hastily gone away; and we do not know where they are. For your information, for your protection I have written to you. May you realize this!

Note here that the sea-borne invaders, like the Vikings in a later age, were perfectly capable of pulling their ships up onto land and proceeding on foot. It was not just sea-borne attacks. This explains why the Hittites summoned land troops from Ugarit (as in the second letter) and how the sea-borne raiders could devastate cities like Carchemish (according to Ramses III) which lay well inland. The reliefs which accompany Ramses III's inscriptions on the invasion actually show the invaders with ox-drawn carts carrying wives and children: an entire people was on the move (J.B. Pritchard, *The Ancient Near East*, II [Princeton, 1975], fig. 44).

rebuild & instant decline

later on, only it was along the coast of the eastern Mediterranean (at least in the three clear cases). In Greece the survivors of the catastrophe were left to rebuild. In those regions of Greece where there is good archaeological evidence, the number of settlements drops sharply from the thirteenth century BC to the twelfth and eleventh. The drastic reduction in the population of Greece provides a testament to the Mycenaean kingdoms' long-term success at maintaining prosperity: without these kingdoms to manage affairs, the steep decline set in. The same holds for the material culture of the survivors. In the Mycenaean period many luxury goods – including items in precious metal – are attested both in the archaeological record (see Figures 2.4 and 2.9) and in the texts. In the period immediately after the catastrophe there are almost no metal objects of any kind in the archaeological record – to say nothing of objects in precious metal.

new peoples settle in Greece

e.g. Dorians

The sharp reduction in population as well as the absence of powerful states capable of keeping intruders out opened the way for new peoples to enter Greece. The most successful of the newcomers were the **Dorians**. They were already in existence in the thirteenth century since the Linear B tablets mention a man called *Dorieus* – i.e., "Dorian" – in the Kingdom of Pylos (Fn 867). Whether this was a genuine name (in much the same way as "Scott" today is a genuine name, rather than an ethnicon for someone from Scotland as it originally was) or still an ethnicon (that is to say, whatever the man's real name was, people just called him "that Dorian fellow"), there is no way of telling. But the name does show that Dorians had some sort of contact with the Mycenaean kingdoms already in the thirteenth century BC.

linguistic evidence

The positive evidence for the entrance of Dorians into the former territory of the Mycenaean kingdoms is linguistic, not archaeological. Although Dorians and Mycenaeans were both Greeks, they spoke different dialects of Greek. In the thirteenth century BC, people wrote (and presumably spoke) Mycenaean Greek on the Peloponnese and Crete; people were speaking and writing Doric Greek in those same places a few centuries later. Doric Greek was a conservative dialect. Among other things it preserved original Greek /ti/ whereas Mycenaean Greek was a progressive dialect in which original Greek /ti/ had already, by **assibilation,** become /si/. Since Doric Greek could not possibly have developed from Mycenaean Greek, Dorians must have immigrated onto Crete and the Peloponnese after the thirteenth century.

Thus far there is no positive archaeological evidence for the entrance of any new peoples into Greece in the period in question. Either the Dorians adopted the material culture of the pre-Dorians on the Peloponnese (and thus remain invisible in the material record) or unambiguous evidence for the former's presence has yet to be found. The archaeological evidence does, however, help suggest a date for the immigration of the Dorians. Two of the most important Dorian cities on the Peloponnese were Corinth and Sparta. Both are new, post-Mycenaean foundations; and both were founded in the second half of the tenth century BC. This suggests that some Dorians, at least in the period 950–900 BC, were settling the areas in which they would thereafter live. The other major Dorian city on the Peloponnese was Argos, but since it was continuously inhabited from Mycenaean times on down, it is impossible to determine at what point in time the Dorians settled there. Another major area of Dorian settlement was the Dodecanese in the southeast Aegean. The two major islands here, Cos and Rhodes, were inhabited in Mycenaean times, but largely deserted in the period immediately following. In the tenth century these islands were resettled, evidently by Dorians. All in all, the evidence suggests that some Dorians were settling the regions which in later times would be theirs around the tenth century BC.

The conventional name for the entrance of the Dorians onto the Peloponnese and elsewhere is the **Dorian Invasion.** This term misleads since the process involved may largely have been peaceful; and other terms such as "Dorian Migration" are not obviously better since many groups of Dorians may have participated in a series of spurts and bursts rather than in one large migration. All the same the positive linguistic evidence simply admits of no other explanation than the entrance of newcomers, however one chooses to imagine the process.

The Dorians, however, did not enter into completely unpopulated lands. Argos, to take one example, had remained settled from Mycenaean times but became "Dorianized" at some point and a glimpse of the process is visible in its tribal structure. The population of a Greek state was usually divided into **tribes.** In almost all Dorian states there still exist traces of the presence of three tribes: **Hylleis, Dymanes,** and **Pamphyli.** In Sparta this system of three tribes was never altered; but in other states (such as Corinth) later tribal reforms sometimes replaced these tribes with new ones, and only a few relics allow one to deduce the original presence of Hylleis, Dymanes, and Pamphyli (in

Corinth's case, for example, the presence of a place called "the Hylleis' Harbor" in one of its colonies, namely Corcyra – Thuc., III 72; for the method, see chap. 5). In Argos there are the three tribes plus a fourth called Hyrnathii (IG IV 517, 600, 601, 602). One can easily imagine that the pre-Dorian inhabitants were ranged next to the Dorians in this fourth tribe. In Sicyon before the sixth century there stood next to the three Dorian tribes a fourth called Aegialeis (**Herodotus**, V 68) – presumably the same thing had occurred as in Argos. In neither case do the pre-Dorians seem to have suffered any discrimination: in Sicyon one member of the Aegialeis accompanied a sacral embassy to Delphi (i.e., served in a prestigious official capacity); and another member allegedly rose to high rank in the course of a successful military career (*BNJ* 105, Fr. 2 and Hdt. VI 126). In these cases the pre-Dorians were simply "Dorianized" and added to the ranks of the Dorians. The Dorians did not always extend this liberality to those whom they conquered (Sparta, notably, deviated from it: see chap. 6), but it does seem to have been deeply ingrained in the Dorians' traditions to accept into their ranks other peoples: the name of the third Dorian tribe, Pamphyli, means literally "people from all (sorts of) tribes" – i.e., it was a catch-all denomination for grouping together people of all manner of origin: the process of Dorianizing non-Dorians had started almost at the very beginning of the Dorians' existence. Finally, the one concrete effect of Dorianization which one can still see was linguistic: the pre-Dorians began speaking Doric Greek (instead of their original dialect of Greek).

The Dorians, however, were not the only newcomers to enter Greece during the so-called **Dark Age** after the downfall of the Mycenaean kingdoms. Along the northern rim of the Peloponnese dwelled in classical times a people called the *Achaïoi* (i.e., Achaians); the region was called *Achaïa* after them. However, another people called *Achaïoi* had settled in another region called *Achaïa* in southeastern Thessaly. This type of settlement pattern – when splinters of the identical people end up in two widely separated regions – arises when a people migrates either at two distinct times (and takes two distinct paths) or when a people splits up at a cross-roads in the course of one migration. In this case, one group of *Achaïoi* wandered southwards along the Pindus Range and onto the Peloponnese while another group of *Achaïoi* crossed the Pindus from west to east and ended up in southeastern Thessaly (see chap. 1).

Migrations Eastward across the Aegean

Another series of population movements brought Greeks to the western coast of Asia Minor. The Hittite texts give a clear picture of the peoples settled in western Asia Minor in the fourteenth and thirteenth centuries, and with the important exception of the Mycenaean outpost of Millawanda, which the Hittites reconquered anyway (see Box 2.4), there was no large-scale Greek settlement there in the Late Bronze Age.

By **archaic** and **classical** times (i.e., from the eighth century BC onwards) this had all changed. By then there lived on the western coast of Asia Minor in the south Dorian Greeks (living in a region called Doris); in the center were **Ionian** Greeks (living in a region called Ionia); and in the north **Aeolian** Greeks (living in a region called Aeolis). In each case, directly opposite the region in Asia Minor, one finds the point of departure for the settlers. Thus, in northern Greece, directly opposite the Aeolis in Asia Minor, lies the Pelasgiotis in Thessaly. In the Pelasgiotis, an **Aeolic** dialect was spoken. In other words speakers of an Aeolic dialect crossed the Aegean from west to east and arrived in northeastern Asia Minor (including the large island of Lesbos just off the coast).

Likewise with Ionia and the Doris. Speakers of an **Ionic** dialect immigrated into the central part of western Asia Minor. Directly opposite Ionia (which includes the large islands of Chios and Samos just off the coast) lie Athens and the island of Euboea where more speakers of an Ionic dialect dwelled. In this case many of the islands (the northern and central Cyclades) which lie between Athens and Euboea on the one hand and Ionia on the other were also settled by speakers of an Ionic dialect.

Meanwhile speakers of a **Doric** dialect immigrated into the southwest of Asia Minor. Directly opposite the Doris (which includes the archipelago called the Dodecanese just off the coast) lie regions in the Peloponnese where Doric was spoken; and, once again, some of the islands (the southern Cyclades and Crete) between the Doris and the Doric regions in mainland Greece were inhabited by other speakers of a Doric dialect.

In brief, the basic outline of the migrations eastwards across the Aegean is not in dispute though the details remain obscure. Interestingly, the settlers who came to Asia Minor were keenly aware of their (even if mostly idealized) status as members of one "tribe" (whether Aeolians, Ionians, or Dorians). The names of the settled regions reflect this (see Box 1.3) as do various other aspects of the settlement. The Ionians settled – at least officially – in twelve cities which formed a **League** which held at the so-called Panionium, a communal sanctuary, an annual League **Assembly** at which League officials such as the (in classical times essentially powerless) "King of the Ionians" were selected (Hdt. I 142 and 148; for the tribal king, see, e.g., *OGIS* 489). The Dorians in the Doris settled in six cities (i.e., instead of the full dozen, a half-dozen) which also held annual assemblies at a communal sanctuary (Hdt. I 144). The Aeolians on the mainland had twelve cities too (Hdt. I 149) and those on the island of Lesbos had six (once again a half-dozen instead of the full dozen) (Hdt. I 151). Strictly speaking it is unknown if the Aeolians also had arrangements for common assemblies, but Herodotus does mention a treaty between the "Ionians" and the "Aeolians" of the mainland as though the Aeolians there too had some organ of government which could conclude treaties on behalf of all their cities (Hdt. I 151).

Moreover, the pattern of the dozen or half-dozen is often repeated in such tribal organizations. The Achaians, for example, a League on the northern rim of the Peloponnese, also settled in precisely twelve cities (Hdt. I 145); the Pylaean Amphictiony, centered on the pass at Thermopylae, was a supratribal League which consisted of precisely twelve tribes (see also chap. 18). (If one looks beyond Greece, there is to the west the Etruscan League which consisted of precisely twelve cities; and to the east dwelled the Israelites who were made up of precisely twelve tribes; also the Ishmaelites [Gen. XXV 13–16] and various others.) Important was the even dozen; but the occasional variation on it also exists such as the half-dozen in the Doris of Asia Minor.

Conclusion

A large number of migrations took place in Greece in the centuries after the destruction of the Mycenaean Kingdoms at the hands of the so-called "sea peoples" around the turn of the thirteenth to the twelfth century BC. These migrations determined the ethnic make-up of Greece in the archaic and classical periods. The migrations took place in a dim inter-historical period – between the reasonably well-illuminated Mycenaean period (roughly the thirteenth century BC on the one hand and the so-called Archaic period which runs from roughly the eighth to the early fifth century BC on the other. The Dorians' migration(s) probably took place, at least in part, in the tenth century BC. The other migrations clearly took place in roughly the same period (eleventh to tenth centuries).

Mycenaean descendents It remains to say a word about the descendants of the Mycenaeans. Many were Dorianized in the course of the migrations, but some of them, organized as a tribe, retreated into the mountains of Arcadia in the central Peloponnese. The Arcadian dialect of Greek was, with some minor qualifications, a descendant of the Mycenaean dialect. This dialect was spoken also on the island of Cyprus in the eastern Mediterranean, so some survivors of the catastrophe fled to that island (which Myceanaean traders had been visiting for some time previous to the catastrophe anyway). Today scholars commonly speak of an **Arcado-Cyprian** dialect.

QUESTIONS FOR REVIEW

1 What is the evidence that the so-called Sea Peoples actually were sea-borne?
2 What points in Ramses III's claims about the Sea Peoples are corroborated by independent evidence?
3 Why are terms such as "invasion" or "migration" problematic for describing the entrance of new peoples into Greece?
4 What makes the Greeks' settlement of the western coast of Asia Minor traceable in outline (even if no details are recoverable)?

QUESTION FOR FURTHER STUDY

What could be known about the so-called Sea Peoples before the publication of the text on the Shikalaeans (Box 3.1), in 1979? How did the publication of that text improve the state of knowledge about the Sea Peoples?

FURTHER READING

The best work on the Sea Peoples is in German:
Lehmann, G.A. (1996) "Umbrüche und Zäsuren im östlichen Mittelmeerraum und Vorderasien zur Zeit der "Seevölker"-Invasionen um und nach 1200 v. Chr. Neue Quellenzeugnisse und Befunde," *Historische Zeitschrift* 262: 1–38.

In English, however, see:
Dothan, T., and M. Dothan. (1992) *People of the Sea: The Search for the Philistines*. New York. (The chief focus is on the Philistines after their arrival in Palestine.)
Drews, R. (1993) *The End of the Bronze Age: Changes in Warfare and the Catastrophe circa 1200 B.C.* Princeton.
Sandars, N.K. (1978) *The Sea Peoples: Warriors of the Ancient Mediterranean, 1250–1150 B.C.* London.

For a survey of the material culture of Greece in the so-called "Dark Age," see:
Desborough, V.R.d'A. (1952) *Protogeometric Pottery*. Oxford.
Desborough, V.R.d'A. (1964) *The Last Mycenaeans and their Successors*. Oxford.
Lemos, I. S. (2002) *The Protogeometric Aegean. The Archaeology of the Late Eleventh and Tenth Centuries B.C.* Oxford.

In regard to the migrations of new peoples into Greece and across the Aegean, it is difficult to recommend anything, let alone something in English.

For the date of the so-called Dorian Invasion, as well as a brief discussion of the linguistic evidence for the entrance of the Dorians, see:
Parker, V. (1995) "Zur Datierung der Dorischen Wanderung," *Museum Helveticum* 52: 130–154.

On the Ionians' migration(s) to Ionia, see:
Sakellariou, M.B. (1958) *La migration grecque en Ionie*. Athens.

4

Greece in the Later "Dark Age" (circa 900–750 BC)

1200–900	900–750	750–600

throughout	*Poleis* arising in Greece
10th century? or later?	Alphabet introduced
in particular in the 8th century	Kingship under threat
steadily throughout 8th century	Material prosperity increases
increasingly in 8th century	Rapid population growth

Evidence and Methodology

The great migrations had brought new peoples into Greece and had expanded the area of Greek civilization. Greek cities dotted the Aegean coastline of Anatolia. Deserted regions such as the Dodecanese were resettled. However, the kingdoms of Pylos, Thebes, and Knosos were no more; and with their glittering courts much had perished. Among other things, in mainland Greece and on Crete literacy ceased: no one remembered anymore how to write in Linear B. In the absence of written documents, it is difficult to provide an historical narrative in any but the broadest terms, and the period is conventionally termed a "Dark Age."

A History of Greece: 1300 to 30 BC, First Edition. Victor Parker.
© 2014 Victor Parker. Published 2014 by John Wiley & Sons, Ltd.

The evidence for historical developments during this period is of a radically different nature from that for the previous two chapters. For the Mycenaean period itself there are the Linear B documents; and various documents from the Near East help to illuminate the downfall of the Mycenaean kingdoms. The great migrations ultimately left such an indelible impression on the Greek landscape that they too can still be described.

But when times become more settled, the absence of a written tradition makes itself felt more keenly. Several avenues of exploration remain open, however. First, one can extrapolate forwards from what is known of the Mycenaean Age and at the same time extrapolate backwards from what is known of the archaic and classical periods. Occasionally, one can make the two lines "meet" and thus cast some light on the period in between. Second, there is still the archaeological evidence. Unfortunately, given the decline in material prosperity after the downfall of the Mycenaean kingdoms, it is patchy and therefore often inconclusive, especially during the earlier part of the "Dark Age." The site of **Lefkandi** on Euboea (see below) makes an exception, however, and as time goes by, the archaeological evidence does become steadily more plentiful as material prosperity picks up again.

Third, even if the glittering courts of the Mycenaean kingdoms perished, one art which they fostered remained: the recitation of epic and **lyric** poetry. People still enjoyed hearing songs in the old style. Moreover, Greek epic poetry as it has come down to us took the adventures of the Mycenaean kings as its subject matter – perhaps precisely because of people's nostalgia for the olden days, when a mighty king yet sat upon a gilded throne in the hall of yonder high palace. The epic poets composed in a highly archaic form of Greek which owes much of its vocabulary to Mycenaean Greek. Many words in Greek epic (and lyric) poetry are attested in Linear B texts, but not elsewhere. The *Iliad* and *Odyssey*, as they exist today, represent the final product of these compositions. While the stories are set in the Mycenaean Age, inevitably they reflect the conditions of the poets' own day. Since later poets continually reworked the older material, the poems, as they now stand, in fact reflect best the conditions of the last poets' age – roughly the eighth century BC or, in the case of the *Odyssey*, a little later (see Box 4.2). The epic poems, therefore, are at their most useful in reconstructing conditions at the very end of the Dark Age.

Political Developments

During the Mycenaean period, officials known as *wanaktes* or "kings" ruled over large states (see chap. 2). Beneath the *wanax* stood a large number of other functionaries, one of whom bore the title *gwasileus*. This official, while clearly not the king himself, often functioned as the leader of a group (Jn 431, 601, and 845). He was commonly wealthy (Jo 438), and his office may have been hereditary (Jn 431). The later Greek form of this word was *basileus*. This was the generic word for "king" in classical Greek; and one can easily imagine a situation in which, when the Mycenaean kingdoms crumbled under the onslaught of sea-borne invaders, local leaders became responsible for rallying the survivors in the aftermath of the catastrophe. These local leaders may often enough have been the *gwasilewes*.

According to the Greeks' own traditions, in the preclassical period their communities had stood under the rule of "kings." The Greeks were correct in this view. First, in some regions of the Greek world kings continued to rule well into the classical period: Sparta, Argos, and Thessaly. The same applies to outlying regions of the Greek world such as Cyprus and the seventh-century colony of Cyrene in North Africa. In fact, the presence of a king in Cyrene attests to the presence of a king in Cyrene's mother-city in Greece, Thera, at the time of Cyrene's foundation (for the methodological basis of this argument see chap. 5). Second, many cities in Greece in which no king ruled during the classical period still had a minor official with the title "king" – without, however, having any of the political functions which one naturally associates with kings. One of the functions of this minor official was to carry out specific sacrifices on behalf of the community ([**Aristotle**], *Ath.Pol.* 57 – with regard to the Athenian **archon basileus** or **King Archon**). Conventionally, this is explained as follows: Custom or unwritten law prescribed that the "king" should make such sacrifices on behalf of the community. Even after the "king" had lost his political role, these sacrifices were still required. The community compromised: it arranged for a minor official to bear the title "king," let him carry out the sacrifices, and thus preserved the letter of the law if not its spirit. One can see the process of the replacement of a genuine king by an annually selected "king in name only" in Argos. As late as 480 Argos stood under the rule of a genuine king (Hdt. VII 149). But by the mid-fifth century the "king" in Argos is an annual functionary who merely bears the title (*GHI* 42, B 43–44 – the dating formula).

Moreover, many stories (granted with varying degrees of credibility) about the downfall of individual kings circulated in later times.[1] These stories in remarkably uniform fashion speak of kings slain and deposed by angry subjects. Next, there are many scenes from Greek epic – depicting life, in general, during the poets' own day, roughly the eighth century BC – in which aristocrats challenge the power of the king. The most spectacular of such scenes comes at the beginning of the *Iliad* when Achilles angrily confronts Agamemnon. Finally, it seems credible *a priori* that the kings should have fought to retain their power rather than meekly giving it up.

To provide a brief methodological summing up at this juncture: The basic method used here is that of attempting to work forwards from what is known of the Mycenaean world (there exist local officials called *gwasilewes*) and then to work backwards from what is known of Greece during the archaic and classical periods (*basileis* are ruling or have ruled in many states). The point of linkage is when local Mycenaean officials such as the *gwasilewes* become the leaders of communities after the catastrophe which destroyed the Mycenaean kingdoms. These *gwasilewes* – or in the later form of the word: *basileis* – continued to rule in a few classical states, but in most of them eventually lost genuine political power, with their title only surviving as that of a minor functionary. In most cases the *basileis* yielded political power after a violent struggle with aristocrats. To underscore, then, the historical conclusion: During the period under discussion, most Greek communities stood under the rule of "kings" whose powers and position within the community, as time wore on, met with increasing challenges.

The Rise of the *Polis*

During the Mycenaean period Greece was divided up into several kingdoms. By the sixth and fifth centuries, however, the more developed regions – central Greece, the eastern Peloponnese, the Aegean islands, and the coast of Asia Minor – are dominated by so-called *poleis* or "city-states." In the less developed regions, especially northern and western Greece, there are so-called *ethne* or "tribe-states" or "league-states." (For working definitions of both, see box 4.1.) The tribe states are the less complicated since they clearly existed even before the rise of the Mycenaean kingdoms and continued to exist on the periphery of the latter. In the Linear B texts tribes appear sporadically as personal appellations (e.g., *Paphlagon*, "the Paphlagonian," in Jn 845), as toponyms derived from the names of tribes (e.g., *Akhaiwia*, in C 914 – named after the tribe of the *Akhaiwoi*), and, as relics of an earlier state of affairs, in the names of possibly specialized military units within the Pylian army (e.g., *Iwas(s)oi* on An 519). The *poleis*, however, are a new development and require explanation.

First, *poleis* are not unique to Greece. Many existed in Asia Minor, already in the Mycenaean period. In Lycia the Hittite texts (e.g., the Tawagalawas Letter – Sommer, 2–4) routinely speak of individual cities (as opposed to large states under kings in Arzawa, Mira, and Seha-River-Land farther to the north). In Lycia (**Strabo**, XIV 3,2–3, Pp. 664–665) and Caria (Hdt. V 118) city-states continued to exist down into the classical period. The presence of a "model" nearby may have encouraged the development of the *polis* among the Greeks, especially among those who settled along the coast of Asia Minor. Very occasionally one can see a *polis* arising in the classical period by copying its neighbors: a few years after 480 BC the Eleans (in the northwestern corner of the Peloponnese) decided to reorganize their community as a *polis*. They built a centrally located town and moved people into it (**Diodorus**, XI 54). This process is known as **synoecism**. Many *poleis* may have arisen in this way, though, strictly speaking, this way of explaining the rise of *poleis* posits the existence of neighboring, pre-existing *poleis*: it requires the presence of models (which may well have existed outside of the Greek world).

Second, within the Mycenaean kingdoms there existed structures which on the surface at least bear a certain resemblance to the classical *polis*. In the Kingdom of Pylos, which was divided into two provinces, these provinces were themselves divided into districts (see chap. 2). These districts are usually named after the chief town within them. In each town stood a functioning

Box 4.1   Poleis *and* Ethne

Poleis (city-states) and *ethne* (league- or tribe-states) were on the Greeks' own analysis the two forms which a Greek state could take. The table below gives a practical working definition for each type of state:

Polis	Ethnos
1 tends to be small	1 tends to be large
2 tends to have one large urban center	2 tends to have several towns on its territory, none of which is the chief city
3 the people are named after the one urban center	3 the territory is named after the people
4 all organs of government tend to be in the one urban center	4 institutions for managing day-to-day affairs are in the various towns; but affairs affecting the entire tribe are dealt with at a tribal assembly which meets annually or as needed at a centrally located sanctuary[2]

When the two types of states have dealings with one another at the diplomatic level no practical distinction exists between them. This can be seen in the superscripts to various treaties as well as in the equal reciprocal clauses in the treaty's body. Here several superscripts:

"an alliance between the Boeotians (an *ethnos) and the Athenians* (a *polis) for all time"* (SVA 223)

"an alliance between the Athenians (a *polis) and the Locrians* (an *ethnos) for all time"* (SVA 224)

"an alliance between the Corcyraeans and the Athenians (both *poleis) for all time"* (SVA 263)

As one can see, *polis* and *ethnos* are treated exactly alike in these superscripts; and likewise the clauses of the treaty themselves make no distinction between the two types of state.

administrative apparatus (one tablet, Jn 829, has a list of various officials present in a district, including a "district administrator" and a "deputy district administrator"). Moreover, especially in comparison to the large Mycenaean kingdoms, the districts – self-contained administrative units, usually named after their chief town (cf. Box 4.1 for the practical closeness of this to the *polis*) – were of about the same size as most classical *poleis*. One can imagine a situation in which, when the Mycenaean kingdoms were destroyed, some of these districts survived. In other words, it is possible, once again, to draw a line forwards from the thirteenth century as well as one backwards from the classical period, such that the two lines meet.

Third, *poleis* occasionally arose in the classical period through the dissolution of older *ethne* or "tribe-states." In a tribe-state one often finds several towns, none of which, however, was markedly larger than the others. However, each town usually had some form of government for regulating the townspeople's day-to-day affairs – see, for example, the compact between two towns from the *ethnos* of the West Locrians (Fornara, Nr. 87). If the tribe-state and its institutions over time became less and less relevant (and concurrently the individual towns were regulating their own affairs more and more) such that at the end the tribe-state for practical purposes ceased to exist, then what remained were the individual towns – indistinguishable from *poleis*. This happened on several occasions: In the mid-fourth century BC, the *ethnos* of the Achaians (on the northern coast of the Peloponnese) still existed (SEG XIV 375), but soon thereafter apparently fell apart (**Polybius**, II 41). The twelve towns which had made up the *ethnos* then emerged as *poleis* in their own right. On another occasion the Lacedaemonians forced the *ethnos* of the Boeotians to dissolve itself in 386 BC. In the place of the old *ethnos*, towns such as Thespiae became fully fledged *poleis* (see chap. 15). On a number of other occasions (for example, in Asia Minor with the settlements in the Aeolis, in Ionia, and in the Doris) similar processes probably took place even if the precise details are irrecoverable.

The development of the *polis*, then, was complex; and a number of developments probably converged to produce a world of scores of often quite tiny *poleis*. That world already dominates, incidentally, in the epic poems the *Iliad* and the *Odyssey* (see Box 4.2).

Contact with the Near East

In this period increased contacts with the Near East (in the form of trade) begin to become apparent. The most obvious sign of this appears on the pottery: the **geometric** motifs (see Figure 4.1) of the tenth and ninth centuries give way in the course of the eighth to motifs taken from Near Eastern art – the new **orientalizing** pottery (see Figure 4.2). In addition, objects imported from the Near East reappear in archaeological sites from this period (e.g., at Lefkandi – see Popham 1980–1996 in Further Reading). These finds show that there was contact with the Near East in this period, but not whether it was direct or indirect.

Fortunately, a good argument exists to show not only that the contact was direct, but also that it had never broken off. For example, the Greeks called the region between Egypt and Phoenicia *Palaistīnē* – an adjectival derivation from the name of the people (*Palaistīnoi* – the biblical Philistines). The Greeks can only have named the region in question when the people in question were

Box 4.2   Poleis *and* Ethne *in "Homer"*

In the epic poems, *Iliad* and *Odyssey*, which tradition attributes to a single blind poet called Homer, there commonly exists a tension between the poets' aim to describe a bygone era and their day-to-day experience with a very different world, that of their own times. For example, the poets repeatedly speak of mighty palaces with hundreds of rooms, yet when they describe a ruler's residence concretely, they do so in the terms of a prosperous farmstead with one main room where guests roast their own meat over the hearth-fire and then, when night falls, stretch out on pelts and rugs laid down in that same room (for example, when Telemachus visits Menelaus at the beginning of Book IV of the *Odyssey*). For all that the poets wish to describe a grand and splendid palace, the ineluctable reality of their own day obtrudes itself whenever they have to speak concretely. A similar situation prevails when they speak of "states." Formally, the poets almost always speak of "tribes" – i.e., tribe-states, *ethne*. The tribe of the *Akhaiwoi* ("Achaians") in the *Iliad* is fighting against the tribe of the *Trōes* ("Trojans"); Odysseus on Ithaca governs the tribe of the *Kephallēnes*; on the fairy-tale island of Scheria dwells the tribe of the *Phaiakoi*. When, however, the poets describe these communities concretely, a different image emerges: the community on Scheria has all of its institutions in one central settlement (*Od.* VI 3sqq. and 255sqq.; see table in Box 4.1 to compare with a *polis*); a herald may summon the community on Ithaca for an assembly which can meet on the same day – that is to say, the community is so small that everyone works within a herald's call and can walk back into the town for an assembly later that day (*Od.*, II 6sqq. and VIII 4sqq.; see table in Box 4.1 to compare with a *polis*); finally, the entire *Iliad* deals with an assault on one single city: the state of the *Trōes* stands or falls with the continued resistance or defeat of one single city, Ilium – that is to say, the state is effectively imagined as having one single city (see table in Box 4.1 to compare with a *polis*).

In other words, as with the prosperous farmsteads, what the poets knew from their day-to-day experience, was life in a *polis*. The literary material with which they were working and which they were reshaping for their own purposes, however, spoke of tribes, of *ethne*. The poets, as they did elsewhere, remained true to the traditional material and continued to speak of *ethne*. But what they wanted to say often enough required them to speak concretely – to speak, say, of a summons to an assembly. So they described this process in the only way in which, in their day-to-day world, it occurred: a herald called to the people who had walked out to work in the fields lying about the town, and everyone finished up the task at hand and then walked back into town for the assembly. That reflects the reality not of the *ethnos* – with its large size and its once-a-year, special-event assembly – but rather that of the small *polis* with its one town and small territory.

Figure 4.1 Geometric pottery from Athens, eighth century BC. Source: photo ©
Ashmolean Museum, University of Oxford, UK / The Bridgeman Art Library

present in it; and the *Palaistīnoi* settled in this region during the twelfth century
BC (see chap. 3). Moreover, the name *Palaistīnē* can have arisen only at a time
when the Philistines were the most powerful people in the region and dominated
it. After the establishment of the Davidic kingdom in Israel in the early tenth
century BC, that was no longer the case; but before then the Philistines had
dominated the entire region, exerting full political control over at least the entire
coastal plain as well as its easternmost extension, the Jezreel Valley, which leads
into the interior (I Sam. XIII 3; n.b. there read "(boundary) marker" rather
than older translations' "garrison"). During that time only – i.e., between the
twelfth and tenth centuries – could the Greeks have begun to call the region
Palaistīnē. In other words, the Greeks were in contact with the Near East even
during the early Dark Age.

To come to another argument: During the Mycenaean period there was
much contact. According to the Linear B texts Cyprus, Egypt, and even Ethio-
pia to the south of Egypt were known to the Mycenaeans (Cn 719, Db 1105,
and Eb 156 respectively). Now the classical Greeks called these same lands by
the same names as their Mycenaean forebears. If one were to assume that the
Greeks during the Dark Age lost all contact with these lands, then it would

Figure 4.2 Orientalizing pottery from Corinth, late seventh century BC. – n.b. the lions and sphinxes, typical motifs borrowed from the Near East. Source: © Marie-Lan, http://commons.wikimedia.org/wiki/File:Olpe_sphinx_Louvre_Cp10475.jpg (accessed 14 January 2013)

surprise that when the Greeks allegedly rediscovered these lands sometime in, say, the eighth century BC, they applied to these lands the exact same names which had been in currency five centuries earlier. Of course, if contact never broke off entirely, then the situation requires no explanation: the Greeks in the Dark Age retained contact with those lands, continued to use the same names for them as the Mycenaean Greeks had; and so did the classical Greeks.

A third argument increases the scope of the contacts in question. *Palaistīnē* is a curious derivation from *Palaistīnoi* – it shows a very rare suffix, *-ē*. That suffix was no longer productive in archaic or classical Greek: that is to say, no name showing this suffix was or could ever have been coined during the archaic or classical periods. A name such as *Libyē* (i.e., Libya, derived from the people's name: *Libyes*) or *Phoinikē* (i.e., Phoenicia, derived from the people's name: *Phoinikes*) must have arisen before the archaic or classical periods – either during the Mycenaean period (in which case the name remained in use during the Dark Age and the same arguments apply as in the paragraph above) or during the Dark Age itself (in which case the same arguments apply as two paragraphs above).

What scholars have commonly spoken of as a renewal of contacts with the Near East during the eighth century, ought instead to be characterized as "reinvigoration" or "intensification": contact never broke off.

Introduction of the Alphabet

At some point during the Dark Age, as has slowly become clear, literacy arose anew in Greece. This time, however, it was not a syllabary, but rather an **alphabet**. The Greek alphabet, as scholars have long realized, is modeled on an alphabet used by the Phoenicians, a Semitic people. The names of some Greek letters reveal this Semitic origin clearly: the names "alpha," "beta," and "delta" are still easily recognizable as the Semitic words for "ox," "house," and "door." The particular alphabet which the Greeks used as a model for their own could originally indicate consonants only (and vowels either not at all or in no unambiguous way). The peculiar Greek innovation was to use certain signs in this Phoenician alphabet to write vowels only. Thus, the signs He and Yodh, used in Phoenician for the consonant sounds /h/ and /y/, in the Greeks' hands became the letters *e(psilon)* and *iota* – and were used for the vowel sounds /e/ and /i/. This idea of using specific signs both for vowels and for consonants was unique in the ancient Mediterranean and Near Eastern world.

Earlier scholarship commonly assumed that the Greeks adopted (and adapted) the Phoenician alphabet in the course of the eighth century. This was in line with the then prevailing view that there had been no contact between Greece and the Near East during the Dark Age. Recently, however, students of Phoenician epigraphy have been pointing out that the actual forms of the various letters in the Greek alphabet bear a far greater resemblance to the letter forms in currency among the Phoenicians during the ninth and tenth centuries. If one were to assume that no contact between Greece and Phoenicia existed during the Dark Age, then that would be an inexplicable situation indeed. If, however, contact did exist, then an explanation for this circumstance lies ready to hand; but the views of the Phoenician epigraphers have yet to win full acceptance among classicists.

Population Growth and Material Prosperity

In his book *Archaic Greece*, Antony Snodgrass collected data to show that the population in Attica and Argos in the eighth century BC was growing rapidly. The tables reproduced below (see Figure 4.3) are taken from him. If the data are taken at face value, then the population grew seven-fold within a century or so. Granted, as the tables show, what Snodgrass was counting were burial sites on the assumption that where there are more people, there are also more deaths. This assumption need not hold true – one might argue that Snodgrass' data mean that owing to disease, famine, or the like people in Attica and Argos were dying at a faster rate than previously.

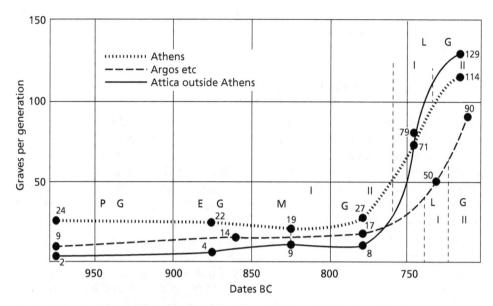

Figure 4.3   Population growth in Greece. Source: Reproduced with permission from Snodgrass, A.M. 1980. *Archaic Greece*. J.M. Dent & Sons, Ltd. Figure 4.4, p. 23

Fortunately, other considerations confirm Snodgrass' overall interpretation, notwithstanding occasional suggestions for refinement (e.g., Morris 1987: 57sqq.). First, it is during this period that Greek communities begin founding colonies throughout the Mediterranean (see chap. 5) – that is to say, there was, *a priori*, population to spare in mainland Greece. Concededly, this argument is to a degree circular since in the next chapter overpopulation will be alleged as the primary factor motivating colonization. Second, investigations on the Cycladic islands of Melos and Ceos have shown on the basis of other evidence (the increased number of settlements) that the population on those islands was indeed growing rapidly during the period in question (see Cherry 1982 in Further Reading). Third, continuing investigation of various regions in Greece such as Knosos on Crete or the southern Argolid has suggested rapid population growth in those regions (see Cavanagh 1996 and Langdon 1995 in Further Reading).

Along with this rapid growth in population – and probably allowing it to a degree – went an increase in material prosperity, especially as seen in the increasing number of metal objects. Below is the table from Snodgrass' book on the number of metal objects found at various sites in Greece (see Figure 4.4). The numbers from the eighth century stand in no proportion anymore to the paltry ones from the ninth, tenth, and eleventh centuries. In the eighth century material prosperity was returning to Greece in a way not seen since the fall of the Mycenaean kingdoms.

Finally, one site from Euboea, Lefkandi (on the eastern edge of the Lelantine Plain between Chalcis and Eretria), requires mention (see Popham 1980–1996

	Eleventh and tenth centuries BC	Ninth century	Eighth century	
Bronze figurines at Delphi	0	1	152	(1969)
Bronze tripods at Mount Ptoön (Boiotia)	0	0	7	(1971)
Bronze dedications on Delos	0	1	19	(1973)
Terracotta figurines at Olympia	10	21	837	(1972)

	Eleventh and tenth centuries BC	Ninth and early eighth	Later eighth and seventh	
Bronze fibulae at Philia (Thessaly)	0	2	1783+	(1975)
Bronze pins at Philia	1	4	37	(1975)
Bronze fibulae at Perachora	7	1	50+	(1940)
Bronze pins at Perachora	0	15	81	(1940)
Bronze fibulae at the Argive Heraion	16	10	88	(1905)
Bronze pins at the Argive Heraion	3	c. 250	c. 3070	(1905)
Bronze fibulae at Lindos (Rhodes)	0	52	1540	(1931)
Bronze pins at Lindos	0	0	42	(1931)

Figure 4.4 Metal objects in the Dark Age and early Archaic period. Source: Reproduced with permission from Snodgrass, A.M. 1980. *Archaic Greece*. J.M. Dent & Sons, Ltd., p. 53

in Further Reading). Here a large building, some 130 feet in length, has been excavated. It apparently dates from the tenth century BC and so far is unique in Greece for that period. The site produced a large number of spectacular finds (including one wealthy burial) out of proportion to anything else of similar date in Greece. Many finds also evinced evidence of contact with the Near East. If Lefkandi should prove truly unique, then the recovery of material prosperity began in Euboea and spread thence to the rest of Greece. However, continuing investigation may eventually discover fully comparable sites elsewhere in Greece.

NOTES

1   Miletus: Conon, *BNJ* 26, Fr. 1,44, and Nicolaus of Damascus, *BNJ* 90, Fr. 52; Corinth: Diod. VII, Fr. 9,6 (cf. Paus. II 4,4); Achaia: Pol. II 41,4–5.

2   Several examples of such assemblies at centrally located sanctuaries: The
     (Peloponnesian) Achaians held their assemblies at the sanctuary of Zeus
     Hamarius (IG V,2,344,8; IvonMagnesia, 39; Paus. VIII 13,2); the Aetolians
     at the Temple of Apollo in Thermon (Pol. IV 37,2; V 8,5–8 und 9,2; Strab.
     X 3,2, p. 463); the Boeotians at the temple of Athena Itonia at Coroneia
     (Strab. IX 2,29, p. 411). For an example of an enactment of such a tribal
     assembly, see *GHI* 20 (*ethnos* of the East Locrians).

QUESTIONS FOR REVIEW

1   What are some of the ways in which *poleis* may have arisen in Greece?
2   What is the evidence for contact with the Near East during the "Dark Age"?
3   How does one distinguish between a *polis* and an *ethnos*?
4   How does the world of the poets' own day intrude on the *Iliad* and the
    Odyssey?
5   What are the signs of reviving prosperity in Greece at the end of the "Dark
    Age"?

QUESTION FOR FURTHER STUDY

Some scholars have denied the existence of a "Homeric" society. Instead they
argue that the epics present a mishmash which cannot convincingly be set in
any one period of time. See Snodgrass (1974) in the Further Reading below.
Other scholars continue to argue that "Homer" portrays a coherent historical
society – see Adkins (1971) and Donlan (1985) in Further Reading. Which view
do you find more persuasive?

FURTHER READING

General (in particular for the archaeological evidence):
Coldstream, N.J. (2003) *Geometric Greece* (2nd edn.). London.
Snodgrass, A.M. (1980) *Archaic Greece: The Age of Experiment*. London.

On the site of Lefkandi:
Popham, M., et al. (1980–1996) *Lefkandi*, Vols. I–III. London.

Kingship:
Carlier, P. (1984) *La royauté en Grèce avant Alexandre*. Strasbourg. (The standard work,
     encyclopedic in scope.)

And in English:
Carlier, P. "Basileus." In: *Brill's New Pauly*, II, 517–523.

Drews, R. (1983) *Basileus. The Evidence for Kingship in Geometric Greece*. New Haven. (A brief treatment arguing that kings did not exist during the Dark Age.)

Contact with the Near East:
Burkert, W. (1992) *The Orientalizing Revolution. Near Eastern Influence on Greek Culture in the Early Archaic Age*. Cambridge, MA.

Homer, Society, and "States":
Adkins, A.W.H. (1971) "Homeric Values and Homeric Society," *Journal of Hellenic Studies* 91: 1–14.
Donlan, W. (1985) "The Social Groups of Dark Age Greece," *Classical Philology* 80: 293–308.
Donlan, W. (1989) "The Pre-State Community in Greece," *Symbolae Osloenses* 64: 5–29.
Finley, Sir M.I. (1954) *The World of Odysseus*. New York. (The "classic" discussion in English).
Gschnitzer, F. (1991) "Zur homerischen Staats- und Gesellschaftsordnung: Grundcharakter und geschichtliche Stellung." In: J. Latacz (ed.), *Colloquium Rauricum, II: Zweihundert Jahre Homerforschung*. Stuttgart. (=*Kleine Schriften zum griechischen und römischen Altertum*, Vol.I, 142–164. Stuttgart, 2001).
Raaflaub, K.A. (1998) "A Historian's Headache: How to Read 'Homeric Society'?" In: N.R.E. Fisher and H. van Wees (eds.), *Archaic Greece: New Evidence and New Approaches*, 169–193. London and Swansea.
Snodgrass, A.M. (1974) "An Historical Homeric Society?" *Journal of Hellenic Studies* 94: 114–125.

Polis:
Hansen, M.H. (2006) *Polis: An Introduction to the Ancient Greek City-State*. Oxford.
Mitchell, L., and P.J. Rhodes (eds.). (1997) *The Development of the Polis in Archaic Greece*. London.
Raaflaub, K.A. (2001) "Zwischen Ost und West: Phönizische Einflüsse auf die griechische Polisbildung?" In: R. Rollinger and Chr. Ulf (eds.), *Griechische Archaik und der Orient: Interne und externe Impulse*, 271–290. Berlin. (Critical of the idea that the development of the Greek polis was due to external influence.)
Sakellariou, M.B. (1989) *The Polis-State: Definition and Origin*. Paris.

Alphabet:
Jeffery, L.H. (1990) *The Local Scripts of Archaic Greece*. Oxford. (Rev. edn. with a supplement by A.W. Johnston.)
Sass, B. (1991) *Studia Alphabetica: On the Origin and Early History of the Northwest Semitic, South Semitic, and Greek Alphabets*. Fribourg/Göttingen.

Population Growth:
Cavanagh, W.G. (1996) "The Burial Customs." In: J.N. Coldstream and H.W. Catling (eds.), *Knossos North Cemetery: Early Greek Tombs*, 651–675. London.
Cherry, J. (1982) "A Preliminary Definition of Site Distribution on Melos." In: C. Renfrew and M. Wagstaff (eds.), *An Island Polity*, 10–23. Cambridge.

Cherry, J., et al. (1991) *Landscape Archaeology as Long-Term History: Northern Keos in the Cycladic Islands*, 245–248 and 328–337. Los Angeles.

Langdon, S. (1995) "The Pottery of the Early Iron and Geometric Periods." In: C. Runnels, et al. (eds.), *Artifact and Assemblage: The Finds from a Regional Survey of the Southern Argolid, Greece*, Vol. I. Stanford.

Morris, I. (1987) *Burial and Society. The Rise of the Greek State*. Cambridge.

figure 4.4

	Eleventh and tenth centuries BC	Ninth century	Eighth century	
Bronze figurines at Delphi	0	1	152	(1969)
Bronze tripods at Mount Ptoön (Boiotia)	0	0	7	(1971)
Bronze dedications on Delos	0	1	19	(1973)
Terracotta figurines at Olympia	10	21	837	(1972)

	Eleventh and tenth centuries BC	Ninth and early eighth	Later eighth and seventh	
Bronze fibulae at Philia (Thessaly)	0	2	1783+	(1975)
Bronze pins at Philia	1	4	37	(1975)
Bronze fibulae at Perachora	7	1	50+	(1940)
Bronze pins at Perachora	0	15	81	(1940)
Bronze fibulae at the Argive Heraion	16	10	88	(1905)
Bronze pins at the Argive Heraion	3	c. 250	c. 3070	(1905)
Bronze fibulae at Lindos (Rhodes)	0	52	1540	(1931)
Bronze pins at Lindos	0	0	42	(1931)

Part II

The Archaic Period: circa 800–479 BC

5

Colonization

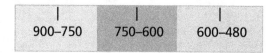

900–750	750–600	600–480

circa 775–750	Earliest colonies in Bay of Naples
730s and 720s	Earliest colonies on Sicily (Naxos, Syracuse)
late 8th century	Corcyra founded by Corinth; Colonies in southern Italy (Taras, Croton)
first half of 7th century	Colonies in Propontis (Byzantium, Cyzicus)
7th century	Colonies on Black Sea
circa 650	Thasos founded by Paros
circa 630	Cyrene founded by Thera
late 7th, early 6th century	Colonies of Corinthian tyrants

Herodotus and the Sources for the History of the Archaic Period

With this chapter the "Dark Age" is left behind and the so-called Archaic period of Greek history begins (roughly from circa 800 BC down to and through the **Persian Wars**). Early in this period the Greeks began to found **colonies** throughout the Mediterranean world, and this movement resulted in a remarkable expansion of the area of Greek civilization. Fortunately, it is also during

A History of Greece: 1300 to 30 BC, First Edition. Victor Parker.
© 2014 Victor Parker. Published 2014 by John Wiley & Sons, Ltd.

colonies & written history

this period that a written tradition starts up again, which allows for discussion of these far-reaching events in greater detail than is the case for the "Dark Age."

A brief introduction of the chief literary source for the Archaic period, the *Histories* of Herodotus, will therefore be useful especially in establishing that Herodotus, although writing in the second half of the fifth century BC, could still recount much valuable information about the eighth and seventh centuries. Herodotus' stories are eminently readable and entertaining even while his work overall has a serious purpose. Here are two programmatic statements from the work:

> Set forth below is the "history" of Herodotus of Halicarnassus, that men's deeds may not fade with the passage of time; that great and marvelous deeds, which both Greeks and non-Greeks acknowledge, may be more widely known . . . (from the proem)

> [I shall treat] the small and the great cities of men alike – for of the ones which were great long ago, many are now small; but some which in my day were great, were small formerly. Wherefore, in the knowledge that among men prosperity never abides long in the same place, I shall speak of both equally. (Hdt. I 5)

good verifiability

While the bulk of Herodotus' work concerns the conflicts between Greeks and Persians during the first two decades of the fifth century, he still has much to say about people and events during the sixth, but progressively less about the seventh and the eighth. This vouches for the information's general reliability; for one ought to expect this of anyone collecting information honestly – more information about earlier periods than later ones would invite skepticism (see **Ephorus**, *BNJ* 70, Fr. 9). *Skepticism cuz of oral sources — unfound*

Nonetheless, scholars who in recent years have discussed Herodotus' use of oral sources have frequently come to depressing conclusions regarding the credibility of the information which he offers for the early period. This discussion, though extremely useful, occasionally relies on a misperception, namely that Herodotus was working with oral sources only – instead of orally recounted traditions edited and arranged according to other written sources which were still available from as early as the mid-seventh century.

Herodotus, in fact, carried out a thorough review of pre-existing Greek literature for historical information which could guide him as he sorted the oral traditions. For example, he mentions Gyges, an historical King of **Lydia** in the mid-seventh century BC (on the Lydian kingdom, see briefly chap. 9). This Gyges is independently attested in the inscriptions of Ashurbanipal, King of **Assyria** (668 – circa 627 BC). Herodotus could not have known of the latter, but he too had a written attestation of Gyges in a poem by **Archilochus** (Fr. 19 West) – see Hdt. I 12. From this Herodotus deduced that Archilochus and Gyges were contemporaries. As an additional token of Herodotus' overall reliability, he states (I 15) that the **Cimmerians** invaded Lydia at about this time. The inscriptions of the Assyrian king Ashurbanipal – notwithstanding various differences from Herodotus' account – attest that same fact.[1]

other signs of reliability

unten
spewl A more important example of Herodotus' use of a written source to guide him comes at V 95 when he cites **Alcaeus** of Mytilene (Fr. 428 Lobel-Page) as his source for a war involving Peisistratus of Athens, Pittacus of Mytilene, and Periander of Corinth (for these sixth-century tyrants, see chap. 7). Just how much of the account derives directly from Alcaeus is unclear, but even if little beyond what happened to Alcaeus in the fighting between Athenians and Mytilenaeans should come from Alcaeus' poem, Herodotus had still read through Alcaeus' poetry and recognized that Alcaeus described events which were the same as those in a series of oral traditions about that war.

Herodotus had likewise read the poems of Alcaeus' contemporary, **Sappho** (see Alcaeus, Fr. 384 Lobel-Page), who ridiculed her brother Charaxus for his dealings with the storied courtesan Rhodopis in the time of Amasis, the historical King of Egypt (570–526 BC; Hdt. II 135 = Sappho, Fr. 202 Lobel-Page). While reading **Solon**'s poems (see chap. 8), Herodotus had noted that Solon in the early sixth century visited the Cyprian town of Salamis when its later king, Philocyprus, was a young man (Hdt. V 113 = Solon, Fr. 19 West). This Philocyprus was the father of a participant in the Ionian Revolt (499–494 BC; see chap. 9). In all of this one can see Herodotus using written sources as historical evidence to make sense of the many oral traditions which he collected.

Thanks to his diligence as well as that of other writers such as **Antiochus of Syracuse** (late fifth century – see also Box 5.2), the colonizing movement largely takes place in the full light of history.

Population Growth and Colonization

overpopulation ∧ hierdny
The rapidly growing population of Greece in the course of the eighth century BC (see chap. 4) meant that many regions in Greece began to experience overpopulation. One should not, however, understand this concept in absolute terms because often enough the overpopulation may have been relative – for example, to the precise use of arable land, to the distribution of the land, to the difficulty of bringing additional land under cultivation, or to the vicissitudes of the weather (Herodotus at IV 151 mentions a seven-year drought which helped motivate the Therans to send out a colony). That is to say, the arable land available to a community may have sufficed for feeding the population, only inequitable distribution of the land meant that much of the population had no access to it or its produce; or a lengthy drought meant that a community which the land could ordinarily support was temporarily badly overpopulated.

However relative overpopulation may have been, its effects on a community were real and the community had to respond or perish. The response of many communities was, crassly, to export the surplus population overseas – to a colony. While some colonies lay as far afield as northern Africa and southern France, most were located in southern Italy and Sicily or around the Black Sea. Other areas heavily affected were the northern Aegean and the eastern coast of the Ionian Sea.

Choosing a Site

A prospective site was usually scouted in advance. For example, when the Therans in the seventh century wished to found a colony, they first sent a party to Crete to see if they could collect information about promising sites from sailors there. Eventually the Therans found a sailor whose ship a storm had blown off course to northern Africa; he told them of the site of Cyrene. Following that lead, the Therans soon sent scouts to the area (Hdt. IV 151).

The presence of edible resources made a site attractive in the first instance. Sometimes the very name of the colony makes this clear: Selinus, founded by Megarians on the southern coast of Sicily, was named after an edible plant, celery, which grew wild there. Colonies such as Sybaris, Croton, and Metapontum in southern Italy lay in grain-producing areas. Metapontum advertised the fact with its coins which displayed on both obverse and reverse an ear of wheat (see Figure 5.1).

Box 5.1   *Foundation "Oath" of the Settlement of Cyrene*

This inscription (Fornara, Nr. 18), from the fourth century BC, was found at Cyrene. It allegedly contains, however, a text from the seventh century, a **decree** of Thera which regulated the settlement of the colony of Cyrene. If this latter text should be genuine, then it is the only extant documentary text contemporary with the colonizing movement of the eighth and seventh centuries. On the authenticity of the text in question, see below.

God. Good fortune.
Damis, son of Bathycles, moved the motion: Concerning what the Therans [i.e., their envoy] Cleudamas, son of Euthycles, said, so that the city (of Cyrene) may prosper and that the People of Cyrene may have good fortune; (the Cyrenaeans) are to grant the Therans citizenship according to the ancestral rules which our forefathers made, both they that founded Cyrene from Thera as well as they that remained on Thera, even as Apollo gave good fortune to Battus and to the Therans who founded Cyrene provided that they abode by the oaths which our forefathers themselves swore to them, when they sent out the colony according to the command of Apollo Archagetes; (wherefore,) for good fortune, be it resolved by the People (of Cyrene):

That the Therans shall continue to have equal citizenship in Cyrene also in accordance with these same rules; that all Therans resident in Cyrene shall swear the same oath which once the others swore; that (the Cyrenaeans) are to induct them into a tribe and a phratry as well as into nine associations; and (the

Cyrenaeans) are to inscribe this decree upon a marble column; to set up the column in the ancestral sanctuary of Apollo Pythius; to inscribe the oath too on the column that the settlers made who sailed to Libya with Battus from Thera to Cyrene; as to the expense necessary for the stone or for the inscribing, let the Managers of the Accounts provide it from Apollo's revenues.

Covenant (literally: oath) of the Settlers:
The Assembly (of Thera) has resolved: Since Apollo of his own accord told Battus and the Therans to found Cyrene, the Therans have resolved to send Battus as Archagetes [i.e., "First Founder"] and King out to Libya and that Therans are to sail as his companions. On equal and like terms are they to sail according to household with one son to be selected . . . [for the space of about twenty letters the text here is either unintelligible or missing] . . . and those who are of age and of the other Therans those who are free . . . [some six letters missing] . . . are to sail. If the colonists establish the colony, then a kinsman [i.e., a Theran] who sails later shall hold both citizenship and (be eligible for) office (in Cyrene) and he shall obtain (a plot of) unowned land. But if they do not establish a colony and the Therans are unable to aid them, but hardships afflict (them) for five years, then from that land are they without fear (of redress) to depart for Thera back to their own property and they are to be citizens (of Thera). But anyone who should refuse to sail when the city sends him out shall be liable to the death penalty and his property shall be confiscated. Anyone that takes him in or that hides him, be he a father (hiding) a son, or a brother (hiding) a brother, shall suffer the same things as he that refused to sail. On these terms they that remain here (on Thera) and they that are sailing to found (a colony) have made a covenant and they have cursed them that should transgress against it and not abide by it, whether amongst them settling in Libya or amongst them remaining here. Having made images of wax they burned them when all had assembled, men, women, boys, and girls; and they made a curse (as follows): "Who should not abide by this covenant, but should transgress against it, may he melt and flow away just as these images, he himself and his descendants and his property; but for them that abide by this covenant, both them that are sailing to Libya and them that remain on Thera, let there be abundance of good things, both for them and for their descendants."

The first two sections of the inscription deal with the grant of full Cyrenaean citizenship (and all which that entailed) to any Therans currently resident in Cyrene and to any Therans who should arrive later. The third section, however, purports to present the seventh-century Theran decree which authorized the foundation of the colony at Cyrene and which contained a provision for the grant of Cyrenaean citizenship to any Theran who sailed to the colony at a later date. Initially, scholars dismissed this "decree within a decree" as a fourth-century forgery ad hoc, but later investigations (see Graham 1960 and Jeffery 1961 in the Further Reading) showed that this dismissal was overhasty, and the decree's content itself does not appear to be faked.

Figure 5.1 Coin from Metapontum. Source: Numismatic Collection Transfer, 2001. Purchased 1963. Acc.n.: 2001.87.456. Photo © Yale Uniersity Art Gallery/Art Resource, NY/Scala, Florence

②defensibility

The next consideration involved defensibility. Because all the early colonies lay in non-Greek regions – only in the fifth century do the Greeks begin to found colonies in Greek areas – conflicts with the non-Greek inhabitants were a real danger. The poet Archilochus, who in the mid-seventh century BC had gone from Paros to the colony Thasos in the northern Aegean, speaks of fighting between the colonists and the indigenous **Thracians** (Fr. 5 West). The Milesian colonists around the Black Sea had to wage war against the **Scythians** (Ephorus, *BNJ* 70, Fr. 183). The first colonists of Metapontum eventually abandoned the site circa 600 BC, allegedly owing to attacks from the indigenous inhabitants of the region (**Strabo**, VI 1,15, p. 264); and the second colonists waged war against the native Oenotreres (Antiochus of Syracuse, *BNJ* 555, Fr. 12).   Carthaginians

In addition to attacks from indigenous populations there were others busily founding colonies who did not desire the competition: the **Carthaginians** and even other Greeks. The Carthaginians from North Africa together with the **Etruscans** from central Italy attacked Phocaean colonists at Alalia on Corsica in the mid-sixth century BC (Hdt. I 166); and the Carthaginians' hostility certainly helped keep the Greeks out of the far West where the former had extensive interests. Meanwhile, Corinthian settlers coming to Corcyra drove out the original colonists from Eretria in the late eighth century (**Plutarch**, *Greek Questions*, 11). It was not just the Oenotreres against whom the Metapontines waged war; they also fought against the Tarantines, Greek colonists from Sparta (Antiochus of Syracuse, l.c.).   many island colonies

In this climate it is not surprising that colonists often settled first on islands just off the coast or an easily defensible headland. The Therans who came to northern Africa first dwelled on the island of Platea (Hdt. IV 153). Syracuse,

Box 5.2 *The Misadventures of Megarian Colonists in Sicily*

Not all colonies survived. Antiochus of Syracuse, who in the late fifth century BC wrote an account of the Greek colonies in the West, mentions failed colonies at both Siris and Metapontum in southern Italy before a second attempt at colonization of those sites succeeded (*BNJ* 555, Fr. 12). The following passage from **Thucydides** recounts the difficulties suffered by Megarian colonists who arrived in Sicily circa 730 BC. They founded two failed colonies before finally succeeding with the foundation of Megara Hyblaea. The passage is also interesting since it gives evidence for friendship between Greek colonists and the indigenous inhabitants; moreover, the people who drove the Megarian colonists from the first two sites of Trotilus and Thapsus may well have been other Greeks – the text itself remains silent on this point.

Thuc. VI 4,1–2
At about the same time Lamis also arrived in Sicily leading out a colony from Megara, and he both settled a certain place called Trotilus on the other side of the Pantacyas River and later on (moved) from there to live with the Chalcidians at Leontini for a brief time. He was driven out by them and founded Thapsus too before dying. But the others driven from Thapsus founded the so-called Hyblaean Megara when Hyblon, the king of the **Sicels,** *handed over land and brought them to it. Now they lived there for two hundred and forty-five years until Gelon, the tyrant of Syracuse, drove them from their city and their land. But before their expulsion, one hundred years after their own foundation, they sent out Pamillus and established Selinus. Now Pamillus came to them from Megara, which was their* **mother-city,** *and carried out the foundation together with them.*

This excerpt comes from a section of Thucydides (VI 1–5) which speaks of the settlement of all the Greek colonies on Sicily. Stylistically, this section of Thucydides is somewhat unusual as in it Thucydides uses phrases and constructions which depart markedly from his normal practice. Moreover, the perspective of the entire section is that of a native Sicilian, in particular a Syracusan – as can be seen even in this small excerpt. First, there is the use of dates relative to Syracuse. The foundation of Megara Hyblaea takes place 245 years before Gelon, the tyrant of Syracuse, destroys it (somewhere between circa 485 and 480 BC – see Hdt. VII 156) – i.e., the relative dates are anchored to an absolute date in the history of Syracuse; that is to say that the reader is expected to know about when Gelon destroyed Megara Hyblaea and thus to be able to work from that. Second, there is the location of Trotilus "on the other side of the river." That wording presupposes a fixed point of reference, i.e., Syracuse, from which the author writes. The author might have phrased it neutrally (e.g., "north of the River Pantacyas"), but Syracuse as a fixed point of reference came naturally to him as well as to his prospective readers who knew the topography of Sicily in relation to Syracuse and therefore understood what "on the other side" of such-and-such a landmark meant. In a word, Thucydides in all likelihood is here incorporating material from none other than Antiochus of Syracuse (mentioned in the opening sentences of this box).

Figure 5.2   Ortygia, the former island, on which Syracuse lay. Source: photo © Tips Images/Tips Italia Srl a socio unico/Alamy

a settlement of the Corinthians circa 730 BC, initially lay on the island of Ortygia ("Quail Island" – see Figure 5.2) in the harbor of the later city (Thuc. VI 3,2). Pithecussae ("Monkey Island"), settled by Chalcidians and Eretrians circa 775 BC (based on the earliest archaeological finds), lay on an island in the bay of Naples (**Livy**, VIII 22,5–6; Strab. V 4,9, p. 247); some years later the settlers transferred the colony to Cumae on the mainland (Thuc. VI 4,5; Liv. l.c.). Zancle, founded circa 700 BC on the Sicilian side of the Strait of Messina, lay on a sickle-shaped promontory (see Figure 5.3). This colony is better known under its later name Messene which it received when Anaxilas, the tyrant of Rhegium, seized the city in the early fifth century (Paus. IV 23). He was a

Figure 5.3   The site of Zancle/Messene. Source: Stefano Barillà, http://en.wikipedia.org/wiki/File:Messina_harbour_-_aerial_view.jpg (accessed 14 January 2013) CC-BY-SA-3.0,2.5,2.0,1.0

descendant of Messenians who settled in Rhegium after the first **Messenian War** (see chap. 6). The Euboean colonies in the Chalcidice, settled in the eighth century BC, lay exclusively on the three prongs protruding from the mainland; each prong was easily defensible against attacks from the mainland.

Finally, there was the matter of a site's suitability for trade. Many colonies lay on or near trade-routes. Thus, Rhegium and Zancle/Messene (both founded circa 700 BC) lay on opposite sides of the Strait of Messina which separates Sicily from Italy. All traffic between the western coast of Italy and Greece flowed through this strait. The island of Corcyra lay in the Ionian Sea to the northwest of Greece proper. The route from Greece to Italy passed by Corcyra since in the ancient world navigation was often a matter of hugging the shore with mariners loath to be out of sight of land for any length of time. For this reason ships bound from Greece to Italy sailed up the eastern shore of the Ionian Sea and made the crossing over to Italy at the southern end of the Adriatic Sea where the passage is briefest. Corcyra and other colonies commanded this route: farther to the south lay additional Corinthian colonies such as Leucas,

Ambracia, and Anactorium; to the north, there where ships headed westwards to Italy, lay the Corcyraean colony of Epidamnus.   *maybe just these places are* traders

Now all of this need not mean that colonists chose a site primarily because it lay on a trade-route. One could explain the location of colonies on such *yeu* routes by noting that potential colonists, when they tried to find out about promising sites, spoke with traders who naturally enough told their questioners of those sites which lay on the trade-routes. All the same, it is difficult to believe that considerations of trade played no role whatsoever in choosing the site.

The curious case of two colonies founded by the Megarians in the seventh century, Byzantium and Chalcedon, best illustrates the matter. Both these cities lay to the north of the Propontis on the Bosporus with Chalcedon on the Asian side and Byzantium on the European side on the site of the later Constantinople (the modern Istanbul). Now the Megarians founded Chalcedon first (Hdt. IV 144). It lay at a spot where the currents made the approach by sea difficult, and it had no good harbor. Yet the fishing was apparently good (**Gellius**, *Attic Nights*, VI 16,5), and this may well have persuaded the Megarians to found a colony there. If the colonists had little to fear from the indigenous peoples, so much the better. Yet across the strait lay the site of Byzantium with its splendid harbor towards which the current bore ships naturally (Strab. VII 6,2, p. 320). When the Persian commander Megabazus (see Hdt. l.c.), while passing through the region, learned that Chalcedon had been founded seventeen years before Byzantium, he said that the Megarians must have been blind – why would anyone have chosen the site of Chalcedon for a city when a far, far better place lay across the strait within view? Megabazus' question, however, presupposes that considerations of trade lay uppermost in the settlers' minds. The realization that that was not the case explains the settlers' actions. Chalcedon had ready access to a supply of food (fish) and, assuming that the indigenous inhabitants were well disposed, may have been the better site for a colony – initially. For the fact remains that seventeen years after the foundation of Chalcedon the Megarians settled the site of Byzantium as well.

In those seventeen years much might have happened to make the settlement of Byzantium feasible. The settlers at Chalcedon might have taken up contact with the indigenous inhabitants on the European side of the strait and so made the peaceful founding of a new colony possible. The contact between the Theran settlers (who after two years on Platea had moved to the mountainous headland of Aziris on the mainland) and the indigenous inhabitants provides a model for such negotiations – for only after such contacts did the Theran settlers move to the site of Cyrene (Hdt. IV 158). To make another suggestion: other circumstances might have caused previous occupants of the site of Byzantium to leave. For example, settlers from Euboea and nearby islands such as Andros had settled the three prongs of the Chalcidice in the eighth century BC. Those three prongs did not have much arable land. Good land lay just to the north, but non-Greek tribes held that land. So the Greek colonists let discretion be the better part of valor and refrained from any attempt to move northwards – until the previous occupants themselves left. Thus, the Greeks at Sane at the northern end of Athos immediately pounced on the site of Acanthus just to the north when they learned that those who had been dwelling there had for reasons of their own left (Plut. *Greek Questions*, 30). Full-scale expansion into the land north of the three prongs, however, did not begin until the early fifth century BC – after the Persians had destroyed the tribe of the Bottiaeans which had held much of the region (Hdt. VIII 127).

Any such scenario can explain why the Greeks declined to settle the splendid site of Byzantium initially, but later on – when presumably it was safe so to do – founded a colony there. Here one sees best the interplay between secondary considerations of trade and the primary considerations of food and safety. The latter two were paramount when choosing a site; the former, although desirable, was an optional extra.

See how considerations of food & safety > trade

Sending Out an Expedition

Step 2: divine approval

Once a promising site had been found, the colonizing city had next to obtain divine approval. For the western colonies application was normally made to Apollo at Delphi; for the colonies on the Black Sea other oracles, such as that of Apollo of Branchidae, may have had a similar role. Although largely a formality – no case of an oracle's withholding the divine assent is attested –, the step was rarely omitted. When the Lacedaemonian adventurer Dorieus in the late sixth century BC allegedly failed to ask for divine approval for an attempt to found a colony in North Africa, Herodotus emphasized this to explain the attempt's eventual failure (Hdt. V 42). The importance of the step emerges from several late examples of colonization. When the Lacedaemonians founded the colony of Heracleia Trachinia in 424 BC, Thucydides records that Delphi officially sanctioned the undertaking (Thuc. III 92). When Ducetius, the heavily Hellenized leader of the (non-Greek) people of the Sicels on Sicily, decided to found colonies in the fifth century BC, he did so unsurprisingly according to the Greek model; and in at least one case, Calacte, he claimed to have received the approval of an oracle (Diod. XII 8,2).

Such approval in the end usually took the form of a command from Apollo to the colonist's leader or to the colonizing city to found the colony (for example, in the foundation decree for Cyrene – see Box 5.1). Parallels exist for this type of reformulation of a request for approval into a direct order to carry out the proposal. Thus, in the fourth century BC when the city of Cyrene wished to carry out a series of cultic reforms, it sought approval from Delphi. The inscription in which these reforms were promulgated (Sokolowski, *LSCG* suppl., No. 115) begins with the words "Apollo spoke: That they may live in Libya making use of regulations for purity, consecration, and supplication forever." These words are in Delphic dialect. There follow over 135 lines of exact regulations – this time in Cyrenaean dialect. That is to say, the entire document, as written in Cyrene, had been placed before Apollo's priests at Delphi for approval who simply added the words quoted as a sort of preamble to indicate that Apollo indeed approved. The important point is that Apollo gave out as his own command what he had merely been requested to approve. So it will have been with the sources' numerous "commands" to found a colony.

On a more human level – once divine approval was forthcoming – prospective colonists were chosen. In some cases prospective colonists volunteered. Poverty at home and the promise of a fresh start – with an allotment of land (see Box 5.3) – in the colony may have sufficed to attract volunteers. Thus the seventh-century BC poet Archilochus of Paros went out to the colony of Thasos, as he himself stated, because he was poor and did not know what else to do (Fr. 295 West).

Occasionally civil unrest at home may have motivated people to go abroad. At Sparta disturbances relating to a group of people called "Partheniae" appear to have caused the latter to be sent out to the colony of Taras in southern Italy circa 700 BC. (the date is based on the oldest finds from the site – see Coldstream, p. 239). Precise details, unfortunately, are irrecoverable (Ephorus, *BNJ* 70, Fr. 216 – with commentary). In the mid-sixth century Arcesilaus, a son of the King of Cyrene, quarreled with his brothers. Apparently a faction within Cyrene backed the latter, who then left with their supporters and founded the nearby colony of Barce (Hdt. IV 160).

In other cases compulsion became necessary. When the Therans sent out their colony to North Africa, they insisted that one man, selected by lot from each household on the island, join – under penalty of death (see Box 5.1). The reluctance to join should not surprise – the perils of a long voyage were real as were those posed by hostile peoples abroad; after all, many colonies (for example, the first settlements at Siris and Metapontum) failed. The Megarians who eventually settled Megara Hyblaea had previously been driven (by unspecified enemies) from two other sites, Trotilus on the River Pantacyas and Thapsus (see Box 5.2). Moreover, clearing land and making it arable was backbreaking labor as was building a new city from the ground up. Unlike Archilochus, many may have preferred poverty at home to perils and hard work abroad even if the latter did offer a chance at a better life.

Given the difficulties involved in finding people willing to go, "joint ventures" often enough took place with more than one community contributing colonists. Thus Gela, founded in the early seventh century on Sicily, had settlers from Rhodes and Crete (Thuc. VI 4). Sometimes the settlers already in a colony were willing to accept others in addition – clearly, a use could always be found for additional hands – as when the Chalcidians at Leontini received Megarian colonists who had been driven out from Trotilus (see Box 5.2).

Next, someone to lead out the colony had to be chosen. This was the **oecist,** the "founder." It fell to him to make all necessary arrangements and to see to it that the colony was properly settled (see also Box 5.3). In the early period he remained in the colony, and when he died he was buried in the colony's marketplace where his fellow colonists errected a shrine to him and where he ever after received heroic offerings (Hdt. VI 38; Thuc. V 11; Diod. XI 49 and 66). The choice of oecist was often a political one. He might be someone whom others at home wished to see gone; or he might be a trusted confidant of a city's leader. To give an example of the former, when Cleomenes became King of Sparta circa 520 BC, his half-brother Dorieus had been a serious rival for the throne. Cleomenes presumably was happy to see Dorieus leave Sparta to found a colony a thousand miles away (Hdt. V 42). The colonies founded by the Corinthians during the tyranny of Cypselus give a good example of the latter phenomenon. Cypselus made his sons Pylades and Echiades the oecists of the colonies of Leucas and Anactorium respectively (**Nicolaus of Damascus**, *BNJ* 90, Fr. 57); the oecist of Potidaea, meanwhile, was Evagoras, the son of Cypselus' successor in the **Cypselid** tyranny, Periander (Nicolaus of Damascus, *BNJ* 90, Fr. 59).

Arrival Overseas

When the colonists finally arrived at the chosen site, assuming that all had gone well on the voyage and that the site could be settled on a permanent basis (this was not always the case – see Box 5.2), land was measured out. All colonists received a plot. Additionally, land was set aside for the construction of temples. These customs are better known from later colonies such as Brea (founded in the fifth century – see Box 5.3), but presumably were the same in the early period.

Box 5.3 *The Athenians Found Brea*

The following inscription (Fornara, Nr. 100) comes from the mid-fifth century. Although the great age of colonization was the eighth and seventh centuries, Greek cities continued to found sporadic colonies in the sixth, fifth, and even fourth centuries. The later colonies are, on the whole, better known owing to more documentary evidence and contemporary historical accounts (for example, that at Thuc. III 92 on the Lacedaemonian colony of Heracleia Trachinia). The distribution of land to the colonists, for example, is specifically attested in the decree for the foundation of Brea. Occasionally it becomes necessary to extrapolate backwards from the fifth-century colonies to the older ones – for example, scholars usually assume that there was some procedure for the division of land in the colonies of the eighth and seventh centuries as well even though it is never explicitly attested. Granted, this method of extrapolation backwards has its risks as the principles of colonization did not remain static (for example, the fifth-century colonies such as Heracleia Trachinia appear to function at times as little more than expressions of the mother-city's geopolitical strategy – that is unknown for the early colonies).

(Continued)

(first three lines here omitted)

*. . . the colonists are to provide . . . for them so as to have good omens for the colony, however many they decide. They are to select ten men as geonomoi [i.e., "land-distributers"], one per tribe. These are to distribute the land. Democleides [i.e., the oecist] shall have full powers to establish the colony however he may best be able. They shall leave the sacred precincts which have been reserved just as they are, and they are to mark off no others. They [i.e., the colonists] are to send an ox and a suit of armor to the Greater **Panathenaea** and a phallus to the Dionysia [i.e., two festivals at Athens]. But if anyone should invade the colonists' land, then the cities shall come to their aid as quickly as possible according to the agreements which were made when [the name is here missing] was secretary (of the **Boule**) concerning the cities in Thrace. (The Athenians) are to write these things on a column and to erect it in the city. The colonists are to provide the column at their own expense. If anyone should propose any decree contrary to the column or any orator speak in the assembly or attempt to persuade (anyone else) to remove or to cancel any one of the provisions (of this decree), he shall lose his citizenship, both he and his children after him; and his property shall be confiscated and a tenth part (of this property) shall be the goddess's [i.e., Athena's], unless the colonists themselves in some way . . . [a few words are missing]. All those enrolled for the colony who are soldiers, after they come back to Athens, within thirty days are to be in Brea as colonists. (The colonists) shall lead out the colony within thirty days. Aeschines shall go with them and shall provide funds.*

(A small addendum, written on the side of the column:)

*Phantocles moved the motion: Concerning the colony at Brea, (let everything be) just as Democleides has moved; but the Erechtheid **prytany** shall introduce Phantocles to the Boule in its first session. As for Brea, the colonists shall come from the **Thetes** and the **Zeugitae**.*

replicate mother city

Everything in the new colony had to be built from the ground up – houses, temples, public buildings. As a general rule the colonists attempted to replicate abroad what they had known at home. They established the same cults to the same gods; they made the same institutional arrangements which they knew from home; they spoke the same dialect and used the same calendar. Changes might occur over time, but in general the newly founded colony was as close to a duplicate of the mother-city as possible. To give one quick example, there was a king (Grinnus by name – Hdt. IV 150) reigning on Thera when Cyrene was founded; so the colony too had to have a king – the oecist Battus became the first King of Cyrene.

Over time institutions in both mother-city and colony could change. The historian Ephorus commented on this already in the fourth century BC (*BNJ* 70, Fr. 149), and those of Cyrene were reformed in the sixth century BC by the **lawgiver** Demonax (Hdt. IV 161). But in many cases the institution or cult which existed in the colony existed also in the mother-city and vice versa.

Relationship between Colony and Mother-city

The new colony was conceived as a fully independent state from day one. The foundation decree of Cyrene (Box 5.1) shows that the colonists ceased to be citizens of Thera with immediate effect (else the decree would not have spoken of the colonists' receiving their citizenship back if the clause allowing their return were implemented).

Nonetheless, the mother-city had obligations, especially in the early years, to its colony. Thera (see Box 5.1) undertook to provide aid to the colonists at Cyrene for five years and agreed to receive the colonists back if such aid were not forthcoming and the colony had to be abandoned. Colonists occasionally invoked this obligation to aid a colony several centuries after the foundation. Thus Syracuse, founded by Corinth in circa 735 BC, requested help from its mother-city when faced with an invasion from Carthage in the mid-340s BC (Diod. XVI 65) (see chap. 17). Taras, founded by Sparta circa 700 BC, applied to its mother-city Sparta for aid, also in the mid-340s BC (Diod. XVI 62,4) (see chap. 17). In both cases the respective mother-city sent what help it could. Sometimes, moreover, it went the other way round. Chalcidian colonists from the Chalcidice returned to Chalcis to help their mother-city in its war against the Eretrians (Plut. *Amatorius*, 17).

A colony for its part owed to its mother-city a degree of deference (especially in religious matters – Thuc. I 25) which becomes manifest in particular when a colony founded a colony in its own right. In this case the existing colony applied to its mother-city to send out an oecist for the new colony. The Megarian colony of Megara Hyblaea did this when it founded Selinus circa 630 BC (see Box 5.2); so did the Corinthian colony of Corcyra when it founded Epidamnus towards the end of the seventh century (Thuc. I 24).

This is not to say that relations between a colony and its mother-city were always good. Corcyra and Corinth in particular fell out with one another on several occasions. The tyrant of Corinth, Periander, conquered Corcyra at one point and appointed his son Lycophron as its governor (Hdt. III 48 and 52). Thucydides records a naval battle between Corcyra and Corinth in the mid-seventh century (Thuc. I 13). Finally, it was Corinth's and Corcyra's bitter dispute over Corcyra's colony Epidamnus that helped touch off the Peloponnesian War (Thuc. I 24sqq.).

For the most part, however, colony and mother-city remained close. Cyrene in the fourth century BC, over three centuries after its founding, offered automatic citizenship to any Theran who chose to settle there. Down to 431 BC,

Potidaea received its annual magistrates from its mother-city Corinth (Thuc. I 56). Miletus and its colony Cyzicus maintained an arrangement of mutual grant of citizenship whereby any Cyzicene who came to Miletus was automatically a Milesian citizen and vice versa (*SVA* 409, 13–16). When the Achaian colonies in southern Italy (founded probably in the late eighth century) were experiencing civic troubles in the late fifth century, they accepted the advice of a commission sent from Achaia, the tribe-state in the northern Peloponnese which had founded these colonies, and went on to reform their constitutions on the model of that of their founders (Pol. II 39).   *tribe states found colonies*

This last example, incidentally, shows that although scholars conventionally speak of "mother-cities," tribe-states could and did found colonies also. The tribe-states of the Western and Eastern Locrians collaborated in founding Locri Epizephyrii in southern Italy in the early seventh century (Pol. XII 5–6); the Eastern Locrians founded the colony of Naupactus on the territory of the Western Locrians in the early fifth (Fornara, Nr. 47).

Alternatives to and Variants on Colonization   *Sparta & Athens: little colonial activity*

Colonization was not the only response to the problem of overpopulation. Two major states are almost entirely absent from the colonizing movement. The first is Sparta which, granted, did found one early colony, that of Taras in circa 700 BC. That foundation, however, came just before the Messenian Wars which practically doubled Sparta's land. After the Messenian Wars (see chap. 6), Sparta had more than enough land to feed its population and hence no need to send out any more colonies.   *Solve overpopulation w/ other ways*

Athens, on the other hand, sent out no colonies in the early period. It too suffered from relative overpopulation, but seems to have overcome the problem in the sixth century through a large-scale redistribution of land (on this, see chap. 8). Athens, moreover, had fought a war against Megara over the rich Plain of Eleusis (Solon, Frr. 1–3 West; Hdt. I 30) and had wrested that region from its neighbor. Accordingly, Athens settled no colonies in the conventional sense until the fifth century BC when it founded Thurii in Italy (Diod. XII 10–11) on the site of Sybaris (destroyed by Croton – Hdt. V 44–45) as well as Brea (see Box 5.3) and Amphipolis in the northern Aegean (Thuc. IV 102 and Diod. XII 32,3). Unlike Athens, Megara, deprived of land, founded colony after colony: Megara Hyblaea in the West (see Box 5.2), Chalcedon and Byzantium in the Propontis, and Heracleia Pontica on the Black Sea (Xen. *Anab.* VI 2,1).

The two Euboean cities of Chalcis and Eretria attempted both strategies to relieve the pressure of overpopulation. Not only did they send out many colonies, but they also went to war over the fertile Lelantine Plain which lay between them (Hdt. V 99; Thuc. I 15). The war lasted for many decades from the late eighth to the mid-seventh century (probably with intermittent periods of peace as with the Messenian Wars – see chap. 6). In this case both cities appear to have worn themselves out in the wars and, although Chalcis won possession of the plain (Hdt. V 77; **Aelian**, *Historical Miscellany*, VI 1), both cities sank into irrelevance thereafter. ⟨trading post⟩

Finally, it was possible to settle abroad for the purposes of trade without founding a colony as such. Probably for as long as they had been plying the seas, Greek traders had occasionally resided in foreign ports. When several traders stayed for prolonged periods of time, an *emporion* or "trading post" may have been established. On the basis of the Greek (specifically Euboean) pottery found there, Al Mina, near the mouth of the Orontes River in Syria, appears to have had a substantial Euboean presence in the second half of the eighth century BC. Yet Al Mina was clearly a Syrian town overall, not a Greek settlement – and certainly not a colony. Al Mina is the oldest known example of a continuing Greek presence in a non-Greek town, yet is later than the oldest colonies. For this reason there is no need to assume that *emporia* provided the idea or model for colonies. Chronologically, *emporia* might have been little more than a variant on the already established model of colonization. The reason for the variant might lie in the existence of well-organized states in the Near East which precluded the establishment of politically self-sufficient colonies. The best-known *emporion*, Naucratis in the Nile delta, supports this idea. Here from the late seventh century onwards (i.e., well after the founding of the oldest colonies), as shown by the earliest Greek pottery from the site, a large Greek trading settlement flourished, clearly with the permission of the rulers of Egypt, who presumably did not desire an independent Greek city on their territory. The trade, however, was mutually beneficial, and Naucratis, drawing its population from across the Greek world, grew to a substantial size – without ever becoming a colony.

NOTES

1 See M. Cogan and H. Tadmor, (1977) "Gyges and Assurbanibal. A study in literary transmission," *Orientalia* 46: 65–85.

QUESTIONS FOR REVIEW

1 What made a site attractive to Greek colonists?
2 What made people wish to go out to a colony? What made them wish to stay at home?
3 What formal procedures were involved in founding a colony?
4 What alternative to colonization were there?

QUESTION FOR FURTHER STUDY

The terms "colony" and "colonization" are conventional; one might speak of "overseas establishments." If so, one could discuss various Athenian extraterritorial possessions (Chersonese, Sigeium, Lemnos, Scyros) as well as the cleruchies which the Athenians imposed in the fifth century (see chaps. 7 and 11). How do the founding cities manage to bind their foundations ever more closely to themselves? Do the Corinthian tyrants' colonies have an intermediate position between earlier colonies and Athenian cleruchies?

FURTHER READING

Many books have been written on Herodotus, and the following is highly selective:

Asheri, D., *et al.* (2007) *A Commentary on Herodotus, I–IV.* Oxford. (English translation of the first four books of the now standard commentary in Italian; the remaining volumes are still being translated, but should soon appear.)

How, W.W., and J. Wells. (1912) *A Commentary on Herodotus.* Oxford. (For many years the standard commentary in English.)

Parker, V. (2007) "Herodotus' Use of Aeschylus' Persae as an Historical Source," *Symbolae Osloenses* 82: 2–29. (A case-study of Herodotus' use of a surviving written source.)

Thomas, R. (1989) *Oral Tradition and Written Record in Classical Athens.* Cambridge.

On colonization in general:

Boardman, J. (1980) *The Greeks Overseas* (2nd edn.). London. (Also with a brief, readable treatment of the emporia.)

Graham, A.J. (1983) *Colony and Mother City* (2nd edn.). Manchester.

Tsetskhladze, G.R. (ed.). (2006) *Greek Colonisation: An Account of Greek Colonies and Other Settlements Overseas.* Leiden.

Tsetskhladze, G.R., and F. De Angelis (eds.). (1994) *The Archaeology of Greek Colonisation: Essays Dedicated to Sir John Boardman.* Oxford.

On specific colonies/areas:–

For Cyrene:

Chamoux, Fr. (1952) *Cyrène sous la monarchie des battiades.* Paris.

Graham, A.J. (1960) "The Authenticity of the ΟΡΚΙΟΝ ΤΩΝ ΟΙΚΙΣΤΗΡΩΝ of Cyrene," *Journal of Hellenic Studies* 80: 94–111.

Jeffery, L.H. (1961) "The Pact of the First Settlers at Cyrene," *Historia* 10: 139–147.

For the West:

Dunbabin, T.J. (1948) *The Western Greeks.* Oxford.

Halloway, R.R. (1991) *The Archaeology of Ancient Sicily.* London.

For the Black Sea:

Tsetskhladze, G.R. (ed.). (1998) *The Greek Colonisation of the Black Sea Area: Historical Interpretation of Archaeology.* Stuttgart.

6

Sparta from the Messenian Wars to the Creation of the Peloponnesian League

| 950–700 | 700–500 | 500–480 |

second half of 10th century	Sparta founded
late 8th century (?)	Great Rhetra promulgated
circa 690–670	First Messenian War, Theopompus king
circa 630–600	Second Messenian War, Tyrtaeus active
mid-6th century	Wars against Argos and Tegea; Peloponnesian League founded

Sparta is Founded and Gains Control of the Laconian Plain

Sparta was founded in the second half of the tenth century BC. Over the course of the next two centuries or so it came to control the entire Laconian plain between Mt. Taÿgetos to the west and Mt. Parnon to the east. It developed one of the most peculiar governmental institutions in Greece, its unique dual kingship whereby two kings from two distinct houses, the **Agiads** and the **Eurypontids**, reigned at any given point in time. It also developed an unusual three-tiered social structure consisting of the **Spartiates** (the so-called "Equals" or full citizens

A History of Greece: 1300 to 30 BC, First Edition. Victor Parker.
© 2014 Victor Parker. Published 2014 by John Wiley & Sons, Ltd.

who alone – at least the males – had political rights); the **Perioeci** (literally "dwellers-about" who were free, but had no political rights); and the **Helots** (whom it is notoriously difficult to define; in antiquity the lexicographer **Pollux**, III 83, classed them as "between free and slave"). Unfortunately, much of this development takes place in a period illuminated by no historical source.

The Perioeci and the Helots presumably arose in the course of the probable conquest of the Laconian Plain, with the former group retaining its freedom while losing all political rights and with the latter group forced to accept an even lower social status. But no one can know for certain how and why these two groups were formed. The dual kingship probably arose through the settlement of Sparta by two groups who eventually were united in one political community, but, again, there is no way to tell for certain.

Finally, a few details of nomenclature need clarification in advance. The city bore two names: "Sparta" (strictly speaking the physical city only) and "Lacedaemon" (the city including its territory in a political sense). The free population (Spartiates and Perioeci) went by the name of "Lacedaemonians." In this book, in accordance with ancient usage, the people will be called "Lacedaemonians." "Sparta," however, will be retained for the city. "Laconia" is the name of Sparta's territory.

Sources for Lacedaemonian History and Society

Reconstructing the history of Sparta involves overcoming two problems. First, already in antiquity many (including the Lacedaemonians themselves) viewed Lacedaemonian society in idealistic terms and mythologized its history (see chap. 10 for discussion of this in regard to the battle of Thermopylae). The process of mythologization, moreover, becomes more pronounced in the later sources. Second, the most comprehensive accounts of Lacedaemonian society and history stand in late sources, in particular Plutarch's biography of Lycurgus. This Lycurgus was the mostly (if not entirely) legendary lawgiver to whom the Lacedaemonians routinely ascribed all their laws, customs, and institutions. There is no early evidence for his existence; even when the late-seventh-century poet **Tyrtaeus** is discussing the Lacedaemonian constitution, he makes no mention of Lycurgus who very much belongs to what E.N. Tigerstedt wrote of under the title *The Legend of Sparta*.

In what follows, for the reconstruction of the early history of Sparta the oldest sources (such as Tyrtaeus or the early treaty in Box 6.1) must have priority. Herodotus has much useful information about events in the sixth and fifth centuries, but with late sources such as **Pausanias** and Plutarch (both second century AD) caution or corroborating argument is in order. Other historians such as Thucydides (late fifth century BC), **Xenophon**, or Ephorus (both fourth century) provide much useful information especially for their own day. Likewise, Aristotle's description of the Lacedaemonian constitution was surely valid in his day (fourth century).

The Messenian Wars and the Helots

To the west of Mt. Taÿgetos lay Messenia or, in the older form, Messene. In classical times this name applied to a large area: the fertile plain of the River Pamisus, the coastal regions to the west and south of that plain, and the thick westernmost of the three prongs jutting southwards off the Peloponnese. Over the course of the seventh century, Sparta conquered this entire region in the two so-called Messenian Wars. These wars used to be conventionally dated to the late eighth and the mid-seventh centuries BC, though the more likely dates are about 690–670 and 630–600 (see below).

The Lacedaemonian poet Tyrtaeus lived in the time of one Messenian War, and his poetry makes it clear that another earlier war had taken place. The chief evidence is the following bit of verse (Fr. 5 West):

. . . *under our King Theopompus, beloved of the gods,*
Through whom we took wide Messene,
Messene good to plow, good to plant.
For it they fought for nineteen years,
Ceaselessly, with ever valiant hearts,
The spearmen fathers of our fathers.
But in the twentieth year (our foes) left their rich fields
And fled from the great mountains of Ithome.

Tyrtaeus dates the first war twice in these lines: it occurred during the reign of King Theopompus and during the lifetime of the current combatants' grandfathers. The latter date has proved more useful to modern historians (since the date of King Theopompus is not directly known), but it can be used only after the date of the second war has been ascertained. Next, the war lasted for twenty years. This could be a round number – i.e., twice ten or double the length of the Trojan War – and mean no more than that the war lasted an especially long time.

Finally, there is a geographical indication of where the war took place. The final line speaks of Mt. Ithome, the high mountain above the plain of the upper Pamisus (see Figure 12.2). On the basis of Tyrtaeus' poem the war could have taken place solely in that plain. The fifth-century Athenian playwright **Euripides** in one passage stated that "Messene" was "inaccessible to sailors" (Fr. 727e Kannicht). If he meant "Messene" in the sense of the later "Messenia," then his words make no sense – Messenia had a very long coastline. But if Euripides meant the plain of the upper Pamisus, then his words are easily explicable. On balance, it seems that the geographical term "Messene" originally referred to that region specifically and therefore that the first Messenian War did indeed involve this region only. Discussion so far has turned almost solely on these seventh-century lines from Tyrtaeus.

The second Messenian War began when those conquered in the first war revolted. These rebels allegedly had allies who included the people from the coastal regions to the west and south – Pausanias (IV 23,1) specifically mentions the Pylians and Methonaeans. Although Pausanias' account of the war is not particularly trustworthy, after the war the Lacedaemonians did annex those regions, so participation of their inhabitants on the Messenians' side can probably be accepted. Given the length of the first war – even if the two decades are merely an approximation –, the second war too should have been long and difficult. Tyrtaeus speaks as if there were many reverses (see, for example, Tyrtaeus, Fr. 11 West, lines 1–10); and according to Pausanias (IV 16,6) he actually wrote his poems to restore the Lacedaemonians' flagging spirits.

Even if no source specifies the length of the second war, a clear statement does exist as to the date of its end. Epaminondas, who restored the independence of the Messenians in 369 BC, stated that he had done so after 230 years of subjection (Plut. *Sayings of Kings and Commanders*, p. 194). That figure probably represents the conversion into years of a count of seven generations (conventionally in Greek historians three generations equal a hundred years with spare generations taken as thirty – e.g., Hdt. II 142), so it should not be construed as absolutely exact. At any rate the figure yields a date of circa 600 for the war's end. The source may be late, but again there is a corroborating argument: on the basis of other evidence the literary historians have dated Tyrtaeus' poetry to about a generation after that of Archilochus who belongs around the mid-point of the seventh century.[1] Tyrtaeus' poetry, therefore, belongs to the closing decades of the seventh century. The second Messenian War was then fought, very roughly, circa 630–600. The first War took place two generations earlier, say, circa 690–670.

The Lacedaemonians' ultimate victory in the second Messenian War resulted in the conquest of the lands to the west and south of the plain of the upper Pamisus, effectively doubling their territory. This made Sparta the largest of all the states in classical Greece and for as long as Sparta held Messenia, Sparta had more than enough land. As late as the year 425 BC when the Athenian general Demosthenes landed near Pylos in western Messenia, he found the region practically uninhabited (Thuc. IV 3). In addition the Lacedaemonians had allegedly resettled refugees from the Argolis on available land during the sixth century (**Theopompus**, *BNJ* 115, Fr. 383; Paus. IV 14,3 – Pausanias is late, but Theopompus did write in the fourth century BC). Unlike many other Greek states, the Lacedaemonians simply stood under no necessity of exporting surplus population; and it need not be coincidence that the single Lacedaemonian colony from the early period, Taras, was founded just before the Messenian Wars began (circa 700 – see chap. 5).

Besides a large amount of land, the Lacedaemonians acquired a great number of conquered people whom they reduced to the status of Helots. While there were already Helots before the Messenian Wars, so numerous were the Helots made after these wars that the two groups – Helots and Messenians – became practically synonomous. Thucydides comments on this in the following passage:

The majority of the Helots were the descendants of the ancient Messenians who were enslaved aforetime; at any rate, they all are called "Messenians." (Thuc. I 101,2).

As mentioned above, the Helots' held an ambiguous position in Lacedaemonian society. They were not exactly "slaves," nor were they "free" (Pollux, III 83). They belonged to the state as a whole, not to any one Spartiate (Xen. *Const. Lac.* 6,3; Ephorus, *BNJ* 70, Fr. 117). They were settled in particular areas on land owned by Spartiates (Ephorus, l.c.), and were required to yield one half of that land's produce to its owners (Tyrtaeus, Fr. 6 West). They possessed certain rights, most obviously the right to retain half of the land's produce (Tyrtaeus, l.c.), but also the important right of inalienability (Ephorus, l.c.) which meant they could not be sold from off the land which they worked and which ensured that, whatever else they suffered, they could not be torn from their homes and families. In the sanctuary of Poseidon on Cape Taenarum – not coincidentally one of the least accessible regions of Laconia (see Figure 6.1) – they were inviolable (Thuc. I 128,1); and here they could also be made free (IG V 1, 1228–1232). Technically they possessed the right to life, but the Lacedaemonians allegedly dodged the law by officially declaring war on them each year so that they might be killed without legal or sacral penalty (Plut. *Lyc.*

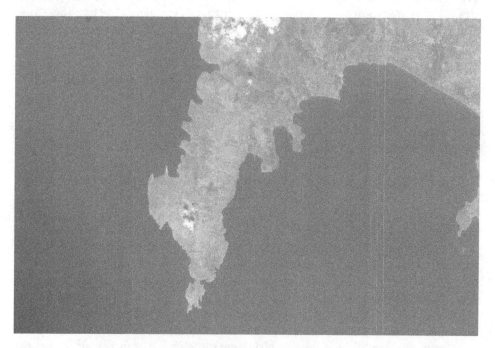

Figure 6.1 Satellite image of Cape Taenarum. Source: Image Science and Analysis Laboratory, NASA-Johnson Space Center. "The Gateway to Astronaut Photography of Earth." <http://eol.jsc.nasa.gov/scripts/sseop/QuickView.pl?directory=ESC&ID=ISS009-E -10425>01/14/2013 16:44:52

28). The Lacedaemonians required them to wear distinctive clothing which made them instantly recognizable (**Myron**, *BNJ* 106, Fr. 2), and privately the Spartiates spied on them through the so-called "**Crypteia**," a sort of secret police which monitored their activities (Plut. l.c.). The Spartiates allegedly subjected them to routine indignities (Tyrtaeus, Fr. 6–7 West; Myron, l.c.) and even allowing for exaggeration, the Spartiates' treatment of them was brutal and harsh.

Additional Lacedaemonian Wars of Expansion

In the decades after their final victory in the Messenian Wars, the Lacedaemonians turned their attentions eastwards and in the mid-sixth century wrested from Argos the regions lying to the east of Mt. Parnon, the Thyreatis and the Cynuria. The decisive battle was noteworthy for the two sides' initial use of a specific tactic to minimize casualties, namely the limiting of the actual combatants to a select number, in this case to three hundred from each side. Both sides agreed to abide by the result of the champions' battle. Unfortunately, that result was itself disputed, and the main armies did meet in a conventional battle which the Lacedaemonians won decisively (Hdt. I 82).

After this battle Argos and Sparta became bitter enemies and remained so, with only brief exceptions, throughout the classical period; and this enmity is an important factor in the various interstate alliances for the next few centuries. Another important result of this battle was Sparta's acquisition of a port on the Aegean Sea, Prasiae, which lay to the east of Mt. Parnon. Sparta's chief port in Laconia proper, Gytheium on the Laconian Gulf, could not serve well as an outlet to the Aegean owing to the difficulty of rounding Cape Malea (see Box 1.1). Prasiae therefore was the naval base from which Lacedaemonian fleets set sail during the Peloponnesian and other wars.

At about the same time as the Lacedaemonians conquered the Thyreatis and Cynuria, they also defeated the Arcadian city of Tegea to the north of the Laconian Plain (Hdt. I 67). In this case they declined to annex the territory of Tegea. Neither did they make any attempt to reduce the Tegeates to the status of Helots. Instead they formed an alliance with the Tegeates, the first of a series of alliances which would become the so-called **Peloponnesian League**.

The Creation of the Peloponnesian League

The Peloponnesian League – or in the ancient formulation: "the Lacedaemonians and their allies" – rapidly became the premier military alliance in Greece. Thanks to the discovery of a treaty between the Lacedaemonians and the small community of the Aetoli Erxadieis (see Box 6.1), the league in the early period is now better known. Smaller, less powerful communities received a reciprocal defensive alliance – if either state were attacked, the other would automatically

Box 6.1 *Treaty between the Lacedaemonians and the Aetoli Erxadieis*

The following treaty dates, probably, from around the year 500 BC. It is the sole epigraphically attested treaty of alliance for the Peloponnesian League. The Lace-daemonians made this treaty with a small, otherwise unknown community, the Aetoli Erxadieis who probably lived somewhere on the Peloponnese, possibly near Mantinea – the Aetoli Erxadieis receive an exemption from ever having to go to war against the Mantineans as though they had earlier made a treaty of alliance with the Mantineans, a treaty which this treaty did not annul; since Mantinea never seems to have exercised much influence beyond its corner of Arcadia, the Aetoli Erxadieis may have dwelled nearby.

> [Trea]ty with the Aetoli E[rxadieis:]
> [they are to] h[ave friendsh]ip and peace [forever]
> [without gu]ile and an alli[ance against others,]
> [exce]pt [against] the Man[tineans] alone, [follow-]
> 5 ing whithersoever the La[cedaemoni-]
> [an]s may lead, both b[y land]
> [a]nd by sea; having th[e same]
> friend and the sam[e enemy]
> whom [also the Lace-]
> 10 daemonians have. No t[ruce]
> may be established without the La[cedaemonians]
> with anyone, ceasi[ng to fight]
> on the same terms as do [the Lacedae-]
> monians. [They are not to receive] exil[es]
> 15 having participa[ted in wrong]
> matters. But if anyone [against the] land
> of the Erxadieis [should make an attack]
> for the purposes of war, [the Lacedaemo]
> nians are to come to their [aid] with all their streng[th according to their ability:]
> 20 but if anyone [should] against th[e] land [of the Lacedaemo-]
> nians make an a[ttack for purposes of wa-]
> r, then the E[rxadieis] are to come to their aid [with all their]
> [strength according to their ability . . .]

(The division into lines follows the Greek as exactly as possible. Matter within square brackets is missing from the stone and has been added by the editor; text after Gschnitzer 1978.)

The significance of this treaty derives from the sheer insignificance of the Aetoli Erxadieis: such a small community was unlikely to have much diplomatic clout in its

(Continued)

negotiations with the Lacedaemonians who in all likelihood simply presented it with a "standard" treaty and requested it to join the League on the standard terms. The Aetoli Erxadieis did win a special clause exempting them from having to go to war against Mantinea – presumably owing to a pre-existing treaty with Mantinea –, but the Lacedaemonians usually allowed precisely this type of exception; that is to say, they did not require an ally to contravene a sacral obligation (such as keeping a treaty duly sworn before the gods).

come to its aid –, an arrangement which in the first instance benefited the smaller community which ran by far the higher risk of attack by another state. In exchange for this promise of Lacedaemonian aid, the smaller community agreed "to follow whithersoever the Lacedaemonians might lead" (cf. Xen. *Hell.* II 2,20, IV 6,2, and VI 3,7) when the Peloponnesian League went to war. That is to say, the Lacedaemonians, provided that they could arrange for the League to go to war (see below), could augment their own forces with the contingents of all the members of the League.

In addition to these basic clauses the Lacedaemonians insisted on several others. The allied community agreed, when there was war, never to negotiate with an enemy behind the Lacedaemonians' back, but always "to have the same friend and the same enemy" as the Lacedaemonians. Second, the Lacedaemonians demanded that the allied community "not receive exiles" who had been involved in "wrongful activities" (the Lacedaemonians apparently knew exactly what they meant by this, so they left it unexplained). The insistence on this is a little surprising, but it is probably explicable with reference to the sole attested clause of the first treaty of the Peloponnesian League, that with Tegea. In that treaty the Tegeates undertook "to expel the Messenians and not to make them 'good'" (Plut. *Greek Questions*, 5). Interpretation of the second clause causes difficulties, but the first is clear: the Tegeates are not to harbor exiles from Messenia, exiles who have either engaged in anti-Lacedaemonian activities or might do so in the future. Many stories attest to the Lacedaemonians' fear of a Helots' revolt, and at least some present this fear as well founded (see, e.g., Plut. *Cim.* 16), so it is understandable that through their alliances the Lacedaemonians should have sought to eliminate any possible refuge for Helots who might rebel or simply flee across the borders.

The Lacedaemonians, however, surely found themselves obliged on occasion to make exceptions from such terms. Not every community that joined the League was a tiny town. Corinth, to take the most noteworthy case, was a large and wealthy city with a colonial "sphere of influence" – several of its colonies (Leucas, Ambracia, Anactorium, Potidaea) maintained close ties with Corinth – and had a powerful navy and army of its own. On several occasions in the history of the League, Corinth displayed an astonishing independence in opposing the Lacedaemonians' wishes (e.g., Thuc. I 40). Twice, in fact, the Corinthians simply refused "to follow whithersoever the Lacedaemonians might lead" as though that clause did not apply to them: in 506 BC (Hdt. V 75 – see chap. 9) and 395 BC (Xen. *Hell.* III 5,17 and 23). Sparta probably had not been able to dictate terms to Corinth and instead had had to negotiate for real so that if the treaty between Sparta and Corinth ever were found, it would probably look very different from the one in Box 6.1.

Finally, the Lacedaemonians usually made one concession to their allies – these were not expected to engage in any war in violation of a sacral obligation (for example, another treaty antedating their entry into the Peloponnesian League). Usually this exception found expression in the catch-all phrase "unless gods or heroes should hinder it" (Thuc. V 30), but the exception could certainly be specified as in the treaty with the Aetoli Erxadieis (Box 6.1). In circa 402 BC the Corinthians and Boeotians availed themselves of this exception (Xen. *Hell.* II 4, 30).

For the early period little is known of how the League was convened or how decisions to go to war were reached. In the second half of the fifth century – by which time the League's institutions may have changed from their forms in the late sixth – the Lacedaemonian assembly first voted to go to war and then convened the League's assembly. There every city's delegation had the right to speak and to cast a ballot. In the end a simple majority sufficed (Thuc. I 40 and 119).

Finally, the role of Sparta's two kings in the League evolved over time. In the early period both kings led out the League's forces, but after a dispute between King Cleomenes and King Demaratus caused a debacle in circa 506 BC (Hdt. V 75), the Lacedaemonians henceforth sent out only one king with the troops. Nonetheless just before the battle of Marathon in 490 BC, the problem with the two kings reared its head once more. King Cleomenes had gone to Aegina, a member of the Peloponnesian League, to demand that the Aeginetans rescind their recent submission to the Persian Empire. An Aeginetan made the telling point that Cleomenes' colleague was absent and that therefore Cleomenes' order had no legitimacy. Cleomenes' reaction shows that he too considered himself caught dead to rights (Hdt. VI 50). Although Herodotus does not explicitly say so, the Lacedaemonians appear to have resolved the matter since this issue never again arises.

Eventually, the Peloponnesian League came to include almost all the communities on the Peloponnese. Argos, an inveterate enemy of Sparta's since the time of the war for the Thyreatis and the Cynuria, was the chief exception. For a brief space only during the Peloponnesian War was Argos ever an ally of Sparta's (Thuc. V 79).

The Great Rhetra and the Lacedaemonian Constitution

The earliest attested constitution of a Greek state is the so-called **Great Rhetra** from Sparta. Although terse, often obscure, and textually difficult, it warrants quotation and brief discussion:

Found a Temple of Zeus Syllanius and Athena Syllania;
*Phyle **phyles** and obe **obes**;*
*Set thirty with Kings as a **Gerousia*** [i.e., a Council of Elders]*;*
At intervals (?) assemble betwixt Babyca and Cnacium;
Thus bring in (i.e., proposals) and dismiss (i.e., assembly [?]);
Let People have final authority (??).
(Plut. *Lyc.* 6)

According to Plutarch sometime later a "rider" was added to the Rhetra under the kings Polydorus and Theopompus (king during the First Messenian War):

But if the People should speak crookedly, then let the Elders and Kings dismiss (them).

Tyrtaeus, in the late seventh century, gives a verse paraphrase of the Rhetra together with the rider:

They listened to Apollo and brought home from Delphi
the god's prophecies and words that came true:
to lead the Council are the god-honored Kings
who care for the lovely city of Sparta –
they and the ancient Elders. But then the men of the people,
obedient to straight arguments,
are both to say fair things and to do everything justly,
nor are they to advise the city crookedly.
Let victory and power lie with the majority of the people
for thus did Apollo speak to the city in these matters.
(Tyrtaeus, Fr. 4 West)

A few points require brief comment. The Lacedaemonians are to institute two cults (otherwise unknown) as they introduce this new constitution; presumably the deities involved are to watch over the process and to guarantee the proper working of the new order. A *phyle* is a tribe; meant are the three Dorian tribes of the Hylleis, Dymanes, and Pamphyli (Tyrtaeus, Fr. 19 West). An *obe* – unlike a *phyle* – is a geographically based subdivision of the Lacedaemonians, that is to say, people of all three *phylai* lived in a given geographically defined *obe*. What the process of "phyling phyles" and "obing obes" involved defies certainty, but Greek states did on occasion carry out tribal reforms whereby the population was redistributed among (new) tribes or the like (Hdt. V 66 and 68; [Arist.], *Ath. Pol.* 21); and something of the sort – perhaps a redistribution among existing tribes – may have happened in Sparta as well. The Gerousia at Sparta did in later times have a fixed membership of thirty and included within the thirty stood the two kings (Hdt. VI 57; Thuc. I 20; Plut. *Lyc.* 5). The two landmarks, Babyca and Cnacium, presumably marked off the field where the assembly took place. The text of the final line of the Rhetra is hopelessly corrupt; translation here is based on a combination of ascertainable general sense and hopeful guesswork.

The translation of the final word of the Rhetra's penultimate line likewise causes difficulty. The "rider" uses the same word ("dismiss") and indisputably refers to a dismissal of the assembly. On the view that one should interpret the obscure in the light of the clear, the above translation of the Rhetra posits that the same thing is meant as in the "rider" – a dismissal of the assembly.

In explanation of this, Plutarch states that initially the assembly could vote only "yes" or "no" to proposals placed in front of it (presumably by the Gerousia collectively or possibly just the kings). Under these circumstances the "rider" seems superfluous. But if, as Plutarch states happened later on, someone within the assembly could "move an amendment" to a proposal, then the "rider" begins to make sense. If such an amendment were transparently a better idea than the original proposal, then well and good. If, however, the Gerousia disliked it and it were defeated in a "procedural" vote, then as far as the Gerousia was concerned, it was a matter of so far, so good. But if such an amendment succeeded, then the Gerousia risked losing control of the assembly as well as the passage of a proposal of which it disapproved. In this case the "rider" empowered it to dismiss the assembly forthwith so as to prevent the passage of any proposal. As debate proceeded in the assembly, the members of the Gerousia at some point had to decide if in their opinion no decision were better than any decision.

The Great Rhetra makes no mention of one important Lacedaemonian institution well known from the fifth century. Although kings continued to reign in Sparta, by then they had lost most of their political power, and a college of five officials called **ephors** had become the genuine executive government of the Lacedaemonians. The ephors were elected (Arist. *Pol.* 1270b–1271b) annually, and one was eponymous – i.e., the Lacedaemonians indicated a year by naming the eponymous ephor for that year (for an example from a Lacedaemonian treaty, see Box 14.1). As emerges not only from the passage in Aristotle, but also from various historical texts (e.g., Thuc. I 132–134), the ephors wielded great power even over the kings. All the same, the kings retained considerable powers when on campaign, and they enjoyed much prestige at home even in peacetime (Xen. *Const.Lac.* 13). Moreover, the kings sat in the Gerousia. The Gerousia, amongst other things, in the third century still set the agenda for the Assembly (Plut. *Agis*, 11), though the ephors presided over its meetings (Thuc. I 87). The Assembly, which consisted of all adult male Spartiates, elected the ephors and the members of the Gerousia by acclamation and also passed decrees in the same fashion (Arist. *Pol.* 1270b–1271a with Plut. *Lyc.* 26; Thuc. l.c.).

Lacedaemonian Society

The society of Sparta has traditionally been portrayed as austere and militaristic, especially given Sparta's military power as well as the regimented system, the *agoge*, for educating Spartiate youth. At age seven, Spartiate boys entered the *agoge* in which they received athletic and military training until reaching full manhood at age 30. The classic description of this tough training (with many gruesome details about beatings and the like) stands at Plut. *Lyc.* 17sqq. Given the late date of this description, much in it may be exaggeration or mythologizing reconstruction. Girls apparently entered the *agoge* as well, though here Plutarch offers fewer details (*Lyc.* 14; cf. **Euripides** *Andr.* 590sqq.). The adult Spartiate males whom the *agoge* produced were supposed to be professional soldiers who lived not from any trade, but from half of the produce from land which Helots worked for them.

Yet there is another side to society in Sparta. For example, it seems that Spartiate males were also enthusiastic singers and members of choirs. Plutarch describes an elaborate three-part male choir (boys, men in their prime, and old men) which presumably turned on the different quality of the male voice according to age (*Lyc.* 16). Various poets attest to the high esteem in which the Spartiates held music and singing (see Plut. *Lyc.* 21), and Sparta produced a number of significant poets such as Tyrtaeus and **Alcman**. The latter's intricate "maidens' hymn," the *Partheneion*, composed for a choir of fifteen girls (possibly divided up into two subchoirs singing in responsion), shows that Spartiate girls too received musical training. So besides training to be soldiers, Spartiates went to choir practice – an artistic side to their society which one might not expect.

Finally, the Spartiates, both men and women, underwent rhetorical training – albeit in a specific kind of rhetoric, namely the art of the "comeback" for which they were renowned (*Lyc.* 19–20). Lesser mortals generally think of the perfect response to a slight or stupid remark while brushing their teeth the next morning. Not so the Spartiates, who time and again immediately replied with devastatingly apt retorts (many of them collected by Plutarch in his *Sayings of Lacedaemonian Kings and Commanders*). Spartiate women also were schooled in this art, as the following selections from Plutarch's *Sayings of Lacedaemonian Women* show. When a naive Athenian lady who was visiting Sparta admiringly noted that Spartiate women were the only ones who could order men around, Gorgo, the daughter of one Lacedaemonian king and the wife of another, told her, "yes, but, then again, we're also the only ones who give birth to men." When a certain foreign man, wearing rather elaborate dress, was making advances to Gorgo, she told him just to go away – "you can't even act like a woman properly, much less a man." One woman, on hearing her son explain that his sword was too short, advised, "try taking a step forwards." And another woman, when a man made her an improper proposal, responded as follows: "When I was a girl, I learned to obey my father. When I became a woman, I learned to obey my husband. So you can run your proposal by him first."

NOTES

1 K.J. Dover. (1964) "The Poetry of Archilochus," *Fondation Hardt* X: 183–212, esp. 190–195.

QUESTIONS FOR REVIEW

1   What role did the Helots play in Lacedaemonian society?
2   What historical evidence can be gleaned from Tyrtaeus' poems?
3   What were the features of a standard treaty of alliance with Sparta?
4   What were the basic institutions of Sparta's government?
5   In what stages did Sparta expand beyond the Laconian Plain?

QUESTION FOR FURTHER STUDY

Sparta was larger than all other *poleis*, had a very unusual social structure, founded few colonies, never had a tyrant (see chap. 7), and had a unique dual kingship which lasted much longer than kingship elsewhere. What factors contributed to Sparta's becoming such an atypical *polis*?

FURTHER READING

Numerous books on Sparta exist, and the bibliography is necessarily highly selective.

General:
Cartledge, P. (2002) *Sparta and Lakonia: A Regional History 1300–362 B.C.* (2nd edn.). London.
Forrest, W.G.G. (1980) *A History of Sparta 950–192 B.C.* London. (A readable introduction, but devoid of references to the sources.)
Huxley, G.L. (1962) *Early Sparta*. London. (Utility is limited to its thorough references to the sources.)
Jones, A.H.M. (1967) *Sparta*. Oxford. (A succinct but still useful political narrative because of the constant reference to the sources.)

On the "myth" of Sparta:
Powell, A. and S. Hodkinson (eds.). (1994) *The Shadow of Sparta*. London.
Tigerstedt, E.N. (1965–1978) *The Legend of Sparta in Classical Antiquity*. Stockholm.

Lacedaemonian Society:
Cartledge, P. (2001) *Spartan Reflections*. London.
Luraghi, N. (ed.). (2003) *Helots and their Masters in Laconia and Messenia: Histories, Ideologies, Structures*. Washington.
Oliva, P. (1971) *Sparta and her Social Problems*. Prague. (A thorough if sometimes involuted discussion of the issues.)

Messenian Wars:
Parker, V. (1991) "The Date of the Messenian Wars," *Chiron* 21: 25–47.

7

Tyranny

| 750–650 | 650–510 | 510–480 |

8th and 7th centuries mostly	decline of kingship
657–584 or circa 630–550	Cypselids rule over Corinth
560s and circa 560–557 and 547–511	Peisistratids rule over Athens
mid-6th century	Pittacus rules over Mytilene
530s – circa 522	Polycrates rules over Samos

The Decline of Kingship in Greece and its Replacement by Aristocracy

In chapter 4, the rule of kings was briefly discussed along with the general decline of that form of rule. That decline mostly took place in the eighth and seventh centuries BC, concurrent with colonization (see chap. 5), rapid population growth, rapid improvement in material culture, and intensification of contacts with the Near East in the form of trade (see chap. 4). In brief, the

A History of Greece: 1300 to 30 BC, First Edition. Victor Parker.
© 2014 Victor Parker. Published 2014 by John Wiley & Sons, Ltd.

kings of the Greek cities faced far-reaching historical developments beyond their control – developments which often placed them before severe challenges.

In particular, economic development meant that many aristocrats grew wealthy enough to challenge a weak king's authority. For example, in the *Odyssey* – reflecting, roughly, the early seventh century BC –, the aristocratic suitors push the ineffectual Telemachus aside even if, in his father's absence, he ought to become the lawful king of Ithaca. Moreover, the rapidly growing population placed intense demands on the king to make new land available. One king of Argos, Meltas, – granted in the sixth century –, was deposed and replaced with a new king after failing to distribute to the Argives land which he had won in a war against the Lacedaemonians. Meltas gave the land to Arcadian refugees instead (Paus. II 19 with Diod., VII, fr. 13,2). While the precise details are irrecoverable, clearly Meltas had badly misjudged the situation as well as overestimating his people's willingness to defer to his authority. In any case, the Argives, like most other communities in Greece, needed extra land. Unlike most other communities, the Argives retained the monarchy – this time –, but the institution probably fared worse in other cities in similar situations as kings failed to see to their people's needs in changed circumstances or otherwise misread situations.

Replacing the kings in most cases were aristocrats who for their part gained a reputation for oppressiveness, greed, and resentment-inducing displays of wealth. The sixth-century Megarian poet **Theognis** bewailed the arrogance of those who ruled over Megara in his day and feared that it would all lead to a **tyrant** in the end:

> . . . *this city is pregnant, and I fear lest she bear a man*
> *who will straighten out our evil outrages* . . .
> . . . *the (city's) leaders*
> *have turned to fall into much evil.*
> *Good men. . . never yet ruined a city,*
> *but when it pleases evil men to work outrages*
> *and they destroy the nation and render unjust judgments*
> *for the sake of profits and power* . . .
> *From these things come civil wars and internecine murders*
> *and a "monarch"* (sc., tyrant) . . .
> (Lines 39–52; in line 52, read against West "monarch" instead of "monarchs.")

To turn to Megara's neighbor, Corinth, when Cypselus was seeking to become "tyrant" of that city in 657 on the traditional or "high" chronology (based on the fourth-century AD chronographer **Eusebius**) or circa 630 BC on the "low" chronology (based on Herodotus), he brought into circulation oracles, allegedly uttered by Delphic Apollo, to denounce the ruling aristocrats of Corinth, the **Bacchiads**, who themselves were supposed to have slain that city's last king (Diod. VII, Fr. 9,6; cf. Paus. II 4):

> *Eëtion* (i.e., Cypselus' father), *no one honors you who are worthy of many honors;*
> *Labda* (i.e., Cypselus' mother) *is with child and will bear a millstone which will fall*
> *Upon the "monarchical" men and bring justice to Corinth.*
> (Hdt. V 92b)

(The positive presentation of the tyrant shows that the oracle was composed before the fall of the tyranny after which nothing positive was said anymore about the Corinthian tyrants – for how they were perceived after their deposition, see the remainder of Hdt. V 92.) Here the would-be tyrant appears as someone who will punish the current rulers and thus bring "justice" to Corinth. This overlaps substantially with the lines from Theognis.

A few more examples may serve to characterize the aristocratic regimes which often replaced kingship. The **Penthilidae** who ruled in Mytilene on Lesbos went about the town hitting people with clubs until a revolt ensued (Arist. *Pol.* 1311b). In Megara wealthy aristocrats were forcing small landholders off the land in order to let their sheep graze there. The man who eventually became tyrant of Megara, Theagenes, gained popularity by slaughtering the aristocrats' flocks (Arist. *Pol.* 1305a).

Luxury goods were inextricably linked with the aristocratic culture of the era. Sappho of Mytilene (mid-sixth century) sang of "golden bracelets, purple robes, intricate bangles, countless silver goblets, and ivory" (Sappho, Fr. 44 Lobel-Page). She appreciated imports from Lydia (Sappho, Fr. 39 Lobel-Page) and lamented it when she could not acquire such finery (Sappho, Fr. 98 Lobel-Page). Yet elaborate displays of wealth such as those by the **Geomori**, the aristocrats on Samos who allegedly had deposed that island's last king (Plut. *Greek Questions*, 57), may well have caused much resentment:

> *When they had combed their locks, they used to go*
> *Into Hera's sacred precinct; wrapped in fair robes,*
> *They covered the ground of the broad earth with their snow-white clothes*
> *On which were golden clasps in the shape of cicadae.*
> *Their hair, in golden fillets, waved in the wind*
> *While they wore wondrously wrought bracelets on their arms.*
> (Asius of Samos, fr. 13 Bernabé; against Bernabé, do not invert lines 4 and 5.)

This sort of conspicuous consumption also appears with the aristocrats who in Erythrae allegedly killed the last king, Cnopus, and thereafter governed the city:

> *They were wrapped in purple coats and tunics with purple borders. They wore sandals with many laces during the summer, but during the winter they went about in women's footwear. They wore their hair long and braided it. As to their heads, they were conspicuous through golden and purple fillets. Additionally, they wore jewelry of solid gold, like*

women. They compelled some of the citizens to carry litters, others to be rod-bearers, and yet others to clean the streets. They had the sons of some brought to their common meetings and ordered others to bring their own wives and daughters . . .
(**Hippias** of Erythrae, *BNJ* 421, Fr. 1)

In the light of all this, one begins to understand why Theognis could view a "tyrant" as someone who would "straighten out" a city and its aristocratic rulers.

The Word "Tyrant" and Defining "Tyranny"

At this point a few remarks on the original meaning of the word "tyrant" in Greek will assist the exposition. *Tyrannos* is not a native Greek word, but rather an import from another language. Its first attested use in Greek comes in a poem by the mid-seventh century BC poet Archilochus who used it to denote – in a positive context – Gyges, the King of Lydia (Fr. 19 West). All the early uses of the word can be interpreted as positive; none is demonstrably negative. The positive connotation of the word still appears in later Greek literature, most noticeably in the works of the tragedians who use *tyrannos* as their standard word for "king" (Fornara, Nr. 8). Herodotus too uses *tyrannos* (and its derivatives) as an occasional synonym for "king" or "ruler." Thus, Periander, the tyrant of Corinth, exhorts his son Lycophron to receive the "tyranny" and to become "king" (Hdt. III 52,3–4). Another example: "Philocyprus, whom of (all) *tyrannoi* Solon . . . praised the most" (Hdt. V 113,2). This Philocyprus ruled as an hereditary king over the Cyprian city of Salamis, yet Herodotus can include him, in an obviously positive context, among the "tyrants." Conversely, Herodotus can refer to rulers traditionally classed as "tyrants" with the word for "king" (V 44,1 and VI 23,1). For Herodotus the two words still function as synonyms, and on the basis of Herodotus' usage no one could possibly distinguish between two classes of rulers – "kings" on the one hand and "tyrants" on the other. That distinction is fully on display in the work of the Athenian Thucydides who consistently uses "king" for hereditary monarchs who lawfully hold their position and "tyrant" for that class of rulers who form the subject of this chapter.

Defining that class was and is difficult, however. Aristotle attempted an analytical definition and distinguished two basic kinds of "tyrant" in Greece, the "elective" tyranny (whereby a "tyrant" was lawfully appointed to his position) and the more normal kind (whereby a "tyrant" gained his position by an unlawful act of his own) (*Pol.* 1285a and 1310b). For the latter Aristotle distinguishes three such unlawful methods of becoming a "tyrant": an ambitious man secures high office for himself and misuses it to make himself a tyrant; a military leader takes advantage of his command and establishes a tyranny; a lawful king oversteps his legitimate authority and so becomes a tyrant. This last method highlights, incidentally, the difficulty in distinguishing "kings" from "tyrants" – Pheidon of Argos was apparently a lawful king (Ephorus, *BNJ* 70, Fr. 115) whom many viewed as a tyrant (e.g., Hdt. VI 127).

However, Aristotle failed to mention one way in which a fair number of Greek tyrants obtained their position: they inherited it from their fathers. Well-known tyrants such as Hippias of Athens and Periander of Corinth came to power in that way. In fact, Aristotle seems completely to have missed one fundamental characteristic of Greek tyranny: its general heritability. When the tyrant had no son, his nearest male relative (a nephew – as in the case of Psammetichus of Corinth who succeeded his uncle Periander [Arist. *Pol.* 1315b]; a brother – as in the case of Hiero of Syracuse who succeeded his brother Gelon [Arist. *Pol.* 1315b]) often assumed power after his death. Moreover, the dynastic nature of the tyranny was apparent to non-Greek observers such as the Persians: When the Persians conquered Samos in the late sixth century, its tyrant Polycrates had been dead for a few years and the tyranny deposed. The Persians promptly appointed a new tyrant, Polycrates' nearest surviving male relative – his brother Syloson (Hdt. III 139sqq.; see also chap. 9). Syloson's son, Aeaces II, would eventually succeed to the tyranny as well (Hdt. VI 13). More tyrannies than the Samian evince this dynastic nature: the Orthagorids, the family of Orthagoras, for example, ruled for a century in Sicyon (Arist. *Pol.* 1315b) – from circa 650 to 550 on the "high" or from circa 610 to 510 on the "low" chronology.

"Tyranny" and "kingship" have this dynastic nature, this heritability, in common. That is to say, etymology and practice coincide in this important point; and from this point discussion should now proceed.

Tyrants' Self-Presentation and Their Subjects' View of Them

The first thing to note now is that no "tyrant" is known ever to have referred to himself by that term or to have been called that to his face by one of his subjects. Herodotus records another "oracle" from the early period of the tyranny in Corinth. The priestess at Delphi allegedly spoke the following words to Cypselus as he entered the shrine there:

> *Blessed is he that enters into my temple,*
> *Cypselus, Eëtion's son, King (basileus) of famous Corinth!*
> (Hdt. V 92 e2; a third line was added after the fall of the tyranny)

The positive presentation of Cypselus, once again, shows that the verses date from the early period of the tyranny. The person who had the most interest in having them circulate was, of course, none other than Cypselus himself who refers to himself as "King of Corinth."

Herodotus, in fact, cannot imagine anyone referring to a tyrant to his face as anything other than "King": In the famous story of the Ring of Polycrates (Hdt. III 42), when the poor fisherman comes into the tyrant's presence, he opens his address to the latter with the words "O King!" Likewise the Athenian ambassador who speaks before Gelon of Syracuse on the eve of the Persian Wars: "O King of the Syracusans!" (Hdt. VII 161).

Moreover, some of the (admittedly late) stories about the tyrants present them in ways which make them seem like kings institutionally as well. The tyrants of Sicyon, according to a story recounted in Nicolaus of Damascus (who incidentally refers to them as *basileis*, "kings") were obligated by their position to carry out certain sacrifices on behalf of the community (*BNJ* 90, fr. 61). This was apparently true of the archaic kings as well (see chap. 4).

The Rise of Tyranny

At this point a few general conclusions may be drawn concerning the rise of tyranny in Greece. First, it is difficult to distinguish "tyrants" from "kings" in any objective way; in fact, the two groups of rulers have much in common. The "tyrants" succeeded aristocratic regimes which had become increasingly unpopular. These regimes had themselves arisen when overmighty aristocrats had successfully challenged the authority of the kings who had ruled even earlier. Did the tyrants – who played on the aristocrats' unpopularity – present their own regimes as the return to an ancestral form of rule which, in hindsight, had begun to look ever better to the subjects of the Bacchiads, the Penthilidae, the Geomori, and so on? This view is not consensus opinion, but it does accord with the evidence which has survived. There is, moreover, one literary depiction of an aristocratic regime in Greek epic, the episodes involving the suitors on Ithaca in the *Odyssey*. The suitors, as has often been pointed out, are irresponsible, oppressive, and abusive (albeit young) aristocrats who have effectively usurped the government of Ithaca. In response, their subjects do nothing so much as to yearn for the return of the rightful king – e.g., the swineherd Eumaeus who "prayed to all the gods that wise Odysseus might return to his home" (*Od.* XX 238–239) – and that the suitors may all receive their just deserts. In the words of the old and tired woman who is still up at dawn grinding grain for the suitors to eat:

> *Father Zeus, who rule over gods and men, . . .*
> *fulfill now even for wretched me this wish which I shall speak:*
> *May the suitors this day for the very last time*
> *take their fine repast in Odysseus' halls . . .*
> *May they sup their last!*
> (*Od.* XX 112–119)

Tyrants' Domestic Policy

Slightly less problematic than the analysis of the rise of tyranny is the description of the tyrants' rule in their communities. First, many tyrants – as one might

Figure 7.1   Hydria from Athens, circa 520, possibly depicting the *Enneakrounos*. Drawing and carrying water, incidentally, was a routine, backbreaking task for women in ancient Greece, one performed each day in the early morning before it got too hot. Cf. *Homeric Hymn to Demeter*, 98–100. Source: Marie-Lan Nguyen, http://commons.wikimedia.org/wiki/File:Public_fountain_MNA_Inv10924.jpg (accessed 14 January 2013) CC BY 2.5

expect after the descriptions of the regimes which preceded them – were genuinely popular at the outset. A salient feature of many tyrants' domestic policy – the construction of large public buildings for their communities – surely helps to explain this initial popularity.

Often such a building's benefit to the community was immediate as with the large fountainhouse, the ***Enneakrounos*** (see Figure 7.1), which the **Peisistratids** in Athens (circa 560s to 511 BC) built in order to secure the city's water supply (Thuc. II 15). Greece is a hot, thirsty place; and especially in the Summer months, when most rivers dry up, access to a dependable source of water is critical for a community. The *Enneakrounos* – the name means "nine heads – i.e., water-spouts" – was a great boon to the Athenians.

Theagenes of Megara (early sixth century BC?) provided the Megarians with a fountainhouse as well (Paus. I 40). One of the great engineering projects of the ancient world, the tunnel of Eupalinus (see Figure 7.2) on Samos (Hdt. III 60; Arist. *Pol.* 1313b) served the same purpose: the tunnel, which ran approximately one mile and connected the city of Samos with a dependable spring, secured Samos' water supply even in the case of a siege by foreign enemies.

There are other examples of investments in what one today might call "infrastructure" to the long-term social and economic benefit of the community.

Figure 7.2 The tunnel of Eupalinus on Samos. Source: Photo (c) imagebroker/Alamy

Box 7.1 *Tyrants and Games*

The tyrants were great patrons of the four Panhellenic festivals (the **Olympic Games** at Olympia, the **Pythian Games** at Delphi, the **Isthmian Games** on the Isthmus, and the **Nemean Games** at Nemea) and avidly participated in the chariot races in which the financial sponsor, as opposed to the driver, was deemed the victor. Cleisthenes of Sicyon, probably in 576, announced his daughter's marriage at Olympia after winning in the chariot race there (Hdt. VI 126–127). Cleisthenes also won in the chariot races at Delphi (Paus. X 7). Pheidon, the king or "tyrant" of Argos depending on one's point of view (Arist. *Pol.* 1310b), actually marched on Olympia, occupied it, and celebrated the games himself sometime in the early sixth century (Hdt. VI 127).

Moreover the tyrants commonly instituted new festivals in their own communities. Thus, Cleisthenes founded Pythian Games in Sicyon (Schol. **Pindar**, *Nem.* 9 inscr.) while Polycrates was planning to found Delian or Pythian Games on Samos when his death intervened (**Suidas**, s.v. Tauta soi kai Pythia kai Delia – "Pythian Games and Delian Games are all one to you"). Peisistratus of Athens instituted the Greater Panathenaean Games at Athens ([Arist.], Fr. 637 alt., Rose). The central event here was a torch relay race.

These games were first of all religious festivals in honor of a god or goddess. Besides the entertainment value of the games and the renown which a tyrant gained when he won in an event, the patronage of these festivals – as indeed the erection of temples and dedications at Olympia and Delphi (e.g., that of Cypselus: Hdt. I 14) – helped to emphasize the tyrants' piety and dutifulness towards the gods.

Figure 7.3   The temple of Zeus in Athens. (For scale, note people next to columns which are circa 55 ft high.). Source: William Neuheisel, http://commons.wikimedia.org/wiki/File:Temple_of_Olympian_Zeus,_Athens.jpg (accessed 14 January 2013) CC BY 2.0

Polycrates, for example, constructed a large artificial breakwater around the harbor of Samos (Hdt. l.c.; Arist. l.c.). Although the benefit here may not have been immediate, improved infrastructure long-term meant increased revenue from the trade which would pass through the "new and improved" facilities.

The economic benefit from the temples which the tyrants erected or planned to erect was indirect, but the enormous scale of the projects shows that the tyrants viewed them as worth the immediate large outlays. Some projects actually saw completion such as the archaeologically attested sixth-century temples of Athena on the **Acropolis** and of Dionysus on the southern slope of the Acropolis – the Peisistratids presumably had both built. Others ultimately proved too much. The temple of Zeus Olympius (see Figure 7.3) to the southwest of the Acropolis exceeded the resources of the city of Athens, and the temple, despite work on it in the early second century BC under the Seleucid king Antiochus IV Epiphanes I, stood uncompleted down into Roman times when the Emperor Hadrian, with the resources of the entire Roman Empire at his disposal, had it finished (Arist. *Pol.*, 1313b; **Vitruvius**, VII 15; Paus. I 18). On Samos Polycrates commissioned the biggest temple in the Greek world, which even in its incomplete state was still impressive enough (Hdt. III 60; Arist. *Pol.* 1313b).

Box 7.2   *Tyrants and the Arts*

The tyrants were great patrons of the arts in their cities. The temples which they built were works of art in their own right; and these and other structures commonly required decoration. Thus, the treasury of the Sicyonians at Delphi, probably erected during the tyranny of Cleisthenes, displayed metopes – relief panels – which depicted scenes from the saga of the Argonauts (for illustrations, see H. Knell, *Mythos und Polis* [Darmstadt, 1990], figures 27–30). Apart from the architectural arts, the tyrants employed sculptors and jewelers. Both Cypselus and his son Periander dedicated a statue at Olympia (Strab. VIII 3,30, p. 353, and Ephorus, *BNJ* 70, fr. 178). Herodotus can actually mention the name of the jeweler – Theodorus, son of Telecles, of Samos – who wrought for Polycrates of Samos the famous ring which Polycrates cast into the sea (Hdt. III 41–42).

The tyrants also fostered the nonvisual arts. Many employed court poets: **Arion** of Methymna worked at the court of Periander of Corinth (Hdt. I 24); **Ibycus** of Rhegium worked at the court not just of Polycrates of Samos (Fr. 1 Page) but also at that of the Sicyonian tyrants (Fr. 308 and 322 Page). The Peisistratids in Athens allegedly sponsored the redaction of the Homeric epics, the *Iliad* and the *Odyssey* (**Cicero**, *De oratore*, III 137; *Anthologia Palatina*, XI 442). During the Peisistratid tyranny the poet **Thespis** also produced the first tragedy at Athens (**Charon** of Lampsacus, *BNJ* 262, Fr. 15; *Marmor Parium*, *BNJ* 239, A ep. 43).

The most spectacular example of the tyrants' sponsorship of poets is probably the victory-ode which Pindar of Thebes, the greatest of the Greek lyric poets, was commissioned to write for Hiero, the tyrant of Syracuse, when the latter won in the chariot race at Olympia – the first Olympian Ode. This complex poem, brimming with praise for Hiero, was probably set to music and performed in Hiero's honor in Syracuse; and the performance was certainly designed to impress Hiero's greatness upon all his subjects. Here it emerges directly that the tyrants commonly expected a return on their investment in the arts. An astonishing amount of early Greek art and poetry is in any case due to the tyrants' willingness to fund such works, whether in their immediate self-interest or not.

The sheer scale of all these projects – temples, fountainhouses, breakwaters, and so on – impresses; as does, in comparison, the absence of such projects from the decades preceding the tyrannies. The tyrants, unlike the regimes which had gone before, must have marshaled their communities' resources for such projects (instead of for "conspicuous consumption"). Several factors aided the tyrants in this design. First, the tyrants occasionally had at their disposal large amounts of property which they had confiscated from their aristocratic opponents. In Athens the Alcmaeonids had owned large estates at the time when they went into exile during Peisistratus' tyranny. This land did not lie fallow for four decades until they returned; and most scholars have generally assumed that Peisistratus disposed of much of this property. Cypselus in Corinth appears to have confiscated much property (Hdt. V 92e), and later historians working from Herodotus' account assumed that it was the property of his opponents, the Bacchiads, whom he deposed, that he confiscated (Nicolaus of Damascus, *BNJ* 90, Fr. 57).

Second, the tyrants in Athens levied a 5% tax on produce (Thuc. VI 54; cf. [Arist.], *Ath.Pol.* 16, where the figure is 10%). Although Thucydides in retrospect characterized this as a modest levy, it may have represented a novelty at the time – because of the absence of coinage (see chap. 8), there may not have been any such tax, at least not a universal one, before the tyrants. In any case, Peisistratus is known to have supported small landholders as best he could, and in later times the countryfolk looked back on his reign as a golden age ([Arist.], l.c.). That detail, given the hatred for the tyrants later on, is unlikely to have been invented and vouches for the essence of the information in the *Ath.Pol.* If Peisistratus really did carry out, as usually supposed, a full-scale redistribution of the land which he confiscated from the Alcmaeonids, then he probably did put many of these small landholders back onto the land, and even a modest 5% tax on the produce from their farms may have brought not just increased, but also regular, amounts into the treasury for the tyrants to disburse.

The tyrants chose, as shown above, to invest these resources to a large extent in extravagant building projects. First, the people who worked to build the temples had to receive remuneration for their labor, and this provided employment for much of the population which was not or no longer involved directly with agricultural production. The workers' pay could then be used to buy food and other goods – that is to say, much of the tyrants' outlay for erecting the temples flowed back into community's economy, especially into the farms. The overall effect, presumably, was to stimulate agricultural production as well as to create demand for manufactured goods which in turn allowed for more specialized employment.

Finally, a few less tangible benefits of all of these projects require at least a brief mention. Large, splendid buildings could easily become a source of pride for the community. When one reads Herodotus' account of Polycrates' splendid buildings on Samos – the Temple of Hera, the breakwater in the harbor, the tunnel of Eupalinus –, one cannot fail to notice Herodotus' local informants' pride in their community's architectural and engineering achievements (Hdt. III 60). The tyrants' building projects helped engender a sense of community.

Tyrants' Foreign Policy

In their foreign policy the tyrants usually sought to keep the peace. The "land-wars" of an earlier age (see chaps. 5 and 6) cease. First, tyrants often owed their position to another tyrant's aid. Thus, a Naxian adventurer, Lygdamis, helped Peisistratus regain the tyranny of Athens in 547 BC (Hdt. I 61). Peisistratus later helped Lygdamis become the tyrant of Naxos (Hdt. l.c.). Lygdamis later on helped Polycrates to become tyrant of Samos (**Polyaenus**, I 23 – granted, the source is late). This mutual aid which tyrants had often given each other fostered peace among them.

The same applies to the tyrants' numerous marriage alliances, both with each other and with prominent aristocratic families throughout Greece. Hippias of Athens in the late sixth century married off his daughter Archedice to the son of Hippocles, the tyrant of Lampsacus (Thuc. VI 59). Proclus of Epidaurus in the early sixth century married off his daughter Melissa to Periander, the son of Cypselus, tyrant of Corinth (Hdt. III 50). An Argive woman named Timonassa, from a prominent family in Argos, was married first to Archinus, apparently the ruler of the Corinthian colony of Ambracia and certainly a member of the Cypselid family which ruled Corinth. Her second marriage was to Peisistratus, the tyrant of Athens ([Arist.], *Ath. Pol.* 17). In circa 576 BC Cleisthenes of Sicyon made a match for his daughter Agariste with Megacles, the future leader of the Alcmaeonid family in Athens (Hdt. VI 126sqq.). Though there were exceptions – for example, Periander of Corinth eventually went to war against his father-in-law Proclus (Hdt. III 52) – these marriage alliances helped keep the peace, and the diplomacy which the women carried out who made these alliances work should not be underestimated. Timonassa, in particular, seems to have been exceptionally good in her role, and Argive troops did indeed help her second husband in gaining control of Athens, so the marriage alliance bore fruit.

If the tyrants were interested in keeping the peace at home, abroad some of them attempted to build up small "empires" – possibly with a view towards trade. Peisistratus of Athens established an outpost on the coast of northwestern Anatolia, Sigeium, just to the south of the Hellespont. As governor of Sigeium Peisistratus appointed his son Hegesistratus (Hdt. V 94). In addition, when the Dolonci, a non-Greek people, on the Chersonnese – the western side of the Hellespont – asked the Athenians to supply them with a ruler, Peisistratus was happy to oblige: Miltiades the Elder was sent out to rule the Chersonese (Hdt. VI 34sqq.). Peisistratus and Miltiades were old opponents, so the arrangement may well have been mutually satisfactory – Peisistratus saw a potential challenger of his rule leave, while Miltiades may well have preferred to play first fiddle abroad as opposed to second fiddle at home. While governing the Chersonnese Miltiades conquered the northern Aegean island of Lemnos (and presumably also Imbros), and it remained ever after an Athenian possession (Hdt. VI 140). Under Peisistratus, then, the Athenians established a strong presence on and near the Hellespont. Athens was already importing a large amount of grain from colonies on the Black Sea, and securing part of the trade-route from the Black Sea to the Aegean may well have helped motivate Peisistratus' interest in maintaining these outposts in the northeastern Aegean.

In the West Cypselus, the tyrant of Corinth, appointed his sons as the oecists of Leucas and Anactorium. His son and successor in the tyranny, Periander, conquered Corcyra, a Corinthian colony from before the time of the tyranny, and brought it within this "empire" (see chap. 5). Another Cypselid, Archinus, apparently ruled the colony of Ambracia ([Arist.], *Ath.Pol.* 17). The Corinthian tyrants were evidently interested in controlling, as a family affair, a small colonial "empire" to the northwest of Greece proper; an "empire" which commanded the eastern end of the trade-route between Greece and the colonies in southern and central Italy and on Sicily.

The Fall of the Tyrannies

Despite their initial popularity, the tyrannies eventually fell. If they may be viewed as the last stage of kingship in Greece, then they were *a priori* hopelessly exposed to the same processes which had been making kingship obsolete in most of Greece. Unlike the older kings, the tyrants' dynasties were young creations which ultimately could not credibly lay claim to the ancestral authority which the kings had once held. Moreover, the circumstances which called forth the tyrants and made them seem an improvement over unrestrained aristocratic rule in course of time passed – ironically, the tyrants' policies had a good deal to do with their passing. After a tyrant had successfully "straightened" a city, what need had the city to continue to submit to his rule? In fact some cities had arranged for the lawful appointment of a "tyrant" and had carefully limited his term in "office." Thus in Mytilene the tyrant Pittacus derived his absolute powers for a term of ten years (**Diogenes Laertius,** I 75 – granted, a late source) from a mandate of the Mytilenaeans:

> They (i.e., the Mytilenaeans) *established the base-born Pittacus as tyrant of the hamstrung and ill-fated city – and cheered him on, all of them together!*
> (Alcaeus, Fr. 348 Lobel-Page)

Alcaeus, a contemporary, bitterly opposed and hated Pittacus – hence his outrage at his townsmen's act. Pittacus, all the same, laid down his position when those ten years were up. Likewise in Athens Solon (see chap. 8) received absolute powers to reform the state, though in his case he only had one year in which to carry out his reforms. Solon himself rejected the label of "tyrant" (Fr. 33 West), and no one in antiquity classed him as one; but ancient opinion need not bind scholarly judgment, and distinguishing credibly between Pittacus' position in Mytilene and Solon's in Athens presents insuperable difficulties. In brief, there were at least two "tyrants" with a fixed term in office.

The other tyrants, however, who had no such fixed term, may well have overstayed their welcome. As their rule went on, they were reluctant to give up power, and if challenged, they had to engage in repressive measures to retain it. The matter is especially clear in the case of the Peisistratids in Athens. Towards the tyranny's end, after his brother's assassination, the final tyrant, Hippias, engaged in repressive measures including judicial executions of those whom he suspected of plotting against him (Hdt. V 55 and Thuc. VI 59). Other tyrants elsewhere may have acted similarly as their subjects began to chafe under their rule. Such actions, of course, could only undermine the tyrants' position even more.

To take one more example: In Asia Minor, in the final years of the sixth century, the tyrants were clinging to power only because the Persians, who had conquered the region in the mid-sixth century, were propping them up, evidently in the mistaken belief that the Greeks themselves preferred them as the traditional form of government (see also chap. 9). The Persians restored at least one deposed tyrant dynasty (Hdt. III 139sqq.) and supported another's desire to be restored (Hdt. V 96); in one case (Mytilene) they actually established a new tyranny (Hdt. V 11). As Histiaeus, then tyrant of Miletus, pointed out to his fellow tyrants in Asia Minor:

> Each one of us rules as tyrant over his city thanks to Darius (the current King of Persia); if Darius' power were removed, neither I myself would be able to rule over the Milesians, nor would anyone else elsewhere. For each of the cities would prefer to be under a democracy than under a tyranny.
> (Hdt. IV 137)

When the Ionian Revolt broke out in 499 BC, it was directed in the first instance against the tyrants, all of whom lost their position as the revolt began (Hdt. V 36–38 and VI 13). One of them, Coës of Mytilene, was actually stoned to death as soon as his erstwhile subjects were able to lay their hands on him (Hdt. V 38). Again, the deep unpopularity of the tyrants' rule in its final stages is palpable.

These final stages remained in the Greek collective memory; and later Greeks viewed the tyrannies through that distorting lens – hence the impassioned denunciations of tyranny at, e.g., Hdt. V 92. Hence also the many tales told of tyrants' atrocities (for example, the hollow bronze statue of a bull in which Phalaris of Acragas allegedly had people roasted alive – e.g., Diod. XIX 108). Few of these stories are credible, but the overwhelmingly negative presentation of the tyrants in later Greek literature, ironically, provides one useful method for identifying genuine information about them: anything positive said about a tyrant is likely to antedate all the negative stories and thus to be contemporary with the tyrannies themselves.

QUESTIONS FOR REVIEW

1 What factors contributed to the decline of kingship in most of Greece?
2 What characterized the aristocracies which preceded the tyrannies in many *poleis*?
3 Why were tyrants initially popular?
4 How did the tyrants redirect their communities' resources?
5 What factors contributed to the tyrannies' eventual downfall?

QUESTION FOR FURTHER STUDY

Another explanation of the phenomenon of tyranny (more usual than the one advanced in the text) views it as an outgrowth of the phenomenon of aristocracy (see Cawkwell in Further Reading). According to this view, aristocrats vied with each other for power, and occasionally one of them outdid all the others. There is much merit to this view. How can one interpret the evidence to support it?

FURTHER READING

The standard reference work on the tyrants remains the following:
Berve, H. (1967) *Die Tyrannis bei den Griechen*. Munich.

In English the following are useful:
Andrewes, A. (1956) *The Greek Tyrants*. London. (Dated, but still useful.)
Lewis, S. (2009) *Greek Tyranny*. Bristol.

Other works on tyranny include:
Anderson, G. (2005) "Before *turannoi* were Tyrants. Rethinking a chapter of early Greek history," *CSCA* 24: 173–222.
Austin, M.M. (1990) "Greek Tyrants and the Persians," *CQ* 40: 289–306.
Cawkwell, G.L. (1995) "Early Greek Tyranny and the People," *CQ* 89: 73–86.
McGlew, J.F. (1993) *Tyranny and Political Culture in Ancient Greece*. Ithaca, NY.
Parker, V. (1998) "Τύραννος. The semantics of a political concept from Archilochus to Aristotle," *Hermes* 126: 145–172.
Parker, V. (2007) "Lawgivers and Tyrants." In: H.A. Shapiro (ed.), *The Cambridge Companion to Archaic Greece*, 13–39. Cambridge.
Waters, K.H. (1971) *Herodotos on Tyrants and Despots. A Study in Objectivity*. Wiesbaden.

8

Athens from Cylon to Cleisthenes

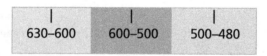

630–600	600–500	500–480

late 7th century (??)	Cylon attempts to establish a tyranny
594? or circa 570?	Solon carries out his reforms
560s	Peisistratus becomes tyrant
circa 560	Peisistratus becomes tyrant again
557–547	Peisistratus' second exile
547	Peisistratus' third tyranny begins
514	Hipparchus assassinated
511	Hippias deposed
end of 6th century	Cleisthenes carries out his reforms

The Cylonian Conspiracy

The first event in Athens which left behind an ineradicable mark on the historical record involved an aristocrat, Cylon, who attempted to establish a tyranny. Herodotus (V 70–71) produced a brief account of the matter, and Thucydides (I 126) a longer one – mostly to correct and pedantically to supplement the

A History of Greece: 1300 to 30 BC, First Edition. Victor Parker.
© 2014 Victor Parker. Published 2014 by John Wiley & Sons, Ltd.

Figure 8.1   The Acropolis of Athens. Source: © Guillaume Piolle, http://commons
.wikimedia.org/wiki/File:Acropolis_-_restoration.jpg (accessed 14 January 2013)
CC-BY-3.0

account in Herodotus. This historiographical circumstance makes the story
reconstructable.

Cylon seized the acropolis (see Figure 8.1) since its possession in the early
period was apparently tantamount to control of Athens itself. Cylon's attempt
failed, however; and he found himself besieged on the acropolis. He and his
fellow conspirators as suppliants claimed sanctuary at the shrine of Athena on
the acropolis, but low supplies compelled them to negotiate with the besiegers
for a safe passage down. These, however, did not keep their end of the bargain
and as the conspirators descended from the acropolis, massacred them. The
circumstances – the besiegers had reneged on their word and the conspirators
had supplicated the goddess – made the massacre a sacrilege, and the blame
fell on one particular leading family of Athens, the Alcmaeonids. The Alcmaeonids had many enemies and rivals, and ever after when the latter saw an advantage in it, they dredged up the old story.

To this basic account, common to both historians, Thucydides adds a few
interesting details, for example, that Theagenes, the tyrant of Megara, was

Cylon's father-in-law and sent troops in aid of his son-in-law's attempt. Tyrants commonly aided each other in this way, and the marriage alliance between a tyrant and a prominent aristocrat has its parallels also (see chap. 7). Cylon's attempt slots neatly in among the other tyrannies of archaic Greece, and it has its uses in providing an example of an attempt at a tyranny which failed. Moreover, Thucydides very carefully corrects a misunderstanding that arises from reading Herodotus' account: Herodotus implies that Cylon died along with his supporters, but Thucydides makes clear that Cylon himself had slipped through the siege before the massacre occurred. Apparently nothing was ever heard of him again.

Finally, there is the difficult matter of the date. Herodotus (V 71) states only that all this happened before the time of the Peisistratid tyranny – i.e., before the 560s BC (see below). The fourth-century AD chronographer Eusebius (I 197–198 Schoene), on the other hand, states that Cylon won in the Diaulos, the double-footrace, in the Olympic Games in 640 BC. If one wishes to trust Eusebius, then Cylon, if he was a young man in 640 and attempted to found a tyranny as a mature adult, should have made his attempt in the late seventh century.

Solon

Some years after the massacre of Cylon's supporters (probably) the Athenians turned in a severe crisis to a man called Solon, evidently an older politician with a reputation for circumspection. Since all sides trusted him, the authority to reform Athens as he saw fit was vested in him – for one year. In principle he held an "elective" tyranny (see chap. 7). More information about Solon and his reforms survived than about Cylon for one simple reason: Solon wrote poetry about his reforms, and writers such as Plutarch and the author of the Pseudo-Aristotelian *Constitution of Athens* (i.e., the *Ath.Pol.*; see Box 8.1) quoted liberally from these poems when describing Solon's achievements. What Solon's poems directly attest is what is most certainly known about the period, and discussion should proceed in the first instance from them. In the second instance it should proceed from what Plutarch and the author of the *Ath.Pol.* say about or on the basis of Solon's poetry for they had the full text in front of them even if they quoted only selected bits.

Finally, as with Cylon, there is some question as to Solon's date. If one views the so-called **Archon** List (see Box 8.3) as accurate for the early sixth century, then the matter is clear: Solon was archon in 594 BC. On the other hand, Herodotus (I 29–30) synchronized Solon's travels in the ten years after his reforms with the reigns of Amasis of Egypt (570 to 526 BC) and Croesus of Lydia (traditionally 561–547). Based on this evidence, the earliest possible date for Solon's travels, then, is 571–561, which places his reforms in circa 572. Most scholars incline to follow the Archon List, though the matter is far from certain.

Box 8.1   *The Pseudo-Aristotelian "Constitution of Athens" (Ath.Pol.)*

Aristotle is known to have written a tract on the constitution of Athens. Unfortunately, the *Corpus Aristotelicum*, the body of Aristotle's works collected in antiquity, contains no such tract. Except for brief fragments, the work appeared irretrievably lost. In 1879 and 1890, however, papyri were found in Egypt which contained a "Constitution of Athens" which overlapped with some of the attested fragments (e.g., *Ath.Pol.* 53,4 with Aristot. Fr. 469 Rose) so scholars naturally enough assumed that Aristotle's long-lost "Constitution of Athens" had finally been found.

Continuing investigation of this text since then has, however, cast doubt on that assumption; most scholars now think that the text is not by the great man himself, but rather by a pupil to whom the master had possibly assigned the task of drawing up a preliminary draft. The text of the attested "Constitution of Athens" – conventionally abbreviated as *Ath.Pol.* for *Athenaion Politeia* – differs in some points from the genuinely Aristotelian *Politics* (e.g., on how **archons** were selected), contains many contradictory statements (e.g., on the eligibility of the Zeugitae for the archonship), and is often unattentive (*Ath.Pol.* 3 contains a late fifth-century blueprint for an oligarchic constitution, but the author mistakes it for a seventh-century text – even though it mentions the Solonian census which according to 7,3 had not even been introduced yet).

Moreover, the *Ath.Pol.* contains bizarre expositions such as the following: According to Herodotus, the third continuous tyranny of Peisistratus and his son Hippias lasted for 36 years, i.e., from 547 to 511 BC (see below in text). The author of the *Ath. Pol.*, however, has the following chronological information to offer about how long each of the three tyrannies lasted:

First Tyranny:	6 years (*Ath.Pol.* 14,3)
Second Tyranny:	7 years (*Ath.Pol.* 15,1)
Third Tyranny:	6 years (Peisistratus) (*Ath.Pol.* 17,1)
	17 years (Hippias) (*Ath.Pol.* 19,6)

Simple mathematics exposes the fraud: $6 + 7 + 6 + 17 = 36$! The author of the *Ath. Pol.* took Herodotus' 36 years and *arbitrarily divided them up among the three tyrannies*.

For these and other reasons, however one feels about this text's authorship, it is a problematic source. The errors, contradictions, and misinterpretations, however, do tend to refer to the early period of Athenian history (i.e., the sixth century – Solon and the tyranny); when the author of the *Ath.Pol.* is describing the situation of the fifth century, which was substantially the same as in his own day, he appears to be far more accurate.

In the text of this chapter the *Ath.Pol.* is continually used as a source, as indeed it must be, but never unsupported by reference to other sources or by argument. Moreover, for methodological reasons the argument generally proceeds from a statement in the *Ath.Pol.* which refers to the later period and reasons backwards to the earlier period. Statements in the *Ath.Pol.* about the earlier period, when they cannot be supported by argument or otherwise, are not used.

The Agrarian Crisis in Athens during the Early Sixth Century

Whatever his date, Solon's poetry sheds much light on the social and economic circumstances of his day, circumstances which led to the Athenians' granting him near-dictatorial powers. First, debt-slavery in Athens had reached critical proportions. In pre-Solonian Athens – as elsewhere in Greece in general – it was possible to borrow using, in lieu of anything else, one's own person as security. In the case of default, the creditor claimed the debtor's person – until such time as the loan was repaid, the debtor remained the creditor's slave. Solon himself describes the steps which he took to address the problem of rampant debt-slavery in Athens:

> To their god-founded native land of Athens I brought back many Athenians who had been sold – some legally, others illegally – as well as those who had fled to escape pressing debt, although they no longer sounded like Athenians when they spoke, so far had they wandered; and others who lived here at home in degrading servitude . . . (Fr. 36 West, lines 8–14)

Several things emerge clearly enough from these verses. First, Solon freed "debt-slaves" in Athens and redeemed those whom their creditors had sold abroad. Second, he allowed those who had gone into exile abroad on account of their debts to return. Solon, then, seems to have carried out a general cancellation of debts – what Plutarch called the *seisachtheia* or "shaking off of burdens." Both Plutarch (*Sol.* 15) and "Aristotle" (*Ath.Pol.* 6) add that Solon also made the use of the person as security illegal in Athens.

One could, of course, borrow using other security than the person; for example, one could take out a loan against one's land. Solon wiped out such debts as well by destroying the proof of the mortgage as a few more verses from the same poem show:

> Let the dark Earth be my witness . . . from whom I pulled out many pegs (apparently mortgage markers, thus Plut. *Sol.* 15) that once in many places had been thrust in – she who once lay in servitude is now free. (Fr. 36 West, lines 3–7).

As a result, the creditor had no way to prove that the debtor owed a thing.

A second piece of evidence is a law of Solon's which prohibited the export from Athens of any natural produce other than olive oil (see Box 8.2). Olive trees are planted on second-rate land which cannot produce staple crops, in particular grain. Solon had no objection to the export of what the second-rate land produced; he was worried about the export of what the first-rate land produced – grain – which he wished to retain in Athens. For it was to obtain grain that people were mortgaging their land or their own persons.

From these two pieces of evidence a picture emerges of a society which was having difficulty feeding itself, not necessarily so much because of the land's inability to produce enough, but because landowners were sending abroad much of what the land did produce in order to acquire other commodities through trade. What grain remained in Athens, by the inexorable law of supply and demand, became even more costly. Whoever had no direct access to the means of production had to purchase through trade or to borrow. Even those who did own some land were having difficulty and were borrowing against what little land they still held.

Driving all of this was the rapid population growth discussed in chap. 4. Greek inheritance customs, whereby all sons inherited equally, compounded the problem. That is to say, if a man had four sons, his land was quartered upon his death. Subdivision over several generations could leave a small landholder in desperate straits if that fragment of an originally sizable estate were now capable of supporting a family in good years only. A bad harvest could force the landholder to borrow against the land itself – thus placing even that remaining fragment at risk. Those who had already lost their land were in an even more difficult position.

Most Greek communities in the eighth and seventh centuries had dealt with the problem of a burgeoning population through colonization (see chap. 5), but in Athens a crisis did not arise until the sixth century. But by Greek standards Athens did possess a large amount of territory to begin with, and, second, war with Megara had gained for Athens the entire Plain of Eleusis, one of the most fertile areas in Greece (see chap. 5). These two factors could not ultimately prevent, but clearly did postpone the crisis.

Solon's response to the crisis, moreover, amounted to nothing more than an additional postponement. He freed the debt-slaves, but did little to address the causes of the debt-slavery. His prohibition of the use of the person as security, ironically, made it even more difficult for those in need to borrow in order to feed themselves. The prohibition of the export of grain is more difficult to judge, but it can only have had efficacy if landowners kept the level of production exactly the same as before – if the level of production, with the removal of an economic incentive to produce (e.g., the value of the grain abroad), actually dropped in response to Solon's law, then matters could well have become even worse. Solon's response may have provided welcome and immediate relief, but clearly did not solve the problem.

That required not an "elective," but rather a conventional tyrant, Peisistratus (see below).

Solon's Political Reforms

Solon's reforms of the Athenian constitution, on the other hand, did have a longer-lasting impact. They involved alterations to the census of classes as well as the introduction of a second executive council for the assembly.

Athenian society in the classical period was divided into four classes, defined in terms of wealth, as follows:

Pentacosiomedimni ("500-Bushel-Men") = Men whose property produced more than 500 bushels of grain or the equivalent

Hippeis ("Horsemen") = more than 300 bushels of grain
Zeugitae ("Yokemen") = more than 200 bushels of grain
Thetes = all others

Although Solon never mentions this class census in his poems, both Plutarch (*Sol.* 18) and "Aristotle" (*Ath.Pol.* 7,3–4) attribute it to him and argument shows the attribution to be plausible. The system assesses wealth in terms of agricultural produce and antedates the introduction of coinage. Only in the absence of coinage would anyone measure wealth in such a clumsy way, and when coinage was introduced, the Athenians, as one might expect, almost certainly redefined the classes in terms of coin at the rate of one **drachma** to the bushel (cf. Plut. *Sol.* 23,3). Now the earliest Greek coins in the western Aegean date from the mid-sixth century (CAH IV^2, Pp. 431–445), so the Athenians' census of classes was designed before then. With that one comes into Solon's time.

Next, the system itself provides a bit of evidence as to how it arose. First, the name of the highest class (Pentacosiomedimni) is an invented name, made up to fit the system being designed. Only after the system of classes defined in terms of bushels of grain had been invented, could a class with the name "500-Bushel-Men" be introduced. The other names ("Horsemen," "Yokemen," and Thetes) antedated the system. The first two names actually imply an earlier system of wealth-based classes, incidentally, for "Horsemen" are those wealthy enough to keep a horse (always a status symbol in Greece) whereas the "Yokemen" are those who at least own two oxen. (The meaning of "Thetes" remains obscure.) At some point an older three-class system based on wealth was modified by redefining the classes in terms of bushels of grain and by the addition of a fourth, highest class. Solon's year in power is almost the only time possible for such a reform.

Solon's other chief constitutional reform requires discussion also. Up until his time, the **Council of the Areopagus** had functioned alone as an executive council to the Athenian assembly, but now Solon introduced a second council usually called after the number of its members the **Council of 400**. It consisted of one hundred men selected in an unknown fashion from each of the four tribes into which the Athenians were then subdivided. Its functions, strictly speaking, are unknown but analogy with its replacement under Cleisthenes (see below) suggests that it to some degree supervised the agenda for a meeting of the Assembly. Which political functions the Council of the Areopagus retained exclusively is obscure, but until the mid-fifth century it held the "guardianship of the **laws**" (Plut. *Sol.* 19; [Arist.] *Ath.Pol.* 25,2). Scholars have traditionally interpreted that phrase as referring to an effective veto-right over any decree made by the Assembly since in the event of a conflict a law overruled a decree – presumably "guardianship of the laws" included the ability to say what the "law" was (see chap. 15). The Gerousia at Sparta held a similar right (see chap. 6), so parallels for such an arrangement do exist. If the Council of the Areopagus held that right until the mid-fifth century (when it lost all political powers – [Arist.] *Ath.Pol.* 25,2), it presumably held the same right in Solon's day also.

Box 8.2   *Solon's Laws*

During his year in power in Athens Solon also made new laws for the Athenians. The pre-Solonian laws were allegedly the product of a mostly legendary lawgiver called Draco whose supposed code became proverbial for its liberal use of the death penalty (Plut. *Sol.* 17). Very little can be said of Draco, though the homicide law (Fornara, Nr. 15) which the Athenians continued to use from Solon's time on down was always ascribed to him.

Although Solon's laws were publicly displayed, no systematic collection has been transmitted in the ancient literature. Moreover, the Athenians were in the habit of attributing any and every law to Solon, whether or not he can have had anything to do with it (for examples, see Hignett 1952: 18–19, in Further Reading). Proving that a particular law attributed to Solon is genuinely Solonian therefore presents challenges, but occasionally an argument can be made in favor of authenticity.

For example, Plutarch speaks of one of Solon's laws as follows:

> Olive oil was the only produce that Solon allowed to be exported, but otherwise he forbade exportation. He decreed that any offender against this law should be cursed by the archon or else should pay one hundred drachmas into the public treasury.
>
> (Plut. *Sol.* 24 = T 5 and Fr. 65 Ruschenbusch)

The two punishments immediately suggest that the text of the law has been tampered with – that is, one punishment is original and the second was added at a later date. In this case the monetary fine has obviously been added because in the time of Solon, who measured wealth in terms of bushels of grain, coinage had not yet been introduced. The genuinely Solonian punishment is the solemn curse by the archon. In a later age, when the Athenians placed less faith in the ability of an archon's curse to deter criminal activity, a new punishment was added to the old law. In fact, the use of the archon's curse as a punishment in and of itself suggests that this particular law was written in the early period, i.e., is highly likely to be genuinely Solonian. This sort of argument, however, has to be made for each allegedly Solonian law one by one.

Solon's purpose in introducing the new Council of 400, according to his own poems, was to give the less wealthy in Athens a share in the government. Plutarch (*Sol.* 19) paraphrases one of Solon's poems which referred to the two councils – the old Council of the Areopagus and the new Council of 400 – as "a double anchor" which would hold the state steady before buffeting from both sides (i.e., rich and poor). The Council of the Areopagus represented the interests of the rich, as it consisted of all former archons (Plut. l.c.), and only the two wealthiest classes, Pentacosiomedimni and Hippeis, were eligible for the archonship ([Arist.] *Ath.Pol.* 26,2; otherwise, however, 7,3). The archons, according to the genuine Aristotle (*Pol.* 1273b–1274a), were moreover elected (otherwise [Arist.] *Ath.Pol.* 8,1). In premodern societies elections are almost entirely a matter of organizing supporters – that is to say, something which only the wealthy can manage. Elections in Athens inherently favored the wealthy and were avoided whenever possible by the later democracy. If either of the two councils, then, was to meet the demands of the "poor," it must have been the Council of 400. Members of the third class, the Zeugitae, could serve on this council (Plut. *Sol.* 18). The Thetes themselves were entitled to attend the Assembly and to serve as **jurors** (Plut. l.c.), but were barred from playing any other role.

This reconstruction accords with Solon's known sentiments that while the "poor" did deserve some say in government, the "rich" deserved a far greater one:

> *For to the People I gave as much power as was sufficient for them, neither taking away from what was owed to them nor adding to it.* (Fr. 5 West, lines 1–2)

> *. . . I did not see fit that the nobles should with the base have an equal share of our country's rich soil.* (Fr. 34 West, lines 8–9)

Solon made no pretence at egalitarianism, and his constitution reflected his bias.

The Tyranny of the Peisistratids

A few years after Solon's year in power an aristocrat called Peisistratus made himself tyrant. He had a regional support base along the coast in northern Attica; and his supporters bore the name *Hyperakrioi*, literally "the people on the other side of the hills" – that is to say, they received that name from people in the city of Athens itself, which lay on one side of the hills in question. Sometime in the mid-560s (for the date, see below) Peisistratus allegedly feigned an assassination attempt and persuaded the Athenian Assembly to provide him with a bodyguard of club-bearers. This put at his disposal a small troop with which he proceeded – like Cylon some decades earlier – to seize the Acropolis (Hdt. I 59).

Unlike Cylon, however, Peisistratus did succeed in making himself tyrant as the Athenians acquiesced in his rule. The difference in the Athenians' reaction can probably be best explained with reference to the intervening "elective tyranny" of Solon who, despite his failure to address the actual causes of the economic crisis, had at least provided some relief. Solon's year as "elective tyrant" had made the idea of submitting to a ruler with absolute power palatable to the Athenians, and Herodotus assures his readers that Peisistratus ruled "wisely and well" and that he altered no existing offices (Hdt. l.c.).

Although Peisistratus – as events would show – was genuinely popular with the majority of the Athenians, his aristocratic opponents, the **Alcmaeonids,** and another prominent clan, the **Philaids**, united against him and expelled him from Attica. The length of his exile is unknown, but he struck an alliance with Megacles, the leader of the Alcmaeonid clan, which allowed his return, an alliance which involved Peisistratus' marrying Megacles' daughter. A cheering populace welcomed Peisistratus back – an indication of his popularity, and in circa 560 (for the date, see below) he became tyrant for the second time. Unfortunately, Peisistratus' and Megacles' relations soon soured. Herodotus tells a scandalous story to account for Peisistratus' and his wife's failure to produce any offspring. The scandal should probably be discounted, but one chronological point may be gleaned: the marriage (and by extension the second tyranny) lasted long enough so that the absence of children began to attract notice (i.e., a few years). In any case, with his alliance with Megacles in tatters, in 557 Peisistratus lost the tyranny a second time (Hdt. I 60–61).

The second exile lasted ten years, and Peisistratus returned to Athens in 547 (Hdt. I 62). This time he came with an army – troops he had hired himself, troops provided by a Naxian freebooter by the name of Lygdamis, and troops provided by his allies in Argos (he now had an Argive wife, Timonassa) (Hdt. I 61; [Arist.] *Ath.Pol.* 17,4). The actual battle was a foregone conclusion, for the majority of the Athenians had no wish to fight against Peisistratus – whose popularity continued unabated. The Alcmaeonids and their supporters fought, but no one else. After the battle the Alcmaeonids went into exile, and Peisistratus ruled for the rest of his life unchallenged. After his death his son Hippias succeeded him and ruled until his deposition at which time the Peisistratids had governed Athens for 36 years (Hdt. V 65). The figure applies to the third tyranny only which according to Herodotus (I 64) was established just before the Persians took Sardis in 546 (Nabonidus-Chronicle, II 15–17, ANET, p. 306).

The government of the Peisistratids has already been discussed in chap. 7; here only a few loose ends need tying up. On the occasion of the Greater Panathenaea (Thuc. VI 56; cf. Hdt. V 56), two men, for private reasons, assassinated Hippias' brother, Hipparchus. The tyranny lasted for three more years, and was deposed in the fourth (Thuc. V 59; cf. Hdt. V 55). In its final stage the tyranny became much more oppressive than before (Thuc. l.c.).

The Alcmaeonids, meanwhile, who had tried to expel the tyrants once before by military means (Hdt. V 62), were now seeking external help. Despite their exile, they retained much wealth, and used it to finance the construction of a new temple of Apollo at Delphi. In gratitude the priests at Delphi agreed to apply pressure on the Lacedaemonians to help the Alcmaeonids. The priests accordingly refused to answer any question which a Lacedaemonian, whether on state or private business, put to the oracle. Whatever the question, the reply was "first liberate the Athenians" (Hdt. V 62–63). Any state business in Sparta which, for form's sake – much like the founding of a colony (see chap. 5) –, required divine approval was blocked. Eventually, the Lacedaemonians gave in to this arm-twisting.

A small force went to Athens, but Hippias was ready. Thessalian cavalry came to his aid, and for the first time Lacedaemonian troops faced horsemen (see chap. 1). Uncertain how to fight against such troops, the Lacedaemonians were defeated. Shortly thereafter, however, Sparta's king, Cleomenes, invaded Attica with more troops. This time the Lacedaemonians were ready for cavalry and defeated their opponents easily enough (Hdt. V 63–64).

Hippias and his closest supporters retreated onto the Acropolis where, having laid in ample supplies, they prepared to wait Cleomenes out. However, they also attempted to smuggle their underage children from the Acropolis and out of Attica. Unfortunately for them, their children fell into the Lacedaemonians' hands. Now they had little choice but to capitulate. Hippias fled to Sigeium, the Athenian outpost in Asia Minor, which he continued to rule (Hdt. V 65).

This took place in the year 511 (Thuc. VI 59; [Arist.] *Ath.Pol.* 32,2). The chronology of the rest of the tyranny is worked out from this date. First, the Greater Panathenaea at which Hipparchus was slain was that of 514. Next, the third, continuous tyranny lasted 36 years, that is, from 547 to 511; and the second exile lasted ten years, that is, from 557 to 547. At this point exact information peters out and guesswork begins. The length of the first exile is unknown; the length of the second tyranny was a few years at least, and there is no reason to suppose that the first tyranny was much shorter. The second tyranny's beginning can fall into about the year 560, and the preceding exile and first tyranny into the 560s. Thus:

First tyranny:	circa mid-560s
First exile:	circa late 560s
Second tyranny:	circa 560 – 557
Second exile:	557–547
Third tyranny:	547–511

The date of Peisistratus' death and Hippias' succession is impossible to determine.

Cleisthenes' Reforms

When Hippias fled to Sigeium, the Alcmaeonids returned to Athens. The leader of the clan was Cleisthenes, who attempted to fill the power vacuum. Other aristocrats in Athens, however, had little desire to see people who had been in exile for a generation return and promptly take charge. One aristocrat, Isagoras, who relied on his personal friendship with Cleomenes, opposed Cleisthenes and attempted to set up a narrow oligarchy (for the concept of **oligarchy**, see Box 13.1) in which three hundred of his supporters alone would have political rights. When Cleisthenes gained the upper hand in the civil strife by "taking the people into his political faction" (Hdt. V 66 – the concrete meaning of this phrase has been endlessly debated), Isagoras appealed for aid to Cleomenes who, underestimating how much opposition he would meet, returned to Athens with but a handful of soldiers. The Athenians, however, rose up against this interference, and Cleomenes in his turn found himself besieged on the Acropolis. He negotiated for his release, and a safe-passage was granted and – unlike in the case of Cylon's supporters many decades earlier – honored (Hdt. V 66, 69–70, and 72).

Box 8.3   *The Archon List and Early Athenian History and Chronology*

The Athenians indicated a date by naming the chief archon for that year. Unless one knew the archons by heart or had a list, such a date made little sense. In the late fifth century BC the Archon List was publicly inscribed in Athens (Cadoux 1948: 77, in Further Reading). Fragments of that publicly inscribed list have been found, but the full list has been transmitted indirectly through authors in antiquity who used it for dating purposes (e.g., the author of the so-called *Marmor Parium* [*BNJ* 239] or Diodorus). In the form in which it has been transmitted it listed annual archons all the way up to the year 683 BC. Then it listed the ten-year archons, next the lifetime archons, and finally the Athenian kings together with the lengths of their reigns till the accession of Cecrops in 1581 BC. No one has ever denied that the early sections of the list are pure myth, yet the archons of the fourth and late fifth centuries are clearly fully historical. At some point between the two ends sound historical information ends, and guesswork and reconstruction begin; but where should that point be set?

Both Herodotus and Thucydides make statements concerning the tyranny which contradict the evidence in the Archon List for that period. Herodotus (VI 123) states that the Alcmaeonid family went into exile from Athens at the beginning of the third tyranny and remained in exile until the tyranny's deposition in 511. Thucydides for his part (VI 54) notes that the tyrants took good care that a member of their family always held the archonship.

Yet a fragment of the public Archon List asserts something rather different, since it enumerates (Fornara, Nr. 23) the following archons in succession:

Hippias (clearly the tyrant, for 526 BC)
Cleisthenes (an Alcmaeonid, for 525 BC)
Miltiades (a Philaid, for 524 BC)

According to this the Alcmaeonids had not only been in Athens during the tyranny, but the most prominent male of the clan had actually colluded with the tyrant. This raises many questions about the reformer Cleisthenes as well as about the tyrants' willingness to allow aristocratic families such as the Philaids and Alcmaeonids to hold office. Moreover, if the Archon List is correct, then both Herodotus and Thucydides are badly mistaken on various points. The other possibility is that the Archon List itself is an inaccurate reconstruction already in the late sixth century. If that is the case, then the Archon List's date for Solon (594 BC) cannot be accepted.

Cleisthenes now had a free hand to reform Athens' constitution. Where the tyrants had left Solon's constitution intact, Cleisthenes altered it radically and introduced many of the features of the classical Athenian **democracy** (whether or not Cleisthenes' constitution should itself be considered democratic). Hitherto the Athenians had been subdivided into four ancestral tribes. Cleisthenes did not abolish them, but he removed their political role and gave it to ten new tribes which he designed to break down any geographical divisions in Athenian society (one need only think of Peisistratus' regional support base in northern Attica – see above). Each of Cleisthenes' new tribes consisted of three *trittyes* with one *trittys* coming from each of three regions of Attica (see Figure 8.2) – the city of Athens and the central plain; the coastal regions including the plain of Eleusis; and the Mesogaia, the interior region. Each new tribe thus combined members from each of these three regions. Each *trittys* was itself subdivided into **demes** ([Arist.] *Ath.Pol.* 21). In the city of Athens itself these demes were neighborhoods or quarters; in the countryside they were old villages or hamlets that had been grouped together. The demes varied in size (for this, see e.g. Thuc. II 19), so that one *trittys* might have more or fewer than another. However, all *trittyes* were apparently of approximately the same size by population ([Arist.] *Ath.Pol.* l.c.). All of Cleisthenes' political reforms turned on this redivision of Athenian society.

Cleisthenes replaced Solon's Council of 400 with a new one of 500 such that fifty members came from each new tribe. These fifty were selected – by lot ([Arist.] *Ath.Pol.* 43) – at the level of the deme ([Arist.] *Ath.Pol.* 62,1). Each deme, based on its population, could select a certain number of councillors. Cleisthenes, finally, allowed the Council of the Areopagus to remain in place.

Next, from now on almost all offices in Athens were filled by lot. However, at least the most important offices – in particular the nine archons – were reserved for members of the top two Solonian census classes which Cleisthenes left intact. When their year in office ended, the nine archons continued to join the Council of the Areopagus which consisted, as it had under Solon's constitution, of all living ex-archons. This Council retained the "guardianship over the laws" – a putative veto-power over the Assembly's enactments.

To summarize Cleisthenes' changes:

Solon		*Cleisthenes*
4 old tribes	→ for political purposes replaced by →	10 new tribes
Council of 400	→ replaced by →	Council of 500 (*Boule*)
Council of the Areopagus	→	Council of the Areopagus

One of the very few exceptions to the general rule that offices were now filled by lot was the tribal generalship ([Arist.] *Ath.Pol.* 61). Each of the new ten tribes carried out an annual election to select a **general** who might be elected two or more years in a row. Moreover, the army now consisted of ten tribally

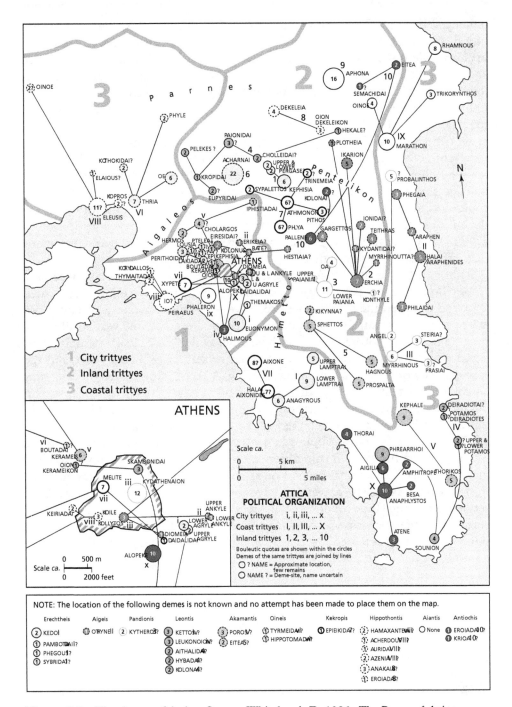

Figure 8.2 The demes of Attica. Source: Whitehead, D. 1986. *The Demes of Attica.* Princeton Univ. Press. p. xxiii

organized brigades. The commander-in-chief, with a deciding vote in the case of a deadlock among the ten tribal generals, was one of the nine archons, the **archon polemarchos** (Hdt. VI 109). The insistence on mixing Athenians from each of the three main regions now becomes clear: whenever the Athenians fought, they did so shoulder-to-shoulder with men from throughout Attica.

It is now necessary to discuss briefly how Cleisthenes intended this system to work. First, all 500 Councillors never met at one time. Only the fifty from a given tribe were in session at a given time, and they were on-call day and night for a tenth of the year, a so-called prytany. During this time they set the agenda for the Assembly and presided over its meetings ([Arist.] *Ath. Pol.* 43); and in practice they functioned as a sort of executive council whenever the Assembly could not meet. They did this without pay, and that is the significant feature of the entire system – one which militates against viewing the new constitution as a democracy (see also Box 13.1) even if Herodotus (V 78) and many Athenians (e.g., Fornara, 39A) saw it that way.

Although technically anyone might be selected by the lot for service as a Councillor, evidently the selection was made from a predetermined list of men who had declared their willingness to serve – because anyone who could not afford to be away from his fields or his work for a tenth of the year would have been ruined if the lot had fallen on his name. Only those of substantial means could afford to serve, and this financial bar to service probably prevented the vast majority of the population from serving. After all, how many people today could forgo a tenth of their salaries and still survive? In Cleisthenes' system public service was an honorary duty reserved for those who could afford it. Power, in other words, was retained in the hands of the wealthy.

The same consideration applies to the other public offices, in particular those which lasted a full year. In the absence of any pay, obviously, only a wealthy man could serve as a tribal general or as an archon. In the case of the archonship, the law expressly prevented anyone from the lower two classes from serving. And since the Council of the Areopagus consisted of ex-archons – that is to say, its membership was drawn exclusively from the top two classes – and since it probably retained an effective right to nullify any decree from the Assembly, even more power was reserved for the wealthy.

QUESTIONS FOR REVIEW

1   What evidence does Solon's poetry provide for the reconstruction of early Athenian history?
2   What makes the Pseudo-Aristotelian *Constitution of Athens* a problematic source?
3   How was the economic crisis in Athens addressed and eventually solved?
4   What are the chief features of Cleisthenes' new constitution?

QUESTION FOR FURTHER STUDY

The conventional reliance on the Archon List for establishing this period's chronology is based on the assumption that documentary evidence is more reliable than the ancient historians' allegedly subjective statements. That assumption, while not absolutely unassailable, is certainly defensible. Should, however, a document such as the Archon List – which was not publicly inscribed until the late fifth century – itself be treated as a subjective historical reconstruction?

FURTHER READING

The following collection of sources is an excellent introduction to the early history of Athens:
Stanton, G.R. (1990) *Athenian Politics, c. 800 – 500 B.C.: A Sourcebook*. London.

The standard work on the Athenian Constitution:
Hignett, C. (1952) *A History of the Athenian Constitution*. Oxford.

On Draco's homicide law:
Stroud, R.S. (1968) *Drakon's Law on Homicide*. Berkeley.

On Solon:
Blok, J.H., and A.P.M.H. Lardinois (eds.). (2006) *Solon of Athens. New Historical and Philological Approaches*. Leiden.
Ruschenbusch, E. (1966) *Solonos Nomoi. Die Fragmente des Solonischen Gesetzeswerkes.* Wiesbaden. (The standard collection of Solon's [alleged] laws.)

On the Pseudo-Aristotelian "Constitution of Athens":
Kapp, E. and K. von Fritz. (1950) *Aristotle's Constitution of Athens and Related Texts*. New York. (An excellent annotated translation.)
Rhodes, P.J. (1981) *A Commentary on the Aristotelian Athenaion Politeia*. Oxford.

On the Peisistratid Tyranny:
Frost, F.J. (1985) "Toward a History of Peisistratid Athens." In: *Festschrift Chester Starr*, 57–78. Lanham, MD.
Heidbüchel, F. (1957) "Die Chronologie der Peisistratiden in der Atthis," *Philologus* 101: 70–89. (Contains the irrefutable demonstration that the chronology of the Peisistratid tyrants in the Ath.Pol. is worthless.)
Lavelle, B. (1993) *The Sorrow and the Pity: A Prolegomenon to a History of Athens under the Peisistratids, c. 560–510 B.C.* Wiesbaden.

On Cleisthenes and his "revolution":
Ober, J. (1996) *The Athenian Revolution*. Princeton.

On Athenian Democracy, many books exist:
Jones, A.H.M. (1986) *Athenian Democracy*. Baltimore. (Rep. of 1957 edition; old but still useful.)

Ober, J. (2008) *Democracy and Knowledge: Innovation and Learning in Classical Athens*. Princeton. (Much more recent.)

On the Archon List:
Cadoux, T.J. (1948) The Athenian Archons from Kreon to Hypsichides," *JHS* 68: 70–123.
Plommer, W.H. (1969) "The Tyranny of the Archon List," *CR* 19: 126–129.

9

Persia and the Ionian Revolt

550–500	500–494	494–480

546	Persian conquest of Lydia (and Ionia)
circa 505	Athens submits to Persia, wards off Cleomenes, and defeats Boeotia and Chalcis
499	Ionian Revolt against Persia begins
498	Ionians defeated at Ephesus
494	Revolt crushed at Lade; Miletus razed to the ground
late 490s	Persian settlement in Ionia

Athens' Submission to Persia

In the year 506 BC, as Cleisthenes and Isagoras vied with each other for control of Athens, the Lacedaemonian king Cleomenes intervened in Isagoras' favor. This misfired badly (see chap. 8), and Cleomenes left Athens under humiliating circumstances. Never one to stomach insults, Cleomenes sought revenge: he

A History of Greece: 1300 to 30 BC, First Edition. Victor Parker.
© 2014 Victor Parker. Published 2014 by John Wiley & Sons, Ltd.

summoned the Peloponnesian League and secured its approval of a military expedition (see chap. 6). Allegedly Cleomenes did so without divulging against whom he planned to lead this expedition. The League's members, however, once they had voted to go to war, had to follow "whithersoever the Lacedaemonians might lead" – and it was to Athens that Cleomenes led them.

On no objective consideration can Cleisthenes and his political allies have had any chance of warding off this invasion. Two third parties made their own view of the probable outcome clear: The Boeotians, to the northwest of Attica, judged the time right to seize a disputed border region between Attica and Boeotia. The Chalcidians, on the island of Euboea to the north, decided to carry out raids along the Attic coast (Hdt. V 74). That is to say, both Boeotians and Chalcidians assumed that the Athenians would lose – the former could snatch some territory and the latter some plunder, both with equal impunity as the Athenians would not be able to do anything about it.

Cleisthenes was no less astute an observer, and his estimation of Athens' chances came equally low, for ambassadors departed from Athens and traveled to Sardis to seek aid from the Persian Empire against the Lacedaemonians. The Persian **satrap** agreed, but only on the condition that Athens submit to Persian rule (Hdt. V 73). The ambassadors, who, given Athens' desperate circumstances, clearly had instructions to do whatever it took to secure an alliance with the Persian Empire, acquiesced. The official ceremony required them to hand over to Persian representatives a bit of Athenian soil and a bit of water from an Athenian well. The ambassadors had these materials ready to hand, that is to say, they had brought them in the expectation that they might be needed. In other words, the possibility that the Persians might demand Athens' submission had been considered in advance. Presumably Cleisthenes had instructed the ambassadors to avoid this step if possible, but to carry it out if necessary. Given Athens' predicament, one can understand such instructions all too well: Cleisthenes, like everyone else, assumed that Athens would lose against the Lacedaemonians – unless, of course, it could secure an ally. So Athens, from the Persians' perspective, officially became a part of the Persian Empire.

Meanwhile events unfolded in Attica in a way which no one could have foreseen. Cleomenes led his troops to Eleusis where the Athenians mustered what they could and prepared for the worst. As battle was about to be joined, the Corinthian contingent walked off the field. Cleomenes had not initially informed his allies of their opponent, and obviously many in his army had deep misgivings about the campaign now that they stood on Athenian soil. The Corinthians had no quarrel with the Athenians and at the crunch refused to fight against them. Seeing the Corinthians leave, Cleomenes' colleague, the other Lacedaemonian king, Demaratus, also walked off the field. According to the rules of the League at the time, the members were obligated to follow only when both kings acted in concert (see chap. 6). More allies than just the Corinthians had misgivings, and Demaratus' exit removed any obligation to remain on the battlefield. One by one the other allied contingents deserted until Cleomenes, bereft of troops, left also (Hdt. V 75).

This sudden deliverance gave the Athenians the opportunity to deal with the Boeotians and the Chalcidians, who clearly had not been expecting any response. The Athenian army marched northwards into Boeotia, engaged the Boeotians near the Euripus, and defeated them soundly. Elated by the victory, the Athenians now crossed over the Euripus to Euboea, engaged the Chalcidians, and, still on the same day, defeated them as well (Hdt. V 77).

Amid the general rejoicing which ensued, the embassy which had gone to Sardis returned and announced that it had secured an alliance with the Persians – at the cost of Athens' submission to the Persian Empire. One can only imagine the insults heaped upon the hapless envoys. The Athenians never revoked their submission, as any revocation would have tacitly admitted that the submission had duly taken place; and in any case this was something which the Athenians preferred to deal with in the time-honored fashion of not talking about it. The "official" story was that the ambassadors had acted on their own initiative (Hdt. V 73) and that therefore their act was not binding upon the state as a whole. The Persian satrap in Sardis, of course, did not share that view.

Persia and the Greeks

At this point it will be as well to look briefly at the Persians and the vast empire which they ruled. In the closing years of the seventh and the opening decades of the sixth centuries BC, the rulers of the **Medes**, an Iranian people in the highlands of what is now northwestern Iran, slowly built up an empire which by 550 BC extended from the Halys River in the west (Hdt. I 72) to at least Parthia in the east (Behistun, col. II 92–98 with 13–17). In the south it bordered on the **Neo-Babylonian Kingdom**. In 550 BC Cyrus, the ruler of Persis (in what is now southwestern Iran) revolted against the Median king Astyages. In the ensuing war, Astyages' army deserted him and went over to Cyrus who became the new ruler (Nabonidus Chronicle, II 1–4, ANET, p. 305; Hdt. I 127). Convention treats Cyrus' revolt as the beginning of a new empire although it was clearly nothing more than a switch from one dynasty to another which happened to be from another Iranian people, the Persians.

After his defeat of Astyages, Cyrus rapidly conquered additional territory. In 546 he defeated King Croesus of **Lydia** (Hdt. I 76–81, 85–86; Nabonidus Chronicle, II 15–17, ANET, p. 306), famed amongst the Greeks for his legendary wealth (e.g., Hdt. VI 125). Croesus and his predecessors had in painstaking work united under Lydian rule all of Asia Minor not under Median rule with the exception of Lycia in the southwest and Cilicia in the southeast (Hdt. I 28). In particular, the Lydians had conquered all the Greek cities on the mainland of Asia Minor (Hdt. I 26–27) with the exception of Miletus which, nearly inaccessible by land, had withstood Lydian attempts at conquest and with which the Lydians in the end concluded a treaty of alliance (Hdt. I 22). At one blow Cyrus reaped all the fruits of the Lydian kings' labors; Cilicia must at about this time have willingly submitted to the Persians. In 539 Cyrus conquered the

Neo-Babylonian kingdom which besides Mesopotamia included Cyprus, Palestine, Phoenicia, and Syria (Nabonidus Chronicle, ANET, p. 306; Cyrus-Cylinder, ANET, pp. 315–316; Hdt. I 178, 190–191). Before his death in 529 Cyrus also added Bactria, the Sogdiane, and eastern Iran up to the Indus River as these are already integral parts of the empire when Darius becomes king in 521 (Behistun, Col. I 16–17) and were not, apparently, added by Cambyses (529–522 BC) to whom Herodotus ascribes the acquisition of Egypt only (Hdt. III 1sqq.).

The political and administrative entity which Cyrus had erected on the foundations which his Median, Lydian, and Babylonian predecessors had laid was still standing, with its borders hardly changed, three and a half centuries later. Its rulers by then were Greco-Macedonians, but no matter – it was still the same empire (see chap. 23). It was by far the largest and the most durable of the empires in the Near East. Its general stability and durability bears witness to Cyrus' achievement in the most authoritative way possible.

With Cyrus' conquest of Lydia, the Persians also began to rule over Greeks. The Persians, as a general rule, retained the established state of affairs in any territory which they conquered and, if at all possible, they retained existing rulers. Thus, the royal dynasty of Cilicia, which evidently had entered the Persian Empire voluntarily, continued to rule over Cilicia, granted, at least officially, as satraps of the **satrapy** of Cilicia (Hdt. I 74, V 118, VII 98). Likewise, the tiny Athenian outpost of Sigeium in northwestern Asia Minor, which was ruled as a family fiefdom by the tyrants of Athens (Hdt. V 94–95), continued under the rule of those tyrants so that Hippias, when he was expelled from Athens, could flee to Sigeium and rule it personally (Hdt. V 65). The same applies to the position of Miltiades the Younger on the Chersonese – he continued to rule this region after its incorporation into the Persian Empire in the late sixth century (Hdt. VI 39 and IV 137). Most of the Greek cities stood under the rule of tyrants at the time of the Persian conquest, and the Persians supported the tyrants' regimes (Hdt. IV 137). Moreover, under the Persians the anomalous status of Miletus continued. It did not stand under the direct authority of the new Persian satrap, but was bound by a treaty of alliance – just now to Persia rather than to Lydia (I 141). The tribute which the Greeks had paid to the Lydians now went to the Persian satrap who did not increase or restructure it in any way until some fifty years later (Hdt. VI 42).

This desire to act in conformity with established tradition fully characterized the Persians' dealings with the Greeks even then when the Persians intervened in the internal affairs of a Greek city. Thus, when the Persians conquered Samos – unlike the Lydians, the Persians did expand onto the Aegean islands –, the old tyrant dynasty had recently been deposed (see also chap. 7). So the Persians installed as the new tyrant the senior surviving male relative of the last tyrant, Syloson, the brother to Polycrates (Hdt. III 139 and 144). In Mytilene the Persians installed Coës as tyrant (Hdt. V 11). Unfortunately, it is not known what situation preceded Coës' installation. All the same, it is clear that the Persians strove to allow the Greeks to be governed in the

Box 9.1   *Persian Administration in Asia Minor:*
The Letter to Gadatas

Comparatively few Persian administrative documents have survived. One of the very few concerning Asia Minor is the following letter (Fornara, Nr. 35) written by King Darius I to the official Gadatas whose exact rank is not known. The Persian Empire was divided up into satrapies which themselves were divided up into districts and subdistricts, and Gadatas, if not a satrap, could have been a district governor or the like. The authenticity of the letter has occasionally been doubted, but most nowadays accept its authenticity.

> *The King of Kings, Darius, son of Hystaspes, speaks to Gadatas his servant as follows: I learn that you are not obeying my orders in all respects. Now inasmuch as you are working my land, in that you plant the fruit trees from 'Beyond Euphrates' in the regions of coastal Asia, I praise your purpose and on account of these things a great favor is laid up for you in the King's house. But inasmuch as you disregard my intentions concerning the gods, I shall give to you, if you do not change, the proof of a wronged heart: for you have levied a tax on the sacred gardeners of Apollo and have given (them) orders to till profane soil, not knowing my fathers' purpose towards the god, who has told the Persians all exact and . . . (the end of the letter is not attested)*

The letter reveals a surprising amount about the Persians and their administration. First, the letter is composed in Greek by a non-native speaker. When dealing with the Greeks, Persian administrators routinely used Greek; and since this letter concerned a Greek temple and was ultimately meant as a public document (it was eventually inscribed on stone and publicly displayed), a non-native speaker wrote it in passable if awkward Greek.

Second, Persian administrators among other duties were expected to cultivate plantations and orchards: Gadatas' planting of fruit trees from the satrapy of "Beyond Euphrates" (roughly Syria, Phoenicia, and Palestine) in the land under his administration in Asia Minor is specifically entered on the credit side of the ledger before Darius proceeds to the debits. It was the peach, incidentally, which the Persians seem to have cultivated preferentially; the Romans called it the "Persian apple" – and as such it is known to this day: "peach" comes from French *pêche*, from Late Latin *persicum (pomum)*, i.e., "Persian (apple)."

Next, this careful recording of credits and debits – and weighing them up against each other before taking any action – was a quintessential part of the Persian national character. Herodotus – who knew the Persians well (see Box 9.3) – states that a Persian master, when wishing to punish a slave, first reckoned up the slave's good deeds and only punished if the slave's errors outweighed the former (Hdt. I 137). Likewise, Diodorus (XV 10–11) records a judicial case when Persian judges voted not to punish a man accused of treason: the accused proved that he had previously rendered services to the king. The first judge voted to acquit because the charges were disputed, but the services agreed upon; and the second judge voted to acquit because even if the charges were true, the services still outweighed them. In the letter under discussion here, Darius reasons in just such a way – albeit in this case the good deed, though duly noted, is outweighed by the error.

Finally, in a dispute between a Persian administrator and a Greek temple, the Persian king intervenes on the side of the temple – because Gadatas has contravened established local custom in levying a tax on the gardeners who worked land owned by the temple and in impressing them for work on lands not belonging to the temple. In matters of religion, the Persian king was even more scrupulous than usual in seeing to it that local customs and traditions were respected.

---

manner which had become customary. What the Persians could not know was that the tyrants were deeply unpopular in their own cities and, had the Persians not propped them up, would have fallen victim to popular revolutions (Hdt. IV 137) (see also chap. 7).

Before this background the next event in Athens' relationship with Persia must be seen. Hippias attempted to enlist the Persians in restoring him to rule over Athens. When a second Athenian embassy visited Sardis (the old Lydian capital, now the seat of the satrap) to protest at Hippias' machinations, the Persian satrap bluntly ordered the Athenians to receive Hippias back as their tyrant (Hdt. V 96). The satrap had every right to make the order – by Persian law, Athens was subject territory –, and his order accorded with Persian policy at the time.

The Ionian Revolt

The proximate cause of the Ionian Revolt allegedly lay in the intrigues of two tyrants of Miletus. King Darius had summoned Miletus' tyrant, Histiaeus, to his court at Susa under ostensibly honorable circumstances (Hdt. V 24) and then appointed as the new tyrant of Miletus Histiaeus' cousin and son-in-law Aristagoras (Hdt. V 30; presumably Histiaeus had no direct male heir and in this case was succeeded by a more distant relative whom, clearly, he had groomed for the part). However, Histiaeus desired to leave Susa, and, according to Herodotus, encouraged his successor to rebel in the hope that Darius would then send him, Histiaeus, back home to deal with the revolt (Hdt. V 35). The truth of this is difficult to judge. Aristagoras, for his part, feared reprisals from Artaphernes, the Persian satrap in Sardis, after a failed attempt to conquer the island of Naxos for the Persians (Hdt. V 30–35). So for his own reasons he too planned to revolt.

The revolt's ultimate cause emerges most clearly from the course which it took. Aristagoras voluntarily laid down his office as tyrant and helped establish a democracy in Miletus. (How "democratic" this democracy was is an open question – see chap. 8 and Box 13.1.) Aristagoras then engaged in a campaign against – not any Persian official, but instead the other tyrants in the various Greek cities, all of whom lost their positions in what can hardly have been other than a large-scale popular uprising. Herodotus explains that most of the tyrants escaped with the loss of their positions only, but that the people of Mytilene stoned their tyrant, Coës, to death (Hdt. V 37–38). In other words the revolt was directed in the first instance against the tyrants, not against the Persian Empire. All the same, the tyrants had ruled as exponents of the Persian Empire which had guaranteed their rule; and once the tyrants had been expelled, the rebellious Greeks had to contend with the inevitable reaction from the Empire.

Even before the Revolt – conventionally called the Ionian Revolt even if it involved all the Greeks in Asia Minor, not just those in Ionia, and additionally extended to Cyprus where various non-Greek towns joined as well – Aristagoras had traveled to mainland Greece to gain supporters. At Sparta King Cleomenes had shown him the door (Hdt. V 49–51 – see also Box 9.2), but at Athens he met with a favorable reception (Hdt. V 97).

Athens, after all, had every reason to desire to undo the Persian position in Asia Minor. Hippias still ruled in Sigeium; and the Persian satrap in Sardis had all too recently ordered the Athenians to accept Hippias as their tyrant. The Persians had been steadily extending their empire into the Aegean – the attempt to conquer Naxos just before the revolt broke out was one of many such steps – and coming ever closer to Athens. So when Aristagoras asked Athens for help in a revolt against the Persians in Asia Minor, he received it. In addition to Athens, one traditional ally of Miletus, the Euboean town of Eretria, sent aid in 499 BC (Hdt. V 99).

It was, then, with troops from Athens (and Eretria) that the rebellious Greeks of Asia Minor marched upon the Persian satrapal capital of Sardis. The revolt had evidently caught the satrap unprepared. The Greeks captured Sardis, except for the strongly defended citadel. Fire broke out and devastated the city. Shortly thereafter, additional contingents arrived to support the satrap, and the Greeks retreated towards the coast. There, at Ephesus, they lost to Persian forces. At this point the Athenians left the others in the lurch and returned home (Hdt. V 100–103).

Meanwhile, the revolt continued to grow. On Cyprus both Greeks and Phoenicians rebelled (only the **Eteocyprian** town of Amathus remained loyal to the Persians and soon found itself besieged by the rebels); Greek forces overran Persian holdings in the Hellespont and even took the important site of Byzantium; various cities in Caria joined the revolt (Hdt. V 103–104). All the same the Persians methodically set about putting the revolt down.

The Phoenicians of the mainland opposite Cyprus had remained loyal; and they provided the fleet on which Persian troops under Artybius crossed over to Cyprus. The rebels had to break off the siege of Amathus and to prepare to fight this army. Even if the rebels' fleet managed to defeat the Phoenician fleet, on land the Persians, despite Artybius' death in battle, had the victory. In an ominous sign for the rebellion, the contingent of one Cyprian town, Curium,

Box 9.2   *Aristagoras' Map of the World*

In Ionia, especially in its largest city Miletus, Greek science had its beginnings as people such as **Thales** and **Anaximander** attempted among other things to explain the natural world. When Aristagoras, the tyrant of Miletus, came to Sparta to enlist King Cleomenes' support for the Ionian Revolt, Aristagoras showed him one of the latest products of Ionian academic endeavor: a map. On the basis of the geographical work of Ionian scholars such as **Hecataeus** of Miletus (*BNJ* 1) who compiled a gazetteer of the known world – a list of the names of peoples and places, complete with ethnographical, botanical, and other information about each place and people – the first maps were being produced.

Herodotus describes some of these early maps (see Figure 9.1):

> *I am amused by all the people who have already drawn maps of the world and not a man of them who has the least notion. For not only do they draw Ocean as a stream which flows around the land (which is so round that it appears to have been made by a compass), but they also make Asia the same size as Europe. But in just a few words I shall now show what size each of them has and how each ought to be drawn . . .* (Hdt. IV 36)

Cartography was still in its infancy, and the Ionian geographers had an overly schematic approach to the shape of the inhabitable world (a circle) as well as to the relative sizes of the landmasses (Europe was the same size as Asia plus Africa).

As one might surmise, these early maps were not necessarily accurate in scale. As Aristagoras expatiated upon the ease with which Cleomenes might lead the Lacedaemonians all the way to Susa, Cleomenes listened with interest – in particular to Aristagoras' description of the Persian Empire and its wealth. Eventually, however, Cleomenes asked his guest about the length of the march from the coast to Susa. When Aristagoras replied that it took three months, Cleomenes threw him out on his ear. Cleomenes, clearly, was nobody's fool, and his inability to apprehend from the map itself the distance to Susa suggests that it had major problems with scale.

switched sides during the battle which quickly became a rout. Thereafter the Persians reconquered the towns of Cyprus one by one (Hdt. V 108–115).

In Asia Minor another Persian commander, Daurises, reconquered much of the territory on the Asian side of the Hellespont in a swift campaign and then turned his attention to Caria. He defeated the Carians and their Greek allies in two major battles before falling victim to an ambush (Hdt. V 116–121). A third Persian commander, Hymaeës, campaigned energetically in the Hellespont until he died of disease (Hdt. V 122). Finally, Artaphernes, the satrap, recaptured Clazomenae in Ionia and Cyme in the Aeolis (Hdt. V 123). The Persians had gained the upper hand by now, and Aristagoras turned his back

Figure 9.1   Reconstruction of the map of the world (Hecataeus'?) which Herodotus ridiculed

on the Ionians and with a few loyal troops fled to Thrace where he managed to conquer a place called Myrcinus. There he ruled until he fell in battle against the Thracians (Hdt. V 124–126).

Meanwhile, Histiaeus, his predecessor as tyrant in Miletus, had returned to Ionia, sent by Darius to help deal with the revolt. Yet Artaphernes suspected Histiaeus of complicity in the revolt and Histiaeus, whether guilty or not, deserted to the rebels and went to Chios. After various adventures and in charge of some troops from Mytilene he gained control of Byzantium – on the European side of the strait (Hdt. VI 1–5). By this time the Persians had brought a large fleet into the Aegean. It consisted of Phoenician, Cilician, Cyprian, and Egyptian contingents and prepared to fight the rebels' fleet, the strength of which, Herodotus states, took the Persians by surprise and made them hesitate to attack (Hdt. VI 6–9).

The decisive battle, in 494, took place off the island of Lade in the inlet of the sea to the north of Miletus (see Figure 1.2). The Persians, apprehensive about engaging the Greek fleet, had secretly made offers to the commanders of various rebellious towns' contingents (Hdt. VI 9–10), and when the battle began the Samian ships sailed away instead of fighting since their commanders had made a deal with the Persians, a deal brokered by Samos' ex-tyrant, Aeaces II (Hdt. VI 13–14). Other contingents followed the Samian example, and the Persian fleet made short work of the few contingents – principally the Milesians and the Chians – which remained to fight (Hdt. VI 14–15). Thereafter the Persians besieged Miletus by land and by sea; when it finally fell the Persians razed it to the ground. Many women and children were enslaved, and many of the surviving men were deported and resettled near the mouth of the River Tigris on the Persian Gulf (Hdt. VI 18–20).

There remained only mopping-up operations. The Carian cities surrendered in short order. Histiaeus engaged in various ineffectual operations on Chios and Lesbos until the Persians captured him near the River Caicus. Artaphernes had him summarily executed. Without any trouble, the Persian fleet, sailing north-wards, took possession both of the islands off the coast as well as the towns on the mainland. The fleet then sailed up the Hellespont and took possession of the towns on the European side. At this time Miltiades, the Athenian ruler of the Chersonese, fled homewards to Athens (Hdt. VI 25–33 and 41).

The revolt had ended; and Persia had re-established its control.

Aftermath of the Revolt

As they had showed, the Persians did not play games when suppressing a revolt. The city of Miletus was a heap of rubble; other Ionian towns lay in ruins as well. Casualties had been high; and Herodotus reports various atrocities (Hdt. VI 32). But now the equally serious business of restoring order and peace began, and the Persian Empire showed another face.

First, the Persians honored their commitment to the Samians and to the Samians' former tyrant, Aeaces II. There were no reprisals on Samos, and Aeaces II became tyrant once again (Hdt. VI 25). Second, Artaphernes summoned representatives from the various Greek cities and forced them to agree to submit any intercity disputes to a special tribunal (rather than settling such disputes in the time-honored manner of war and raids). Artaphernes was clearly attempting to minimize the chances for any additional conflict in his satrapy. Third, Artaphernes carried out a thorough review of the system of taxation in the Greek cities – as though suspecting that resentment at too high taxes had contributed to the revolt. The Persians had simply taken over, without any review, the system which the Lydians had installed. The Persians resurveyed all the Greek cities' territories and adjusted the level of tax accordingly. The result

Box 9.3   *Herodotus and the Persians*

Herodotus was born a Persian subject, probably sometime in the early fifth century about the end of the Ionian Revolt. No doubt he heard many stories about the revolt during his childhood. By his own claim he also traveled widely in the western half of the Persian Empire (as well as in other places), and he knew the Persians and their empire well (see also Box 9.1).

He provides a long account of Darius' rise to the throne by means of a conspiracy together with six other Persian noblemen against an alleged pretender to the throne (III 68sqq.). A second account of that conspiracy also exists, composed by Darius himself and carved into the cliff-face at Behistun in Iran.

Figure 9.2   Darius' inscription at Behistun.   Unlike with modern monuments such as Mt. Rushmore or Stone Mountain, people were not actually meant to view the inscription or the reliefs since they cannot be seen from the plain below. Source: Hara1603, http://commons.wikimedia.org/wiki/File:Bisotun_Iran_Relief_Achamenid_Period.JPG (accessed 14 January 2013)

Both Herodotus and Darius name the six co-conspirators:

Herodotus	Darius
Intaphrenes	Vindafarnā
Otanes	Utāna
Gobryas (i.e., /Gobruwas/)	Gaub(a)ruva
Hydarnes	Vidṛna
Megabyxos	Bagabuxša
Aspathines	Ardumaniš

Herodotus' Greek versions – with one exception – are fair renderings of the original Persian forms. The sixth name, however, is almost, but not quite correct, and the mistake reveals how Herodotus came by this particular piece of information.

A high-ranking nobleman by the name of Aspacanā did exist at Darius' court, only he was not one of the co-conspirators. (DNd Kent; the letter "c" here represents the sound "tch" in "match"; Herodotus reproduced it with "th" in Greek). What happened here was that Herodotus' immediate source, who relayed the information to Herodotus orally and clearly knew the story as inscribed at Behistun, was relying on his memory instead of looking it up. Five names he rattled off accurately, but, stuck on the sixth, racked his brains and in the end came up with the similar-sounding name of another nobleman associated with Darius. The mistake was the sort which only a well-informed source could have made, and it shows that Herodotus gathered information from well-informed sources.

For precisely this reason Herodotus' material on the Persian Empire (as well as on the ancient Near East by extension) must be taken seriously. Mistakes and misrepresentations there are, but much sound information as well.

left the overall tribute, Herodotus says, more or less the same as before (Hdt. VI 42). The Persians did not, then, impose any punitive indemnity on the defeated Greeks.

Finally, Darius' new military commander in the region, Mardonius, established democracies (how "democratic" they were is, again, an open question – see chap. 8 and Box 13.1) in the Greek cities, excluding Samos however. Herodotus concedes that many of his readers may view this claim skeptically, but insists that this is indeed what happened (Hdt. VI 43). In other words, the Persians who, as Artaphernes' actions demonstrate, were concerned to get at every possible root of the revolt, eventually decided that the ultimate cause of the revolt had nothing to do with the intrigues of Aristagoras and Histiaeus, but rather with the unpopularity of the tyrants' regimes which they themselves had been propping up. This the Persians now sought to address. Their actions do them and their empire credit and show more clearly than anything else why this particular empire enjoyed greater stability and longer life than any other in the Near East.

QUESTIONS FOR REVIEW

1 How did Athens and the Persian Empire develop such a hostile relationship?
2 What factors contributed to the Ionian Revolt?
3 What made the Persians' response to the revolt so slow?
4 What changes did the Persians make in their governance of Ionia after the Ionian Revolt?

QUESTION FOR FURTHER STUDY

Considering how the Persians governed Ionia, would it have made much difference to the Greeks of the mainland if the Persians had conquered it in the Persian Wars?

FURTHER READING

For Near Eastern and Persian texts the collections most easily accessible to the English-speaking student are the following:
Kent, R.G. (1953) *Old Persian. Grammar Texts Lexicon* (rev. edn.). New Haven.
Pritchard, J.B. (ed.). (1969) *Ancient Near Eastern Texts Relating to the Old Testament* (3rd edn.). Princeton.

For the Persian Empire the following are useful:
Briant, P. (2002) *From Cyrus to Alexander. A History of the Persian Empire*. Winona Lake, IN.
Dandamaev, M.A. (trans. W.A. Vogelsang) (1989) *A Political History of the Achaemenid Empire*. Leiden.
The volumes of the series *Achaemenid History* (Leiden: 1987–).

For the Greeks and the Persians see:
Burn, A.R. (1984) *Persia and the Greeks* (2nd edn.). London. (Still the standard survey.)
Cawkwell, G.L. (2005) *The Greek Wars: The Failure of Persia*. Oxford.

10

The Persian Wars

| 530–490 | 490–478 | 478–431 |

490	Battle of Marathon
483	Athens begins to build 200 triremes
480	Thermopylae, Salamis, and Himera
479	Battle of Plataea
474	Battle of Cumae

Persian Expansion in Europe and the Marathon Campaign

To the Persians, the Ionian Revolt signified little more than a minor interruption in what for them was the irresistibly proceeding expansion of their empire. Each king since the death of Cyrus the Great in 529 BC had added to the empire. Cyrus' son, Cambyses (529–522 BC), had added Egypt. For several years after his succession, Darius I had had to contend with various revolts, but after he and his allies had suppressed them all, he led an army across the Hellespont and conquered a large swath of Europe from the North Aegean up to the Danube (Hdt. IV 83–143). Additional minor campaigns brought numerous Aegean islands (such as Samos, Chios, and Lesbos) into the empire.

A History of Greece: 1300 to 30 BC, First Edition. Victor Parker.
© 2014 Victor Parker. Published 2014 by John Wiley & Sons, Ltd.

Following the Ionian Revolt, the Persians returned to setting their empire's bounds wider still and wider. In the year after the revolt's end, Mardonius' fleet added the island of Thasos to the empire, and a campaign on land brought the Thracian tribe of the Bryges to heel. Alexander II of Macedon sent earth and water and thus surrendered his kingdom (Hdt. VI 44–45). Persian heralds went to most of the Aegean islands to demand submission. Various states made the required gesture – among them Aegina within sight of Athens (Hdt. VI 48–49).

The Athenians, since Aegina belonged to the Peloponnesian League, complained to Sparta. From one point of view it was the height of hypocrisy since Athens, a few years earlier, had committed the same crime as Aegina. Moreover, the person to whom the Athenians made their complaint, was none other than King Cleomenes whom they had humiliated when they had besieged him on the Acropolis (see chap. 8) and who had suffered an even greater humiliation the next year when his army dissolved before his very eyes as he led it against the Athenians (see chap. 9).

All the same, Cleomenes listened to the Athenians' representations and then went to Aegina to order the Aeginetans to rescind their submission – a step, incidentally, which the Athenians had never undertaken. An Aeginetan, Crius, pointed out that Cleomenes' colleague, Demaratus, had not come and that therefore Cleomenes had no right to give the Aeginetans orders (Hdt. VI 49–50; see also chap. 6). Cleomenes had no immediate answer to that, but upon his return to Sparta he contrived Demaratus' deposition. Gossip about Demaratus' birth and legitimacy was dredged up, and Cleomenes suborned the Delphic Oracle to confirm his colleague's illegitimacy (Hdt. VI 61–66). Demaratus, thus deposed, eventually made his way to the Persians, who gave him two cities in the Troad as fiefdoms (Xen. *Hell.* III 1,6). He would stand at Xerxes' side when the latter invaded Greece (Hdt. VII 101–105). In the meantime Cleomenes returned to Aegina with his new colleague, Laotychidas II, and forced the Aeginetans to repudiate their submission and to provide hostages against their future good behavior. These hostages Cleomenes turned over to the Athenians for safekeeping (Hdt. VI 73).

Cleomenes' actions are perhaps best understood as a clear-sighted recognition of where the real danger was coming from and as an attempt to patch up a quarrel with Athens in advance. The Persians' empire now extended to the border of Thessaly in the north and, in theory at least, to western Aegean islands such as Aegina. That the Persians would soon appear in Greece proper required no particular clairvoyance. In fact, the Athenians' active rebellion, as it must have appeared to the Persians, during the Ionian Revolt and participation in the burning of Sardis made this a certainty. Cleomenes would not live to see it – he died in 491 (Hdt. VI 75) –, but he helped the Greeks prepare for it.

In 490 a Persian fleet crossed the Aegean with an army to punish Athens as well as Eretria which had also sent aid to the Ionians. The Persians sailed up the strait between Attica and Euboea and dealt with Eretria first (Hdt. VI 98, 100–101). The city they took and razed to the ground. Then they ferried their troops across the strait and landed in northern Attica near Marathon. With them came Hippias, by now extremely aged and infirm, but still eager to rule Athens once again (Hdt. VI 102–103). Marathon lay where the Peisistratids many years ago had had their regional support base (Hdt. I 59 and 62), and Hippias may have believed that he could rally the people living there to his standard once again.

The terrified Athenians had sent to Sparta for aid, but the Lacedaemonians could not march immediately since tradition obligated them to celebrate a festival first (Hdt. VI 106; the festival is the Carneia – see VII 206). This was no self-serving excuse – the Lacedaemonians were always punctilious in their observance of religious rites. The second the festival ended, the Lacedaemonians marched. Meanwhile the Athenians prepared to meet the Persians alone – or all but alone; the tiny Boeotian town of Plataea, just across the border from Attica, sent a handful of troops (Hdt. VI 108). The Athenians never forgot the gesture (Hdt. VI 111).

The Persian troops who had landed at Marathon outnumbered the Athenian army, albeit not by much. Moreover, the Persian strength lay in archery and cavalry. The Athenians in this period had no cavalry and relied, as did most Greek states, on heavily armed infantrymen, so-called **hoplites** (see Box 10.1). Bows are long-range weapons, and hoplites were vulnerable to arrow fire until they came to close quarters. Moreover, they were vulnerable to cavalry from behind and from the sides. Until the hoplites closed with the Persian archers, they were exposed to arrow fire; but if cavalry continually attacked them so that they kept having to wheel about to protect themselves, then they had little chance of closing with the archers.

The Athenians, however, learned that the Persians were brigading their cavalry separately – such that the Athenians might be able to attack before the Persians had the cavalry in position. Some Ionians with the Persians allegedly apprised the Athenians of this circumstance (Fornara, Nr. 48). Miltiades the Younger, who after his return to Athens from the Chersonese had procured his election as one of the ten tribal generals (see chap. 8), drew up a daring plan to take advantage of this unforeseen opportunity. His plan involved thinning out the Athenian center and strengthening the wings. Then, to minimize the amount of time the Athenians were exposed to arrow fire, he proposed to have the hoplites advance "at a run" (Hdt. VI 111–112). Given that a hoplite carried some forty pounds of armor, this was a harsh demand. It also meant that the hoplites would have to even up in the ranks and files of the phalanx under stressful conditions just before engaging with the enemy. Miltiades gambled that the hoplites would succeed in this.

Miltiades convinced four of his fellow tribal generals of his plan's efficacy. The other five viewed the risks as too great. In such a deadlock, the Archon Polemarchus cast a deciding vote, and Callimachus, who held the post in this year, to the eternal glory of Athens voted with Miltiades (Hdt. VI 109), whose gamble in the event paid off handsomely. The Athenian hoplites rose to the physical challenge, evened up the phalanx quickly enough before engaging, and closed with the Persian troops. The strengthened wings pushed the opposing

Box 10.1   *The Hoplite*

In the classical period the hoplite carried on his left arm a large, round shield (the *hoplon*). With his right he held a thrusting spear, 8–10 feet in length. He also wore a helmet, a breastplate of stiffened linen, and greaves. The helmet limited his vision to what lay straight ahead. Finally, he commonly carried a small sword in case his spear should break (Hdt. VII 225). In battle he stood in a **phalanx**, shoulder to shoulder with his fellows in a "rank" (Tyrtaeus, Fr. 11 West); before and behind him were his fellows in a "file."

Opposite stood the enemy phalanx. The duty of those in the respective front ranks was to thrust with their spears upperhand (as on the Chigi Vase below) or underhand (Tyrtaeus, Fr. 10 West) at the man directly in front. The *hoplon* protected the hoplite's left side well and extended a bit beyond his left, but left his right exposed. A given hoplite, by taking a half-step to the right, commonly tried to move behind the protruding bit of the shield of the man on his right. The man at the right, of course, was trying to do the exact same thing with the man on his own right, and so on down the rank. Thucydides comments:

The following happens to all armies: during battles they are thrust out somewhat on their right wings, and both overlap their opponents' left side on their own right since each man out of fear places his exposed right side as much as possible behind the shield of the man stationed at his right . . . (Thuc. V 71)

As a rule, both sides attempted to push the other backwards in a sort of reverse tug-of-war (see Figure 10.1): once one side did begin to force the other backwards, that momentum was difficult to reverse (Thuc. IV 96). Since the right wing, as Thucydides explains, might come to protrude past the opposing phalanx's left, it was the right that could attempt to outflank (Thuc. V 71; Xen. *Hell.* IV 2, 18–19). Generals accordingly took steps to shore up their left (Thuc. l.c.), and such considerations dictated many tactics on the battlefield, which, incidentally, was almost always a plain since on broken ground the phalanx tended to lose cohesion.

While there was still experimentation in the eighth and seventh centuries (note swords rather than spears in Archilochus, Fr. 5 West; cf. Tyrtaeus, Fr. 11 West), the hoplite battle became "set" by the early sixth. Thereafter, experimentation was largely confined to lightly armed infantry and cavalry with the aim of finding ways to break the phalanx by attacks on the flank (Thuc. VII 6) or by hindering the phalanx's movement (Thuc. VI 70).

Finally, the hoplite owned his own arms (Alcaeus, Fr. 357 Lobel-Page). Since these were expensive, fighting as a hoplite implied high social status – a point of pride as the following poem by the Cretan Hybrias (**Athenaeus**, XV, p. 695) shows:

The great spear and the sword are my riches, and the fair shield which saves one's skin. With this I plow, with this I harvest, with this I drink the sweet wine

Figure 10.1 Two hoplite phalanxes meet circa 650 BC, on the Chigi Vase from Corinth. Note the arms – shields, helmets, corslets, greaves, and thrusting spears held upperhand. Source: Museo Etrusco di Villa Giulia, Rome, Italy. Photo © De Agostini Picture Library / The Bridgeman Art Library

from a cup; and because of this I am master of slaves. For slaves dare not hold spear and sword, and the fair shield which saves one's skin – they all fall down and kiss my knee and call me "master" and "great king."

Persians back with ease. The Athenian center, on the other hand, was itself pushed in the other direction. As the Persians on the wings began to flee, the Athenian wings themselves swung round inwards and attacked the Persian center from the rear. The Persian center, beset in front and in behind, dissolved in a rout (Hdt. VI 113). The Athenians had repulsed the Persians. In a dramatic break from hallowed practice the dead were piled into a large, collective grave over which a mound of earth was heaped – the so-called *soros* (see Figure 10.2).

Figure 10.2 The *soros* at Marathon. "*There is a public memorial in Athens' fairest suburb, and always do the Athenians there lay to rest those who have fallen in war – with the exception of those who fell at Marathon: for they deemed their valor pre-eminent and made even their tomb there . . .*" Thuc. II 34). Source: Ryvinios, http://en.wikipedia.org/wiki/File:Hill_where _the_Athenians_were_buried_after_the_Battle_of_Marathon.jpg (accessed 14 January 2013)

Shortly thereafter the Lacedaemonians arrived, but could do little more than to congratulate the Athenians on a job well done (Hdt. VI 120).

In the Athenians' collective memory, Marathon always remained the battle that counted. At Marathon, but for a handful of Plataeans, the Athenians had withstood the great Persian Empire alone. The playwright **Aeschylus**, who won thirteen prizes for his tragedies (*Vit.* p. 333 Page) and who fought at Salamis as well (**Ion of Chios**, *BNJ* 392, Fr. 7), held all that cheap against his participation at Marathon. The one thing which he wanted commemorated on his grave was that he too had fought that day at Marathon (Paus. I 14).

Athens and Aegina

From the Greeks' perspective the danger had now passed: the Persians had invaded, suffered defeat, and gone. So far as the Greeks were concerned, they could get back to fighting each other instead of a foreign enemy. A few years after Marathon, war broke out between Athens and Aegina. These two states were enemies from way back, and the events just before Marathon had only served to exacerbate matters. Aegina was a major naval power in those days and actually had the upper hand against the Athenians. Allegedly in 483, however, luck came to the Athenians' aid.

In southeastern Attica lay silver mines, and in that year the Athenians discovered the richest lode of them all at Laureium. Suffering from a sudden embarassment of riches, the Athenians had little idea what to do with the silver. One idea was simply to distribute the money at the rate of ten drachmas per man. A politician called Themistocles – who, as Herodotus states, had recently come to prominence – argued, however, that the Athenians should use the money to construct a fleet of two hundred warships of the latest model, the **trireme** (see Figure 10.3) (Hdt. VII 144; [Arist.] *Ath.Pol.* 22,7 with date albeit with different details). Themistocles' proposal carried the day, and the Athenians undertook to build a fleet of two hundred triremes – a fleet which, as it turned out, was ready just as the real Persian invasion began.

Figure 10.3 Modern reconstruction of an ancient trireme. Source: photo © Private Collection / Ancient Art and Architecture Collection Ltd. / Mike Andrews / The Bridgeman Art Library

Xerxes' Invasion

For as far as the Persians were concerned, the Marathon campaign had been a minor punitive expedition. King Darius had died in 485 BC, and his son Xerxes was initially occupied with a revolt in Egypt (Hdt. VII 7). But thereafter preparations for the full-scale invasion of Greece began and according to Herodotus (VII 20) lasted for four years. These preparations reveal a different empire from that of earlier generations. Where Cyrus the Great had engaged in swift campaigns straight into enemy territory, his third successor Xerxes was not prepared to take the risks of the founding generation. Xerxes prepared slowly, systematically, and in keeping with an empire whose watchwords now were stability and prudence.

Land and sea forces were to cooperate throughout the campaign, and Xerxes – or rather the administrators who planned the operation – felt it advisable to take steps against any foreseeable risk. For example, in 493 a fleet active in the northern Aegean had been shipwrecked, with heavy loss of life, off Mt. Athos (Hdt. VI 44). Determined that no such disaster should befall them again, the Persians dug a canal across the base of the peninsula so that their fleet could pass safely – without having to sail southwards along Mt. Athos' treacherous eastern face (Hdt. VII 22–23). In addition, a bridge was built across the River Strymon which the Persian army would have to cross on its way to Greece (Hdt. VII 24). Such prudence had its downside, however, for it advertised to all in Greece that the real invasion was now imminent and gave them precious time to prepare.

In 481 BC the Greek states sent delegates to a conference on the Isthmus (Hdt. VII 172–175). Old quarrels – in particular that of Athens and Aegina – were patched up (Hdt. VII 145). Since the Persians planned to have army and fleet cooperate, so too did the Greeks. Arrangements were made for a united command under the leadership of the Lacedaemonians, both by land and by sea (Hdt. VII 148–149). The Argives refused to accept this and took no part in the defense of Greece; the Athenians, even if they were providing the bulk of the fleet, accepted a Lacedaemonian commander even by sea. This was only realistic as many states – in particular those on the Peloponnese – were already used to following "whithersoever the Lacedaemonians might lead" (see chap. 6). The Peloponnesian League already had a command structure in place for the management of a common campaign; and additional states' introduction into this structure presented fewer difficulties than the invention of an entirely new one.

Even if the first Greek historians of the Persian Wars, and in their train Herodotus as well, relentlessly overestimated the numbers in the Persian army (see Box 10.2), there can be little doubt that the Greeks were badly outnumbered. Otherwise, the Lacedaemonian commanders would not initially have opted for a purely defensive strategy. The commanders first investigated the possibility of fending the Persians off at the Tempe Pass which led from Macedonia (already

Figure 10.4 Thermopylae today. In ancient times, the coastline lay much closer to the mountains. Source: tyler, http://commons.wikimedia.org/wiki/File:Thermopylae_ancient _coastline_large.jpg (accessed 14 January 2013) CC BY-SA 3.0, 2.5, 2.0, 1.0

Persian) into Thessaly, but decided that holding that pass was not militarily feasible (Hdt. VII 172–173). So they left the Thessalians to shift for themselves and concentrated on the defense of the pass between northern and central Greece – Thermopylae, the "Hot Gates," named after the hot springs in the area (see chap. 1 and Figure 10.4).

The narrowness of this pass meant that a small number of troops could hold it indefinitely against a much larger army, and it was the only route from Thessaly into central Greece which a large army could easily use. A small track – the Anopean Path – did lead around the pass, but it was easily defended and impracticable for an army to use anyway. Moreover, since fleet and land forces had to cooperate, a perfect position lay nearby for the fleet. Thermopylae lay on the Malian Gulf, part of the calm, sheltered waters to the west of the island of Euboea. The east coast of Euboea was devoid of harbors and prone to storms as was the east coast of Magnesia just to the north (see Box 1.1). A narrow strait led from the Aegean between Magnesia and Euboea towards the Malian Gulf. A small cape on northern Euboea, Artemisium, provided sufficient shelter for a fleet just to its west, a fleet which could guard the entrance to the strait (Hdt. VII 175–176). No fleet approaching from the north could find shelter, either off Magnesia or off Euboea, without passing Cape Artemisium. In other words, if the Persians hesitated to attack immediately – and they had hesitated at Lade (see chap. 9) –, then they would have to anchor at a place exposed to storms. The Greeks' plan then was entirely defensive and took hardheaded advantage of the region's topography and weather.

Early in 480 BC the Persian host, led by King Xerxes himself, crossed the Hellespont thanks to a feat of engineering which took the Greeks' breath away – a bridge of boats, yoked together by flax and papyrus ropes (Hdt. VII 33–36). When the Persians reached Thessaly, the Thessalians submitted earth and water and joined the expedition against their fellow Greeks who had deserted them (Hdt. VII 172–174). At Thermopylae, however, the Persian juggernaut ground to a halt. The fleet came to anchor off Cape Sepias, to the north of Cape Artemisium.

Box 10.2   *The Strength of the Persian Army*

The Persians brought to Greece the largest army the Greeks had ever seen. Even before Herodotus many had speculated as to the size of this enormous host. Herodotus himself quotes an inscription displayed at the battlefield of Thermopylae:

> *Four thousands here from Pelops' Land*
> *Against three millions once did stand.*
> (Hdt. VII 228; trans. after de Sélincourt)

(Pelop's Land is the Peloponnese; that is to say, 4,000 Peloponnesians stood among the Greek troops at Thermopylae to hold the pass against the Persians.) Herodotus had various other such written sources for the numbers on both sides. Thus, at Sparta an inscription recorded by name each of the three hundred Spartiates who fell in the famous last stand at Thermopylae (Paus. III 14,1).

Meanwhile, another source of Herodotus' – evidently a written one again – purported to give the numbers for the Persians at that point in time when they crossed the Hellespont – at the impressive total of 1,700,000 (Hdt. VII 60; VII 184). That figure conflicts with the even more wildly inflated figure in the epigram at Thermopylae quoted above. Herodotus attempted to reconcile the two figures with a series of mostly dubious assumptions at VII 184–185. By counting the fleet with the army and by adding some 300,000 infantry between the Hellespont and Thermopylae, Herodotus raised the total from 1,700,000 to 2,641,610 which was close enough to the 3,000,000 in the epigram.

Despite Herodotus – who took both the epigram as well as the other source seriously –, both figures (3,000,000 and 1,700,000) are obviously wild guesses. Yes, the Persian host appeared enormous, but so large an army was, first, an utter impracticality and, second, could not possibly have lost to a Greek force at Plataea which numbered a mere 38,700 hoplites (Hdt. IX 29).

As the Greeks had no doubt hoped, the Persians at Cape Sepias – despite outnumbering the Greeks opposite – hesitated to attack. The weather, too, worked in their favor for the Persians also lost a number of ships in a storm (Hdt. VII 188). At this point the Persians gambled. Wary of meeting the Greeks at Artemisium in a straightforward sea battle, they opted to send a squadron around the eastern coast of Euboea. This squadron would then sail up the strait. The plan evidently was then to launch a concerted attack from two directions on the Greek fleet (Hdt. VIII 6–7). The Greeks were, in fact, reckoning with the possibility, since an Athenian contingent had remained near southern Euboea (Hdt. VIII 14) – so the gamble was not reckless, but calculated. Unaware of the departure of that squadron, the Greeks at Artemisium now attempted to provoke the Persians to battle by attacking (Hdt. VIII 10). The weather, moreover, went hard against the Persians again, and the entire Euboean squadron went down in a catastrophic storm off the "Hollows of Euboea" – probably a particularly dangerous if unfortunately unidentifiable stretch of coastline. The same storm buffeted the Persian fleet to the north of Euboea as well (Hdt. VIII 12–13). After additional skirmishes, the Persian fleet finally did attempt a straightforward battle against the Greeks. Herodotus describes the ensuing battle as a closely run affair, but at the end of the battle the Persians had failed to dislodge the Greeks from their position at Artemisium (Hdt. VIII 14–18). The naval arm of the Greeks' forces had fought the invaders to a standstill.

Where the fleet had failed, the Persian army, however, succeeded. Although the Persians could not push through the pass at Thermopylae, they learned about the narrow track which ran around the pass (Hdt. VII 213); and slowly they sent small detachments along that path during the night (Hdt. VII 217). The Phocian troops, whom the Greeks' commander, the Lacedaemonian king Leonidas, had sent to guard against this eventuality, failed in their task (Hdt. VII 218). At dawn on the third day of the fighting at Thermopylae, Leonidas learned that a Persian army was on the Greeks' side of the pass and that he would soon be surrounded. He ordered the bulk of the army to retreat while this was still an option. He himself with 300 Spartiates as well as 1,100 unsung Boeotians from Thespiae and Thebes remained behind (Hdt. VII 219–222 with 202) – possibly to cover the retreat of the rest.

The legend which arose around the last stand of the 300 erased whatever the truth may have been. The famous Thermopylae epigram best encapsulates the legend:

Go tell the Spartans, passer-by,
Obeying orders, here we lie. (Hdt. VII 228)

Because Leonidas' orders were to hold the pass, he himself – so the legend goes – declined to retreat with the others; and the Spartiates with him preferred a fight to the death over the ignominy of retreat. The last stand at Thermopylae enshrined the legend of Sparta forever.

Meantime, the retreat of the army compelled the retreat of the fleet. The Greek fleet now sailed down the strait between Euboea and the mainland, rounded Attica, and took up its new position in the sound between Attica and the small Saronic island of Salamis. The land army moved to the south of the Isthmus, the next logical place at which to make a stand (Hdt. VIII 40). As at Thermopylae and Artemisium, fleet and land army took up corresponding positions. Salamis was, however, not so ideal as Artemisium had been; and the Greek commanders debated whether or not to move (Hdt. VIII 56sqq.).

The retreat from Thermopylae placed the inhabitants of central Greece into the same situation as the Thessalians after the decision not to hold the pass at Tempe. The Boeotians, with two exceptions (Thespiae and Plataea), submitted earth and water and in the next year fought on the Persian side (Hdt. VIII 50). The Phocians refused to submit, and Xerxes let his army plunder their land thoroughly (Hdt. VIII 32–33) with the exception of Delphi which Xerxes probably spared for his own reasons though legends soon arose about how the gods themselves had defended the oracle (Hdt. VIII 36–39). In Athens the assembly voted to evacuate the women and children to Troezen on the other side of the Saronic Gulf. All men who could fight went to the island of Salamis where the fleet lay (Hdt. VIII 41). The Persians entered a practically deserted Athens and, in revenge for the destruction of Sardis in 499, burned it to the ground (Hdt. VIII 51–55).

It was now autumn, and the campaigning season would soon be over. The Persian fleet had lost a fair number of ships to storms (both at Cape Sepias and off Euboea) and had come off second-best in the actual fighting at Artemisium when it had had more ships than now. For some reason, however, the Persians decided to risk all on an attack upon the Greek fleet at Salamis. The explanation which arose in the immediate aftermath of the battle was that Themistocles, the Athenian statesman and commander by whose counsels the Athenians had built 200 triremes and who had argued strenuously for keeping the fleet at Salamis, had sent a secret message to Xerxes to promise him, in effect, that what had happened at Lade would now happen again (Aes. *Pers.* 355–360; cf. Hdt. VIII 75). In any case Xerxes, in full confidence of a great victory, had a special viewing platform built on a hill overlooking the stretch of water where the battle would take place (Aes. *Pers.* 465–467; cf. Hdt. VIII 90). The assurances of dissension among the Greeks – if historical – must have been particularly persuasive.

The actual course of the battle is hotly contested among historians, but the result, fortunately, is clear-cut. The Greek fleet, far from dissolving as at Lade, held together and won a resounding victory as Xerxes, struck dumb, gazed on from his throne (Aes. *Pers.* 353–471; Hdt. VIII 84–95). Themistocles, the Athenian commander, was the hero of the day (Hdt. VIII 123–124). On the Persian side Herodotus, though clearly proud of the Greeks for their victory, cannot help but make much of Artemisia, the ruler at the time of Halicarnassus, his hometown, in addition to the islands of Cos, Calydna, and Nisyros. She, according to him, displayed greater skill and courage than the other captains in the Persian fleet (Hdt. VIII 87–88; cf. VII 99 and VIII 68).

Box 10.3   *Herodotus' Sources for the Battle of Salamis*

When Herodotus wrote his account of the Battle of Salamis, people were still alive who had fought in the battle or had heard their fathers talk about it. Herodotus, however, did not restrict himself to oral interviews with veterans and their children. He also had a written eyewitness account composed by the tragedian Aeschylus (Ion of Chios, *BNJ* 392, Fr. 7) for his play the *Persae* ("Men of Persia") which was performed only eight years (*Arg. Pers.*) after the battle in front of an audience which included thousands who had participated in the battle just as Aeschylus had.

While these circumstances do not mean that Aeschylus provided an absolutely accurate version of the battle, the presence in the audience of thousands of veterans who had been there set certain limits to any "artistic" reworking of the battle. Herodotus would have been remiss if he had not consulted this eyewitness account, and, fortunately, he very clearly did. In one passage Aeschylus wrote of how many ships the Persians had. A Persian messenger is speaking:

> *Xerxes – and I know it for a fact – had 1,000 ships, but in speed two hundred and seven were superior . . . (Pers. 341–343)*

Did Xerxes have 1,000 ships (i.e., the 207 fast ships are included within the 1,000) or 1,207 ships in all? The statement is frustratingly ambiguous, but Herodotus, for reasons of his own, interpreted it as meaning 1,207 (VII 184). Its unroundness, incidentally, makes it certain that Herodotus was using Aeschylus, since no two people could possibly have hit upon that figure independently. Other ancient commentators, incidentally, read the passage in Aeschylus as meaning "1,000" (e.g., **Plato**, *Laws*, 669; **Ctesias**, *BNJ* 688, Fr. 13.30).

Yet Herodotus did not use Aeschylus slavishly; his figures for the Greeks' fleet, for example, differ markedly from Aeschylus' (Aes. *Pers.* 337–340; Hdt. VIII 42–48). For Herodotus had many other sources for the battle – and not just veterans' orally recounted memories. On the island of Salamis itself various inscriptions were displayed for all to see – for example, that which recounted the Corinthians' contribution during the battle (IG I³ 1143) and to which Herodotus may well refer at VIII 94. Throughout Greece stood additional inscriptions for example, that of the Corinthian general Adeimantus who, on his tomb, spoke of his participation in the battle (e.g., Plut. *On the Malice of Herodotus*, p. 870). Each little community in Greece, insofar as it had taken part in the great collective effort to repel the Persian invader, had its own monument to the glorious dead (for Megara, see Fornara, Nr. 60). The inscriptions on these monuments commonly contained historically useful information – see also Box 12.1 for another such memorial to the fallen of later wars and consider its importance for reconstructing events of the 450s BC.

With Salamis the campaigning season of 480 ended (Hdt. VIII 109). The rump of the Persian fleet sailed across the Aegean to Cyme (Hdt. VIII 130); Xerxes returned to Persia (Hdt. VII 113–117); and Mardonius, whom he left behind as commander, went into winter quarters in Boeotia (Hdt. VIII 113).

The next year the Greeks dispatched the Persian land forces, as it turned out, easily enough. In the spring the Lacedaemonians, under Pausanias (regent for Pleistoanax, Leonidas' underage son) marched northwards from their position south of the Isthmus (Hdt. IX 10), some ten thousand strong, with Spartiates and Perioeci in roughly equal numbers. All the members of the anti-Persian alliance contributed however many they could. The total came to 38,700 hoplites (Hdt. IX 27–28). Herodotus' somewhat confused account of the battle (Hdt. IX 47–65) precludes detailed reconstruction, but, as at Marathon, the Greek hoplite proved his superiority over the Persian bowman. In the early stages of the battle, the Greeks did suffer heavy losses to arrow fire (Hdt. IX 61), but once the hoplites came to close quarters the battle quickly became a rout.

The comparative ease with which the Greeks won at Plataea perhaps suggests that they need not have been so cautious initially. Yet one must reckon with the effects of Salamis on both sides – sapping the Persians' morale while boosting the Greeks'. Additionally, after Salamis it became easier to persuade more states to send troops to fight the Persians. This bolstered the Greeks' numbers, whereas the Persians may well have been steadily losing troops owing to attrition, desertion, and Xerxes' departure with some men. The situation in 479 may have differed radically from that of 480.

The Persians were now in full-scale retreat even if mopping-up operations would go on for some time. Those operations belong, more properly, however to an account of the **Pentecontaetia** (see chap. 12) since a growing dissension between the Athenians and the Lacedaemonians characterizes them – a dissension which would lead to the establishment of an Athenian-led alliance in the place of one led by the Lacedaemonians. Moreover, both for the Greeks and for the Persians the battles of Salamis and Plataea marked an epoch.

For the Persian Empire, the "Greek Wars" were the last known attempt at major expansion. Its future wars would be about the suppression of rebellions or the warding off of invaders. From this moment forwards the empire was mostly concerned with maintaining itself in its existing boundaries; and it did so for another century and a half until Alexander the Great conquered it.

For the Greeks, on the other hand, the "Persian Wars" consolidated a nascent nationalism. Many Greek states had cooperated to defeat the Persians – and talk arose of how a "Greek" army (Hdt. IX 30) alongside of the "Greeks'" fleet (e.g., Hdt. VIII 1) had waged a "Greek" war (Thuc. I 128). It encouraged reflection on who "Greeks" were and what made them different. Herodotus' *Histories* from a certain point of view are nothing other than an extended reflection on a definition of "Greekness." By continually describing non-Greeks' customs throughout his work, Herodotus slowly circumscribes "Greekness." Such reflection took on concrete form as well. A "Greek" war ought by rights to be waged on behalf of all "Greeks" – including those in Asia Minor and on

Cyprus who currently stood under Persian rule and had done so, the Ionian revolt notwithstanding, for six or seven decades. That issue would, however, remain unsettled until the time of Alexander the Great.

Sicily

While the Greeks of the mainland were repulsing the Persians, the Greeks on Sicily had to face a threat of equal proportions. Greek cities on that island had coexisted – usually peacefully enough, but always somewhat uneasily – with a number of Carthaginian strongholds in the island's northwestern corner. Tensions between the Carthaginians and nearby Greek colonists occasionally flared up into open war – such as when the Lacedaemonian adventurer Dorieus attempted to found a colony at Heracleia which lay rather too close to what the Carthaginians considered their sphere of influence. The Carthaginians quickly drove the Lacedaemonian colonists from the area (Hdt. V 43–48).

In the late 480s the Carthaginians – on Herodotus' presentation – intervened in ongoing conflicts among the Greek cities on the island. Terillus, the tyrant of Himera (a colony founded by Zancle/Messene), had just lost a war against Theron, the tyrant of Acragas (a joint Rhodian and Cretan colony). Terillus, driven from Himera, sought aid from Carthage, and in this Anaxilas, the tyrant of the Chalcidian colony of Rhegium on the Italian side of the strait, opposite Sicily, supported him. The Carthaginians responded with a full-scale invasion of the island under the command of Hamilcar; Herodotus (VII 165; cf. Diod. XI 20) puts their numbers at 300,000, but this too is surely an inflated figure (if not so inflated as his figures for the Persians' army).

At least one Greek colony actively backed the Carthaginians – Selinus (Diod. XI 21) – and there may have been others (cf. Diod. XI 26). Gelon, the tyrant of the Corinthian colony of Syracuse, however, backed Theron in the ensuing war (Hdt. VII 166). When the Greeks of mainland Greece sent ambassadors in 481 to Syracuse to ask Gelon to send help against the Persians, Gelon's hands were tied (cf. Hdt. VII 165). With the Carthaginians about to invade Sicily, he could not afford to send troops to Greece itself. In 480 – according to Herodotus on the exact same day as the battle of Salamis and according to Diodorus on the exact same day as Thermopylae (both are too good to be true) – the combined armies of Gelon and Theron decisively defeated Hamilcar's forces at Himera (Hdt. VII 166; Diod. XI 22–24). The repulse of the Carthaginians inaugurated a long period of peace between Greeks and Carthaginians on the island.

The simultaneousness of the Carthaginians' invasion of Sicily and the Persians' of mainland Greece made no particular impression on Herodotus who obviously viewed the two events as serendipitous. Not so later historians who – in large part under the influence of the very nationalism which the Persian Wars had engendered – saw a nefarious plot by the Greeks' enemies, east and west, to blot Greek civilization from the map with carefully coordinated attacks

(Ephorus, *BNJ* 70, Fr. 186; cf. Diod. XI 1 – based, ultimately, on Ephorus). That plot, though some modern scholars have viewed it as historical, is pure fiction – Herodotus, in particular, knows nothing of it. The story of the plot probably arose after him.

Gelon, at any rate, died in 478 and was succeeded as tyrant by his brother Hiero (Diod. XI 38). In 474 the Chalcidian colony of Cumae (see chap. 5) on the Bay of Naples appealed to Hiero for aid against the Etruscans who dominated much of central Italy at the time. The Etruscans had attacked Cumae once before in the late sixth century (**Dionysius of Halicarnassus**, *Rom.Ant.*, VII 3); moreover, Carthaginians and Etruscans had in the past cooperated against the Greeks (Hdt. I 166). Hiero responded to the appeal and in 474 the combined fleets of Syracuse and Cumae defeated the Etruscans off Cumae (Diod. XI 51; cf. Pind., *Pyth.* I, and Fornara, Nr. 64).

The Syracusan tyrants had thus shored up the position of the Greeks in the West against their two most powerful opponents.

QUESTIONS FOR REVIEW

1   What advantages did the Persian military have over the Greeks, and vice versa?
2   How did the Greeks take advantage of weather and topography in their fight against the Persians?
3   Why did Marathon and Thermopylae become significant battles for Athens and Sparta respectively whereas Salamis and Plataea did not?
4   How did the Persian and Carthaginian invasions encourage Greek nationalism in both East and West?

QUESTION FOR FURTHER STUDY

Herodotus occasionally evinces an awareness that his comments on the Persians are controversial (e.g., at VI 43). Likewise, in his account of the battle of Salamis he pointedly contradicts the Athenians' story of the Corinthians' cowardice. Moreover, he defends Pausanias against accusations of Medism and the like (see V. Parker, "Pausanias the Spartiate as Depicted by Charon of Lampsacus and Herodotus," *Philologus* 149 [2005] 3–12). What do such things presuppose about writing on the Persian Wars before Herodotus?

FURTHER READING

For the Persian Wars in general:
Blösel, W.T. (2004) *Themistokles bei Herodot*. Stuttgart. (Contains long sections on Artemisium and Salamis with up-to-date bibliography.)

Burn, A.R. (1984) *Persia and the Greeks* (2ⁿᵈ edn.). London. (Still the standard survey.)

Cawkwell, G.L. (2005) *The Greek Wars. The Failure of Persia.* Oxford.

Wallinga, H.T. (2005) *Xerxes' Greek Adventure: The Naval Perspective.* Leiden. (On the campaign at sea.)

On hoplites and hoplite warfare:

Hanson, V.D. (2000) *The Western Way of War: Infantry Battle in Classical Greece.* Berkeley.

Krenz, P. (2007) "Warfare and Hoplites." In: H.A. Shapiro (ed.). *The Cambridge Companion to Archaic Greece,* 61–84. Cambridge.

On the battle of Salamis and associated topographical issues:

Hammond, N.G.L. (1973) "The Battle of Salamis." In: *Studies in Greek History,* 251–310. Oxford.

Pritchett, W.K. (1959) "Towards a Restudy of the Battle of Salamis," *AJA*: 251–262.

Strauss, B. (2004) *The Battle of Salamis: The Naval Encounter that Saved Greece – and Western Civilization.* New York.

Wallace, P.W. (1969) "Psyttaleia and the Trophies of the Battle of Salamis," *AJA* 73: 293–303.

On Herodotus' sources for his narrative of the Persian Wars:

Parker, V. (2007) "Herodotus' Use of Aeschylus' Persae as an Historical Source," *Symbolae Osloenses* 82: 2–29.

Parker, V. (2009) "Zu dem ersten Epigramm auf die Schlacht bei den Thermopylen als historischer Quelle Herodots," *Classica & Mediaevalia* 60: 5–26.

Part III

The Classical Period: 479–323 BC

11

The Athenian Empire

| 480–479 | 478–431 | 431–404 |

479	Battle of Cape Mycale
winter of 479–478	Athenians take Sestos
478–477	Delian League formed
466 (?)	Battle of the Eurymedon
466–465 (?)	Siege of Naxos
465–463 (?)	Siege of Thasos

The Creation of the Delian League

If the victories at Salamis and Plataea in the autumn of 480 and in the spring of 479 BC respectively had decided the ultimate outcome of the Persian Wars, there remained any number of outstanding problems. First, the Persians continued to hold territory in Europe, including strategic sites such as Byzantium on the Bosporus. Second, many Greeks still lived under Persian rule in Asia Minor and on Cyprus. The residual operations would go on for a number of

A History of Greece: 1300 to 30 BC, First Edition. Victor Parker.
© 2014 Victor Parker. Published 2014 by John Wiley & Sons, Ltd.

years. In line with this, towards the end of 479 the Greek fleet under the command of the Lacedaemonian king Laotychidas II surprised the rump of the Persian fleet in east Aegean waters, off Cape Mycale. The Greeks had gone on the offensive and were now bringing the war to the Persians.

Greek triremes carried some infantry on board, so-called **epibatai**. During the Persian Wars the *epibatai* allegedly numbered fourteen hoplites and four archers (Plut. *Them.* 14). Since the Persian ships off Cape Mycale refused to fight and sought protection from nearby land forces, Laotychidas let his *epibatai* disembark and led them against the land forces, which he defeated (Hdt. IX 99–106). The Greeks had brought the war to the mainland of Asia Minor itself. The Ionian Revolt lay a mere fifteen years in the past: memories of the Persian suppression of the revolt lingered, and now that a Greek army stood in Ionia, many – though by no means all – of the Greeks in Asia Minor took the opportunity to revolt again (Hdt. IX 104). However, it was already autumn and the campaigning season was ending. Storms made sailing perilous during the winter, so Laotychidas, in keeping with standard procedure, after a brief expedition to the Hellespont made ready to sail home. The majority of the triremes under his command came from Athens, however, and the Athenians wanted to remain in Asia Minor and to continue the fight to liberate all Greeks from Persian rule (Hdt. IX 106 and 114; Thuc. I 89).

When Laotychidas sailed home, the Athenians stayed behind. Completely on their own they besieged and took the town of Sestus on the European side of the Hellespont (Hdt. IX 114–115; Thuc. I 89). For the first time in the war they were acting independently. When the spring of 478 arrived, the Lacedaemonians returned to prosecute the war with a new commander, Pausanias, the victor of Plataea. Instead of invading Ionia, he led the Greek forces – including the Athenians – to Cyprus (Thuc. I 94). The choice of target is revealing.

Herodotus records that in these years the Lacedaemonians were proposing that a campaign against the Persians in Asia Minor be avoided; instead, the Greeks who lived there should be resettled in mainland Greece on the territory of the states which had fought on the Persian side (in particular Thessaly and Boeotia – the plan presupposes, incidentally, the expulsion of the Thessalians and the Boeotians) (Hdt. IX 106). This Lacedaemonian reluctance to fight against the Persians in Asia Minor manifested itself in Pausanias' decision to attack the Persians on Cyprus. The Lacedaemonians were willing to wage war against the Persians, just not in Asia Minor. Considerations of military feasibility surely played a major role in this strategic decision to focus on areas (Europe, Cyprus) where the Persians, given their lack of adequate naval support, simply could not respond.

After an allegedly successful campaign on Cyprus, Pausanias led the Greek fleet into the Propontis again. Here he captured Byzantium on the European side of the Bosporus (Thuc. I 94), but despite these successes Pausanias was growing increasingly unpopular (Thuc. I 95, 128–130). Even Herodotus, who defends him against the more fanciful accusations (Hdt. IX 78–82), confirms his arrogant behavior (Hdt. VIII 3). Late in 478 Pausanias was, in fact, recalled to Sparta where he was convicted of various offenses against individuals – but acquitted of all other charges (including treason) (Thuc. I 95). He was not sent out as commander again. His extreme unpopularity became, as Herodotus puts it, the pretext by which the Athenians took over the leadership of the anti-Persian alliance (Hdt. VIII 3). Herodotus also presents the Athenians as actively seeking the leadership. This is surely more credible than Thucydides' presentation of the Athenians as entirely passive (Thuc. I 95). According to him, the Ionians placed themselves under the Athenians' protection and the Athenians merely acquiesced in this. This surprising thesis of essential Athenian passivity in the acquisition of power will recur later on in Thucydides (see below).

However it had come about, the Athenians now commanded the anti-Persian alliance which they reorganized according to their views. Besides now providing the military commanders, they put in place for the first time arrangements for financing the alliance's campaigns. The Lacedaemonians had apparently been doing this on an *ad hoc* basis and problems had presumably arisen repeatedly. Significantly, the members of the alliance had no objections to the Athenians' proposal for a common treasury and for individual payments into that treasury, payments which in total amounted to 460 talents per annum. Finally, these treasurers were called **Hellenotamiai**, "Greek Treasurers," a title which reveals that those who created this structure still viewed the alliance as a Greek one, waging a Greek war on behalf of Greeks. The Athenians appointed the treasurers, and the treasury was located on the Cycladic island of Delos where meetings of the member states took place as well (Thuc. I 96).

This choice of location points up, however, a gap between the claim to be a "Greek alliance" and the reality of the membership. The Lacedaemonians – together with their supporters, i.e., the Peloponnesians – were absent from an alliance, members of which hailed mostly from the Aegean islands and from Asia Minor. They were to a large extent Ionian, and various sanctuaries with special significance for Ionians lay on Delos, the place that gives the alliance its conventional name: the **Delian League**.

The Lacedaemonians, meanwhile, did not meekly accept all this, even if that is what Thucydides claimed. In fact, in the spring of 477 they sent out a successor to Pausanias, a man called Dorcis whom, however, the other Greeks simply refused to follow (Thuc. I 95). Moreover, roughly concurrent with these events (478 to 477 BC), King Laotychidas II led out an expedition to Thessaly (Hdt. VI 72; Paus. III 7; Plut. *Them.* 20). The Lacedaemonians can only have been intending to expel the Thessalians so as to prepare the way for the proposed resettlement of the Ionians in Thessaly. Laotychidas failed miserably to achieve anything (allegedly Thessalians bribed him), but, clearly, the Lacedaemonians in these years were actively pursuing their own plans in the war against Persia. In 477 all this activity ceases abruptly and with considerable acrimony. Despite Thucydides, the Lacedaemonians, much against their will, were rudely elbowed aside.

The Development of the Delian League into the Athenian Empire

With the Lacedaemonians out of the way, the Athenians, at the head of the Delian League, prosecuted the war against Persia. To show how the League developed under Athenian leadership, Thucydides selected four events from the first twelve years or so of its history. First, the League expelled the Persians from Eion (Thuc. I 98; Ephorus, *BNJ* 70, Fr. 191, fr. 4; Diod. XI 60). The League's sworn purpose was to wage war against the Persians (Thuc. III 10) and at Eion it did so. Eion lay in the northern Aegean near the mouth of the River Strymon far to the west of the Hellespont. While Eion may have been an isolated base, it is nonetheless possible that the Persians still held much territory in Europe and that the League had a fair amount to do before it had confined them to Asia.

Second, the League captured the island of Scyros in the northern Sporades (ll.cc.), probably in 470. There were no Persians on Scyros, but the island was a notorious pirates' nest (Plut. *Cim.* 8). When the League cleaned that nest out, it may not have been adhering to its sworn goal of fighting the Persians, but it was certainly doing everyone in the Aegean a favor. Third, the League attacked the Euboean town of Carystus. This was a Greek town which had not joined the League and which had fallen afoul of the other Euboeans (Thuc. I 98). Carystians had fought for the Persians at Salamis, and perhaps they had cooperated with the Persians more than strictly necessary. Soon after the Greek victory at Salamis, Themistocles had actually led forces against Carystus and had extorted money from it (Hdt. VIII 112), so just possibly a case was advanced that the Carystians were collaborators who deserved what they got. All the same, the League was this time fighting neither against the Persians nor against a common pest, but against a Greek community, albeit one outside of the League.

Fourth, Thucydides mentions the League's campaign against Naxos (Thuc. I 98), a campaign which was ongoing in 465 (Thuc. I 137). Naxos had been a member of the League; its sin was that it had tried to leave the League. For the first time, the League took action against a member state, and the suppression of the Naxian Revolt showed that this was no longer an alliance of free states, but one under the dominion of Athens (cf. Thuc. III 10) which clearly would not countenance a departure from the League. Thucydides then explains that the allies were themselves responsible for their fate: they had the option of contributing ships to the common campaigns or, in lieu of ships, money. Most preferred to send cash and to let the Athenians do the lion's share of the actual fighting. The Athenians, fairly enough, expected such allies to meet their fiscal obligations and when they failed so to do, took action to see that they did. Since the allies had been shirking their duty in the fighting, they were woefully under-prepared to fight against the battle-hardened Athenians who, after all, were merely insisting that the allies pay what they had undertaken to pay into the common treasury so as to finance a war which the Athenians were waging on behalf of them all (Thuc. I 98).

Thucydides' analysis contains, however, an historiographical sleight of hand which calls it into question. Just before Naxos revolted (on this, see Box 11.1), the Athenians under the command of Cimon, the son of Miltiades the Younger, had defeated the Persians in a "double battle," first by sea and then by land near the mouth of the River Eurymedon in Pamphylia (Thuc. I 100; Ephorus, *BNJ* 70, Fr. 191, frr. 9–13; **Callisthenes**, *BNJ* 124, Fr. 15). The battle probably took place circa 466 and effectively brought hostilities between Persia and the Athenian-led alliance to an end. The Persians for now accepted that they had lost control of most of the Greek-settled regions in Asia Minor. In other words, the war was over and the Delian League had achieved its goal. What reason was there for the member states to continue making payments into a common treasury to finance a war which was no longer being waged?

So, shortly after the Battle of the Eurymedon, Naxos ceased making the payments. Yet the Athenians were loath to forgo the 460 talents annually deposited into a treasury that Athenian-appointed treasurers controlled. In effect the Athenians were now demanding that the members of the League pay the Athenians money to protect them from an enemy which was not threatening them anymore. The Delian League had become, in essence, a protection racket; and the Athenians were willing and able to exact severe vengeance on anyone who possessed the effrontery not to pay the demanded protection money. The Delian League, originally an alliance of independent states united to fight the Persians, had been transmogrified into the Athenian Empire – a collection of subject states united for the greater glory of Athens.

Next, around this time the Athenians probably concluded a formal peace with the Persians, the so-called Peace of Callias, named after the chief Athenian negotiator (see Plut. *Cim.* 13). Callias was Cimon's brother-in-law (Plut. *Cim.* 4), and presumably Cimon supported the making of a peace treaty. While Callias' travel to Persia is clearly attested by a fifth-century source (Hdt. VII 151), the Peace itself is not (see Fornara, Nr. 95). Like Herodotus, Thucydides too fails to mention it, probably because it did not serve his purposes to point out that the war against Persia ended about this time. The paucity of clear early attestations of the Peace of Callias has caused an endless debate on the matter in modern scholarship (see Badian 1993 in the Further Reading).

Finally, Thucydides' is not the sole surviving account of the early years of the Delian League. A parallel account exists in Diodorus and the surviving fragments of Ephorus, Diodorus' source (see *BNJ* 70, Biographical Essay, section II F). Comparison of Thucydides' and Diodorus'/Ephorus' accounts shows that both are actually based on the same source, **Hellanicus** (*BNJ* 4), a late-fifth-century BC writer on Athenian history (see Rainey 2004 in Further Reading and commentary to Ephorus, *BNJ* 70, Fr. 191).

Although Diodorus presents the material erratically (see Box 18.1), his account is occasionally more detailed (e.g., Diod. XI 88 vs. Thuc. I 112) and probably more faithful to the original source – especially there where Thucydides had a specific ax to grind. Thus there is in Diodorus no trace of the thesis that the allies themselves were responsible for their eventual subjection by

Box 11.1 *Thucydides and his Methods for Constructing an Argument*

Thucydides was an Athenian who wrote an account of the Peloponnesian War (431–404 BC). Very little is known about his personal life – he held a military command in the early years of the war (IV 104), was relieved of his command, and went into exile. He lived to see the end of the war (V 26), but died before he could finish his work which breaks off in mid-sentence in the final chapter. Book I includes matter which bridges the gap from where Herodotus' work ends (478 BC) to where the Peloponnesian War begins. These sections are among the trickiest in Greek historical writing, mostly owing to the way in which Thucydides arranged and composed his material so that his readers would draw (or not draw) certain conclusions. Ernst Badian elucidated Thucydides' methods in a series of articles (see Further Reading), and discussion must now proceed from that seminal work.

A case in point for the way in which Thucydides arranged material to serve a specific argument comes when he dates the Revolt of Naxos and the Battle of the Eurymedon in the mid-460s (Thuc. I 98–100). In his narrative he discusses three events in the following order: the Athenians' attack on Carystus, the Revolt of Naxos, and the Battle of the Eurymedon. But he dates the latter two events relative to the attack on Carystus only: Naxos revolts "after the events" at Carystus, and the Battle of the Eurymedon takes place "also after the events" at Carystus. When Thucydides wishes to express two events' contemporaneity, he does so with the phrase "at (about) the same time" (e.g., I 107), but here he chooses to say something entirely different. The point of his curious phrasing ("also after the events" at Carystus) indicates his departure from a chronologically arranged narrative. Assuming that the correct order of events was Carystus, then Eurymedon, then Naxos, if Thucydides had wished to switch the order of Eurymedon and Naxos without committing himself to an out-and-out lie, the only way to do it was to say that both took place after the attack on Carystus. Thucydides, by removing the Revolt of Naxos from its correct historical context after the Battle of the Eurymedon, made the revolt appear to take place while the war against the Persians was still going on.

He also added a piece of exposition by which he attempted to show that the allies became subjects of Athens through their own grievous fault – rather than through the Athenians' refusal to allow members of the League to leave after it had served its purpose. This view follows naturally from Thucydides' earlier thesis that the Athenians had been passive in their assumption of the leadership of the anti-Persian alliance a few years earlier (see above). Thucydides was, after all, an Athenian; and he was not above repainting his city's history in softer hues.

Athens. That thesis appears to be Thucydides' personal contribution without any basis in his source material.

The Administration of the Athenian Empire

Because of the way in which the Athenian Empire had arisen, it was a heterogeneous affair with an almost haphazard administration. First of all, some states retained a considerable degree of independence. They had their own fleets, kept their fortifications in good repair, and, in the case of a revolt, would prove difficult to defeat. For example, when Thasos revolted in 465, the Athenians' siege of the Thasians lasted into the third year after an initial naval battle (Thuc. I 101; Diod. XI 70). The revolt of Samos in 440 nearly brought the empire to its knees (Thuc. I 115–117; Diod. XII 27–28). Athens always managed to keep control of its empire after such revolts, but they were frightening enough that allies with strong fleets and good fortifications retained considerable latitude in regulating their internal affairs. Mytilene maintained such a position down to the year 428 (Thuc. III 2sqq.); Chios and Methymna down until 411 when they finally revolted (Thuc. VII 57 and VIII 14 and 22).

Even states of far less importance than Mytilene and Chios could have such a position. The insignificant town of Potidaea, down to 432, still received its annual magistrates from its mother-city, Corinth (Thuc. I 56) – whether Athens allowed this anomaly for diplomatic reasons (relations with Corinth) or because Potidaea was too small for much concern, and as long as it paid the required tribute, the Athenians let it be. Potidaea's position, even if strictly speaking unparalleled within the empire, is still compatible with the empire's wide-ranging heterogeneity of administration; and it shows that other small cities, of which little is known, might still have possessed much freedom in regulating their own affairs.

Next, the Athenians tended to impose tighter control on individual states on a case-by-case basis rather than by uniform application of a rule. There was a garrison in some states (e.g., Erythrae – Fornara, Nr. 71), but not in all. Some states had Athenian governors (e.g., Miletus – Fornara, Nr. 92) or *episkopoi*, i.e., "inspectors" (e.g., Erythrae – Fornara, Nr. 71). The Athenians tended to impose or to restore democratic constitutions (e.g., in Eryrthrae – Fornara, Nr. 71; or on Samos – Diod. XII 28,4; cf. generally Diod. XIII 48,4). A few states (e.g., Histiaea – Thuc. I 114; Naxos and some cities on the Chersonese – Diod. XI 88,3) suffered perhaps the most hated penalty, namely the confiscation of land and the settlement of Athenians – a so-called **cleruchy** – on that land. But in no state were all of these things (garrison, governors, inspectors, democracy, cleruchy) to be found.

Despite this considerable heterogeneity some general conditions did apply. First, by the eve of the Peloponnesian War almost every state paid the tribute; and the Athenians had the authority to regulate the payment of the tribute (Fornara, Nr. 98) and to set its level (Fornara, Nr. 136). Second, the Athenians could and did ban the importation of goods from Megara into the empire (Aristoph. *Ach.*, 517–522); later on the Athenians banned the entrance of the Megarians personally into the empire (Aristoph. *Ach.* 530–534; Thuc. I 67 and 139). Third, the Athenians could at least attempt to regulate currency throughout the empire (Fornara, Nr. 97); had they been successful in this, the empire would effectively have had a uniform currency.

Finally, as regards the assessment of the tribute, the Athenians by 442 BC had organized the tribute-paying members of the League (or Empire) into five districts (Carian, Ionian, Hellespontine, Thracian, and Island – see Meiggs 1972, Map I.i–vi). Regular **tribute** lists (Fornara, Nr. 85) recorded what each town was to pay annually, down to the obol (approximately half of one man's daily wage at the time). Not for nothing did Thucydides call the Athenians "exact" in these matters (I 99).

The Benefits of Empire

The Athenians drew tangible benefits from the possession of an empire. Thucydides places the following words into Pericles' mouth in the justly famous Funeral Oration:

> On account of our city's greatness all things from all the world are available to us, so that we enjoy other peoples' products with just as much pleasure as we enjoy our own country's. (Thuc. II 38).

Athens was the empire's chief port and marketplace; and here people could buy anything they wanted.

More importantly, the Athenians had the advantage of the 460 talents which came in from the empire each year. In spite of controversy Pericles used the money on the construction of the Parthenon and the Propylaea, the entrance onto the Acropolis (Plut. *Per.* 12–14) (see Figure 11.1). The building accounts for the Propylaea survive and record how the *Hellenotamiai*, the treasurers of the League, steered funds towards its construction (Fornara, Nr. 118B). The exploitation of the allies – in what was, as has been suggested, effectively a vast state-run protection racket – paid for the enduring monuments of Athens.

Moreover, during these years philosophers and scholars flocked to Athens. Anaxagoras of Clazomenae, Protagoras of Abdera, Gorgias of Leontini, and many others of the so-called sophists arrived; so did a man from Halicarnassus called Herodotus. Here they found audiences willing to pay for their lectures because Athens – as Pericles describes in the Funeral Oration above – had become a wealthy city in these days, and the Athenians wanted the good things which the wider world had to offer. This included first-rate lectures from the leading thinkers of the day. Likewise, the leading sculptors and artisans arrived because the construction and decoration of, for example, the Parthenon created lucrative opportunities for them.

Figure 11.1   The Acropolis of Athens. The Propylaea, partially obscured by scaffolding, is at the left; the Parthenon is at the center. The allies' tribute to Athens paid for both. Source: Harrieta171/Grèce, http://commons.wikimedia.org/wiki/File:2004_02_29_Ath%C3%A8nes.JPG (accessed 14 January 2014) CC BY-SA 3.0, 2.5, 2.0, 1.0

After humble beginnings in the time of the Peisistratid tyranny (see Box 7.2) the art of tragic drama, buoyed by the general cultural and economic upswing, reached new heights in the fifth century as well. The three greatest tragedians – Aeschylus, **Sophocles**, and Euripides – produced play after play for the festival of the Greater Dionysia on the southern slope of the Acropolis. They too as Athenians were proud of their city and its institutions, and even if they generally drew their subject matter from mythology, they still found opportunity to praise Athens and the Athenian way of life. In his play *Oedipus at Colonus*, Sophocles depicts an encounter between the mythological kings of Athens and Thebes, Theseus and Creon respectively. When Creon attempts unjustly to lay hands on Oedipus, who has taken refuge on Athenian soil, Theseus stops him in his tracks with an affirmation of Athenian values and a reminder that Athens stood ready to defend them:

> *You have come to a city which obeys justice and which does nothing unauthorized by law. You have flouted this land's sovereignty bursting in here, seizing what you want, and*

Figure 11.2 The theater of Dionysus (initially built in the fourth century BC) on the slope of the Acropolis. Source: Glenlarson, http://commons.wikimedia.org/wiki/File:Theatre_of_Dionysus_01382.JPG (accessed 12th February 2013)

using violence. You apparently think that my city is bereft of men or servile. (Soph. *OC* 913–918)

In this time of prosperity and cultural achievement Athens had confidence in itself and its citizens, and it answered to no one but justice and its own laws.

QUESTIONS FOR REVIEW

1 What factors contributed to the Lacedaemonians' failure at leading the Greeks against the Persians in the years after 479?
2 How did the Delian League develop into the Athenian Empire?
3 What are some of the problems with Thucydides' account of events in these years?
4 What mechanisms did the Athenians use to keep control of their "empire"?

QUESTION FOR FURTHER STUDY

Given how heterogeneous the Athenian Empire actually was, is the term "empire" even appropriate? Or is such heterogeneity (including a high degree of local **autonomy**) perfectly compatible with contemporary concepts (e.g., the Persians') of rule over others?

FURTHER READING

On the Delian League/Athenian Empire in general:
Meiggs, R. (1972) *The Athenian Empire*. Oxford.
Meritt, B.D., et al. (1939–1953) *The Athenian Tribute Lists*, Vols. 1–3. Princeton.

On Thucydides as a source for these years:
Badian, E. (1993) *From Plataea to Potidaea*. Baltimore. (Containing the following articles: "The Peace of Callias" (pp. 1–72); "Toward a Chronology of the Pentecontaetia down to the Renewal of the Peace of Callias" (pp. 73–108); and "Thucydides and the Outbreak of the Peloponnesian War: A Historian's Brief" (pp. 125–162).)
Rainey, S. (2004) "Thucydides, 1.98–118, and Diodorus, 11.60–12.28, and their Common Source." *Athenaeum* 92: 217–236.

On Thucydides in general:
Gomme, A.W., et al. (1945–1981) *Commentary on Thucydides*. Oxford. (The older commentary in English, but still useful.)
Hornblower, S. (1991–2008) *A Commentary on Thucydides*. Oxford. (The newer commentary in English.)

On matters of chronology:
Badian, E. (1993) (See above.)
Parker, V. (1993) "The Chronology of the Pentacontaetia from 465 to 456 B.C.," *Athenaeum* 81: 129–147.

12

Sparta and Athens during the Pentecontaetia

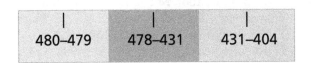

| 480–479 | 478–431 | 431–404 |

470s	Pausanias in Hellespont
early 460s	Pausanias dies
465	Themistocles flees to Persia
465–456	Helots' revolt and siege of Mt. Ithome
465–463	Thasian Revolt
462/1	Reforms of Ephialtes
460–454	Egyptian Expedition
456	Battles of Tanagra and Oenophyta
446	Battle of Coroneia; Revolts of Megara and Euboea; Thirty Years' Peace sworn
440	Revolt of Samos

A History of Greece: 1300 to 30 BC, First Edition. Victor Parker.
© 2014 Victor Parker. Published 2014 by John Wiley & Sons, Ltd.

Pausanias and Themistocles

Relations between Athens and Sparta were inevitably strained by the circumstances under which the Athenians had gained the leadership of the anti-Persian alliance. An ugly affair involving Pausanias and Themistocles, the victors of Plataea and Salamis respectively, oddly enough may have helped to ease matters.

Pausanias' opponents in 478 had accused him of "Medizing" – of betraying the Greeks to the Persians or, as these were commonly known in Greece, the "Medes." As discussed in Chapter 11, Pausanias secured acquittal on those charges, but the Lacedaemonians never sent him out as a commander again. Eventually he left Sparta in a private capacity, gained a following in the Hellespontine region, captured Byzantium, and held it, allegedly, for seven years (Thuc. I 131; **Justin**, IX 1,3). Expelled by the Athenians under Cimon, he went to Colonae in the Troad (Thuc. l.c.; Ion of Chios at Plut. *Cim.* 9). The rumors of his Medism persisted, however; and the Lacedaemonians summoned him thence for a second trial. Pausanias indeed returned to Sparta, but when matters began to look grim for him, he took refuge in the sanctuary of Athena Chalcioecus there. The ephors had him walled up and let him starve (Thuc. I 134; Diod. XI 45). The date should be in the early 460s BC.

The "evidence" (the letters which Thucydides quotes at I 128–129 are forgeries, as has long been seen) which the ephors had gathered in the course of their investigations allegedly implicated Themistocles too – then living in Argos. In the years following Salamis, Themistocles' enemies had used a curious tool to end his political career – an **ostracism**. The Athenian constitution allowed for an annual vote ([Arist.] *Ath.Pol.* 43) to banish any Athenian from Athens for ten years (Plut. *Per.* 10). When the ten years were up, the man could return home with no additional consequences (Arist. *Pol.* 1284 – granted, by implication only). Cleisthenes supposedly introduced this institution; allegedly it was antityrannical in inspiration and enabled the Athenians to send into exile any man who was about to establish a tyranny ([Arist.] *Ath.Pol.* 22). In reality it gave the dominant faction in Athens a weapon with which to destroy any politician whom it regarded as a threat (cf. Arist. *Pol.* l.c.). Themistocles fell victim to such an ostracism (see Figure 12.1) and left Athens for Argos.

Lacedaemonian ambassadors now traveled to Athens and presented their "evidence" to officials there. The Athenian authorities agreed to cooperate in the matter and sent to Argos commissioners charged with arresting Themistocles (Thuc. I 135; cf. Diod. XI 54–55). In all likelihood Themistocles' enemies in Athens, having already gotten him ostracized, were now availing themselves of an opportunity to kick a man who was already down. Themistocles, however, got wind of what was afoot and fled from Argos. After various narrow escapes – e.g., he passed by Naxos just as the Athenians were besieging it in 465 BC – he arrived at Ephesus, a port then in Athenian hands. Leaving Ephesus, he traveled up-country all the way to Susa where he met with King Artaxerxes I, the son of the man whom he had helped defeat at Salamis. Themistocles was a clever man,

Figure 12.1 An *ostrakon* with the inscription "Themistocles of (the deme) Phrearhi." Many of these, often in the same handwriting have been found, so Themistocles' opponents were organized and ready, handing out prewritten "ballots" against him. Source: G.dallorto, http://commons.wikimedia.org/wiki/File:3164_-_Sto%C3%A0_of _Attalus_Museum_-_Ostracism_against_Themistokles_(480s_BC)_-_Photo_by_Giovanni _Dall%27Orto,_Nov_9_2009.jpg?uselang=en-gb (accessed 12th February 2013)

and he rose to the challenge of a personal interview with the King of Persia who, in the end, awarded him with three cities in Asia Minor: Lampsacus, Magnesia on the Meander, and Myus (Thuc. I 136–138; cf. Diod. XI 56–57).

More important in the current context, however, was the official cooperation in the persecution of Themistocles by Sparta and Athens. Whatever lay behind the allegations of Medism against Pausanias and Themistocles, the authorities in Athens (probably for reasons of their own) took it seriously when the Lacedaemonian embassy arrived with charges against Themistocles. But the cooperation itself may have left an impression in Sparta and have done much to dispel the lingering bitterness over events at the end of the Persian Wars. It may also help explain a surprising request which the Lacedaemonians made of the Athenians just a few years after Themistocles' flight.

The Helots' Revolt

Shortly after the revolt of Naxos in circa 465, Thasos too revolted (Thuc. I 100–101; Diod. XI 70,1), and although the Athenians defeated the Thasians' fleet easily enough in an initial battle, the Thasians were evidently prepared for a long siege. Thucydides states that the siege lasted into "the third year" – since Thucydides works with seasonal years which end with the winter (Thuc. V 20), he apparently means "past a second winter"; that is, that the siege took up parts of three seasonal years. The chronology of this period is difficult, but, as will emerge below, it appears that the Thasian revolt ended before the year 462. If so, then it could have begun after the suppression of the Naxian revolt – i.e., in late 465 – and lasted past a second winter into 463.

Thucydides claims that the Lacedaemonians had made a "secret" promise to the Thasians that they would invade Attica in support of the revolt (Thuc. I 101). Thucydides never explains how he found out about this "secret" promise about which no one in Athens could have known for many years (see below). He states that the Lacedaemonians were prevented from fulfilling their promise by an earthquake which struck Laconia in the time between the making of the promise and that for its fulfillment. This severe earthquake ripped several peaks from Mt. Taÿgetos and left only five houses in Sparta standing (Plut. *Cim.* 16) and was the occasion of a large-scale rising of the Helots (Thuc. l.c.; Diod. XI 63; Plut. l.c.).

Such a revolt had long been the Lacedaemonians' national nightmare, as seen, e.g., in their treaties of alliance (see chap. 6). The nightmare now became reality. Although the Lacedaemonians soon gained control of the countryside, some Helots retreated to Mt. Ithome where they prepared for a siege (Thuc. l.c.; cf. Diod. XI 64,4). The natural strength of the mountain (see Figure 12.2)

Figure 12.2   The natural fortress of Mt. Ithome seen from the city of Messene at its foot. Source: Stefan Artinger, http://en.wikipedia.org/wiki/File:Ithome1.jpg (accessed 12th February 2013). CC0 1.0

made it untakeable in antiquity, and, even worse for the Lacedaemonians, there was sufficient land near the summit for the rebels to sow a crop.

The Lacedaemonians, used to straight battles, had no experience in siege-warfare and quickly came to their wits' end. So they took the step of appealing to Athens precisely because the Athenians had skill at sieges (Thuc. I 102). Presumably the Athenians' reputation, following the successful end to the siege at Thasos, stood high enough that even the proud Lacedaemonians could call upon them without shame.

The most prominent Athenian statesman after Themistocles' demise, Cimon, the current leader of the Philaid clan and the victor in the Battle of the Eurymedon, had always had philolacedaemonian sympathies. His political opponents held other views, however, so it was against some opposition that Cimon persuaded the Athenian assembly to vote in favor of an expedition to Mt. Ithome (Plut. *Cim.* 16). Cimon then led troops to aid the Lacedaemonians (Thuc. I 102).

Unfortunately for Cimon, the Athenians too found the siege of Mt. Ithome tough. In the Greek world, whenever a state sent troops to fight on behalf of another state and on that state's territory, the latter state provisioned those troops (see Thuc. VI 47 and VII 27; cf. Xen. *Hell.* III 2,1). As long as the Athenians remained at Mt. Ithome, they were eating the Lacedaemonians' produce. At some point it became clear that the Athenians too were unable to end the siege, so the Lacedaemonians cut their losses and dismissed them. Thucydides, however, insists that the Lacedaemonians sent the Athenians away owing to the suspicion that the revolution-loving Athenians sympathized with the rebellious Helots (Thuc. I 102). Given Cimon's views and the likelihood that it was his supporters who had gone on this expedition, Thucydides' assertion misses the mark – but it does fit with his general thesis of Lacedaemonian fear and distrust of Athens (see also chap. 13). In Athens this dismissal was taken as a grave affront, and Cimon, since he had staked his own reputation when persuading the Athenian assembly to vote in favor of this expedition, was spectacularly embarrassed when his "friends" sent the Athenians packing (Thuc. l.c.).

A far-reaching constitutional change in Athens attended upon Cimon's loss of prestige. The Council of the Areopagus, which consisted of all former archons (see chap. 8), appears to have been closely allied to Cimon during this period (cf. Plut. *Cim.* 15). Cimon's political opponents – chief among them a man called Ephialtes – therefore strove to reduce the authority of the Council of the Areopagus. Ephialtes had already made a name for himself prosecuting members of the Council of the Areopagus for corruption ([Arist.] *Ath.Pol.* 25). Presumably he targeted close allies of Cimon's. Either during Cimon's (and his supporters') absence at Ithome or just possibly after the expedition's ostensibly humiliating return, the Athenian Assembly, at the instigation of Ephialtes, stripped the Council of the Areopagus of all political powers in 462–61 ([Arist.] *Ath.Pol.* 25). Presumably the Council was cowed into acquiescence and, especially if Cimon and many of his supporters were away at the time, too frightened to avail itself of its "guardianship of the laws" to nullify the decree. When Cimon attempted to undo the reforms, his opponents silenced him with an ostracism

(Plut. *Cim.* 15 and 17). Ephialtes and his allies had broken Cimon's political dominance and had also removed an important antidemocratic check in the Athenian constitution.

Athens' Imperial Ambitions in Greece and Abroad

Meanwhile, the Helots' Revolt dragged on; it had begun at about the same time as the Thasian Revolt (i.e., 465). Sparta was effectively hamstrung for its duration: with an unsettled revolt at home, no Lacedaemonian army dared leave Laconia. As long as the Lacedaemonians had their own revolt to deal with, Athens had the freedom to develop its own empire without interference from Sparta. Athens' ambitions in this period knew no bounds, and the Athenian Empire reached its high water mark.

First, Megara was involved in a border dispute with its neighbor Corinth. Failing to get any assistance from the otherwise occupied Lacedaemonians, the Megarians turned to Athens and entered the Athenian Empire (Thuc. I 103; Diod. XI 79). An erstwhile member of the Peloponnesian League had decided that Athens would protect its interests better than Sparta, and the Athenian Empire had begun to expand by land as well as by sea. The Athenians promptly began fortifying various places in Megara, through which the roads from the Peloponnese into central Greece led.

Second, in 460 an Athenian fleet set sail for Cyprus to liberate the island (once again) from Persian rule, clearly nullifying the Peace of Callias (see chap. 11). While on Cyprus the commanders of the fleet learned that Egypt had revolted from the Persian Empire. They decided to sail on to Egypt and to aid the revolt there (Thuc. I 104; Diod. XI 71,4sqq.). A brief but highly significant inscription (see Box 12.1) shows that in addition to Cyprus and Egypt the Athenians also fought in Phoenicia during these years. The Athenians, then, were fighting against the Persians on three fronts – hundreds of miles from home, all along the eastern Mediterranean. Twenty years earlier the Persians had been invading Greece; now that Greek city which had gone on the offensive against them and had taken the Aegean coast of Asia Minor from them was challenging them for supremacy throughout the eastern Mediterranean. For a brief time the Palestinian city of Dor, south of Mt. Carmel, actually appears as a tribute-paying member of the Athenian Empire (*ATL* I, p. 483).

In 457 war broke out again between Athens and its old enemy Aegina. This time the Athenians quickly defeated the Aeginetans' fleet and besieged Aegina (Thuc. I 105; Diod. XI 70 and 78). Athens was now fighting on a fourth front. At this point the Corinthians, in the belief that Athens would be unable to respond, attacked the Megarians in order to settle the border dispute. Yet Athens did respond. The "oldest and the youngest" – the men in the age brackets 50–60 (**Lycurgus**, *Leoc.* 39–40) and 18–19 (**Aeschines**, II 167) who ordinarily were not called upon to go to war – marched out and in two battles decisively defeated the Corinthians (Thuc. I 105–106; Diod. XI 79,3–4).

Box 12.1   *The Erechtheid Casualty List*

The following inscription comes from a war memorial of one of the ten Athenian tribes, Erechtheis. Its brevity belies its historiographical significance for it shows how much historically significant information could stand in a mundane memorial inscription:

Of (the tribe) Erechtheis the following men died fighting in Cyprus, in Egypt, in Phoenicia, at Halieis, on Aegina, in Megara in the same year: . . . (Fornara, Nr. 78; below the superscript stand three columns of names)

Most important are the words "in the same year" – clearly the large number of fronts on which the Athenians were waging war made an impression even at the time. In fact, these words in the inscription are written larger than the others and take up an entire line by themselves. Thucydides mentions much of this fighting, but he says nothing of any fighting in Phoenicia. The brief inscription provides this piece of highly valuable information. Moreover, it is this inscription which shows that the fighting at Halieis and in Megara as well as the siege of Aegina all took place during the Egyptian expedition (460–454). Accordingly, the inscription plays an outsize role in establishing the chronology of these years.

Towards the end of the year 457 the Phocians invaded the Doris (Thuc. I 107; Diod. XI 79,4–5), a small region in central Greece, which counted as the ancestral homeland of all the Dorians (including the Lacedaemonians) (see chap. 3). The Doris may have been insignificant, but it meant something to the Dorians as a whole; and the Phocians' invasion of it shocked the Lacedaemonians who, still bogged down with the siege at Mt. Ithome, finally realized that they had to do the hitherto unthinkable: negotiate with Helots. Greek states commonly kept collections of oracles (Hdt. V 90 and VI 57), and the Lacedaemonians searched their own collection until they found an oracle which they thought might serve them in their present need. The oracle spoke of releasing "the suppliant of Ithomaean Zeus"; so even if many Helots (not just one) were involved, the Lacedaemonians employed the oracle as a face-saving device and consented to let the Helots on Mt. Ithome go – on condition that they indeed went and never came back (Thuc. I 103; Diod. XI 84). This occurred, probably, very early in the year 456 – so the Helots' Revolt and the Siege of Ithome ended "in the tenth year," having begun in 465.

Free of the siege, a Lacedaemonian army of 1,500 Spartiates and 10,000 allies in the spring of 456 was ferried across the Gulf of Corinth to Phocis. The Phocians, who had never expected such a response, immediately came to terms (Thuc. I 107; Diod. XI 79). The Athenians – though still heavily committed in the eastern Mediterranean and on Aegina – marched out against the largest

Lacedaemonian army in central Greece since 479. The two sides came together
at Tanagra, a small town in Boeotia. Here the two sides fought each other to an
effective draw, and both apparently counted themselves fortunate to have escaped
a clear defeat. For after the battle the Lacedaemonians were mostly concerned
to get back to the Peloponnese quickly, and the Athenians for their part did not
attempt to prevent the Lacedaemonians from going as they too had no desire for
another battle (Thuc. I 108; Diod. XI 80 – see below). Special commendations
were due to the partisans of the ostracized Athenian politician Cimon – at his
encouragement they had fought exceptionally and ostentatiously well. The Athenians, in a special dispensation, recalled Cimon from his ostracism early (Plut.
Cim. 17), before five years had elapsed (Theopompus, *BNJ* 115, Fr. 88).

Meanwhile the Lacedaemonian army was at a loss as to how to return to the
Peloponnese – the Athenians controlled Megara and the roads leading through
it (Thuc. I 107); and crossing the Gulf of Corinth was no longer an option
since, in a bold maneuver, an Athenian fleet had circumnavigated the Peloponnese (see also Thuc. I 108). Tolmides, who commanded this fleet, had carried
out raids along the way, and, although Thucydides does not say so, had apparently also managed to pick up the Helots who had left Mt. Ithome. He was
now present in the Gulf of Corinth (Thuc. I 107 and 108; Diod. XI 84). In the
end the Lacedaemonians decided to return by land, and, as noted above,
the Athenians had little inclination to hinder their departure (Thuc. I 108).
In the absence of a Lacedaemonian army to oppose them the Athenians invaded
Boeotia, defeated the Boeotians at Oenophyta a mere 61 days after Tanagra,
and conquered Boeotia. Additionally, they gained control of Phocis and Eastern
Locris (Thuc. l.c.; Diod. XI 81–83). Athens' land empire – Megara, Boeotia,
Phocis, Eastern Locris – had grown large indeed.

The Athenians now took a hundred of the wealthiest Eastern Locrians as
hostages (Thuc. I 108) and demanded the strategic port of Naupactus which
lay on West Locrian territory just within the bottleneck of the Corinthian Gulf.
The Eastern and the Western Locrians were related and always maintained close
ties (see chap. 1); the Eastern Locrians had founded Naupactus in the early
fifth century on Western Locrian territory (Fornara, Nr. 47), but the Western
Locrians had recently come into possession of the colony (Thuc. I 103). Now,
to relieve the pressure on the Eastern Locrians, they surrendered it to the Athenians who settled in it the Helots with Tolmides' fleet (Thuc. l.c.; Diod. XI 84;
see also Badian 1993, in the Further Reading to Chapter 11, pp 163–169).
Athens had gained an important base on the Gulf of Corinth and had settled
in it people whose hatred of Sparta was absolute. The "Messenians in Naupactus" – that is their technical name – were reliable Athenian allies during the
Peloponnesian War. To cap the year 456, the Aeginetans too surrendered, and
Aegina became a tribute-paying ally (Thuc. I 108; Diod. XI 79). The Athenian
Empire stood at the height of its powers.

Unfortunately, it was all too good to last. In 454 the Persians reconquered
Egypt and crushed the Athenian army there (Thuc. I 109–110; Diod. XI 77).
After Pericles' minor campaigns in Sicyon and Acarnania (Thuc. I 111; Diod.

XI 88), Athenian expansion ground to a halt. In fact, Thucydides announces that he is leaving the next three years blank (Thuc. I 112), apparently for want of anything significant to report. The parallel account in Diodorus, however, mentions the establishment by Pericles and by Tolmides of cleruchies in the Chersonese and on Naxos respectively (Diod. l.c.).

In 451 the Athenians and the Lacedaemonians negotiated a peace for five years. Thereupon the Athenians made another expedition to Cyprus so as to liberate the island yet again from Persian rule (Thuc. I 112; Diod. XII 3). (The Cyprians, incidentally, appear to have fought against their would-be liberators – what the Athenians called "liberation" may well have seemed more like "conquest" to the Cyprians.) Cimon, who was advanced in years by now, commanded the expedition and died during the campaign, but his fleet still managed to defeat the Persians in a major sea battle. Thereafter the fleet returned home (Thuc. l.c.; Diod. l.c.), and it appears that the Peace of Callias was renewed (Diod. XII 4; **Aristodemus**, *BNJ* 104, Fr. 13; Fornara, Nr. 95 L – all based on Ephorus).

The Revolts of 446 and the Thirty Years' Peace

In 446 the five years' peace expired. A small Lacedaemonian expedition to Phocis appears to have had no real effect on Athenian control of the area (Thuc. I 112), but a revolt was brewing in Boeotia. It began in the towns of Orchomenus and Chaeroneia. When an Athenian force under Tolmides attempted to put down the revolt, the Boeotian rebels surprised it near Coroneia, inflicted a severe defeat, and took a number of Athenians prisoner. All Boeotia now rose in revolt and, in order to secure the release of their prisoners, the Athenians acknowledged Boeotian independence. They lost control of Phocis and Eastern Locris at the same time (Thuc. I 113; Diod. XII 6).

Megara and Euboea revolted as well, and in the absence of a peace treaty a large Lacedaemonian army under King Pleistoanax invaded Attica in support of the revolts (Thuc. I 114; Diod. XII 5 and 7). Pericles, whose long ascendancy in Athenian politics had by now been established, reached an accommodation with Pleistoanax (Ephorus, *BNJ* 70, Fr. 193): if the Lacedaemonians withdrew from Attica, the Athenians would not challenge Megara's withdrawal from the Athenian Empire; in exchange the Athenians were to receive a free hand on Euboea. This settled, Pericles suppressed the Euboean revolt and established a cleruchy in Histiaea (Thuc. I 114; Diod. XII 7). Athens' land empire had disappeared, and Pericles had restricted the Athenians to a sea-borne one. Pericles now negotiated a formal peace treaty with the Lacedaemonians. It was meant to last for thirty years (Thuc. I 115; Diod. XII 7). Pericles apparently viewed the land empire as impracticable in the long term, and by committing Athens to a peace treaty of thirty years' duration he presumably hoped to prevent any attempts to regain control of lost territory in central Greece. Athens was supposed to have three decades to concentrate on the more practicable – and lucrative – sea-borne empire.

Thucydides, for reasons of his own, declines to quote the text of the Thirty Years' Peace, but, fortunately, the diplomatic debates which preceded the Peloponnesian War allow a partial reconstruction of the treaty's clauses:

1   The treaty contained a list of allies of both Sparta and Athens;
2   Both Sparta and Athens were able to make alliances with neutral states;
3   Athens (and probably Sparta also) undertook to guarantee its allies' "autonomy" (whatever was meant concretely) – see Box 12.2;

Box 12.2   *Reconstructing the Clauses of the Thirty Years' Peace*

The clauses of the Thirty Years' Peace can be reconstructed out of the diplomatic debates before the beginning of the Peloponnesian War (see chap. 13). The two most controversial are the autonomy clause and the free-access clause. When various delegations arrived at Sparta to complain about Athens, Thucydides records that a delegation from Aegina played a considerable role behind the scenes. The Aeginetans alleged that the Athenians were not granting them the autonomy which the treaty enjoined (Thuc. I 67). According to Thucydides, Pericles responded to this assertion with the following comment:

> . . . *we will give the cities their autonomy if they had it when we swore the treaty . . .* (Thuc. I 144)

Pericles' words admit that the treaty enjoined the Athenians to grant their allies autonomy, but suggest that this applied only under certain circumstances.

Another charge leveled at the Athenians during the initial conference in Sparta had to do with an Athenian decree which banned the Megarians personally from entering any port in the Athenian Empire. Thucydides makes no mention of an initial decree which banned the importation of Megarian goods, mostly woolen textiles, into the Athenian Empire, but Aristophanes, the contemporary playwright, attests to the existence of such an earlier decree (Aristoph. *Ach.* 517–522). The Megarians – as the lines from Aristophanes show – were circumventing the first decree by smuggling, hence passage of the second decree intended to enforce the first (*Ach.* 530–534; Thuc. I 67 and 139). Although the Megarians might have complained about both decrees, they did so concerning the second only because presumably here they had a case. Again according to Thucydides, Pericles rebutted the accusation with the blunt assertion that the decree did not violate the treaty (and if it did, then the Lacedaemonians too were violating it – Thuc. I 144), but without knowledge of the treaty's text there is no way to judge who was right.

What no one disputed was that the treaty required arbitration if one side thought that the other was violating another of its clauses (Thuc. I 78 and 85; cf. I 144). Without the text of the treaty, however, no one can know what sort of arbitration it envisaged, since Thucydides withholds that information.

4   The treaty contained a clause which, on one interpretation, allowed members of one alliance to travel freely into the other – see Box 12.2;

5   In the case of a dispute the treaty enjoined arbitration upon Sparta and Athens (though it remains murky what sort of arbitration) – see Box 12.2.

The first challenge to the treaty came in 440 when Samos revolted from Athens (Thuc. I 116–117; Ephorus, *BNJ* 70, Fr. 195; Diod. XII 27–28). The Lacedaemonians viewed the Athenians' actions in suppressing the revolt as a violation of the treaty (presumably the autonomy clause), and the Lacedaemonian assembly must have voted accordingly. At a subsequent assembly of the Peloponnesian League, however, the Corinthians argued strenuously that the Athenians should be allowed to deal with their own allies as they saw fit (Thuc. I 40). The Lacedaemonians let the matter drop, and the Athenians reconquered Samos, albeit barely: Pericles personally led the Athenians in a difficult campaign which saw the Athenians employ new-fangled siege machinery (Ephorus, l.c.; Diod. l.c.). Rumors of the imminent arrival of a Persian fleet unnerved the Athenians, but fortunately for them no such fleet ever materialized (Thuc. I 116; Diod. XII 27) and the Athenians brought the siege to a successful conclusion, and returned home.

The Thirty Years' Peace remained in force and probably achieved exactly what Pericles had hoped for – it kept Lacedaemonians and Athenians in their separate dominions.

Athenian Democracy

The reforms of Ephialtes, as discussed earlier, removed one of the antidemocratic checks (the retention by the Council of the Areopagus of the "guardianship of the laws") which Cleisthenes had retained in his constitutional reforms (see chap. 8). At about the same time as these reforms (462/1) another constitutional reform took place. Its instigator this time was not Ephialtes – who fell victim to an assassination shortly after his reforms' passage ([Arist.] *Ath.Pol.* 25) –, but a younger associate of his, Pericles.

Pericles' reform seems modest: pay for jury duty ([Arist.] *Ath.Pol.* 27; Plut. *Per.* 9). The pay was initially set at two obols per day (Schol. Aristoph. *Wasps*, 88a), evidently a standard daily wage back then. With this he introduced the concept of pay for public office, and although no source explicitly attests it, the concept was quickly expanded to include the other offices. As soon as people began receiving a daily wage for holding an office, everyone could serve, because now no one suffered financially for being away from work, and another antidemocratic check in the Cleisthenic constitution fell away.

One, however, remained. The ten generalships were filled each year by election. Originally, each tribe elected one general, but eventually the voters as a whole elected ten generals ([Arist.] *Ath.Pol.* 61). Elections in ancient Greece always counted as undemocratic for the simple reason that the rich and famous could and did manipulate them. Securing election to a generalship required money and organization. Moreover, unlike with other offices in Athens, there was here no prohibition against serving more than one year in a row. The politically ambitious and wealthy Athenian aristocrats concentrated on the generalship and spurned the other offices which could be held for just one year and were filled by lot. As a consequence the generalship was the most important office in Athens from the mid-fifth century on, and the aristocrat Pericles held this office again and again (Plut. *Per.* 18sqq.). It functioned as the concrete base of his power and allowed him to dominate politics in Athens to such an extent that Thucydides could later write that under Pericles "what was in name a democracy was in reality rule by the best man" – Athens under Pericles was practically a monarchy (Thuc. II 65). No matter how hyperbolical Thucydides' comment may be, the dominance of the generalship by the wealthy made for a strong antidemocratic element in the Athenian constitution during the fifth century (see also Box 13.1).

This is not to say that the Athenian government was fully undemocratic, and from Thucydides' narrative it emerges clearly enough that the Assembly, at which in theory all adult male citizens were present and had an equal voice, had the final say in all major questions in the second half of the fifth century. The *Boule* (the Council of 500) and the jury-courts for their part were filled with a random cross-section of adult male citizens. In fact, routine participation in the Assembly, in the jury-courts, and in the *Boule* as well as the occasional holding of magistracies in these days became an important part of the lives of many male citizens who viewed it as their patriotic duty to do their part in the governance of their city. Aristophanes, in his comedy the *Wasps*, parodies the ideal of the dutiful male citizen with an hilarious portrait of an obsessive-compulsive juror, a meddler, who simply cannot stop attending the law-courts. Aristophanes' audience must have recognized the character type instantly, an officious busybody who took this sort of thing far too seriously. Behind the parody, though, one can still discern the civic ideal. However, many people in the state of Athens lived in the countryside, away from the city proper. For them this sort of regular participation at the Assembly or in the jury-courts was impossible owing to the distances involved. Granted, there was still the possibility for participation at the level of the deme where regular deme assemblies and the like took place ([Arist.] *Ath.Pol.* 42 and 59).

Next, even if female citizens could not participate in the Assembly or hold most offices, they could hold some, in particular those of a religious nature. An inscription from 424 BC. (Fornara, Nr. 139) shows what arrangements the Athenians made for the appointment and pay of the Priestess of Athena Nike, whose temple lay on the Acropolis to the south of the entry-way. That this priestess received a salary at public expense shows that she held a public office just as any man did who served on the *Boule*. In fact, one of the most important and visible public officials in Athens was the Priestess of Athena in the Parthenon, the chief temple on the Acropolis. When the Athenians decided to evacuate Attica in 480 as the Persian army entered central Greece, it was she who gave the final all-clear for the evacuation to begin – a highly public act with far-reaching consequences (Hdt. VIII 41).

Finally, the discussion of citizens' duties under the democracy in the second half of the fifth century raises the question of how in Athens the body of citizens was defined in those days. In 451 Pericles arranged for a new law, by which citizenship was restricted to those whose parents were both Athenian citizens ([Arist.] *Ath. Pol.* 26; Plut. *Per.* 37 – previously just an Athenian father had sufficed). Male citizens were registered in their deme on a roll kept by the **demarch** (**Demosthenes**, XLIV 37 and LVII 60), so in cases of doubt this document attested one's father's citizenship. One proved one's mother's citizenship with a document as well, the ***engyesis***-contract which recorded her father's transfer of a dowry into her fiancé's possession (**Isaeus**, III 8 and 53; VIII 9). Since as a general rule Greek states restricted marriage to citizens, the *engyesis*-contract showed that one's mother, since she could enter into a legal marriage, was indeed a citizen.

Pericles' law of citizenship enforced this general rule in Athens. Before the rise of the Athenian "empire," with few exceptions, Athenian men almost always married Athenian women for reasons of simple practicality. Exceptions were rare and therefore negligible. But in the time of the "empire," when people from abroad were coming to Athens in droves and Athenians were constantly traveling abroad on business and even living there as cleruchs or stationed in garrisons, marriages between Athenians and non-Athenians became too frequent to be overlooked. At Pericles' instigation a law was made which deprived of citizenship the children of any such marriage and so made them illegitimate. As Demosthenes (LIX 122) remarked in a famous passage, "marriage is this, that a man begets children and enrolls his sons in a **phratry** and a deme and gives his daughters as his own to men in marriage" (i.e., both sons and daughters are publicly and officially acknowledged as legitimate and as Athenians). The Athenians thus maintained a distinct civic identity rather than merging through intermarriage with the other peoples in the "empire."

QUESTIONS FOR REVIEW

1   How did internal political struggles help to produce Athenian democracy?
2   How did internal political struggles affect Athenian relations with other states such as Sparta or the Persian Empire?
3   How are the terms of the Thirty Years' Peace reconstructed in the absence of a text of the treaty itself?
4   How was the Thirty Years' Peace supposed to reduce tension between Athens and Sparta?

QUESTION FOR FURTHER STUDY

Although the government of Athens in the second half of the fifth century is usually described as a "radical democracy," just how democratic was the Athenian government when one considers the limitations on participation by gender, by census class, by status as free or unfree, by citizenship as well as by the effective exclusion of most of the people in the Attic countryside who simply could not routinely travel to attend a meeting of the assembly?

FURTHER READING

In addition to the works listed at the end of Chapter 11, see also the following:
de Ste. Croix, G.E.M. (1972) *The Origins of the Peloponnesian War*. London.
Kagan, D. (1969) *The Outbreak of the Peloponnesian War*. London.

On Athenian democracy:
Ober, J. (1989) *Mass and Elite in Democratic Athens*. Princeton.
Ober, J. (1996) *The Athenian Revolution*. Princeton.

13

From the Outbreak of the Peloponnesian War to the Peace of Nicias

| 478–431 | 431–421 | 421–404 |

late 430s	Civil war in Epidamnus; War between Corinth and Corcyra
431	Peloponnesian War breaks out
430	Plague in Athens
428–427	Revolt of Mytilene
425	Athenians capture Pylos
421	Peace of Nicias

The Origins of the War

Thucydides writes that the "truest cause" of the great war between Athens and Sparta was "the growth of Athenian power and the fear which this caused in Sparta" (Thuc. I 23). His judgment in the matter has impressed modern scholars since he uses genuinely historical analysis in seeking the roots of the war deep in the past. Evaluating Thucydides' judgment, however, causes difficulties – how, after two and a half millennia, can one estimate to what degree fear determined Sparta's politics? Athenian power is a different matter; and here one can

A History of Greece: 1300 to 30 BC, First Edition. Victor Parker.
© 2014 Victor Parker. Published 2014 by John Wiley & Sons, Ltd.

at least say that the Athenian Empire of the 430s was actually smaller than in the 450s.

The contemporary playwright Aristophanes, on the other hand, saw Pericles' difficulties in Athenian politics (*Peace*, 603–611) and his personal involvement in a dispute with Megara (allegedly Megarians had kidnapped two prostitutes owned by Aspasia, Pericles' influential mistress [*Ach.* 515–539]) as the causes of the war. The late fourth-century BC historian Ephorus found this general view more convincing than Thucydides' and, quoting various passages from Aristophanes, elaborated on them (while deleting the material regarding Aspasia and the prostitutes). According to Ephorus, Pericles drove Athens into war simply to escape from political problems (his enemies' prosecution of his friends; a looming audit of his accounts which was likely to show misuse of funds) because he felt that in wartime the Athenians would focus on his competence – as opposed to worrying about details in a financial audit (Ephorus, *BNJ* 70, Fr. 196). Even if most scholars have looked down on Ephorus' discussion, one needs to remember that enough modern leaders have sought through sabre-rattling to distract public attention from their domestic difficulties. His contemporary Aristophanes would have placed Pericles among them.

Finally, Thucydides includes a long discussion of disputes which diplomatic negotiations failed to resolve and which – in his view: proximately – led to the outbreak of the war. This discussion, interestingly, shows how much influence on events second-tier states such as Corinth could have and in the end calls into question the accuracy of conventional presentations of Greece as polarized between the two "superpowers" Athens and Sparta. Despite Thucydides, one could suggest that the war's ultimate causes lay in disputes away from Athens and Sparta.

The spark which would kindle the war came from civil strife between democrats and oligarchs (see Box 13.1) in Epidamnus, a Corcyraean colony on the eastern coast of the Adriatic Sea. The losers in this conflict, the oligarchs, had gone into exile and made common cause with non-Greek peoples living in the interior. Together they made an attack on Epidamnus, which did what any Greek colony did when it felt itself threatened: it appealed to its mother-city for aid (Thuc. I 24; see also chap. 5). The Corcyraeans, however, turned the Epidamnians down – Thucydides does not explain why, but perhaps the Corcyraeans had been backing the exiled oligarchic party in the Epidamnian civil war. An oligarchy governed Corcyra at the time (Thuc. III 72), and the exiled Epidamnian oligarchs and the Corcyraeans did fight side by side later on (Thuc. I 26). Corcyra was itself a colony of Corinth's; and in accordance with ancient custom, as Thucydides says, the oecist of Epidamnus had actually come from Corinth (Thuc. I 25 – see also chap. 5). So, from a certain point of view, Epidamnus was a Corinthian colony. Accordingly, Epidamnus appealed next to Corinth. Corinth always took its responsibilities as a mother-city seriously (cf. its aid to Syracuse in the 344 – see chap. 17) and promptly sent aid to Epidamnus; settlers from Corinth and two Corinthian colonies on the Ionian Sea, Ambracia and Leucas, went overland to Epidamnus by way of yet another Corinthian colony, Apollonia (Thuc. I 26).

Box 13.1   *Oligarchy*

Although the Greek form of government most often discussed is democracy (i.e., "rule by the people"), the most common form of government at any point in time during the classical period was probably the much less discussed oligarchy – "rule by a few." Oligarchies could be defined officially by the number of people who held political rights. Thus, the four oligarchies which governed Athens in the last years of the fifth century were known as the "400," the "5,000" (both in 411–410 – see chap. 14), the "30," and the "3,000" (both just after the Peloponnesian War ended – see chap. 15). Often enough, however, no number was specified. The government of Sparta may justly be deemed an oligarchy since adult male Spartiates, who in 479 made up about a ninth of the adult male population overall (Hdt. IX 28), reserved political rights for themselves. Yet there never was a set number of Spartiates.

Even when a number was specified, it could be an approximation. Thus, membership in the "5,000" in Athens depended on ownership of hoplite arms (Thuc. VIII 97; [Arist.] *Ath.Pol.* 33). But the registrar charged with enrolling those who had them later on claimed to have enrolled a full 9,000: [**Lysias**], XX 13). In other words, a specific criterion – ownership of hoplite arms – determined the issue.

Two constitutional features characterized an oligarchy: absence of pay for office and the use of elections to fill office. Absence of pay appears with the "5,000" in Athens (Thuc. VIII 97). In an oligarchy the holding of office was the preserve of those with substantial means. Elections – and not the lot – were the rule in Sparta (Arist., *Pol.* 1265b and 1271a). Elections, too, favored the wealthy since they alone possessed the means to organize and to canvass for votes.

The sources repeatedly speak of civil conflict between oligarchic and democratic factions in various cities (see, e.g., Thuc. III 69–85 – the long and justly famous description of the civil war between oligarchs and democrats on Corcyra in 427); and such strife was so common that normally no details needed to be given – the author simply expected his readers to understand. Thus Thucydides mentions not one single constitutional detail in his account of the conflict.

Even if the sources routinely present such conflict as clear-cut, often enough a given constitution was a "blend" of democratic and oligarchic elements on a broad spectrum, the difference between a democracy and an oligarchy residing in the position at which a given constitution sat on that spectrum. Thus in the constitution of the Boeotian League before 386 BC, arrangements are made for the pay of the councilmen (democratic), but not for the highest-ranking officials, the Boeotarchs, who were presumably unpaid (oligarchic) (***Hellenica Oxyrhynchia***, XVI 3, *BNJ* 66). Assuming that [Arist.] *Ath.Pol.* 30 describes the constitution of the "5,000" in Athens, then in this government the higher offices were filled by election (oligarchic), but the lot was used for the lower ones (democratic). Even the Athenian "democracy" contained oligarchic elements: the generals were elected, and the archonship was the preserve of the three wealthiest classes.

The participation of three Corinthian colonies in this venture emphasizes, first, the location of all these events within a Corinthian colonial "sphere of influence" – away from Athens and Sparta. Second, it shows the spectrum of relations between states within that area. Corinth and its colony Corcyra had a strained and difficult history – Corcyra had been founded in the time of the Bacchiads, the other colonies in the time of the tyrants who envisaged their colonies as having closer links to the mother-city (on all this, see chap. 5). When Corinth responded to Epidamnus' appeal, Corcyra reacted badly and Thucydides actually states that one of the Corinthians' chief motives in aiding Epidamnus was hatred of the Corcyraeans (Thuc. I 25). The historical bad blood between Corinth and Corcyra soon boiled over into open war. Corcyra possessed a larger fleet than Corinth (120 triremes to 30 – Thuc. I 25 and 27), so the Corinthians organized a combined fleet to which Megara, Epidaurus, Hermione, Troezen, Leucas, Ambracia, and Pale on the island of Cephallenia contributed a total of 38 ships with additional funds coming from Thebes, Phleius, and Elis (Thuc. I 27). Corinth managed this impressive alliance on its own and without any recourse to Sparta. Unfortunately for Corinth, the Corcyraeans easily defeated this hastily cobbled together fleet and, in a separate action, captured Epidamnus itself (Thuc. I 29).

The Corinthians now redoubled their efforts. They built new ships for a total of ninety; and their allies contributed even more ships than the last time. The new combined fleet would reach 150 ships in all (Thuc. I 46). The Corcyraeans, in alarm at the preparations in Corinth, sought an alliance with Athens (Thuc. I 31). At this point events which had been taking place entirely within Corinth's sizable colonial "sphere of influence" intruded into the affairs of one of Greece's two alleged "superpowers."

The Athenians could have let the Corcyraeans and Corinthians sort out their own problems, but made an alliance with Corcyra instead. The Thirty Years' Peace (see chap. 12) self-evidently allowed either Sparta or Athens to make an alliance with a state which hitherto had been neutral, and advantages of an alliance with Corcyra were obvious: it had a sizable fleet (some 110 triremes at this point – Thuc. I 47) and lay at a strategic point on the trade-route which led from Greece to Italy (Thuc. I 44; see chap. 5). The disadvantage of such an alliance was a breakdown in relations between Athens and Corinth, and this the Athenians accepted.

In the ensuing sea battle, near an island group called Sybota, the combined fleet of Corinth and its allies fought the Corcyraean fleet, supported by an Athenian contingent, to an effective draw. However, the Corinthians did capture a fair number of influential Corcyraeans and held them as hostages (Thuc. I 48–55). Thereafter hostilities between Corinth and Corcyra died down; the hostages would later return to Corcyra and agitate for the nullification of Corcyra's alliance with Athens (Thuc. III 70). Indeed Athens never had much benefit from that alliance since civil war – between democrats supported by Athens and oligarchs supported by Corinth – was soon roiling Corcyra (Thuc.

III 70–85). But the disadvantage of the alliance – hostility between Corinth and Athens – would linger.

The Athenians took the next step in aggravating that hostility. Up until now, the Athenians had allowed the city of Potidaea – a small Corinthian colony on Pallene, the westernmost of the Chalcidice's three prongs – a fair degree of autonomy, especially as regards the practice of receiving its annual magistrates from its mother-city Corinth. This, the Athenians now demanded, had to cease (Thuc. I 56). The Potidaeans, with full backing from Corinth, refused. Meanwhile the Corinthians and Perdiccas II, the Macedonian king, entered into negotiations which involved other Athenian allies in the Chalcidice as well. The result was a full-blown revolt on the Chalcidice against Athens (Thuc. I 57–60). Corinth actually sent troops to Potidaea to assist the Potidaeans in their revolt. Corinth was going head-to-head with Athens in the northern Aegean. Moreover Corinth, keen to make matters worse for Athens, sent ambassadors to Sparta to argue that the Athenians were in violation of the Thirty Years' Peace (Thuc. I 67), thus drawing Sparta into the conflict.

The long, tortuous chain which leads from a civil war in Epidamnus to a conflict between Athens and Sparta demonstrates just how unlikely an event the Peloponnesian War really was. Slightly different decisions at any point, such as an Athenian refusal to make an alliance with Corcyra, or slightly different outcomes, such as a Corinthian victory in the initial encounter with the Corcyraeans, in all likelihood would have kept the chain from ever reaching as far as Sparta. If Corinth – which on any interpretation emerges as a fiercely independent state with interests and policies fully its own and with an iron will to implement those policies – had not approached Sparta, the conflict might have remained one between an Athenian alliance and a Corinthian one. And Corinth's ability to go up against Athens shows, finally, how heavily qualified a status as "superpower" Athens had.

In 432, then, the Corinthians succeeded in persuading the Lacedaemonians to vote that the Athenians had, *prima facie*, violated the Thirty Years' Peace treaty: the exact wording of the motion ran "that the treaty had been broken and that the Athenians were in the wrong" (Thuc. I 87). The Thirty Years' Treaty under such circumstances enjoined "arbitration," but Thucydides never states what "arbitration" entailed concretely (see Box 12.2).

The first Lacedaemonian embassy soon went to Athens. In accordance with Greek diplomatic protocol, it simply sought to gain the moral high ground for Sparta by asserting that Athens was guilty of religious impropriety. The Athenians countered this by calling attention to corresponding Lacedaemonian sacrileges (Thuc. I 126–138). This over, the negotiations on the substantive issues could begin. Embassies from Sparta traveled back and forth to Athens (Thuc. I 126 and 139) and focused on three demands: that the Athenians lift the siege of Potidaea (alleged violation of the treaty's autonomy clause – see Box 12.2); that the Athenians grant Aegina autonomy; and that the Athenians rescind the second Megarian decree (alleged violation of the treaty's free-access clause – see Box 12.2). During the negotiations the Lacedaemonians backed down from the first two demands, but insisted on the third. The Athenians, however, remained unyielding (Thuc. I 139; Aristoph. *Ach.* 538). Pericles, in particular, was adamant, and he bore the chief responsibility for the Athenians' refusal to rescind the Megarian decree (see esp. Plut. *Per.* 31). Frustrated by the Athenians' absolute inflexibility, the Lacedaemonians sent one last embassy which merely delivered an ultimatum designed to be unacceptable (Thuc. I 139). In the next spring, the war began.

The Archidamian War (431–421 BC)

In the year 431, as the wheat ripened for the harvest in the spring, King Archidamus II of Sparta (from whom this phase of the war receives its name) led a Lacedaemonian army into Attica (Thuc. II 19). The Lacedaemonians expected a standard hoplite battle, but the Athenians, on Pericles' advice, refused. The Lacedaemonians had demonstrated their military skill at Plataea (479) and more recently at Tanagra (456), and Pericles may reasonably have viewed them as the probable victors in a battle. At Mt. Ithome, on the other hand, the Lacedaemonians had shown their ineptitude at siege warfare (465–456) – and in the end had negotiated a settlement there. Athens was heavily fortified; the so-called Long Walls connected the city itself to its port, the Peiraeus, which had its own fortifications. As long as the Athenian fleet retained control of the Aegean, Athens could supply itself by sea. In principle Pericles' plan was nothing other than the time-honored tactic of retreating behind one's city's walls before an invader whom one could not reasonably expect to beat. So the Athenians evacuated the Attic countryside and brought everyone into the city of Athens itself (Thuc. II 14). Faced with the prospect of an interminable siege, the Lacedaemonians torched the Athenians' fields and left (Thuc. II 23).

Meanwhile, an Athenian fleet of a hundred ships sailed around the Peloponnese to carry out raids. The tactic again was based on experience: Tolmides' successful *periplus* or circumnavigation in 456. The Athenian fleet in 431 almost succeeded in capturing the city of Methone in the southwestern Peloponnese. The officer who managed to save Methone, Brasidas, would go on to a spectacular career (Thuc. II 23 and 25). Finally, the Athenians, led personally by Pericles, unsuccessfully invaded Megara with the largest Athenian land force up to that time. Had the invasion succeeded, the Athenians could have warded off any future Lacedaemonian army at the Isthmus (Thuc. II 31).

The first year of the war had a sobering effect on the Lacedaemonians, who in the second year of the war altered their tactics to respond to the Athenians' strategy of refusing battles by land. Granted, the Lacedaemonians invaded Attica again with the same results as last time (Thuc. II 47). But they also put together a fleet of one hundred ships, collected from their allies, and attacked the island of Zacynthos (Thuc. II 66) which the Athenians in 431 had used as a base for naval operations. The Lacedaemonians were trying to deprive the Athenian fleet of way-stations for its annual *periplus* (which took place in 430 as well). Second, the Lacedaemonians had realized that without a fleet with which they could challenge Athens' supremacy in the Aegean, they could not win the war. However, they lacked the financial resources to construct and to maintain a fleet of adequate size. Accordingly, they did the unthinkable: they sent an embassy to Persia, the putative enemy of all Greeks, to negotiate for money. The Athenians by chance intercepted the embassy when it arrived at the court of the Thracian king Sitalces whom it had additionally hoped to persuade to support the ongoing revolts against Athens in the Chalcidice (Thuc. II 67). The Lacedaemonians, in sum, engaged in three innovative tactics already in the war's second year: deprive the Athenian fleet of bases from which to raid Laconia; weaken Athens by helping its allies to revolt; and negotiate for money from Persia. The latter two strategies in particular would bear fruit in the end.

The year 430 in Athens, on the other hand, was marked by the outbreak of the Plague (see Box 13.2). Despite the Plague Pericles, after the Lacedaemonian invasion of Attica had ended, led out a major sea-borne expedition to Epidaurus opposite Athens on the Saronic Gulf, just to the southeast of the Isthmus. As with the previous year's invasion of Megara, the expedition presumably had a defensive aim ultimately – control of the isthmus (Thuc. II 56). Another fleet circumnavigated the Peloponnese and carried out raids. Also, in the winter of 430 to 429 Potidaea finally surrendered to Athens (Thuc. II 69–70).

When the third year (429) of the war began, King Archidamus once again led out the Lacedaemonian army – past Attica and into Boeotia to attack Plataea (Thuc. II 71). Boeotia was a league-state (see Box 4.1) – granted, one which the largest Boeotian city, Thebes, was gradually coming to dominate – to which Plataea belonged. But Plataea, relying on support from Athens, had left the league and had been at war against troops from Thebes since 431 (Thuc. II 2–6). Archidamus had given up on futile invasions of Attica and concentrated instead on eliminating a nearby Athenian ally. The Plataeans prepared for a siege; and even if Plataea was a small city and its fortifications makeshift (Thuc. II 75–76), the Lacedaemonians' clumsiness at sieges showed. They would not take Plataea until 427 (Thuc. III 52).

Meanwhile, the Athenians settled down to the business of suppressing the revolts in the Chalcidice (Thuc. II 79). The Lacedaemonians, having left a small force to besiege Plataea, began a major expedition in the west. They sought to conquer Acarnania as part of a wider plan to deprive the Athenians of bases in the west (Thuc. II 80). Yet the Acarnanians fought the Lacedaemonians to a standstill. Meanwhile, the Athenian commander at Naupactus, Phormio, succeeded in defeating the supporting fleet which the Lacedaemonians had sent into the Corinthian Gulf (Thuc. II 81–92). One other significant event occurred in the course of this year: Pericles, the leading statesman in Athens for the past three decades or so, died (Thuc. II 65).

In 428 Mytilene and most of the island of Lesbos, with the exception of Methymna, revolted against Athens (Thuc. III 2). Suppression of the revolt – as at Samos in 440 and Thasos in 465 – proved difficult; not until 427 did the Athenians manage to put the revolt down (Thuc. III 27). The Lacedaemonians

Box 13.2   *The Effect of the Plague on Athens*

In the year 430 the Plague broke out in Athens. Thucydides composed both a fascinating psychological portrait of a beleaguered city under attack by an invisible enemy (Thuc. II 51–54) as well as a detailed clinical account of the disease itself (Thuc. II 49). Despite this wealth of clinical detail no modern attempt at identifying the disease has succeeded – it may well be that this particular disease does not exist today, at least not in the specific form it had in 430. Thucydides indicates that even in his own time no one had ever seen any disease like this one. He also notes that while the plague did appear in other places, it raged most virulently in Athens (Thuc. II 47–48) where the crowding caused by the evacuation of people from the countryside must have provided perfect conditions for the transmission of the disease.

Although a first reading of Thucydides' account gives the impression of high rates of contagiousness as well as mortality, the overall historical context shows that the Plague's impact was limited. Later on in the year 430 the Athenians, after the Lacedaemonians had departed from Attica, were still able to send an expedition of some 4,000 hoplites and 300 cavalry against Epidaurus (Thuc. II 56); and the Plague did not prevent the Athenians from sending a fleet of 20 ships around the Peloponnese (Thuc. II 69). 20 triremes, if fully manned, had a combined crew of 4,000. So there remained enough healthy men of fighting age in Athens to continue with the war. Thucydides does say (III 87) that 4,400 Athenian hoplites in all died of the plague – out of a total of 13,000 in 431 (Thuc. II 13 and 31). This seems a large proportion (roughly one third), but possibly the largest number of fatalities came among the older hoplites who were going to leave active service in a few years anyway.

Nothing in Thucydides' accounts of the following years suggests that the Athenian population experienced such a steep decline as one might expect after reading about the virulence with which the Plague raged in the city. This should not, however, detract from the genuine suffering of those who contracted the disease nor from the terror which it induced in the population as a whole – and Thucydides' description of that terror makes for riveting reading even today.

Thucydides himself fell ill, but was one of those who recovered (Thuc. II 48). He notes that most of those who recovered never caught the disease again and that with the few who did it was never fatal (II 51). A few years later, in the winter of 427 to 426, there was a second major outbreak of the Plague in Athens (Thuc. III 87) – the fact suggests that there was a considerable reservoir of people in Athens who had not contracted it the first time round.

failed to get effective aid to the Mytilenaeans (Thuc. III 26 and 29) since the Athenian fleet in the Aegean made it too difficult. The Lacedaemonians did invade Attica both in 428 and 427, but to no effect (Thuc. III 1 and 26).

When Mytilene finally capitulated in 427, Thucydides records that the Athenian assembly voted to put all men in Mytilene to death and to enslave all the women and children. The next day, ostensibly after the Athenians had had time to feel the pangs of conscience, the assembly again convened to re-debate the matter. For this, the Mytilenian debate, Thucydides composed two speeches which he placed into the mouth, first, of Cleon – the leading politician after Pericles' death and one whom Aristophanes mercilessly pilloried in his play, the *Knights* – and, second, that of Diodotus (otherwise unknown). It is Thucydides' own ideas and views which the speeches present; and, against all humanity, they depict an Athens beyond conscience: the Athenian assembly votes to rescind the original Mytilenaean decree on the basis of purely utilitarian reasoning (Thuc. III 36–49). Moreover, Thucydides lets the assembly's "mood swings" speak for themselves.

To sum up, now, the rest of the events from the year 427. First, Plataea finally surrendered (Thuc. III 52); second, on Corcyra a civil war broke out between the governing oligarchy and the democratic faction (see Box 13.1). Thucydides describes this civil war as exceptionally bitter and destructive (Thuc. III 70–85).

In 426 the Lacedaemonians began to invade Attica. Whether because they understood several earthquakes occurring during the march as a sign of divine disapprobation (Thuc. III 89) or because they were hardly convinced of the efficacy of such an invasion to begin with, they turned back and, thinking outside of the box, conceived another plan. They decided to found a colony, Heracleia Trachinia, at a strategic location near Thermopylae to provide both a way-station for an army marching northwards as well as a staging post for attacks on the nearby island of Euboea (Thuc. III 92). One can see in this plans for attacks on Athenian possessions in the north (where the Athenians were still fighting to suppress the revolt of many Chalcidian cities). In addition, since Euboea lay close to the mainland, it was usually not too difficult to bring an army over to the island even without full naval support. Athenian naval supremacy had hindered the Lacedaemonians from aiding the Mytilenaean revolt and from campaigning effectively in Acarnania and had additionally made the Lacedaemonian invasions of Attica useless. The strategic colony of Heracleia might allow for campaigns that could work around that naval supremacy. A large degree of hardheaded planning characterizes a Lacedaemonian strategy directed at achieving specific, attainable goals.

This applies less to Athenian actions in these years. Thucydides records particularly irrelevant campaigns on Sicily of all places (Thuc. III 86 and 88) as well as an expedition, launched from Naupactus, against the Aetolians whom the war had hitherto left unscathed (Thuc. III 94–98). All the same, in the winter of 426 to 425 the fighting in Acarnania began to go the Athenians' way (Thuc. III 105–114); and in 425 the Athenians, who each year had been carrying out a *periplus* of the Peloponnese, scored a spectacular success and captured Pylos, a small town on the north of the Bay of Navarino. Across the mouth of this wide bay, almost closing it off from the sea entirely, lay the long, heavily wooded, and uninhabited island of Sphacteria (Thuc. IV 3–5).

The Lacedaemonians, now under the command of Archidamus' son Agis II, had invaded Attica in 425, but as soon as they learned of the capture of Pylos, they returned to Laconia forthwith and attempted to recapture that town

(Thuc. IV 6–8). In the course of the operations, however, a small Lacedaemonian detachment became trapped on Sphacteria (Thuc. IV 8 and 14). Since Athenian ships patrolled the waters around the island, the detachment on Sphacteria had no means of provisioning itself despite desperate attempts. Among other things, the Lacedaemonians promised immediate emancipation to any Helot who could get food to the island. Although the Athenians were summarily executing anyone whom they caught trying to get through, such was the Helots' desire for freedom that there was no shortage of volunteers (Thuc. IV 26).

With what Helots could smuggle in and with typical Lacedaemonian hardiness in combat, those trapped on the island held out better than the Athenians expected. The difficulty in defeating these trapped Lacedaemonians led to another spectacular meeting of the assembly in Athens. There Cleon roundly assailed the commanders who had failed to bring the affair on Sphacteria to a successful conclusion – until one of them, Nicias, in a moment of frustration suggested that if Cleon were so smart, why did he not take over the command himself? Cleon, who had little military experience, had painted himself into a corner – without complete loss of face he could not turn down the offer. So the assembly, in one of many erratic decisions, gave the command to Cleon (Thuc. IV 27–29). Beginner's luck, however, came to Cleon's aid, and, happily for the Athenians, under his command the trapped Lacedaemonians were compelled to surrender (Thuc. IV 30–38).

Among the Lacedaemonians stood 120 Spartiates (Thuc. IV 38). The legend of Thermopylae (see chap. 10) – that Spartiates never surrendered, but always fought to the death (cf. Thuc. IV 40) – had nowhere found such ready belief as at Sparta itself. The surrender, not just of Lacedaemonians but of Spartiates themselves, dealt the legend, as well as Lacedaemonian morale, a severe blow. After the loss of Sphacteria the Lacedaemonians practically ceased fighting and concentrated on negotiating a settlement to the war which would involve, above all, the release of the 120 Spartiates (see Box 13.3).

The Athenians, too, were having their difficulties despite the capture of Pylos in 425. In the official year 425–24, they carried out a steep upward reassessment of their allies' tribute (Fornara, Nr. 136). Wars are expensive to wage, and naval warfare with triremes (with 170 rowers on board all of whom had to be paid a daily wage) especially so. As the war went on, the Athenians simply needed more cash. Although Thucydides does not mention this reassessment, he too was acutely aware of the financial requirements imposed by war (see, e.g., I 141–142 and II 13). Even the Lacedaemonians had to meet such requirements as the so-called War Fund inscription (Fornara, Nr. 132: whatever its precise date – probably during this phase of the war) and Polybius' perceptive analysis (VI 49) both show. Such efforts to secure financing, even if they cannot often be documented in such detail as the Athenians' reassessment of the tribute, surely accompanied the war throughout.

By 424 the war, even with financial matters left aside, was indeed going badly for Sparta. The Athenian raids had taken their toll, and despite the

Box 13.3   *The 120 Spartiates and Spartiate Society*

The impact which the capture of a mere 120 Spartiates had on Sparta's war effort seems, at first glance, disproportionate. Yet this mistakes the nature and size of the Spartiates' society. In the year 479 there were approximately 5,000 adult male Spartiates of fighting age (presumably between the ages of 20 and 60 – Hdt. IX 28; Xen. *Hell.* V 4,13). The loss of 120 out of 5,000 can be keenly felt.

Adult male Spartiates formed a closely knit group within the larger Lacedaemonian society in which they were a tiny minority – and as a minority, they always had to be on their guard (Xen. *Hell.* III 3,4–7; Plut. *Cim.* 16; *Lyc.* 28). They alone held political rights. It was, moreover, difficult to become a Spartiate. Each Spartiate had gone through the *agoge* – the system of military training which a Spartiate boy entered at age seven and in which he remained until he was thirty (Plut. *Lyc.* 17sqq.; see chap. 6). The *agoge*, with all its rigors was for the Spartiates a vast, shared experience of twenty-three years' duration which shaped them as a class and formed their collective attitudes.

The final step to becoming a Spartiate was admission into a **syssition** (Plut. *Lyc.* 12). This was almost a fraternity or club. In theory an adult male Spartiate took each evening meal at his *syssition* with some fifteen companions. Each evening the eldest man present, after all were foregathered, pointed at the doors and said, "what is said here does not pass those." Men here could speak openly and trust each other not to repeat anything. When a fresh graduate of the *agoge* applied for membership, a vote was held and only a unanimous result was sufficient for admission. Each member had to be fully certain in his mind that he could trust the applicant absolutely – that the applicant was genuinely "one of us."

This sort of thinking – the concept of "one of us" – characterized the Spartiates' society. "One of us" had gone through the *agoge*; "one of us" could be trusted in a *syssition*; "one of us" would stand his ground in battle and come back with his shield or on it; "one of us" held the proper attitudes; and so on. And now, after their surrender on Sphacteria in 425 BC, one hundred and twenty "of ours" were in prison in Athens. Every Spartiate still in Sparta probably knew most of the prisoners personally and had at least heard of the rest – cf. the comments of Thucydides at V 15. Given the nature of Spartiate society, the loss of 120 Spartiates loomed large; and the paralyzing horror which it caused is all too comprehensible.

Lacedaemonians' best efforts to deprive them of bases, they now actually had more rather than fewer. With Sphacteria, Pylos, and Cythera (captured in 424: Thuc. IV 54), the Athenians now held bases all round the Peloponnese and could raid anywhere at will. In Acarnania, where the Lacedaemonians had had high hopes of frustrating the Athenians' raids, the war had turned decisively in the latter's favor. Owing to the Lacedaemonian inability to challenge the Athenians' naval supremacy in the Aegean – and even in the Gulf of Corinth –, all attempts to foster and to support revolts against Athens had failed miserably and the invasions of Attica had proved a waste of time.

All Lacedaemonian effort, careful planning, and genuine creativity had counted as nothing. But the Lacedaemonians had one more card to play, and this time they would win the trick. In 424 Brasidas, who had distinguished himself on various occasions already, marched northwards with an army of 1,000 mercenaries and 700 Helots armed as hoplites (Thuc. IV 78 and 80). The composition of this force requires comment. The Lacedaemonians commonly availed themselves of Helots for filling minor roles in the army, but had hitherto declined to allow them to serve as hoplites. Besides the issue of the prestige associated with fighting as a heavily armed infantryman (see Box 10.1) – a prestige incompatible with the Helots' degraded status –, the last thing which the Lacedaemonians wanted was Helots with military experience. Yet in desperation the Lacedaemonians gave arms to Helots (whom they later freed – Thuc. V 34) and hired mercenaries – another first for them.

Brasidas first led his troops to Heracleia Trachinia where he waited while he negotiated with various Thessalian clans for permission to march through Thessaly. The negotiations were tricky since the Thessalians were on good terms with the Athenians at the time, but Brasidas' diplomatic skills proved equal to the challenge, and he obtained passage through Thessaly (Thuc. IV 78). He arrived in Macedonia to a warm reception from King Perdiccas II, an old enemy of the Athenians. Granted, Perdiccas had his own motives – he wanted help in conquering the region of Lyncestis in the mountains to the west of Macedonia proper (Thuc. IV 79). Presumably Brasidas, in exchange for permission to pass through Macedonia, had to promise to aid Perdiccas against Lyncestis later on.

Various Chalcidian cities were still in revolt, and Brasidas was determined to foster even more rebellions. In this, diplomacy served him better than force of arms, and Thucydides grudgingly does him the honor of stating that "he was not a bad speaker – for a Lacedaemonian" (Thuc. IV 84). At Acanthus Brasidas entered the town alone, addressed its assembly, and spoke persuasively enough that the Acanthians revolted and threw in their lot with him (Thuc. IV 88). The situation for the Athenians in the north was worsening rapidly.

Late in 424 fighting flared up again between the Athenians and the Boeotians. At Delium, the Boeotians inflicted a heavy defeat on the Athenians in one of the very few major land battles during the Peloponnesian War (Thuc. IV 89–101).

In the winter of 424 to 423 Brasidas, meanwhile, achieved his greatest success. Near the mouth of the River Strymon lay Amphipolis, a large Athenian colony which had been founded in 436 (Thuc. IV 102; Diod. XII 32). The Athenians had recruited the majority of the colonists from places other than Athens so when Brasidas appeared in the neighborhood with an army and offered generous terms, many Amphipolitans lent a ready ear. The city capitulated without a fight (Thuc. IV 106).

The loss of revenue for Athens was substantial, since Amphipolis provided access to silver and gold mines in the interior. A curious circumstance of

Amphipolis' founding made the loss particularly galling to the Athenians: when they founded this colony, the Athenians apparently retained ownership of the land on which the physical city of Amphipolis stood. Legally – and the Athenians insisted on this for decades afterwards (see chap. 18) – it was their land which Brasidas had taken. Moreover, Brasidas had won for Sparta a bargaining chip in the negotiations for the return of the 120 Spartiates, and finally the Athenians began to negotiate. The first fruit was a one year's truce, sworn in 423 (Thuc. IV 117).

Meanwhile, other cities had joined Brasidas, including Torone (Thuc. IV 110–114) and Scione (Thuc. IV 120–121). Scione, however, had joined close to the day on which the armistice was made: the Athenians insisted that it had surrendered to Brasidas after, the Lacedaemonians with equal stridency that it had done so just before the day in question (Thuc. IV 122). In this atmosphere neither side observed the truce in the north. Brasidas accepted the surrender of an additional town, Mende (Thuc. IV 123); and the Athenians sent troops to recapture it and Scione (Thuc. IV 122). At Mende they met with success, and they began to besiege Scione (Thuc. IV 130–131).

Elsewhere, however, the truce held. When it expired in 422, Cleon persuaded the Athenian assembly to send to the Chalcidice an army some three to four thousand strong with himself as commander. Upon arrival Cleon managed to capture Torone. He then sailed around Mt. Athos towards Amphipolis (Thuc. V 2–3). Here Brasidas and Cleon met in battle, and Cleon (and the assembly that had sent him) learned the hard lesson that beginner's luck applies only once. His troops were routed with heavy loss of life (including his). Brasidas, however, fell in the battle as well (Thuc. V 6–11).

The Peace of Nicias

With Cleon and Brasidas dead and with the war in the north over, negotiations for a more lasting peace than the one year's truce began. The negotiations went on for the winter of 422 to 421, and the Peace of Nicias, named after the chief Athenian negotiator, was sworn early in 421. Thucydides cites the text verbatim (Thuc. V 18–19).

Its chief terms were that the Lacedaemonians should return Amphipolis to the Athenians while the Athenians should return all Lacedaemonian prisoners (with a corresponding return by the Lacedaemonians of any Athenian prisoners). Specific arrangements were made for the cities in the Chalcidice which had rebelled against Athens: Argilus, Stageirus, Acanthus, Scolus, Olynthus, and Spartolus were to pay the tribute (as fixed in the year 477), but be neutral. They could, however, become allies of Athens again at their own desire. In all of these cities (including Amphipolis) all inhabitants retained the right to leave with their (movable) property. The Athenians, however, had a free hand in any city on the Chalcidice which they already held (including Torone and Scione). Finally, the Athenians were to return to Sparta Pylos (called Coryphasium in the treaty; including, obviously, Sphacteria), Cythera, and various other places.

Lots were cast to see which side would begin the exchange of places and prisoners, and Sparta was chosen. At this point it became clear that neither side had reckoned with the host. The Amphipolitans refused to leave – and declined to be handed over to Athens. And the Lacedaemonian commander after Brasidas' death, Clearidas, would not use force (Thuc. V 21), quite possibly because it was not a realistic option. Without Amphipolis, Athens would not hand over the 120 Spartiates.

So the Lacedaemonians renewed negotiations. Up until now they had been negotiating on behalf of the Peloponnesian League as well; this time they negotiated behind their allies' backs and agreed to a treaty of alliance between themselves and the Athenians (Thuc. V 22; text of treaty 23–24). News of the alliance sent shockwaves throughout the Peloponnesian League, and a number of members, most prominently Corinth, left it (Thuc. V 27). But the Athenians, while they held on to Pylos (including Sphacteria), Cythera, and the other places until such time as they should receive Amphipolis, did release the 120 Spartiates. With this the first phase of the Peloponnesian War ended (Thuc. V 24).

QUESTIONS FOR REVIEW

1   What factors may have helped cause the Peloponnesian War?
2   What innovative tactics did the Lacedaemonians adopt in the Archidamian War?
3   How did internal political struggles impinge on the Athenians' ability to wage war successfully?
4   What things brought both Sparta and Athens to the bargaining table for the Peace of Nicias?

QUESTION FOR FURTHER STUDY

Thucydides states (I 23) that the diplomatic disputes in 432 were all for show and actually obscured the real causes of the Peloponnesian War. Why, then, does he spend so much time discussing these disputes? Of what does he wish to convince his readers?

FURTHER READING

Kagan, D. (1974) *The Archidamian War*. Ithaca, NY.
Kagan, D. (1981) *The Peace of Nicias and the Sicilian Expedition*. Ithaca, NY.
(However, one does best first to read Thucydides.)

On financing the war, see:
Kallet, L. (1993) *Money, Expense, and Naval Power in Thucydides'* History *1–5.24*. Berkeley.
Loomis, W.T. (1992) *The Spartan War Fund*. Stuttgart.

14

From the Peace of Nicias to the Surrender of Athens

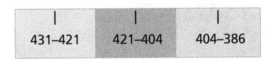

431–421	421–404	404–386

418	Battle of Mantinea
416	Melian Dialogue
415–413	Sicilian Expedition
411	Treaty between Persia and Sparta
411–410	Oligarchies in Athens
410	Battle of Cyzicus
406	Alcibiades exiled after Notium
406	Battle of the Arginussae
405	Battle of Aegospotami
404	Athens surrenders

From the Unraveling of the Peace of Nicias to the Melian Dialogue

The way in which it had come into being meant that the Peace of Nicias stood on shaky foundations. After ten hard years of war, bad feelings lingered on both sides. The chief wish of the Athenians had been that they should receive

A History of Greece: 1300 to 30 BC, First Edition. Victor Parker.
© 2014 Victor Parker. Published 2014 by John Wiley & Sons, Ltd.

Amphipolis back – yet they had not and, rightly or wrongly, blamed Lacedae-monian recalcitrance. The Lacedaemonians for their part cast a worried eye on the presence of Athenian bases around Laconia, especially Cythera and Pylos.

Moreover, in many ways the diplomatic situation in Greece was, precisely because of its lack of clarity, far more dangerous than it had been in the period before the war. Many members of the Peloponnesian League (in particular Corinth) had deserted Sparta in the aftermath of Sparta's unilateral swearing of an alliance with Athens. The Corinthians along with other states on the Peloponnese – e.g., Mantinea – began negotiations with Argos, which hitherto had stood aloof from the war (Thuc. V 27 and 29). These negotiations might have led to a fundamental realignment of alliances in Greece which could have shunted both Athens and Sparta to one side. Neither Athens nor Sparta could have watched these negotiations with equanimity.

In 420 the Lacedaemonians added to the atmosphere of suspicion by the way in which they fulfilled a minor condition in the Peace of Nicias (the handing over of a fortification in Boeotia along with the release of Athenian prisoners held by the Boeotians). On the Athenian view of events the Lacedaemonians had not quite upheld the spirit of the treaty, while the Lacedaemonians for their part felt that they had indeed carried out the letter. To make matters worse, the Lacedaemonians had also negotiated an alliance with the Boeotians (Thuc. V 42). Since the Boeotians and the Athenians were enemies of long standing, the latter viewed this alliance with deep suspicion.

Shortly thereafter, the Athenians began to negotiate with Argos. According to Thucydides, Alcibiades, a rising politician in Athens, drove these negotiations for personal reasons (Thuc. V 43) though one can easily suggest others – in particular, the way in which Argos appeared to be putting together a large alli-ance could have made some in Athens wish for good terms with this rising power. The negotiations between Athens and Argos, on the other hand, cannot have failed to alarm the Lacedaemonians. Still, nothing in the text of either the Peace of Nicias or in the alliance between Athens and Sparta prevented either party from swearing an alliance with a neutral third party, and in the end Athens made an alliance with Argos and two Argive allies, Mantinea and Elis (Thuc. V 47). All main parties had negotiated on behalf of any allies under their control as well. This move left Sparta perilously isolated diplomatically and probably increased the likelihood of a renewal of the war.

The affair which would cause the Peace of Nicias to break apart was com-paratively trivial. Argos and Epidaurus, Argos' neighbor to the north, had a long-standing quarrel concerning a temple of Apollo Pythiaeus on the border between the two states (Thuc. V 53). Athens' treaty with Argos obligated it to render the Argives assistance in case of war. Epidaurus, for its part, had remained within the Peloponnesian League. What was bound to happen, did, and soon enough Athens and Sparta were at war again.

As this second phase of the war began, the Athenians gave up entirely on Pericles' strategy of never meeting the Lacedaemonians in the field. This time, relying on their alliance with Argos, Mantinea, and Elis, the Athenians marched to the Peloponnese. The two sides met at Mantinea in 418. The result bore out the wisdom of Pericles' strategic judgment. Although the Athenians nearly won, in the end Lacedaemonian experience and training paid off. With the Lacedaemonian victory (Thuc. V 66–74), the entire diplomatic landscape shifted dramatically. The chastened Argives quickly concluded a treaty with Sparta whereby they for the first time ever entered the Peloponnesian League (Thuc. V 77–79). Various other states hastened to join or rejoin the Peloponnesian League, which now stood in a far stronger position than at the beginning of the Archidamian War.

For the remainder of 418 and all of 417 Thucydides has practically nothing to record of Athenian activities. The loss at Mantinea seems to have demoralized the Athenians completely. In 416, however, they made a minor expedition to the small Cycladic island of Melos. This island was one of the very few in the Aegean which had remained outside of their empire. A place of no real consequence, the Athenians had never bothered with it much in the decades preceding the Peloponnesian War. During the war itself, there had been raids on Melos, but, again, the island was too insignificant to become the target of a major expedition. Until now.

Having failed at Mantinea, the Athenian military leadership, desperately in need of a victory to boost morale, planned an expedition against Melos. The Melians had no chance of withstanding such an attack and succumbed rapidly enough. Thucydides, however, used this occasion as the subject of one of the most intriguing sections of his work, the so-called Melian Dialogue.

This fictional debate takes place between anonymous Athenians and anonymous Melians. The Athenians advance purely pragmatic reasons both for why the Melians should surrender and for why the Athenians should force them so to do. The Melians respond with considerations of justice – considerations which the Athenians brusquely push aside. The dialogue revolves around the same major issue as the Mytilenaean Debate (see chap. 13), only this time the Athenians had no change of heart; after they conquered Melos, they put the men there to death and enslaved the women and children (Thuc. V 84–116).

The campaign on Melos, if its purpose was to restore Athenian morale, succeeded admirably. In 415 the Athenians voted in favor of the biggest expedition which they had ever undertaken. It had nothing to do with Sparta. Instead, the Athenians planned to conquer the island of Sicily.

The Sicilian Expedition

The great advocate of this expedition was the same Alcibiades who had persuaded the Athenian assembly to make the alliance with Argos. Nicias, who had a long record of distinguished service to Athens both as a soldier and as a diplomat and after whom the Peace of Nicias was named, spoke against the expedition. Thucydides places into his mouth two speeches, one in which he advanced arguments against the expedition – he preferred, with some logic, to concentrate on unsettled affairs such as the suppression of the long-running revolts in the Chalcidice (Thuc. VI 9–15) –; and a second in which he sought to make the Athenians aware of what enormous preparations the Sicilian expedition would entail (Thuc. VI 20–23). Neither speech succeeded in dissuading the Athenians.

Perversely, the Athenian assembly, in fact, appointed Nicias as one of the commanders of the expedition alongside Alcibiades and another man named Lamachus (Thuc. VI 8). Before the expedition began, however, a scandal rocked Athens. All over Athens stood stereotyped images of the god Hermes, so-called **herms** (see Figure 14.1). They consisted of a square pillar surmounted by the god's head; but their most prominent feature was an erect phallus protruding from the pillar a little below the god's face. One morning in 415 the Athenians awoke to find that all over town someone had mutilated their herms. Thucydides says that it was the "faces" which had been mutilated (Thuc. V 27), and one may take that literally (the less common interpretation, though a perfectly defensible one) or as a euphemism. In any case a person (or persons) unknown

Figure 14.1   A herm in front of an altar on an amphora (circa 465 BC). Source: photo Museum of Fine Arts, Boston, Massachusetts, USA / Gift of Landon T. Clay / The Bridgeman Art Library

had committed a terrible sacrilege. Suspicion, rightly or wrongly, fell on Alcibiades, and rumors of another sacrilege committed by him, this time a mocking re-enactment of the **Eleusinian Mysteries,** surfaced as well (Thuc. VI 28).

He sailed out with the expedition, but before the campaign on Sicily could begin, the Athenians recalled him to Athens to stand trial for impiety. Alcibiades, who clearly trusted little in Athenian justice, defected to the Lacedaemonians (Thuc. V 61). Since he knew a great deal about the Athenians' military capacity generally as well as about the Sicilian expedition specifically, he surely gave the Lacedaemonians much helpful information.

Meanwhile Nicias and Lamachus brought the Athenian army (some 4,000 hoplites supported by a fleet of 100 triremes – Thuc. V 31) to Sicily and began operations against Syracuse. In an initial battle outside of Syracuse in 415, the Athenians were successful, but because of the onset of winter, they withdrew northwards to Naxos and Catane. The vastness of the undertaking was making itself manifest to the commanders who realized that they needed more cavalry and more allies on Sicily itself in order to provision their army (Thuc. VI 62–72). During the winter they did manage to collect cavalry from home and from their allies on the island (Thuc. VI 96 and 98), but the longer they remained, the more of a burden they were to their allies and the more difficult it became to maintain their army.

In the spring of 414, the Athenians after some skirmishing took possession of Epipolae ("The Heights"), some high ground overlooking Syracuse. Skirmishing continued as the Athenians set about erecting a wall around the city in order to besiege it while the Syracusans busily erected a counter-wall (Thuc. VI 94–103). Meanwhile the Lacedaemonians sent aid to Syracuse. The Lacedaemonian commander Gylippus arrived in Sicily with troops and collected additional ones on the island before traveling to Syracuse (Thuc. VII 1–2). On Gylippus' advice the Syracusans began with the construction of a wall at an angle to the wall which the Athenians were building – such that, if the Syracusans could complete this cross-wall, the Athenians would be unable to complete theirs (Thuc. VII 4). Despite vigorous attacks by the Athenians, Gylippus succeeded in building his wall past the Athenians' (Thuc. VII 6). There would now be no siege of Syracuse.

Nicias, however, had already begun with the construction of forts on a headland at the entrance to the harbor of Syracuse. He hoped to gain an advantage in naval actions as he slowly despaired of a victory by land (Thuc. VII 4). However, at sea as well matters were growing grim for the Athenians. Ships from Sparta's allies in mainland Greece were arriving, and the Syracusans themselves were making their own fleet battle-worthy (Thuc. VII 7).

Back in Greece, in the spring of 413, the Lacedaemonians invaded Attica again and this time fortified the town of Decelea, in sight of Athens, and established a permanent base there (Thuc. VII 19). This meant more than the resumption of full-scale warfare in mainland Greece for up until now the chief loss incurred by the Athenians during a Lacedaemonian invasion was the torching of the crop. Annoying as this was, the Athenians could always sow a new one. But now the Lacedaemonians deprived them of access to their livestock. Some 20,000 skilled slaves deserted – a tremendous loss of manpower and as such a severe blow to the Athenian economy (Thuc. VII 27). The fortification of Decelea had brought warfare in Attica to a new level.

In Sicily, meanwhile, both sides were receiving reinforcements from mainland Greece. The Athenians sent some 73 ships and 5,000 hoplites, collected mostly from allies (Thuc. VII 42). Their commander, Demosthenes, correctly realized that the Athenians could not postpone matters any longer. The Syracusans had captured the forts which Nicias had built near the harbor, effectively cutting the Athenians off by sea (Thuc. VII 22–23) (see Figure 14.2). More reinforcements

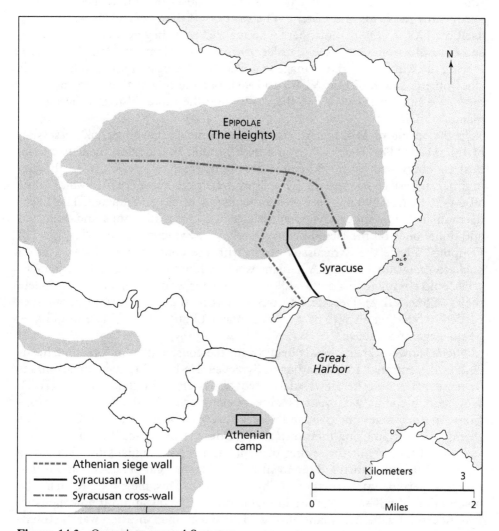

Figure 14.2 Operations around Syracuse

from Athens would not be forthcoming; and the Syracusans were more easily able to supply themselves. Demosthenes opted for an attack by night on the Syracusan cross-wall, but the Athenians had the worst of it in the fighting (Thuc. VII 42–44).

After this failure Demosthenes wished to evacuate while there was still a chance (Thuc. VII 47), but Nicias, with peculiar stubbornness, refused. Thucydides, who seems to have found Nicias' refusal out of character – after all, not much earlier Nicias had asked to be relieved of the command (Thuc. VII 15), and he had felt that the expedition was a mistake right from the start –, suggests that Nicias trusted too much in the messages which an allegedly pro-Athenian faction within Syracuse was sending to him. (As always with a Greek state, Syracuse had its political divisions; and one faction within the city evidently hoped to gain power after an Athenian conquest and was prepared to cooperate with the Athenians.) Thucydides, in any case, characterizes the result not as resolution, but as inertia: the Athenians stayed, but did not do much else (Thuc. VII 48–49).

The situation steadily grew worse for them. In the naval fighting in the Great Harbor of Syracuse the Syracusan fleet was having the better of it (Thuc. VII 51–55); and the Syracusans hit upon the idea of trapping the entire Athenian fleet by closing the entrance to the harbor with a chain of boats. When the Athenians saw this, Nicias realized that everything would now come down to one great battle in the Harbor in which the Athenians would either win or perish. The Athenians brought as many men as possible onto every ship which would still float, some 110 in all, and opened the engagement. Thucydides tells the story of the battle from the point of view of those Athenians who were still on land and were watching the fighting, which went on for a long time without any clear indication of who was winning. But at last the Syracusans gained the victory, and the majority of the Athenians on land gave way to blind panic (Thuc. VII 56, 60, 70–71).

Nicias and Demosthenes attempted to lead out a retreat in the next few days, but the Syracusans harried the retreating troops every step of the way so that the retreat soon became a rout. Casualties under the circumstances were high: some 7,000 or so of the Athenian and allied troops, by Thucydides' estimation, were imprisoned in stone quarries near Syracuse. Both Nicias and Demosthenes surrendered; the Syracusans had them both put to death. The entire expedition had perished (Thuc. VII 72–87).

The Aftermath of the Sicilian Expedition

The destruction of the Sicilian Expedition in 413 had consequences in Aegean Greece. First, many of Athens' subjects revolted over the next few years – Chios and Erythrae; Miletus; Methymna, Mytilene, and Eresus on Lesbos; Cnidus; Rhodes; Thasos; Byzantium; all Euboea (Thuc. VIII 14–95). Cos still stood under Athenian control early in 411 (Thuc. VIII 108), but apparently revolted a little later (Diod. XIII 42,3). Andros, close to Attica, had revolted by 407 (Diod. XIII 69,4; Xen. *Hell.* I 4,22). By way of an exception, Samos remained loyal. The Athenians, in gratitude, voted to restore Samos' autonomy (Thuc. VIII 21).

Second, the Persians, seeing Athens' weakness, were now ready to take advantage by aiding Sparta. The Persians' aims appear most clearly in their negotiations with the Lacedaemonians in 411 BC. Of the territory lost to the Greeks in war over the last seven decades, the Persians sought to recover as much as possible. In the end they settled for Asia Minor, and in exchange the Lacedaemonians won financing for a fleet.

Box 14.1   *The Treaty between King Darius II of Persia (423–405) and the Lacedaemonians in 411 BC*

Thucydides quotes two drafts (Thuc. VIII 18 and 37) as well as the final version of this treaty (Thuc. VIII 58). He mistakes the drafts for actual treaties, but the presence of a prescript with date shows that only the third text is a treaty. Such a prescript is missing from the two drafts, the first of which contains the following proposal which, since it benefits the Persians only, shows that they put it forward:

> However much land and (however many) cities the King holds and the King's fathers held, shall be the King's . . . (Thuc. VIII 18)

This meant that the Lacedaemonians were supposed to acknowledge Persian sovereignty over all of Asia Minor, all the Aegean islands, and all of mainland Greece right up to the Isthmus, the farthest extent of the Persians' march in 480 BC. Moreover, the draft makes no mention of anything the Persians are prepared to do for the Lacedaemonians. So the Lacedaemonians negotiated.

The next draft (another Persian document) shows that the Persians were adjusting their demands:

> However much land and (however many) cities are King Darius' or were his father's or his ancestors', against this (land) and these (cities) neither the Lacedaemonians nor the Lacedaemonians' allies shall march for purposes of war or harm; neither the Lacedaemonians nor the Lacedaemonians' allies shall levy tributes from these cities. (Thuc. VIII 37)

Moreover, it mentions the Persians' providing something for the Lacedaemonians:

> However many troops may be on the King's land at the King's request, the King shall provision them. (Thuc. VIII 37)

In exchange for a Lacedaemonian promise to give the Persians a free hand all the way up to the Isthmus, the Persians will undertake to provision the Lacedaemonians'

(Continued)

troops that, at the king's request, are in those same regions. The Lacedaemonians are being asked to acknowledge Persian sovereignty in those regions *de facto* only. In addition they get something for doing so. But negotiations continued.

The final version of the treaty shows the Persians settling for what, presumably, they had truly wanted all along and which in any case was actually feasible:

> *The land of the King's, however much is in Asia, shall be the King's . . .* (Thuc. VIII 58)

The Lacedaemonians, meanwhile, were willing to acknowledge that much, especially since they too received something which they desperately needed:

> *Tissaphernes shall provide maintenance for the ships which are now present according to the arrangement* (probably that mentioned in Thuc. VIII 29) *until such time as the King's ships arrive. Once the King's ships arrive, the Lacedae-monians and their allies may, if they should wish, provide maintenance for their own ships on their own. But if they desire to receive maintenance from Tissa-phernes, Tissaphernes shall provide it, but the Lacedaemonians and their allies, when the war ends, shall pay back to Tissaphernes however much money they may have borrowed.* (Thuc. VIII 58)

In the end the Lacedaemonians agreed to acknowledge Persian sovereignty in Asia Minor; and the Persians agreed to pay for the Lacedaemonians' fleet.

Third, the Athenian democracy's failure in managing the war had become apparent throughout Athens. Many Athenian aristocrats had always preferred an oligarchy anyway, and they now had practical arguments with which to buttress their views. The leadership of the army and navy proved a fertile breeding ground for such sentiment (Thuc. VIII 47), presumably because the commanders, after some twenty years of the Assembly's capricious decisions, were simply tired of going about the serious business of warfare at the direction of dilettantes. The first steps towards the dissolution of the democracy took place among the captains of the fleet as it lay off Samos; and from there an aristocrat named Peisander was sent to Athens to arrange for the establishment of an oligarchy (Thuc. VIII 49).

Alcibiades, meanwhile, apparently weary of aiding the Lacedaemonians, now desired to return home. However, as he was wary of the democracy, he too conspired for an oligarchy (Thuc. VIII 47), and his support strengthened the oligarchs' case. Much discussion took place as to what sort of an oligarchy Athens should receive. Eventually, the oligarchs put forward a blueprint for an oligarchy in which 5,000 were to have political rights with arrangements for a provisional government of 400 charged with implementing the blueprint

([Arist.] *Ath.Pol.* 30–31). When the time came, the oligarchs met with little opposition. The Assembly meekly voted to dissolve the democracy and ceased to meet. The 400 then entered the chamber where the members of the *Boule* were sitting, dismissed them, and paid them their wages on the way out (Thuc. VIII 69).

Although the 400 were charged with establishing the government of the 5,000, once in power, they preferred to stay that way. In Athens they initially succeeded by simple delay, but they met with strict opposition from the men in the fleet. The rowers in the fleet – 170 to a trireme with a full crew – were drawn from the lowest and most numerous class in Athens, the Thetes (who had no money to buy Hoplite armor, but could hold an oar in a trireme against pay). Most of the triremes at this point lay off Samos and here resistance to the rule of the 400 was strongest. In fact, the men with the fleet called an assembly at which they deposed all commanders whom they suspected of having connived in the establishment of an oligarchy back home. They elected new commanders – ironically using the oligarchic means of filling an office – and effectively set up a parallel government (Thuc. VIII 75–76) which stole a march on the government in Athens by recalling Alcibiades from exile almost immediately (Thuc. VIII 81).

In Athens, meantime, opposition to the 400 grew as well. The 400 attempted to make peace with Sparta (Thuc. VIII 70) and thereby probably undermined themselves more effectively than anyone else could have. The antidemocratic sentiment in Athens had largely resulted from a desire to win the war and from the realization that the democracy was failing in this task. The attempts at peace by the 400 were probably perceived as collusion and in any case met with no success. Within four months of the establishment of the 400, the next revolution came ([Arist.] *Ath.Pol.* 33). The Assembly met, voted to depose the 400, and established the oligarchy of the 5,000 (Thuc. VIII 97).

Thucydides has unqualified praise for this new government and calls it a "moderate blend between oligarchy and democracy" (see Box 13.1). The 5,000, once they had taken charge of Athens, led the city back from the brink of disaster in the war (Thuc. VIII 97). In fact, they brought the city almost to the point of victory. The 5,000 secured the loyalty of the fleet at Samos with the mediation of Alcibiades (Thuc. VIII 86), whose recall from exile they confirmed (Diod. XIII 42) under the guidance of Theramenes, a prominent moderate oligarch. Moreover, Thucydides' statement about the leadership which the 5,000 provided in the prosecution of the war makes it almost certain that the Battle of Cyzicus (see below) occurred on their watch.

Continuations of Thucydides' History

Unfortunately, Thucydides' history breaks off at this point. Presumably he died before he could finish it. Given that Thucydides' history in a sense continued Herodotus', it was perhaps natural that someone should continue his. At least three, possibly four, people did so. Xenophon of Athens, whose work, the *Hellenica* or *Res Graecae*, survives in its entirety; Theopompus of Chios, the surviving fragments of whose work (also called *Hellenica*) stand at *BNJ* 115; the anonymous author of the so-called *Hellenica Oxyrhynchia* which survives on papyrus scraps from the village of Oxyrhynchus in Egypt (*BNJ* 66); and **Cratippus** of Athens (*BNJ* 64) of whose work almost nothing survives unless, of course, he should be identical with the anonymous author of the *Hellenica Oxyrhynchia*.

Theopompus' work, since so little of it survives, is for practical reasons alone the least useful. This verbose work (*BNJ* 114, Fr. 21) covered in twelve books the period from 410 to the Battle of Cnidus in 394 (*BNJ* 115, T 14).

The *Hellenica Oxyrhynchia* – the **Oxyrhynchus Historian** is a common way of referring to its author – is a work of considerable historiographical merit. It covered the years from 410 down to, probably, 386. Its author gathered much detailed information about major battles such as Cyzicus, Arginussae, Aegospotami, and Sardis. The phrasing at Diod. XIII 98,5 (based on the *Hell. Oxy.* – see below and Box 15.1) about the Battle of the Arginussae suggests that much of this information came from eyewitnesses: "[the unusual formation at the battle] in many respects caused great amazement *for those watching.*" The Oxyrhynchus Historian was moreover intensely interested in individual cities' internal politics and their influence on these cities' external relations. His detailed description of the constitution of the Boeotian League (col. XVI, 2–4) exceeds anything of the sort in Herodotus, Thucydides, or Xenophon. Continuing investigation of the history of the period has led to a generally high opinion of the Oxyrhynchus Historian (see Further Reading).

Unfortunately, most of the work is lost. Indirectly, however, it survives in Diodorus through the medium of Ephorus, who used it and whose work Diodorus excerpted (see *BNJ* 70, Biographical Essay, section II F). The account of the Battle of Notium (*HellOxy*, col. VI and Diod. XIII 71 – cf. with these Xen. *Hell.* I 5,10–15) in particular shows that the information in Diodorus for the years 410 to 386 is based on the account of the Oxyrhynchus Historian. Unfortunately, Diodorus is a sloppy and often incompetent excerptor. His presentation of the material commonly lacks coherence; the chronology is notoriously erratic and he omits important information (see Box 18.1). The historiographical value of the material itself, however, owing to its source, is high.

Finally, there is the work of Xenophon. For various reasons this work was traditionally taken as the basis for any historical narrative of the period it covers, from 410 to 362 (the second Battle of Mantinea). In particular, it has survived in its entirety, and it presents a coherent narrative with a sound chronology (unlike Diodorus). Over the decades, however, especially as investigation of issues concerning the *Hellenica Oxyrhynchia* has proceeded, Xenophon has slowly slipped in scholars' esteem *vis-à-vis* the *Hellenica Oxyrhynchia*. All the same, his work is still indispensable in reconstructing the history of the period (especially in matters of chronology and where Diodorus omits material), and it has many other good qualities: an experienced soldier and commander, he understood battles, campaigns, and the business of command with the marrow of his bones. Although an Athenian, he spent long years in Sparta or in the company of Lacedaemonians and so possessed an insider's knowledge of Sparta as well as Athens. He knew many of the leading commanders and statesmen of the period – most prominently King Agesilaus of Sparta (reigned circa 400 to 360 BC) – personally.

Any reconstruction of Greek history after the year 410 must therefore work with both Xenophon and the *Hellenica Oxyrhynchia*. Finally, the switch from Thucydides' work to the continuations causes various problems since the continuators had their own interests and did not follow every narrative thread in Thucydides to its conclusion. Xenophon, for example, never says how or when the 5,000 in the end lost power to a restored democracy. If the other continuations were attested in full, it might be possible to smooth out this particular unevenness which hinders comprehension of events during the years 411 and 410.

The Battle of Cyzicus and the Ionian War

In the year 410, shortly after the point at which Thucydides' work breaks off in mid-sentence, the Battle of Cyzicus took place, and it reversed fortunes in the war. The Lacedaemonians, using Persian money, had collected a fleet of approximately 120 ships which they had divided into two squadrons. One was active in the western Aegean near Euboea under the commander Agesandridas (Thuc. VIII 91), and the other in the Propontis under the overall commander Mindarus (Thuc. VIII 99). The Athenian fleet surprised this second Lacedaemonian squadron. Mindarus immediately sent a message to Agesandridas to sail into the Propontis as quickly as possible (Diod. XIII 41). The route which this squadron took led it along the coast of the northern Aegean and around Mt. Athos (see Box 1.1) where a catastrophic storm caused some fifty ships to sink. Of the crews on those ships – 10,000 in all if one assumes that each trireme's crew was at full strength – only twelve men survived (Ephorus, *BNJ* 70, Fr. 199). A handful of ships made it into the Propontis (Xen. *Hell.* I 1,1 and 3,17), but the vast majority now lay on the bottom of the Aegean. Consequently, when the Athenians' and the Lacedaemonians' fleets met at Cyzicus, the latter's was at approximately half the strength it otherwise would have had. A squadron of twenty Athenian ships under Alcibiades succeeded in tricking the Lacedaemonian commander, Mindarus, who still had eighty ships, into attacking – unaware that two additional Athenian squadrons were lying out of sight. These two squadrons came in behind the Lacedaemonian fleet as it pursued Alcibiades' squadron; and Mindarus was beset from all sides (Diod. XIII 50; cf. Xen. *Hell.* I 1,16–18, with a different account). The Athenians either captured or destroyed every ship in what remained of the Lacedaemonians' fleet (Diod. l.c.; Xen. *Hell.* I 1,18), and the Lacedaemonians sent an embassy to Athens to offer terms of peace on the basis of the *status quo* (Diod. XIII 52).

Given the losses which the Athenians had suffered in the Sicilian expedition and given the large number of revolts which they still had to suppress, they would have been well advised to accept. That they took the very poorest advice – to continue the war (Diod. XIII 53) – could suggest that in the aftermath of the great victory at Cyzicus the oligarchy of the 5,000, which in Thucydides' opinion had brought Athens back from the brink, was replaced by the restored democracy. Granted, oligarchies had as much skill as democracies in making bad decisions, but the Athenian democracy was particularly capable in this regard – and its inability to accept terms of peace except under the direst stress will be on spectacular display later on.

In the meantime the Athenians got on with suppressing revolts throughout the empire. The revolts on Lesbos they had mostly suppressed even before the Battle of Cyzicus (Thuc. VIII 23); Eresus alone remained unconquered (Thuc. VIII 100). Theramenes reconquered Paros in 410 if Diodorus has the date right (Diod. XIII 47), while on the mainland of Asia Minor the Athenians had also recaptured Clazomenae (Thuc. VIII 23) and Cyzicus (Thuc. VIII 107). After the Battle of Cyzicus, with Alcibiades once again fighting for the Athenians, the suppression of the revolts began in earnest. The town of Colophon on the mainland of Asia Minor surrendered peaceably to the Athenian commander Thrasyllus in 409 (Xen. *Hell.* I 2,4). In the next year Alcibiades managed to recapture the important city of Byzantium (Diod. XIII 66–67; Xen. *Hell.* I 3); a consequential campaign in the Hellespont brought all the cities there with the exception of Abydus back under Athenian control (Diod. XIII 68). In 407 Thrasybulus campaigned along the Thracian coast and put down the revolts there; he also brought the large and important island of Thasos back under Athenian control (Diod. XIII 72; Xen. *Hell.* I 4,9). Alcibiades recaptured Andros off the southern tip of Euboea in the same year (Diod. XIII 68; Xen. *Hell.* I 4,22–23).

Much of the coast of Asia Minor, however, was still in revolt (Ephesus, Erythrae, Miletus) as were many islands in the Aegean (Chios, Cos, Rhodes, Euboea) and in 409 the Lacedaemonians finally recaptured Pylos (Diod. XIII 64; Xen. *Hell.* I 2,18). The Persians had also obligingly financed the construction of a new fleet for the Lacedaemomians and were continuing to pay the rowers in it (Xen. *Hell.* I 1,24–26). Notwithstanding, the war was definitely going the Athenians' way again. The Athenian assembly, however, was unwilling to accept that in the long process of suppressing the revolts, minor setbacks were bound to occur.

In a minor battle off Cape Notium near Ephesus, a detachment of the Athenian fleet suffered such a setback. Alcibiades had left the detachment off Cape Notium to keep watch over the Lacedaemonian fleet at Ephesus while he himself went to Clazomenae. In his absence – according to standard policy – the helmsman of his ship, Antiochus, took over the command. Even though Alcibiades had given strict instructions not to engage the Lacedaemonian fleet, Antiochus did so anyway; and in the ensuing engagement the Athenians lost 22 ships (*Hell. Oxy.* col. IV; Diod. XIII 71; cf. Xen. *Hell.* I 5, 10–14). Such an unnecessary setback must have frustrated the Athenians, but as an isolated incident it did not signify much.

Yet the Athenian assembly made much of it anyway. Diodorus, following Ephorus who was a native Cymaean, also records an account of Alcibiades' attack on Cyme and claims that Alcibiades' operations in Cyme incurred additional unpopularity back home. Ephorus, ever the patriotic Cymaean, may have exaggerated a bit here, but Diodorus also mentions that various private individuals had brought lawsuits against Alcibiades. Xenophon, when discussing the affair at Notium, states that the Athenians attributed the loss to Alcibiades' "heedlessness and want of self-control" – and he may mean roughly the same thing as that to which Diodorus refers. That is to say, the affair at Notium may have been minor, but various other episodes involving Alcibiades had preceded it; and at some point the cup ran over. When the Athenians elected their ten generals that year, Alcibiades was not among them. In a fit of pique he defected again. This time he struck out on his own in the Chersonese (Diod. XIII 73–74; Xen. *Hell.* I 5,16–17). An official sentence of banishment followed (**Isocrates,** XVI 37).

In the absence of Alcibiades – who despite all was a competent commander – the Lacedaemonians with a fleet that eventually comprised 170 ships (Diod. XIII 76 and 78; Xen. *Hell.* I 6,3, 17, and 26), began to make some headway under their commander Callicratidas. In 406 they surprised an Athenian detachment of seventy ships under the command of Conon off Lesbos, defeated it, captured thirty ships, and blockaded the rest in the harbor of Mytilene (Diod. XIII 77–79; Xen. *Hell.* I 6,16–18). On Lesbos meanwhile the Lacedaemonians captured Methymna (Diod. XIII 76; Xen. *Hell.* I 6,13). In this situation the Athenians made an extraordinary effort to man the largest fleet possible. Everyone – from slaves at the bottom of the social scale to wealthy aristocrats who normally served in the cavalry at the top – clambered aboard to serve as rowers (Diod. XIII 97; Xen. *Hell.* I 6,24).

In the end the Athenians had 150 ships. Eight of the ten generals sailed with the fleet towards Lesbos to relieve Conon. Callicratidas left behind thirty ships to continue the blockade and sailed with 140 to meet the Athenians. The two sides engaged near a group of islets to the south of Lesbos, the Arginussae. The islands precluded a single battle line; effectively, one battle became two with, for practical purposes, four fleets fighting in what for number of ships was the greatest naval battle of Greek against Greek up to that time (Diod. XIII 97–98; cf. Xen. *Hell.* I 6,25–33). The result was an unqualified disaster for Sparta. Callicratidas himself died, and the Lacedaemonians lost 77 ships (Diod. XIII 100; cf. Xen. *Hell.* I 6,34). Effectively the Lacedaemonians had managed to lose a second, Persian-financed fleet. As after the Battle of Cyzicus, the Lacedaemonians probably offered terms of peace to the Athenians. The offer is attested only at [Arist.] *Ath.Pol.* 34 which for the late fifth century is generally well informed, though, unfortunately, some doubt must remain in the point (on the *Ath.Pol.* as a source, see Box 8.1).

The Athenians too had lost ships at the Arginussae, some 25 in all. Shortly after the battle a storm had arisen, and under the circumstances the generals decided to bring the 125 other ships to safety quickly – instead of staying behind to rescue the survivors from the wrecks (Diod. XIII l.c.; Xen. *Hell.* I 6,34–35). Given that the Athenians could ill afford to lose ships – unlike the Lacedaemonians they had no backers with bottomless pockets to keep building ships for them –, the generals clearly made the right decision. All the same, a number of shipwrecked sailors survived the storm and came ashore alive. Upon their return to Athens, they complained bitterly about the callous generals who had left them to drown; and the Assembly wished to put the generals on trial. Chairman of the *Boule* on that day, and thus responsible for putting any motion to the Assembly for debate, was none other than the philosopher **Socrates** (Xen. *Mem.* I 1,18 and IV 4,2), the teacher of both Plato and Xenophon. On a legal technicality Socrates refused to put the motion (Xen. *Hell.* I 7, 9–15), so the Assembly waited one day ([Plat.] *Ax.* 368) and under a more pliant chairman passed a sentence of death on all the generals. Two had already gone into exile in anticipation of the verdict, while the other six took the proffered cup of hemlock (Diod. XIII 101–102; Xen. *Hell.* I 7). The Athenian Assembly had just decapitated Athens' military leadership.

In 405 the Lacedaemonians sent out Lysander as commander. He received another generous subsidy from the Persians and set about building new ships to replace the ones lost off the Arginussae (Diod. XIII 103; Xen. *Hell.* II 1,10–12). As long as the Persians remained willing to finance fleet after fleet for Sparta, the Lacedaemonians could continue the fight indefinitely. If Athens, on the other hand, lost a battle on the order of magnitude of Cyzicus or Arginussae, it had no way to recover. By 405, however, Athens had with a few exceptions (in particular Conon) deprived itself of almost all competent commanders. Under the circumstances errors were likely, and a major one might easily mean the end. In the Hellespont in 405, the Athenians erred.

After a siege, Lysander captured Lampsacus from the Athenians in that year just before the Athenian fleet could arrive to relieve the town. Therefore Lysander's fleet lay in a good harbor at Lampsacus. The Athenian commanders, however, brought their fleet to a place called Aegospotami opposite Lampsacus (Diod. XIII 104–105; Xen. *Hell.* II 1,18–21). In the absence of a harbor, the Athenians had to pull their triremes up onto the beach for the night. Bringing a trireme back into the water takes time, and during the process the trireme is hopelessly exposed to attack. Under the circumstances extraordinary watchfulness was required so that the Athenians could get their ships ready in case of attack, but the commanders, with the exception of Conon, did not understand just how much care was needed in such a risky situation.

An Athenian commander made an inadequately supported sortie with thirty triremes while the other triremes remained on the beach. Lysander, forewarned by deserters, was ready and responded with a full-scale attack, easily defeated the first thirty triremes of the Athenians, and caught most of the rest on the beach (Diod. XIII 106; cf. Xen. *Hell.* II 1, 27–28 with a different account).

In the end Lysander captured some 170 Athenian triremes. A few under the command of Conon, who had kept the ships under his direct command ready, managed to get away. One of them was the *Paralus*, one of the Athenians' two messenger triremes, especially fast ships always kept in perfect repair. This ship Conon sent on to Athens with the terrible news while he himself with the others headed eastwards (Diod. XIII 106; Xen. *Hell.* II 1,29). Athens was no longer a place to which Conon wished to return; he took service with Evagoras, the king of the Greek city of Salamis on Cyprus which still stood under Persian control. A highly competent commander, Conon did well for himself first in the employ of Evagoras and then in that of the Persian king himself, Artaxerxes II, whose fleet he would eventually command (Diod. XIV 39; Xen. *Hell.* II 1,29 and IV 3,12).

Meanwhile, the *Paralus* arrived in Athens with its ill tidings. The game was up for Athens, even if the Assembly refused to acknowledge the fact. As the Lacedaemonian fleet made its way to blockade Athens by sea in addition to the blockade by land, the Athenian Assembly, at the suggestion of Cleophon (Aesch. II 76; Lys. XIII 8), passed a decree that made it a capital crime even to suggest surrendering. The Athenians stubbornly put off the inevitable until the pressure of starvation became too great (Xen. *Hell.* II 2,1–15). In mid-404, Theramenes, a guiding light of the 5,000 who had retained his influence even under the restored democracy and who whatever his faults maintained a firm grip on reality, eventually contrived to get the Athenians to see sense. Athens surrendered on terms and the war was over (Xen. *Hell.* II 2,16–24).

QUESTIONS FOR REVIEW

1 How was the Peloponnesian War restarted?
2 What contributed to the destruction of the Sicilian Expedition?
3 How did the Lacedaemonians finally manage to win the Peloponnesian War?
4 What problems does the ending of Thucydides' work in the middle of 410 cause?

QUESTION FOR FURTHER STUDY

In the text, where Diodorus and Xenophon diverge, Diodorus has been followed. Is this an overhasty abandonment of the traditional view that Xenophon should be followed? For this view, see Gray (in Further Reading). Compare, however, the studies in the Further Reading list which argue for following Diodorus.

FURTHER READING

Kagan, D. (1981) *The Peace of Nicias and the Sicilian Expedition*. Ithaca.
Kagan, D. (1987) *The Fall of the Athenian Empire*. Ithaca.

On the Oxyrhynchus Historian:
Bruce, I.A.F. (1967) *An Historical Commentary on the Hellenica Oxyrhynchia.* Cambridge.
McKechnie, P., and S.J. Kern. (1987) *Hellenica Oxyrhynchia.* Warminster.

On Xenophon:
Gray, V. (1989) *The Character of Xenophon's Hellenica.* London.
Gray, V. (ed.). (2010) *Xenophon. Oxford Readings in Classical Studies.* Oxford.
Tuplin, Chr. (ed.). (2004) *Xenophon and his World.* Wiesbaden.

In the absence of a commentary on Xenophon's *Hellenica*, the following translation with copious notes by G.L. Cawkwell may be recommended:
Xenophon. (1979) *A History of My Times.* (Trans. R. Warner.) Harmondsworth.

Select studies comparing Xenophon's account with that of the *Hell. Oxy.*:
Andrewes, A. (1974) "The Arginousai Trial," *Phoenix* 28: 112–122.
Andrewes, A. (1982) "Notion and Kyzikos: the Sources Compared," *Journal of Hellenic Studies*: 15–25.
Ehrhardt, Chr.Th.H.R. (1970) "Xenophon and Diodorus on Aegospotami," *Phoenix* 24: 225–228.
Gray, V. (1987) "The Value of Diodorus Siculus for the Years 411–386 B.C.," *Hermes* 115: 72–89. (Dissenting from the *communis opinio*.)

15

The Lacedaemonian Ascendancy in Greece

421–404	404–386	386–362

404	Athens surrenders to Sparta
404–401	Civil war in Athens
404–397	Decarchies in many Greek cities
401	Cyrus the Younger rebels
399	Lacedaemonians invade Asia Minor
396	Agesilaus crosses over to Asia Minor
395	Battle of Sardis
394–386	Corinthian War
394	Battle of Cnidus
386	King's Peace

The Aftermath of the Peloponnesian War

Given the length and bitterness of the war, the Lacedaemonians offered the Athenians surprisingly lenient terms: Athens had to surrender its empire; to pull down the Long Walls which connected the city itself with its port, the

A History of Greece: 1300 to 30 BC, First Edition. Victor Parker.
© 2014 Victor Parker. Published 2014 by John Wiley & Sons, Ltd.

Peiraeus; to give up its fleet save for twelve ships; and to become a member of the Peloponnesian League with the obligation to follow "whithersoever the Lacedaemonians might lead." Beyond that the Lacedaemonians inflicted no harm (Xen. *Hell.* II 2,20; Diod. XIV 3).

Far more harmful to Athens was the ensuing civil war. The democracy had spectacularly failed in the final years of the Peloponnesian War and, once again, an oligarchy replaced the failed democracy (Xen. *Hell.* II 3,2–3; Diod. XIV 4). Thirty men were elected to write a new oligarchic constitution, only – as had happened with the 400 under similar circumstances (see chap. 14) – once in power the 30 declined to give it up (Diod. l.c.; Xen. *Hell.* II 3,11). However Theramenes was one of the 30, and he convinced them to draw up a list of 3,000 who were supposed to assume power eventually (Xen. *Hell.* II 3,18). Working against Theramenes, however, was Critias, an extremist bent on vengeance against prominent democrats. Xenophon tells the dramatic story of the final showdown between the two when Critias surrounded the council chamber with armed assassins and stage-managed Theramenes' execution (Xen. *Hell.* II 3,24–56; Diod. XIV 4–5). With the influential moderate Theramenes dead, nothing hindered Critias and his allies from inaugurating a reign of terror in which they had their political and private enemies murdered (Diod. IV 5; cf. Xen. *Hell.* II 3,17, 21, and 39, who improbably puts the reign of terror before Theramenes' death). The terror, of course, speedily undermined the regime of the 30.

Meanwhile Thrasybulus, a distinguished commander from the final years of the Peloponnesian War, whom the 30 had exiled and who had been living in Thebes, returned to Attica with Boeotian assistance and established himself at a fortress near Athens called Phyle (Diod. XIV 32; Xen. *Hell.* II 4,2). Thrasybulus' aim was the restoration of the democracy, and he rapidly collected some twelve hundred supporters. With these he carried out a daring night-time march to the Peiraeus which he seized. The 30 led out troops to retake the Peiraeus, but were defeated. Critias himself fell in the fighting (Xen. *Hell.* II 4,10–19; Diod. XIV 33). Shortly thereafter the 3,000 managed to depose the 30 who withdrew from Athens to Eleusis while the 3,000 took over in Athens itself (Diod. l.c.; Xen. *Hell.* II 4,23–24).

Three factions were now contending for power in Attica: the 30 (who held Eleusis); the 3,000 (who held Athens); and the democrats with Thrasybulus (who held the Peiraeus). Both the 30 and the 3,000 appealed to Sparta. In the end King Pausanias came and effected a settlement between the 3,000 and the democrats in the Peiraeus – a settlement which, surprisingly, saw the democrats enter Athens and re-establish the old democracy there. The 30 were allowed to continue ruling in Eleusis for the time being (Xen. *Hell.* II 4,28–43; Diod. l.c.).

On Xenophon's presentation, Pausanias favored the democrats for the simple reason that he was locked in a bitter power struggle with Lysander, the victor of Aegospotami. Lysander wanted to keep some sort of an oligarchy in charge in Athens, therefore Pausanias saw to it that a democracy gained control. Yet purely pragmatic reasons for Pausanias' support of the democracy existed –

most prominently the inability of the 30 to govern Athens effectively. Moreover, Pausanias may have legitimately formed a dim assessment of the prospects of the 3,000 to do much better: both the 30 and the 3,000 had sent embassies to Sparta, and each embassy may well have made the case that the other government was illegitimate and inept too persuasively. Finally, while Pausanias was in Athens, the democrats in the Peiraeus, allegedly at his encouragement, sent their own embassy with proposals for peace – possibly this embassy simply made a rather better impression. The result, in any case, bore out Pausanias' decision.

Pausanias' settlement, however, had left the 30 still in Eleusis. A little later the restored democracy removed this last remnant of Athens' second experiment with oligarchy. When the 30 attempted to raise an army of mercenaries, the democracy's army marched out against them. When the generals of the 30 appeared at a conference for negotiations, they were seized and put to death; and their rule in Eleusis dissolved. A full amnesty was declared for any crimes committed during the three-way struggle for control of Athens, and the Athenians all took a simple oath to abide by this amnesty: "I will not remember" (Xen. *Hell.* II 4,43).

By now it was 401 BC; three years had passed since Athens had surrendered in the Peloponnesian War, thirty since the war had begun.

The Development of the Athenian Democracy in the Fourth Century

Two direct experiments with oligarchy had failed, and the old democracy had been restored. Yet even if the basic constitutional forms at Athens remained the same, seemingly minor changes over the next few decades imposed limits on the democracy and effectively shifted it towards the oligarchic end of the constitutional spectrum (on this, see Box 13.1). For example, the Assembly, instead of making its own erratic and hasty decisions, now sometimes requested the Council of the Areopagus first to submit an *apophasis*, a report, on the matter (e.g., **Dinarchus**, I 4–7). The gentlemen on the Council, mostly distinguished pillars of the community, took the time to reach a considered judgment, and the Assembly acted on their recommendations. An oligarchic "brake" was thus added back into the constitution.

The failure to raise the daily rate of pay for holding office achieved much the same in the early decades of the fourth century. With inflation, the three obols on offer per day since the 420s (Schol. Aristoph. *Wasps*, 88a) no longer sufficed to allow every Athenian male to hold an office or to sit on a jury. The effect on the jury rolls is especially noticeable. In the fifth century more than the necessary 6,000 placed their names on the rolls so that lots were cast to see who would serve on a given day (Arist., *Pol.* 1274a). In the fourth century this was no longer necessary ([Arist.] *Ath.Pol.* 63) since fewer than 6,000 names stood on the rolls for the simple reason that poorer people could no longer afford to serve. Office, according to the oligarchic ideal, once again became a benefaction rendered to the community since the pittance which one received for service was mostly a token. It was a second oligarchic brake on the democracy.

Special importance accrued to the men on the jury rolls in these days because of their role in making laws – as distinct from decrees. The Assembly enacted and revoked decrees at will (see, for example, the Mytilenaean Debate in chap. 13), but laws ideally were permanent, and the Assembly could not act contrary to them. Therefore a carefully crafted law could dramatically constrain the Assembly's ability to make policy.

In the fourth century **Nomothetai**, appointed by lot from the jury rolls (**Andocides** I 84; Dem. XXIV 26) made laws in a special vote designed as a trial of the old law. Any adult male citizen might suggest a new law and "prosecute" the old one. The Assembly appointed five **syndikoi** to "defend" the old law, and at the end of the trial the *Nomothetai* voted either to "convict" the old law (i.e., to replace it with the new one) or to "acquit" it (Dem. XXIV 21, 23, 25, and 33). The decision of the *Nomothetai* could be challenged, but in the law-courts by bringing against the law's author a charge of "making an inappropriate law" ([Arist.] *Ath.Pol.* 59). Controlling the entire procedure, then, were those on the jury rolls. Since for practical reasons only the wealthy placed their names on the rolls, from a certain point of view the making and judging of laws had been ceded to an oligarchy within the larger framework of a democracy.

The law which made it a capital offense to move a decree contrary to law (a **graphe paranomon**) in the Assembly safeguarded this oligarchy's powers. The first attestation of such a law is in 411 (Thuc. VIII 67; [Arist.] *Ath.Pol.* 29), but such prosecutions became commonplace during the fourth century, and they made it difficult for any politician to get around a law which was tying the Assembly's hands (e.g., Demosthenes at I 19–20). The most famous of all Greek orations – Demosthenes' *On the Crown* – is actually a defense against a charge of having made a *graphe paranomon*.

While the democratic forms, as known from the fifth century, all remained, behind the façade over the course of the fourth century much changed to make the democracy less "democratic" and more "oligarchic." The oligarchic criticisms of the democracy found their concrete expression in this way rather than in an actual oligarchy.

Initial Lacedaemonian Efforts at "Empire"

This, however, is looking several decades ahead. During the period of the civil war in Athens (404–401), when Athens lay prostrate in the aftermath of the Peloponnesian War, the general who had defeated them, Lysander, dominated Lacedaemonian politics. Under his leadership the Lacedaemonians strove to establish what amounted to an "empire" of their own, a sort of dominion which scholars, in line with ancient usage (e.g., in Diod. XV, based on Ephorus), have commonly called **hegemony**.

In the cities under his control Lysander established **decarchies** – boards of ten (see, e.g., Xen. *Hell*. III 4,7), the members of which he chose from the Sparta-friendly faction within each city (Plut. *Lys*. 13). Overseeing decarchies were the Lacedaemonian-appointed **harmosts** or "governors" (Xen. *Hell*. III 5,13). The harmost sometimes commanded a garrison also (Xen. *Hell*. II 3,14). The two institutions – decarchies and harmosts – went hand-in- hand (see, e.g., Paus. VIII 52; IX 6 and 32). The decarchy, then, which consisted of hand-picked locals, formed the government of the city in question, but remained subject to the supervision of a Lacedaemonian governor who could call upon a garrison at need.

Very little is known about the decarchies beyond that they elicited near universal opprobrium from their subjects; in fact, Isocrates (XII 54) states that the decarchies were so obviously unjust that to enumerate their crimes would be a redundant exercise. Accordingly, denunciations of them and the harmosts abound: e.g., Isoc. IV 110 and 117; XIV 13. The speech which Xenophon places into the mouth of the Boeotian ambassador in Athens in 395 surely exaggerates when it asserts that the Lacedaemonians appointed Helots as harmosts (Xen. *Hell*. III 5,12), but the exaggeration does give an indication of the general contempt which those compelled to live under harmosts reserved for them.

The harmosts (and presumably also the decarchies) in Asia Minor were apparently still in place in the year 397 (Xen. *Hell*. III 2,20), but the ephors shortly thereafter ordered the decarchies there (and presumably also the harmosts) abolished (Xen. *Hell*. III 4,2). The decarchies in Asia Minor had indeed mostly disappeared by the time of Agesilaus' expedition in 396 (Xen. *Hell*. III 4,7) when Lysander wished to re-establish them (Xen. *Hell*. III 4,2). All the same, some harmosts and decarchies evidently lingered, whether there or elsewhere. The Boeotian ambassador's speech mentions decarchies and harmosts in the context of the year 395 (Xen. *Hell*. III 5,13), and Xenophon speaks of the expulsion of harmosts after the Battle of Cnidus in 394 (*Hell*. IV 8,1; see also Paus. VIII 52). Harmosts in Methymna and Abydos are attested in the late 390s (Xen. *Hell*. IV 8,29 and 32), while the second-century AD writer Pausanias speaks of the suppression of both decarchies and harmosts after the Battle of Leuctra in 371 (Paus. IX 6).

Even if a few decarchies managed to survive down to the 370s – and possibly Pausanias in Roman times was simply laboring under a misapprehension –, this Lacedaemonian attempt at establishing an "empire" met with little success overall. The person most closely associated with the attempt in its initial stages was Lysander, and he inspired strong emotions even in Sparta. The Lacedaemonian king Pausanias undid Lysander's arrangements in Athens; the ephors abolished the decarchies in Asia Minor between 397 and 396. Moreover, the other Lacedaemonian king, Agesilaus, pointedly thwarted all Lysander's wishes in Asia Minor in 396 (Xen. *Hell*. III 4,8–9).

It is, however, difficult to tell to what extent personal hostility towards Lysander motivated internal Lacedaemonian opposition to his policy – given the general unpopularity of the decarchies which Lysander had installed, opposition to them may have stemmed from purely pragmatic concerns. As the heavy Lacedaemonian military involvement in Asia Minor from 399 to 395 and even later shows, the Lacedaemonians had no objections to "empire" in Asia Minor *per se*. Likewise, whatever else the Lacedaemonians may have done in Athens in 401, Athens remained one of Sparta's allies and upon request dutifully supplied troops that followed "whithersoever the Lacedaemonians might lead" (Xen. *Hell.* III 1,4 and 2,25). Details might have changed, but the essence remained the same: the Lacedaemonians were determined to establish their dominance throughout the Greek world.

Lacedaemonian imperial ambitions in Asia Minor of course ran counter to the treaty which the Lacedaemonians had made with King Darius II in 411. At that time in exchange for money the Lacedaemonians had handed over all Asia Minor to the Persians. Selling fellow Greeks out to Barbarians always struck most people in Greece as a foul bargain. In 391 the Athenians would actually reject a peace treaty simply because it involved acknowledgment of Persian rule over Greek cities (**Philochorus**, *BNJ* 328, Fr. 149a); and the assertion that such-and-such a power in Greece was betraying Greeks to a Barbarian always hit home with some trenchancy (e.g., Isoc. VI 27 – here a Lacedaemonian levels the accusation against the Boeotians in 366). So when the Lacedaemonians reneged on their sworn obligations to the Persians, they were reverting to traditional Greek sentiments; and if they were attempting to establish their own rule in the place of the Persians', they were doing no more and no less than the Athenians had done in the 470s and 460s.

The Lacedaemonian Invasion of Persia

In 404 BC, as the Peloponnesian War in Greece ended, in Persia King Darius II died. His death set in train a series of events which would lead to the full-scale Lacedaemonian invasion of Asia Minor already alluded to in the previous section. First, Darius II's son, Artaxerxes II, ascended the throne to the displeasure of his half-brother, the so-called younger Cyrus. During the Peloponnesian War, at Darius II's behest, Cyrus had coordinated efforts with the Lacedaemonians to defeat the Athenians in Asia Minor (Xen. *Hell.* I 4,3sqq.). This work had left him with good contacts in the Greek world, and here he gathered some 10,000 mercenaries (among them the historian Xenophon of Athens) for a rebellion against his brother. Troops loyal to Artaxerxes II, however, smashed the rebellion in the Battle of Cunaxa, on the banks of the River Euphrates, in 401 BC. Cyrus the Younger perished, but the 10,000 Greek mercenaries, under the inspired leadership of Xenophon, fought their way back to Greece. Xenophon records the story of the march of the 10,000 in the *Anabasis* ("a march up-country"), a fascinating tale of swashbuckling endeavor which manages to present an inglorious retreat as a triumph over bumbling Persians. This presentation of the Persians would prove highly influential among the Greeks (see chap. 19).

Artaxerxes II, however, secured his rule all the same. As the satraps in Asia Minor – primarily Pharnabazus of Hellespontine Phrygia and Tissaphernes of Lydia – finally set about re-establishing Persian rule in the Greek-settled regions of Asia Minor shortly thereafter, many cities there feared reprisals, in particular for their support of the younger Cyrus' rebellion. Since many cities stood under the control of Lacedaemonian harmosts and decarchies at the time, they appealed to Sparta for help (Diod. XIV 35; Xen. *Hell.* III 1,3).

The Lacedaemonians sent out a commander, Thibron, to wage war against the Persians on behalf of the Greeks of Asia Minor. He arrived in 399 BC with some 1,000 **Neodamodeis** (Helots freed against their future military service) from Sparta, 4,000 troops from Peloponnesian allies, and 300 cavalrymen from Athens (Xen. *Hell.* III 1,4; cf. Diod. XIV 36). Thibron made very little headway, however. He briefly held Magnesia on the Meander and attempted to besiege Tralles in Caria (Diod. l.c.). Pergamum and a few other places surrendered to him, but the taking of even so minor a town as Larissa in the Troad proved too difficult (Xen. *Hell.* III 1,6–7). The cities on whose behalf Thibron was fighting were expected to provision his troops, but this became problematic during the winter of 399 to 398 (Xen. *Hell.* III 2,1). Complaints about Thibron's troops' rapacity poured in to Sparta (Xen. *Hell.* III 1,8 and 2,6–7), and in 398 Dercylidas arrived to replace him (Diod. XIV 38; Xen. *Hell.* III 1,8).

Dercylidas, although more vigorous than Thibron, made little progress as well, taking only a handful of towns in the Troad and the Aeolis (Diod. l.c.; Xen. *Hell.* III 1,16–28). He did at least hit upon a solution to the problem of provisioning his troops over the winter: for the winter he made a truce with Pharnabazus, the satrap of Hellespontine Phrygia, and moved his army to Bithynia. The Bithynians were in revolt from Pharnabazus who was perfectly happy to see Dercylidas plunder their land (Xen. *Hell.* III 2,1–5). When the winter ended, Dercylidas and Pharnabazus agreed to extend the truce. Dercylidas spent most of 397 either fighting on the Chersonese against the Thracians (Diod. l.c.; Xen. *Hell.* III 2,9–10) or besieging the town of Atarneus in Asia Minor. The siege of this minor place, held by Chians, took eight months (Xen. *Hell.* III 2,11). On two occasions the ephors ordered Dercylidas to invade Caria, but he never did (Xen. *Hell.* III 1,7 and 2,12). In fact, by the end of 397 Dercylidas was negotiating with both Pharnabazus and Tissaphernes, the satrap of Lydia. This produced a proposal whereby the Persians would allow the Greek cities autonomy if the Lacedaemonians withdrew their harmosts (Xen. *Hell.* III 2,20). Dercylidas sent the proposal on to Sparta (Xen. *Hell.* III 2,19–20; Diod. XIV 39).

The ephors responded by relieving Dercylidas of his duties, by abolishing the decarchies which Lysander had installed, and by sending out King Agesilaus in 396 with a force of 30 Spartiates, 2,000 Neodamodeis, and 6,000 allies (Xen. *Hell.* III 4,2; cf. Diod. XIV 79). With the troops already in Asia Minor Agesilaus had some 13,000 at his disposal, more than double what Thibron and Dercylidas had had. For the first time the Lacedaemonian general commanded troops sufficient for major campaigns. The reversal of Lysander's specific policies did not entail a retreat from Asia Minor; far from it, the Lacedaemonians were redoubling their efforts.

Tissaphernes, alarmed at the size of this new Lacedaemonian army, played for time. He negotiated with Agesilaus while secretly requesting a large army from Artaxerxes II. Tissaphernes received his army, but Agesilaus, correctly guessing that Tissaphernes would not use it for the benefit of Pharnabazus, left Lydia and invaded Hellespontine Phrygia instead (Xen. *Hell.* III 4,6 and 11–12; cf. Diod. l.c.). Tissaphernes and Pharnabazus detested each other (cf. Xen. *Hell.* III 1,9), and Agesilaus exploited their enmity.

While Agesilaus made little progress in Hellespontine Phrygia, Pharnabazus had no army sufficient for defeating him (as emerges from Xen. *Hell.* III 4,13–14). The stand-off did, however, buy Agesilaus time to remedy one weakness in his forces, a lack of cavalry, through recruitment and training (Xen. *Hell.* III 4,15). In 395, having built up his cavalry, he invaded Lydia and marched on Sardis. Tissaphernes, with an army of (allegedly) 10,000 cavalry and 50,000 infantry, opposed him every step of the way. Near Sardis, at a place called Thybarnae, Agesilaus set a trap for Tissaphernes (see Box 15.1 for discussion of the sources). Some 1,400 troops were hidden near thick woods as an ambush. Agesilaus led the Persian troops (mostly cavalry) which were harassing him past that place. When the ambush was sprung, Agesilaus turned and attacked. The result was a modest victory over the Persians. Tissaphernes fled to Sardis while Agesilaus briefly contemplated an invasion of the satrapy of Greater Phrygia to the east (*Hell.Oxy.* col. VII; Diod. XIV 80).

Tissaphernes' failure had consequences. Artaxerxes II had him arrested and executed (Diod. XIV 80; Xen. *Hell.* III 4,25); his replacement was Tithraustes, who himself could think of nothing better to do than to bribe Agesilaus to invade Hellespontine Phrygia again (Xen. *Hell.* III 4,26). Meanwhile Pharnabazus sent a Rhodian by the name of Timocrates to Greece to bribe politicians in various states to attack Sparta at home – in the hope that Agesilaus would be recalled to mainland Greece. Timocrates liberally distributed fifty silver talents in Athens, Boeotia, Corinth, and Argos (*Hell.Oxy.* coll. VI–VII; cf. Xen. *Hell.* 5,1–2, with different details). The bribes' efficacy is debatable. According to Xenophon they worked like a charm, but according to the Oxyrhynchus Historian they were wasted since the politicians who took them hated the Lacedaemonians anyway and were already fomenting war. In either case Agesilaus did have to return to mainland Greece when Athens, Boeotia, Corinth, and Argos all united against the Lacedaemonians (Diod. XIV 83; Xen. *Hell.* IV 2,1–2).

Although Agesilaus left 4,000 troops behind in Asia Minor (Xen. *Hell.* IV 2,5), the Lacedaemonians' war to "liberate" the Greeks of Asia Minor had come to an end. As a final codicil, Conon, the former Athenian commander who had gone to the Persians at the end of the Peloponnesian War (see chap. 14),

Box 15.1 *The Battle of Sardis (395 BC)*

Three accounts of this battle between Lacedaemonians and Persians exist: *Hell.Oxy.*, col. VI, 4–6; Diod. XIV 80; and Xen. *Hell.* III 4,12–25 (see Table 15.1). Comparison of the three accounts shows that the account in Diodorus is ultimately based on that of the Oxyrhynchus Historian. Agesilaus is marching through Lydia:

Table 15.1 Three accounts of the Battle of Sardis

Hell. Oxy. (4th century BC)	Diodorus (1st century BC)	Xenophon (4th century BC)
(*The Papyrus is very fragmentary here, but in essence clearly recounts the same thing as Diodorus.*)	Tissaphernes' army (50,000 foot and 10,000 horse) harasses the Lacedaemonians every step of the way.	Tissaphernes has stationed both his infantry and his cavalry in Caria; the cavalry eventually returns to Lydia to oppose the Lacedaemonians.
Agesilaus has 500 light infantrymen and a certain number of hoplites (the exact number is missing) lie in ambush.	Agesilaus has 1,400 troops in all lie in ambush.	*No correspondence to the ambush.*
He puts the Spartiate Xenocles in charge.	He puts the Spartiate Xenocles in charge.	*No correspondence to the ambush.*
He leads his main army – and thus the pursuing Persians – past the ambush.	He leads his main army – and thus the pursuing Persians – past the ambush.	*No correspondence to the ambush.*
Xenocles attacks the Persians.	Agesilaus attacks the Persians.	Some Persian cavalry attack the Lacedaemonians. Agesilaus orders up the Lacedaemonian cavalry, and the Persians draw up all their cavalry.
The Persians panic.	Xenocles attacks the Persians.	Agesilaus draws up his infantry too and attacks with all arms at once.
Agesilaus attacks the Persians.	The Persians panic.	The Persians panic.
600 Persians killed. Tissaphernes withdraws to Sardis	6,000 Persians killed. Tissaphernes withdraws to Sardis.	*No indication of casualties.* Tissaphernes was in Sardis when the battle took place.

The account in Diodorus closely follows that of the *Hellenica Oxyrhynchia*. The few minor differences are easily explained: Diodorus was not using the *Hellenica Oxyrhynchia* directly, but was summarizing the work of Ephorus (late fourth century BC) instead. Ephorus, for his part, had based his account of the battle on the *Hellenica*

(Continued)

Oxyrhynchia. In other words, two points exist at which a bit of confusion may have arisen as to the order in which Xenocles and Agesilaus attacked the Persians – Ephorus could have made a careless mistake in the matter, but Diodorus (who is notoriously capable of faulty summarizing of his sources – see Box 18.1) might have been careless too. The divergence in number – 600 vs. 6,000 casualties – is probably due to a copyist's error somewhere along the way (already in antiquity authors commented on how copyists made errors in transcribing cardinal numbers – see Ephorus, *BNJ* 70, Fr. 218).

had by now risen to command the Persian fleet. He surprised a Lacedaemonian fleet of 85 triremes near Cnidus in 394, defeated it, and captured fifty triremes (Diod. XIV 83; Xen. *Hell.* IV 3,10–12). This time there was no financial backer present to pay for a new fleet so the defeat at Cnidus spelled the end of Lacedaemonian naval power.

Although the Lacedaemonian invasion of Persia came to nothing, an indelible memory of it remained in Greece. Agesilaus departed still undefeated in the field and had actually beaten the Persians in one modest battle. He had played two satraps for fools; and the only way the Persians could think of to get rid of him was to bribe Sparta's opponents in Greece. Agesilaus appeared to have shown that the Persian Empire was weak and ripe for the taking for someone with the proper resources.

The Corinthian War

Agesilaus in the meantime turned to the prosecution of Sparta's war against Boeotia, Athens, Corinth, and Argos. This war has received the conventional name "Corinthian War" because much of the fighting took place near Corinth (Diod.XIV 86). In addition the anti-Lacedaemonian alliance maintained a council at Corinth to oversee its efforts (Diod. XIV 82). A word now on terminology: In the following the political term "Boeotia" will be strictly used although Xenophon's *Hellenica* almost always speaks of "Thebes," the chief city of Boeotia. Boeotia was a league-state, and league-states both in theory and in practice functioned on terms of parity with city-states (see Box 4.1).

The initial fighting, before Agesilaus' return, went against the Lacedaemonians. At Haliartus in Boeotia, a Boeotian army had defeated a small Lacedaemonian force under Lysander, who himself had fallen in the fighting. Athenian troops arrived to reinforce the Boeotians just before King Pausanias could lead a second Lacedaemonian force to Haliartus. Pausanias opted to conclude a truce rather than to fight, and upon his return to Sparta the ephors put him on trial for his life (Xen. *Hell.* III 5,17–25; Diod. XIV 81). Pausanias went into exile and, presumably as an act of vengeance, composed a tract on the poor quality of Sparta's laws (Ephorus, *BNJ* 70, Fr. 118).

Determined to win the war, the Lacedaemonians mobilized in full and met their opponents' army at Nemea, near Corinth, in 394 BC. This time the army of Spartiates carried the day (Xen. *Hell.* IV 2,14–23; Diod. XIV 83). Meanwhile Agesilaus had arrived in Boeotia and defeated the anti-Lacedaemonian coalition in a remarkable battle at Coroneia a little later in the same year (Xen. *Hell.* IV 3,15–23; Diod. XIV 84). All the same, neither battle was decisive and the war continued with the fighting centered on Corinth, where the anti-Lacedaemonian coalition had its base, and Sicyon, which the Lacedaemonians used as theirs (Xen. *Hell.* IV 4,1).

Over the next few years both sides stayed bunkered down in their bases. They spared their own citizens and relied heavily on mercenaries (Xen. *Hell.* IV 4,14). Of potentially far greater consequence than any fighting was a curious political experiment of the Argives and the Corinthians who in 393 formed a **sympolity** – a political union which did not involve the physical relocation of either or both cities. There was a common citizenship so that the former Corinthians were now "Argives" (Xen. *Hell.* IV 4,2–6; Diod. XIV 92). The new state dominated the northeastern Peloponnese and controlled the Isthmus' southern portion. If this new state had endured, it might have had a greater effect on developments in Greece. In Athens, meanwhile, Conon, though in Persian employ, used his crews as laborers to help the Athenians rebuild their Long Walls between the city and the Peiraeus (Xen. *Hell.* IV 8,9–10; Diod. XIV 85).

Additionally, negotiations for a peace treaty were underway. The Lacedaemonians approached the Persians with a view towards securing the withdrawal of Persian support for Conon's activities and went on to suggest a peace treaty (Xen. *Hell.* IV 8,12–14). The Persians also had a vested interest in establishing peace in the Aegean region and so attempted to broker this treaty. First, Lacedaemonian troops still stood in Asia Minor and, under the command of Thibron, were carrying out raids (Xen. *Hell.* IV 8,17–19; Diod. XIV 99). Second, the Athenian commanders Thrasybulus and Iphicrates were actively campaigning in the Propontis, including on the Asian side, in an attempt to re-establish Athenian control over this strategic area (Xen. *Hell.* IV 8,25–39; Diod. XIV 99). Finally, the Persians wanted once and for all to restore their control over the Greek regions in Asia Minor – and to have the Greeks *all* acknowledge it (that is, not just the Lacedaemonians as in 411 or the Athenians as in the Peace of Callias).

That final Persian wish proved the sticking point. The Athenians refused to hand over fellow Greeks to Barbarians, so the Persians' first attempt to establish peace (in 391 BC) came to nothing (Philochorus, *BNJ* 328, Fr. 149). The war continued in a desultory fashion for an additional five years during which neither Diodorus nor Xenophon has much to report. By the year 386, however, all warring parties were ready to make peace – whether they had to acknowledge Persian overlordship of Asia Minor or not (cf. Diod. XIV 110).

Box 15.2   *The Decline in the Number of Spartiates*

In these years a precipitous decline in the number of Spartiates first becomes apparent. It forced the Lacedaemonians to become creative in how they put armies together, and allied troops and even mercenaries played an ever-increasing role in Lacedaemonian armies as Spartiates became too precious to use except when truly necessary. Thus besides 6,000 other troops the Lacedaemonians sent only 30 Spartiates to campaign in Asia Minor in 396. Additionally, in a major development within Lacedaemonian society the class of the Neodamodeis (Helots freed against future military service) grew dramatically as the scarcity of Spartiates opened up a pathway to freedom for many Helots. Even more importantly, this decline set the stage for the end of Sparta as a military power in Greece, so it merits some attention in its early stages. The immediate cause for the drop in numbers was high and sustained casualties during the Peloponnesian War (431–404), but for the systemic causes which prevented a recovery, see Box 16.2.

At the Battle of Plataea in 479 BC, some 5,000 Spartiates had fought alongside of an equal number of Perioeci (Hdt. IX 27–28). Herodotus reckons with seven Helots to a Spartiate, so the following overall ratio emerges:

1   Spartiate : 1 Perioecus : 7 Helots

Given the situation in 479 BC, this was a maximum levy. Even if the figures must be taken with some salt – the numbers of Spartiates and Perioeci are round and the ratio of Helots to Spartiates seems just a plausible guess –, they ought to be approximately accurate.

The next probable maximum levy recorded is that from the Battle of Nemea in 394 BC during the Corinthian War. Here a total of 6,000 Spartiates and Perioeci took the field (Xen. *Hell.* IV 2,16). The number of Lacedaemonians, then, according to the available figures, had dropped by approximately 40% in just over eight decades.

If Spartiates and Perieoci still stood at a ratio of 1:1 in 394, then there were 3,000 Spartiates at the battle of Nemea. However, another piece of evidence suggests that there were even fewer Spartiates than that. In 399 BC, shortly after Agesilaus' accession, the ephors got wind of a conspiracy to overthrow the government in Sparta. A man called Cinadon had taken a potential confederate into the marketplace at Sparta and had asked him to count the number of Spartiates – it came to somewhat over 40. Then he estimated the non-Spartiates at 4,000 (Xen. *Hell.* III 3,5). The figures may be exaggerated for effect, but they seemed plausible to someone who knew Sparta as well as Xenophon. If so, then the ratio of Spartiates to everyone else in Sparta in 399 approached 1:100 (as opposed to 1:8 in 479). The number of Spartiates was almost surely lower than 3,000 in 394.

The King's Peace

Xenophon quotes verbatim the text of an edict from King Artaxerxes II:

King Artaxerxes considers it just that:

1 *The "cities" (poleis) in Asia and, of the islands, Clazomenae and Cyprus should be his;*
2 *But that the other Greek "cities" (poleis), both small and large, should be left "autonomous" –*
3 *With the exception of Lemnos, Imbros, and Scyros which should be the Athenians', as in the past.*
4 *And whichever party does not accept this peace, I together with those who desire these things will wage war against that party both on the land and by sea, both with ships and with money.*

(Xen. *Hell.* V 1,31; the numbers of the clauses are added for the sake of greater transparency in the following discussion. Diod. XIV 110 contains an abbreviated version of the edict.)

This edict formed the basis of the treaty eventually sworn. In the case of Athens, a special clause was added to the effect that the Athenians were to take down the gates at the entrance to the Peiraeus. The absence of these gates left the Peiraeus open to attack such that an enemy of Athens, at the outbreak of a new war, might seek to seize the Peiraeus and thus prevent the Athenians from supplying themselves by sea in the event of a siege. In other words, the Athenians were requested unilaterally to deactivate a portion of their defenses in the interests of peace, and they did so (on this, see Cawkwell 1973: 54). The case of Athens shows that clauses tailored to the specific situation of individual states may have existed in other cases as well.

The king's edict contains a number of specific details and brief discussion of them is in order. Clause 1 establishes Persian control of the mainland of Asia Minor and in lawyerly fashion clarifies two potential points of dispute. The island of Cyprus, which fleets from mainland Greece had attacked on several occasions in the past, belonged to the king. Next, the small Greek town of Clazomenae had been for purposes of defense physically relocated from the mainland onto some small islands just off the coast (Strab. XIV 1,36, p. 645). The Clazomenians' fields still lay on the mainland, so there was potential for dispute – was Clazomenae an island or part of the mainland? The edict mentioned Clazomenae specifically to achieve clarity in the matter.

Clause 3 lists some specific exceptions to Clause 2. The exceptions concern three islands currently in Athens' possession, but which in the past had evidently been "autonomous" in the terms envisaged by the treaty. However, the pre-Athenian inhabitants of the islands were long gone, and no one had any interest in bringing them back. So the treaty confirms Athens' continued possession of the islands in case any objection on the basis of Clause 2 were to arise. Clause 4 makes provisions for the treaty's enforcement. King Artaxerxes undertakes – at least officially – to enforce the treaty, but accepts all help which others may give. This last would have practical consequences as the Lacedaemonians took it upon themselves to enforce the treaty or rather their interpretation of it.

Clause 2 was the explosive part of the treaty. The treaty spoke of *poleis* – "cities," "city-states," or, freely, just "states." All *poleis* were to be "autonomous" – but which definition of *polis* did one take when deciding which communities the treaty was speaking of? That the word itself was ambiguous becomes clear when representatives of the Boeotian League desired to swear the treaty. King Agesilaus insisted that *polis* be taken as "city" – the cities within the Boeotian League, which had never been city-states in the way in which Athens, for example, clearly was, were now supposed to be "autonomous." Then there was the question as to what "autonomy" was concretely. Its most literal definition was "to make one's own laws for oneself." By this view a league-state such as Boeotia was depriving the *poleis* within it of their "autonomy" by making laws for them.

Agesilaus wielded the Lacedaemonian interpretation of Clause 2 against the Boeotians with devastating effect. He isolated them diplomatically by threatening them with a continuation of the war (by virtue of Clause 4) against them alone. The other Greek states declined to get involved as Agesilaus began to mobilize the full Lacedaemonian army for a campaign against the Boeotians. Bereft of any support, the Boeotians capitulated. They dissolved the centuries-old Boeotian League, and over a dozen cities became autonomous city-states. Duly authorized representatives of each one swore the treaty (Xen. *Hell.* V 1,32–33). It was a policy of "divide and conquer" – the newly autonomous city-states were much smaller and consequently much weaker than the old Boeotian League. Most importantly, the Lacedaemonians could play them off against each other.

It was the Corinthians' and the Argives' turn next. Agesilaus isolated the sympolity of those two states and insisted that if the sympolity were not dissolved, then Sparta would mobilize against them – and them alone. Once again, all others stood by and did not get involved, and once again Sparta got its way. Corinth regained its "autonomy." Concurrent with this process, those Corinthians who had objected to the sympolity and had, as commonly happened when a faction lost out in a power struggle, gone into exile, now returned and evidently with Lacedaemonian support formed the new government of Corinth. The Lacedaemonians had succeeded in taking a formidable political entity and splitting it into fragments which they could far more easily deal with. In the case of Corinth the factionalism of internal politics actually delivered a new ally (Xen. *Hell.* V 1,34 and 36).

Duly authorized representatives from both Corinth and Argos now swore the King's Peace. It was the first so-called **koine eirene** or Common Peace in that it was a multilateral treaty which, in theory, encompassed the entire Greek world and established peace throughout it. According to an Athenian decree, Persian representatives swore the Peace as well (Harding, Nr. 31). However, it raised a number of new issues, most prominently how to define "autonomy" concretely as well as what political entities could be recognized under such a Peace. Those issues would vex Greek diplomats for some years to come.

QUESTIONS FOR REVIEW

1 How did Athens' second experiment with oligarchy fail?
2 How did the Athenians in the end modify their democracy to make it more "oligarchic" (without actually turning it into an oligarchy)?
3 What social factors at home made it increasingly difficult for the Lacedaemonians to wage war effectively and to play a major role in interstate affairs?
4 What did both sides – Greeks and Persia – gain from the King's Peace?

QUESTION FOR FURTHER STUDY

Why are there so many differences between Xenophon's account and that of the Oxyrhynchus Historian? Is this a case of two witnesses seeing the same event slightly differently, or are both Xenophon and the Oxyrhynchus Historian better informed about some events than others?

FURTHER READING

On Greece after the Peloponnesian War:
Cartledge, P. (1987) *Agesilaos and the Crisis of Sparta*. London.
Strauss, B. (1987) *Athens after the Peloponnesian War*. Ithaca, NY.
Tritle, L.A. (ed.). (1997) *The Greek World in the Fourth Century*. London.

On the Battle of Sardis:
Anderson, J.K. (1974) "The Battle of Sardis in 395 B.C.," *California Studies in Classical Antiquity* 7: 27–53. (Preferring the account of Xenophon.)
Bruce, I.A.F. (1967) *An Historical Commentary on the Hellenica Oxyrhynchia*. Cambridge. (Pp. 150–156; preferring the account of *Hell. Oxy.*)
Gray, V.J. (1979) "Two Different Approaches to the Battle of Sardis in 395 B.C.," *California Studies in Classical Antiquity* 12: 183–200. (Also preferring the account of Xenophon.)

On the oligarchies in Athens, the following monograph in German exists:
Lehmann, G.A. (1997) *Oligarchische Herrschaft im klassischen Athen: zu den Krisen und Katastrophen der attischen Demokratie im 5. und 4. Jahrhundert v. Chr.* Opladen.

On "law" and the new Athenian Democracy:
Hansen, M.H. (1991) *The Athenian Democracy in the Age of Demosthenes*. Copenhagen.
Ostwald, M. (1986) *From Popular Sovereignty to the Sovereignty of Law*. Berkeley.

On the King's Peace, the following are useful:

Badian, E. (1991) "The King's Peace" In: *Georgica: Festschrift Cawkwell* = *Bulletin of the Institute of Classical Studies* Suppl. 58: 25–48. London.

Cawkwell, G.L. (1973) "The Foundation of the Second Athenian Confederacy," *Classical Quarterly* 23: 47–60, esp. p. 54.

16

The Boeotian Ascendancy in Greece and the Second Athenian League

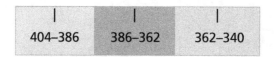

| 404–386 | 386–362 | 362–340 |

385	Dioecism of Mantinea
382	Lacedaemonians seize the Cadmeia
382–380	Lacedaemonian war against Chalcidian League
winter of 379–378	Thebans retake the Cadmeia
377	Charter of the Second Athenian League
374	First Renewal of King's Peace
371	Second Renewal of King's Peace; Battle of Leuctra
370	Messenia becomes independent
366	Third Renewal of King's Peace
362	Battle of Mantinea; Final renewal of the Peace

A History of Greece: 1300 to 30 BC, First Edition. Victor Parker.
© 2014 Victor Parker. Published 2014 by John Wiley & Sons, Ltd.

Sparta Enforces the King's Peace

The Lacedaemonians, having wielded the autonomy clause in the King's Peace as a potent weapon twice already, did so at least twice again in the years that followed its swearing. A peace treaty between Sparta and Mantinea had expired in 388 (Thuc. V 81; Xen. *Hell.* V 2,2 with incorrect date), and this left Mantinea exposed. In 385 the Lacedaemonians issued an unacceptable ultimatum, and when the Mantineans rejected it, the Lacedaemonians mobilized and attacked. After defeating the Mantineans (Xen. *Hell.* V 2,1–6; Diod. XV 5), they inflicted upon Mantinea what the pamphleteer Isocrates (VIII 100) termed a "**dioecism**" – the opposite of a "synoecism." A synoecism was a political union of two or more cities such that only one city existed thereafter: either the residents of one city moved into the other or all involved in the synoecism moved into one new city. In the course of time Mantinea had grown through such unions with smaller towns in the vicinity (see Box 16.1), and these smaller towns had ceased to exist as political entities in their own right.

By a strict interpretation of the autonomy clause in the King's Peace, Mantinea had through these synoecisms violated the autonomy of the smaller towns. It did not matter if these smaller towns had voluntarily ceded their autonomy – what mattered to the Lacedaemonians was that all cities, small and great, were autonomous. The Lacedaemonians accordingly split Mantinea up into five autonomous cities (Ephorus, *BNJ* 70, Fr. 79 with Diod. XV 5 and 12,1–2; cf. Xen. *Hell.* V 2,7 with the number four, but with the detail which proves "autonomy": the Lacedaemonians sent a ***xenagos***, a mustering official, to each city). Each new town was more easily managed than just Mantinea. All, incidentally, became members of the Peloponnesian League.

Box 16.1   *The Sympolity of Mantinea and Heliswon*

The following inscription, SEG 37, Nr. 340, published in 1987, records the sympolity of Mantinea with the nearby small town of Heliswon (probably in the early fourth century). In this case the city-state of Heliswon (line 5 – *polis* in the sense of "political entity") will be incorporated into Mantinea though the physical city of Heliswon (line 6 – *polis* in the sense of "physical city") will still exist. The inscription moreover shows that Mantinea – as presupposed by the Lacedaemonians' "dioecism" of it – did indeed grow through unions with nearby communities. Granted, a sympolity is not a synoecism; in the case of a synoecism all the Heliswasians would have moved to Mantinea. Whether the erstwhile Heliswasians were later on relocated to Mantinea so that the sympolity became a synoecism is pure speculation. In either case the Lacedaemonian "dioecism" should have brought the town of Heliswon along with its "autonomy" back into being.

The inscription, translated immediately below, finally shows how much thought went into regulating the technical details of such a political union. Lines 8–10 confirm that the sympoly will have no effect on religious observances in Heliswon. Lines 10–16 explain how lawsuits between Mantineans and former Heliswasians will be handled and confirm the validity of all contracts made between Heliswasians. Lines 16–24 deal with the registration of the Heliswasians as Mantinean citizens.

Gods! Good fortune!
Compact of the Mantineans and the Heliswasians . . .
. . . which the Mantineans and the Heliswasians have ratified. The
Heliswasians shall be Mantineans, equal and alike, having in common all
5.   things which the Mantineans too have, incorporating their land and their *polis*
into Mantinea according to the laws of the Mantineans, while the *polis*
of the Heliswasians remains just as it has for all time, with the Heliswasians
being a village of the Mantineans. There shall be sacral ambassadors from
Heliswon just as from other *poleis*. They shall sacrifice in
10. Heliswon and shall receive oracles according to their ancestral traditions.
Lawsuits
the Heliswasians and the Mantineans shall prosecute against each other by the laws
of the Mantineans, now that the Heliswasians have become Mantineans, for the future;
but matters from before then may not be the subject of lawsuits. As many contracts
as the Heliswasians happen to have among themselves from before they became
15. Mantineans, they shall be valid according to the laws which they themselves had when
they came to Mantinea. All the Heliswasians shall register themselves with the
Epimeletai in Mantinea by their father's name according to age within ten days of when
the scribes come. But the *Epimeletai* shall take the registered names away
to Mantinea and shall register them with the **Thesmotoaroi** under
20. Nices, the **Damiorgos**; and the *Thesmotoaroi*, once they have written (the names) on tablets,
shall display them at the Council Chamber. But if anyone of those registered should deny
that someone is a Heliswasian, then he may denounce (him) before the *Thesmotoaroi* in
the year after that in which Nices was *Damiorgos*. But the person who is denounced shall
plead his case before the 300 themselves . . .

Fresh off the success at Mantinea, the Lacedaemonians in 382 turned their attention to the Chalcidian League in the north. Various towns on the Chalcidice had by this time joined forces in a league-state with a common citizenship. According to Xenophon, ambassadors from two cities on the Chalcidice, Acanthus and Apollonia, in 382 arrived in Sparta to protest against their forced inclusion in the Chalcidian League. They claimed that all they wished was to live by their own laws and to have their own citizenship to themselves (Xen. *Hell.* V 2,11–19). The Lacedaemonian assembly voted to send an army to disband the Chalcidian League owing to its alleged violation of other cities' autonomy. Over the next two years the Lacedaemonians fought against the Chalcidians and compelled the temporary dissolution of the league (Xen. *Hell.* V 2,20–21; 2,37–3,9; and 3,18–26). (By the mid-370s it had re-established itself – Harding, Nr. 35).

From one perspective the Lacedaemonians' actions both at Mantinea and on the Chalcidice just enforced the letter of the autonomy clause in the King's Peace. From another perspective the Lacedaemonians violated that same Peace's spirit. Thus Diodorus, following Ephorus, writes: "the Lacedaemonians decided to make war against Mantinea, paying no heed to the existing treaties [i.e., the King's Peace]" (XV 5,1). Isocrates says that the Lacedaemonians "sacked Mantinea even though Peace had already been established" (IV 126).

What allowed the Lacedaemonians to get away with all this? When the Lacedaemonians attacked Mantinea, other Greeks expressed outrage, but when it came to doing something, they all, like Athens (Diod. XV 5), looked the other way even though the more perspicacious in Greece surely realized that, given how the Lacedaemonians were acting, it might be their turn next.

The Theban Revolt and the Second Athenian League

When the Lacedaemonians marched northwards to attack the Chalcidians, they passed by Thebes, the largest city in Boeotia. As so often in a Greek city, there was factional strife there. The leader of one of two competing factions, Leontiades, approached the Lacedaemonian commander, Phoebidas, with an offer: if Phoebidas assisted Leontiades in gaining power in Thebes, then Leontiades would betray to the Lacedaemonians the **Cadmeia**, the citadel of Thebes. The Cadmeia was untakeable in antiquity and, as such, a prize which Phoebidas could not possibly refuse. Accordingly, the two did the deal and shortly thereafter, at midday in the middle of summer – i.e., when everyone was having a siesta – Leontiades led Lacedaemonian troops onto the Cadmeia and, with the backing of the Lacedaemonian troops, carried out a coup d'état (Xen. *Hell.* V 2,25–31; Diod. XV 20). Phoebidas' act violated the King's Peace (Xen. *Hell.* V 4,1). Even at Sparta the act aroused controversy (Xen. *Hell.* V 2,32), but while the Assembly there sentenced Phoebidas to a fine (Diod. l.c.), it did not remove the garrison from the Cadmeia.

In the five years after the swearing of the King's Peace, the Lacedaemonians had achieved a dominant position in Greece by diplomacy and by the careful isolation of selected foes. Ruthlessly, they had pursued a policy of splitting other states into small, manageable fragments and hindering the creation of alliances. But during these same years the diplomats of one state, realizing full well that it might stand next on the Lacedaemonians' list, found the key to undoing the latter's diplomatic success. It was the Athenians, and what they did initially attracted no notice. In 384, shortly after the dioecism of Mantinea, they negotiated with the Chians for an alliance. The decree (Harding, Nr. 31) which ratified the alliance in Athens specifically stated that the contractants would preserve the "oaths and treaties . . . which the King, the Athenians, the Lacedaemonians, and the other Greeks swore." Chios and Athens, moreover, formed the alliance "on terms of freedom and autonomy." Here, then, was a military alliance of two states such that no objection on the basis of the King's Peace might arise. The Chian alliance was unobtrusive; the Lacedaemonians raised no objections. In the next few years Byzantium and Methymna made an alliance with Athens on the same terms (Harding, Nrr. 34 and 37; for the date, see Cawkwell 1973: 50–51 [see Chapter 15, Further Reading]). The Athenians were collecting allies in case the Lacedaemonians should turn against them next.

The Athenians also played an active role in the event which undid the Lacedaemonian position in Greece militarily. Over the winter of 379 to 378, they colluded with Thebans plotting a revolution. When the time came, the plotters carried out a series of assassinations by night, and at daybreak the Lacedaemonian garrison on the Cadmeia found itself under siege (Xen. *Hell.* V 4,2–9; Diod. XV 25). Meanwhile, two Athenian generals – who just happened to have troops on the border to Boeotia – rushed to the rebels' aid (Xen. *Hell.* V 4,9; cf. Diod. l.c. with a version revised to make the Athenian support for Thebes appear official). When the Lacedaemonians thereafter sent a relief force northwards, it had to travel from Megara to Boeotia by one of two roads: the first led directly from Megara into Boeotia, and a Theban force was blocking it; the second led from Megara across a corner of Attica and then into Boeotia – and an Athenian force just happened to be blocking that one too (Xen. *Hell.* V 14). The relief force pushed on past the Boeotian blockade, but the garrison commander had already surrendered (Diod. XV 27; Plut. *Pel.* 13; cf. Xen. *Hell.* V 4,11 – chronologically vague). King Cleombrotus, who had led the relief force, could do little now. He shored up the Lacedaemonians' position in Boeotia as best he could and left behind a man called Sphodrias as the commander of a Lacedaemonian garrison in Thespiae (Xen. *Hell.* V 4,15).

The Athenian Assembly had not authorized any of the Athenian aid. As so often, the executive council, the *Boule*, had taken the Assembly out of the loop: covert aid for a secret coup d'état was a matter better not discussed in front of several thousand Athenians (for a parallel, see chap. 18). But the Lacedaemonians, having connected the dots all the same, sent an embassy to Athens to complain (Xen. *Hell.* 4,22 – not stating the embassy's purpose). As it happened, the

Athenian assembly, when the Lacedaemonian relief force was in Boeotia, had panicked and had condemned the two commanders who had rushed to Thebes in aid of the coup d'état (Xen. *Hell.* V 4,19). So the Athenian explanation to the Lacedaemonian ambassadors adverted to two things: first, the generals' acts had not been authorized; second, the generals had already received just punishment. Still, the fact remained that the Lacedaemonians had, with Athenian connivance, lost their garrison on the Cadmeia, and that fact rankled.

So King Cleombrotus suggested – off the record, of course – to Sphodrias, the garrison commander at Thespiae, that he carry out an unauthorized raid on Attica (Diod. XV 29; otherwise Xen. *Hell.* V 4,20). Early in 378, Sphodrias planned to seize the Peiraeus in a night-time march. In keeping with their obligations under the King's Peace, the Athenians had removed the gates from the Peiraeus' fortifications (see chap. 15), so it was an obvious target.

Unfortunately for Sphodrias, he lost his way during the night. At sunrise he was nowhere near his goal, and his plan had failed (Xen. *Hell.* V 4,21; Diod. XV 29). The Lacedaemonian ambassadors were still in Athens, and Sphodrias' raid embarrassed them greatly. They insisted that the raid had been unauthorized (just as believably as the Athenians had been doing) and that the Lacedaemonians would punish Sphodrias. With that the embassy traveled back to Sparta where, however, Sphodrias secured an acquittal (Xen. *Hell.* V 4,21–24; Diod. XV 29). When that news arrived in Athens, the Athenian assembly voted that "the treaties were no longer in force" (Diod. l.c.), and war between Athens and Sparta began again.

For this conflict the Athenians had laid the diplomatic groundwork well. An appeal, the text of which survives (Harding, Nr. 35; see also Diod. XV 28 and 30; Xenophon omits entirely), went out to the entire Aegean world, insofar as it did not stand under Persian control (that is to say, the appeal avoided an offense against the first clause of the King's Peace), that whoever wished might join the Athenians' alliance on the same terms as had the Chians. The appeal also stated the express purpose of the alliance: "that the Lacedaemonians will permit the Greeks to live in peace, with freedom and autonomy." The Lacedaemonians' violations of the spirit of the King's Peace (however scrupulously they claimed to have been upholding the letter) were thus turned against them as the Athenians and their allies undertook to maintain individual states' "autonomy" against the Lacedaemonians.

Moreover the Athenians for the first time proposed a practical working definition of "autonomy":

1   No interference in a state's constitution
2   No garrison
3   No governor
4   No payment of tribute.

The definition's second element is obviously directed against the Lacedaemonians' putative violations of states' autonomy, for the Lacedaemonians had commonly maintained garrisons on other states' territories (e.g., that of Thebes). The third element might have referred to the Lacedaemonian harmosts, governors whom the Lacedaemonians had installed in cities under their control (see chap. 15).

However, not just the Lacedaemonians had a history of violating other states' autonomy. The states to whom Athens was offering membership in this alliance were often the same states which Athens had subjected to the tyranny of the Athenian Empire in the fifth century. And the memory of the imposed democracies, the garrisons, the governors, and the tribute lingered. These states had all been burned once before, and they required assurances to overcome their shyness the second time around. The Athenians' proposed definition of autonomy ruled out those abuses too.

In addition, the Athenians offered potential allies the assurance that no Athenian might own land in any allied city (any existing deeds for such land were to be destroyed), and Athens' allies this time would have a council in which only they had representation. Effectively, the Second Athenian League (as it is conventionally termed) had two governing bodies: the Council of the Allies (see most clearly Diod. XV 28) and the Athenian Assembly, such that both bodies had to approve any action of the League. Moreover, the League undertook to finance its common expeditions not through a compulsory tribute, but from *syntaxeis* (contributions) voluntarily given by the members (Harding, Nr. 36 – for discussion, see chap. 18).

The assurances worked, and resentment at the Lacedaemonians' abuses of the autonomy clause drove states into Athens' open arms. Over the next few years several dozen states joined (some sixty names eventually stood on the public list [Harding, Nr. 35], which, however, the Athenians after a while ceased to update), with seventy (Diod. XV 30) or more than seventy-five (Aesch., II 70) members in the League's heyday.

The Renewal of the Boeotian League

The creation of the Second Athenian League was a severe blow for the Lacedaemonians. Even worse, the Thebans steadily rebuilt the Boeotian League over the next few years. In 378, shortly after Sphodrias' failed raid, Agesilaus led out the Lacedaemonian army against Thebes. Thanks to the Athenian general Chabrias' intervention, the Thebans escaped destruction (Xen. *Hell.* V 4,35–41; Diod XV 32–33). Agesilaus left Phoebidas behind as commander of the garrison at Thespiae; and the Thebans gained a surprising victory over him during a raid in Thespian territory (Xen. *Hell.* V 4,41–45; Diod. XV 33). At this, so Xenophon vaguely states, "the Thebans' affairs began looking up" (Xen. *Hell.* V 4,46). In all likelihood the Thebans began to rebuild the Boeotian League in the winter of 378 to 377.

In 377 Agesilaus again invaded Boeotia, but neither Xenophon (*Hell.* V 4,47–55) nor Diodorus (XV 34) offers much information about the Thebans' activity. Agesilaus devastated the territory to the east of Thebes as far as Tanagra which, Xenophon notes, "Hypatodorus, who was pro-Lacedaemonian, still held" – as though this needed mentioning because the Thebans had brought part of eastern Boeotia back into the League.

The next year (376) Agesilaus was confined to his bed, so King Cleombrotus led out the army against Thebes. However a strong Athenian and Boeotian force held the road into Boeotia, and he returned to Sparta. Having failed at this, the

---

Box 16.2   *The Revival of Federal Leagues*

One of the salient characteristics of political development during the fourth century in Greece is the steady eclipse of the *polis* – the city-state – which is traditionally portrayed as the quintessentially Greek way to organize a community, so much so that Aristotle could famously write "man is a political animal," by which he meant, to render it more exactly if less elegantly, that human beings are animals whom nature has designed to live in a *polis*. Even if many city-states did survive into later times (for example, most prominently Sparta and Athens), in the fourth century, when Aristotle was writing those words, the *polis* was becoming outmoded.

Although the Lacedaemonians fought tooth and nail against them, league-states steadily came to dominate the political landscape in Greece as the fourth century wore on. Not only were old Leagues revived, but new ones came into being. For the (new) Chalcidian and the (old) Boeotian Leagues, see in the text. In 370 to 369, with assistance from the Boeotians, the Arcadian League was also revived (Diod. XV 59 and 62; cf. Xen. *Hell.* VII 1,22–24 – though many now view this league as a new structure). The Thessalian League always remained in existence, yet its most important office, that of the *tagos* (an elective king), had long since fallen into abeyance when Jason, the Tyrant of Pherae, revived it circa 375 (Xen. *Hell.* VI 1 and 4,20–32). The Achaian League clearly still existed in the fourth century when it made a treaty with Corone (SEG XIV 375), but it had disintegrated by 280 when four cities re-formed it (Pol. II 41,12–13). The other original eight cities rejoined the League soon enough, and in the course of time it would encompass almost the entire Peloponnese (see chaps. 21–23). The Phocian League rose to prominence in the fourth century as well (see chap. 18), and the Aetolian League would do so in the third.

Unfortunately, a quirk of Greek usage can make it difficult to notice the rise of the leagues in this period. Most major texts were written by *polis*-dwellers for whom it came naturally to call any state by its chief city. Thus Demosthenes (II 6) speaks of a proposed alliance between the Athenians and the "Olynthians" after Olynthus, the Chalcidian League's largest city. The treaty between the League and Philip of Macedon survives (Harding, Nr. 67), and the text says what Demosthenes ought to have said: the "Chalcidians." Xenophon plays the same trick in the *Hellenica*, almost always saying the "Olynthians" or the "Thebans" rather than the constitutionally correct the "Chalcidians" or the "Boeotians."

Lacedaemonians next undertook a naval campaign. They collected enough triremes from their allies to attempt to prevent transport ships with grain from reaching the Peiraeus. The Athenians in response manned some 83 triremes and defeated the Lacedaemonian fleet of 65 in the sound between the islands of Paros and Naxos (Diod. XV 34; Xen. *Hell.* V 4,60–61). During this year the Thebans – possibly one should already say "Boeotians" – could have made considerable progress with the rebuilding of the Boeotian League.

In his account of the year 375, when the Lacedaemonians again did not invade Boeotia, Xenophon remarks that the Thebans "went to war against the cities of Boeotia and once more gained control over them" (*Hell.* V 4,63). Diodorus (XV 37) does record an attack on Orchomenus around this time, but Xenophon (*Hell.* VI 4,10) probably implies that Orchomenus was still fighting against the Boeotians' forces in the late 370s. The Boeotians, moreover, did not take Plataea until late 373 (Paus. IX 1). Xenophon (*Hell.* VI 3,1) implies that Thespiae was still outside of the Boeotian League just before the Battle of Leuctra in 371, and according to Pausanias (IX 14) the Boeotians did not conquer it until after the battle. The reconstruction of the Boeotian League proceeded, then, in stages down to just after Leuctra in 371. Despite Xenophon's statement, it cannot all have taken place in 375.

In 375, however, the Athenian commander Timotheus did circumnavigate the Peloponnese. He persuaded the Corcyraeans, Acarnanians, and Cephallenians to join the Second Athenian League (Harding, Nr. 41 and 42) and defeated another Lacedaemonian fleet off Alyzeia near Leucas (Xen. *Hell.* V 4,63–66). Since the dissolution of the King's Peace in the aftermath of Sphodrias' raid, the Lacedaemonians had fared badly in the fighting. In the summer of the next year, 374, the Persians, possibly at the Lacedaemonians' request, brokered a renewal of the King's Peace (Philochorus, *BNJ* 328, Fr. 151; Diod. XV 38; cf. Xen. *Hell.* VI 2,1 who, however, speaks of a Peace limited to Athens and Sparta). The Boeotian League – insofar as it had been rebuilt – remained outside of the Peace though the Boeotian city of Plataea, which stood outside of the League, did swear it (Isoc. XIV 5).

The new Peace, however, fell apart almost immediately, as fighting began again in the west on Zacynthos and Corcyra. In 373, one Lacedaemonian attack on Zacynthos and two on Corcyra failed miserably (Diod. XV 45–47; cf. Xen. *Hell.* VI 2,2–39). The Boeotians, meanwhile, captured Plataea and razed it (Diod. XV 46; for the date: Paus. IX 1; cf. Xen. *Hell.* VI 3,1). Once again, the war was going badly for the Lacedaeomonians, who again turned to diplomacy in an attempt to restore the situation. In 371 they participated in a second Persian-brokered renewal of the King's Peace (Diod. XV 50 [see also Dion. Hal. *Lys.* 12]; cf. Xen. *Hell.* VI 3,18–20). This time they accepted at least part of the Athenians' practical working definition of autonomy, namely the withdrawal of all governors and garrisons. Once again the only major state to remain outside of the Peace was the Boeotian League.

In 371 the Lacedaemonians marched against the Boeotians for the first time since the spring of 376, and the Boeotians faced them alone. The two armies met at Leuctra. The Lacedaemonians' troops outnumbered the Boeotians' (see Diod. XV 53 and 56 – probably exaggerating, however), so the issue ought to have been a foregone conclusion. Commanding the Boeotians, however, was Epaminondas, the most brilliant military innovator of the period (whom Xenophon contrives to delete from his account of the battle). The Lacedaemonians under King Cleombrotus drew up their ranks and files in the traditional order, with files twelve men deep and the king on the right wing. Epaminondas thinned out most of his line in order to put a wedge fifty men deep opposite the place where Cleombrotus stood (Xen. *Hell.* VI 4,12; cf. Diod. XV 55). Xenophon argues that the troops around Cleombrotus initially had the better of it in the fighting, but even he cannot deny that all the Lacedaemonian troops in that section of the battlefield were soon hurled back under the weight of the Boeotian files, fifty men deep, and that the entire Lacedaemonian left wing gave way as well as it saw the right being destroyed. Of 700 Spartiates present, 400 (including Cleombrotus) had fallen, as well as 600 others (Xen. *Hell.* VI 4,15; Diod. XV 56 exaggerates and says 4,000). The loss of 400 Spartiates meant that there now were fewer than a thousand of them left (Arist.*Pol.* 1270a).

Leuctra destroyed Sparta as a major power in Greece even as it raised the Boeotian League to pre-eminence. Shortly after Leuctra, surely, whichever Boeotian towns had not yet rejoined the League (Thespiae is the only one known), were forced to do so.

From the Liberation of Messenia to the Battle of Mantinea

In 370 Epaminondas led a Boeotian army onto the Peloponnese and into Laconia. No one had ever done this before, and the cowed Lacedaemonians did nothing. Their army (augmented by 6,000 newly freed Helots) stayed in Sparta and watched as the Boeotians burned fields and plundered villages (Diod. XV 62–65; Xen. *Hell.* VI 5,22–52). Epaminondas then led his army across Mt. Taÿgetos and liberated Messenia. Messenians from Messene on Sicily and from Naupactus (Paus. IV 31) returned to their ancestral homeland which had lain subjugated to the Lacedaemonians for 230 years, and Messenia became an independent state once again (Diod. XV 66; Plut. *Sayings of Kings and Commanders*, p. 194 [23]). Thereby the Lacedaemonians lost roughly one half of their arable land and much of their unfree labor force. In exchange they received a bitter enemy at their back just in case they should ever attempt a major campaign north of the isthmus again, which they never did. The Boeotians, meanwhile, campaigned on the Peloponnese again in 368 (Xen. *Hell.* VII 1,15–22; Diod. XV 68–69) and in 367 (Diod. XV 75; cf. Xen. *Hell.* VII 1,41–42).

The Boeotians had changed the political landscape in Greece dramatically: they had re-established the Boeotian League; they had refounded Messenia; they had, moreover, helped to revive the Arcadian League (see Box 16.2). These achievements still lacked, however, to use a modern term, diplomatic recognition. The Common Peace of 366 supplied this want. As usual, the Persians brokered

Box 16.3   *Systemic Causes for the Decline in Spartiate Numbers*

Spartiate numbers continued to decline in the second and third decades of the fourth century (for their numbers in the 390s, see Box 15.2). No matter how much the Lacedaemonians strove to use non-Spartiate troops whenever possible and no matter how successfully they used diplomatic means to achieve their aims without fighting, Spartiate numbers did not recover. Because it took twenty-three years in the *agoge* and thereafter admittance to a *syssition* (see Box 13.3) to make a Spartiate, whenever a Spartiate died young, there was no immediate replacement.

A Spartiate, as a professional soldier, had no trade: his sole income was half of what the Helots on his land produced (Plut. *Lyc.* 24). Out of this income the Spartiate paid his membership dues to his *syssition* (Plut. *Lyc.* 12), and if he could not pay them, then he lost his membership, dropped out of the ranks of the Spartiates, and became a so-called **hypomeion**, an "inferior" (for the term, see Xen. *Hell.* III 3,6) Here the absence of primogeniture comes into play. If a Spartiate had, say, four sons, then each son inherited a quarter of his land. If a quarter were not large enough for sustaining a family and paying the dues to a *syssition*, then all four sons dropped out of the Spartiate class. In other words, even if a given Spartiate did have a large number of sons, they would not necessarily have been replacing a Spartiate who had died without producing a son.

Moreover, even if in theory all Spartiates held equal plots of land and in theory each Spartiate male at birth was assigned to one such plot (Plut. *Lyc.* 16), in reality the land was very unevenly distributed, and sons inherited their father's land (thus, plainly, Arist. *Pol.* 1270b). The lack of primogeniture worked unevenly over time to produce such a distribution. Additionally, although it was illegal to sell land in Sparta, there were ways to circumvent the law such that a few families eventually acquired large landholdings even as most were restricted to the smallest of plots (Arist. *Pol.* 1270a). For example, if a poor Spartiate could not pay his dues to his *syssition* in bad years, he might "borrow" from a wealthy landholder – to whom he might then "give" a bit of land. Technically, he had not "sold" any land; and while he may have secured his status as a Spartiate for his lifetime, he had probably ruined any chance which his son might otherwise have had. The "giving" of land in this way worked to produce an uneven distribution also. Aristotle (l.c.) impatiently notes that the Lacedaemonians ought to have made the very transfer of land illegal – not merely the selling of it.

Aristotle also comments that if the Lacedaemonians' land had been evenly distributed so as to maximize the number of Spartiates, it could have supported 30,000 infantrymen and 1,500 cavalrymen to boot. As it was, Aristotle continues, after the Battle of Leuctra in 371 (in which Spartiate casualties were high), the number of Spartiates dropped to below a thousand.

this peace, the third renewal of the original one (Diod. XV 76; cf. Isoc. VI 27, confirming Persian involvement; Xen. *Hell.* VII 1,36–37, records the initial terms proposed by the Boeotians; VII 4,6–11, speaks of the Peace itself). For the first time, duly authorized representatives of the Boeotian League swore the Peace – that is to say, the Boeotian League won full diplomatic recognition. Also swearing the Peace were the Messenians, whose new independence was thus recognized (Diod. XV 81 and 90). The Lacedaemonians remained aloof as they could not bear to swallow this bitter pill. Their allies, however, they permitted to make the peace (Xen. *Hell.* VII 4,9): Corinth, Phleius, and Epidaurus are known to have done so (Isoc. VI 91). Of the Lacedaemonians' enemies, Argos (Xen. *Hell.* 4,11) and Athens also (Dem. XIX 137; cf. Xen. *Hell.* VII 4,1) swore this Peace. Others surely did as well. It was a spectacular achievement for the Boeotians and their chief diplomat, Pelopidas.

The Boeotians now built a fleet of a hundred triremes and challenged the second Athenian League on the sea (Diod. XV 79; Isoc. V 53; Dem. XIV 22; Plut. *Phil.* 14). Diodorus reveals little of this fleet's activities though it was apparently active in the Propontis near Byzantium (Isoc. l.c.). The Athenians under Timotheus, allegedly in 364, relieved a siege of Cyzicus in the Propontis (Diod. XV 81) – it may have been the Boeotians besieging Cyzicus, but Diodorus does not say. Despite the Boeotians' ambitions, little came of their attempt at naval power; and the expenses of a fleet may well have exceeded their long-term financial capacity.

In 364 the Boeotian League destroyed one of the cities in the League itself, Orchomenus. Orchomenus had been brought into the League much against its will in the late 370s and prominent Orchomenians had allegedly been plotting against the League in 364. The Boeotians responded by razing Orchomenus to the ground, slaying the men, and selling the women and children into slavery (Diod. XV 79). The other Greeks never forgot the act; when Alexander the Great had Thebes itself razed in 335, he took good care to present his act as just retribution, decreed by other Greeks, for what had happened to Orchomenus in 364 and Plataea in 373 (**Arrian,** *Anab.* I 9).

Meanwhile the Boeotian ascendancy had made firm allies of two erstwhile foes, Athens and Sparta. Thebes had actually been one of the first members of the Second Athenian League (Harding, Nr. 35), but regardless of whether or not it ever officially withdrew, its membership had effectively ended by 373 at the latest with the destruction of Plataea. Already in the aftermath of Leuctra (in 371), Athens and Sparta had made an alliance (Xen. *Hell.* VI 5,1–2). The Athenians sent troops to the Peloponnese in support of the Lacedaemonians in 369 (Xen. *Hell.* VI 5,49), renewed their alliance with Sparta in 368 (Xen. *Hell.* VII 1,1–14), and fought against the Boeotians on the Peloponnese in that year (Diod. XV 68–69; Xen. *Hell.* VII 1,15–21). When the Boeotians invaded Thessaly in 368, the Athenians assisted the Thessalians (Diod. XV 71). Thus, when the Boeotians invaded Arcadia in 362 – intervening in a quarrel within the Arcadian League on behalf of Tegea against Mantinea – the Mantineans and those Arcadians allied with them promptly appealed to both Athens and Sparta for aid (Xen. *Hell.* VII 4,33–5,3; Diod. XV 82). Both responded.

In 362, the Boeotians and their allies fought at Mantinea against the Lacedaemonians, the Athenians, and their allies. The result was in theory a victory for the Boeotians as great as Leuctra (Xen. *Hell.* VII 5,4–25; Diod. XV 82–87 [Xenophon's account of the battle is better; for criticism of that in Diodorus, based on Ephorus, see Pol. XII 25f]), but Epaminondas himself fell in the fighting, and the Boeotian troops did not pursue their fleeing opponents after the battle. In the opinion of Ephorus (*BNJ* 70, Fr. 119; see also Diod. XV 79,2 and Pol., VI 43,6) the Boeotian dominance in Greece had rested on the ability of Epaminondas alone, and with his death it ended.

After the Battle of Mantinea, one last Common Peace came into being. For once Persian involvement is not attested; as the Messenians swore this Peace too, the Lacedaemonians refused to participate (Diod. XV 89).

QUESTIONS FOR REVIEW

1 How did the Lacedaemonians manipulate the terms of the King's Peace to their advantage?
2 What way around the Lacedaemonians' interpretation of the King's Peace did the Athenians find?
3 How did the Athenians' proposed definition of autonomy serve two purposes?
4 What new and old *ethne* are rising to prominence in this period?
5 What changes to the political landscape in Greece did the Boeotians make from 371 to 362?

QUESTION FOR FURTHER STUDY

Why did the diplomacy of the period from 386 to 362 fail so spectacularly at establishing a lasting peace? Did the diplomatic documents produced actually create more uncertainty and more opportunities for conflict? Or was the diplomacy of the period merely an instrument for gaining an advantage in ongoing conflicts?

FURTHER READING

In addition to the works listed at the end of Chapter 15 under the heading "general," see also the following:
Stylianou, P.J. (1998) *A Historical Commentary on Diodorus Siculus Book 15.* Oxford.

On the second Athenian League:
Cargill, J. (1981) *The Second Athenian League: Empire or Free Alliance?* Berkeley.

On Boeotia and the Boeotian Hegemony:
Buckler, J. (1980) *The Theban Hegemony.* Cambridge.
Buckler, J. (2008) *Central Greece and the Politics of Power.* Cambridge.

17

The West from the Sicilian Expedition to the Campaigns of Timoleon

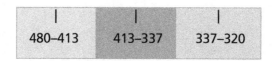

480–413	413–337	337–320

Introduction

The Sicilian Expedition (see chap. 14) brought the political history of the West into dramatic contact with that of mainland Greece, and the Syracusans' defeat of the Athenians materially affected developments on the mainland. Such

A History of Greece: 1300 to 30 BC, First Edition. Victor Parker.
© 2014 Victor Parker. Published 2014 by John Wiley & Sons, Ltd.

Figure 17.1   Third-century BC theater of Syracuse. Source: Victoria from London, UK, http://commons.wikimedia.org/wiki/File:Theatre_at_Syracuse,_Sicily.jpg (accessed 12th February 2013) CC BY 2.0

conjunctions between West and mainland were rare, however, and tend to be limited to military interventions by mainlanders in Western affairs (e.g., the campaigns of Pyrrhus – see chap. 22). The long periods without such an intervention should not, however, lead to the conclusion that the West and mainland Greece were separate entities in other respects. On the contrary, both West and mainland belonged to the same culture (see Figure 22.2) and shared in the same sense of "Greekness."

Architecturally there is little which is so quintessentially Greek as a theater (see Figures 1.6, 1.8, 11.2, and 12.2), and no Greek city in the West could dispense with one. The dramas performed in the theater of Syracuse (see Figure 17.1) were often the latest from the Athenian stage (see chap. 11); and many of the finest depictions of scenes from Attic tragedy come from Sicilian vases (see Figure 17.2). In fact, the Syracusans enjoyed Euripides' plays so much, that after the defeat of the Sicilian Expedition in 413 fleeing Athenians were allegedly spared if they could quote at length from these plays (Plut. *Nic.* 29).

Figure 17.2   A scene from Euripides' *Alcmene* (the title character sits between the gods Zeus and Hermes) on a Sicilian crater from the mid-fourth century). Source: akg-images / Erich Lessing

As far as religion went, the Westerners were again Greek (see briefly chap. 2); and they built temples to the same gods in the same architectural styles as on the mainland (see Figure 17.3; cf. Figures 1.8, 7.3, and 11.1). Moreover, the Panhellenic festivals and sanctuaries in Greece proper meant just as much to the Westerners as to the mainlanders. Westerners attended and competed in the Olympic Games (see, for example, Pindar's *Second* and *Tenth Olympian Odes* in honor of Theron of Acragas and Hagesidamus of Locri Epizephyrii; Diod. XIV 109) and made dedications there (Hdt. I 170; Fornara, Nr. 64; Diod. XVI 57).

The same intellectual currents flowed in the West and on the mainland. Historians from Aegean Greece (e.g., Ephorus of Cyme – *BNJ* 70) included the West in their works; and the West produced important historians of its own (e.g., **Timaeus** of Tauromenium – *BNJ* 566). When Dio sought a benign advisor for his nephew, the Syracusan tyrant Dionysius II, he invited the philosopher Plato to journey from Athens to Sicily. The distances which tended to keep the political history of the West discrete from that of the mainland had no effect on matters of culture.

Figure 17.3   Fifth-century temple of Hera at Acragas. Source: poudou99, http://commons.wikimedia.org/wiki/File:Agrigente_2008_IMG_1909.JPG (accessed 12th February 2013) CC BY-SA 3.0

There was, however, one political link which not even distance could sever. All the cities in the West were colonies of cities in Aegean Greece (see chap. 5). The ties that bound mother-city and colony remained vital for centuries. Even in the fourth century a Syracusan might, as Dionysius II indeed did in his retirement, return "home" to Corinth, Syracuse's mother-city; and a colony in distress in any case turned to its mother-city as unerringly as the needle to the pole.

Sicily after the Defeat of the Sicilian Expedition

The impetus for Athenian involvement on Sicily during the Peloponnesian War had come from the Elymian city of Segesta (or Egesta) in the island's northwest. Segesta had been quarreling with the nearby Greek city of Selinus over some disputed land and asked Athens for aid (Thuc. VI 6; Diod. XII 82–83). With the collapse of Athens' great expedition (see chap. 14), the Segestans, bereft of allies, yielded the land to Selinus. However, this no longer satisfied the Selinuntians, who demanded more, with the result that the frightened Segestans now appealed to Carthage (Diod. XIII 43).

There had been peace between Greeks and Carthaginians on Sicily for two generations, but Hannibal, the grandson of Hamilcar, the losing general at Himera in 480 (see chap. 10), happened to be one of the two **suffetes** ("judges" – the chief executives of Carthage) in that year. Hannibal persuaded the Carthaginian Council to grant him an army (Diod. XIII 43–44), some 100,000 strong, against Selinus in 409 (Timaeus, *BNJ* 566, Fr. 103). Against so large an army the Selinuntians could do little, and Hannibal took their town and destroyed it (Diod. XIII 54–59). Then he marched on Himera and destroyed it as well. Having avenged his grandfather, he returned home (Diod. XIII 60–62), but a long series of wars between Greeks and Carthaginians had begun.

In 409 and 408 Hermocrates, a Syracusan politician, undertook a private war against the Carthaginians. With mercenaries he occupied Selinus and began raiding Carthaginian territory (Diod. XIII 63). In 406 the Carthaginians responded with a second invasion. Hannibal and a cousin, Himilco, led 120,000 troops (Timaeus, *BNJ* 566, Fr. 25) over to Sicily. They landed on the southern coast and marched on the Greek city of Acragas which they besieged. Plague in the Carthaginian camp (Hannibal himself died) as well as a Syracusan relief force's victory over a detachment of the Carthaginian army almost derailed the Carthaginian offensive. However, the cautious Greek generals refused to follow up that victory; and just as it seemed that hunger would destroy the Carthaginians, with forty ships Himilco intercepted Greek ships bringing supplies to Acragas. Now it was the Acragantines' turn to starve. With supplies running low, they evacuated the city. (Diod. XIII 80–90).

The Rise of Dionysius I, Tyrant of Syracuse

In the meantime the political situation at Syracuse had altered. Shortly after the death of Hiero, the victor of Cumae (see chap. 10), in 467, the tyranny in Syracuse had yielded to a democracy. Now the Syracusans consented once more to live under a tyranny. A man called Dionysius became tyrant in 406 (Diod. XIII 91–92), and it was he who would lead the Greeks against the Carthaginians over the next four decades.

After taking Acragas, Himilco next marched on Gela (405). Here 30,000 Syracusan troops (Timaeus, *BNJ* 566, Fr. 107) including allies from Italy made a combined attack which, however, failed when Dionysius could not carry out his part of the plan. Dioynsius then decided to evacuate Gela and to bring its population, together with the refugees from Acragas, to Syracuse. Camarina, which lay on the coast to the east of Gela, was evacuated as well. These actions incurred great unpopularity (the Syracusan cavalry revolted against the tyrant) (Diod. XIII 108–113), but Dioynsius may have judged them necessary before an overwhelming Carthaginian army. In late 405 Dionysius and the Carthaginians made peace. The treaty allowed the refugees from Selinus, Acragas, Himera, Gela, and Camarina to return to their cities which, however, were to remain unfortified and to pay tribute to Carthage. The Carthaginians' sovereignty over their colonies on the island as well as over the non-Greek Elymians and **Sicanians** was confirmed. Dionysius was to hold Syracuse, and the other cities and peoples on Sicily (named are the non-Greek Sicels as well as the Greek cities of Leontini and Messene) were to have their freedom (Diod. XIII 114). With that, Himilco returned to Carthage.

Dionyius used the time which he had won well. He constructed massive fortifications on the island of Ortygia, where the original settlement of Syracuse had lain (see chap. 5); he put down a revolt (Diod. XIV 7–8); and with the help of traitors he seized the Greek cities of Catane and Naxos and sold their inhabitants into slavery. Leontini fared a little better; its people were merely relocated to Syracuse (Diod. XIV 15). With the exception of Messene, with which he made an alliance (Diod. XIV 40), Dionysius had brought what was left of Greek Sicily under his control. He next rebuilt the Syracusan army from the ground up with special emphasis on siege artillery (Diod. XIV 41–43).

Box 17.1   *The Younger Tyrants*

In the fourth century tyrannies appeared again. Dionysius I was the most successful of these so-called younger tyrants who came to power mostly in response to the fourth century's endemic warfare. Dionysius I provides a clear instance of this since the period when no tyrants reigned in Syracuse (467 to 406) largely coincided with an unbroken era of peace. When hostilities with the Carthaginians flared anew, Dionysius I became tyrant; and his reign (406–367) consisted largely of wars against them.

In mainland Greece as well, tyrants rose again, so in both the West and the mainland trends coincided even if developments took place discretely. Jason and his successors ruled over the Thessalian city of Pherae as tyrants from the 370s to the 350s. Jason's assassination in 370 may have ended his ambitious plans for conquest, and his successors such as his nephew Alexander and sons Tisiphonus and Lycophron may have had little success miltarily given whom they had to contend against (e.g., Epaminondas), but the Pheraean tyrants too appear to have functioned principally as warlords. Euphron of Sicyon (368–366), after his election as a general, made himself tyrant at the head of mercenaries he had hired (Xen. *Hell.* VII 1,44–46; 2,11; 3,1–12). Other tyrants such as Themison of Eretria (mid- to late 360s; Diod. XV 76) are too poorly known for much comment under this aspect.

Other than in their pronounced military role, these younger tyrants did not differ materially from their older predecessors. The same sorts of vicious stories that circulated about the older tyrants were told of them too. Moreover, they too viewed their rule as hereditary, and successful tyrants passed it on to a son or at least kept it in the family. There were successful tyrant dynasties in Heracleia Pontica (**Memnon**, *BNJ* 434, Fr.1.1–4) as well as in a far-flung corner of the Greek world, in Panticapaeum and

Phanagoreia (old Milesian and Megarian colonies respectively) on the Cimmerian Bosporus, the so-called Kingdom of the Bosporus (Diod. XII 31). In theory and vocabulary Plato (and others such as Xenophon) may have distinguished between "tyrants" and "kings," but in practice Plato made no distinction and could envision his "philosopher-king" as coming from either group (see Box 17.2).

Underpinning these new tyrants' rule intellectually was the era's prevailing political thought. The soldier and historian Xenophon held up before his readers numerous monarchs as ideal rulers in a profusion of literary genres. First, there was the biography of Agesilaus, the King of Sparta from circa 400 to 360. The strong idealizing tendency of this tract emerges in comparison with the treatment of Agesilaus in Xenophon's *Hellenica*. Second, Xenophon composed a philosophical dialogue, the *Hiero*, with that tyrant of Syracuse (478 to 467) as an ideal ruler. Finally, there is the sprawling historical romance, the *Cyropaedia* ("Education of Cyrus"), with the non-Greek Cyrus the Great incorporating the ideal.

Xenophon was not alone in looking up to kings and tyrants. The pamphleteer Isocrates presented Evagoras, the king of the Cyprian city of Salamis, in much the same fashion (e.g., *Evagoras*). And a far more sophisticated thinker than either Xenophon or Isocrates, the philosopher Plato, conceived of the ideal state as ruled by a monarch, the "philosopher-king." His ideas influenced many tyrants. Clearchus of Heracleia Pontica even studied under him (Memnon, *BNJ* 434, Fr. 1.1). Finally, Plato traveled to Syracuse to turn Dionysius II into a "philosopher-king" (see Box 17.2).

Dionysius I and the Carthaginians

In 397 Dionysius was ready. He led an army of 80,000 across the island; won Camarina, Gela, Acragas, Himera, and Selinus over; and laid siege to the Carthaginian city of Motya in the northwest. The Sicanians as well as the city of Eryx joined him, and he raided the few cities which remained loyal to the Carthaginians (Diod. XIV 47–48). A Carthaginian fleet sent out to assist the Motyans could do little, and Dionysius took the city. His army began to slaughter the inhabitants, but Dionysius intervened so that he could convert the survivors into cash on the slave market (Diod. XIV 50–53).

In 396, however, Himilco reappeared in Sicily with an army even larger than Dionysius' – 100,000 with an additional 30,000 levied on Sicily (Timaeus, *BNJ* 566, Fr. 108). Himilco landed near Panormus on the northern coast, marched to Eryx which he took by treachery, and thence to Motya. Before so large an army Dionysius, who had been besieging Segesta, retreated to Syracuse (Diod. XIV 55).

Himilco then marched across the island to Messene. When the inhabitants fled into the hills, Himilco razed the city. Then he founded a new city near the old site of Naxos, Tauromenium, and settled Sicels there (Diod. XIV 56–59). As Himilco moved southwards with his army and fleet, Dionysius led his own

army and fleet northwards. The two fleets fought off Catane, but the numerically superior Carthaginians, with 500 or 600 (Diod. XIV 56) ships, defeated
the Greeks easily (Diod. XIV 59–60). Thereupon Dionysius retreated behind
the walls of Syracuse (Diod. XIV 61), the sole bit of Sicily not yet under
Carthaginian control.

Like Nicias some years earlier (see chap. 14), Himilco now laid siege to Syracuse (Diod. XIV 62–63). But the walls were strong, and the Carthaginians were
weakened by an outbreak of plague (Diod. XIV 70–71). But what broke the
siege was an attack, as daring as it was ruthless, which Dionysius personally
led. On a moonless night, he brought 1,000 mercenaries with his cavalry to the
west of the Carthaginian camp. The mercenaries thought that the Syracusan
cavalry would support their attack, but Dionysius was throwing their lives away
in a diversion. When the mercenaries attacked, Dionysius left them in the lurch
(the Carthaginians annihilated them), rode round the camp with his horsemen,
and then led the real attack in the east against the Carthaginian forts by the
harbor (see Diod. XIV 63). In the meantime the Syracusans' fleet fell on
the Carthaginians' in another surprise attack. Dionysius captured the forts, and
large numbers of Carthaginian ships were destroyed before they could be
manned (Diod. XIV 72–74).

After this reverse, Himilco negotiated with Dionysius who, against receipt of
300 talents, let Himilco, together with all Carthaginians in his army, withdraw
by sea in some forty ships that remained of the Carthaginian fleet (Diod. XIV
75). Although it had been a closely run affair, Dionysius had succeeded in
breaking the Carthaginians' dominion over much of the island, a dominion
established by the treaty of 405 which he himself had concluded with them.
Now the Carthaginians were confined to the northwest of the island; at some
point they founded the city of Lilybaeum to replace the destroyed Motya (Diod.
XV 73).

In the next few years Dionysius strengthened his grip on the island's east.
He rebuilt Messene. He captured a few towns of the Sicels as well as the
Carthaginian colony of Solus (Diod. XIV 78), but an attack on Tauromenium
failed (Diod. XIV 87–88). In 393, however, Mago, now the Carthaginian
commander in northwestern Sicily, improved the Carthaginians' position.
He accepted refugees from Dionysius' dominions, made alliances with the
Sicels, and even raided Messene. But Dionysius' army was evidently larger than
Mago's, and under such circumstances Dionysius was happy to give battle,
easily defeating Mago (Diod. XIV 90). The Carthaginians in response sent
80,000 troops to Sicily. With these Mago was at least a match for Dionysius,
but neither side desired to risk everything in one battle. Dionysius' troops were
deserting him, and Mago was apparently having difficulty supplying his own.
A peace treaty was concluded whereby this time Dionysius had sovereignty over
the Sicels; moreover Tauromenium was ceded to him (Diod. XIV 95–96). No
other provisions are attested, but the peace was clearly efficacious since in the
next few years Dionysius campaigned in Italy with no fear of Carthaginian
attacks on Sicily.

Dionysius I in Italy

As early as 393 Dionysius had attacked Rhegium on the Italian side of the strait, opposite Messene. The attack had failed, but since the non-Greek Lucanians were menacing the Greek cities in Italy anyway, many of the latter formed a defensive alliance – both against the Lucanians and against Dionysius (Diod. XIV 90–91).

In 391 Dionysius, his back guarded by the treaty with the Carthaginians, brought an army across the strait to Italy. He had apparently secured Locri Epizephyrii (just up the coast from Rhegium on the east) as an ally, so he landed there, marched on Rhegium, and besieged it. Other Greek cities in Italy (Croton and Thurii are named or implied) stood by Rhegium and sent a fleet to hinder the siege. Eventually Dioynsius was forced to retreat to Messene. He then formed an alliance with the Lucanians and, it seems, persuaded them to attack Thurii. Dionysius' brother, Leptines, commanded the Syracusan fleet in the next year and was supposed to assist the Lucanians by sea, but after Leptines had picked up some Thurian survivors from a battle which the Thurians had lost against the Lucanians, he negotiated an armistice between the two. Dionysius, not surprisingly, relieved his brother of the command shortly thereafter (Diod. XIV 100–102).

Dionysius went on the attack again in 389. This time he laid siege to Caulonia, a small Achaian colony a little up the coast, on the west, from Rhegium. Another Achaian colony, Croton, sent aid to Caulonia, but Dionysius surprised and defeated those troops. In fact, he managed to capture some 10,000 prisoners whom he – for once – graciously set free. The magnanimous gesture worked, and most of the Greek cities in Italy now made peace with Dionysius. This left him free to capture Caulonia in 398 as well as, in the next year, Hipponium (a Locrian colony, opposite Caulonia, on the eastern coast). He transferred the inhabitants of both cities to Syracuse and awarded their territory to the Epizephyrian Locrians. In 387 Dionysius besieged Rhegium, now bereft of allies, and after an eleven months' siege, he took it. He allowed those Rhegines who had the money to ransom themselves, the rest he sold into slavery (Diod. XIV 103–112).

In the next few years Dionysius founded several colonies on the Adriatic Sea – Lissus and Issa on the eastern side, Ancona and Hadria on the western side. Additionally, he assisted the Parians in founding a colony on the island of Pharos (Diod. XV 13) near Issa. Dionysius also took the city of Croton (Dion. Hal. *Rom.Ant.*, XX 7). The paucity of the evidence hinders analysis of this activity, but one may suggest two possible motives: profit from trade in the Adriatic and access to a pool of Celtic mercenaries. Dionysius had need of both. Unfortunately for him, the peace with Carthage which had allowed this tremendous expansion of his power was now fraying.

Dionysus had made alliances with some cities which the Carthaginians regarded as dependent on them, and the Carthaginians responded by making alliances with Greek towns in Italy not under Dionysius' control. In 379 the two sides came to blows. Two battles were fought, the first at an unknown place called Cabala (a Syracusan victory) and the second at Cronium near Panormus. This time the Carthaginians won decisively and in the negotiations for peace Dionysius agreed to pay a thousand talents to the Carthaginians as well as to accept the River Halycus (midway between Selinus and Acragas on the southern coast) as a boundary between the Carthaginian and the Syracusan dominions (Diod. XV 15–17). In Italy the Carthaginians wrested Hipponium from Dionysius and gave it back to the previous inhabitants (Diod. XV 24).

The next ten years are a blank. In 368, however, Dionysius tried one last time to dislodge the Carthaginians from Sicily. He won Selinus and even captured Eryx in the northwest, but his attempt at besieging Lilybaeum failed. Additionally, the Carthaginians captured much of his fleet while it lay in Eryx' harbor. Dionysius died that same year after ruling Syracuse for 38 years (Diod. XV 73).

As a ruler he appears never to have enjoyed popularity (*Seventh Letter*, Pp. 331d–332c), and frequent mutinies always kept him on his guard – he is the tyrant who in the famous story of the sword of Damocles continually sat with a sword suspended over his head by a single thread (**Cicero**, *Tusc.* V 61). An acute need for money characterizes his administration, and financing his wars must have imposed great hardships on his subjects. Yet his overall success speaks for itself. To his son, also called Dionysius, he left behind an empire which stretched from the Halycus on Sicily across the straits and into southern Italy, with outposts on the Adriatic Sea. Finally, Dionysius also fancied himself a poet. He wrote tragedies, one of which, *The Ransom of Hector*, even won the first prize at a festival in Athens (Diod. XV 74; Snell, *TGF* 76, T. 3). Too little of his poetry survives to form an opinion on its quality now, and one may doubt that ancient critics, given who Dioynsius was, judged it dispassionately. All the same, it shows another side of the tyrant; and his participating in the dramatic festivals at Athens as well as staged recitals of his poetry at Olympia (Diod. XIV 109) shows that he maintained contact, at least culturally, with mainland Greece.

The Successors of Dionysius I

Dionysius II is best known as the rather unwilling pupil of the philosopher Plato who vainly attempted to turn him into the "philosopher-king" envisaged in the dialogue *The Republic* (see Box 17.2). Despite Plato's efforts, Dionysius II became a cruel and unpopular ruler, and the empire which he had inherited soon broke apart. His father had also bequeathed to him an overbearing and ambitious advisor in his uncle Dio as well as the unpleasant task of securing peace with the Carthaginians after the last inconclusive war. In 367 he concluded peace. He also sent Dio into banishment (Diod. XVI 5–6; Plut. *Dio*, 14). Over the next few years Dionysius II expanded Syracusan power in the

---

Box 17.2 *The Seventh Platonic Letter and the "Philosopher-King"*

The so-called *Seventh Letter* of Plato deals with Plato's attempts in the 360s to educate the young Dionysius II. If genuine, the letter is of incalculable value both historically and autobiographically. Even if forged, it is still valuable historically since it was apparently written close to the events which it describes. The argument is complicated (and here omitted), but the historian Ephorus, who cannot have been writing later than the 330s, already knew the *Seventh Letter*.

Plato, like most aristocrats, nursed an abiding distrust of democracy. After all, the restored democracy in Athens had in 399 executed his teacher Socrates. Plato's tract, the *Apology*, gives a moving version of Socrates' defense which among other things makes the democracy appear brutal and capricious for executing so wise and noble a man. In his best-known dialogue, the *Republic*, Plato designs an ideal state – a monarchy with a philosopher-king as its ruler. In one passage he reflects on the possibility of such a ruler existing in reality: either a philosopher would have to become a ruler or "by some divine inspiration a true love of true philosophy might arise either in one of the current dynasts or kings or in one of their sons" (*Rep.* 499b).

In the *Seventh Letter* Plato's undertaking to educate Dionysius II is justified as follows:

> If ever anyone were to make the attempt to achieve the things which I had in mind regarding laws and constitutions, the time to try was now: for I would sufficiently accomplish all good things if I won over one single man . . . Mostly I was ashamed lest I should appear to myself to be just a theorist and unwilling to set my hand to any deed. (*Seventh Letter*, 328b–c).

In 366 Plato came to Syracuse and attempted to win Dionysius II over. Unfortunately for Plato, Dionysius II was not exactly an apt pupil and the *Seventh Letter* recounts Plato's disappointment at Dionysius II's inability to comprehend philosophy. Moreover, Dio and Plato esteemed each other highly, and this grated on Dionysius II who was quarreling with Dio. Plato left Dionysius II on bad terms and returned to Athens after about a year. In 361, however, Dionysius II invited him back, and Plato journeyed to Syracuse again to make one last attempt. It met with the same success as the first, and Plato was lucky to escape with his life.

Adriatic and Italy with foundations of colonies in Apulia and with a war against the Lucanians (Diod. XVI 5 and 10). None other than Plato helped him form ties with the philosopher and politician Archytas of Taras (Plut. *Dio*, 18).

If Dionysius II had let his exiled uncle Dio live out his days abroad in peace, his rule might have continued longer. Instead, Dionysius II confiscated Dio's estate and even forced Dio's wife, who had remained in Syracuse, to marry another man (Plut. *Dio*, 18–19 and 21). Provoked beyond endurance, Dio decided to make his own play for power.

He returned to Sicily in 357 with a handful of mercenaries and landed on the southern coast, to the west of the River Halycus. He collected supporters as he marched towards Syracuse. Fortunately for him, Dionsysius II was away with the fleet in Italy, so when Dio entered Syracuse, he easily gained control of the city, except for the heavily fortified island in the harbor (Diod. XVI 9–12; Plut. *Dio*, 25–29). Although fighting against Dionysius II's supporters on the island went on for some time, the actual issue was settled. When Dionysius II's fleet sailed against Syracuse, a Syracusan fleet loyal to Dio defeated it (Diod. XVI 16). Dionysius II withdrew to Locri Epizephyrii in Italy, where he continued to rule as the rest of his empire fell apart (Strab. VI 1,8, p. 260).

In Syracuse Dio ruled as a tyrant, but only briefly as Callipus assassinated him in 354 (Plut. *Dio*, 56–58). Callipus himself was tyrant for a year (Diod. XVI 31), before Hipparinus, a son of Dionysius I's by his second marriage, returned and seized control. Hipparinus ruled for two years (Diod. XVI 36), and his brother Nysaeus thereafter for another five or so (Plut. *Tim.* 1). In 346 Dionysius II decided to exploit the confused circumstances in Syracuse and returned from Locri Epizephyrii. The Epizephyrian Locrians, meanwhile, rose up against the garrison which he had left behind, and regained their independence (Strab. l.c.).

Timoleon on Sicily

In 344 the Syracusans, devastated by the civil wars and the near anarchy – and worried by the presence of a Carthaginian fleet – appealed to their mother-city, Corinth, for help (Diod. XVI 67). It seemed a hopeless appeal since Philip, the King of Macedonia, having just brought the Phocian War to an end, was busily tightening his grip in Greece (see chap. 18). Yet Corinth always took its maternal obligations seriously, and sent what it could: a thousand mercenaries under the command of the aristocrat Timoleon, who lived under a curious shadow in Corinth. He had slain a would-be tyrant (and so won his fellow citizens' praise) who, however, was his own brother (and so incurred opprobrium as a slayer of kin). As Timoleon left Corinth, it was said that if his mission in the West prospered, then he would have slain a tyrant; but if it failed, then he would have murdered his brother (Diod. XVI 65).

With his modest troop of mercenaries, Timoleon set sail for the West. When he put in at Rhegium, he found both a Carthaginian fleet and envoys from a man called Hicetas waiting for him. Hicetas, having in the meantime gained control over Syracuse as tyrant and having shut Dionysius II up on the island of Ortygia, had reached an accommodation with the Carthaginians. So Timoleon was politely asked to return home. With equal politeness, Timoleon insisted on discussing matters in the Rhegine assembly. Here, with the Rhegines' active connivance, Timoleon wasted both the envoys' and the Carthaginian commanders' time while his troops got his ships under sail. Timoleon himself left the assembly just in time to leap aboard the last ship – the Carthaginian commanders realized too late what had happened.

Timoleon next put in at Tauromenium. A civil war had broken out in the nearby Sicel town of Hadranum, and factions there appealed both to Hicetas and to Timoleon. Hicetas arrived first, but Timoleon on arrival caught Hicetas' troops unawares and attacked them. With an easy victory behind him, Timoleon took control of Hadranum (Diod. XVI 68; Plut. *Tim.* 9–12). At this point Dionysius II, whose once mighty empire had shrunk to Ortygia, wearied of living trapped in the fortress there. He offered Ortygia to Timoleon in exchange for permission to go to Corinth to live out his days in peace. Timoleon acquiesced and thus gained Ortygia without the striking of a blow (Plut. *Tim.* 13; cf. Diod. XVI 70).

Hicetas still held Syracuse, but it was mostly thanks to Carthaginian support: 150 Carthaginian ships lay in the harbor and a Carthaginian force stood in the city itself (Plut. *Tim.* 13 and 16–17; otherwise Diod. XVI 68–69). However, whatever assignment the Carthaginian commander, Mago, did have, it was not to prop up Hicetas indefinitely. When Mago took his fleet back to Carthage, Hicetas lost control of Syracuse (Diod. XVI 69; cf. Plut. *Tim.* 18). Timoleon established democracy in the city, restored its population (depleted by the civil wars) by advertising for immigrants from mainland Greece, and suppressed tyrants in the other Greek cities on the island (Diod. XVI 70, 72–73; Plut. *Tim.* 22–24).

In 339 the Carthaginians finally invaded. They brought an army of (allegedly) 70,000 infantry and 10,000 cavalry to the island's west (Diod. XVI 77; Plut. *Tim.* 25); against this host Timoleon could muster (allegedly) a mere 12,000, of whom a thousand shortly deserted anyway (Diod. XVI 78–79; Plut. *Tim.* 25, has even smaller numbers). That the numbers have been shaded a bit to emphasize the David-and-Goliath nature of the contest is eminently probable. The two armies met at the River Crimisus near Entella. As luck would have it, Timoleon's troops caught the Carthaginians as they were crossing the river (Diod. XVI 79; Plut. *Tim.* 27). Initially the Greeks were winning, but as more and more Carthaginian troops reached the opposite bank, the latter gained momentum. Then a blinding rainstorm blew up – behind the Greeks and into the Carthaginians' faces. Since the Carthaginians were wearing heavier armor, in the wet and mud they fought at a distinct disadvantage (Diod. XVI 80–81; Plut. *Tim.* 28). However much the story's details may have been adjusted for dramatic effect, the fact remains that Timoleon returned victorious to Syracuse (Diod. XVI 81; Plut. *Tim.* 30).

He had to confront several tyrants again (including Hicetas who had set himself up in Leontini), but, as one might expect, defeated them. Peace was arranged with Carthage (Diod. XVI 82–83; Plut. *Tim.* 31–35), and Timoleon, to whom the Syracusans granted an estate near their city (Plut. *Tim.* 36), retired there and died in 337 (Diod. XVI 90).

The Greeks in Italy

About the same time as Syracuse appealed to Corinth, the Tarantines, whom the non-Greek Lucanians were now attacking, sought help from their mother-city, Sparta. By 345, Sparta's best days were long past, and men such as King Archidamus III chafed at the want of opportunities to display their martial talents. So Archidamus, gathering together some mercenaries left over from the Phocian War (see chap. 18), departed from Sparta for Taras to seek fortune and glory there. He led the Tarantine forces for some seven years before falling in a battle against the Lucanians in 338 (Diod. XVI 62–63 and 88).

Deprived of one defender, Taras in 334 appealed to Alexander of Epirus (brother-in-law to Philip and uncle to Alexander the Great) for help. Alexander, it seems, had more success than Archidamus. He defeated the Tarantines' foes and then turned to rescue other Greek cities such as Heracleia on the Gulf of Taranto and Terina on the western coast. The new rising power in central Italy, Rome, which had slowly displaced the Etruscans as the major power there, even made a treaty with him. When a Lucanian exile assassinated Alexander in 331, it made little difference to the overall result – he had succeeded in shoring up the Greek cities' position against the Italian tribes in the interior (Liv. VIII 3, 17, and 24; Just. XII 2).

Away to the north, however, the Greeks on the Bay of Naples, where Euboean settlers had founded Cumae in the mid-eighth century (see chap. 5), fared more poorly. After the successful conclusion of a war in Campania the dominion of the new Italian power, Rome, extended to the territory of Neapolis (Naples), a daughter-city of Cumae's, which by now was the most important Greek city in the region (Liv. VIII 22). War broke out between Neapolis and Rome in the 320s. Although the Romans gained the upper hand, they could not take the fortified city by storm and, lacking a fleet, had no means to conduct an effective siege. The Neapolitans, however, apparently had little desire to see hostilities continue indefinitely. Unlike in 474, no Hiero appeared to deliver them from a central Italian enemy (see chap. 10). In negotiations the Romans proved reasonable, and the Neapolitans accepted their terms. Thus they became the first Greeks to fall under Roman dominion (Liv. *Per.* VIII).

QUESTIONS FOR REVIEW

1   What sorts of things show that the Greeks of the West shared the same culture as the Aegean Greeks?
2   In what stages did Dionysius I repel the Carthaginian threat and then consolidate his control over the Greeks of the West?
3   Why were there so many prominent tyrants/monarchs throughout the Greek world in this period?
4   How did Dionysius I's empire break apart under his successor?

5   How much of Timoleon's apparent success may be due to genuine luck and how much may be due to the sources' revising the material to make him appear luckier than he actually was?

QUESTION FOR FURTHER STUDY

Is the portrayal of Dionysius I in this chapter a fair one? Diodorus' account (see Pearson in Further Reading and commentary to *BNJ* 70, Frr. 219–221) is based on Timaeus' (*BNJ* 566) who for reasons of his own was unrelentingly hostile to Dionysius I and everyone associated with him, such as Philistus (*BNJ* 556) who actually wrote positively about Dionysius I. To what extent is the negative impression which Dionysius I makes the result of Timaeus' hostile presentation?

FURTHER READING

Caven, B. (1990) *Dionysius I: War-lord of Sicily*. New Haven.
Pearson, L.I.C. (1987) *The Greek Historians of the West. Timaeus and his predecessors.* Atlanta.
Talbert, R.J. (1975) *Timoleon and the Revival of Greek Sicily, 344–317 B.C.* Cambridge.

On the younger tyrants overall:
Berve, H. (1967) *Die Tyrannis bei den Griechen*. Munich.

On the *Seventh Letter* of Plato:
Edelstein, L. (1966) *Plato's Seventh Letter*. Leiden. (Inauthentic.)
Solmsen, F. (1969) Review of Edelstein 1966, *Gnomon* 41: 29–34. (Authentic.)

18

Philip of Macedon and the Conquest of Greece

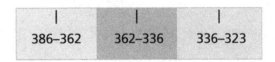

| 386–362 | 362–336 | 336–323 |

360	Philip II becomes ruler of Macedonia
357	Philip II makes alliance with Chalcidians
mid–350s	Social War
355–346	Phocian or Third Sacred War
349	Philip II conquers Chalcidians
346	Peace of Philocrates
338	Battle of Chaeroneia

Macedonia and the Macedonians

Macedonia lay on the periphery of the Greek world to the north of Thessaly (chap. 1). Leaving aside the difficult question of whether or not they were Greek, the Macedonians, in the eyes of their neighbors to the south, were a backward folk (Dem. IX 31) even if the splendid golden objects (see Figure 18.1) found at Vergina (ancient Aegae) suggest an aesthetically sophisticated society.

A History of Greece: 1300 to 30 BC, First Edition. Victor Parker.
© 2014 Victor Parker. Published 2014 by John Wiley & Sons, Ltd.

Figure 18.1   Gold ossuary from Philip II's tomb at Aegae; n.b. the sixteen-pointed "Star of Vergina" on the lid. Source: photo © Gianni Dagli Orti/Corbis

However that may be, the Macedonian aristocracy had long shown an interest in the "higher" culture down south. At the invitation of the Macedonian king Archelaus, the Athenian tragedian Euripides had spent his final years there (Diod. XIII 103; Paus. I 2,2), and years later a Macedonian officer could be represented, even in heated argument, as quoting Euripides (Plut. *Alex*. 51). When Philip II was looking for a tutor for his son, he chose Aristotle who gave the boy, Alexander the Great, a copy of the *Iliad* which he had personally annotated (Plut. *Alex*. 7–8) and from which Alexander could allegedly quote (Plut. *Alex*. 28). By the mid-fourth century aristocrats in Macedonia spoke standard Greek well enough, even if most Greeks could not understand "Macedonian" (**Curtius**, VI 9,35), and some Macedonians clearly understood "Macedonian" better than standard Greek (Plut. *Alex* 51). For whatever the cultural pretensions of the standard-Greek-speaking aristocracy, the soldiers in Philip's and Alexander's armies were rough mountaineers (from Upper Macedonia) and hardy farmers (from Lower Macedonia) who probably did not often quote from Euripides and "Homer."

Up until the fourth century the sources mention Macedonia only in passing – for the simple reason that events in Macedonia for the most part passed notice south of the Tempe Pass. However, the Macedonians had occasionally come into conflict with the Chalcidian League (chap. 16), as well as with Athens, which held outposts in the northern Aegean (chaps. 13–14). They were moreover involved in affairs in Thessaly in 369 (Diod. XV 61) with the result that when the Boeotians intervened in Thessaly, their commander, Pelopidas, had to deal with the Macedonians also (Diod. XV 67). Both the Boeotians and the Athenians intervened in dynastic struggles in Macedonia over the next few years (Plut. *Pel.* 26; Aesch. II 29), and conflicts between the Macedonians and the Athenians grew (Aesch. II 30). In the late 360s the Macedonian king, Perdiccas III, seized the old Athenian colony Amphipolis, to which the Athenians had never given up their claim (see chap. 13), and installed a garrison there (Diod. XVI 3).

Philip's Accession

In 360 BC Perdiccas III fell in battle against the Illyrians (Diod. XVI 2) and was replaced by his brother Philip whose accession was soon enough seen as a pivotal event. Theopompus (*BNJ* 115) began his major work, the *Philippica*, at this point, and, as the work's title shows, Theopompus, though no admirer of Philip, viewed him as the epoch's dominant figure. Philip initially was regent for Perdiccas' minor son, Amyntas IV (Just. VII 5,9–10; Arr. *BNJ* 156, Fr. 9.22), whom he later displaced on the throne. The Paeonians, whom the Macedonians had recently subjugated, exploited the confused circumstances to revolt against Macedonia, and, to make matters worse, two pretenders to the throne, Pausanias and Argaeus, challenged Philip's authority.

The Thracians backed the first and the Athenians the other (Diod. XVI 2). Perdiccas had brought much territory (including Amphipolis) east of the River Axius under Macedonian control, and this expansion eastwards had aroused the ire of the Thracians; and the taking of Amphipolis that of the Athenians. Both Athenians and Thracians were expecting something in return for their backing in the event of success: the Thracians wanted territory east of the Axius and the Athenians wanted Amphipolis back.

To each challenge Philip rose in turn, but he needed to buy time. He emptied his treasury to bribe the Thracians to pull the rug out from under Pausanias and the Paeonians to cease from hostilities against Macedonia. He put off the Athenians by withdrawing the Macedonian garrison from Amphipolis, thus affording them a fair opportunity to retake it. In return, the Athenians withdrew support from Argaeus whom Philip then defeated easily. Next, Philip made a surprise attack on the Paeonians and defeated them too. Finally, it was the Illyrians' turn and in a great battle Philip smashed their forces (Diod. XVI 3–4). This unsurpassed combination of military talent and diplomatic skill would aid him throughout his career.

In ca. 357 Philip reoccupied Amphipolis. This act alarmed the Chalcidian League and angered Athens so that both considered an alliance against Philip, but Philip offered the Athenians a deal first. The Athenians held two cities on the Macedonian coast, Pydna and Methone, which shut the Macedonians off from the sea. Philip accordingly proposed to swap the Athenians Amphipolis for Pydna. The Athenian *Boule* handled the matter in secret because the deal's success depended on the Pydnaeans' (and presumably the Amphipolitans') ignorance of what was about to happen. At the same time, members of the *Boule*, believing that they were getting from Philip what they most wanted, rejected the Chalcidians' proposal for an alliance (Dem. II 6 with Harding, Nr. 61; Diod. XVI 8).

Philip, however, double-crossed the Athenians. He retained Amphipolis while capturing Pydna by force and, additionally, the city of Potidaea, another Athenian possession. He offered the latter to the Chalcidians in exchange for an alliance and the Chalcidians, rebuffed by Athens, accepted (Harding, Nrr. 61 and 67; Diod. XVI 8). It was an ominous harbinger of things to come.

The Social War and the Development of the Second Athenian League

While Philip was consolidating his grip in Macedonia and making it a formidable power, the major states in Greece were steadily weakening. Sparta never recovered from the loss at Leuctra in 371, and after the Battle of Mantinea in 362 its king, Agesilaus, who had spent nearly four decades fighting to maintain Sparta's position, left Sparta and took service as a mercenary in the army of Tachos, the ruler of Egypt (Diod. XV 92–93) which had been in rebellion against the Persians for close on four decades (Diod. XIV 35 and 79). The Boeotian League, meanwhile, without the military genius of Epaminondas proved incapable of meeting the challenge which the Phocian War (see below) posed. The Athenians for their part had come off second best in their initial confrontation with Philip and were soon enough occupied by a major revolt among their allies, the so-called **Social War**. Byzantium, Chios, Cos, and Rhodes all revolted from the Second Athenian League, probably early in the year 356 (see Box 18.1). Mausolus, the Persian satrap of Caria, helped the rebels. The Athenians sent the generals Chabrias and Chares to Chios to besiege the city. However, the Chians broke the siege and defeated the Athenian infantry under Chares as well as the Athenian ships under Chabrias in the harbor; Chabrias himself fell in the fighting (Diod. XVI 7). For the moment, the rebels had free rein. With a fleet of a hundred ships they raided the Athenian islands of Imbros and Lemnos and actually besieged Samos. They apparently carried out other attacks on members of the Second Athenian League, but Diodorus gives no details. The Athenians managed to outfit sixty ships in addition to the sixty which had survived the engagement at Chios and sent them all against Byzantium. At this the rebels broke off the siege of Samos (Diod. XVI 21). The Athenian fleet then left the Propontis and sailed southwards towards Samos. However, just as a battle was being joined in the sound between Chios and the mainland, a major storm blew up (**Nepos**, *Timoth.* 3; Poly. III 9,29; on Diod. XVI 21, see Box 18.1). One Athenian general, Chares, wished to continue with the engagement, but his fellow commanders, Timotheus and Iphicrates, outvoted him. A furious Chares accused them of treason, and the Athenian assembly did indeed vote to remove them from office (probably in the winter of 356 to 355) (Diod. XVI 21).

Box 18.1   *Diodorus'* Historical Library *and the Difficulties with Using It*

Diodorus' vast compilatory work, the *Historical Library*, purports to give a complete history of the ancient Mediterranean world down to Diodorus' own day, the first century BC, in a year-by-year format. The entry for a given year begins with the Athenian archon and the Roman consuls for that year. This matter comes from Diodorus' so-called "Chronographic Source," a sort of almanac of rulers, dates, and important events. After the chronological matter, Diodorus places an account of events allegedly from the year in question. This account is an excerpt from whatever author Diodorus was using as his source for a given period or area. Diodorus did little original work, but produced condensed versions of others' books (see most clearly commentary to Ephorus, *BNJ* 70 Fr. 191; Ephorus was Diodorus' source for books XI to XV, minus the sections dealing with Sicily).

When using Diodorus, one has to distinguish between the material itself and Diodorus' arrangement of it. The latter causes problems. Until 362, when Xenophon's narrative ends, a second narrative source exists which either makes Diodorus redundant or allows for corrections. From 362 to 336 and from 323 until the 270s (insofar as his work has itself survived) Diodorus is the only surviving narrative source, so here the problems with his narrative become acute.

First, Diodorus' chronology is erratic. His statements on the Social War are a case in point. At XVI 7,3, in his entry for the year 358/57, Diodorus states that the Social War began and lasted for three years (i.e., with exclusive counting, from 358/57 to 355/54). In his entry for this last year, however, there stands no notice of the Social War's end. Instead, that notice comes at XVI 22,2, in the entry for 356/55 – with the additional remark that the war had lasted for four years (i.e., from 360/59 to 356/55).

Second, Diodorus' abridging can distort his source's account. According to Diod. XVI 21, an abortive battle between the Athenians and their opponents in the Social War took place in the Propontis, near Byzantium. Yet the battle (probably in 356) took place at Embata near Erythrae opposite Chios (Poly. III 9,29; Nep. *Timoth.* 3 – both based, like Diodorus, on Ephorus). Diodorus began with an account that proceeded thus:

1   the Athenians sailed into the Propontis and achieved nothing
2   the Athenians sailed southwards towards Samos and on the way met their
    opponents' fleet near Embata between Erythrae and Chios
3   the abortive battle took place

Diodorus omitted step two (so that the battle then appeared to take place in the Propontis), drew this false conclusion, and summarized accordingly.

Third, Diodorus' work contains frequent "doublets" – descriptions of one and the same event as though it had occurred twice. In ancient authors doublets arise either through faulty combination of two sources or when one source described the same event in two different contexts. In his narrative of the Phocian War, Diodorus has Philip conquer Methone once in his entry for 354/53 (XVI 31 – possibly from the "Chronographic Source") and again in his entry for 353/52 (XVI 34). Yet Philip clearly took Methone once only.

All of this makes using Diodorus frustrating. The material, as continuing investigation has repeatedly shown, is often sound since it comes from good sources, but Diodorus' presentation of the material commonly obscures its value.

Chares now had a free hand to prosecute the war as he saw fit; unfortunately, he had no money. So probably in 355 he joined forces with Artabazus, the satrap of Hellespontine Phrygia, who had revolted against the Persian king Artaxerxes III Ochus, and defeated royal troops in battle. In exchange for this aid, Artabazus provided Chares with the funds necessary for waging war against Athens' rebellious allies. But before Chares could begin with this, ambassadors from the king arrived in Athens and threatened that the Persians would soon attack Athens with a fleet of three hundred ships. The overawed Athenian assembly decided to end the Social War (Diod. XVI 22; Harding, Nr. 72), and presumably during 354 peace treaties between Athens and its rebellious allies were concluded (Diod. XVI 22).

On the basis of these treaties, Byzantium, Chios, Cos, and Rhodes all withdrew from the Second Athenian League (Isoc. VIII 16). In the treaties the Athenians apparently acknowledged that the cities involved were "autonomous" (Harding, Nr. 71; Dem. XV 26). The acknowledgment of the cities' "autonomy" raises the question of how the Second Athenian League had developed since the time of its founding in 377 – whether or not Athens had lived up to its promise, explicitly made in the League's Charter, to respect the allies' freedom and autonomy (see chap. 16). That document (Harding, Nr. 35) had defined the following as infringements of autonomy: the levying of tribute, the imposition of a garrison, the imposition of a governor, and interference in the choice of constitution.

To take the points in order: The Second Athenian League had to finance its military expeditions somehow, and it did so through the collection of *syntaxeis*, voluntary contributions, from its members. Yet the question remains just how voluntary this "contribution" was (see Harding, Nr. 36). For example, in the 330s Alexander the Great released the town of Priene from payment of a *syntaxis* – which is to say that the payment otherwise was obligatory (Harding, Nr. 106). Additionally, Demosthenes, in a disarmingly frank passage, explains that a large Athenian fleet was rather more successful in collecting a sizable *syntaxis* than a small one (Dem. VIII 25). The more firepower the collectors were packing, the more freely the money flowed. In other words, it was extortion; and the Athenians' treaty with Ceos in 362 shows how unsentimentally the Athenians proceeded with the collection of any money which they considered due them:

> *If they* [i.e., the Iulietae on Ceos] *do not pay at the prescribed time, then let those whom the (Athenian) Assembly has chosen to collect money collect (it) from them however they can* . . .
> (Harding, Nr. 55, lines 11–14.)

Garrisons, meanwhile, sprouted up all across the Second Athenian League. As early as 376 Chabrias had installed one in Abdera, a member of the League, albeit under circumstances which surely excused the action – heavy fighting against the Thracians to the north (Diod. XV 36). Nothing of the sort, however, excused the garrison present on Corcyra in 361 (**Aeneas the Tactician**, 11,13; Diod. XV 95). In 356, granted during the Social War when the rebellious allies were carrying out attacks all around the Aegean, the Athenians installed a garrison on Andros (Harding, Nr. 69). At the very least, all of this formally violated the League's Charter. The appointment of Athenian governors (on Amorgos and Andros – see Harding, Nrr. 68 and 69) during the Social War was another such violation; and even if the external situation made the installation of a garrison advisable, appointing Athenian governors did not logically follow from that. The same applies to the interference in an ally's internal affairs attested on Corcyra (Diod. XV 95) and on Ceos (Harding, Nr. 55). All of the states mentioned were members of the Second Athenian League (Harding, Nrr. 35, 41, and 42).

Meanwhile the Athenians had once again begun installing cleruchies. The earliest known cleruchy from the time of the Second Athenian League was that on Samos in 365 (Diod. XVIII 18). The Athenians sent out a second cleruchy to Samos in 361–60 and a third in 352–51 (Harding, Nr. 77 with note). At the time of the third cleruchy, all the original Samians were expelled; they did not return until 322 BC (Diod. l.c.). The Athenians additionally sent out cleruchs to Potidaea in 361–60 (Harding, Nr. 58) and to various cities on the Chersonese in 353 (Diod. XVI 34). No evidence exists that these cities were members of the League, but these acts demonstrated how Athens could exert its power when it chose, and they made clear both what might happen to a state which did not join the League as well as what might happen to one that dared leave.

The Athenians in the time of the Second Athenian League became oppressive and high-handed just as in the time of the First League. When they captured

Sestus in 353, they slew the men and enslaved the women and children (Diod. l.c.) as they had at Melos in 416. It is no wonder that states such as Byzantium, Chios, Cos, and Rhodes eventually rebelled and that by the end of the Social War some 75 states left the League (Aesch. II 70).

The Social War reduced this new Athenian Empire to a few remaining members of the League (e.g., Ceos, Amorgos, and Andros) and some possessions outside of the League both in the north (e.g. Methone) and in the Aegean (Lemnos, Imbros, Samos, and Euboea). In addition to this, Cersobleptes, the king of Thrace, in 353 gave the Athenians the Chersonese (except for the town of Cardia) in exchange for Athenian support against Philip (Diod. XVI 34,3–4). This was still a sizable "empire" even if only a shadow of either the First or the Second Athenian Leagues in their heyday. Far worse was the parlous state of Athens' finances once the *syntaxeis* ceased to flow in.

The Phocian or Third Sacred War

As for the Boeotian League, it suffered the most from the Phocians' attacks in what the Greeks called a Sacred War. Such a war was waged in defense of a shrine, in particular that of Apollo at Delphi. The Phocian War was the third such war. The second was a minor affair during the Pentecontaetia (Thuc. I 112), but two results of the more important First Sacred War in the early sixth century (see Box 18.2) have relevance for the beginning of the third war: First, the valley beneath Delphi (see Figure 1.8) down to the Gulf of Corinth was dedicated as land sacred to Apollo after the First Sacred War – land which could not be plowed, but which might be used for grazing animals or planting trees (Aesch. III 107–112). Second, after the First Sacred War jurisdiction over Delphi fell to the **Pylaean Amphictiony** (Strab. IX 3,7, p. 420), an organization of twelve "tribes" living on both sides of Thermopylae – Thessalians, Boeotians, Dorians, Ionians, Perrhaebians, Magnesians, Locrians (both western and eastern together), Oetaeans (=Aenianes), Phthiotic Achaians, Malians, Phocians (Aesch. II 116), and the Dolopians (with Paus. X 8 and Diod. XVI 29 – the Epirotic Athamanians mentioned there were not members in the fourth century).

Delphi had been the most important Panhellenic sanctuary since at least the seventh century when even foreign potentates such as Gyges of Lydia began to pay honor to it (Hdt. I 14). Year in, year out pilgrims – some extremely wealthy – made dedications there, often in precious metals. In the ancient world sanctuaries moreover functioned as banks where both states and individuals deposited funds under the gods' protection. Many of the buildings on the site of Delphi were not shrines but so-called treasuries (see Figure 18.2), and down to the year 355 the money had remained safe.

In 355, however, the Boeotians brought a charge of sacrilege – allegedly of cultivating the sacred land in the valley below Dephi – against the Phocians (Diod. XVI 23). Since the same charge of sacrilege which the Boeotians allegedly made against them recurs at the start of the Fourth Sacred War (see below),

Figure 18.2 The treasury of the Athenians at Delphi. Source: Ian W. Scott, http://commons.wikimedia.org/wiki/File:Athenian_Treasury.JPG (accessed 12th February 2013) CC BY-SA 3.0

where it is more credibly attested, one may legitimately wonder if its occurrence at the start of the Third Sacred War too is an historiographical construct. All the same, Greece was heavily overpopulated in the fourth century, and many communities surely felt pressure to take nearby marginal land under cultivation in order to obtain food. All along the edges of the valley below Delphi communities may have been doing this, especially if no one knew exactly where profane land ended and sacred land began. In any case, to what degree the Boeotians' accusation against the Phocians was political is now irrecoverable, but the Amphictionic Council did indeed saddle the Phocians with an astronomical fine (Diod. l.c.; cf. 29). Thereafter the entire affair rapidly became political.

The Phocians responded by electing an aristocrat named Philomelus as general with authority to implement a plan for asserting Phocian – as opposed to Amphictionic – control over Delphi (Diod. XVI 23). Philomelus received money and covert support from Sparta, since the Lacedaemonians detested the Boeotians, who had pressed the original charge. Philomelus recruited among

Box 18.2   *Delphi, the Amphictiony, and the First Sacred War (Early Sixth Century BC)*

Various sources recount how the city of Cirrha or Crisa (the older form), which lay on the Gulf of Corinth at the bottom of the valley below Delphi, had once controlled the sanctuary there. According to them the Pylaean Amphictiony from 595 to 586 waged the First Sacred War against Crisa for control of Delphi. In 591 the Amphictiony captured Crisa after having poisoned its water supply during a siege. Some Crisaeans, however, took to the hills and fought on until 586. Thereafter the members of the Amphictiony dedicated the land in the valley below Delphi to Apollo so that it became sacred land which might not be plowed. Finally, after the war's end the victors reorganized the Pythian Games, the Panhellenic festival which took place at Delphi, so that it now included athletic contests (Aesch., III 107–112; Callisthenes, *BNJ* 124 Fr. 1; Paus. X 37,4–5; Arg. Pind. *Pyth.* b and d).

Because none of these sources antedates the late fourth century, one scholar has argued that the story of the war arose then. However, as others immediately pointed out, Isocrates (XIV 31) referred to the war in the 370s (without, however, many details), so this extreme view has since been abandoned.

Moreover, certain elements in the stories of the First Sacred War can be corroborated, in particular the existence of a powerful city called Crisa which lay on the Corinthian Gulf which, however, had originally been called the "Crisaean Gulf" (thus consistently still in Thucydides). Yet that name cannot have arisen after the sixth century, because the name of the city itself had changed by then. Initially, it was "Crisa," but in the mid-sixth century the form was "Cirsa" (Alcaeus, Fr. 7 Lobel-Page), and by the fifth it was "Cirrha" (the usual form in Pindar and Aeschines). The name "Crisaean Gulf" was coined while the city was still called "Crisa." The gulf was not named after some insignificant hamlet, but rather after the most important city on it – as when it was renamed after Corinth later. A mighty city called Crisa really did exist ca. 600 BC.

Next, the Amphictiony, which administered the sanctuary in classical times, was initially centered on another sanctuary, that of Demeter of Anthela at Thermopylae (Hdt. VII 200). During the archaic period it must have expanded to gain control over Delphi. It continued to hold meetings at Thermopylae, but thereafter at Delphi also (Strab. IX 3,7, p. 420). Its secondary acquisition of Delphi, then, is demonstrable and confirms another element in the story of the First Sacred War.

Third, the Amphictiony, perhaps rueing its poisoning of Crisa's water supply, later instituted a rule that none of its members might cut off another member's access to water (Aesch. II 115). This prohibition against a member's cutting off another's water supply was in existence as early as 479. In that year the Greeks at Plataea swore an oath which included this prohibition despite its irrelevance to the situation at Plataea (Tod, GHI II, Nr. 204). This oath therefore cannot have been written for the occasion, but had been borrowed from elsewhere. The only other context in which this prohibition occurs concerns the Amphictiony, i.e., the oath was borrowed from the Amphictiony's files in 479.

(Continued)

Finally, the first Pythian Games with athletic contests took place in 582 (*Marmor Parium, BNJ* 239, A ep. 38), and the date is probably based on a list of victors. The story of the First Sacred War dates that war to just before then when a powerful city called Crisa still existed. The Amphictiony gained control over Delphi somehow, and while it need not necessarily have been by war, people living in the area could point out the ruins of Crisa and tell stories about how the city had fallen in a war.

the Phocians, hired mercenaries, and seized Delphi. The Locrians, another tribe in the Amphictiony and the Phocians' nearest neighbors, sent troops to recapture the sanctuary, but Philomelus' mercenaries defeated them easily (Diod. XVI 24; cf. 29).

Both the Phocians and the Boeotians now prepared for full-scale war. The latter arranged for the Amphictionic Council to declare a sacred war against the Phocians, while these sent envoys throughout Greece to proclaim the justice of their cause. They found a ready ear among the Athenians and Lacedaemonians, the Boeotians' traditional enemies (Diod. XVI 27–28; cf. 29). The Boeotians, for their part, had well-trained troops at their disposal as well as the active support of the Thessalians and Locrians, but Philomelus, in possession of the largest reserve of precious metal in Greece, offered mercenaries half again the going rate and quickly collected a sizable army (Diod. XVI 25; 30).

Accordingly, Philomelus invaded Eastern Locris in an attempt to keep his opponents from uniting against him. He managed to defeat the Locrian and Boeotian forces in a cavalry battle and then the Thessalians, but when the Thessalians joined up with the Boeotians and Locrians, he withdrew to Phocis. Here, at Neon to the north of Mt. Parnassus, the Boeotians inflicted a severe defeat and Philomelus himself died (Diod. XVI 30–31; Paus. X 2). The battle probably took place toward the end of the year 355.

The Boeotians presumably thought the war effectively over (Diod. XVI 32) as they arranged for their leading general, Pammenes, to take an army of 5,000 troops to Asia Minor to fight for Artabazus, the satrap of Hellespontine Phrygia, who was still in revolt against the King of Persia (cf. Chares' campaigns during the Social War). Pammenes actually managed to defeat the king's troops in two battles (Diod. XVI 34) even while he was sorely needed at home.

Philomelus' second in command, Onomarchus, had survived the Battle of Neon. Over the winter of 355 to 354 he rallied the Phocians and, availing himself of the reserves in Delphi, hired mercenaries in superabundance and lavishly distributed bribes among the Thessalians to secure their absence from the campaign in the next year. In 354 Onomarchus took the field and in a series of vigorous campaigns captured the city of Thronium in Eastern Locris, sacked the cities of the Doris, and, turning towards Boeotia, managed to capture

Orchomenus. After an attempt to besiege Chaeroneia, he withdrew again to Phocis (Diod. XVI 32–33).

In Thessaly, meanwhile, civil war had broken out between the two main cities, Larissa in the north and Pherae in the south. In 354 the Larissaeans – at least claiming to represent the full Thessalian League – asked Philip of Macedonia for help against the Pheraeans (Diod. XVI 14 [cf. XV 61] and 35), and Philip did not hesitate. He had just taken Methone (Diod. XVI 31 and 34 – see Box 18.1), the last Athenian outpost in the northwestern Aegean, and now marched into Thessaly. The tyrant of Pherae, Lycophron, asked Onomarchus for help against Philip, and Onomarchus sent his brother Phaÿllus with 7,000 troops. Philip beat him, so Onomarchus himself went to Thessaly. No Greek other than Onomarchus ever defeated Philip, and Onomarchus did it twice.

Having driven Philip from Thessaly, Onomarchus returned to Phocis. In the next year (353) he invaded Boeotia, defeated the Boeotians in a major battle, and captured Coroneia. In 353, however, Philip entered Thessaly again and marched on Pherae. Onomarchus hastened to its aid, only this time Philip had gathered an army big enough (20,000 foot) to match Onomarchus' (also 20,000 foot). The difference lay in the cavalry: here the numbers (3,000 to 500) favored Philip, who had apparently called up every available cavalryman in all Thessaly with the exception of Pherae. Onomarchus and the Phocians finally met their match, and 6,000 Phocian troops fell, Onomarchus among them (Diod. XVI 35).

The issue now was effectively settled, but the Phocians still had vast reserves of cash, and now their allies in Greece were both free of other conflicts and willing to help – if perhaps not so much to aid the Phocians' cause as to prevent the Boeotians from winning. The Athenians, having just come to terms in the Social War, bought the Phocians precious time by occupying the pass at Thermopylae and preventing Philip from following up his victory with an invasion of Phocis (Diod. XVI 38). The Athenians also sent a full 5,000 foot and 400 horse, the Lacedaemonians 1,000 foot, and the Peloponnesian Achaians an additional 2,000. Moreover, the tyrant of Pherae, Lycophron, even if Philip had forced him from Pherae, still had 2,000 mercenaries with whom he joined the Phocians. Onomarchus' brother, Phaÿllus, having survived the terrible defeat at Philip's hands, now assumed command and hired mercenaries to make good the losses.

Phaÿllus, however, lacked his brother's military talent, and when he invaded Boeotia he suffered three defeats (Diod. XVI 37). An invasion of East Locris fared a little better, but in 352 he died of disease, and Onomarchus' son, Phaleucus, took over the leadership. After some initial success the Boeotians defeated him twice (Diod. XVI 38,3–7), and by now the Phocians' cause was obviously lost. In the next years the Phocians finally began to run out of cash, with many recriminations amongst their leaders as to who had wasted what or misappropriated how much (Diod. XVI 56), but the war had sapped the Boeotians' resources as well. To gain money, the Boeotians supplied troops for the Persians' latest attempt to reconquer Egypt (Diod. XVI 40 and 44), and this surely prevented them from gaining a decisive victory over the Phocians in the next few years as the war continued in desultory fashion.

The Phocian War accomplished for Boeotia what the Social War had for Athens, namely a severe diminution of power just when Philip of Macedonia was building his own empire in the north. As for Phocis, the war devastated it (see below). The Phocians may have declined as swiftly as they had risen, but if circumstances had been a little different, Onomarchus might have erected a Phocian "empire" in central Greece. That it was a league-state and not a city-state which had brought itself into such a position is characteristic for the period.

Philip's Successes against the Chalcidians and Athens

Following his defeat of Onomarchus and the Phocians in 353, Philip turned his attention to the north (Illyria, Epirus, Thrace) in campaigns about which little is known (Dem. I 13). But in 349 the reckoning with the Chalcidian League – deferred by an alliance in 357 – came due. Philip invaded, defeated the Chalcidians in two battles, and shut them up in their chief town Olynthus (Diod. XVI 52–53). The Athenians came to the Chalcidians' aid (Philochorus, *BNJ* 328, Frr. 49–51), but Philip had anticipated that.

The Athenians still held the island of Euboea where, however, many were ready to revolt. Philip had long since taken up contact with would-be rebels (Dem. IV 37) and, as the Athenians sent aid to the Chalcidians, a revolt on Euboea broke out (Plut. *Phoc.* 12–14). If the Athenians had concentrated all their forces in one theater, they might either have beaten Philip or have retained Euboea, but they tried to do both, and lost twice. Olynthus was betrayed into Philip's hands (Diod., l.c.), and the Euboean towns became independent.

Thereafter Philip consolidated his influence in northern and central Greece. In Thessaly he arranged for his election as *tagos* (Just. XI 3,2; cf. Diod. XVII 4) and thenceforward ruled the kingdoms of Thessaly and Macedonia in personal union. He installed partisans of his as "tetrarchs" of the Thessalian **tetrads** (Dem. IX 26; Theopompus, *BNJ* 115, Fr. 208) and expelled the rulers of various cities (Diod. XVI 69). Philip then turned to the north again and waged war against Cersobleptes, the king of Thrace (Aesch. II 81 with Harding, Nr. 76).

In 346 Philip and the Athenians swore a treaty, the Peace of Philocrates, on the basis that each party should "hold what it held" – i.e., respect the territorial *status quo* (Dem. XIX 143 and VII *passim*). Athens thereby hoped to secure its possession of the Chersonese which Philip threatened; Philip in the short term wished to deprive Cersobleptes of an ally in the Athenians. Moreover, Philip wanted a free hand in central Greece to deal with the Phocians permanently – the terms of the Peace of Philocrates expressly excluded Phocis from the Peace (Arg. B to Dem. XIX, p. 337). Philip already had an alliance with the Boeotians (Diod. XVI 59) and with Athenian neutrality could settle matters in Phocis to

Box 18.3   *Demosthenes and Aeschines as Historical Sources*

The most important check on and supplement to Diodorus' insufficient and often incoherent narrative of events during these years are the political speeches of two Athenians, Demosthenes and Aeschines. Demosthenes (384–322), although he stuttered as a child (Plut. *Dem.* 11), grew to become the greatest of the Greek orators. Whatever the wisdom of his politics, his speeches already in antiquity were seen as models of the craft. Aeschines (390–315) for his part has had the eternal misfortune of being "opposing counsel" to the rhetorically more accomplished Demosthenes. Yet both of them helped shape Athenian policy in these decades (however much each may have overstated his role), and in their speeches they often argue on the basis of historical detail. Their speeches are thus rich sources of information.

However, neither orator was composing an historical treatise with events in succession and order. Historical events in the speeches can stand without any context or indication of date. For example, at XV 9 Demosthenes notes that the Athenian commander Timotheus captured Samos. The only way to anchor that fact in an historical narrative is through Diod. XVIII 18, which attests the Athenians' expulsion of some Samians from Samos in 365 – i.e., Timotheus' conquest of the island must have taken place a little earlier. If the passage from Diodorus fixes the event in time, Demosthenes attests what no one could have guessed from Diodorus' mention of the expulsion: not just who conquered Samos, but whom he conquered it from – the Persians, who a little earlier had evidently repossessed themselves of a bit of territory which they had last held in 479.

The orators were also speaking before Athenian audiences who sometimes knew exactly what the orator was talking about, such that, on the one hand, he could allude to a matter briefly and pass on. At II 6, Demosthenes reminds his auditors of "a well-known secret that was much talked about once" without bothering to explain it (in this case Harpocration's first-century AD lexicon to the ten canonical Athenian orators as well as a marginal notation in a manuscript explain what Demosthenes was referring to – see Harding, Nr. 61). On the other hand, if most in the audience had only a dim notion of the circumstance at issue, the orator could play fast and loose with the facts if it suited his purposes. In oration XXIII (from the year 352) Demosthenes portrays Cersobleptes, the king of Thrace, as a persistent enemy of Athens although Cersobleptes, if only for fear of Philip, at the time was a reliable ally.

Most importantly, both Demosthenes and Aeschines were trying to argue a case persuasively – not necessarily to produce an accurate and historically intelligible account. Distortions, stretched points, and self-promoting assertions abound; and one may legitimately wonder, for example, whether Demosthenes had quite as much influence on, e.g., the formation of the Peace of Philocrates as he claims. Diodorus, on the other hand, never mentions this treaty. The omission underscores the importance of the speeches as historical sources.

his liking. First, however, Philip defeated Cersobleptes and, as a token of dependence, compelled him to send his son to Philip's court as a hostage even though Thrace remained formally independent (Harding, Nr. 76A). Then Philip, honoring a Boeotian request, marched into central Greece to settle matters with the Phocians. Their leader, Phaleucus, had no chance, so he simply negotiated Phocis' capitulation on the condition of his and some 8,000 mercenaries' safe passage to the Peloponnese (Diod. l.c. – for these mercenaries' later adventures, see below and chap. 17). Philip now arranged for a meeting of the Amphictionic Council to decide Phocis' fate.

As *tagos* of Thessaly, Philip controlled the Thessalians' two votes. But since six additional votes lay in the hands of the Thessalians' so-called perioecic or subject peoples (Magnesians, Perrhaebians, Phthiotic Achaians – Thuc. II 101, IV 78, and VIII 3), Philip actually held eight. Given Philip's currently friendly relations with the Boeotians (two votes) and the Locrians (two votes), Philip could count on their four votes for twelve in all. Since the Phocians were not represented on the Council anymore, there were at this time twenty-two votes in all, so with twelve on his side Philip could simply dictate the decision. He left the Phocians in possession of their land, but had their cities razed and the inhabitants relocated to villages of fewer than fifty houses apiece. Their arms and horses were confiscated, and they were forbidden to rearm until such time as they should restore in installments of sixty talents a year all that they had taken from Delphi. Any Phocians guilty of robbing the sanctuary at Delphi were subject to arrest, but the rest might live in peace (Diod. XVI 60).

The Fourth Sacred War and Chaeroneia

During the first few years after the Phocian War Philip collected allies in Greece. For example, when the Lacedaemonians pointlessly attempted to (re)conquer Messenia, Philip took the opportunity to make alliances with Messenia and Argos (Dem. VI 13 and 15) as well as with the Arcadians (Dem. XIX 261). Not every diplomatic endeavor of Philip's met with success, however; an attempt to send troops to Megara to intervene in civil strife there and to cement an alliance with that state failed when the Athenian general Phocion intervened first (Dem. XIX 295; Plut. *Phoc.* 15). Nothing makes it particularly probable that every such effort of Philip's receives a mention in the sources; but the ones that are mentioned give an indication of how frenetically Philip's agents were working throughout Greece.

Militarily Philip continued to tighten his grip on the lands to the north and northwest of Greece. He invaded Epirus, expelled its king, Arybbas, and installed his brother-in-law Alexander, Arybbas' nephew, on the throne (Diod. XVI 72). In 342 and 341 Philip fought a long, successful campaign in Thrace, after which he annexed it (Diod. XVI 71).

The conquest of Thrace alarmed the Athenians whose possessions on the Chersonese it threatened. The Athenian commander there, Diopeithes, attacked the town of Cardia, a Macedonian ally, and made raids on Thracian territory. At the urging of Demosthenes, the Athenians refused to condemn Diopeithes ([Dem.] XII 3 and 11; Dem. V 25 and VIII *passim*). Instead, with Demosthenes at the forefront, they formed an alliance with Byzantium (Dem. XVIII 302). Rhodes and Chios, moreover, apparently promised aid (Dem. IX 71) and on Euboea, the Athenians with support from Chalcis and Megara took Oreus and won Eretria as an ally. Chalcis, Eretria, and Oreus now formed a new league-state which allied itself with Athens (Aesch. III 94–105 and Schol. to III 85).

As the Athenians strove to put a coalition together that could defeat Macedonia, Philip, fresh off the conquest of Thrace, in 340 moved to attack Perinthus, an ally of Byzantium's on the Chersonese. With help from Byzantium and from Arsites, the satrap of Hellespontine Phrygia, the Perinthians managed to repel Philip (Diod. XVI 74–76). Philip then marched on Byzantium. Up until now Philip and the Athenians had, at least officially, been at peace, but now the Athenians formally voted that Philip had broken the Peace. With Athenian aid the Byzantines repelled every Macedonian attempt to take their city, and Philip, at long last, gave up (Dem. XVIII 87). He had suffered one of the few setbacks of his career. He remained in Thrace over the winter of 340 to 339, and in the spring carried out a long campaign to the south of the Danube's delta (Just. IX 2,3,1–3).

The Athenians meanwhile made all possible preparations for the coming war (Aesch. III 22; Philochorus, *BNJ* 328, Fr. 53–55). By now Athens' finances had recovered dramatically from their nadir after the Social War. In 341 the annual revenues had reached 400 talents (up from 130 in the late 350s) (Dem. X 38; Theopompus, *BNJ* 115, Fr. 166). This recovery was due primarily to the unfortunately obscure work of one man, Eubulus, who through unclear processes had brought most of Athenian financial administration under the control of one board, the **Theoric Commission** (Aesch. III 25; Plut. *Precepts of Statecraft*, p. 812sq). Moreover, a law prevented the use of the funds under the Theoric Commission's control for military purposes (Dem. I 19–20; III 10–11), so money had steadily been collecting. By 339, however, the law had apparently been modified, and, with Demosthenes moving the motion, the stockpiled money was now applied to the coming war against Philip (Philochorus, *BNJ* 328, Fr. 56a).

Philip for his part was laying the diplomatic groundwork for a campaign against Athens. In the Amphictionic Council, which Philip dominated, one of his allies, the Locrians, in 340 accused the Athenians of sacrilege: while the Phocians held Delphi the Athenians had restored an old dedication there which the Plataeans had made "out of the booty from the Medes and the Thebans, when they fought against the Greeks" (Aesch. III 116). Technically the Athenian act, because of when it had taken place, was a sacrilege. The accusation, moreover, was calculated to secure Boeotian support – the Thebans did not care for reminders of how they had fought for the Persians against the Greeks. Philip planned to have the Amphictiony declare a Sacred War against Athens.

However, the "tribe" of the Ionians had two votes on the Council, and since the Athenians, as Ionians, by custom held one of those two votes, an Athenian delegation was present at the Council when the Locrians made their accusation. The head of the Athenian delegation, Aeschines, parried it by pointing out that citizens of the West Locrian town of Amphissa were plowing the sacred land of Apollo in the valley south of Delphi. He then demanded that the Amphictionic Council take immediate action. Aeschines had caught the Locrians red-handed, and the Council voted in favor of his proposal (Aesch. III 107–124).

Early in 339, the Council declared the Fourth Sacred War against Amphissa, but proved incapable of forcing Amphissa to pay a fine (Aesch. III 128–129; Dem. XVIII 151). Philip meanwhile had decided that any Sacred War was sufficient pretext for bringing an army into central Greece. The Amphictionic Council, no doubt with Philip's active connivance and against the Athenians' wishes, voted to appoint Philip commander of the war against Amphissa (Aesch. III 128–129; Dem. XVIII 151). Although the season by now was advanced, Philip, having completed his campaign on the Danube, marched southwards. The Boeotians held Thermopylae (Didymus, trans. Harding, Pp. 83–85), but Philip went around it (presumably following the course of the Asopus River – cf. Hdt. VII 199 and 216) and entered the Doris (Philochorus, *BNJ* 328, Fr. 56). No one in Greece had expected him to appear so quickly, much less by another route than the pass at Thermopylae.

The next few months saw frantic negotiations between Philip and Boeotia on the one hand and Athens and Boeotia on the other (Dem. XVIII 169–179; Philochorus, l.c.; Didymus, l.c.). Which side would the Boeotians take? Formally, they were allied to Philip, and for a generation the Athenians had been their bitter enemies. But if they aided Philip against Athens, it was plain that Philip would dominate Greece, to their detriment as well as to everyone else's. The Boeotians cast in their lot with Athens.

Early in 338 the Athenian army joined up with the Boeotian army; together with additional troops from other Greek states they entered Phocis while a mercenary army under the command of Chares and Proxenus took possession of Amphissa (Poly. IV 2,8). In two minor battles the Greeks did prevent Philip from entering Phocis, but they could not drive him from the Doris (Dem. XVIII 216). Finally, Philip exploited the physical division of his opponents' forces. With his entire army he marched from the Doris into Western Locris, fell upon the mercenary army, and cut it to pieces (Aesch. III 146–147). Amphissa surrendered, and Philip occupied Delphi.

Now Philip marched into Phocis, around the Athenians' and Boeotians' army, and forced it to make a tactical retreat to Chaeroneia in western Boeotia. To keep Philip from Boeotia, the Greeks would have to fight him here and they did so. With some 30,000 battle-hardened professional troops Philip faced his opponents' citizen armies. Commanding on Philip's left – which led the attack – stood Philip's eighteen-year-old son Alexander; and this teenager broke through the Boeotian line opposite. The Boeotians' ensuing flight allowed Alexander to attack the Athenians (on the Greek right) from behind, and when Philip himself advanced, the affair dissolved into a rout (Diod. XVI 85–86).

Philip had achieved what had eluded Xerxes a century and a half earlier. At Chaeroneia he crushed the last Greek army capable of resisting his. For years his agents had been active diplomatically all across Greece, so in every state prominent politicians were ready to make a sensible and realistic settlement with the Macedonians or, depending on one's point of view, to collaborate with the occupying army. Both the Boeotians and the Athenians accepted Philip's terms and surrendered. Athens had to give up whatever was left of the second Athenian League (Paus. I 25), though it retained Lemnos, Imbros, Scyros, and Samos ([Arist.] *Ath.Pol.* 61 and 62; Diod. XVIII 56).

The League of Corinth

Philip next proceeded to Corinth and summoned representatives of all the Greek states. Here he formed a military and to some degree political structure to encompass all Greece: the **League of Corinth**. Philip arranged for his election as the League's *hegemon* ("leader, commander"). A Council, to which the member states sent delegates, later on made decisions for the League (Arr. I 9,9; Diod. XVII 14) and exercised some judicial functions (Harding, Nr. 107). Each member in the League was responsible for contributing a certain number of troops if the League declared war; the total came to 200,000 infantry and 15,000 cavalry. The representatives of the League, on behalf of their states, also swore loyalty to Philip (Just. IX 5; Harding, Nr. 99A).

The Thessalian League's presence in the new structure underscores the intricate nature of Philip's "empire": Macedonia itself was a distinct kingdom; Philip was *hegemon* of the League of Corinth, a second distinct structure with a very different organization; and within the League of Corinth Philip remained *tagos* of Thessaly. Little information survives about the arrangements in other parts of Philip's "empire," but there too matters may have been complicated. Sparta alone remained outside of the League of Corinth (Just. l.c.; cf. Arr. *Anab.* I 16,7). Philip neglected to compel it to join the League not out of any respect for it, but because he considered it negligible.

Philip's Military Reforms

During his long reign Philip reworked the Macedonian army from the ground up, and Philip's success in conquering Greece (and Alexander's in conquering Persia) rests in large measure on reforms which turned on the use of a new weapon – the **sarissa**, a heavy thrusting spear, some fifteen feet long (Pol. XVIII 29; **Asclepiodotus**, 5), which Philip had introduced (Diod. XVI 3) and which one had to hold with both hands (Pol. l.c.). A *sarissa* was made from the trunk of the cornelian cherry tree which had no heart-wood; that is to say, a *sarissa* made from wood near to the exterior of the trunk still had the same density and toughness as one from wood near to the core (**Theophrastus**, *Enquiry into Plants*, III 12).

Holding and thrusting with the *sarissa* required large amounts of physical training. Second, since Macedonian soldiers fought in phalanx (just as hoplites), if a unit of **sarissophoroi** were to have any maneuverability, the men had to be drilled exactly. If a unit were to make, say, a 90° turn, all men in it had to raise their *sarissai* perpendicular to the ground in unison, execute the 90° turn in unison, and line up exactly so that they could then lower their *sarissai* parallel with the ground – without hitting each other in the head as they did so. The maneuver, obviously, worked only if every man, once the turn was completed, stood in the proper place relative to everyone else. It took practice; and under combat conditions, obviously, the faster and the more smoothly it could be done, the better. Additionally, the more such maneuvers an army could execute, the safer it was in combat (see, e.g., Arr. *Anab.* I 6,1–4).

It took years for an army to learn how to use the *sarissa*, and an army accustomed to fighting otherwise was apparently difficult to retrain. When Alexander decided to have a Persian army trained in the use of the *sarissa*, he started with new recruits – teenaged boys not used to fighting in any other way (Arr. *Anab.* VII 6,1). Moreover, experience counted for a lot in fighting with the *sarissa*. In the wars of the **Diadochi** after Alexander's death, the best soldiers were Alexander's superannuated veterans. They were mostly in their seventies; but even if their knees no longer bent properly and their eyesight wavered, they could still hold a *sarissa* because they had been doing that from before anyone else had been born and, when the signal came, could execute the necessary maneuvers with a perfection born of forty years' practice. These redoubtable septuagenarians several times cleared the field of armies with an average age some thirty years lower than theirs (Diod. XIX 28, 30, 41, 43 – see chap. 20).

This army was many years in the making. Much experimentation had gone into the armor worn by the *sarissophoros*. Because the *sarissophoros* carried a great deal of weight already, any piece of armor that he could dispense with was a welcome relief. But he still had to have some defensive armor – it was only through experimentation that Philip learned that a helmet and greaves were necessary, but that a breastplate need not be worn (Poly. IV 2,10). Since the *sarissa* kept both hands occupied, the *sarissophoros* could not hold a large hoplite-shield in his left hand. But experimentation presumably showed that some sort of shield was still necessary, so eventually Philip hit upon a small shield that could be strapped to the upper left arm (Asclep. 5). Since when holding a *sarissa* one naturally turns one's left shoulder towards the foes, only the narrowest portion of one's own upper body is exposed – so a small shield actually serves the purpose well enough.

Next, a Macedonian file was sixteen men deep. Its name, however, was **dekas**, literally "group of ten" (Arr. *Anab.* VII 23,3–4), so surely it had once consisted of ten men. At some point its composition was changed, but the old name stayed. Now, in a file of *sarissophoroi* the *sarissai* of just the first five men protruded past the first rank (Pol. XVIII 29; Asclep. l.c.). The back eleven held their *sarissai* at about a 45° angle. These *sarissai* then functioned as a reasonably effective screen against arrow fire (Pol. XVIII 30). Only through long – and utterly brutal – experimentation could Philip have known that eleven such *sarissophoroi* were required rather than, say, five or eight.

The Macedonian army was a fighting machine without peer in its day. The fifteen-foot *sarissa* was half again as long as the longest hoplite spear, so no hoplite phalanx could withstand a charge of *sarissophoroi*. Until the early second century BC, when it finally succumbed to the Roman manipular legion (see chap. 24), it held the field.

QUESTIONS FOR REVIEW

1 How did Philip use diplomacy to achieve his ends?
2 How did Philip's military innovations rework the phalanx from the ground up?
3 Did the Second Athenian League become as oppressive as the First?
4 How did the Phocians almost manage to establish their own ascendancy in Greece?
5 What were the institutional bases of Philip's power?

QUESTION FOR FURTHER STUDY

Is the Macedonian conquest of Greece attributable solely to Philip's military, political, and diplomatic talents? Or did the Greek ingrained preference for small states (notwithstanding the contemporary trend to larger *ethne* in place of smaller *poleis*) make them hopelessly weak against a determined and ultimately more powerful opponent? Why did Philip succeed where Xerxes had failed?

FURTHER READING

On Philip, many biographies exist; the following are given *exempli gratia*:
Cawkwell, G.L. (1978) *Philip of Macedon*. London.
Ellis, J.R. (1976) *Philip II and Macedonian Imperialism*. London.
Hammond, N.G.L. (1994) *Philip of Macedon*. Baltimore.

On both the Social and the Phocian Wars, the following is still well worth reading:
Beloch, J. (1922) *Griechische Geschichte*, III.1: 211–262. Berlin.

On the Phocian War, see also:
Buckler, J. (1989) *Philip II and the Sacred War*, pp. 148–195. Leiden.
Hammond, N.G.L. (1937) "Diodorus' Narrative of the Sacred War," *Journal of Hellenic Studies* 57: 44–78.

On the Second Athenian League:
Cargill, J. (1981) *The Second Athenian League: Empire or Free Alliance?* Berkeley. (Taking the opposite view to that espoused in the text.)

On the work of Eubulus:
Cawkwell, G.L. (1963) "Eubulus," *Journal of Hellenic Studies* 83: 47–67.

On Demosthenes and Aeschines:
Harris, E. (1995) *Aeschines and Athenian Politics.* Oxford.
Sealey, R. (1993) *Demosthenes and his Time.* Oxford. (Sealey's title consciously reprises that of an older work: Schäfer, A., *Demosthenes und seine Zeit* [Leipzig, 1885–1887] which is still eminently useful.)

19

Alexander the Great and the Conquest of Persia

362–336	336–323	323–301

336	Alexander becomes King
334	Alexander invades Persia
333	Battle of Issus
331	Battle of Gaugamela
329–327	Sogdian Revolt
326	Mutiny on the Hyphasis
323	Alexander's death

Philip's Death and Alexander's Accession

After establishing the League of Corinth, Philip proceeded to his next project: an invasion of the Persian Empire, many times the size of his own. Philip, as his entire career shows, was no wild dreamer, but a hard-headed – and hard-working – realist. Why should he have believed the invasion of the Persian Empire a realistic undertaking?

A History of Greece: 1300 to 30 BC, First Edition. Victor Parker.
© 2014 Victor Parker. Published 2014 by John Wiley & Sons, Ltd.

The answer lies in how the Greeks had learned to perceive the Persian Empire. Xenophon's story of the march of the 10,000 out of Persia in 401 BC had portrayed the Persians as weak and easily outwitted (see chap. 15). Agesilaus of Sparta had invaded Persia in 396, made fools of two satraps, defeated the Persians in one battle, and considered a march into the satrapies farther inland. The Persians never defeated him and instead bribed his opponents in Greece to cause enough trouble for the Lacedaemonians so that they would recall him (see chap. 15). Egypt's rebellion in the late fifth century (Diod. XIV 79) and the Persians' repeated failure to reconquer this province (e.g., in the 370s – Diod. XV 41–43) spoke poorly of Persian military prowess; the rebellion of Artabazus, the satrap of Hellespontine Phrygia, just made the empire look unstable – especially when Greek generals such as the Athenian Chares and the Boeotian Pammenes could invade Asia Minor in support of Artabazus and defeat imperial troops (see chap. 16). Other events contributed to this overall picture, for example, the rebellion of Evagoras, the king of Salamis on Cyprus in the 380s (Diod. XIV 98, 110, XV 2–4, 8–9) and the so-called Great Satraps' Revolt of the 360s (Diod. XV 90–91).

One may question the accuracy of this view of the Persian Empire as weak and ripe for the plucking. By the time Artaxerxes III Ochus (circa 359–338) became King of Persia, the Great Satraps' Revolt had ended, and Ochus reformed the satrapal administration throughout the Empire (Diod. XVI 50 and 52). The best-known measure, greatly conducive to the empire's internal peace, compelled satraps to disband their mercenary armies (Harding, Nr. 72A). The vigorous Ochus also oversaw the reconquest of Egypt in 343 (Diod. XVI 40–52) and set the empire on a new foundation.

Philip, however, knew nothing of such revisionism. His view of the Persians was that which Isocrates propounded in countless pamphlets (e.g., IV 140–149) – an effete and feeble people. In 336 Philip sent an advance force under his second-in-command Parmenio across the Hellespont (Diod. XVII 2) and prepared for the coming campaign. Before he could attack, however, one of his bodyguards, Pausanias, who may or may not have been acting alone, assassinated him (Diod. XVI 94). Many people wished to see Philip dead or stood to gain from his death – disaffected Macedonian noblemen (Arr. *Anab.* I 25,1), rebellious Greeks (Arr. *Anab.* I 1,3; cf. I 7,3), Persian officials (Arr. *Anab.* II 14,5), his estranged wife Olympias, and his ambitious son Alexander (Plut. *Alex.* 10) –, so numerous conspiracy theories arose.

The most intriguing one turned on a bitter quarrel within Philip's family. Philip had contracted numerous political marriages as he pieced together his "empire" – one ancient writer, **Satyrus**, remarked that Philip married according to whatever war he was waging at the time (Athen. XIII, p. 557). Among his numerous wives, Olympias, the sister of the king of Epirus, apparently occupied a privileged position until her son, Alexander, fell out with his father on the occasion of Philip's last marriage with a Macedonian noblewoman called Cleopatra.

At the wedding feast her uncle Attalus, who was giving her away, proposed a toast wishing for legitimate sons to issue from the marriage. Perhaps he chose his words poorly (all present had been drinking heavily), but Alexander responded angrily to the imputation of his illegitimacy and in a drunken rage flung his cup into Attalus' face. Attalus was the guest of honor, and hospitality obliged the inebriated Philip to defend his guest. Philip rose, drew his sword, and lunged at his own son, but tripped over his own two feet and collapsed in a drunken heap on the floor. The next day Alexander and Olympias fled. Some time later Alexander and Philip patched up their quarrel, and Alexander returned to Macedonia. Olympias, however, remained with her people in Epirus (Plut. *Alex.* 9).

Alexander's position at court was ambiguous. He might have been his father's preferred heir for now, but the Macedonian royal house had never practiced strict patrilinear succession. Alexander also had an elder half-brother, Philip surnamed Arrhidaeus. Arrhidaeus was feebleminded (Plut. *Alex.* 77), but in Macedonia this did not disqualify him from the succession (n.b. Plut. *Alex.* 10) and Arrhidaeus would actually become king after Alexander's death in 323 (see chap. 20). Meanwhile Philip's new wife, Cleopatra, was pregnant (see Paus. VIII 7), and Philip, a vigorous sixty, showed no signs of slowing down any time soon. Time was not necessarily on Alexander's side: Cleopatra might come to occupy the position at court which Olympias had once held and a son of Cleopatra's might displace him as preferred heir (see chap. 21 for a parallel for this situation). Additionally, the quarrel between Alexander and his father had been patched up rather than laid to rest. Olympias, who wielded much influence over Alexander, never made up her quarrel with Philip nor could she forgive Cleopatra (she would in fact have Cleopatra and her infant son murdered later on [Paus. l.c.]) and when Philip fell victim to an assassin's dagger, people had their suspicions about Olympias and Alexander.

Whatever the case, once Philip lay dead, the first order of business for the nobles present was to arrange the succession. With a surprising swiftness, which itself has aroused suspicion, the nobles closed ranks behind Alexander and proclaimed him king. He was barely twenty years old.

Alexander first had to assume all his father's positions in a multistate empire. He went to Thessaly where the Thessalian League elected him *tagos* (Diod. XVII 4). At Corinth the Council of the League of Corinth recognized him as the League's leader (Diod. XVII 4 – using the word **autocrator**, "sole ruler," instead of *hegemon*). Philip's empire, however, encompassed more than just Greece, so in the spring of 335 Alexander began a long campaign in the north to assert his authority there. The campaign took him through Thrace to the Danube's delta and, briefly, even across that river; and from there through Illyria (Arr. *Anab.* I 1,4–6,11).

While Alexander was away in the north, a rebellion broke out in Thebes with Athenian support. Towards the end of 335, Alexander marched from Illyria into Thessaly and onwards into Boeotia where he appeared before the Thebans even knew that he was on his way. Fearing lest the rebellion spread rapidly, Alexander dealt with it severely. He took Thebes by storm, and his troops carried out a massacre. Afterwards Alexander – acting through the Council of the League of

Corinth – had Thebes razed to the ground (Arr. *Anab.* I 7–9; Diod. XVII 8–14). From the sale of prisoners into slavery and other booty he also collected 440 talents (**Cleitarchus,** *BNJ* 137, Fr. 1; Diod. XVII 14). The example worked: the Athenians sent him an official note of congratulations (Arr. *Anab.* I 10,3). Alexander had consolidated his rule over his father's empire and could now undertake his father's work – the invasion of Persia.

From the Granicus to the Eve of Issus

In the spring of 334 Alexander crossed into Asia with approximately 30,000 infantry and 5,000 cavalry (Arr. *Anab.* I 11,3; slightly different figures at Diod. XVII 17 and Plut. *Alex.* 15,1). He marched eastwards past various Greek cities which for now remained loyal to the Persians. At the River Granicus Alexander met the combined army of the satraps of Hellespontine Phrygia, Lydia, Cilicia, and Cappadocia. Theirs was a forlorn cause: although responsible for the defense of their satrapies, Artaxerxes III Ochus' satrapal reforms had deprived them of the ability to hire sufficient numbers of mercenaries to do the job. Alexander's juggernaut rolled over this satrapal levy with ease (Arr. *Anab.* I 13–16; Diod. XVII 18–22).

Alexander appointed Calas the new satrap of Hellespontine Phrygia, secured the satrapal capital at Dascyleium with its enormous treasury (Arr. *Anab.* I 17,1–2), and proceeded southwards into Lydia. Its satrap, Spithridates, had fallen at the Granicus, and the garrison commander in Sardis, with next to no troops at his disposal, simply surrendered. In possession now of two gargantuan satrapal treasuries any problems which Alexander may have had with the financing of his expedition were well and truly over. Asander became the new satrap of Lydia, but, significantly, in a departure from Persian administrative practice, Alexander did not entrust him with its financial administration and appointed a separate treasurer (Arr. *Anab.* I 17,3–8).

From Sardis, Alexander turned towards the coast. He entered the Greek city of Ephesus and, on the basis of affairs in this city, altered his policy towards the Greek cities in Asia Minor. Hitherto he had treated Greeks and non-Greeks the same; now he intervened in the constitutions of Greek cities, insofar as he could, and replaced the ruling oligarchies with democratic governments bolstered by the return of exiles whom the oligarchs had banished – exiles who owed their return to Alexander alone and whom Alexander might reasonably expect to show him some gratitude on this account (Arr. *Anab.* I 18,1–2; Harding, Nr. 107). He awarded these cities "freedom and autonomy" (Arr. l.c.; Harding, Nr. 106) and relieved them of the obligation to pay a "tribute" (**phoros**) (Arr. l.c.). The words were fair; but the reality was that the Greek cities continued to pay an obligatory *syntaxis* ("contribution") (Harding, Nr. 106). Moreover, the interference in their constitutions and judicial affairs (Harding, Nr. 107) as well as Alexander's imposition of garrisons (Harding, Nrr. 106 and 107) demonstrates that the façade of "freedom and autonomy" under Alexander's regime was as hollow as ever it had been under the Second Athenian League.

To the south of Ephesus lay the Greek city of Miletus. Here Alexander met with stiff resistance, but in the end took the city after a difficult siege. By chance Alexander's fleet had occupied the city's harbor before a Persian fleet could arrive; this circumstance alone prevented the Persians from supporting the city's defense by sea. Still at Miletus, Alexander disbanded his fleet (Arr. *Anab.* I 18,3–20,1; Diod. XVII 22–23) in an egregious strategic error which allowed the Persian fleet free rein in the Aegean and which Alexander within a few months strove to undo by forming a new fleet (see below).

From Miletus Alexander entered the satrapy of Caria. The satrapal capital of Halicarnassus, a Greek city, resisted energetically and, thanks to Alexander's error, this time the Persians could supply it by sea. Alexander managed to take the city itself, but not the harbor which had its own fortifications and which remained in Persian hands. If Alexander ever envisaged any grand strategy of defeating the Persian fleet on land by steadily depriving it of ports (thus Arr. *Anab.* I 20,1), he abandoned it here when he left Halicarnassus' harbor untaken. As satrap of Caria he left behind an elderly lady called Ada. She was a member of the Carian satrapal dynasty whose younger brother Pixodarus had displaced her even though her elder brother (and husband) Hidreus had wished her to succeed him as satrap (Arr. *Anab.* I 20,2 –23,9; Diod. XVII 23,4–27,5 – for Pixodarus' lineage, see Diod. XVI 74).

Alexander proceeded into Lycia, part of the satrapy of Greater Phrygia, before turning northwards into the heart of the satrapy. A mere 1,100 troops garrisoned the satrapal capital of Celaenae. The low number gives an indication of how few troops the satraps had with which to defend their satrapies. The garrison agreed to surrender at a specified date if no help were forthcoming by then. Alexander accepted the offer, left 1,500 troops as a guard, and appointed as satrap Antigonus Monopthalmus ("one-eye" – the name Antigonus was common, and the Macedonians were unsentimental about nicknames to distinguish people with the same name) (Arr. *Anab.* I 29,1–3). It was now the winter of 334 to 333, and Alexander moved northwards to Gordium back in Hellespontine Phrygia (Arr. *Anab.* I 29,3–5). By now, Alexander had reversed his disbanding of his fleet, thus correcting his error (Curt. III 1,19).

In the spring of 333, Alexander left Gordium and swiftly passed through the satrapy of Cappadocia on the Taurus and marched towards the so-called Cilician Gates (see Figure 19.1), the chief pass through the Taurus Range into the satrapy of Cilicia. Owing to the pass's narrowness, a small contingent can hold it indefinitely. Alexander's wish to enter Cilicia probably explains the swiftness of his march through Cappadocia on the Taurus – he had to appear in Cilicia before its satrap, Arsames, could barricade the Gates against him. Arsames fled when he learned of Alexander's approach (Arr. *Anab.* II 4,1–6). Cilicia was a small but wealthy satrapy, both in terms of agricultural produce and shipbuilding timber. In the ancient world armies lived off the land (less sentimentally: they stole from the natives), and Cilicia was one of the few places where

Figure 19.1   The Cilician Gates today. Source: Teogomez, http://commons.wikimedia.org/wiki/File:Puertas_Cil%C3%ADcias.jpg (accessed 12th February 2013)

Alexander might be able to provision his army for a considerable time. Once in Cilicia, Alexander took possession of Tarsus, the capital (with its own wealthy treasury). Alexander arrived in the spring; he stayed there until the Battle of Issus in November of 333 – a period of up to eight months, depending on the exact time of his arrival. The illness from which Alexander suffered at this time can account for the delay only partially.

The Persian Counter-offensive

The Persian counter-offensive helps explain Alexander's situation during those months in Cilicia. Since the western satraps were failing to defend their satrapies, the central administration responded. Darius III Codomannus appointed a Greek, Memnon of Rhodes, commander of the Persian fleet (Arr. *Anab.* II 1,1). Under Memnon's leadership the Persians began an extensive campaign in the Aegean during which they reconquered islands which the Empire had not ruled for over a century.

The Persians never gave up their claim on any territory which they once had held. In 411 BC, as the Persians negotiated with the Lacedaemonians, their initial negotiating position had been to ask for all land back which they had ever controlled in Asia Minor, the Aegean, and mainland Greece, before eventually settling for all the land on the continent of Asia Minor (see Box 14.1). In the King's Peace of 386 BC, they had adhered to that basic position, but whenever an opportunity arose to reconquer an island or two off the coast, the Persians never hesitated to take it (see Box 18.3). So, when Memnon brought a large fleet into the Aegean in 334, he used it to reconquer Aegean islands. In the years 334 and 333, the Persians took the Cyclades, Tenedos, Lesbos, Chios (Arr. *Anab.* II 1–2), Samos (Arr. *Anab.* I 19), Cos (Arr. *Anab.* II 5,7 and Curt. III 1,19), most of Crete (Diod. XVII 48,2), and Rhodes (Arr. *Anab.* II 20,2).

Since Alexander was conquering Asia Minor (and well on his way to overrunning the Persian Empire), the Persians' minor campaigns on Aegean islands initially appear frivolous, but this view relies on two misconceptions. First, it never occurred to the Persians that Alexander genuinely threatened their empire. They had drawn the exact opposite conclusion to that drawn by the Greeks from the invasion of Agesilaus, the march of the 10,000, and other such events. For the Greeks these events had shown the Persian Empire up as weak, but for the Persians the invasion of Agesilaus had simply demonstrated that these western warlords came and went – the empire endured. By this reasoning, Alexander would soon go away as his kind always did.

The second misconception is that Alexander had actually conquered Asia Minor. Cappadocia on the Taurus, for example, remained unconquered until 322 (Diod. XVIII 16). A quick survey of Asia Minor on the eve of the Battle of Issus (Nov. 333) shows how little of it Alexander truly controlled: he had never entered the satrapies of Armenia and Cappadocia on the Pontus; Bithynia remained unconquered (Memnon, *BNJ* 434, Fr. 1.12); Lycaonia, and Paphlagonia (Curt. IV 5,13) were not conquered until after Issus; and the Persian fleet disembarked troops in Lycia early in 333 and, despite the assumptions of some commentators, marched them overland across southern Asia Minor, through the Cilician Gates just ahead of Alexander, to Syria (Arr. *Anab.* II 2,1 – n.b. Brunt's Loeb translation), so southern Asia Minor with the exception of Cilicia still stood under Persian control. Moreover, the Persians were snatching back other portions of Asia Minor: they recaptured Miletus (Curt. l.c.); various places on the mainland opposite Cos (Arr. *Anab.* II 5,7); and were at least attempting to reconquer the Hellespontine region (Curt. l.c.). Shortly after Issus, Antigonus Monophthalmus, Alexander's satrap of Greater Phrygia, repelled a major Persian land offensive in central Asia Minor (Curt. IV 1,34–35 – accidentally calling Antigonus the satrap of Lydia).

Alexander's position, then, in Cilicia during most of 333 was precarious. The Persian fleet held the Aegean; retreat meant surrender and was not even an option if the Cappadocians were holding the Cilician Gates from the north (for a parallel, see Plut. *Demetr.* 47); and going forwards meant either proceeding straight into Syria or entering Phoenicia with a dozen heavily fortified cities which were highly unlikely to surrender. The first option was to follow in the footsteps of the younger Cyrus' doomed expedition (not a good precedent – see chap. 15), and the second involved a series of sieges, each one of which could take several months. So Alexander waited as long as he could, in the one place where he could keep an army for an extended period of time.

Box 19.1 *Arrian's Use of Ptolemy*

Arrian wrote his history of Alexander (called *Anabasis* after Xenophon's work) in the second century AD, almost half a millennium after Alexander's death. However, his use of works written by Alexander's contemporaries permits use of his work today as an historical source. Arrian himself states that he relied primarily on two authors, both participants in Alexander's expedition: **Aristobulus** of Cassandreia (*BNJ* 139) and **Ptolemy**, the first Hellenistic king of Egypt (*BNJ* 138). Arrian's principal method was to assume that where his two chief sources agreed, he could accept as fact what they said (Proem, 1). That Arrian could compose a history of Alexander's conquest out of the overlap between Ptolemy and Aristobulus establishes one essential fact about those two authors: their works stood very close to one another, and this closeness distinguished them from the rest of the herd (Callisthenes of Olynthus [*BNJ* 124], **Chares** of Mytilene [*BNJ* 125], **Onesicritus** of Astypalaea [*BNJ* 134], **Nearchus** of Crete [*BNJ* 133], etc.).

In fact, the suspicion immediately arises that either Aristobulus or Ptolemy was using the other's work. The evidence for determining who was copying whom is slight, but coheres with the aprioristic argument that Ptolemy, the king of Egypt, had little reason to tailor his account after Aristobulus', but that Aristobulus may gladly have availed himself of a king's authority in difficult questions. Moreover, Ptolemy is far more likely than Aristobulus to have supplied the archival material present in Arrian (see below) and this consideration also suggests that Aristobulus had a reason to consult Ptolemy's work. If so, then the overlap between Aristobulus and Ptolemy is just Ptolemy; and Arrian then effectively purports to be following Ptolemy's account.

Moreover, various passages in Arrian reveal him to be a reasonably faithful copier of his sources: compare Arr. *Ind.* 11–12, with Diodorus, II 40–41 and Strabo, XV 1,39–41, 46–49, pp. 703–704, 707 (all copied from **Megasthenes**, *BNJ* 715, Fr. 4); or Arr. *Anab.* IV 12,3–5 with Plut. *Alex.* 54 (both taken from Chares of Mytilene, *BNJ* 125, Fr. 14). With certain qualifications Arrian's account in the main faithfully reproduces Ptolemy's. When Arrian departs from Ptolemy, he commonly marks the departure by a phrase such as "it is also said that . . ." or "there is also the story that . . ." (e.g., IV 12,3). The phrase, however, does not mark every departure from Ptolemy; nor does its presence in every single instance mark a departure from Ptolemy. Its presence or absence is a strong indicator, just not necessarily an inerrant one.

Ptolemy's use of archival material gives his work great value. For example, in his account of Alexander's march from Persepolis to Ecbatana Arrian preserves one unsolicited and false intelligence report (*Anab.* III 19,3), one obviously solicited report which debunked the false report (*Anab.* III 19,3–4), and one intelligence debriefing (*Anab.* II 19,4–5). The second report and the debriefing are dated to the day – i.e., had been filed with "date stamp." This highlights the strength of Ptolemy's account: he gets names, dates, and places right. Every modern account of Alexander's life inevitably relies heavily on Ptolemy through Arrian's transmission.

On the other hand, Ptolemy owed his career and his kingdom to Alexander. Often enough Ptolemy may have suppressed unpleasant material (e.g., Cleitarchus, *BNJ* 137, Fr. 25, mentions a massacre of 80,000 Indians, absent from Arrian) or purposely white-washed Alexander's deeds. Ptolemy, moreover, had risen through the ranks, and he was suspiciously involved in some of the less savory incidents during the campaign (Arr. *Anab.* IV 13,7–14,1). Most modern historians have gradually accepted that they must read Arrian's account, especially when Alexander's reputation is concerned, with skepticism. This does not, however, detract from the many good qualities of Arrian's (i.e., Ptolemy's) account.

From Issus to the Decision at Gaugamela

Fortunately for Alexander, Darius III spared him the need to make a decision one way or the other. Darius himself led out an army to crush Alexander, withdrawing resources from his fleet in the Aegean for the expedition (Arr. *Anab.* II 2,1). He thus hobbled a promising counter-offensive in the far west and delivered to Alexander an opportunity to show the world that he could meet the Great King in the field and win.

Before the battle Darius actually managed to outmaneuver Alexander. Through disinformation Darius made Alexander think that he was about to enter the Cilician Plain from Syria through the southern of two passes across the intervening mountains, the so-called Assyrian Gates. Alexander marched southwards into the tapering section of the plain (Arr. *Anab.* II 6,1–2), between the Mediterranean and the Lebanon range, in order to meet Darius there, but Darius instead entered the Cilician Plain through the northern pass, the so-called Amanic Gates, and marched southwards behind Alexander (Arr. *Anab.* II 7,1). The lack of any guard on the Amanic Gates casts the colossal failure of Alexander's intelligence into even starker relief.

Nonetheless, on the field itself Alexander prevailed. The narrowness of the battlefield worked against Darius who could not bring much of his army into the actual battle; nor could his cavalry ride around Alexander's army (on the Macedonian left) because the field was not wide enough with the Mediterranean on one side and the Lebanon range on the other. Even so, the result was not a foregone conclusion. Greek mercenary hoplites in the Persian center came close to exploiting a gap in the center of the Macedonian phalanx. But on the

Macedonians' right, Alexander with the Macedonian cavalry (the so-called "Companions") broke through the Persian ranks; and then with the rest of his right wing he turned leftwards against the Persian center even as the Macedonian center regained coherence and moved forwards.

The result was a rout of the Persians' army. Darius fled (Arr. *Anab.* II 8–11). The counter-offensive ended completely (Arr. *Anab.* II 13,5–6), and Alexander's lieutenants in Asia Minor made good any losses (Curt. IV 1,34–35 and 5,13–18). After Issus, Darius withdrew to the Empire's heartland, where he waited and made extensive preparations for Alexander's inevitable march into Mesopotamia.

Alexander meanwhile appointed the Macedonian Meno as satrap of Syria (Arr. *Anab.* II 13,7), and moved southwards into Phoenicia. The Phoenicians had hitherto refused to break faith with Darius without a clear sign that Alexander might prevail against him. With Issus they received their sign. One by one the cities of Phoenicia, with the exception of Tyre, surrendered (Arr. *Anab.* II 13,7–8; 16,6). What happened next demonstrates why Alexander had declined to enter Phoenicia without a sign that he might win: it took Alexander seven months to take Tyre by siege (Diod. XVII 46; Plut. *Alex.* 24; Curt. IV 4,19). A dozen such sieges would have ground Alexander and his army to powder. As it was, Tyre just delayed Alexander on his march to Egypt.

After Tyre, Alexander continued his southwards march. Batis, the garrison commander at Gaza on the Egyptian border, decided to resist and succeeded in holding Alexander up for an additional two months (**Josephus**, *Ant.* XI 8,4 [325]). Then Alexander entered Egypt, which Artaxerxes III Ochus had reconquered a decade earlier after some six decades of independence. Egypt was not reliably pacified, and its satrap had no choice but to surrender.

After founding Alexandria (the most successful of the cities bearing his name) (Arr. *Anab.* III 1), Alexander visited the oracle of the Egyptian god Ammon at Siwah in the desert to the west of the Nile (Arr. *Anab.* III 3–4). Although an Egyptian sanctuary, at the time it had more importance in the Greek world. Most of its visitors came through the old Greek colony of Cyrene (see chap. 5) to consult a god whom the Greeks identified as Zeus (e.g., Pind. *Pyth.* IV 28 or Hdt. II 42). Mythological heroes such as Perseus and Heracles had also consulted Zeus here (Callisthenes, *BNJ* 124, Fr. 14). When Alexander went to Siwah, he did so as a sign to Greeks. According to Callisthenes (l.c.), at the time Alexander's official historian (Arr. *Anab.* IV 10,2; Just. XII 6,17), the priest at Siwah expressly stated that Alexander was a son of Zeus (see also chap. 20). This was one of a series of flattering oracular pronouncements about Alexander which, procured at this juncture, were aimed at burnishing his image in Greek eyes.

Simultaneously, the oracle of the Branchidae, near Miletus, which had lain dumb since the Persian Wars, found its voice again and broadcast oracles concerning Alexander's birth and coming triumphs. Good things come in threes, and a woman in Erythrae, where long ago a sybil had supposedly dwelled, claimed to be that sybil, risen anew, and made prophecies in Alexander's favor

(Callisthenes, l.c.). All three prophetic incidents belong together, and Callisthenes in his character as propagandist indeed reported all three together for the benefit of Greek readers. A revolt against the Macedonians had either begun or was threatening to begin in Greece (see below), hence Alexander's wish for a burst of positive publicity in Greece.

None of this has anything to do with the Egyptians, even if Alexander's new divine sonship does admit of an interpretation in an Egyptian context. The Pharaoh of Egypt, while alive, was traditionally considered a son of Ammon (i.e., "Zeus" to the Greeks), and an Egyptian priest, in respect of Alexander's conquest of Egypt, might have accorded to Alexander all ranks and titles due to a legitimate pharaoh. Alexander later on presented himself as the legitimate Pharaoh in an inscription in a shrine at Karnak (P. Barguet, *Recherches d'Archaéologie, d'Philologie et d'Histoire* 21, 1962, pp. 194–195), and he may have welcomed the priest's address. In fact, Alexander was never officially invested as Pharaoh – only the so-called **Alexander Romance**, recension a, I 34, makes this assertion, and this fantastical text of uncertain date (it was in existence by the third century AD) has no claim to historical accuracy. Granted, the Alexander Romance probably arose in Egypt, so it could attest a native Egyptian view which arose after the fact – cf. the Persian version of the Alexander Romance below.

After returning from Siwah to Memphis Alexander made detailed arrangements for dividing up the administration of Egypt among several men (Arr. *Anab.* III 5); but one of them, Cleomenes, who received the task of managing the finances, later took over the entire government (Arr. *Anab.* VII 23). Alexander left Egypt in the spring of 331 and retraced his path northwards into Syria.

There, in a radical departure from Persian administrative practice, he set up a financial hierarchy. He appointed Philoxenus to be in charge of the revenues from Asia west of the Taurus. Coeranus, meanwhile, assumed a similar position in Phoenicia (i.e., Syria) and, although Arrian does not mention it, presumably Cilicia. Harpalus, as chief treasurer, oversaw Philoxenus and Coeranus and, apparently, Cleomenes in Egypt though Arrian does not add this (Arr. *Anab.* III 6,4). Alexander then turned eastwards, crossing the River Euphrates at Thapsacus. He continued in this direction until he crossed the River Tigris. Here, at a place called Gaugamela, Darius III had chosen to fight (Arr. *Anab.* III 6–8).

Darius III had learned from his mistakes at Issus. This time he had selected a broad plain which he had in advance scoured of obstacles which might have obstructed his cavalry (Arr. *Anab.* III 8,7; Curt. IV 9,10). Here he could make his line as long as he wanted, and his cavalry would have every opportunity to ride around the Macedonians. On his field of choice Darius simply waited for his opponent.

Alexander, for his part, drew up an ingenious plan. At an angle to the Persians' line the Macedonian phalanx advanced with its right wing thrust forward and its left, commanded by Parmenio, pulled back. This invited the Persians to outflank him on his right (their left). Darius III noted this and obligingly shifted troops leftwards (from his perspective). During the battle the Persian cavalry strove to ride around Alexander's right wing; some of Alexander's mercenary and allied cavalry units rode to block them. Meanwhile the Macedonian cavalry, with Alexander at its head, remained beside the advanced right wing of infantry. In the Persian lines opposite, as Alexander had hoped, Darius kept shifting units leftwards so as to outflank Alexander's perilously exposed right and during these shifts, a gap opened in the Persians' line. Into this gap Alexander led the Macedonian cavalry which then bore leftwards (from Alexander's perspective) towards the Persian centre where Darius himself stood. Alexander outflanked the Persians in the center of their line, not, as convention would dictate, on a wing. The Persian center collapsed under this assault, and once again Darius fled (Arr. *Anab.* III 13–14,3).

Here, at this point, even if no participant could have known, the issue was decided. The Persian cavalry was undefeated; the Persian right (as it turned out) on the brink of victory (Arr. *Anab.* III 14,6–15,1); and the Persian left had not even joined battle. But the center had not held and Darius had fled. Alexander had won, and neither Darius III nor anyone else would prove able to rally an army for a third battle. Gaugamela was decisive.

With minor qualifications of the academic sort, the Persian Empire passed whole into Alexander's hands. It had stood, once Egypt is removed from the picture, with approximately the same borders for over two hundred years – stable, prosperous, and quietly governed. In the rare cases of popular revolt (for example, in Ionia at the end of the sixth century – see chap. 9) the Persians had sought to address the cause of the revolt; in Ionia certainly with ultimate success. What few problems had arisen with satraps' revolts in the fourth century Artaxerxes III Ochus had systematically addressed and solved. Alexander's conquest did not impinge on the Empire's political unity or administrative stability, and to the vast majority of its subjects, whether a Persian or a Macedonian king happened to be ruling did not matter. People paid their taxes and went about their daily lives.

In fact, from a certain point of view, Alexander's conquest might as well have been the successful internal revolt of a frustrated prince such as Cyrus the Younger. One or two battles, and the king changed. The later tradition in Iran actually did take this view: in Ferdowsi's eleventh-century AD epic, the *Shahnameh* ("Book of Kings"), Sekandar (=Alexander) is just a half-brother to Dara (=Darius III), whom he replaces on the throne after a revolt. This presentation dervives, however indirectly, from a version of the so-called Alexander Romance which survives in Syriac, but which was originally written in Persian.

Greece during Alexander's Expedition

Because of the sources' understandable focus on Alexander and because the League of Corinth with one exception kept Greece quiet, little is known of

Greece during these years. That one exception was the revolt of Sparta's king, Agis III. Sparta had not joined the League, and during the Persian counter-offensive in the Aegean Agis III began to prepare a revolt. Shortly after Issus (Nov. 333) the counter-offensive ended, but, before they sailed away, Darius' generals in the west gave Agis money (Arr. *Anab.* II 13,6; Diod. XVII 48). With better financing or more direct Persian support, the revolt might have succeeded. As it was, many states (including Athens – Diod. XVII 62), mindful of the terrible example of Thebes, stood aloof, and the rebels' forces soon became bogged down in the siege of Megalopolis (Curt., VI 1,20) which remained loyal to the Macedonians (see chap. 18).

Alexander had left as regent in Macedonia the veteran marshal Antipater, who was not the man to lose his head in a crisis; and even if he had denuded Macedonia of men of fighting age when he sent reinforcements to Alexander, he still had funds (Arr. *Anab.* III 16,10) with which to hire mercenaries. Antipater collected an army while the rebels were engaged in the siege, marched southwards (Diod. XVII 63,1), and crushed the rebels at Megalopolis. Agis fell in the fighting, and the revolt ended (Diod. XVII 63,4; Curt. VI 1,13–15). The battle allegedly took place on the same day as Gaugamela (Plut. *Ages.* 15), but this sort of programmatic simultaneity occurs too often in Greek historiography (see chap. 10) to have credibility. When exactly the Battle of Megalopolis took place is a vexed question, but presumably within a few months of Gaugamela.

The Conquest of the East and Alexander's Death

No one on the battlefield at Gaugamela that day in October of 331 could know that the rest would just be epilogue. After the battle Darius fled to Ecbatana, the summer capital of the Persian kings (Xen. *Anab.* III 5,15; *Ezra*, VI 1–2), where he strove earnestly to raise another army for a third contest (Arr. *Anab.* III 16,1 and 19,1–2; Diod. XVII 64; Curt. V 8,1). Alexander, meanwhile, entered Babylon (another capital of the Persian kings – *Ezra*, l.c.) where the satrap, Mazaeus, surrendered and in a clear sign of continuity was straightaway reappointed satrap (Arr. *Anab.* III 16,4 with III 8,6 and Curt. V 1,17). After resting his army there for a month, Alexander proceeded to the Susiane and the old Elamite capital of Susa, yet another capital of the Persian kings (DSf Kent; Aes., *Pers. passim*; *Esther*, I 2). Here he reappointed the old satrap, Abulites, who had surrendered peacefully (Arr. *Anab.* III 16,9; Diod. XVII 65; Curt. V 2,8 and 17). It was the winter of 331 to 330, and Alexander moved forwards to Persepolis, yet another imperial capital (for Persepolis as an administrative center, see most clearly the Elamite *Persepolis Fortification Texts* and *Treasury Tablets*) as well as the capital of the satrapy of Persis – the Persians' homeland. The old satrap, Ariobarzanes, had attempted to block Alexander's entrance into his satrapy and so could not be reappointed, but Alexander did appoint another Persian nobleman, Phrasaortes (Arr. *Anab.* III 18,1–11). The old satrapal governing class was, by and large, lining up behind Alexander as it accepted that

Box 19.2 *Cleitarchus and the "Vulgate"*

After Arrian, the two most important surviving accounts of Alexander's expedition, are Diodorus, Book XVII, and a history written by Q. Curtius Rufus, probably in the first century AD. Anyone reading Diodorus' and then Curtius' account is immediately struck by their substantial identity. E. Schwartz, (1901), "Curtius, 31," *RE* 4.2: 1873–1874, provides a full list of the exact correspondences. Both Diodorus and Curtius were clearly using the same source, by common consent Cleitarchus. The decisive evidence is Cleitarchus, *BNJ* 137, Fr. 25 (=Curt. IX 8,15) when compared with Diod. XVII 102. Cleitarchus probably wrote in the middle of the third century BC, two generations or so after Alexander's death though other dates remain possible. Whatever his date, Cleitarchus relied heavily on written sources for his subject matter.

Although Cleitarchus does not appear to have used Ptolemy (Curt. IX 5,21), he did use a number of other accounts written by contemporaries of Alexander's expedition: Callisthenes of Olynthus (cf. *BNJ* 124, Fr. 14 with Diod. XVII 49,5 and Curt. IV 7,15); Onesicritus of Astypalaea (cf. *BNJ* 134, Fr. 3 with Diod. XVII 75,6 and Curt. VI 4,22); Nearchus of Crete (cf. Arr. *Ind.* 30 and 42, which with near certainty derive from Nearchus, with Diod. XVII 105–106 and Curt. X 1,10–12); and Aristobulus of Cassandreia (cf. *BNJ* 139, Fr. 15 with Diod. XVIII 52 and Curt. IV 8,1–6, in respect of Alexander's return journey from Siwah). This heavy use of contemporary sources makes Cleitarchus valuable. Diodorus provides a condensed version of Cleitarchus, and Curtius one contaminated by the use of other sources such as Ptolemy (Curt. IX 5,21) and Curtius' own thoughts.

Cleitarchus' work enjoyed immense popularity in antiquity; Plutarch in his *Life* of Alexander relied on it heavily, as did Pompeius Trogus in the universal history of which Justin produced an abridgment. Scholars commonly use the term **"vulgate"** to denote the Cleitarchan version of Alexander's expedition as seen especially in Diodorus and Curtius; but the term sometimes includes Plutarch and Justin/Trogus as well.

The most noticeable characteristic of Cleitarchus' account is its raciness. Cleitarchus enjoyed purveying legendary material (for example, Alexander's meeting with the Queen of the Amazons – Cleitarchus, *BNJ* 137, Fr. 16; cf. Diod. XVII 77 and Curt. VI 5,24–32) as well as salacious gossip (for example, Alexander's "consorting" with the Queen of the Amazons for thirteen days). But Cleitarchus, unlike Ptolemy, had no reason to spare Alexander's reputation. Thus Cleitarchus recounted many stories which reflect discreditably on Alexander (for example, Alexander's burning of the palace at Persepolis in a drunken frenzy at the encouragement of an Athenian prostitute called Thaïs – Diod. XVII 72; Curt. V 7; Plut. *Alex.* 38; for another possible motive, see in text).

An older generation of scholars dismissed the "vulgate" as inferior to Arrian and discounted its stories, especially when these portrayed Alexander uncharitably. Few today, however, would maintain that stance. Even if Arrian (i.e., Ptolemy) will always be fundamental, no one now ignores the information in Cleitarchus; often it provides a much needed corrective or supplement.

a new dynasty had taken over the empire. For the time being it served Alexander's purposes that it thought that it still had a role to play: he needed it and the skills which it possessed to help him run the Empire at least until enough Macedonians had acquired the knowledge necessary to fill the old elite's shoes.

In a much discussed act, Alexander, before leaving Persepolis in the late spring of 330, burned three buildings (all built by Xerxes) in the palatial complex there. In all likelihood he intended the gesture to signify to the Greeks – both back home and in his army – that he had taken revenge on Xerxes, the man who had invaded Greece and burned Athens (Arr. *Anab.* III 18,10–12; Diod. XVII 72; Curt. V 7; Plut. *Alex.* 38). From Persepolis Alexander marched north-westwards to Ecbatana, prepared to fight again against Darius III who, however, unable to raise an army, fled eastwards. At Ecbatana Alexander appointed a Persian, Oxydates, as satrap in place of Atropates, the old satrap – whom, however, Alexander would soon enough reappoint (a telling sign of his need for experienced administrators with specialized knowledge of affairs in their satrapies) (Arr. *Anab.* III 8,4; Curt. VI 2,11; Arr. *Anab.* IV 18,3). Alexander now dismissed part of his army and stationed the bulk of the remainder in Ecbatana with Parmenio as commandant (Arr. *Anab.* III 19,5–8). The war was over now, and he knew it.

With the Macedonian cavalry and picked infantry units (Arr. *Anab.* III 20,1) he proceeded eastwards behind Darius III. A relative of Darius', Bessus, the satrap of the enormous double satrapy of Bactria and the Sogdiane as well as the commander of the Persian cavalry at Gaugamela (Arr. *Anab.* III 8,3), was accompanying him. Bessus, realizing that Darius III had failed, had him murdered (Arr. *Anab.* III 21,10). Bessus never posed a threat to Alexander who for now did not even bother to pursue him. Alexander instead took possession of the double satrapy of Hyrcania and Parthia and briefly installed a new Persian satrap before reappointing the old Persian satrap, Phrataphernes (Arr. *Anab.* III 22,1; 23,4; and 28,2).

While in Parthia Alexander received word that Bessus had proclaimed himself king, with the regnal name Artaxerxes, and was wearing the upright tiara and other royal garb (Arr. *Anab.* III 25,3). To Alexander's surprise, just as the old satrapal governing class had mostly come over to his side, he now had a rival for its affections. Moreover, Bessus' dressing up for the part cast into relief Alexander's own failure hitherto to look like a King of Persia. This he now remedied. The sources differ slightly as to the exact details, but all agree that Alexander adopted a half-Persian, half-Macedonian costume. He refused, for example, to put on Persian trousers, since some things were just too outlandish, but he did wear the diadem, a fillet about the head (Plut. *Alex.* 45; Diod. XVII 77; Curt. VI 6,4). Persian kings had kept harems, so Alexander now instituted a harem with as many concubines as Darius III had had (Diod. and Curt. ll.cc.). The Macedonian troops' opposition to their king's "going native" would cause conflict over the next few years, but Alexander was the Persians' (and other Asians') king too. Political considerations aside, Alexander may have liked Persian finery as well.

In the meantime, however, Alexander still had to wrap up the conquest of the East. From Parthia Alexander proceeded southwards into the satrapy of Aria where again he reappointed the old satrap, Satibarzanes. Here Alexander had to contend with a minor, though genuinely popular, revolt as the Arians themselves attempted to shake off the rule of the new king. After a false start, Alexander eventually suppressed the revolt (Arr. *Anab*. III 25; a Macedonian, Stasanor, in the end became satrap: Arr. *Anab*. III 29,5) and moved eastwards into the double satrapy of the Drangiane and Arachosia. The satrap, Barsaentes, fled and Alexander appointed a Macedonian, Meno, to take command (Arr. *Anab*. III 21,1; 25,8; 28,1). Here an alleged conspiracy, with Philotas, Parmenio's son, as ringleader, was reported to Alexander. Although to modern historians the conspiracy seems little more than a frame-job, it was credible to the Macedonian soldiers. Many must have been murmuring against Alexander in the camp, so it surprised no one unduly when someone accused a particular officer of conspiring. Philotas was executed, and assassins were dispatched to murder Parmenio as well (Arr. *Anab*. III 26).

Early in the year 329 Alexander approached the Hindu Kush from the south. He appointed as satrap of the district, Paropamisadae, a Persian called Proexes (Arr. *Anab*. III 28,4). From there Alexander crossed the Hindu Kush and entered Bactria, whence Bessus, the would-be Artaxerxes IV, promptly fled across the River Oxus (Arr. *Anab*. III 28,8–10). Alexander followed him across the river into the Sogdiane, a large, sparsely inhabited satrapy of mostly desert and mountains. Here the Sogdian clan chiefs handed Bessus over to Alexander who had him tortured and put to death (Arr. *Anab*. III 29,6–30,5). To all appearances the Sogdian chiefs accepted Alexander as their new king, and Alexander proceeded to the River Jaxartes. He then learned that behind him a full-scale popular revolt had broken out in the Sogdiane (Arr. *Anab*. III 30,6–IV 1), and unlike in Aria where in the end he had dealt with the revolt easily enough, he spent the rest of this year with mixed success attempting to stamp it out. He captured seven towns in an initial campaign (Arr. *Anab*. IV 2–3,5) and appeared to have settled matters. He even took time to fight against some Scythian nomads to the north of the Jaxartes and to found the city of Alexandria Eschate ("the last/farthest Alexandria" that marked the extent of his Empire in this direction) on the Jaxartes (Arr. *Anab*. IV 4–5,1; cf. IV 1,3; for the name, see App. *Syr*. 57, and **Claudius Ptolemy**, VI 12). Another section of his army, however, had suffered a defeat before the walls of Maracanda, the Sogdian capital (Arr. *Anab*. IV 5,2–6,2; cf. 3,6–7).

Alexander went into winter quarters in Zariaspa (Bactra) in the reliably pacified Bactrian satrapy (Arr. *Anab*. IV 7,1). Here he sought a solution to a ceremonial problem which impinged on his ability to appear as a legitimate Persian king. For the Persians *proskynesis*, prostration, was a polite, respectful gesture (rather like a bow or a curtsey) which one performed before a social superior. Greeks and Macedonians, however, prostrated themselves before gods only. To the Persians it appeared that the Macedonians were showing disrespect to the king when the latter did not prostrate themselves – at worst it even suggested that Alexander was not fully king. To the Macedonians, however, the Persians were at best ludicrous (Curt. VIII 5,22) and at worst blasphemous (Arr. *Anab.* IV 11) when they made this gesture. Alexander now attempted to impose a uniform ceremony, and perhaps significantly he chose (instead of the alternative) to have the Macedonians prostrate themselves before him. The elaborate ceremony which Alexander, probably with the help of his majordomo Chares of Mytilene, staged to secure the Macedonians' acquiescence, might have succeeded had not his court historian, Callisthenes, bungled matters and wrecked the ceremony (Chares of Mytilene, *BNJ* 125, Fr. 14). Alexander let the matter drop and put up with two modes of behavior at court well enough – so well, in fact, that one wonders if he had really needed to bring the matter up in the first place. Callisthenes shortly thereafter was implicated in a "conspiracy" and died under unclear circumstances (Arr. *Anab.* IV 14).

Alexander spent all the next year (328) putting down the Sogdian Revolt. It was a year of hard, boring campaigning in the desert; of installing garrison after garrison in an attempt systematically to deprive guerrillas of bases. In the course of this year, Alexander compelled the surrender of Sogdian refugees on a natural citadel, the so-called Sogdian Rock (Arr. *Anab.* IV 18,4 with wrong date of 327; Curtius, VII 11 with correct date – see Bosworth, 1981). He then married one of the erstwhile refugees, Rhoxane, the daughter of Oxyartes, the chief of a prominent clan (Arr. IV 19,5). Although the sources present the marriage as a love match, the political motivation for it is transparent. Like his father, Alexander had married according to which war he was waging (Athen. XIII, p. 557). With Oxyartes' help Alexander persuaded other Sogdian refugees on another natural citadel to surrender (Arr. *Anab.* IV 21,6–7); and with Oxyartes at his side, presumably, other clan chiefs slowly came round.

In 327, Alexander finally left the Sogdiane. He had initially named a Persian, Artabazus, as satrap, but by now the Macedonian Amyntas had replaced him (Arr. *Anab.* IV 17,3). There would be no more Persian satraps, as the need for them had passed. Alexander would eventually make his father-in-law (who as a Sogdian was indeed an Iranian, just not a Persian) the satrap of Paropamisadae (Arr. *Anab.* VI 15,3), but otherwise all new appointments were Macedonian or Greek. Granted, the next three satrapal appointments were in northern India which the Persians had never conquered; but in the next few years Alexander would replace a large number of satraps with Greeks or Macedonians, including in places where he might have appointed Persians.

Continuing his conquest, Alexander recrossed the Hindu Kush from north to south. He spent 327 in hard campaigning along the River Cophen in the satrapy of Paropamisadae, where he appointed Tyriespes as the new satrap (Arr. *Anab.* IV 22,5), and in the modern regions of Bajaur and Swat, where he appointed Nicanor as satrap of a satrapy conventionally known as "India I" (Arr. *Anab.* IV 28,6). In the spring of 326 Alexander crossed the River Indus. The local ruler, Omphis – often called by his title Taxiles –, who had long since taken up contact with Alexander (Diod. XVII 86,4; Curtius, VIII 12,5), was confirmed by Alexander in his position. As satrap of the region between the

Indus and the River Hydaspes to the east ("India II") Alexander appointed a Macedonian, Philip, son of Machatas (Arr. *Anab.* V 8,2–3). Alexander then crossed the River Hydaspes where the local ruler, Porus, chose to fight. Alexander defeated him in a battle memorable for the Indians' heavy though unsuccessful reliance on war elephants (Arr. *Anab.* V 14–18). From there Alexander marched eastwards across the Rivers Acesines and Hydraotes until he came to the River Hyphasis.

Here, still in the year 326, Alexander's troops famously mutinied and refused to go one step farther (Arr. *Anab.* V 25–28). Alexander had gathered sound information on the regions farther to the east and drawn up plans for their conquest (see Bosworth 1996: 74–78) and a man eminently qualified to render an authoritative verdict in the matter, Chandragupta Maurya (in Greek: Sandracottus) who shortly thereafter conquered the region himself, viewed Alexander's aim as feasible (Plut. *Alex.* 62). All the same, without anyone to follow him, even Alexander was helpless, and one of his officers, Coenus, even talked back to him before the assembled troops (Arr. *Anab.* V 27). The Hyphasis became the eastern boundary of Alexander's empire, and Coenus died, allegedly of a disease, shortly thereafter (Arr. *Anab.* VI 2,1).

The conquest was over. Alexander returned to the Hydaspes and, late in 326, traveled downriver, first along the Hydaspes and then the Indus. To accompany the army on its march downriver Alexander had a fleet constructed and named Nearchus, a man from Crete, its commander (Arr. *Anab.* VI 1,6 and 2,3–4). The campaigns on land were brutish and marked by massacres (Arr. *Anab.* VI 3–17), the worst of which saw an alleged 80,000 lose their lives (Cleitarchus, *BNJ* 137, Fr. 25). Even allowing for exaggeration, the "body count" must have been terrifying. Having "organized" these regions ("India III") Alexander appointed Peithon as satrap (Arr. *Anab.* VI 15,4).

Having arrived in the Indus Delta, Alexander ordered Nearchus to sail westwards along the coast while he himself would lead the army back by land (Arr. *Anab.* VI 21). In mid-325 Alexander, having badly underestimated the difficulties, journeyed through the Gedrosian Desert. He emerged with a battered and ravaged army in the winter of 325 to 324 (Arr. *Anab.* VI 23–26). Alexander had just appointed Apollophanes as satrap of Gedrosia (Arr. *Anab.* VI 22,2); he now replaced him with Thoas. Thoas himself soon died and the new satrap of Carmania, Sibyrtius, was appointed satrap of the new double-satrapy of Arachosia and Gedrosia. Tlepolemus became the new satrap of Carmania (Arr. *Anab.* VI 27,1), which satrapy Alexander entered in early 324 (Arr. *Anab.* VI 27,3).

The rapid changes in the satrapal administration at this point have their parallels elsewhere in the Empire. In the years 325 and 324 no fewer than nine satrapies changed hands. Other satraps were summoned to Alexander's court and occasionally kept there; others had to send their sons. A number of executions took place (for the details, see Badian 1961: 16–18). Whatever the justice in these actions, they led to the emergence of a new governing cadre which was Macedonian and Greek (with two Persians and one Iranian clinging on) and which must have come from the ranks of the junior officers – of many newly appointed satraps such as Sibyrtius (first Carmania, then Arachosia plus

Box 19.3   *Onesicritus, Nearchus, and the Age of Discovery*

Nearchus of Crete, a boyhood friend of Alexander's (Arr. *Anab*. III 6,5; Plut. *Alex*. 10), was one of Alexander's officers on the expedition. In 326 Alexander appointed him commander of a fleet of ships on the Indus River. This fleet, augmented along the way, eventually sailed from the Indus delta along the northern coast of the Arabian Sea and into the Persian Gulf. Onesicritus of Astypalaea, evidently an experienced sailor, served as chief helmsman (Plut. *Alex*. 66). Both Onesicritus and Nearchus wrote books about their service under Alexander. Onesicritus, however, wrote first and since the commander's helmsman by tradition was the second-in-command of the fleet and, when the commander had little nautical experience, the real commander, Onesicritus presented himself, possibly with some justice, as commanding the fleet (*BNJ* 134, Frr. 13 and 27). Nearchus wrote, at least in part, to refute this "lie" (see in particular *BNJ* 133, T 1 = 134, Fr. 27).

Little of Onesicritus' work is preserved, but the fragments suffice to show that Onesicritus reveled in descriptions of all the exotic things which the soldiers encountered on the expedition: the enormous banyan trees of India (*BNJ* 134, Fr. 22); another tree, in Hyrcania, which exuded honey (Fr. 3); unusual climates (Fr. 8); strange customs (Frr. 5, 17, and 21); marvelous animals such as whales (Fr. 31), giant serpents (Fr. 16), and Indian elephants (Frr. 13–14), and so on. Onesicritus also offered detailed discussion about various battles (see Fr. 19) as well as legendary material (T. 8 and Fr. 1), but few fragments on these subjects survive.

Far more, however, survives of Nearchus' work. Arrian used it extensively in his tract, the *Indica*, and also relied on it frequently in the *Anabasis* from Book VI onwards. For example, Arrian gives two accounts of the crossing of the Gedrosian Desert (a so-called doublet – see Box 18.1). The first (VI 23–24,1) is dry, spare, and gives no indication of the privations which the troops suffered. This is Ptolemy's account. The decision to march through the desert did not reflect well on Alexander, and Ptolemy did not choose to dwell overlong on the episode. The second account (VI 24,1–27,1) is vivid and colorful and stylizes the march as an heroic struggle of man against nature. This is what Nearchus wrote, and Arrian, recognizing its high literary merit, could not omit it.

Besides correcting Onesicritus at various points (see, e.g., *BNJ* 133, Fr. 21, on the Indus Delta), Nearchus sought to outdo him. Nearchus' account of Greek sailors' first encounter with whales (Arr. *Ind*. 30) indisputably excels what Onesicritus had had to say on the matter (Fr. 31). Where Onesicritus had focused on the whales' size which he exaggerated (about 100 yards long, he claimed), Nearchus composed a vivid and engaging story of the sailors' battle against these monsters of nature – Nearchus had the sailors give the signal for battle and row directly at the whales which in response dived under the ships.

The attention which both Onesicritus and Nearchus paid to exotic beasts and plants highlights an aspect of Alexander's expedition which often escapes notice: it was a tremendous age of discovery. In addition to all the fighting, people were writing about how large banyan trees were and excitedly telling stories about a bird which could mimic human speech (Nearchus, *BNJ* 133, Fr. 9).

Gedrosia) almost nothing is known before they were suddenly propelled into the Empire's highest posts.

Alexander visited Persepolis (Arr. *Anab.* VI 30,1) and Susa (Arr. *Anab.* VII 4,1) in the spring of 324. At Susa he married a daughter of Darius III's and one of Artaxerxes III's (Arr. *Anab.* VII 4,4). From Susa Alexander marched westwards and then northwestwards up the River Tigris. Here at Opis his troops mutinied once again (Arr. VII 8), only this time he was ready. He threatened to replace them with Persians (among other things, he had earlier arranged to have some 30,000 Persian teenagers trained in the Macedonian style of fighting; this corps was now almost ready – Arr. *Anab.* VII 6,1), and the Macedonian veterans caved in. Alexander had no need for them anymore, and he dismissed some 10,000 of them homewards. Alexander retained any sons whom they had sired while on the expedition and promised to raise these in the Macedonian manner (Arr. *Anab.* VII 11–12) – surely as another corps of soldiers loyal to Alexander alone. Alexander was laying the foundations of a new imperial army.

From Opis Alexander journeyed to Ecbatana. Here Hephaestion, his **chiliarch** or "vizier" and perhaps his last true friend, died, and Alexander's grief was immense (Arr. *Anab.* VII 14). From Ecbatana, in the spring of 323, he returned to Babylon where in June he died in his thirty-third year (Arr. *Anab.* VII 28,1). Because of his youth rumors that someone had poisoned him immediately arose (Arr. *Anab.* VII 27,1), but given that he had spent the last thirteen years of his life in nonstop warfare during which he had continually pushed himself to the uttermost limits of human endurance; suffered repeated injuries, many life-threatening; contracted several severe illnesses; and abused alcohol far too heavily and far too often; the question really should not be why he died so young, but rather how he had managed to live so long.

Because of his outsize achievements, even his contemporaries viewed Alexander in legendary terms and attributed to him an outsize personality. It is easy to subscribe to this legend and to see Alexander as some sort of titan. Yet need Alexander have been more than a hard-drinking (e.g., Arr. *Anab.* IV 8 where he murders his friend Cleitus in a drunken rage), hard-driving soldier with tactical talent, an army with superior weaponry, and ruthless, political cunning? As the mutinies and the grumbling against him show, his ability to inspire men had its limits. He committed egregious errors (e.g., before Issus), and Nearchus states bluntly that he led his army through Gedrosia out of "ignorance" of the difficulty (*BNJ* 133, Fr. 3a). Because he died just after the conquest, his governmental and administrative ability remains largely unknown. So much of what later authors said about Alexander's personality appears contrived (e.g., Plutarch on Alexander's literary refinement – *Alex.* 8). The famous Alexander bust shows another contrived image with its dreamy, philosophical gaze (see Figure 19.2). Could any man who had gone through thirteen years of nonstop fighting actually look like that? Coins show a somewhat different portrait and are perhaps more realistic (see Figure 20.1). In the end Alexander must be judged not by dubious and unverifiable stories about his character, but by the

Figure 19.2   The Alexander bust (Roman copy of Greek original). Source: Gunnar Bach Pedersen, http://commons.wikimedia.org/wiki/File:Aleksander-d-store.jpg (accessed 12th February 2013)

deeds which he demonstrably did – deeds which, taken on their own terms, are surely impressive enough with or without value judgments.

QUESTIONS FOR REVIEW

1   In what ways did Alexander attempt to manipulate Greek opinion?
2   How was the Persians' counter-offensive meant to work?
3   How did the satrapal class change under Alexander as his needs changed?
4   What caused the tension between Alexander and his army and how was it resolved?

QUESTION FOR FURTHER STUDY

Is one justified in viewing Alexander the Great as unique – as someone who, by virtue of extraordinary endowments, "changed history"? Can one instead

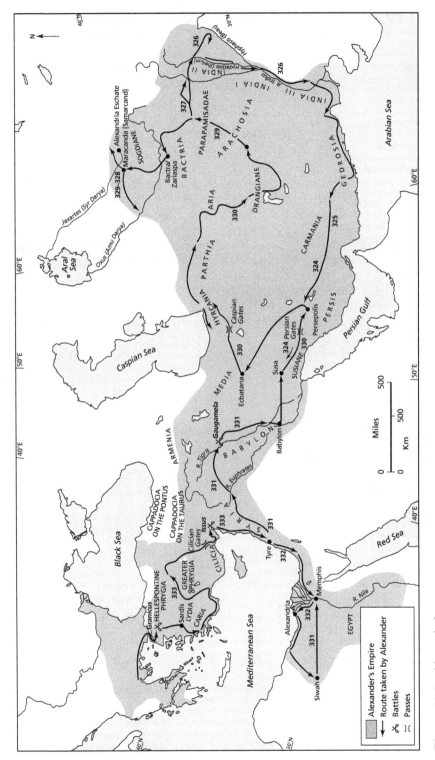

Figure 19.3 Alexander's conquests

make the argument that all that Alexander did was to carry out the plans which his father had made with the army which his father had trained – that Alexander's accomplishments are owed solely to Philip who, had he lived, would just have done the same thing? (That is to say, the conquest of Persia was no "unique" accomplishment by any "unique" individual.)

FURTHER READING

Many biographies of Alexander have been written. As far as the basic narrative of the conquest is concerned, most will serve the student's purpose – though the student requiring just the basic narrative is in many ways better advised simply to read Arrian's *Anabasis*.

The "classic" biography in English is the following, though its idealistic portrait of Alexander is, to speak charitably, dated. Nonetheless, it was influential in its day and is still a good read:
Tarn, W.W. (1948) *Alexander the Great*. Cambridge.

The biography in English nowadays in widest circulation as a textbook is probably the following:
Bosworth, A.B. (1993) *Alexander the Great: Conquest and Empire*. Cambridge.

More recent is:
Heckel, W. (2008) *The Conquests of Alexander the Great*. Cambridge.

In a highly influential series of articles, Ernst Badian debunked previous generations' hagiographical conception of Alexander. Some of the most important are:
"Alexander the Great and the Unity of Mankind," *Historia* 7 (1958): 425–444.
"The Eunuch Bagoas," *Classical Quarterly* 8 (1958): 144–157.
"The Death of Parmenio," *Transactions of the American Philological Society* 91 (1960): 324–338.
"Harpalus," *Journal of Hellenic Studies* 81 (1961): 16–43.
"Alexander the Great and the Greeks of Asia." In: *Festschrift Ehrenberg*, pp. 37–69. Oxford, 1966.

Indispensable for any work on Alexander is the following reference work:
Berve, H. (1926) *Das Alexanderreich auf prosopographischer Grundlage*. Munich.
(Each person associated with Alexander receives a number; scholars frequently cite by "Berve-Number" – e.g., for Parmenio, see Berve, Nr. 606.)

For several of the major sources on Alexander the Great, there exist good, if partial commentaries:
Atkinson, J.E. (1980–1994) *A Commentary on Q. Curtius Rufus' Historiae Alexandri Magni*. Amsterdam. (Only Books III–VII 2.)
Bosworth, A.B. (1980–1995) *An Historical Commentary on Arrian's History of Alexander*. Oxford. (Only Books I–V.)
Hamilton, J.R. (1968) *Plutarch, Alexander: A Commentary*. Oxford.

On Ptolemy:
Fundamental is the following study in German:
Strasburger, H. (1934) *Ptolemaios und Alexander*. Leipzig. (Rep. in *Studien zur Alten Geschichte* I, Hildesheim, 1982: 83–147.)

On Cleitarchus:
Parker, V.L. (2009) "Source-Critical Reflexions on Cleitarchus." In: P. Wheatley and R. Hannah, *Alexander and His Successors*, 28–55. Claremont.

On Philip's assassination:
Badian, E. (1963) "The Death of Philip II," *Phoenix* 17: 244–250. (Arguing that Alexander may well have had a hand in his father's assassination.)
Fears, J.R. (1975) "Pausanias, the Assassin of Philip II," *Athenaeum* 53: 111–135. (Arguing that Pausanias was a "lone nut" after all.)

On the burning of Xerxes' palace in Persepolis
Badian, E. (1967) "Agis III," *Hermes* 95: 170–192. (First connecting the burning with Agis III's revolt.)
Morrison, G.L. (2001) "Alexander, Combat Psychology, and Persepolis," *Antichthon* 35: 30–44.

On Alexander's campaigns in the East:
Bosworth, A.B. (1996) *Alexander and the East*. Oxford.

On the Alexander Romance and other noncanonical material on Alexander:
Davies, D. (trans.) (2007) *Shahnameh*. Harmondsworth.
Nöldeke, Th. (1890) "Beiträge zum syrischen Alexander-Roman," *Denkschriften der Österreichischen Akademie der Wissenschaften* 38. Vienna.
Stoneman, R. (1994) "The *Alexander Romance*: From History to Fiction." In: J.R. Morgan and R. Stoneman (eds.). *Greek Fiction. The Greek Novel in Context*, 117–129. London.
Stoneman, R. (1997) *The Greek Alexander Romance*. Harmondsworth.

Part IV

The Hellenistic Period: 323–30 BC

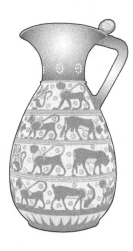

20

The Wars of the Diadochi

336–323	323–301	301–276

323	Perdiccas becomes Regent; Ptolemy becomes Satrap of Egypt
winter of 323–322	Lamian War
321	Antipater becomes Regent; Seleucus becomes Satrap of Babylon
319	Death of Antipater
318–317	Cassander gains control of Greece and Macedonia
317–316	Antigonus Monopthalmus gains control of Asia
312	Seleucus returns to Babylon
311	Diadochi make peace; Cassander kills Alexander IV
307	War begins anew; Diadochi take the royal title
301	Battle of Ipsus; Antigonus' kingdom divided

A History of Greece: 1300 to 30 BC, First Edition. Victor Parker.
© 2014 Victor Parker. Published 2014 by John Wiley & Sons, Ltd.

The Inheritors of the Empire

Because Alexander left behind no clear successor and at his death was in the process of replacing the "old guard" with "new talent" promoted from lower down the ranks, the empire fell to a diverse group: the survivors from the "old guard" – long-serving officers such as Craterus, Perdiccas, and Polyperchon; Antipater, his regent in Macedonia; Antigonus Monophthalmus, the satrap of Greater Phrygia – as well as new faces such as Ptolemy (who became satrap of Egypt just after Alexander's death), or Seleucus (who at the same time obtained his first major command) or Eumenes of Cardia (the chief archivist under Alexander and the satrap of Cappadocia on the Taurus later on). By convention they are collectively known as the Diadochi, the "Successors," and they would fight it out among themselves to see who would rule. The "royalist" nature of the age, moreover, allowed the female members of Alexander's family – his mother Olympias, his niece (Philip's granddaughter) Eurydice – to become players in a way in which they had not been in the period immediately preceding; and these first Hellenistic queens paved the way for the later ones such as Cleopatra VII of Egypt.

Alexander's Deification and the Hellenistic Ruler Cult

Two acts of Alexander's at the end of his life spilled over into the world of the successors. The first, and more important one long-term, concerned his apparent wish that the Greeks deify him. This inaugurated the cult of the ruler so characteristic of the Hellenistic world. The second – the Exiles' Decree –, however, had immediate consequences in Greece.

Shortly before the end of his life, various Greek cities deified Alexander (Arr. *Anab.* VII 23,2 – see Badian 1981 in Further Reading). Debates on the matter are attested in Athens (Din. I 94; **Hypereides**, *Dem.* fr. 7; Athen. VI, p. 258) and Sparta (Plut. *Sayings of Lacedaemonians*, p. 219). Although scholars once strove to see the roots of Alexander's deification in the Near East, in no Near Eastern kingdom had a ruler hitherto been worshipped as a god while still alive. Moreover, no evidence that any of Alexander's non-Greek subjects deified him exists, whereas the Greek world provides evidence of rulers who just before Alexander were approaching deification.

The Eresians on Lesbos, for example, had instituted a cult to a god called "Zeus Philipp*ios*" (Harding, Nr. 112B). The italicized "i" holds the key. In its absence the god would be "Zeus (who is) Philip," but instead the god is "Philip's Zeus, the Zeus who is closely associated with Philip." In Syracuse the tyrant Dio (see chap. 17) had once received *heroic* honors (Diod. XVI 20 describing heroic honors; cf. Plut. *Dio*, 46, saying "god" – see Badian 1981 in Further Reading). Yet in Greek religion heroes were not gods, and mortals, albeit after they died, could become heroes (oecists, for example – see chap. 5). Both Philip and Dio had gone right up to the line, but had shrunk back from crossing it.

Alexander too had come close to the line on several occasions. At Siwah the priest had proclaimed him the "son of Zeus." Divine sonship, though close to divinity, still stops short of it. Likewise, when Alexander had attempted to introduce *proskynesis* among the Macedonian troops, paths for explaining why this was not truly deification lay open – it was just a Persian custom, it did not actually mean what it appeared to mean, and so on.

When in his last year Alexander suppressed his own hesitations and strode across the line, he brought to conclusion a peculiar cultural development within the Greek world – one which just a generation later found its purest expression in the so-called Ithyphallic Hymn to Demetrius Poliorcetes, the son of Antigonus Monophthalmus (Athen. VI, p. 253), sung as that ruler entered Athens in 291:

> *The greatest and dearest gods are here in the city, for the occasion has hither brought*
> *Demeter and Demetrius together . . . He is gracious, as a god should be, and handsome*
> *and smiling . . . other gods are far away or have no ears or do not exist or pay no atten-*
> *tion to us . . . but you* [sc. O Demetrius] *we can see are present, not made of wood or*
> *stone, but real; so we pray to you . . .* (Athen. VI, p. 253)

Although Alexander's deification at the time caused much soul-searching, replete with many rationalizations ("if Alexander wishes to be *called* a god, then let him" – Plut. *Sayings of Lacedaemonians*, p. 219), in the end most went along with it however reluctantly (e.g., Demosthenes – Din., I 94; Hyp. *Dem.* fr. 7). The next time, however, was easier; and the time after that easier still; and soon enough rulers like Demetrius were routinely recognized as gods because they were present and could, much as a god, intervene from above in their subjects' lives. The cult of the ruler became an integral part of the social and political fabric of the Greek world.

The Mercenaries and the Exiles' Decree

Towards the end of his life Alexander had also promulgated a decree, extremely conducive to his empire's stability, requiring his satraps to dissolve their mercenary armies (Diod. XVII 111). Like Artaxerxes III Ochus (Harding, Nr. 72A), Alexander had recognized the danger in allowing some twenty satraps to command personal armies of mercenaries. The dismissal of the mercenaries, however, caused a new problem: thousands of armed men at large in the empire (Diod. l.c.). Compounding the problem was a mercenaries' revolt in Bactria which began in 325 (Diod. XVII 99; Curt. IX 7,1–11).

To solve these problems Alexander sought to facilitate what many mercenaries most wanted to do – to return home. Since many were exiles for one reason or another, Alexander had a proclamation made at the Olympic Games of 324 that all exiles from any Greek city should be allowed to return home (Diod. XVIII 8). Moreover, as a decree (Harding, Nr. 122) from Tegea in Arcadia shows, Alexander intended the returning exiles to receive a house and a plot of land in their hometowns. With a bit of luck the mercenaries, once settled back home, might show some gratitude to Alexander for having effected their return. Alexander did not live to see the benefits of the policy; but the Diadochi saw some of the disadvantages.

The Regency

On Alexander's death, the Macedonian army had to decide who would succeed him. One of his wives, Rhoxane, was pregnant and her confinement imminent. A number of officers apparently wished to see if the child should be a boy and, if so, to proclaim him king (Plut. *Eum.* 3). The rank and file, however, preferred Alexander's elder half-brother, Philip Arrhidaeus, who though feebleminded, was alive and present. In the end all agreed to a compromise: Arrhidaeus should become king (Diod. XVIII 2), but if Rhoxane bore a son, he should become co-king (from XVIII 18 onwards Diodorus speaks of two kings; he omitted the material explaining the compromise). A few weeks later Rhoxane did indeed give birth to a boy called Alexander.

A regency, however, was required in any case. Since Alexander's generals could not agree on a single regent, they settled on a transparently unworkable arrangement whereby four veteran officers Antipater, Craterus, Perdiccas, and Meleager (as Perdiccas' deputy) were to share power (Arr. *BNJ* 156, Fr. 1,1–3; Diod. XVIII 2 just gives the effective result). However, since Antipater was in Macedonia and Craterus was currently leading the 10,000 veterans whom Alexander had discharged at Opis back to Macedonia (Diod. XVIII 4) (see chap. 19), for the moment Perdiccas took over the command and redistributed the satrapies and other high offices (see Box 20.1). Noteworthy were the appointments of Ptolemy as satrap of Egypt and of Seleucus as commander of the "Companions," the Macedonian cavalry.

Thereafter Perdiccas, who did not wish to have his hands tied by Alexander's notebooks, contrived to have annulled all outstanding orders and plans left over from when Alexander was alive. At an assembly of the troops, Perdiccas read out the late king's last plans (presumably he had "edited" them to achieve the desired effect), and their preposterousness caused the troops to vote to carry out none of them. His hands free, Perdiccas turned to practical matters of state. He eliminated some enemies, including Meleager, and suppressed the mercenaries' revolt in Bactria (Diod. XVIII 4).

Ptolemy meantime took over his satrapy (Diod. XVIII 14). His effective predecessor, Cleomenes, was to remain in charge of the finances (**Dexippus**, *BNJ* 100, Fr. 8; Just. XIII 4,11), but Ptolemy quickly eliminated his rival (Paus. I 6). In hindsight Ptolemy had received the one satrapy which could most easily be severed from the empire (as Egypt had been for six decades in the fourth century) and converted into an independent kingdom. If Ptolemy wanted, or even realized, this in 323 can no longer be ascertained, but Egypt would eventually become one of the chief Hellenistic states.

Box 20.1   *The Division of the Empire at Babylon (323)*
and at Triparadeisus (321)

By an irony of history the Persian Empire's administrative structure can be viewed in full after its conquest only. Two archival lists stand at Diod. XVIII 3 (Perdiccas distributes the satrapies at Babylon in 323) and XVIII 39 (Antipater distributes the satrapies at Triparadeisus in 321). **Hieronymus of Cardia**, Diodorus' source in Books XVII–XXII, preserved these documents. In Table 20.1, the satrapies are presented according to the order of the division at Babylon:

Table 20.1   Persian satrapies

	Babylon (323)		Triparadeisus (321)	
	Satrapy	**Satrap**	**Satrapy**	**Satrap**
1.	Egypt	Ptolemy	Egypt	Ptolemy
2.	Syria	Laomedon	Syria	Laomedon
3.	Cilicia	Philotas	Cilicia	Philoxenus
4.	Media (Greater)	Peithon	Media (Greater)	Peithon
5.	Cappadocia	Eumenes	Cappadocia	Nicanor
6.	Greater Phyrgia	Antigonus	Greater Phrygia	Antigonus
7.	Caria	Asander	Caria	Asander
8.	Lydia	Menander	Lydia	Cleitus
9.	Hellespontine Phrygia	Leonnatus	Hellespontine Phrygia	Arrhidaeus
10.	(Thrace	Lysimachus)		
11.	(Macedonia	Antipater)		
12.	India I + II	Taxiles	India I + II	Taxiles
13.	India east of Hydaspes	Porus	India east of Hydaspes	Porus
14.	India III	Peithon	India III	Peithon
15.	Paropamisadae	Oxyartes	Paropamisadae	Oxyartes
16.	Arachosia + Gedrosia	Sibyrtius	*accidentally omitted*	
17.	Aria + Drangiane	Stasanor	Aria + Drangiane	Stasander
18.	Bactria + Sogdiane	Philip	Bactria + Sogdiane	Stasanor
19.	Parthia + Hyrcania	Phrataphernes	Parthia (+ Hyrcania)	Philip
20.	Persis	Peucestas	Persis	Peucestas
21.	Carmania	Tlepolemus	Carmania	Tlepolemus
22.	Media (Atropatene)	Atropates	*accidentally omitted*	
23.	Babylon	Archon	Babylon	Seleucus
24.	Mesopotamia	Arcesilaus	Mesopotamia	Amphimachus
25.	*accidentally omitted*		Susiane	Antigenes

(Continued)

One must consider both lists side by side in order to get a complete list of satrapies owing to accidental omissions in both. The first list treats Thrace and Macedonia (Nrr. 10 and 11) with the other satrapies (*de facto* justified) while the second omits them since these territories were not historically satrapies.

Both lists also show that long-term historical trends, from the Persian period, were continuing. The Persians often split overlarge satrapies into smaller ones. Thus Caria stood under the satrap of Lydia during Agesilaus' invasion of Asia Minor in the 390s (see chap. 15), but shortly thereafter it had its own satrap (see chap. 19). In 323 the old Persian satrapy of Babylon was split into two satrapies, Mesopotamia and Babylon, and the old Persian satrapy of Media was split into Greater Media and Media Atropatene. Paradoxically, the Persians also grouped together satrapies, which had not proved viable alone, to form "double-satrapies." This too continued under Alexander and his successors with some new arrangements of double-satrapies (Arachosia + Gedrosia and Aria + Drangiane – Nrr. 16 and 17 respectively).

Finally, the list of satraps shows the old Persian satrapal class – at Alexander's death already reduced to three if one includes Oxyartes – continuing to lose ground. In 323 half of Atropates' satrapy (Media) was taken from him, and in 321 a Macedonian replaced Phratapherenes in Parthia and Hyrcania.

The Lamian War

In Greece, however, a rebellion had broken out. An Athenian commander, Leosthenes, acting with the clandestine approval of the Athenian *Boule* (Diod. XVII 111), was collecting mercenaries returning from Asia (Paus. I 25; VIII 52) after their dismissal by the satraps on Alexander's orders. Leosthenes hired some 8,000 whom he brought to Athens (Diod. XVIII 9). Together with 5,000 Athenian hoplites, 2,000 additional mercenaries, and troops from various allies (Diod. XVIII 11), Leosthenes now had an army capable of rebelling credibly against Macedonian rule.

It fell to Antipater, who as regent of Macedonia had quelled Agis III's revolt a decade earlier, to deal with this one as well. Needing more troops he sent to Craterus (marching towards Macedonia at the head of 10,000 veterans) and to Philotas, the satrap of Hellespontine Phrygia, for help. Meanwhile, he marched southwards with what troops he had. Near Thermopylae Leosthenes defeated him, and Antipater, with the winter drawing on, retreated into the nearby fortress of Lamia. During the ensuing siege, Leosthenes was killed (Diod. XVIII 12–13). In the spring of 322 Macedonian reinforcements arrived, and the Greeks lifted the siege. Next Craterus arrived with even more troops. He yielded the command to Antipater, who now made short work of the rebels (Diod. XVIII 16–17). Thereafter Antipater instituted oligarchies throughout Greece in the hopes of thereby avoiding additional revolts – for the oligarchs would owe their position to the Macedonians. In Athens 9,000 men with property valued at 2,000 drachmas or more took charge of the government (Diod. XVIII 18; see also 55). Events in Asia, however, prevented Antipater from settling matters in Greece entirely, and he broke off a campaign against the Aetolian League (Diod. XVIII 24–25).

Antipater Becomes Regent

In Asia Minor Perdiccas had undertaken the conquest of Cappadocia on the Taurus. The old Persian satrap, Ariarathes, who had since become king, could not withstand this offensive (Diod. XVIII 16), and Eumenes of Cardia, Alexander's archivist, whom in 323 Perdiccas had appointed as satrap, now took charge of his satrapy. Next Perdiccas turned to Pisidia, a mountainous region that had not yet been pacified, and brought it under the empire's control (Diod. XVIII 22). In 323 and 322, Perdiccas had consolidated the empire's position in Asia. However, as Perdiccas' grip on the empire grew steadily firmer, the other marshals began to cooperate against him. Antigonus Monophthalmus, the satrap of Greater Phrygia, met with Antipater and Craterus and convinced them that Perdiccas would soon act against them. Thereupon they contacted Ptolemy who agreed to cooperate against Perdiccas (Diod. XVIII 25).

In the spring of 321, Perdiccas marched against Egypt while he sent Eumenes, the satrap of Cappadocia, to hold the Hellespont against Antipater and Craterus (Diod. XVIII 29). The archivist Eumenes, who was nearly untested militarily, was going up against some of the most experienced Macedonian generals. As a Greek, his control over Macedonian troops was tenuous at best (see Diod. XVIII 32; 40; 60), yet in battle Eumenes defeated Craterus who himself fell (Diod. XVIII 30–32). Meanwhile, Perdiccas became bogged down in fighting at Pelusium on the Egyptian border where his officers with Ptolemy's connivance assassinated him (Diod. XVIII 33–36).

Since Ptolemy stayed in Egypt and both Craterus and Perdiccas were dead, Antipater had no rival left, excepting Eumenes, who as a Greek hardly counted. He calmly proceeded to Triparadeisus in Syria, secured his election as regent by the troops, and redistributed the satrapies (see Box 20.1). Noteworthy was the promotion of Seleucus as satrap of Babylon. Antipater also appointed Antigonus Monopthalmus as commander of the army in Asia and his own son, Cassander, as **chiliarch** or vizier. Thereafter he returned to Macedonia with the co-kings Philip III Arrhidaeus and Alexander IV (together with his mother, Rhoxane). Antigonus remained in Asia Minor to deal with the outstanding matter of Eumenes.

Eumenes' cavalry having deserted him, Antigonus defeated him easily in 320. During the winter of 320 to 319 Antigonus besieged Eumenes in the fortress of Nora, somewhere in the Taurus range. Antigonus, in charge of the largest army in the empire and with access to the revenues of his and Eumenes' satrapies, now set his sights higher (Diod. XVIII 40–41). Ptolemy too, however, was conceiving ambitions and towards the end of 320 he seized control of the so-called **Hollow Syria,** the southern portion of the Syrian satrapy together with Phoenicia (Diod. XVIII 43).

In 319 the by now very old Antipater died, but not before appointing Polyperchon, a veteran officer of Alexander's, as regent (Diod. XVIII 48). This reset the board. Antigonus now made peace with Eumenes and began his own play for power (Diod. XVIII 50 and 53). Cassander, Antipater's son, bitter because he had not become regent, conspired with Antigonus and Ptolemy against Polyperchon (Diod. XVIII 54). For his part Polyperchon offered Eumenes money, and Eumenes, reneging on his alliance with Antigonus, accepted. With the money Eumenes began to raise an army, and, in the name of the Kings Philip III Arrhidaeus and Alexander IV, Polyperchon wrote to satraps and treasurers throughout the empire to order them to assist Eumenes (Diod. XVIII 57–58). Although Antigonus and Ptolemy tried to hinder him, Eumenes collected a large army and in a perilous march led it into the so-called **Upper Satrapies** in the eastern half of the empire (Diod. XVIII 59–63 and 73).

In Greece, meanwhile, Polyperchon reversed Antipater's policy of backing oligarchies and ineffectively threw his support behind democracies (Diod. XVIII 55–56). Many oligarchies (e.g., in Megalopolis) thereupon sought support from the still-embittered Cassander (Diod. XVIII 68). Nicanor, the commander of the Macedonian garrison in the Peiraeus, welcomed Cassander when he appeared with a fleet (Diod. XVIII 64–65 and 68). Polyperchon's lackluster attempts at besieging both the Peiraeus and Megalopolis (Diod. XVIII 68–72) merely eroded his support in Greece, and by the end of 318 Cassander had won over most of the Greek cities, including Athens (Diod. XVIII 74).

Shortly thereafter, Eurydice, Philip's granddaughter and the wife of the feebleminded Philip III Arrhidaeus, acting in the name of her husband, removed Polyperchon from the regency and assumed it herself (Just. XIV 5; Diod. XIX 11). It was the first bold assertion of power by a Hellenistic queen, yet Eurydice had precious little support among the soldiers. When Polyperchon (together with Olympias, Alexander's mother and a rather more formidable queen) approached with an army, Eurydice's troops deserted (early 317). Polyperchon handed Philip III Arrhidaeus and Eurydice over to Olympias who saw to it that both died (Diod. l.c.). This left in Olympias' keeping a six-year-old boy as titular king, but from now on there was no (generally recognized) regent. Where Perdiccas and Antipater had succeeded, Polyperchon had failed; and his failure delivered the empire into the hands of the warlords.

Antigonus in Asia

The eastern satrapies of the empire had remained remarkably quiet during the preceding years. However, the satrap of Greater Media, Peithon, had made war upon his neighbor, the satrap of Hyrcania and Parthia, whom he replaced with his own brother, Eudamus. This had united the remaining eastern satraps

Box 20.2   *Athens under Demetrius of Phalerum*

In 317, shortly after he had taken Athens, Cassander appointed as its governor an Athenian called Demetrius, from the deme of Phalerum (Diod. XVIII 74). Demetrius, once in charge of Athens, justified the confidence which Cassander placed in him. Impeccably loyal to his benefactor, he secured for Athens a decade of peace. Not everyone, however, could approve of an Athenian serving as a foreign power's puppet governor (e.g., **Demochares**, *BNJ* 75, Fr. 7).

But for now Demetrius' position was unassailable. Since he himself served as eponymous archon in 309 (Diod. XX 27), this office was probably filled by election in this period (unless by improbable coincidence the lot fell on the name of the man who happened to be the Macedonian-appointed governor). Seven **nomophylaces** ("law-guardians"), with wide-ranging powers to make sure that other officials were acting in accordance with the laws (Philochorus, *BNJ* 328, Fr. 64; see Pollux, VIII 102 for the link with Demetrius, though Pollux speaks of eleven nomophylaces), were also probably elected (cf. Xen. *Oec.* IX 14). The Council of the Areopagus moreover had augmented judicial powers (Diog.Laert. II 101 and 116) and was partially responsible for enforcing Demetrius' sumptuary laws (Philochorus, *BNJ* 328, Fr. 65; cf. Cic. *de Leg*. II 66). In other words it was a mostly oligarchic constitution even if the Assembly and the *Boule* otherwise functioned as under the classical democracy.

Demetrius, moreover, for the first time ever carried out a census in Athens (**Ctesicles/Stesicleides**, *BNJ* 245, Fr. 1). Normally maximum military levies (e.g., the 13,000 Athenian hoplites attested at Thuc. II 13 and 31 for the year 431) provide the only clue to a state's population, but for once the demographer has actual data, even if the figures have been rounded off: 21,000 citizens (presumably adult males over 18) and 10,000 resident aliens (again, presumably adult males). The figure given for slaves (400,000) is, unfortunately, impossibly high, so probably there has been an error in the transmission of the numeral.

Demetrius also improved Athens' financial situation. He reduced expenditure where he could, but probably his keeping Athens out of war helped most of all. Athens' annual revenue rose to 1200 talents (**Duris** of Samos, *BNJ* 76, Fr. 10), and Demetrius boasted of the low prices of goods during his tenure (Demetrius, Fr. 90 Fortenbaugh).

Demetrius, finally, was a man of letters as well. He studied philosophy under Aristotle's successor in the so-called Peripatetic school, Theophrastus (**Cicero**, *de Fin*. V 54) and, given the timeframe, presumably also Aristotle himself. Demetrius wrote widely on many topics, and two and a half centuries later Cicero would write that Demetrius alone of the Greeks was both a scholar and a statesman (*De leg*. III 14).

Nonetheless, given the ongoing wars of the Diadochi, sooner or later war would come to Athens again no matter what Demetrius did. When Demetrius Poliorcetes, Antigonus Monophthalmus' son, took Athens in 307, Demetrius of Phalerum had to flee (Plut. *Demetr*. 8–9). He stayed with his patron Cassander for a decade and after Cassander's death found refuge with Ptolemy I Soter in Alexandria (Strab. IX 1,20, p. 398; Diod. XX 45).

against Peithon, and for this reason Eumenes, upon his arrival in the east in 317, found a large army already gathered (Diod. XIX 14). It took all of Eumenes' diplomatic skill to manage the individual satraps so as to gain control of this army for his own purposes.

Antigonus, meanwhile, with his own army pursued Eumenes into the eastern satrapies, and there ensued a game of cat and mouse as each sought to out-maneuver the other. Towards the end of 317 the two armies met in the region Paraetacene on the marches between Media and Persis (Diod. XIX 34). Eumenes was once again going up against one of the most experienced generals of the time. Antigonus had some 28,000 infantry, 8,500 cavalry, and 65 ele-phants; fighting against them on Eumenes' side were 35,000 infantry, 6,100 cavalry, and 114 elephants. Among his infantry stood some 3,000 of Alexander's veterans, all at least sixty by now, many seventy and some even older; but fight-ing with a *sarissa* gave the edge to experience, and these elderly veterans, at the heart of Eumenes' phalanx, carried the day in the center. Eumenes himself led light cavalry in a highly successful flanking maneuver on his right wing, put Antigonus' left wing to flight, and pursued it. With a desperate maneuver Antig-onus managed to avert total defeat. As Eumenes' center advanced, a gap opened up between it and Eumenes' left, and through this gap Antigonus led a cavalry charge which, unexpected as it was, nearly routed Eumenes' left wing. Eumenes broke off his pursuit and returned to rescue his left wing, but by then it was nearly night, and the battle ended. Antigonus remained in possession of the battlefield, so, technically, could claim the victory though his losses (3,700 infantry, 54 cavalry, 4,000 wounded) greatly exceeded Eumenes' (540 infantry, hardly any cavalry, and 900 wounded) (Diod. XIX 27–31). Anxious to avoid any more such "victories," Antigonus soon retreated into Media and went into winter quarters (Diod. XIX 32).

Eumenes himself went into winter quarters in the nearby region of Gabene, where, owing to the scarcity of provisions, he had to divide his army into many parts such that some detachments were six days' march from others. A twenty-five days' march through inhabited country separated the two armies; but a nine days' march through a desert (Diod. XIX 34). About the time of the winter solstice Antigonus led his army towards Eumenes' camp by the shorter route hoping to catch Eumenes by surprise. Eumenes, however, got wind of Antig-onus' march in time (Diod. XIX 37–39), and a second full battle took place. Once again the 3,000 elderly veterans cleared the field in front of them (Antig-onus allegedly lost some 5,000 men), but Eumenes himself, fighting this time with his cavalry on the left wing, was badly beaten by Antigonus who even managed to capture Eumenes' camp. (Diod. XIX 40–43).

Only with difficulty had Eumenes retained control of an unwieldy army com-manded by various satraps, none of whom liked him, and the Macedonian troops in the army had never quite willingly followed a Greek. After this humili-ation and the capture of his camp, Eumenes' standing with the satraps and the troops was destroyed. They seized him and handed him over to Antigonus, who had his opponent put to death (Diod. XIX 43–44), ending one of the most remarkable careers of the era. In early 316 Antigonus, despite two effective defeats, became master of the Asian part of the empire. He distributed the eastern satrapies anew (Diod. XIX 48) and appeared to be well on his way to uniting the entire empire under his control.

The War against Antigonus

Meanwhile, Cassander had gained control of Greece, and when he learned that Olympias had put Philip III Arrhidaeus to death, he hastened from the Peloponnese northwards (317). Since the Aetolian League held Thermopylae, Cassander got his troops to Euboea and thence to Thessaly on barges. He marched on Pydna, where Olympias had taken refuge. She sought aid from Epirus and Polyperchon, but the latter was a spent force, and his army deserted; meanwhile a revolution in Epirus brought that land into alliance with Cassander. Olympias thus found herself besieged in Pydna with no hope of aid, and in 316 she surrendered. Cassander had her killed and took possession of Alexander IV, the seven-year-old titular king. For the remainder of the year Cassander fought against Polyperchon's son, also called Alexander, on the Peloponnese and consolidated his grip on that region (Diod. XIX 35–36 and 50–54).

Meanwhile, in Asia Antigonus grasped for power too quickly. He expelled Seleucus from the satrapy of Babylon and thus drove him to Egypt into Ptolemy's arms. Seleucus and Ptolemy wrote to Cassander and won him over to an alliance against Antigonus. In late 316, the three presented Antigonus with a list of demands, which he rejected out of hand (Diod. XIX 55–57). Antigonus now formed an alliance with Polyperchon and Polyperchon's son Alexander; Antigonus moreover sought to stir Greece up against Cassander by promulgating an edict whereby all Greece was to be "free and autonomous" and without garrisons (Diod. XIX 60–61). Cassander, however, retained control of the situation and made Alexander, Polyperchon's son, a better offer than Antigonus had. Alexander joined Cassander while his father apparently went into retirement (Diod. XIX 63–64). Practically the only supporters of Antigonus now left in Greece were the Aetolians. In 314 and 313 Cassander and his general, Philip, carried out successful campaigns in western and northwestern Greece and inflicted severe defeats on the Aetolians (Diod. XIX 67 and 74). In 313 Antigonus sent a general, Ptolemy (not the satrap of Egypt), to invade Greece. Ptolemy landed with his fleet in Boeotia and campaigned in central Greece (Diod. XIX 78) while Antigonus himself marched towards the Hellespont hoping to get his army across with ships from Byzantium. That city, however, remained scrupulously neutral, and since the year was advanced, Antigonus went into winter quarters (Diod. XIX 77).

In Asia, as well, things had been going badly for Antigonus. In 315 Asander, the satrap of Caria, had joined the coalition against him (Diod. XIX 62), and in 314 and 313 Antigonus was compelled to dispatch troops to fight against Asander (Diod. XIX 68 and 75). There was also Ptolemy to guard against in the south. In 314 Antigonus stationed his son, Demetrius, in Syria to face any attack from Egypt (Diod. XIX 69). Demetrius seems to have recaptured Hollow Syria from Ptolemy in 314 or 313, but late in 313 Ptolemy, operating from Cyprus, captured a few cities in Cilicia before sailing back to Egypt. In the spring of 312, while Antigonus was still on the Hellespont, Ptolemy invaded Hollow Syria and defeated the overwhelmed Demetrius (Diod. XIX 79–86). Antigonus thereupon marched into Syria, and Ptolemy decided to give up Hollow Syria without a fight rather than to risk all in one engagement (Diod. XIX 93). There had been no decisive battle, but Cassander still held Greece and Macedonia and Ptolemy still held Egypt. Antigonus had nothing to show for his efforts, and his authority in Asia was crumbling.

Box 20.3   *Legitimating the Rule of the Diadochi*

The position of the Diadochi in their respective kingdoms was long ambiguous. Although Ptolemy had been ruling Egypt as its king *de facto* since 323, he did not feel secure enough to advertise this publicly. For a number of years documents during his reign were dated according to the formula attested at *Pap.Eleph.* 1 1–2: "in the seventh year of King Alexander, son of Alexander, and in the fourteenth year of Ptolemy the Satrap" (i.e., 310; the regnal years of Alexander IV are counted from Philip III Arrhidaeus' death in 317). Officially, then, Ptolemy maintained the fiction that Alexander IV was ruling a unified empire in which he, Ptolemy, was merely a satrap. The fiction existed in the first instance for the benefit of the Macedonians in Ptolemy's employ, especially the soldiers – Ptolemy was sure of their adherence to the house of Alexander the Great, less sure of their adherence to him.

The same principle emerges from the coins Ptolemy minted in these years (see Figure 20.1). Coins, because they got into everyone's hands, were rulers' best means of putting out their message in an age without "photo ops," "sound-bites," and press releases. And the message which Ptolemy put out until circa 307 can be seen on the top right coin in Figure 20.1.

The legend on the coin reads "of Alexander," and the head is that of Alexander the Great himself, who is wearing an elephant scalp (a reference to the conquest of India). Alexander the Great was dead, but not forgotten by the Macedonians in Egypt who honored his legacy and were willing to obey the man who governed them as a satrap in the empire which Alexander had fashioned and over which Alexander's son now reigned. Because Ptolemy's rule rested on the fact of Alexander's conquest, it should not surprise that Ptolemy drew on Alexander's achievements in order to legitimate his own rule in the eyes of his (Macedonian and Greek) subjects.

The other Diadochi followed much the same pattern, as the coins of Seleucus and Antigonus Monopthalmus in Figure 20.1 show. On both coins Alexander wears a lion's skin as Heracles; the inscription reads "of Alexander."

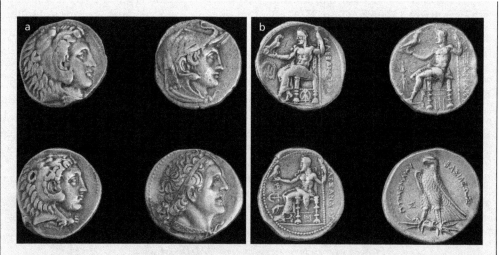

Figure 20.1 Four coins of the Diadochi: the obverse ("heads") of a given coin in the left-hand image corresponds to the reverse ("tails") in the same position in the right-hand image. Clockwise from top left: tetradrachm of Antigonus Monophthalmus (Mørkholm, Nr. 84, circa 307; inscription on reverse: "of Alexander"); tetradrachm of Ptolemy I Soter (Mørkholm, Nr. 90, circa 319–315; inscription on reverse: "of Alexander"); tetradrachm of Ptolemy I Soter (Mørkholm, Nr. 97, after circa 307; inscription on reverse: "of King Ptolemy"); tetradrachm of Seleucus I Nicator (Mørkholm, Nr. 87, after 312; inscription on reverse: "of Alexander"). Source: National Museum of Denmark

The coins, incidentally, are far more than just historical evidence. They are works of art, prime examples of portraiture. When the Hellenistic kings began putting their own images on coins, the art of portraiture quickly reached impressive heights.

The Rise of Seleucus

Also in 312 Ptolemy sent Seleucus with a small force back into his old satrapy of Babylon. Seleucus had built up a loyal base there during his time as satrap and easily regained control. When Nicanor, who commanded troops loyal to Antigonus in Media, opposed this, Seleucus defeated him in a surprise attack. Nicanor's army deserted to Seleucus who succeeded in bringing Media, the Susiane, and some neighboring satrapies (possibly Aria [cf. Diod. XIX 92,4 with 48,2] and the Persis [see Diod. l.c.]) under his control (Diod. XIX 90–92). Seleucus had laid the foundation for the greatest of the Hellenistic states, the so-called **Seleucid** Kingdom.

In 311 Cassander, Ptolemy, and Antigonus made a peace treaty, whereby Cassander received Europe, Ptolemy Egypt, and Antigonus Asia (Diod. XIX 105,1). The absence of Seleucus is glaring, and Diodorus probably omitted a critical piece of information. Either Seleucus participated in the treaty directly or he and Antigonus had a separate arrangement. Although the treaty envisaged a division of the empire, technically it still existed under the rule of the young Alexander IV who at the age of twelve was now close to attaining his majority. Should he have lived that long, he might have threatened the arrangements which the Diadochi had just made for themselves. Cassander, deciding that this particular charade had gone on long enough, had Alexander IV and his mother Rhoxane murdered (Diod. XIX 105,2).

Despite the peace treaty, the Diadochi continued to maneuver for advantage against each other. Between 310 and 308 matters rarely flared into open warfare, and the most notable episode of those years in the west involved the ex-regent Polyperchon who in 310 came out of retirement to produce a seventeen-year-old boy, called Heracles, whom he presented as an illegitimate son of Alexander's. Cassander through various promises won over the old ex-regent, whose political perspicacity had never been great, and induced him to murder the hapless youth (Diod. XX 20 and 28).

In the east, however, Seleucus' power was growing. A campaign against Bactria is attested (Just. XV 4, 11), and Seleucus eventually controlled the Sogdiane as well as all territory up to the River Indus (App. *Syr.* 55). He even crossed the Indus and waged war against Chandragupta Maurya (Sandrocottus in Greek) (App. *Syr.* 55; Just. XV 4,12), so he must have attempted to reconquer those regions too which Alexander had held east of the Indus. A few years before the Battle of Ipsus (in 301), however, he made peace with Chandragupta Maurya (App. l.c.) from whom he received 500 war-elephants (Plut. *Alex.* 62; Strab. XV 2,9, p. 724 – mentioning Seleucus' cession of some land west of the Indus as well). A bare half-sentence in Diodorus (XX 53,4 – for the year 307) gives just a hint at his activities in these years: "Seleucus, who had recently gained control of the upper satrapies . . ." Diodorus' zeal to abridge may have caused the loss of his source's material on perhaps the historically most significant events of these years.

In 307 war broke out again in earnest. Antigonus sent his son Demetrius with a fleet against Athens. Demetrius succeeded in taking Cassander's garrison in the Peiraeus by storm and soon captured Athens. With his fleet Demetrius then sailed for Cyprus, then under Ptolemy's control, and routed Ptolemy's commander there. He took the city of Salamis on Cyprus by siege and did his nickname "Poliorcetes" or "Besieger of Cities" credit. Ptolemy sailed with a fleet of 140 **quinqueremes** and **quadriremes** (triremes, by now, were mostly outmoded) but Demetrius appears to have had more at his disposal though the number is unclear. The result was a complete victory for Demetrius (Diod. XX 45–52).

Politically, the Diadochi all took a major step forward in 307 or thereabouts: Antigonus took the title "King" and set the diadem upon his head, and he allowed his son Demetrius to do the same. Thereupon Ptolemy, Cassander, Seleucus, as well as Lysimachus (the ruler of Thrace, a minor Diadochus up until now, but his day would come) all took the title of king (Diod. XX 53). Ptolemy had hitherto displayed the image of Alexander on his coins (see

Box 20.3) but now coins appeared bearing his own image with the proud inscription "of King Ptolemy" (see Figure 20.1, bottom right).

In the next year, Antigonus by land and Demetrius by sea attempted a full-scale invasion of Egypt, but Ptolemy had long since fortified the approaches heavily. Antigonus made little headway, and Demetrius found no unguarded landing place for his fleet. In the end Antigonus was forced to retreat with nothing to show for his efforts (Diod. XX 73–76). Yet Antigonus was nothing if not determined, and in 305 he sent Demetrius against Rhodes. Despite its small size, Rhodes was an important naval power (see Box 23.2) and at the time allied with Ptolemy. Demetrius used all possible means to take the city by siege, but had not done so after about a year. A treaty was arranged whereby the Rhodians became allies of Antigonus except when Antigonus was fighting against Ptolemy (Diod. XX 81–88 and 91–100). The Rhodians, thankful to have survived the siege, erected the storied Colossus of Rhodes in commemoration (**Pliny**, *NH* XXXIV 17).

Free of the siege of Rhodes, Demetrius, still in 304, undertook a major campaign against Cassander. He landed on Euboea, seized the strategic site of Chalcis, and won over the Boeotian League (Diod. XX 100). In 303 he proceeded to the Peloponnese and took various cities there including the strategic site of Corinth (Diod. XX 102–103). Cassander appeared unable to stop Demetrius and appealed for help to Ptolemy, Seleucus, and Lysimachus, the King of Thrace. In 302 Lysimachus invaded Asia Minor while Cassander marched southwards into Thessaly where Demetrius too arrived (Diod. XX 106–110). At first Antigonus was confident in his ability to repel Lysimachus, but when he learned that Seleucus was marching from the east with a great army, he ordered Demetrius to return to Asia. Demetrius hastily came to terms with Cassander and went to join his father (Diod. XX 111). Seleucus soon arrived in Cappadocia with an army of 20,000 infantry, 12,000 cavalry, and 480 elephants (Diod. XX 113). The last two numbers are particularly impressive: Seleucus had grown mighty indeed.

The Battle of Ipsus and its Aftermath

Lysimachus and Seleucus joined their armies; together they had some 64,000 infantry. Antigonus and Demetrius had approximately the same numbers in infantry, but were hopelessly outnumbered in cavalry and elephants (of the latter they had only 75) (Plut. *Demetr.* 28–29). Ptolemy, meanwhile, had advanced into Hollow Syria, however when he received a false report that Lysimachus and Seleucus had been defeated, he withdrew to Egypt, leaving behind garrisons in Hollow Syria (Diod. XX 113). Thus it came about that Ptolemy was absent when Lysimachus and Seleucus fought the decisive battle against Antigonus at Ipsus, near Synnada in Greater Phrygia.

Seleucus' cavalry and elephants won the day. Demetrius, having defeated the opposing cavalry on one wing, pursued it too far and left his and his father's infantry hopelessly exposed to Seleucus' cavalry (Plut. l.c.). Antigonus Monoph-thalmus, in his eighties by now, fell fighting to the last. Until the end he had fought for possession of the entire empire of Alexander the Great; lesser Dia-dochi had been content to carve out of it kingdoms for themselves – Ptolemy in Egypt, Cassander in Macedonia and Greece, Lysimachus in Thrace. Seleucus alone perhaps still harbored ambitions like to those of Antigonus, but he was circumspect in the matter.

After Antigonus' death the victors of Ipsus divided up his kingdom. Lysima-chus took northern Asia Minor east of the Taurus, Seleucus took Syria, and Pleistarchus, a brother of Cassander's, took southern Asia Minor from Caria to Cilicia (Plut. *Demetr.* 30–31; Pol. V 67; App. *Syr.* 55; Diod. XXI 1).

QUESTIONS FOR REVIEW

1 What attempts did the regents make initially to keep the empire together?
2 How did some Diadochi begin to concentrate on establishing their rule in a part of the empire?
3 How did the alliances among the Diadochi shift in order to prevent one of them from gaining the entire empire?
4 In what stages did the Diadochi gradually emerge from Alexander's legacy?

QUESTION FOR FURTHER STUDY

Does Antigonus Monophthalmus deserve his reputation as a commanding figure among the Diadochi? After all, he lost every major battle in which he fought; he seems to have had next to no political skill, and to have underesti-mated all his main opponents (Seleucus, Ptolemy, Cassander, etc.). Is his repu-tation due solely to the historiographical quirk that the main source for the history of the epoch, Hieronymus of Cardia (*BNJ* 154), was a close associate of his?

FURTHER READING

Hieronymus' account is reasonably well preserved in Diodorus' abridgment, down to just before the Battle of Ipsus. In many ways, Books XVIII and XIX of Diodorus are the best way to approach this period. However, recent biographies of some Diadochi exist:

Anson, E.M. (2004) *Eumenes of Cardia: A Greek among Macedonians.* Leiden.
Billows, R.A. (1990) *Antigonus the One-eyed and the Creation of the Hellenistic State.* Berkeley.
Ellis, W.M. (1994) *Ptolemy of Egypt.* London.
Grainger, J.D. (1990) *Seleukos Nikator: Constructing a Hellenistic Kingdom.* London.
Lund, H.S. (1992) *Lysimachus: A Study in Early Hellenistic Kingship.* London.

On Hieronymus of Cardia, the chief source for the period:
Hornblower, J. (1981) *Hieronymus of Cardia*. Oxford.

On Alexander's deification, see:
Badian, E. (1981) "The Deification of Alexander the Great," *Ancient Macedonian Studies in Honor of C.F. Edson*, 27–71. Thessaloniki.

On Athens in this period, see:
Habicht, Chr. (1997) *Athens from Alexander to Antony*. Cambridge, MA.

On the coinage of the Diadochi, see:
Mørkholm, O. (1991) *Early Hellenistic Coinage*. Cambridge.

21

The Creation of the Hellenistic States

| 323–301 | 301–276 | 276–206 |

A History of Greece: 1300 to 30 BC, First Edition. Victor Parker.
© 2014 Victor Parker. Published 2014 by John Wiley & Sons, Ltd.

The Hellenization of Asia

In the aftermath of the Battle of Ipsus the political map of the Hellenistic world began to take shape. Egypt under Ptolemy already had its basic borders, but Seleucus' kingdom had yet to reach its full extent. And it was still unclear what state would form in Greece and Macedonia. All the same, in Asia things were settling down, and Seleucus and Ptolemy devoted more and more of their energy to the administration and development of their respective kingdoms. Hand in hand with the establishment of the Hellenistic states went the process of Hellenization, whereby the indigenous peoples of Asia came under the influence of Greek language and culture. The Hellenistic kings drove this process along through the steady importation of Greeks (and Macedonians) into their kingdoms. Sometimes they founded genuinely new cities with these immigrants (e.g., Antioch – see below), but on other occasions they merely placed the immigrants into an existing non-Greek city which then received a new Greek name (e.g., Philadelphia, the older Amman – see below). New foundations were fully Greek from the start, but the renamed cities often had just a core of Greek settlers to which, however, the old inhabitants could assimilate. Both the new and the renamed cities then spread Greek language and culture into the surrounding countryside.

Alexander the Great had led the way with his foundation of the new city of Alexandria in Egypt (Arr. III 1,5–2,2) and with the settlement of Greek mercenaries in existing cities (e.g., in Bactria – Curt. IX 7,1) or in smaller outposts (e.g., Arr. VII 21,7). Since the Diadochi invested most of their energy in wars against each other, they initially founded few cities. But Antigonus Monophthalmus did found Antigoneia on the River Orontes (Diod. XX 47) and settled it with Athenians (**Malalas**, p. 201). The Mesopotamian town of Carrhae had Macedonian settlers in 312 B.C. (Diod. XIX 91), whichever Diadochus settled it. Some cities in these regions, not known to have been founded by Alexander or by the Seleucids (i.e., Seleucus and his successors) could be Antigonus' foundations (e.g., Alexandria near Issus).

Ptolemy and his successors, meanwhile, founded a few cities (e.g., Ptolemaïs in Upper Egypt [Strab. XVII 1,42, p. 813], Ptolemaïs in Palestine, and Philadelphia in Transjordan). In addition they welcomed immigrants into Alexandria, including the families from Syracuse whom Theocritus describes and whose Doric dialect grated on the ears of some (XV 87–95). Yet the Ptolemies' activity pales before the Seleucids'.

Seleucus, already before the Battle of Ipsus, had built Seleuceia on the Tigris, presumably as his capital (Strab. XVI 1,5, p. 738), but after Ipsus he treated Syria as the heartland of his kingdom, and there on the River Orontes he founded a new capital, Antiocheia ("Antioch," named after his father) (Diod. XX 47,6 – though Diodorus accidentally writes "Seleuceia"). A little upstream lay Apameia, and at the mouth of the Orontes lay the port of Seleuceia. Laodiceia was farther south on the coast (Strab. XVI 2,4, p. 749). Where the road from Antioch reached the Euphrates Seleucus founded another Seleuceia which a

bridge connected with another Apamea on the river's eastern bank. This Seleuceia was known as "Seleuceia by the bridge" or simply as Zeugma ("bridge")
(Plin. *NH* V 86).

In Mesopotamia, where few cities existed, the Seleucids founded a large
number (Plin. *NH* VI 117). Besides the aforementioned Apamea, there were
Edessa and Nicephorium, both foundations of Seleucus I (App. *Syr.* 57). A satrap
of Mesopotamia by the name of Nicanor founded Europus (Plin. l.c.; **Isidore
of Charax**, *BNJ* 781, Fr. 2). Even in the satrapy of Babylon, where many cities
already existed, Seleucus I also founded Apollonia to the east of the Tigris, and
his successors founded others (Plin. *NH* VI 117, 129, 132, 146; Strab. XVI 1,18,
p. 744).

After Seleucus' conquest of Asia Minor to the west of the Taurus (see below),
his son and grandson, Antiochus I Soter ("savior") and Antiochus II Theos
("god"), founded Apameia (the older Celaenae) (Strab. XII 8,15, p. 577),
Laodiceia on the River Lycus, and Stratoniceia in Caria (**Stephanus of Byzantium**, ss.vv.) and, probably, Antiocheia on the Meander, and Antiocheia near
Pisidia (foundations *per se* unattested, but only a king named Antiochus is possible as founder). Emigrants from Magnesia on the Meander helped to settle
the last-named city (Strab. XII 8,14, p. 577).

Even in the Upper Satrapies the Seleucids were active. Media received a
number of Greek cities (Pol. X 27,3): Europus (the older Rhagae), yet another
Apameia, and yet another Laodiceia are known (Strab. XI 13,6, p. 524;
Plin. VI 43). Seleucus himself settled Greek colonists in Ecbatana (Plin. l.c.).
In the Persis there lay yet another Antiocheia with settlers from Magnesia
on the Meander (Burstein, Nr. 32); Antiochus I founded Antiocheia Margiane
to the north of Aria (Strab. XI 10,2, p. 516), and **Appian** (*Syr.* 57) names a
series of additional Greek cities in Parthia.

Even when many inhabitants of these cities were not Greek originally, there were
usually enough Greeks to "Hellenize" the rest, provided that the city stood under
Greek rule long enough, for the administration of the cities functioned in Greek;
the officials, the local grandees, as well as the social elite all spoke Greek; and
Greek festivals were celebrated. The king who ruled spoke Greek, and his coins
bore Greek legends. The cities had Greek names, and whatever the ethnic origin of
the inhabitants, in course of time Greek language and Greek culture prevailed.

Even beyond the cities the effects of Hellenization were felt. Much is occasionally made of references in the literary sources (e.g., **John Chrysostomus**,
Homilies 19, p. 184) to the way in which the people living around so thoroughly
Greek a city as Antioch still spoke a language other than Greek as late as
the fourth and fifth century AD, and doubtlessly Aramaic always remained the
predominant language throughout the countryside in Syria. But this does not
exclude an easy bilingualism whereby many speakers of the "native" language
could at least make do in Greek.

In time even the fashions of the big city pervaded the countryside to the
farthest corners of the Empire. Thus by the mid-second century in the sleepy
district of Judea, people were adopting Greek names in addition to their native

ones (for example, the High Priests Jason and Menelaus – Yeshua and Yohannon respectively before they changed them); and much to the disgust of traditionalists were wearing Greek hats and practicing Greek sports such as discus-throwing (II Macc. IV 12–14). This Greek influence can only have come from neighboring Greek cities such as the nearby Ptolemaïs. When a revolt against the Seleucids broke out in Judea in the 160s (see chap. 24), historical texts were composed to record that revolt; what survives is all in Greek. II Maccabees was actually composed in Greek originally, and it is merely the abridgment of a longer work, by one Jason of Cyrene, who had taken a Greek name and wrote in Greek. Judea lay off the beaten track for the main road between Egypt and Syria ran along the coast to the west of the Judean Hills. Few people from outside, besides merchants and the occasional sportsman looking for game (for the evidence, see below), ventured up into those hills. Yet the influence of Greek culture and Greek language was very real in Judea; and that will have been the case throughout Syria and Asia Minor – as well as in Iran as long as the Seleucids held it.

Hellenization, however, had its limits. Indigenous languages, as indicated above, held their ground and the introduction of Greek sports and fashions in Judea, for example, raised the hackles of many who then pushed back hard. Greek visitors, moreover, sometimes received firm instruction in matters on which the "natives" would not compromise. To remain with Judea, Greeks wishing to see the Temple precinct in Jerusalem could read a sign (Jos. *Ant.* XII 3,4 [145–146]) which explained, among other things, that they could not have on their persons body parts of horse, ass, or mule; and leopard, fox, or hare. The list of animals is instructive in that it indicates what sort of people were entering Jerusalem from the outside world. The animals of transport are unexceptional, since any visitor might be using them; but leopard, fox, and hare are animals of the chase. The concrete problem which the "natives" faced was sportsmen who had been out coursing hares and who, since they were in the Judean hills anyway, came into Jerusalem to see the sights.

Demetrius in Europe after the Battle of Ipsus (301)

While Antigonus Monophthalmus lay dead at Ipsus, his son, Demetrius Poliorcetes, survived to pick up the pieces of what had once been a mighty kingdom. On account of his successes against Cassander just before Ipsus (see chap. 20), Demetrius' prospects were still reasonably bright. He controlled most of central and southern Greece, including the stronghold of Corinth as well as Athens, still important as a naval base. Since Greece provided the bulk of the mercenary armies on which the Diadochi relied, holding Greece had greater importance than holding Asia. Asia may have been wealthier, but the soldiers who held it came from elsewhere. Finally, a sizable fleet still stood under Demetrius' command, and he controlled a number of important ports such as Ephesus, Tyre, and Sidon as well as Cyprus and various Aegean islands (Plut. *Demetr.* 30–33).

Box 21.1 *Plutarch's Biographies as Historical Sources*

Plutarch in the second century AD wrote a large number of so-called lives – biographies – of important figures from Greek and Roman history. Plutarch, though he read rather less than he claimed, nonetheless read widely and collected much information about his subjects from good sources. His biographies are useful for the entire period of Greek history, but nowhere so much as here, where his *Life of Demetrius Poliorcetes*, because Book XXI of Diodorus is attested in fragments only, becomes the chief narrative source. Just enough of Diodorus, however, is attested to show that Plutarch frequently relied on the same source, Hieronymus of Cardia. The transition from Diodorus to Plutarch does not then involve a true switch in source.

Plutarch, however, was writing biography, not history. He himself made this point in his *Life of Alexander*:

> I am not writing histories, but biographies. For virtue and vice do not always manifest themselves in the most eminent deeds, but rather a small matter such as a quip or a joke may illuminate character better than battles with thousands of casualties, than complicated military formations, and sieges of cities. Just as portrait painters take their likenesses from the face and the expression of the eyes, by which character is shown, but pay the least attention to other body parts, so must I concentrate more on what reveals the soul and in this way depict the life of each; while leaving mighty deeds and battles to others. (*Alex.* 1)

Plutarch, who wished to depict character, thus set himself a different goal from that of the historian. Granted, he worked with historical material, but he selected those details which served his purpose so that his exposition often lacks historical clarity. Thus, at *Demetr.* 32 Demetrius holds Cilicia, but at *Demetr.* 47 it is in Seleucus' hands without so much as a word of explanation. After the battle of Ipsus, Pleistarchus received southern Asia Minor, including Caria (see chap. 20). However, at *Demetr.* 46 Lysimachus holds Caria with no explanation of what had become of Pleistarchus' realm in the meantime. Surely Hieronymus of Cardia had explained all that, but Plutarch was unconcerned. Neither does Plutarch provide much in the way of chronology even though Hieronymus had presented events in an annalistic framework, carefully noting the beginning of each successive winter (e.g., Diod. XIX 34; 37; 56).

Plutarch's focus on character moreover leads to some unusual conclusions. For example he tells how Demetrius planned to invade the Upper Satrapies, part of Seleucus' empire, and then entered into Cilicia, another part of Seleucus' empire; but when Demetrius negotiated with Seleucus, Plutarch actually attributes Seleucus' ill-temper towards Demetrius to the churlish advice of Seleucus' unchivalrous advisor (*Demetr.* 47–48) – as though Seleucus might otherwise have taken kindly to Demetrius' invasion of his kingdom!

On the other hand, Plutarch did preserve material in his biographies which historians overlooked. Some of the best-loved and best-remembered stories about Alexander the Great – for example how the boy Alexander was able to ride the great, black horse Bucephalus when he noticed that the horse was spooked by its own shadow – are absent from Arrian, who was far too busy describing military formations and battles in which countless thousands died, but survive thanks to Plutarch (*Alex.* 6).

Nonetheless things got worse for Demetrius before they got better. Athens annulled its alliance with him, and Demetrius, in no position to besiege it, simply had to accept this. Other cities followed suit, and Demetrius' dominion in Greece shrank to a few cities around the Isthmus. Seleucus now threw Demetrius a lifeline (Plut. l.c.). The victors at Ipsus had awarded all of Syria to Seleucus (Pol. V 67), yet Ptolemy still held Hollow Syria. Even if Seleucus forewent any action against Ptolemy, he had no intention of seeing Hollow Syria an Egyptian possession for ever (Diod. XXI 1,5). In like fashion Seleucus was not willing to countenance Lysimachus' and Pleistarchus' rule over Asia Minor. But Seleucus, who knew how to bide his time, was equally unwilling blatantly to upset the balance of power which had come into being after Ipsus. Any open attempt at seizing land from Lysimachus, Pleistarchus, or Ptolemy would merely create a coalition of warlords against him who in the end, because together they were stronger than he, would bring him down. But Demetrius – who had little to lose from an attack on Cassander, Lysimachus, Pleistarchus, or Ptolemy – might prove a useful tool in this regard. So Seleucus extended his hand to Demetrius Poliorcetes who grasped it with alacrity. Seleucus' marriage with Demetrius' daughter Stratonice sealed the alliance.

Demetrius was soon carrying out plundering raids in the Chersonese, part of Lysimachus' kingdom. Moreover, Demetrius seized Cilicia (presumably the eastern "smooth Cilicia" as distinct from the western "rough Cilicia") from Pleistarchus (Plut. *Demetr.* 31–32) and Samareia in southern Syria from Ptolemy (Euseb. II 118 Schoene). However, it appears that Seleucus expected Cilicia from Demetrius and grew angry when it was not forthcoming (Plut. *Demetr.* 32). What exactly Demetrius and Seleucus had agreed upon privately is unknown, but Demetrius was no pliable tool in Seleucus' hands.

Cassander's death in 298 opened up additional opportunities for Demetrius. Cassander's son, Philip IV, died soon after his father; and Cassander's remaining two sons, Antipater and Alexander, were still minors for whom their mother Thessalonice, a daughter of Philip II's, apparently assumed the regency (Euseb. I 231 Schoene). In the absence of any rival in Greece the time was ripe for Demetrius to regain lost ground. Civil war had broken out in Athens (Paus. I 25,7; Plut. *Demetr.* 33), and Demetrius sought to capitalize on this. Failing at taking Athens immediately, he turned to the Peloponnese and captured Messene. From there he returned, captured Eleusis and blockaded Athens itself. Starvation forced the Athenians to surrender, and Demetrius garrisoned both Athens as well as the Peiraeus in 294 (Plut. *Demetr.* 33–34).

While Demetrius was winning Greece, Ptolemy, Lysimachus, and Seleucus made common cause against him everywhere else. Lysimachus captured ports in western Asia Minor, while Ptolemy captured Cyprus (Plut. *Demetr.* 35). Cilicia was in Seleucus' possession a few years later (Plut. *Demetr.* 47); presumably Seleucus had meantime taken by force what he viewed as rightfully his anyway. When the news of Cyprus' loss arrived, Demetrius withdrew from Sparta, which he was on the verge of capturing, and Sparta remained independent (Plut. *Demetr.* 35).

Events in Macedonia, however, played into Demetrius' hands. Antipater, Cassander's eldest surviving son, had had his mother Thessalonice murdered. A civil war had broken out between him and his younger brother Alexander who had pled with both Demetrius and Pyrrhus, the King of Epirus, for help. Pyrrhus had responded more quickly; and together with Lysimachus, the King of Thrace, had helped negotiate a treaty according to which the two brothers were to divide Macedonia into halves. When Demetrius finally arrived, all was settled, so Alexander attempted to dismiss Demetrius, but Demetrius had him assassinated instead. Antipater's rule was anything but firmly established, and his matricide and murder of Philip II's last remaining child did little to endear him to his people. Demetrius persuaded the Macedonian army to come over to his side, and Antipater fled to Lysimachus. He, however, was involved in a difficult war against the Getae in the north, and so could not stop Demetrius who for his part was willing to make peace with his neighbor. Lysimachus, still in 294, recognized Demetrius as the new King of Macedonia (Just. XVI 1; Plut. *Demetr.* 36–37; Euseb. I 231 Schoene).

A quick campaign against the Boeotians brought them under his control (Plut. *Demetr.* 39), and Demetrius stood unchallenged as the ruler of Macedonia and Greece (bar Sparta on the Peloponnese and the Aetolians in the west). He founded a new centrally located capital for his kingdom, Demetrias, on the site of Pagasae, Thessaly's chief port (Strab. IX 5,15, p. 436). Demetrius, however, not content with what he had won, began massive preparations for an invasion of Asia (Plut. *Demetr.* 43).

Seleucus Gains Asia Minor

The other kings – Lysimachus in Thrace, Pyrrhus in Epirus, Ptolemy in Egypt, and, of course, Seleucus – promptly joined forces against Demetrius who, although his kingdom was far smaller than theirs, now controlled the lands which provided the armies upon which they all depended. They struck hard and first. In 288 Lysimachus invaded Macedonia from the east, Pyrrhus from the west; and Ptolemy sent his fleet into the Aegean (Plut. *Demetr.* 44).

What happened next reveals that Demetrius was merely a general, no ruler of a nation. Without any obvious reason for why this should be so, Demetrius' army, apparently even in Demetrius' estimation, stood ready to go over to Lysimachus' side if Demetrius should try to lead it against him. Lysimachus was an old brother-in-arms of the great Alexander's so Demetrius opted to lead his army instead against Pyrrhus for whom the Macedonian army ought to have had less sympathy. Demetrius miscalculated. His army mutinied and went over to Pyrrhus anyway (Plut. *Demetr.* 44). As a ruler Demetrius had failed; after so many years of constant warfare he simply could not make the transition to governing and to winning the long-term loyalty of his subjects. Plutarch writes of his remoteness from his people, his love of elaborate ceremony, and general vanity (*Demetr.* 41–42).

So he lost most of his kingdom once again. Lysimachus and Pyrrhus split Macedonia between them, and Athens revolted from Demetrius and allied itself with Pyrrhus. Pyrrhus and Demetrius made a treaty whereby Demetrius apparently agreed to forgo Macedonia and Athens (with the exception of the strongly garrisoned Peiraeus) while Pyrrhus recognized Demetrius as ruler of Thessaly and whatever else was left of his kingdom in Greece (Plut. *Demetr.* 46 and *Pyrrh.* 12.

Demetrius, unbowed by it all, began his planned invasion of Asia in 287 with some 11,000 troops anyway. Fortunately for him, Lysimachus' rule in Asia Minor – as the reaction to Demetrius' invasion showed – rested on shaky foundations. Miletus, Sardis, and other cities promptly took his side, and some of Lysimachus' officers deserted with their troops to him. But in 286 Demetrius avoided battle against Lysimachus' son, Agathocles, and marched eastwards through Greater Phrygia into Cappadocia. He planned to pass through Armenia into Media and to gain control of the Upper Satrapies, but he had not reckoned with the difficulty of the passage. He lost a large number of troops crossing the River Lycus and even more when disease broke out in his camp. He turned southwards and entered Cilicia, then in Seleucus' possession, and attempted to negotiate with that monarch (Plut. *Demetr.* 46–47).

When the negotiations failed, Seleucus blocked the passes from Cilicia into Syria and, although he had a large army with him, refused to fight. Unlike Darius III in a similar situation half a century earlier (see chap. 19), Seleucus would not give Demetrius the opportunity to win a battle, for Seleucus understood that time was working against his opponent. Demetrius' troops were beginning to desert. Even when Demetrius forced his way through the Amanic Gate into Syria, Seleucus would not be lured into a fight. As the two armies stood opposite each other, Seleucus rode out before his troops, dismounted, removed his helmet so that Demetrius' troops could see who he was, and exhorted them to desert to him. They did so (Plut. *Demetr.* 48–49).

Demetrius attempted to escape, but soon gave up. He surrendered to Seleucus who gave him a palace in Apameia and allowed him to live there in the manner to which he was accustomed. Seleucus spurned the pleas of Demetrius' son to release his prisoner; but he also ignored Lysimachus' demands to kill him. Demetrius took to drink and died some three years later in 283 (Plut. *Demetr.* 50–52).

In Greece, meanwhile, Demetrius' son Antigonus – surnamed "Gonatas" (the epithet is unclear) – inherited what remained of his father's possessions. He had already lost Thessaly with the exception of the heavily fortified Demetrias to Pyrrhus (Plut. *Pyrrh.* 12; *Demetr.* 53). However, the news of Demetrius' imprisonment by Seleucus brought Antigonus a reprieve. Pyrrhus' and Lysimachus' alliance had as its sole basis their common fear of Demetrius, but once Seleucus had rendered Demetrius harmless, Lysimachus' dominance in Europe made Pyrrhus seek an alliance with Antigonus (**Phoenicides**, Fr. 1 Kassel-Austin). As Pyrrhus had expected, with Demetrius out of the way, Lysimachus moved to take all Macedonia. In 284 Lysimachus marched against Pyrrhus

Box 21.2 *Financial Administration in Lysimachus' Kingdom*

Plutarch wrote biographies of Demetrius Poliorcetes and Pyrrhus, both of whom spent most of their lives engaged in ultimately useless military adventures. Demetrius eventually fought his kingdom away before drinking himself to death, and Pyrrhus spent five years fighting in the West (see chap. 22) with nothing to show for it before getting himself killed in street fighting in Argos (see chap. 23). Other Diadochi, however, such as Lysimachus, Ptolemy, and Seleucus left off adventuring and settled down to the much harder and more worthwhile business of governing kingdoms, yet Plutarch evidently found this less congenial and declined to write their biographies. If Plutarch had written these works or if Hieronymus of Cardia were better attested for the period in question, more might be known of how these Diadochi administered their kingdoms. What is known of Lysimachus' kingdom gives at least some idea of what the successful Diadochi concentrated on doing.

For example, when Lysimachus died there were some 9,000 talents stored up in the treasury at Pergamum alone (Strab. XIII 4,1, p. 623). Two additional treasuries happen to be attested – in Sardis (Poly. IV 9,4) and Tirizis in Thrace (Strab. VII 6,1, p. 319) – and more probably existed. Unless the situation in Pergamum should be seriously misleading, during his long reign Lysimachus had paid careful attention to the financial affairs of his kingdom – and the money had piled up. Demetrius Poliorcetes found this distinctly unkingly, however, and scoffed that Lysimachus was just a "money-counter" (Plut. *Demetr.* 25) – which goes a long way towards explaining why Demetrius failed where Lysimachus succeeded. In the long term money-counting accomplished more than military campaigns.

All the same, Lysimachus' careful husbanding of his kingdom's financial resources may have had its drawbacks. According to one inscription (Burstein, Nr. 23 – a letter from, probably, Antiochus I) the city of Erythrae had been "exempt from payment of tribute under Alexander and Antigonus (i.e., Monophthalmus)" – but not apparently under Lysimachus. Even if Erythrae's exemption from "tribute" had been mostly formal (that is, Erythrae had had to pay something such as a *syntaxis*, just not a "tribute" *per se* – see chap. 19), the phrasing still implies that Lysimachus drew the financial reins more tightly than had his predecessors. When Demetrius Poliorcetes invaded Asia Minor in 287, many cities there joined his side with an alacrity which suggests strong dissatisfaction with Lysimachus' rule. After Demetrius had left and Lysimachus had regained control, Lysimachus exacted indemnities from those cities which had revolted – at least 25 talents from Miletus alone (*IvonMilet* 138). These exactions may account for why many of the cities in Asia Minor revolted again a few years later when Seleucus invaded in 281.

whose Macedonian troops proved unwilling to fight against a Macedonian who had fought beside the great Alexander. Although Antigonus sent aid (Paus. I 10), Pyrrhus would not risk a battle, withdrew to Epirus, and ceded his half of Macedonia to Lysimachus (Plut. *Pyrrh.* 12). Pyrrhus, expelled from Macedonia, soon turned west for new adventures (see chap. 22). Lysimachus, meanwhile, became king of all Macedonia in addition to Thrace. He controlled all of Thessaly (Euseb. I 241 Schoene), excepting Demetrias, as well as the better part of Asia Minor west of the Taurus. However, he was an old man now and could no longer keep his house in order. He had his eldest son and logical successor, Agathocles, executed, allegedly owing to the intrigues of his young wife, Arsinoë (daughter of Ptolemy I Soter) who wanted to place her own young son upon the throne. Arsinoë was an ambitious and clever woman with a long career of courtly intrigue and imperial politics ahead of her (see chap. 23 for the next installment), and she may well have made short work of a hapless Agathocles. His many friends, however, resented what had happened, and the aged Lysimachus resorted to additional executions to stifle their murmuring. His rule in Asia Minor, moreover, had never been popular (as Demetrius' invasion had demonstrated), and some officials, such as Philhetaerus, the officer in charge of the treasury at Pergamum, were secretly sending out feelers to Seleucus (Just. XVII 1; Strab. XIII 4,1, p. 623; Paus. I 10) who now sensed that his time had come (Memnon, *BNJ* 424, Fr. 1.5.7).

In 281 Seleucus invaded. Some cities revolted from Lysimachus (Poly. VI 12), and Seleucus, meeting no resistance, marched to Sardis where the commandant of the citadel surrendered (Poly. IV 9,4). Lysimachus crossed the Hellespont to fight it out with Seleucus, and the two armies met at Cyrupedium, "the plain of (the River) Cyrus," just to the north of Magnesia by Sipylus. Seleucus won, and Lysimachus fell (Just. XVII 2; App. *Syr.* 62 and 64; Euseb. I 234 Schoene). Seleucus then took possession of Lysimachus' former dominions in Asia Minor. When Lysimachus' widow, Arsinoë, attempted to hold Ephesus, the city revolted as Seleucus approached (Poly. VIII 57).

Some forty years after he had first become satrap of Babylon, Seleucus was now in a position to gather under his rule not just all Alexander's Empire, but all the lands the Persians had ever held. He even compelled Armenia, a Persian satrapy that Alexander had never conquered, to recognize his overlordship (App. *Syr.* 55) and to pay tribute (Pol. VIII 25). He also sent one of his generals to conquer Cappadocia on the Pontus, a Persian satrapy which neither Alexander nor any other Diadochus had ever attempted to take; here, however, the Cappadocians under their king Mithridates defeated his army (**Trogus**, *Prol.* 17; Memnon, *BNJ* 424, Fr. 1.7.2). Seleucus himself crossed the Hellespont to take possession of Macedonia (App. *Syr.* 62), and no one, neither Pyrrhus nor Antigonus Gonatas, could realistically oppose him. The only other part of Alexander's Empire which was not yet under his rule was Egypt, and Seleucus had plans for that land as well.

Ptolemy I Soter had died in early 282. A few years earlier he had disowned his eldest son, Ptolemy Ceraunus ("Thunderbolt"), in favor of a younger son, conventionally known as Ptolemy II Philadelphus ("Sibling-loving"), who did in the end ascend the throne of Egypt. Ptolemy Ceraunus had left Egypt and was now with Seleucus, who had promised him aid in regaining his paternal throne (Just. XVI 2,7–9; Memnon, *BNJ* 424, Fr. 1.8.2; App. *Syr.* 62). One may however doubt how sincerely Seleucus had meant that promise. After all, if Seleucus conquered Egypt, what would stop him from ruling Egypt himself? And it was doubtful that Ptolemy II Philadelphus alone would be able to withstand an invasion by Seleucus.

Seleucus had worked patiently and quietly for forty years. He had never striven obviously for complete dominion as Antigonus Monophthalmus had. He had never engaged in rash invasions (such as those of Demetrius Poliorcetes) nor had he waged war for the sake of small goals (for example, winning Hollow Syria back from Ptolemy I Soter). Only when large things were at stake was he willing to fight, and he did so with careful preparation. Now in 281 he stood at the threshold of the ultimate goal. Early in 280, however, Ptolemy Ceraunus, who had ambitions beyond being Seleucus' tool, had Seleucus I Nicator ("victor") assassinated (Memnon, *BNJ* 424, Fr. 1.8.3; App. l.c.; Just. XVII 2,4). Even if Seleucus died before he could reunite all Alexander's Empire, he had still attained more than any other Diadochus.

At his death, his realm – with a few minor qualifications– was coextensive with that of Cyrus the Great. Out of all the wars of the Diadochi and out of Alexander's expedition itself there had emerged, at long last, practically unaltered the old Persian Empire – under a new dynasty to be sure, but in many ways still the old Empire (see chap. 23). Unlike Ptolemy I Soter and Lysimachus, Seleucus had moreover kept his own house in order. He was succeeded by his eldest son, Antiochus I Soter ("savior"), whom he had made co-regent by the end of 292 (Parker–Dubberstein, p. 19) and put in charge of the Upper Satrapies (Plut. *Demetr.* 38; App. *Syr.* 59).

Antigonus Gonatas and the Celts

Seleucus' kingdom survived his sudden death. While Antiochus I Soter dealt with affairs in the central and eastern satrapies, a Seleucid general, Patrocles, held Asia west of the Taurus for his king (Memnon, *BNJ* 424, Fr. 1.9.1). In Macedonia Ptolemy Ceraunus seized power. In a treaty with his half-brother Ptolemy II Philadelphus he gave up all claim to Egypt; in exchange Ptolemy II recognized him as King of Macedonia (Just. XVII 2,9). Antigonus Gonatas attempted to invade Macedonia by sea, but Ptolemy Ceraunus defeated him (Memnon, *BNJ* 424, Fr. 1.8.4–6; Just. XXIV 1,8). Antigonus' defeat encouraged revolts in his dominions in Greece: the Athenians regained control of the Peiraeus around this time (Paus. I 26), and the Boeotians, who still stood under Antigonus' control in 280 (Memnon, *BNJ* 424, Fr. 1.8.6) probably revolted around this time as well as they are independent by late 279 (Paus. X 20). Antiochus I Soter made peace with Ptolemy Ceraunus (Trog. *Prol.* 17; Just.

XXIV 1), presumably on the basis of the *status quo* – that is to say, Antiochus I would hold what his father had conquered in Asia Minor and Ptolemy Ceraunus would hold Macedonia.

However, Ptolemy Ceraunus would not enjoy his kingdom for long. In 279 Celtic tribes, the so-called Galatians, who had been migrating southwards down the Balkan peninsula, entered Macedonia. Since only half the migrating Galatians were men of fighting age, entire tribes with women and children were clearly on the move (Liv. XXXVIII 16). They intended to win new land and to settle there. Ptolemy Ceraunus fell in battle against them, and the Galatians overran Macedonia (Just. XXIV 5; Diod. XXII 3–4).

In Greece and Asia Minor, meanwhile, Antigonus Gonatas and Antiochus I Soter were at war. Antiochus I had by now come to his westernmost satrapies and was attempting to subjugate the Bithynians, but Antigonus took the Bithynians' side (Memnon, *BNJ* 424, Fr. 1.10.2; Trog. *Prol.* 24). When the Galatians invaded and moved from Macedonia into Greece, neither Antigonus nor Antiochus I sought to do much. The central Greek states – in particular the Aetolians – organized their own defense and managed, with help from heavy snowfalls, to force the Galatians from Greece during the winter of 279–78 (Paus. X 19–23).

Box 21.3 *The Growth and Constitution of the Aetolian League*

Of little importance during the classical period, the Aetolians rose to prominence in the third century. They resisted Macedonian domination after Alexander's death and began to increase their territory. In 290 they controlled Delphi (Plut. *Demetr.* 40), and control of Delphi probably presupposes control of Western Locris. In 280 they also gained control of Heracleia Trachinia near Thermopylae (Paus. X 20).

In 279 they had their finest hour. In that year a horde of Galatians under the chieftain Brennus invaded central Greece, and the Aetolians played the chief part in warding them off. The principal account stands at Paus. X 19–23. When describing actual fighting, the account speaks principally of the Aetolians and it represents Brennus as deciding that if he could separate the Aetolians from the main army, he would easily defeat the rest (22). The Galatians were repulsed, and the proud Aetolians erected statue after statue at Delphi in celebration (Paus. X 15, 16, and 18). The League's coinage advertised the feat as well (*Cat. Gk. Coins,* Thessaly to Aetolia, pp. 194–195). The prestige which they gained established the Aetolians as the predominant state in Greece north of the Peloponnese: Phocians, Locrians, and Boeotians (Pol. XVIII 47 and XX 5) soon all belonged to the Aetolian League which also held the eastern part of Acarnania (Pol. II 45).

(Continued)

The Aetolian League held two assemblies each year. At the fall meeting in Thermum the assembly elected the League's annual officers, the most important of whom was the *Strategos* ("General") (Ephorus, *BNJ* 70, Fr. 122a; Pol. V 8). A second meeting took place in the spring at Naupactus (IG IX^2 1,1,192; Liv. XXXI 29; the time of year emerges from the general account in Liv. XXXI 28–33). Between meetings of the Assembly a council, the **Synhedrion**, managed the League's affairs. All the towns within the League (Just. XXXIII 2), proportionally to their size (IG IX^2 1,1,188), annually sent councillors (IG IX^2 1,1,192, line 13). The total number of councilors varied according to the size of the League, but appears to have been high: no fewer than 550 of them were banished in 167 BC. (Liv. XLV 28). Because of its size, the Council, though it did sometimes meet in its entirety (IG IX^2 1,1,188, lines 32–33), was usually represented by a standing committee of at least thirty **Apokletoi** (Pol. XX 1; Liv. XXXV 34) which met at the request of the *Strategos* who chaired its meetings (Pol. XX 9–10; Liv. XXXV 35 and XXXVIII 8). The *Apokletoi* and the *Strategos* ran the League on a day-to-day basis.

The constitution of the League allowed it to grow in a way in which a city-state could not. When another community (whether a city-state or another league-state) was incorporated into the League, its citizens became "Aetolians." On official Aetolian documents, those from originally Aetolian territory as well as those from regions added over the course of time are listed in the same way, with the person's name followed by the town of origin (whether or not the town in question had previously been a city-state or belonged to a league-state): for example, in IG IX^2 1,1,3, lines 16–17, the three main Aetolian officials are listed in a dating formula: "the *Strategos*, Polycritus of Callium" (an Aetolian town originally), "the Cavalry Commander, Philo of Pleuron" (an Aetolian town originally), and "the Secretary, Neoptolemus of Naupactus" (a West Locrian town originally). These newly enfranchised Aetolians could become officials of the Aetolian League, and all towns, whether originally Aetolian or not, were proportionally represented in the *Synhedrion*. The guarantee of political rights within the League on a par with older members made joining the League attractive, and the system of proportional representation on the *Synhedrion* made the League's political structure flexible – new communtities could easily be added.

In 278 Antigonus and Antiochus I made peace (Just. XXV 1). On his way back to Greece from Asia Minor Antigonus annihilated a horde of some 18,000 Galatians near Lysimacheia (Trog. *Prol.* 25; Just. XXV 1–2; Diog. Laert. II 141). He then entered Macedonia which since Ptolemy Ceraunus' death had been in a state of near anarchy (Diod. XXII 4), defeated various minor contenders for the throne (Poly. IV 6,17), and then captured Cassandreia around 276 (Trog. *Prol.* 25; Poly. IV 6,18). With the reputation which he had established through his destruction of the Celtic horde at Lysimacheia he easily won recognition as king from the Macedonians. Since Antiochus I was willing to recognize him as king, he had no challengers to his authority.

Antigonus thus established a stable dynasty in Macedonia, the first since the death of Alexander the Great in 323. With this the three chief dynasties of the Hellenistic World, and their three kingdoms, were finally all in place: the Ptolemies in Egypt, the Seleucids in the old Persian Empire; and the **Antigonids** in Macedonia. As for Alexander's generals, all that generation had by now passed away; and its sons (Ptolemy II Philadelphus; Antiochus I Soter) or grandsons in the case of Antigonus Gonatas had finally inherited the Empire in three main parts. Notwithstanding various wars, for the next few generations the three kingdoms effectively coexisted in a sort of equilibrium until the coming of Rome (chap. 24).

Some of the Galatians, however, to follow that thread of the narrative to its conclusion, with the Bithynians' help crossed over into Asia Minor in 278 (Memnon, *BNJ* 424, Fr. 1.11; Liv. XXXVIII 16; for the date Paus. X 23). After terrorizing the inhabitants of Asia Minor, they eventually settled in Greater Phrygia on the River Halys in a region which ever after would be called "Galatia" (on their political organization, see Strab. XII 5,1–2, p. 567). Other Celts settled in Thrace and established their own nation there (Pol. IV 46).

QUESTIONS FOR REVIEW

1 How did Hellenization begin and by what stages did it proceed?
2 How did Demetrius Poliorcetes manage to lose his kingdom?
3 What enabled Seleucus to achieve more than the other Diadochi?
4 How did the Aetolian League achieve its rise to prominence in this period?

QUESTION FOR FURTHER STUDY

Plutarch's decision to focus on the unsuccessful Diadochi (Demetrius, Pyrrhus) results in a scarcity of information about what the successful ones (Ptolemy, Lysimachus, Seleucus) were doing as they settled down to the business of administering a kingdom as opposed to waging war. What made the unsuccessful ones so attractive to him and the successful ones so unappealing?

FURTHER READING

On Hellenistic History in general:
Errington, R.M. (2008) *A History of the Hellenistic World*. Malden, MA.
Green, P. (1993) *From Alexander to Actium*. Berkeley.

On Ptolemaic Egypt:
Bevan, E.S. (1968) *The House of Ptolemy* (Repr.). Chicago. (The classic history in English.)
Hölbl, G. (2001) *A History of the Ptolemaic Empire*. London.

On the Seleucid Kingdom:

Bevan, E.S. (1966) *The House of Seleucus* (Repr.). London. (The classic history in English.)

Kuhrt, A., and S. Sherwin-White. (1993) *From Samarkhand to Sardis*. Berkeley.

On Antigonus Gonatas:

Gabbert, J.J. (1997) *Antigonus II Gonatas. A Political Biography*. London.

22

Sicily and the West from Agathocles to the First Punic War

414–337	337–263	263–240

337	Death of Timoleon
319	Agathocles becomes ruler of Syracuse
310–307	Agathocles in North Africa
306	Agathocles takes royal title
290s	Agathocles campaigns in southern Italy
289	Death of Agathocles
mid-280s	Mamertines seize Messene
280–278	Pyrrhus campaigns in Italy
278–276	Pyrrhus on Sicily
274	Pyrrhus returns to Epirus; Romans control southern Italy
264–241	First Punic War; Sicily becomes Roman province

A History of Greece: 1300 to 30 BC, First Edition. Victor Parker.
© 2014 Victor Parker. Published 2014 by John Wiley & Sons, Ltd.

Agathocles becomes King of Sicily

As the Hellenistic kingdoms of the East arose after Alexander's death, yet another kingdom was being established in the West, on Sicily. Timoleon's victory there over the Carthaginians in 339 had achieved a welcome respite for all Greek Sicily (see chap. 17). By the 320s, however, civil war had begun anew in Syracuse. An oligarchy, led by a man called Sostratus (or Sosistratus), seized power. When a democratic revolution followed, the exiled oligarchs sought aid from the Carthaginians, who went to war against the Syracusans. The democrats in the city, however, apparently appealed to Corinth for another leader such as Timoleon. By this time Corinth stood under Macedonian overlordship, and Antipater, who as Alexander's regent in Macedonia had been governing Greece since 336, had installed oligarchies throughout Greece in the late 320s (see chap. 20). The man whom the Corinthians sent out, Acestorides, accordingly supported the Syracusan oligarchs. He re-established peace with the Carthaginians, banished the democrats, and handed Syracuse back over to the oligarchs (Diod. XIX 3–5).

Among the banished democrats, however, stood a man of pre-eminent military talent, Agathocles. In Morgantina, in the Sicilian interior, he succeeded in establishing his own power base. He captured Leontini and waged war against the Syracusan oligarchs (Just. XXII 2) who this time could hope for no help from mainland Greece since Antipater's successor as regent, Polyperchon, was supporting democracies (see chap. 20). Even within Syracuse the oligarchs had little support and so accepted a necessary compromise (which the Carthaginians helped negotiate), whereby Agathocles returned to Syracuse in 319. He pledged to support the existing government – a nominal democracy – which in return made him general (Diod. XIX 5; Just. l.c.).

When, however, Agathocles judged the time right, he massacred the leading oligarchs (Diod. XIX 6–9). In the next few years he gained possession of other Greek cities on Sicily: Tauromenium by 312 (Diod. XIX 102); Camarina and Catane by 311 (Diod. XIX 110). In 315 he was besieging Messene. Carthaginian intervention, however, compelled him to desist and to make peace with Messene instead (Diod. XIX 65).

Agathocles' opponents in Greek Sicily had by now recognized the bleakness of their long-term prospects and accordingly sought help from mainland Greece. Given the situation there, with the Greek cities hopelessly subject to the whims of the Diadochi, one might surmise that little help would be forthcoming. Yet a Lacedaemonian called Acrotatus, the son of King Cleomenes II and an officer with exquisite military training and no opportunity for using it, paid for a few ships out of his own pocket and sailed to Taras, which placed an additional twenty at his disposal. He arrived in Acragas early in 315 and assumed command of the forces gathered against Agathocles. However, Acrotatus, whom apparently even the Lacedaemonians considered a stern disciplinarian, soon caused a mutiny from which he scarcely escaped with his life. Taras recalled its twenty ships, and nothing now remained for Agathocles' enemies but to make their peace with him. In a peace which the Carthaginians helped negotiate, all recognized the Carthaginians' possession of the northwest of the island whereas the Greek cities elsewhere remained "autonomous," albeit under Syracusan "hegemony" (Diod. XIX 70–71; cf. XIX 102 regarding Messene's inclusion in this peace).

Despite the treaty, Agathocles' steady consolidation of his position as ruler of Greek Sicily eventually led to war with the Carthaginians. Acragas proved the stumbling block. Presumably as Acragas insisted on its "autonomy" and Agathocles with equal stridency on Syracuse' "hegemony," conflict arose, and Acragas sought support from Carthage. In 312 Agathocles marched on Acragas, but broke off the attack when a Carthaginian fleet appeared. Instead Agathocles marched into Carthaginian territory itself. Meanwhile his old political opponents in Syracuse, led now by a man called Deinocrates, revolted with Carthaginian support, and the Carthaginian fleet sailed into the harbor of Syracuse itself while Carthaginian land forces occupied a position near Gela (Diod. XIX 102–104).

Over the winter both sides prepared for a major war. In early 311 the Carthaginians had some 40,000 infantry and 5,000 cavalry encamped near Gela. Agathocles marched against them and seized control of Gela itself. Neither side, however, wished to give battle, but the Carthaginians did repel an attack on their camp. When Agathocles withdrew after this failure, he lost large numbers of men as the Carthaginian cavalry harassed his retreat. Agathocles brought the survivors into Gela in the expectation of a siege, but Hamilcar, the Carthaginian general, marched into the interior instead – correctly guessing that news of the battle would weaken Agathocles' hold over the Greek cities. These all indeed joined Hamilcar's side, and Agathocles himself hastened to Syracuse to save what he could there (Diod. XIX 106–110).

Now a siege was inevitable, and given the situation in mainland Greece (see chap. 20) no help would come from that quarter. Agathocles, however, had no intention of waiting for his opponents to besiege Syracuse. While he still could, he went on the offensive where they least expected it. With sixty ships and some 13,500 troops he slipped past the Carthaginians' blockading fleet and, in one of the most dramatic moves in ancient warfare, in 310 invaded their homeland in Africa which they had denuded of troops in order to wage war on Sicily. Before marching inland, to demonstrate to his troops that there was no turning back, he burnt his ships behind him. With no effective opposition he took town after town and led his army to the gates of Carthage itself. On Sicily, Hamilcar had had little success against Syracuse where Agathocles had left behind part of his army under the command of his brother Antander. Hamilcar now hastily sent 5,000 troops from Sicily to Africa, but Agathocles caught them by surprise and destroyed them (Diod. XIX 3–18).

In 309 Hamilcar attempted to besiege Syracuse, but Antander led troops out of the city and inflicted a severe defeat on the Carthaginians. Hamilcar himself fell into the Syracusans' hands and was tortured to death. Many Greek cities on Sicily now deserted the Carthaginians and formed an alliance among themselves under the leadership of Acragas and with that the Carthaginian invasion of Greek Sicily was at an end (Diod. XX 29–32). In Africa, meanwhile, Agathocles, after various minor successes (Diod. XX 33–34, 38–39), had formed an alliance with Ophellas, one of Alexander's old officers and now the ruler of Cyrene, who still in 308 led some 10,000 troops westwards to Agathocles' camp. Although Agathocles had promised him the rule of Carthage's territory, the two soon quarreled, and Agathocles had Ophellas assassinated. Ophellas' troops, far from home, had little choice but to take service with Agathocles, who thereby effectively doubled his army (Diod. XX 40–42).

Agathocles now captured the important city of Utica as well as the port of Hippu Acra. Other cities in the interior joined him so that he soon controlled almost all Carthaginian territory in Africa – with the exception of Carthage itself. As long as the Carthaginian fleet controlled the seas, however, a siege was impracticable and in any case a Carthaginian fleet was still blockading Syracuse. So Agathocles arranged for the construction of a fleet (cf. App. *Lib.* 110) and early in 307 returned to Sicily (Diod. XX 54–55). He landed near Selinus in Carthaginian territory and quickly brought most of the northwest of the island under his control – granted without Lilybaeum and Panormus, the two most important cities (Diod. XX 56).

Agathocles, however, had less success against the Greeks on Sicily. Deinocrates had collected some 20,000 troops, and Agathocles, badly outnumbered, retreated before them. In Africa, meanwhile, the Carthaginians had collected some 30,000 troops and divided them into three detachments. This forced Agathocles' deputy, his eldest son Archagathus, to follow suit, but two of his divisions shortly met with catastrophic defeats. With this the Carthaginians regained most of their territory (Diod. XX 57–61). Even Agathocles' return to Africa could not restore the situation, and when an attack on a strongly defended Carthaginian position failed, Agathocles' troops began to desert or to mutiny. In late 307 Agathocles returned to Sicily. What remained of his army in Africa, including Archagathus, he left to fend for itself; the army murdered Archagathus and made what terms it could with the Carthaginians (Diod. XX 64–69).

Back on the island Agathocles faced two enemies – the Carthaginians and his Greek opponents under Deinocrates. Agathocles offered terms of peace first to the latter (who stupidly refused them) and then to the former (who, weary of a long and senseless war, accepted them). Agathocles in 306 gave them their territory in the northwest back, and they gave him 150 talents and 200,000 bushels of grain (Timaeus, *BNJ* 566, Fr. 120; Diod. XX 77–79). Now Agathocles could focus on Deinocrates. Even if Deinocrates had far more troops at his disposal and Agathocles a mere 5,800, Agathocles correctly assumed that his battle-hardened troops would win any pitched battle. After they had done so, Agathocles was once again master of Sicily east of the Halycus. Agathocles offered all exiles the right to return to their homes and in exchange he won general recognition of his rule (Diod. XX 89–90).

Firmly ensconced as lord of Greek Sicily, Agathocles followed the example of the Diadochi in assuming the royal title (Diod. XX 54 – n.b. that for Agathocles Diodorus surely has too early a date [307] –; cf. Plut. *Demetr.* 25). In their political culture, the Sicilians were now aligned with the rest of the Hellenistic world; and all rulers on Sicily who sought to follow in Agathocles' footsteps (Phintias, Pyrrhus, Hiero II) would call themselves kings. Sicily had become a Hellenistic kingdom.

Agathocles in Italy

In Italy in 303, Taras came into conflict yet again with an Italian power (see chap. 17), this time Rome and its allies, the Lucanians. As usual Taras desperately required help from abroad and as on previous such occasions the lack of opportunities for displaying martial valor at Sparta aided the Tarantines. Cleonymus, Acrotatus' younger brother, used the Tarantines' money to hire mercenaries in Greece and Italy. With the Tarantines' regular levy he had an army of 22,000. Faced with an army of that size, the Lucanians decided to make peace (Diod. XX 104), and even Rome, busy elsewhere, made a treaty with Taras whereby the Romans agreed "not to sail past (i.e., from a westerly direction) Cape Lacinium" near Croton (App. *Samn.* 15).

Cleonymus, deprived of one war, now looked for other outlets for his energy. He captured Corcyra and began raiding in the Adriatic, but was driven from Corcyra in circa 300 (Diod. XX 104–105; Liv. X 2; Trog. *Prol.* 15).

In Italy, meanwhile, Taras was under attack again. This time the Tarantines appealed to Agathocles (Strab. VI 3,4, p. 280) who defeated their Italian foes. Agathocles too then turned aside to Corcyra. After Cleonymus' departure from the island, Cassander, the King of Macedonia (see chaps. 20 and 21), had decided to seize it himself. Perhaps desiring to prevent so powerful a ruler from establishing a foothold on the Adriatic, Agathocles defeated a Macedonian fleet which was blockading Corcyra. Thereafter Cassander withdrew his troops and Agathocles took the island (Diod. XXI 2), presumably just before Cassander's death in 297. In 295 Agathocles would present Corcyra as a dowry to his daughter Lanassa whom he gave in marriage to Pyrrhus, the King of Epirus (Plut. *Pyrrh.* 9; Diod. XXI 4). The diplomatic marriage betokened Agathocles' integration into the world of the Hellenistic kings.

But in the meantime matters in Italy required his attention again. He suppressed a mutiny among his mercenaries there, but the non-Greek Brettians in southwestern Italy, his erstwhile allies, inflicted a severe defeat (Diod. XXI 3). Agathocles, undeterred, seized control of Croton in 295 and made an alliance with some of the Iapygians (Diod. XXI 4). This ought to have concerned the Romans, but as the **Samnite Wars** were occupying them at the time, the Romans left him in peace. In 293 Agathocles crossed over to Italy again with an army 33,000 strong and wrested Hipponium from the Brettians. They for their part acknowledged him as overlord, but only for as long as he remained

Box 22.1   *The City of Taras*

Taras was founded by the Lacedaemonians circa 700 BC (see chap. 5). It lay in the region Apulia, on a peninsula with the open sea to the south and a lagoon to the north, in possession of the sole good harbor on the Gulf of Taranto (Pol. X 1; Strab. VI 3,1, p. 278) (see Figure 22.1). The standard trade-route between Sicily and the Greek mainland continually brought ships past the site. The fishing, moreover, was good (Arist. *Pol.* 1291b), and the land roundabout fertile (Strab. VI 3,5, p. 281). In many ways Taras had the ideal position for a Greek colony.

Although it never obtained the might and wealth of Syracuse, Taras did grow to become the most important Greek city in southern Italy. Originally governed by kings (Hdt. III 136) and aristocrats, a democracy was established a little after the Persian Wars (Arist. *Pol.* 1303a). Taras' splendid port always secured it economic advantages, and it boasted a thriving pottery industry during the fourth century as the numerous archaeologically attested vases made at Taras show (see Figure 22.2).

It was also a cultural center during this period, when it produced notable philosophers such as the statesman Archytas whom the Tarantines elected as general seven times (Diog. Laert. VIII 79). A prolific inventor (Arist. *Pol.* 1340b; Gell. X 12), he maintained contacts with Plato (Plut. *Dio*, 18; Diog.Laert. VIII 80–81) who refers to

Figure 22.1   The site of Taras today. Source: Kadellar, http://commons.wikimedia.org/wiki/File:Taranto-Aerial_view-2.jpg (accessed 12th February 2013) CC BY-SA 3.0, 2.5, 2.0, 1.0

Figure 22.2   Apulian bell crater, ca. 355–340 BC, depicting a mythological scene, the Judgment of Paris, which helped cause the Trojan War – Western and Aegean Greeks shared the same cultural heritage (see chap. 17). Source: Ashmolean Museum, University of Oxford, UK / The Bridgeman Art Library

some of his geometrical work (*Rep.* 528 – cf. Diog.Laert. VIII 83). More important was Aristoxenus, a distinguished pupil of Aristotle (Cic. *Tusc.* I 19), who allegedly expected Aristotle to name him, instead of Theophrastus, as successor in the Peripatetic School (Suid. s.v. Aristoxenos). Of Aristoxenus' many works, only one, *The Elements of Harmony*, a systematic description of music, has survived; it is indispensable for modern discussions of Greek music.

Despite its economic and cultural importance, Taras never succeeded in extending its power far into the interior and this would prove its undoing, as failure in wars against the Italian tribes there characterizes its history from start to finish. Both Herodotus (VII 170) and Aristotle (*Pol.* 1303a) speak of bloody defeats at the hands of Italian tribes already in the early fifth century. Although their general Archytas was allegedly never defeated in battle in the mid-fourth century (Diog.Laert. VIII 82), the Tarantines as a general rule, whenever threatened, had to turn to mainland Greece or to Sicily for help (see in text as well as in chap. 17 for the numerous instances). When the Tarantines brought about a war with Rome, they called upon Pyrrhus, the King of Epirus, to protect them but when his intervention finally failed, they had no choice but to accept Roman dominion. The other Greek cities in southern Italy, much less powerful than Taras, had to follow suit.

in Italy (Diod. XXI 8). Still, Agathocles retained control over most of the coast-line of southern Italy from Hipponium to Taras.

Satisfied with how matters in Italy now lay, Agathocles, although by now an old man, planned one last war against the Carthaginians. In 289 he made an alliance with Demetrius Poliorcetes, who had just become King of Macedonia (see chap. 21), and had a fleet of 200 warships built. Unfortunately, Agathocles died before he could carry out his plan. Quarrels within his family made it impossible for him to arrange for one of his descendants to succeed him as king, so on his deathbed he gave the Syracusans their freedom back (Diod. XXI 15–16).

Sicily after Agathocles

Agathocles' realm did not long survive his death. A man called Hicetas took over the leadership of the newly proclaimed Syracusan democracy, but not of Agathocles' mercenary army. One of Agathocles' officers, Meno, eventually gained control of it. He, however, hesitated to attempt a pitched battle against the Syracusans and instead sought aid from the Carthaginians. The resultant treaty dissolved Agathocles' kingdom. The Greek cities all became independent again (as emerges from the following) and the Syracusans granted Agathocles' mercenaries land in Syracuse (Diod. XXI 18). By default the Carthaginians became the dominant power on the island.

Within Syracuse itself conflict soon broke out between the original Syracu-sans and the newly settled mercenaries (mostly Campanians from Italy). Even-tually the mercenaries agreed to sell their land and to leave. On their way back to Italy, however, they seized the city of Messene in the mid-280s, killed or expelled the inhabitants, and established themselves as the new masters of the strait (Diod. XXI 18). These mercenaries, who called themselves the Mamer-tines (after their native god of war), were soon engaged in plundering raids up and down the eastern half of Sicily (Pol. I 8). They destroyed Gela and Cama-rina on the southern coast (Diod. XXIII 1) and brought the northeastern section of the island under their control.

Internecine wars, moreover, did little to improve the situation of the Greeks on the island. The new tyrant of Acragas, Phintias, settled the survivors from Gela in a new city named after himself, brought much of the southern coast under his control, and actually proclaimed himself king (Diod. XXII 2; Cat. Gk. Coins, Sicily, p. 22). Hicetas, the ruler of Syracuse, alarmed by all this, went to war against Phintias, defeated him, and so put an end to any dream of an Acragantine empire. Hicetas then carried out an ill-advised attack on the Carthaginians, who defeated him near Leontini (Diod. l.c.). Thereafter (279) he fell victim to a coup d'état led by Thoenon who replaced him as ruler of Syracuse. But a revolt in Syracuse forced Thoenon to withdraw to the heavily fortified island in the harbor. In the ensuing civil war the Syracusans appealed to Sostratus (or Sosistratus) who had taken control of Acragas after Phintias' death. Determined to prevent Sostratus from gaining control over both Acragas and Syracuse, the Carthaginians sent troops and a fleet to besiege Syracuse and it appeared as though the hopelessly divided Greeks on Sicily were finally about to succumb (Diod. XXII 7–8).

Pyrrhus' Invasion of Italy and Sicily

In Italy too Agathocles' death in 289 had had severe consequences. In the mid-280s the Brettians again took Hipponium (Strab. VI 1,5, p. 256), and the Lucanians attacked Thurii. The Thurians, as expected, required help from another power only this time the appeal went neither to Sicily nor to mainland Greece, but to Rome. In 282 a Roman army under C. Fabricius defeated the Thurians' enemies (Pliny, *NH* XXXIV 32; Dion. Hal. *Rom.Ant.* XIX 13; Liv. *Per.* XI) and placed a Roman garrison in Thurii itself (App. *Samn.* 15). Rhegium and Locri Epizephyrii, caught as they were between the Mamertines' Scylla and the Brettians' Charybdis, also saw their best hope for survival in a Roman garrison. Both cities duly received one; that in Rhegium was composed of Campanians, i.e., countrymen of the Mamertines on the other side of the strait (Dion. Hal. *Rom.Ant.* XX 4; Just. XVIII 1). In addition to all that, ten Roman ships sailed past Cape Lacinium in distinct violation of the treaty with Taras. This rapid Roman expansion perhaps highlights best Agathocles' accomplishment in retaining Greek control of the region.

The furious Tarantines in any case sank four of the offending Roman ships, marched on Thurii, and forced the Roman garrison there to capitulate (App. *Samn.* VII). With full-scale war with Rome looming, the Tarantines again looked for a protector. This time it was Pyrrhus, the King of Epirus. He had just ceded Macedonia to Lysimachus, the King of Thrace (see chap. 21), and, thwarted in one direction, now sought a new outlet for his energies in the West. In the spring of 280 Pyrrhus landed in Taras with 20,000 foot soldiers, 3,000 cavalrymen, 2,500 light troops, and – a novelty in the West – twenty elephants. At Heracleia, on the coast between Thurii and Taras, Pyrrhus defeated the Romans under P. Valerius Laevinus (Plut. *Pyrrh.* 15–17). The elephants were decisive as the Roman cavalry fled before them. The Romans lost some 7,000 men, but Pyrrhus' losses too were high – some 4,000 (**Hieronymus**, *BNJ* 154, Fr. 11). Italian tribes such as the Brettians, Lucanians, and Samnites now joined Pyrrhus (Plut. *Pyrrh.* 17), as did the Epizephyrian Locrians who even delivered their Roman garrison into his hands (Just. XVIII 1). The Campanian garrison in Rhegium, evidently fearing the same fate, seized control of the city after slaying or driving out the inhabitants (Dion. Hal. *Rom. Ant.* XX 4; App. *Samn.* 19). Pyrrhus for his part followed up his victory at Heracleia with a march on Rome itself (he came within forty miles of the city – App. *Samn.* 24; Plut. *Pyrrh.* 17), but since the Romans' allies in central Italy stayed loyal, Pyrrhus gave up any thought of attacking the city and withdrew to winter quarters.

In 279, with support from his new Italian allies, he marched into Apulia on the Adriatic coast. There he met the Romans in a second battle in which he won another dearly bought victory. The Romans lost some 6,000 and Pyrrhus, according to his own notebooks, exactly 3,505 (Hieronymus of Cardia, *BNJ* 154, Fr. 12). This was the famous "Pyrrhic victory" after which Pyrrhus, contemplating his losses, allegedly remarked, "one more such victory will ruin me" (Plut. *Pyrrh.* 21). Negotiations between Pyrrhus and the Romans began, and for a moment it appeared as though the Greeks in southern Italy might find security from Roman encroachment.

At this juncture events in Sicily supervened. The Carthaginians were besieging Syracuse, and the Syracusans desperately needed help. The Galatians had just invaded Macedonia and Greece (see chap. 21), so no help could possibly come from that quarter; as things stood, Pyrrhus alone could bring aid. For Pyrrhus, who, like Demetrius Poliorcetes, was just a useless adventurer, this promised a new stage for even grander displays of valor, so he prepared to go to Sicily. The Carthaginians and the Romans thereupon made an alliance against their common enemy (Pol. III 25), and that alliance sealed the fate of the Greeks in Italy.

Pyrrhus landed at Tauromenium late in 278 with about 10,000 troops. The Carthaginians withdrew from Syracuse, and Thoenon and So(si)stratus handed it over to Pyrrhus. He received the support of the various other tyrants (Diod. XXII 8) and was proclaimed King of Sicily (Pol. VII 4).

In 277 Pyrrhus, at the head of some 30,000 infantry plus cavalry, marched westwards and captured all Carthaginian Sicily with the exception of the heavily fortified Lilybaeum. Carthage offered peace on the basis of the status quo, but Pyrrhus demanded the surrender of Lilybaeum also. At that the Carthaginians balked, so Pyrrhus began a siege which, however, given the city's strength he gave up within two months (Diod. XXII 10; Plut. *Pyrrh.* 22). Meanwhile, the Romans were making headway against Pyrrhus' Italian allies, and late in 276 Pyrrhus returned to Italy. He marched against Rhegium, but the Carthaginian fleet sailed against his, and in the strait it won a decisive victory: 70 of Pyrrhus' 110 ships were lost. (App. *Samn.* 29).

This cut Pyrrhus off from Sicily, and the Greek cities there hastened to make their peace with Carthage (Just. XXIII 3). Pyrrhus for his part gave up the attack on Rhegium, fought his way through an army which the Mamertines had sent to southern Italy, and returned to Taras for the winter (Plut. *Pyrrh.* 24). In 275 he fought against the Romans one last time in Lucania (Plut. *Pyrrh.* 25). The result was a draw (Pol. XVIII 28, whose opinion trumps all others'), but by now Pyrrhus was out of money and in any case weary of an "adventure" which was proving far too much hard work. He returned to Epirus in 275 (Plut. *Pyrrh.* 26) and in the next year went to war against Antigonus Gonatas, the new King of Macedonia (see chap. 23) from whom he hoped to win glory more easily.

However, Pyrrhus had left some troops in Italy under the command of his son Helenus, who evidently managed to hold the Romans back for well over a year until his father recalled him to Greece in 273 (Just. XXV 3). In 272 Pyrrhus died fighting in Argos (see chap. 23), and his son Alexander, who succeeded him in Epirus, had no interest in western adventures.

Taras now bowed to the inevitable and came to terms with Rome. The other Greek cities in southern Italy, also made their peace with Rome at this time (Liv. *Per.* 15; **Zonaras**, VIII 6).

The First Punic War

After Pyrrhus' departure from the West, the Mamertines as well as their countrymen in Rhegium had taken up their raids again, both on Sicily (Pol. I 8) as well as on the mainland where they destroyed Caulonia (Paus. VI 3) and captured Croton. In the latter city they also annihilated a Roman garrison (Zon. l.c.). This act provoked a response from Rome, and in 270 a Roman army marched against Rhegium and took it by siege. The Campanians were executed, and the previous inhabitants received the city back, albeit subject to Rome (Pol. I 7).

Meanwhile, a new tyrant had arisen in Syracuse, Hiero II, who took up the war against the Mamertines, defeating them decisively in 264 (Pol. I 8–9). The Mamertines, if they were to continue to hold Messene, now needed help against Hiero II, even if they had little cause to expect any from their possible allies: Carthage or Rome. Division of opinion ran deep, but the appeal finally went out to Carthage. It succeeded, and the Carthaginians installed a garrison in Messene. Hiero II swiftly broke off his campaign against the Mamertines for he could not risk a war against the Carthaginians. But he had at least united the Greek cities of Sicily under Syracusan control, and he was now proclaimed King of Sicily.

However, now that a Carthaginian garrison resided in Messene, second thoughts arose even among those Mamertines who had previously preferred an alliance with Carthage to one with Rome. So an appeal also went out to Rome. After some hesitation the Romans accepted it, and a Roman army marched towards Sicily to receive Messene's submission. The Carthaginian garrison commander evidently deemed his position too weak to fight and simply withdrew (Pol. I 10–11).

Alarmed at this sudden turn in events, the Carthaginians sent an army and a fleet against Messene, and with that the First **Punic War** between Rome and Carthage began. The story of that conflict need not be told here; in what follows the fate of the Greeks in Sicily is the sole concern. For Hiero II, who now saw the opportunity to drive the hated Mamertines from Sicily forever, made an alliance with Carthage. Together Carthaginians and Syracusans began to besiege Messene early in 263.

By the end of that year, however, Roman troops forced both Carthaginians and Syracusans to break off the siege and a Roman army moved southwards through Greek Sicily (Pol. I 11–12). The Carthaginians were not prepared for a major campaign, and Hiero II alone could not meet the Romans in the field. Most of the other Greek cities hastened to find an accommodation with the Romans, and when the Romans began to besiege Syracuse (Pol. I 12) Hiero II too had second thoughts about his alliance with the Greeks' ancestral enemies on the island, the Carthaginians, against whom so many of his predecessors had fought for so long.

Hiero II switched sides and made peace with Rome. The price was a hundred talents and the loss of all Greek cities which had already submitted to the Romans. Hiero II did, however, retain Tauromenium and a handful of towns near Syracuse (Pol. I 16; Diod. XXIII 4). But for all that Syracuse was effectively now subject to the Romans. In 241 the Romans finally won the First Punic War, and the Carthaginians consented to pay an enormous indemnity (3200 talents) and to withdraw from Sicily entirely (Pol. I 62–63). Thereafter the Romans placed Sicily under the control of, effectively, a governor, and Sicily thus became the first Roman province. Both Syracuse and the Mamertines in Messene remained formally independent, but both answered to the Roman governor.

Retrospect

The Greeks in the West, both those on the coasts of Italy and those on Sicily, had finally fallen under the dominion of others. Half a millennium had passed since the establishment of the first Greek colonies in the West; and considering that Greek settlement, especially in Italy, had never penetrated far into the interior – that is to say that the Greek colonies there always remained isolated enclaves in a land mostly held by others –, it is perhaps remarkable that the Greeks managed to hold on for so long. Much of the Greeks' success rested on superior military technology and a political organization which allowed them to wage war more effectively than their more numerous neighbors. These for their part, however, did not stand still in time. As the centuries passed they too developed – not least according to the model which their Greek neighbors held up – such that they began to compete with the Greeks on a level field, or rather on one which would have been level had they not badly outnumbered the Greeks. Hence the Greeks' eventual need for help from outside, whether from Sicily or mainland Greece, whenever they came into conflict with the Italian tribes in the fourth and third centuries BC It was, then, only a matter of time before they succumbed when such help was not forthcoming.

On Sicily the Greeks always had to compete with Carthage such that their position on the island was never wholly secure, and on several occasions the Carthaginians came within a hair's breadth of overwhelming the Greeks. In the end, however, it was the rise of Rome which spelled the end of the Greeks' independence on the island. Their compatriots in mainland Greece and in the East would, over the next two centuries, suffer the same fate (see chap. 24).

QUESTIONS FOR REVIEW

1 What did Agathocles do to shore up the position of the Greeks on Sicily against the Carthaginians?
2 How did Agathocles and Pyrrhus delay Roman domination of southern Italy?
3 How did the Romans slowly establish their dominion over southern Italy?
4 To what extent did the fate of the Western Greeks turn on the actions of Campanian mercenaries such as the Mamertines?

QUESTION FOR FURTHER STUDY

Given how easily, in the end, the Romans established mastery over the entire island of Sicily, why had the Carthaginians failed at doing this for so long? Or was it mere chance that events such as Pyrrhus' invasion of the island prevented them from doing so?

FURTHER READING

On the wars against Carthage and Agathocles:
Miles, R. (2010) *Carthage Must Be Destroyed. The Rise and Fall of an Ancient Mediterranean Civilization*. London.
Warmington, B.H. (1969) *Carthage*. London.

Also:
Berve, H. (1953) *Die Herrschaft des Agathokles*. München.
Lehmler, C. (2005) *Syrakus unter Agathokles und Hieron II: Die Verbindung von Kultur und Macht in einer hellenistischen Metropole*. Frankfurt am Main.

On the First Punic War:
Lazenby, J.F. (1996) *The First Punic War: A Military History*. Stanford.

23

The Hellenistic World in Equilibrium

| 301–276 | 276–206 | 206–168 |

mid-270s	Galatians settle in central Asia Minor; First Syrian War
272	Pyrrhus killed in Argos
late 260s	Pergamum becomes fully independent
250s	Second Syrian War
245	Third Syrian War
243	Achaian League captures Acrocorinth
mid-230s	Rebellion of Antiochus Hierax in Asia Minor
late 230s	Seleucus II loses Parthia and Bactria
mid-220s	Attalus I drives Hierax from Asia Minor
227	Macedonian garrison leaves Peiraeus
220	Antiochus III crushes revolt in Media
217	Battle of Raphia
214	Antiochus III defeats Achaius
210–206	Antiochus III regains Parthia and Bactria

A History of Greece: 1300 to 30 BC, First Edition. Victor Parker.
© 2014 Victor Parker. Published 2014 by John Wiley & Sons, Ltd.

Historiographical Characterization of the Hellenistic World

While in the West the Hellenistic kingdom on Sicily had fallen under Roman domination by the mid-third century, the Hellenistic kingdoms of the East were still enjoying their heyday. In fact, after Antigonus Gonatas established a stable dynasty in Macedonia, these kingdoms settled into a self-contained equilibrium. They dealt mostly with each other since with few qualifications they had no neighbors whom they either had to take seriously or with whom they had serious conflicts. They were evenly matched at war so that the various **Syrian Wars** which the Seleucids and the Ptolemies fought achieved hardly anything.

An historical narrative of the period moreover comes across as a recitation of details for two reasons. First, there has survived from antiquity no coherent historical narrative which could assist in evaluating the significance of individual events. Second, because the Hellenistic states were so evenly balanced in a self-contained world, their history is difficult to relate to larger concerns. One Ptolemy, one Antiochus or Seleucus follows the other; one Syrian War ends much the same as the previous one.

And yet the Hellenistic World in these decades was hardly devoid of excitement. The Seleucid Kingdom appeared to be about to go under at one point, but just as all seemed lost, its greatest king since Seleucus I Nicator, Antiochus III Megas, seized the helm and steered the kingdom back to its full glory. For all that it affirmed the *status quo*, for sheer drama the Battle of Raphia has few peers – with Ptolemy IV Philopator leading an untested phalanx of native Egyptian recruits to victory over veteran Greeks and Macedonians.

Moreover, if one views the Seleucid Kingdom as the continuation of the Persian Empire (see next section), then certain larger concerns do emerge. For example, both the Persian Empire and the Seleucid Kingdom display a tendency to crumble at the edges as satraps, who on a day-to-day basis were independent anyway, either revolted or incrementally paid less attention to the king. The six Syrian Wars could be compared with the various wars which the Persians waged to reconquer an independent Egypt during the first sixty years of the fourth century (Diod. XV 41–43; 92–93; XVI 40–50).

Finally, even if none of the countless battles ever seems to resolve anything, they meant something to people at the time. Little is known about the victory which Attalus I of Pergamum won over the Galatians in the 230s, and the battle might easily disappear in a litany of dates and wars had it not inspired a spectacular sculptural program at Pergamum, the best-known piece of which is the famous statue of the defeated Galatian warrior who, having just slain his wife so that she will not fall into the enemy's hands, in a final act of heroic defiance commits suicide (see Figure 23.1). The considerable dignity which the sculptor imparted to these Galatians in defeat immediately catches the eye. Attalus took his enemies seriously and paid the sculptor good money to provide a serious treatment. In the end, it was all for Attalus' greater glory since these noble foes had succumbed to him.

Figure 23.1   The so-called Ludovisi Group; Roman copy of original from Pergamum circa 220s BC. Source: Jastrow, http://commons.wikimedia.org/wiki/File:Ludovisi_Gaul _Altemps_Inv8608_n3.jpg (accessed 12th February 2013)

To go beyond the confines of this chapter, when the Rhodian fleet helped defeat the Seleucid fleet off Myonnesus in 190 BC, the Rhodians commemorated the deed by commissioning the statue now known as the Winged Nike of Samothrace (see Figure 23.2). One can appreciate this victory's significance for the Rhodians even without a description of the battle by an historian of note, which, however, one does need for a full historical evaluation of the battle.

The Seleucid Kingdom

The largest and wealthiest Hellenistic Kingdom was that of the Seleucids. In many ways this kingdom, practically coextensive with the old Persian Empire, was merely the same empire under new management. Thus it shared many curious institutional aspects with its predecessor: For example, it had no official name. "Persian Empire" and "Seleucid Kingdom" – as well as titles such as

Figure 23.2   The Winged Nike of Samothrace, circa 190 BC. Source: Marie-Lan Nguyen, http://commons.wikimedia.org/wiki/File:Nike_of_Samothrake_Louvre_Ma2369.jpg (accessed 12th February 2013)

"King of Persia" – are modern or foreign appellations. For the Persian ideology of rule was one of universal dominion: the king was, in the words of Darius I himself, "the Great King, the King of Kings, the King of lands with all manner of men, the King of this great Earth far and wide . . ." (Kent, DNa lines 8–15). Next to the universal titles a Persian king might use an additional geographically limiting title when it had relevance locally – e.g., "King of Babylon" in Babylon itself: "I am Cyrus, King of the world . . . King of Babylon . . . King of the four corners of the Earth (from the Cyrus Cylinder, a Babylonian text, line 20, *ANET*, p. 316). In Asia at least the Seleucids followed suit as an inscription of Antiochus I's from Babylon shows with its use of universal titles along with the relevant local one: "I am Antiochus, the Great King, the rightful King, the King of the world, the King of Babylon, the King of all lands . . ." (Austin, Nr. 189). To the Greeks, moreover, the Persian king was always just that – the "King" without qualification. Seleucus I Nicator and each of his successors likewise bore no geographical title – he was merely the "King."

In other respects also the old Persian ways continued. The Seleucid Kingdom's Persian roots appear in some of its administrative terminology, for example the word for "treasury," *gazophylakion* (II Macc. III 24), respectively a half-Persian and half-Greek compound. Many satrapies remained unaltered from Persian into Seleucid days and even where alterations took place, they merely continued a Persian trend – the subdivision of large satrapies. Thus the entire fertile crescent from the head of the Persian Gulf to the border of Egypt had been one satrapy in the late sixth century, but was soon split by the Persians themselves into two, Babylon (east of the Euphrates) and Ebir Nari ("Beyond the River" – i.e., the Euphrates). By 323 Babylon had been split into Mesopotamia and Babylon (see Box 20.1), and the trend continued into Seleucid times. Ebir Nari now became four satrapies with satrapal capitals at Antioch, Laodiceia, Apameia, and Seleuceia (**Poseidonius**, *BNJ* 87, Fr. 65; with RC 70, line 7 and Diod. XXXIII 28); Parapotamia was split off from Mesopotamia (Pol. V 69,5); and the satrapy of the "land by the Red Sea (Persian Gulf)" from the satrapy of Babylon (Pol. V 48). Persian Kings had often grouped multiple satrapies together under the oversight of a royal appointee (e.g., Diod. XVI 50) and had sometimes placed a strategically important satrapy under a close relative (e.g., Hdt. IX 113). Seleucus I's grouping of the Upper Satrapies under the authority of his son and co-regent Antiochus I Soter was merely a logical development from that.

But there were also differences. The Persians had worked with a system of four imperial capitals: Babylon, Ecbatana, Susa, and Persepolis (see chap. 19). Seleucus, however, founded as sole capital Antiocheia in Syria, much farther to the west and much closer to Macedonia and Greece. The additional foundations of cities here show that he intended for Syria to be the heartland of his empire. This directed the empire toward Greece and the Mediterranean and away from its roots in Iran. Accordingly, the retention of the somewhat neglected Upper Satrapies in Iran and farther afield in central Asia and on the Indus would eventually cause Seleucus' successors many problems. Finally, the Seleucids insisted on Greek as the language of administration (unlike the Persians who had never attempted to impose Persian), and their foundations of cities with attendant Hellenization find no precedent in Persian times.

Box 23.1　*The Library at Alexandria*

During the reigns of Ptolemy I Soter (323–282) and Ptolemy II Philadelphus (282–246), the famous library at Alexandria was founded. The latter Ptolemy in particular gained renown both as a patron of the arts (e.g., **Theocritus**, XVII 112–116) as well as for his own academic virtuosity (Athen. XI, p. 493), and large numbers of books were procured for the library in his days (Jos. *Ant.* XII 2,1 [11–12]). Alexandria rapidly became a center not only for scholarship, but also for literature, for in the Hellenistic age the two went hand in hand.

The greatest of the Hellenistic poets, Philadelphus' contemporary **Callimachus**, was presumably head of the library in Alexandria and certainly compiled its first catalogue (Suid., s.v. Kallimachos). The learned, scholarly character of his poetry (his *Aitia* – "origins" – are practically pieces of research) comes as perhaps no surprise given his work in the library. Callimachus strongly preferred small poems and declared that "a big book was a big evil." His insistence on this principle led to a dispute with the most important of his pupils, one **Apollonius**, allegedly a successor of his at the library (*POxy* X 1241).

Apollonius, who was willing to attempt composition on a large scale, eventually left Alexandria for Rhodes (hence his surname "of Rhodes") where he published his masterpiece, a long epic poem on Jason and the Argonauts (*Vita* A). Although replete with adventure as the Argonauts sail in search of the Golden Fleece, it too drips with erudition and scholarship. For the Hellenistic world, not just the Ptolemies in Alexandria, valued learning even in its staler forms; and its greatest literary achievements accordingly arose amidst stacks of books. Nor was it just the Ptolemies who collected. The rulers of Pergamum allegedly built up a library of some 200,000 volumes (Plut. *Ant.* 58), and there were surely others across the Hellenistic world.

Where Callimachus and Apollonius had still composed original works, their successors in Alexandria gradually became pure scholars concerned especially with critical editions of the classical Greek poets. Aristophanes of Byzantium (late third, early second century BC) edited the texts of Homer, Hesiod, Alcaeus, Alcman, and Pindar. Other scholars such as Aristarchus concerned themselves with editions of tragedies and comedies also. This preoccupation with the literary heritage of classical Greece reinforced a sense of Greek identity in lands far from "home." Along with the foundation of Greek cities, it helped ground "Greekness" in Egypt and elsewhere, and it was not limited to scholars: the housewives in Theocritus' fifteenth idyll appreciate learning as well (XV 146) and use their own knowledge of Greek mythology to vindicate their "Greekness" (XV 90–92).

The library at Alexandria remained a center for learning long past its heyday in the third and second centuries BC. In the second century AD the impossibly learned Athenaeus worked there, and the countless quotations from obscure books in his sprawling work, the *Deipnosophistae* (roughly "professors at dinner"), give some indication of how many books the librarians had brought together from across the ancient world. The total number eventually rose to an alleged 700,000 (**Ammianus Marcellinus**, XXII 16,13).

The library's fate is unclear. Although some sources claim that **Julius Caesar** accidentally burnt it in 48 BC (Plut. *Caes.* 49; Amm.Marc. l.c.), the library was still standing for Strabo to see a few years later (Strab. XVII 1,8, pp. 793–794) and for Athenaeus to use. It was apparently no longer there, however, during the reign of the Roman emperor Julian the Apostate (AD 361–363) (Amm.Marc. l.c.).

Antiochus I and the Beginning of the Struggle against the Ptolemies

When Ptolemy Ceraunus assassinated Seleucus I Nicator in 280 BC, Antiochus I Soter succeeded in orderly fashion. Initially affairs in the Upper Satrapies fully occupied the new king. Upon his arrival in the west he attempted to bring the Bithynians, whom the Persians had struggled to govern (Xenophon, *Hell.* III 2,2) and whom even the great Alexander had left unconquered, under control, but Antigonus Gonatas took their side and they remained independent (Memnon, *BNJ* 424, Fr. 1.9–12). The Galatians' entrance, with the Bithynians' assistance, into Asia Minor in 278 unsettled the entire region.

The absence of a reliable narrative source makes itself felt acutely as one works through Antiochus I's reign. For example, with the help of his elephants Antiochus I defeated the Galatians in a major battle (App. *Syr.* 65; **Lucian**, *Zeuxis*, 8–11). The battle, however, remains undateable, and one can advance aprioristic arguments for dating it as early as 277 or 276 (doing something about these marauders should have been an absolute priority for Antiochus I) or for some time later in the 260s (since by the time of the battle the Galatians appear to have established themselves in the Greater Phrygian highlands too firmly for even a major defeat to dislodge them). All the same Antiochus had brought the situation under some degree of control.

Antiochus moreover conceded a fair degree of autonomy to Philhetaerus, who under Seleucus I had become the ruler of Pergamum. While Philhetaerus lived, no problems arose. He coined in his own name, but he placed Seleucus' image on the coins (*Cat. of Gr. Coins, Mysia*, p. xxix) and otherwise maintained friendly relations with Antiochus I (Strab. XIII 4,1, p. 623).

The overall picture which emerges somewhat resembles that under the Persians. These too put up with the occasional district that was independent *de facto* (Bithynia, for example); with more or less independent tribes in mountainous terrain (the Uxii in Iran – Arr. III 17); and with a local ruler whom they allowed near complete autonomy as long as he paid the tribute and preserved the trappings of formal subordination, for example the city-king Evagoras of Salamis [Diod. XIV 98; 110; XV 2–4; 8–9].

A slightly different matter was Ptolemaic possession of land (e.g., Hollow Syria) which the King claimed as his. As in the previous generation, the current Ptolemy (II Philadelphus) had problems within his own house; and like Seleucus before him, Antiochus I planned to turn this to his advantage. Ptolemy I Soter had made Ptolemy II's half-brother, Magas, the governor of Cyrene but after their mother's death the two half-brothers had a falling out. In the mid-270s Magas entered into negotiations with Antiochus I who gave Magas his daughter Apame in marriage. In 276 Magas revolted and marched on Alexandria, but a revolt by his Libyan allies forced him to retreat. Antiochus I ought to have invaded Hollow Syria simultaneously with Magas' march on Alexandria, but failed to muster his troops in time, and Ptolemy II – now that Magas had turned back – launched a pre-emptive strike (the beginning of the First Syrian

War). Ptolemy II apparently managed to take the important city of Damascus before Antiochus with the help of troops from the Upper Satrapies retook the city (Paus. I 7; Poly. II 28,2 and IV 15; Austin, Nr. 141 with date). If the Ptolemaic holdings in southern Asia Minor (see Box 23.2) did not antedate the First Syrian War, then they were established now. Granted, no fighting in Asia Minor is attested during this war, but given how poorly attested the war is, that is neither here nor there.

Antiochus I and Ptolemy II eventually made peace, evidently on the basis of the *status quo* and Ptolemy II presumably agreed to tolerate Magas' rule in Cyrene. Especially if Ptolemy II had made substantial gains in southern Asia Minor, the First Syrian War had ended badly for Antiochus I. Worse was to follow, however, in 263 when Philhetaerus, the ruler of Pergamum, died. His nephew and adoptive son, Eumenes I, revolted against Antiochus I and defeated him in a battle near Sardis (Strab. XIII 4,2, p. 624). With that Pergamum became fully independent. Ephesus, meanwhile, revolted as well and became part of Ptolemy II's dominions; Ptolemy II appointed his adoptive son and co-regent, also called Ptolemy, as governor (see below). Shortly thereafter Antiochus I Soter died (261). His younger son and co-regent, Antiochus II Theos ("god"), succeeded to the throne and his first task was to restore Seleucid authority in Asia Minor. His interest in so doing coincided with that of Antigonus Gonatas in expelling the Ptolemies from the Aegean.

Antigonus Gonatas and the Revival of Macedonia

When Antigonus Gonatas united Macedonia under his authority in 276, he took over a desolate land in near anarchy. It took Antigonus years to restore it to some semblance of its former self. Antigonus first had to fend off a challenge from Pyrrhus, the King of Epirus, who had just returned from his western adventure (see chap. 22) and who, in 274, invaded Macedonia. When Antigonus led out his army to meet Pyrrhus, some 2,000 of his troops deserted. When Pyrrhus later attacked Antigonus' retreating army in a narrow pass, the rest of Antigonus' phalanx deserted as well. Supported by his fleet, Antigonus managed to retain the coastline of Macedonia and Thessaly, including Demetrias (Plut. *Pyrrh.* 26). Antigonus raised another army, but suffered another defeat, this time at the hands of Pyrrhus' son, Ptolemy (Just. XXV 3).

Pyrrhus' easy success encouraged disloyalty in Antigonus' Greek possessions, and Pyrrhus, who could do nothing against Antigonus' fleet, marched onto the Peloponnese to seize what Antigonus held there (272). After transporting his troops across the Gulf of Corinth, Pyrrhus rapidly gained allies, both among Antigonus' enemies such as Achaia (Just. XXV 4) and Elis (Paus. VI 14) as well as allies such as Megalopolis. However Pyrrhus for unclear reasons turned aside from his actual task in order to attack Sparta. This attack served to bring Sparta's King Areus I and Antigonus together, and when Pyrrhus failed to take

Box 23.2   *The Ptolemies in Asia Minor*

The two chief pieces of evidence for the Ptolemies' control of southern Asia Minor in the first half of the third century are a few lines from the poet Theocritus as well as an inscription of Ptolemy III Euergetes' from Adulis (Burstein, Nr. 99). Theocritus, the founder of the genre of bucolic poetry, is best known for his pastoral idylls, but he also wrote poetry in praise of his patron Ptolemy II Philadelphus:

> *He has cut off for himself parts of Phoenicia, Arabia, Syria, and Libya; and he rules over the dark Ethiopians, all the Pamphylians, the spearmen Cilicians, the Lycians, the warlike Carians, and the Cycladic Islands.* (Theoc. XVII 86–90)

Ptolemy II clearly ruled over much of southern Asia Minor though one must allow for poetic license: the Seleucids, for example, always retained the eastern "Smooth Cilicia" (since they had access from Syria to Asia Minor through the Cilician Gates), so Ptolemy II can have held the western "Rough Cilicia" only.

When exactly the Ptolemies came into the possession of these regions is unclear. In the early 290s Ptolemy I Soter wrested Cyprus from Demetrius Poliorcetes (Plut. *Demetr.* 35) and could have seized territory in Asia Minor as well. Ptolemy II could have taken advantage of Seleucus I's assassination (280) to establish control over the seaboard of southern Asia Minor. Finally, in the late 270s Ptolemy II may have waged war in southern Asia Minor against Antiochus I during the so-called First Syrian War. Perhaps the Ptolemies seized territory on all three occasions.

Inscriptions (discussed in Ma 1999: 40–42) shed less light on the situation than one might hope. The inscription *SEG* XXVII 929 shows Ptolemaic control of the Lycian coastal town of Limyra, but the inscription is dated to "year 36" of Ptolemy – if Ptolemy I Soter, then 288 BC (that is to say, Ptolemy I must have seized some of Lycia in the 290s), but if Ptolemy II Philadelphus, then 247 BC (that is, Lycia need not have come under Ptolemaic control until the First Syrian War in the late 270s). The inscriptions do, however, make one thing clear: Ptolemaic control (whenever established and for however long retained) was not limited to the coast (see Ma, l.c.). Overall, the inscriptions bear out Theocritus' lines.

However, Ptolemy II lost much of this territory to Antiochus II during the so-called Second Syrian War (mid-250s). The inscription from Adulis lists the lands which Ptolemy III Euergetes inherited from his father:

> *. . . he inherited from his father rule over Egypt, Libya, Syria, Phoenicia, Cyprus, Lycia, Caria, and the Cycladic Islands . . .*

Pamphylia and Rough Cilicia are missing, so Ptolemy II had presumably lost them.

In the Third Syrian War (245 BC), however, Ptolemy III Euergetes reconquered Pamphylia and (Rough) Cilicia as the inscription from Adulis claims ("he gained control of Cilicia and of Pamphylia . . .") and with the possible exception of Pamphylia, the Ptolemies held these regions until the time of Antiochus III Megas who reconquered them towards the end of the third century BC (see chap. 24).

Sparta by storm (Plut. *Pyrrh.* 26–29), Areus and Antigonus cooperated in destroying him.

When Antigonus brought his army to Argos, Pyrrhus marched northwards to meet him. Thereupon Areus, with 1,000 Cretan mercenaries and a handful of Spartiates, also marched towards Argos and joined Antigonus. Neither army initially entered Argos, but some within the city offered to betray it to Pyrrhus. As Pyrrhus' troops entered under cover of darkness, others in Argos, realizing what was happening, sent to Antigonus for help, and Antigonus' and Areus' troops entered the city through another gate. At dawn, with two armies inside, street-by-street fighting ensued in which Pyrrhus himself was slain (Plut. *Pyrrh.* 32–34).

With his one major opponent in Europe removed, Antigonus had time and leisure to establish his rule firmly. Over the next few years he saw to it that his allies became the rulers – commonly termed "tyrants" – of most Greek states (Pol. II 41 and IX 29). In addition, strong garrisons held a few important sites such as Corinth and Chalcis – along with Demetrias the so-called "Fetters of Greece" (Liv. XXXII 37; App. *Mac.* 9).

All the same, now that Pyrrhus was dead, Areus again worked against Antigonus. Areus concluded alliances with various Peloponnesian states and established friendly relations with Ptolemy II Philadelphus. In 269 or 268 one Chremonides moved a motion in the Athenian assembly that Athens should join Areus in an alliance against Macedonia (Burstein, Nr. 56). The modern name for the war which ensued is the **Chremonidean War**.

Antigonus promptly marched against Athens and occupied Attica. Ptolemy II Philadelphus sent a fleet to the tip of Attica, but it did nothing (Paus. I 1). Areus attempted to march across the Isthmus (Paus. III 6), but Antigonus' troops blocked it. A mutiny among his Galatian mercenaries in Megara briefly brought him into serious danger, but he crushed the mutineers in battle (Trog. *Prol.* 26; Just. XXVI 2). Thereafter Areus marched back to Sparta (Paus. l.c.), only to march out again the next year, and this time Antigonus met him in battle and defeated him (Trog. l.c.; Plut. *Agis,* 3). Antigonus now besieged Athens and forced it to surrender; thereafter he installed a garrison in the Peiraeus (Paus. l.c.) as well as one in Athens itself, where he either abolished the offices or filled them with his own appointments (Apollodorus, *BNJ* 244, Fr. 44; Athen. IV, p. 167).

By the mid-260s, then, Antigonus had restored Macedonian dominion over most of Greece. His rule in Macedonia itself was securely established. Yet Ptolemy II Philadelphus, who had supported Sparta and Athens in the Chremonidean War, still controlled the Cyclades and other Aegean islands, especially Samos (Burstein, Nr. 92), and would remain a threat for as long as he did so.

Ptolemaic Losses in the Aegean and in Asia Minor

Ptolemy II Philadelphus' control of the Aegean irked not just Antigonus. Antiochus II Theos, who ascended the Seleucid throne in 261, also wished to see a diminution of Ptolemaic power in the region. So Antigonus Gonatas and Antiochus II Theos made common cause against Ptolemy II Philadelphus; the marriage of Antiochus' sister Stratonice with Antigonus' son Demetrius apparently sealed the alliance (Euseb. I 249 Schoene; Just. XXVIII 1). Stratonice is just one example of the talented and ambitious women whose task it was to make alliances work and who played important diplomatic and political roles in the Hellenistic world. Stratonice would later on show that she possessed the drive to rule in surpassing measure, but for now her job was to facilitate her brother's and husband's alliance against Ptolemy II.

Ptolemy II Philadelphus' inability to keep the peace within his house gave his foes their opportunity. In the early 250s Philadelphus' adoptive son and co-regent, also called Ptolemy, whom he had installed as governor at Ephesus (Athen. XIII, p. 593), revolted against him (Trog. *Prol.* 26). This Ptolemy was the son of none other than Arsinoë, the daughter of Ptolemy I Soter and the widow of Lysimachus (see chap. 21). After Lysimachus' death the ambitious Arsinoë had returned to Egypt where she married her brother Ptolemy II Philadelphus. There had been marriages between close kin within the Macedonian royal house, but never one between brother and sister. Yet such a marriage did correspond to ancient Egyptian royal custom, and for Arsinoë and Philadelphus this sufficed. That son whom Arsinoë had once wished to make King of Macedonia she now attempted to set upon the throne of Egypt. Philadelphus adopted him and made him co-regent over his biological son, the eventual Ptolemy III Euergetes. Philadelphus' favoring of his adoptive son clearly caused conflict within his house, and Philadelphus himself seems eventually to have had second thoughts in the matter. When he began to favor his biological son again, he packed his adoptive son off to a provincial posting where the latter soon revolted.

The war that began with this revolt in the mid-250s went badly for Philadelphus. The Rhodians, who had joined the coalition against him, beat back his fleet's attempt to capture Ephesus by sea (Poly. V 18); Timarchus, evidently an ally of the rebel Ptolemy's, captured Samos, an important Ptolemaic possession (**Frontinus**, *Strat.* III 2,11 – there read "Samians" instead of "Sanians"); and Antigonus Gonatas, at the head of the numerically inferior Macedonian fleet, inflicted a severe defeat upon Philadelphus' commanders near Cos (Plut. *On Self-Praise*, p. 545; *Sayings of Kings and Commanders*, p. 183). The rebel Ptolemy's rule in Ephesus ended when he fell victim to a mutiny (Athen. XIII p. 593), and this allowed Antiochus II Theos with Rhodian help to recapture Ephesus for the Seleucids (Front. *Strat.* III 9,10). Antiochus II captured Miletus from Timarchus as well (App. *Syr.* 65) and, since Timarchus held Samos, may well have taken it also.

Antiochus II Theos also wrested control of Pamphylia and Rough Cilicia from Ptolemy II Philadelphus (Burstein, Nr. 99). Given how poorly events in this period are attested and given the extent to which the Ptolemies were losing ground, Antiochus II Soter may well have made additional conquests in the other regions under Ptolemaic control in Asia Minor (Caria and Lycia). Although

Box 23.3   *Rhodes in the Hellenistic Age*

Most Greek states cut a pathetic figure in the period between the death of Alexander the Great in 323 and the rise of the Achaian League in the 240s and 230s. Occasional rebellions notwithstanding, the Diadochi and the early Hellenistic Kings seem to have done whatever they wished with cities such as Athens and Corinth or, in Asia Minor, with Miletus and Ephesus. There were, however, some exceptions: for example, Byzantium and Heracleia Pontica regained their independence after Lysimachus' death at Cyropedium in 281 and held it against the Seleucid Kingdom, against the Galatians, and against Pergamum. The most spectacular exception is surely the island of Rhodes. Although it was minuscule when compared even to Antigonid Macedonia, it routinely challenged Hellenistic kings in the pursuit of its own policies.

As a general rule, the Rhodians sought to keep any one Hellenistic king from attaining a dominant position on the sea. Thus, in 315, at a time when Ptolemy I Soter's fleet dominated, the Rhodians assisted Antigonus Monophthalmus with the construction of a fleet so that he could compete with Ptolemy (Diod. XIX 57–59). In 306 Antigonus' son, Demetrius Poliorcetes, destroyed Ptolemy's fleet in a battle off Salamis on Cyprus. Rhodes then allied itself with Ptolemy and fought against Antigonus and Demetrius (see chap. 20). In the period after Ipsus, Antigonus' son Demetrius Poliorcetes slowly lost his naval superiority in the Aegean. By the 270s Ptolemy II Philadelphus dominated those waters, so the Rhodians allied themselves with his opponents, Antiochus II Theos and Antigonus Gonatas (see in text).

Rhodes, moreover, lay on several important trade-routes. All traffic from Egypt or Syria to Greece or northwards to the Black Sea (and the reverse) passed by Rhodes, and this made Rhodes a wealthy city. The Rhodians accordingly fought to keep trade-routes open. When Byzantium imposed a toll on traffic through the Bosporus, Rhodes promptly went to war and forced Byzantium to remove the toll (Pol. IV 38sqq.). In addition, the Rhodian fleet provided a valuable service to all merchants in the eastern Mediterranean: the suppression of piracy (Diod. XX 81,3; Strab. XIV 2,5, 652; Pol. IV 19,8).

The Rhodians clearly maintained their ships well since they achieved all this with what appears to be a fleet of modest size. The only attested figures come from the war against Antiochus III Megas in 190 when the Rhodians initially sent 36 ships against the Seleucids. When 31 of these were destroyed, the Rhodians replaced the lost ships quickly (Liv. XXXVII 9,11,12, and 23), so they must have had at least about 70 on call. These sufficed to guarantee Rhodes' independence in an age when most Greek states lost theirs.

it is not entirely clear that any fighting took place in Syria, this period of warfare between Antiochus II and Ptolemy II is conventionally known as the Second Syrian War. It ended in circa 252 when the two kings made a treaty with one another and sealed it with Antiochus II's marriage to Ptolemy II's daughter, Berenice (Porphyry, *BNJ* 260, Fr. 43).

While southern Cappadocia remained in the possession of the Seleucids, probably during Antiochus II's war against Ptolemy II a man called Ariarathes established himself as the ruler of part of Cappadocia on the Taurus (Diod. XXXI 19). This Ariarathes was allegedly a descendant of that Ariarathes who had been the last Persian satrap of Cappadocia on the Taurus and who had continued to rule the region until Perdiccas conquered it in 322 (see chap. 20). Whether Ariarathes II was fully independent or continued to acknowledge Seleucid overlordship (if only formally) is unclear. Antiochus II, fully occupied with the war against Egypt, may simply have had to tolerate the situation.

Antiochus II's effective cession of a part of Cappadocia on the Taurus as well as the independence of Pergamum were partially offset by a surprising gain. Probably after the treaty with Egypt, Antiochus II conquered portions of Thrace (Poly. IV 16).

The Achaian League and Macedonia

By the late 260s Antigonus Gonatas appeared to have consolidated Macedonian rule over Greece. City states such as Athens and Sparta may have had a glorious past, but as the Chremonidean War had shown, even when they united they were no match for a Hellenistic king. The league-states, however, were a different matter entirely. They were larger to begin with and, owing to their federal structure, eminently capable of expansion (see Boxes 21.3 and 23.4). A state such as the Aetolian League, which stretched from the Adriatic to the Aegean, might resist the King of Macedonia. Yet Antigonid Macedonia's most dangerous opponent came from the northern Peloponnese. Here, in Achaia, a league of twelve cities had existed in the fourth century, but it had become defunct. In 280, however, four of the original towns – Dyme, Patrae, Tritaea, and Pharae – renewed the League and in the next few years the remaining eight towns rejoined (Pol. II 41). But the Achaian League's true rise began in 251 when conspirators in neighboring Sicyon seized power from the tyrant Nicocles. The conspirators' leader was a young Sicyonian called Aratus who understood that the city-state of Sicyon was too small to survive in this age (Plut. Arat. 4–9).

Antigonus' nephew Alexander, who had been his governor in Corinth and on Euboea, had just rebelled, and Antigonus and he were at war (Trog. Prol. 26; Plut. Arat. 12 and 17). Since Nicocles had been an ally of Alexander's, Sicyon too was at war against Alexander. Rather than let Sicyon be destroyed by a war for which it was too small, Aratus persuaded his fellow citizens to join the Achaian League (Plut. Arat. 9) which soon negotiated an alliance with Alexander against Antigonus (circa 250; Plut. Arat. 18). Aratus meanwhile traveled to Egypt and persuaded Ptolemy II Philadelphus to support this alliance financially (Plut. Arat. 12–14).

Because the Aetolians held Thermopylae and because a good part of the Macedonian fleet must have been in Alexander's hands in Chalcis and Corinth, Antigonus' ability to send an army onto the Peloponnese was compromised, and his control over many Peloponnesian cities through the tyrants whom he had installed was crumbling. Some Arcadian towns, for example, soon made alliances with the Achaian League (Paus. VIII 10,6). In the early 240s Alexander died, and his widow, Nicaea, assumed control. This princess, reversing her husband's policy, acted to shore up Antigonid Macedonia's position in Greece. She offered Demetrius, Antigonus Gonatas' son, her hand. Demetrius was already married to a Seleucid princess, Stratonice, the daughter of Antiochus I Soter, but the reasons for making that alliance had passed, so Demetrius divorced her and married anew according to the current diplomatic situation (Plut. *Arat.* 17). Stratonice returned to Syria. She did not meekly acquiesce in her abrupt removal from a position of power, but instead waited until such time as she might be able once again to play a political role. Thanks to Nicaea's decisive action, however, Antigonus Gonatas regained control of Euboea and the northeastern Peloponnese.

The newly restored Antigonid position would, however, be shattered in 243, when Aratus, with the help of traitors in the Macedonian garrison, succeeded in seizing Acrocorinth, the citadel of Corinth, in a daring raid by night. The deed made him famous, secured him the leading position in the Achaian League until his death, and established the Achaian League as the dominant state on the Peloponnese since not only Corinth, but also Megara, Epidaurus, and Troezen soon joined (Plut. *Arat.* 18–24).

Box 23.4   *The Constitution of the Achaian League*

The Achaian League, before its dissolution in the late fourth century, had traditionally held its assemblies at the centrally located sanctuary of Zeus Homarius near Aegium (IG V,2,344,8; IvonMagnesia, 39). Aegium was not one of the four cities which reformed the League in 280, but as soon as it did rejoin in 275 (Pol. II 41), assemblies once again took place at the sanctuary there (Strab. VIII 7,3, p. 385). However, from 189 BC onwards assemblies began to take place in all member cities in rotation (Liv. XXXVIII 30). For the first 25 years of the reformed League (280–255), each member city in rotation annually elected a Secretary and two *Strategoi* as the League's chief officers. From 255 onwards the entire League annually elected a single *Strategos* as its chief officer (Pol. II 43; cf. Strab. l.c.). Immediate re-election was not allowed, so Aratus of Sicyon, the League's most prominent statesman, for much of his career was *Strategos* every other year (Plut. *Cleom.* 15,1). Other League officials were the Cavalry Commander and the Naval Commander (Syll. 3, 490).

For the League's first few decades the Assembly, at which in theory all male citizens above the age of thirty were present (Pol. XXIX 24), met at set times (Pol. IV 7), although an extraordinary meeting, a **Synkletos**, could be held if needed (Pol. XXIX 24). By 185, however, the Assembly was convened only in certain situations: to vote

(Continued)

on matters of war and peace or at the request of the Roman Senate (Liv. XXXIX 33; cf. Pol. XXIII 5).

Polybius often mentions a League Council (e.g., Pol. XXIX 24), but gives few details. Analogy with the Aetolian League's Council suggests that it had many members, presumably taken proportionally from all member cities (see Box 21.3). The presence of a standing committee for the Council, the *Damiourgoi*, also suggests that that the Council's membership was large, that is to say, it could not easily meet in its entirety. Presumably after the Assembly stopped meeting under normal circumstances the Council elected the officers.

In 198 there were ten *Damiourgoi* (Liv. XXXII 22). These arranged for meetings of the Assembly (Liv. XXXVIII 30) and presumably the Council. They also chaired the Assembly's meetings and put questions to the vote (Liv. XXXII 22). In 183 the Roman commander T. Quinctius Flamininus wrote to the *Strategos* and the *Damiourgoi* to request a meeting of the Assembly (Pol. XXIII 5). In other words a request could be delivered to the *Damiourgoi* (as to the *Strategos*) at any time. Another body, called the **Synarchiai**, which met in secret (Pol. XXVIII 13) could make executive decisions for the Achaian League (Pol. XXVII 2). The *Strategos* was a member of this body (Pol. l.c.) to which surely the *Damiourgoi* too belonged. It is not known whether other officials such as the Cavalry Commander did also. It may be that the *Synarchiai* were simply the League's annual officers plus the *Damiourgoi*. The day-to-day administration of the League in any case resided with these officers, the *Damiourgoi*, and anyone else who happened to belong to the *Synarchiai*.

Like the Aetolian League (see Box 21.3) the Achaian League had a flexible structure which allowed it easily to incorporate new members. As with the Aetolian League, the immediate award of political rights served as an inducement to join. In the Assembly, each new member city (unless the Assembly in 198 was anomalous) received one vote on a par with all those cities which were already members and in addition could proportionally to its size send members to the Council. Someone from a city not originally Achaian (such as Aratus of Sicyon) could hold office in the League.

Desperate to regain Corinth, Antigonus made an alliance with the Aetolian League; the Achaians meanwhile sought aid from Ptolemy III Euergetes (who gave Aratus a subsidy of six talents per year) and Sparta. In 241, Sparta's King Agis IV led out an army to help the Achaians ward off the expected Aetolian attack, but Agis IV and Aratus soon quarreled. Aratus wished to avoid a full-scale battle while Agis IV desired one and when the Aetolians finally attacked, Agis IV had already returned home. They went past Corinth and Sicyon and seized the Sicyonian town of Pellene, but Aratus' troops surprised them while they were plundering the city and drove them out. The Aetolians lost some 700 men and, having little desire to continue a proxy war for Antigonus, returned home (Plut. *Arat.* 31–32; *Agis*, 13–15). The Aetolian and Achaian Leagues now made peace (Plut. *Arat.* 33).

In 239 Antigonus Gonatas died. He had built up the Macedonian supremacy in Greece in the late 270s and early 260s, only to watch it dissolve in his old age. When his son Demetrius II succeeded him, the only Antigonid possessions left in central Greece and the Peloponnese were Euboea (with a strong Macedonian garrison at Chalcis), Athens (with a Macedonian garrison in the Peiraeus), and Argos which the tyrants Aristomachus and, after his assassination, Aristippus held for Macedonia (Plut. *Arat.* 25).

The Aetolian and Achaian Leagues now formed an alliance (Plut. *Arat.* 33; Pol. II 44). Since the Aetolians held Thermopylae, it was difficult for Demetrius II to launch any attack against them; but he still held Chalcis connected by a bridge to Boeotia. From Chalcis then he presumably crossed over into Boeotia. Faced with a Macedonian army in their land the Boeotians deserted the Aetolians (Pol. XX 5). Demetrius II, however, in the so-called **Demetrian War** found himself unable to achieve any signal victory against the Aetolians, whom the Achaians supported.

On the Peloponnese, meanwhile, Aratus strove to capture Argos, the chief remaining Macedonian bastion in the area. In 235 he led out the Achaian army against Aristippus, the tyrant of Argos, who initially defeated him, though Aratus did take the town of Cleonae. While Aristippus was attempting to retake it, Aratus sprang a surprise attack. Some 1,500 Argives, including Aristippus, fell with allegedly not one single casualty on the Achaian side. The victory was impressive, even if a second tyrant called Aristomachus gained control of Argos before Aratus could seize it (Plut. *Arat.* 27–29; Pol. II 59). Shortly thereafter, Lydiadas, who had recently seized power in Megalopolis, voluntarily stepped down from his position, and at his urging Megalopolis joined the Achaian League (Plut. *Arat.* 30).

By 231 Demetrius II was fighting a difficult war against the Dardanians to the north of Macedonia (Trog. *Prol.* 28; Liv. XXXI 28), and he had to desist from wars in Greece. The Achaians for their part could not dislodge him from Argos or Athens. But in 229 Demetrius II died, leaving behind a young boy, Philip, for whom his cousin Antigonus Doson ("the one who will give" – because Doson tended to promise that he would do something rather than simply doing it) became regent. Doson soon made himself king, but he adopted his ward and thus preserved the Antigonid line of succession (Plut. *Paul.* 8; Just. XXVIII 3,9–10). Macedonia in any case was still at war against the Dardanians.

Given Macedonia's problems, it probably went unnoticed that around this time pirates under the Illyrian queen Teuta became such a disturbance that the Romans for the first time intervened in the eastern Adriatic. In 229 a Roman fleet arrived to put a stop to the piracy. In the end, Rome placed various Greek cities in the Adriatic (including Corcyra) under its protection and although Rome assumed no direct or even indirect control over these regions, it did establish a certain sphere of influence (Pol. II 2–12; III 16 and 18–19).

Macedonia had more pressing concerns elsewhere. In Greece, Aristomachus, the tyrant of Argos, opened negotiations with the Achaian League. He laid down his position, and Argos joined the League, with the tyrants of Hermione and Phleius shortly following suit (Pol. II 44 and 60; Plut. *Arat.* 34–35). That eliminated the last vestige of Macedonian authority on the Peloponnese. In Athens Diogenes, the commander of the Macedonian garrison, agreed to leave provided that he received 150 talents to pay his troops. It took time to raise the sum, but in the end Athens' freedom was bought (Plut. *Arat.* 34). The Boeotians, meanwhile, regained their independence from the Macedonians as well (Pol. XX 5). By 227, with the exception of Euboea and Thessaly, all of mainland Greece was independent for the first time since the Battle of Chaeroneia in 338. Yet much had changed in 110 years – two gigantic leagues, Achaia and Aetolia, both of which had been backwaters in the classical period, now dominated. They had ingested many smaller leagues and indeed many city-states including once powerful towns such as Corinth and Argos. A few city-states remained, however – most prominently Athens with its glorious past and Sparta which despite all still had ambitions. But it had been the Aetolians and the Achaians who had proved capable of resisting the Macedonians and of restoring the freedom of the Greeks.

The Crisis of the Seleucid Kingdom

As Antigonid rule was crumbling in Greece, the Seleucid Kingdom experienced its own crisis. In 246, when Antiochus II Theos lay dying prematurely (Euseb. I 251 Schoene), the empire still stood intact with only minor losses in the far northwest. The independence of Pergamum and of Cappadocia on Taurus may have galled, but the Seleucids had won back much land lost in the First Syrian War and gained possessions in Europe and in the Aegean. On his deathbed Antiochus II made arrangements for the succession; his son by the Ptolemaic princess Berenice was only a few years old, but his eldest son from his first marriage was approximately twenty. Antiochus chose the latter option and his eldest son, Seleucus II Callinicus ("Glory through victory") ascended the throne. Berenice, however, in her young son's name now made her own play for power. She held Antioch briefly, but a revolt broke out in which both she and her son lost their lives (Poly. VIII 50; Just. XXVII 1). At this Ptolemy III Euergetes, who had become king upon his father's death in 246, invaded Syria.

According to Euergetes' own account, in 245

> he marched forth into Asia with infantry, cavalry, a fleet, and both Troglodytic and Aethiopic elephants . . . After he had made himself lord of all countries within (i.e., west of) the Euphrates, of Cilicia, Pamphylia, Ionia, the Hellespont, and Thrace; and of all troops in these lands and of Indian elephants, and after he had made all the rulers in these lands his subjects, he crossed the River Euphrates; and he made Mesopotamia, Babylon, the Susiane, Persis, Media, and everything else as far as Bactria subject to him . . .
> (Burstein, Nr. 99) (See also the papyrus at Austin, Nr. 220.)

The confused circumstances at the Seleucid court meant that Ptolemy III met with little resistance during this dramatic campaign, the opening of the Third

Syrian War (sometimes called the **Laodiceian War** after Seleucus II's mother, Laodice). However problems at home apparently caused Ptolemy III to return to Egypt (Just. XXVII 1), and Seleucus II meanwhile had won Mithridates II, the King of Cappadocia on the Pontus, as an ally. A marriage had sealed the alliance, for Mithridates married Seleucus II's sister Laodice. In addition Seleucus II ceded Greater Phrygia (Euseb. I 251 Schoene; Just. XXXVIII 5). With the Cappadocian king's backing, Seleucus II won back all that Ptolemy III had captured to the East of the Taurus. West of the Taurus, however, Ptolemy III's conquests, concentrated on the coast as far north as the Hellespont and Thrace (Pol. V 34), were more durable since the Ptolemies still held much territory in those regions when Antiochus III Megas set about restoring Seleucid authority some three decades later (see chap. 23). Finally, Ptolemy III retained possession of Seleuceia at the mouth of the Orontes (Pol. V 58). Circa 240 Ptolemy III Euergetes and Seleucus II Callinicus made peace on the basis of the *status quo* (Just. XXVII 2).

The restoration of Seleucid authority in Asia Minor was now pressing. Seleucus II had already appointed his brother, Antiochus, to take charge of Asia west of the Taurus. This initially appears no different from Seleucus I's appointment of his son to a similar position of authority in the Upper Satrapies (see chap. 20), but Antiochus – surnamed Hierax, "the hawk," because he dived headlong into things – was only fourteen years old (Just. XXVII 2,6–8); presumably their mother was to rule as Antiochus Hierax' regent (Plut. *On brotherly love*, p. 489). Yet relations between the two brothers soured, and Seleucus II, inaugurating a bitter civil war, marched against his brother a few years later.

Seleucus II attacked both Sardis and Ephesus, but failed at taking either city (Euseb. I 251 Schoene). Near Ancyra, Hierax defeated his brother (Just. XXVII 2; Trog. *Prol.* 27) in a major battle (circa 235). Hierax had received support both from his brother-in-law Mithridates, the King of Cappadocia on the Pontus (Euseb. l.c.), as well as from the Galatians, who, however, soon turned against him and began plundering his dominions (Just. XXVII 2). Near Magnesia, Antiochus Hierax defeated them with Ptolemaic help. Hierax' alliance with Mithridates also broke apart, and Hierax won Greater Phrygia from him. In the meantime Ptolemy III Euergetes sent troops to attack Damascus (Euseb. l.c.), but apparently achieved little.

The situation was grim for Seleucus II, but Hierax' wars against Mithridates and the Galatians gave him an opportunity to recover. Whether or not he swore a formal peace with his brother, in the next few years he felt secure enough to march into the Upper Satrapies where Seleucid rule had been growing shaky. Antiochus II Theos had spent almost his entire reign in Asia Minor and Syria and had let the satraps in the East rule as they saw fit.

In Bactria, the satrap Diodotus had by now proclaimed himself king (Just. XLI 4; Strab. XI 9,2, p. 515 – mistakenly writing "Euthydemus"). For decades Media Atropatene had acknowledged Seleucid overlordship at best formally only (Strab. XI 13,1, pp. 522–523; Pol. V 55). The exact circumstances in other satrapies are unclear, but Seleucus II's defeat at Ancyra as well as the recent expedition of Ptolemy III Euergetes cannot have done much for the Seleucids' authority in these parts. Arsaces, an Iranian chieftain to the north of the empire, invaded Parthia, defeated its satrap Andragoras (who himself fell in the battle), and established his own kingdom to which he soon added Hyrcania. Diodotus I of Bactria was succeeded by his son, also called Diodotus (Just. XLI 4).

Seleucus II marched against Arsaces in the late 230s (and probably also Diodotus II, who allied himself with Arsaces). Even if Arsaces achieved a minor victory against Seleucus II, in the end he still had to flee into the steppes to the north whence he had come. Seleucus II, however, received no opportunity to deal with Bactria or even to re-establish Seleucid authority in Parthia and Hyrcania since a revolt had broken out in Antioch itself. Seleucus II returned to Syria, and Arsaces re-entered Parthia and established his rule there firmly (Just. XLI 4–5).

Meanwhile, in Antioch Stratonice, Seleucus II's aunt and the ex-wife of Demetrius II of Macedonia, had decided that her time had come. She had never resigned herself to her removal from the high game of imperial politics, and she now attempted to seize power. Seleucus II suppressed the revolt (Agatharchides, *BNJ* 86, Fr. 20a), but the Seleucids lost the northern half of the Upper Satrapies.

Meanwhile Antiochus Hierax was faring even worse in Asia Minor. The current ruler of Pergamum, Attalus, had defeated the Galatians in battle (Burstein, Nr. 85, nr. 276; Pol. XVIII 41; Strab. XIII 4,2, p. 624; see also Figure 23.1). These now sought help from Hierax who gladly seized the opportunity to make an end of Pergamene independence. Yet Attalus defeated Hierax and his allies (Burstein, Nr. 85, nr. 275; IvonPergamum, Nr. 247) and went on to win three more victories against him (Burstein, Nr. 85, nrr. 274, 278, and 279; Euseb. I 253 Schoene – dating them to the early 220s). Thereafter Attalus took possession of all Seleucid Asia Minor (Pol. IV 48; Just. XXVII 3 – though Justin erroneously calls him "Eumenes, King of Bithynia") and proclaimed himself "king" (see Pol. l.c.). Hierax, after various misadventures, ended up in Thrace where he fell in a battle against the Galatians (Euseb. I 253 Schoene; Trog. *Prol.* 27).

In 225 Seleucus II died and left to his young son, Seleucus III Soter ("savior"), an empire in deep crisis. Yet this empire still possessed great resources. It had recovered from the Great Satraps' Revolt in the 360s and it would eventually recover from the current crisis as well. In the company of an experienced commander, Achaius, Seleucus III marched into Asia Minor where, however, he fell victim to an assassination in 223 (Pol. IV 48). His twenty-year-old brother, Antiochus III, succeeded him and in Asia Minor Achaius took command.

Antiochus III Begins the Restoration of the Seleucid Kingdom

In Asia Minor Achaius prosecuted the war against Attalus with vigor and soon had him confined to his original territory (Pol. l.c.). In Greater Media, however, a revolt had broken out. Its satrap, Molon, declared himself independent in 322; his brother Alexander, the satrap of Persis, joined him, as did Artabazanes, the ruler of Media Atropatene. Molon defeated the first imperial army sent against him and took the Apolloniatis on the east bank of the Tigris. In the next year he defeated a second imperial army, crossed the Tigris, and seized the satrapy of Babylon (Pol. V 41–48).

Now Antiochus III personally assumed command. He crossed the Tigris from west to east and marched southwards, behind Molon. To avoid being cut off from Media, Molon recrossed the Tigris as well and attempted to retreat to Media, but Antiochus III had been too fast. Antiochus III had by far the larger army and he was the king. Most of Molon's army deserted, and the revolt was crushed in early 220 (Pol. V 48–54). Antiochus III then turned his attention to Media Atropatene. At his arrival its ruler, Artabazanes, hastened to reach an accommodation with the king (Pol. V 55). Presumably Artabazanes recognized the king's authority and possibly agreed to pay a tribute. Antiochus III did not care to press for more; Parthia and Bactria he left as they were for the time being and returned to Syria.

In Asia Minor, Achaius, having guessed that Antiochus would fail in the East, had proclaimed himself king (Pol. V 57), but there was also the unfinished business with Egypt in Hollow Syria. Ptolemy III Euergetes had died in 221, his son Ptolemy IV Philopator had just become king, and this gave Antiochus III an opportunity to settle matters with the house of Ptolemy. Antiochus III let Achaius be for now and in 219 marched against Egypt instead – the Fourth Syrian War.

After initial successes (he recaptured Seleuceia; Tyre and Ptolemaïs were surrendered to him), his offensive ground to a halt. The Egyptians began to negotiate, and Antiochus unwisely consented to a four months' truce for the winter of 219 to 218. But Ptolemy IV Philopator was playing for time, and in 218 the war continued. Antiochus III defeated a Ptolemaic army near Sidon, but failed to take the city itself. In the meantime he consolidated his grip on Hollow Syria all the way down to the border of Egypt. In 217 Ptolemy IV marched into Palestine with an army of some 70,000 infantry, 5,000 cavalry, and 73 elephants; Antiochus III had 62,000 infantry, 6,000 cavalry, and 102 elephants. The two armies met at Raphia. It was the largest pitched battle since Ipsus. While Antiochus's army was superior in point of cavalry and elephants, Ptolemy had a larger phalanx – but it contained 20,000 native Egyptian recruits whose loyalty to a Macedonian king was untested in battle (see Box 23.5). Antiochus stationed himself on his right, with 4,000 riders; Ptolemy stood opposite on his left with some of his own cavalry. The Seleucid cavalry with Antiochus gained the upper hand quickly, but while Antiochus pursued the retreating Egyptian riders, Ptolemy rushed to the phalanx in the center of his line. He rallied the troops and, leading raw recruits against veterans, charged against the smaller Seleucid phalanx, which gave way. Antiochus' losses were high – 10,000 killed and 4,000 captured –, and he gladly accepted Ptolemy's offer of peace. Although he had to accept Ptolemaic control of Hollow Syria for now, his campaign had achieved one gain: Seleuceia, Antioch's harbor town, was back in Seleucid hands (Pol. V 59–71, 79–87).

Box 23.5   *Internal Problems in Egypt after Raphia*

The Hellenistic kingdoms insisted on Greek as the administrative language. Inevitably this caused tension between the non-Greeks and the Greek-speaking elite. Theocritus during the reign of Ptolemy II Philadelphus can depict Greek housewives looking down on native Egyptians as thieving rabble (XV 47–50). A letter (mid-third century BC) from a native Egyptian to a Ptolemaic official named Zeno has survived; in it he complains that Greek officials have treated him badly "because I am not Greek" and "because I do not 'Hellenize'" (Austin, Nr. 245). Whatever precisely this last term means (dress? manners? proficiency in Greek?), this native Egyptian was clearly suffering what today would be called racial discrimination. To get along in Egypt, one had to "Hellenize."

During the Fourth Syrian War, however, in a desperate situation, Ptolemy IV Philopator enlisted 20,000 native Egyptians for his phalanx. This was apparently the first time that the Ptolemies had recruited among the native population. As it turned out, it was Ptolemy IV's phalanx which won the day at Raphia. Polybius notes:

> Immediately after these events Ptolemy (IV) waged war against the Egyptians. For this King, when he armed the Egyptians for the war against Antiochus (III), made a decision which was advantageous in the short term. In the long term, however, he was making a mistake. For the Egyptian soldiers owing to their pride in their victory at Raphia no longer took orders. Instead they sought out a leader and a representative since they were capable of looking out for themselves. Not long after they succeeded in this. (Pol. V 107)

Polybius later on states that Ptolemy IV had to contend with a guerilla war after a revolt:

> Late (i.e., in his reign) circumstances compelled him to wage war as already noted. This war, apart from both sides' brutality and lawlessness, involved no pitched battles, naval engagements, or sieges, nor anything else worth mentioning. (Pol. XIV 12).

Another reference to this revolt occurs in the most famous Egyptian inscription of them all, the Rosetta Stone, from the year 196 BC. (Burstein, Nr. 103; see lines 19–28). The inscription – a decree in honor of Ptolemy V Epiphanes – is much more noticeably "Egyptian" in tone (for example, the continual references to Egyptian deities) than a similar decree in honor of Ptolemy III (Austin, Nr. 222). If appearances do not mislead, then the Ptolemies were now "Egyptianizing" a bit.

The revolt – as a hieroglyphic inscription from the Ptolemaic temple of Horus at Edfu shows (C. de Wit, *Chronique d'Égypte*, 36, 1961, pp. 73–75 and 287–289.) – began around the year 207 BC in Upper Egypt and lasted until Ptolemy V Epiphanes finally suppressed it in 186 BC.

Antiochus III now moved to deal with Achaius in Asia Minor. Before crossing the Taurus, he made an arrangement with Attalus, the King of Pergamum (Pol. V 107). Although Achaius and Attalus had been fighting each other, the danger existed that they might unite in the presence of a common enemy. Presumably Antiochus III offered recognition, with credible guarantees, of Pergamene independence since he avoided ceding any land to Attalus. In 216 the campaign began. Polybius' account of the first two years of the war is missing, but in 214 Antiochus III had Achaius' forces trapped in Sardis which he soon took (Pol. VII 15–18). What Achaius had held, Antiochus III regained for the empire: this included Hellespontine Phrygia (with the exception of Pergamene territory, obviously), Greater Phrygia, and Lydia, as well as adjacent territories.

Antiochus III appointed Zeuxis, a trusted official, over the satrapies of Asia Minor west of the Taurus (see most clearly Ma, Nr. 29). In 212 he campaigned in Armenia and reduced that land to tributary status once more. Antiochus III let its king, Xerxes, retain his throne and gave him a daughter of his, Antiochis, in marriage (Pol. VIII 23).

In 210 Antiochus III invaded Parthia. Arsaces II, the Parthian king, fled before him, and Antiochus easily enough took possession of Hecatompylus, the chief town in the region. From there Antiochus III marched northwards and took Tambrax, the chief town of Hyrcania (Pol. X 28–31). Arsaces II he left in power, presumably against payment of tribute (Just. XLI 5,7).

From Parthia Antiochus proceeded to Bactria. In 208 he defeated its king, Euthydemus, in battle (Pol. X 49), but allowed Euthydemus to continue to rule. However, he did make arrangements for Euthydemus' son, Demetrius, to marry a daughter of his. Before leaving Bactria in 206, Antiochus III requisitioned all Euthydemus' elephants. Antiochus III then crossed the Hindu Kush from north to south to enter what had once been the satrapy of Paropamisadae. Its current ruler, an otherwise unknown Indian called Sophagasenus, agreed to pay tribute and handed over more elephants, so that Antiochus III now had 150 of them. From here Antiochus proceeded through Arachosia and the Drangiane to Carmania where he went into winter quarters (Pol. XI 34). There was no fighting in those three regions, nor did Antiochus have to deal with any independent rulers. Apparently, and despite all, those satrapies had loyally remained within the empire all this time. Polybius concludes his account of Antiochus III's expedition as follows:

> So ended Antiochus' campaign in the Upper Regions, by which he made not only the Upper Satraps subject to his rule, but also the coastal cities and the rulers to the west of the Taurus. In sum, he made the Kingdom secure and impressed all his subjects with his courage and hard work. Owing to this expedition he was shown to be worthy of his Kingdom – not just to those in Asia, but even to those in Europe. (Pol. XI 39)

As to Antiochus III's leaving existing dynasties in place (for example, in Parthia or Armenia), there was perfectly good Persian precedent for this – in the sixth century the Persians had allowed the kings of Cilicia to continue to rule there (see chap. 9). As for his permitting Euthydemus to remain satrap even after revolting, the Persians had done much the same in the case of Evagoras of Salamis (see chap. 19).

Antiochus III had brought the Seleucid Kingdom through its worst crisis yet; and the best was still to come.

QUESTIONS FOR REVIEW

1   In what respects was the Seleucid Kingdom the successor state of the Persian Empire?
2   What are the possible historical contexts for the establishment of Ptolemaic possessions in southern Asia Minor?
3   What means did Antigonus Gonatas employ to secure Macedonian domination in most of Greece?
4   In what stages did the Achaian League destroy Macedonian domination in Greece?
5   How did Antiochus III restore the Seleucid Kingdom's flagging fortunes?

QUESTION FOR FURTHER STUDY

Traditionally the claims that Antiochus III "restored" Seleucid authority in the Upper Satrapies have been viewed with skepticism. What arguments can one advance in favor of that position?

FURTHER READING

In addition to the works listed at the end of Chapter 20, see also the following:
Berthold, R.M. (2009) *Rhodes in the Hellenistic Age*. Ithaca, NY.
Ma, J. (1999) *Antiochos III and the Cities of Western Asia Minor*. Oxford.

24

The Coming of Rome

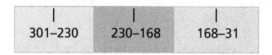

301–230	230–168	168–31

228–222	Cleomenean War
214–206	First Macedonian War
200	Battle of Panium; Antiochus III takes Hollow Syria
200–197	Second Macedonian War
197	Battle of Pydna
197–196	Antiochus III campaigns in Asia Minor
192	Antiochus III invades Greece
190	Battle of Magnesia by Sipylus
188	Peace of Apameia
171–168	Third Macedonian War
170–168	Sixth Syrian War

Macedonia and Greece

The Achaian and Aetolian Leagues had cooperated in destroying Macedonian control of Greece by the early 220s. Once the external enemy was banished,

A History of Greece: 1300 to 30 BC, First Edition. Victor Parker.
© 2014 Victor Parker. Published 2014 by John Wiley & Sons, Ltd.

however, old quarrels flared anew. Moreover, one city state in Greece still had ambitions: Sparta. A few Arcadian towns (Tegea, Mantinea, Orchomenus) were allied to Sparta (Pol. II 46) and Elis too made an alliance (Plut. *Cleom.* 5). Given, finally, an old border quarrel between Sparta and Megalopolis (Plut. *Cleom.* 4), a member of the Achaian League, the ground was well prepared for an eventual war between Lacedaemonians and Achaians.

When Sparta's king, Cleomenes III, seized some land from Megalopolis, the so-called **Cleomenean War** spluttered into being in 228. The Ephors called it off once; when an Achaian and a Lacedaemonian army finally faced each other near Pallantium in southern Arcadia, Aratus, the chief statesman of the Achaian League (albeit without any official position at the time) avoided battle. In 227, however, Aratus (once again in office) led out the League's army against Elis, and Cleomenes III marched to stop him. The two armies met near Megalopolis where the Lacedaemonians won. Aratus himself was believed dead, but taking advantage of the rumor, he gathered some troops for a surprise attack on Mantinea where no one expected him. The attack succeeded and to a degree made good the loss in the field (Plut. *Arat.* 36; *Cleom.* 5; Pol. II 57). But the Achaians lost a second battle near Megalopolis, and Cleomenes followed up the victory by capturing several Arcadian towns (Plut. *Cleom.* 6–7).

In 226 Cleomenes recaptured Mantinea and then invaded Achaia itself. Once again he defeated the Achaians in a pitched battle, and now negotiations for peace began. Cleomenes bluntly demanded the leadership of the League – that is to say, that the Achaian League come under Lacedaemonian control. Aratus, who had declined to put his name forward for election as *strategos* for 225, now watched from the sidelines as the Achaians voted to hand the League over to Cleomenes III (Plut. *Cleom.* 14–15).

However, illness hindered Cleomenes from formally taking over the League, and so Aratus, who had been elected *strategos* for 224, received one last opportunity to avert the Lacedaemonian takeover. A calculated affront to Cleomenes III near Argos caused him to seize Pellene and several nearby towns in Arcadia as well. He then marched on and captured Argos. One by one the cities of the northeastern Peloponnese deserted the Achaian League to join Sparta – Phleius, Cleonae, Epidaurus, Troezen, Hermione, even Corinth (with the exception of Acrocorinth which an Achaian garrison held). The Achaians managed to hold on to Sicyon which Cleomenes III was soon besieging (Plut. *Cleom.* 17–19; Pol. II 52).

Desperate situations call for desperate remedies. For the Achaian League the remedy was to ask Antigonus Doson, the King of Macedonia, for help and to offer what Aratus had snatched from Macedonia two decades earlier: Acrocorinth. Aratus had long foreseen that this might be necessary, and negotiations with Doson were already underway (Pol. II 47–50; Plut. *Arat.* 38; *Cleom.* 17). For his part, Doson had an army ready, and as soon as matters were arranged with the Achaians, he led it through Euboea into Boeotia in 223.

Cleomenes III took up a strong defensive position on the Isthmus. Doson was initially unable to force his way through, but the Achaians managed to seize

> ## Box 24.1 *Attempts at Land Reform in Sparta*
>
> In the late third century, several Lacedaemonian kings attempted to carry out a redistribution of land. Without such a reform an increase in the numbers of the Spartiate class was not possible (see Boxes 15.2 and 16.3). By the reign of Agis IV (244–241), there were only 700 Spartiates left, 100 of whom held most of the land (Plut. *Agis*, 5). Agis proposed to redistribute the land into 4,500 plots, each for a Spartiate, with an additional 15,000 plots for Perioeci (Plut. *Agis*, 8). He underestimated the ability of the largest landholders to fight his plan, however, and neglected to eliminate opposition in advance. While Agis was away on campaign, they undermined his position at home and on his return had him put to death (Plut. *Agis*, 13–20).
>
> Agis IV's son-in-law Cleomenes III made the next attempt. Cleomenes had learned from Agis' failure. Before even proposing any reform, he first made certain of his political position. When his colleague in the kingship, the young boy Eudamidas III, died, Cleomenes saw to it that a political ally, Agis IV's brother Archidamus V, replaced him. Next, in the so-called Cleomenean War Cleomenes III achieved signal victories against the Achaians in 227. This made his position at home unassailable. Then he had four of the five ephors assassinated to remove any official opposition and the next day he sent eighty Spartiates into exile (obviously the largest landowners – cf. the 100 or so of them in Agis IV's day). Now, finally, Cleomenes carried out a redistribution of the land and raised the number of Spartiates to 4,000 (Plut. *Cleom.* 5–11). Cleomenes' extraordinary success against the Achaian League in the next few years rests on his restoration of the Spartiate levy.
>
> Unfortunately, Cleomenes III succeeded all too well against the Achaians, who in the end made an alliance with Antigonus Doson of Macedonia. After defeating Cleomenes at Sellasia, Antigonus Doson reversed all Cleomenes' reforms and restored Sparta's "ancestral constitution" (Pol. II 70).

Argos behind Cleomenes. When he failed to retake the city, Cleomenes was forced to leave his position at the Isthmus, and Doson marched on Corinth. Here the Achaian garrison handed over Acrocorinth, and Macedonia once again held all three "fetters of Greece." From Corinth Doson marched on Argos which Cleomenes III was trying to recapture, and Cleomenes fled. Doson followed him through Arcadia and took all his outposts there (Pol. II 52–54).

Towards the end of 223, Doson went to the meeting of the Achaian Council at Aegium. Thither he summoned representatives of his other allies (Thessalians, Boeotians, Phocians, Locrians, Euboeans, and others), and presided over the establishment of a mutual defensive alliance (Pol. II 54; IV 9; XI 5). What is perhaps most striking is the complete absence of city-states – it was all leagues now.

In early 222, Cleomenes III marched towards Argos where Doson had gone into winter quarters and carried out several raids. But a little later Doson collected his army and led it, some 30,000 strong, into Laconia. Cleomenes had only 20,000 to set against this army, so he chose a strong defensive site, Sellasia, at which to await his opponent. All the same, Doson won a complete victory, Sparta was crushed and forced to enter the Macedonian alliance, and Cleomenes III fled to Egypt (Pol. II 64–70). In a few short years Antigonus Doson had brought most of Greece under Macedonian domination again.

One of Doson's allies at Sellasia was Demetrius, the ruler of Pharos, a fourth-century Parian colony on an Adriatic island off the Illyrian coast (see chap. 17). In addition to Pharos Demetrius held a number of cities on the Illyrian mainland (Pol. II 65). When the Romans suppressed the Illyrian pirates in 229 (see chap. 23), he too had been compelled to desist from such activity. Now, however, he had a powerful ally in the Macedonians with whom he shared a common enemy, the Illyrians, who had invaded Macedonia while Doson was in Sparta. In 221 Doson defeated them as well (Pol. II 70), and Demetrius of Pharos, confident of Macedonian support, began carrying out raids in the Adriatic (Pol. III 16).

Later on in 221 Antigonus Doson succumbed prematurely to illness. His adoptive son, Philip V, the biological son of Demetrius II, now became king (Pol. II 70). This encouraged some in the Aetolian League to attempt to reverse Doson's successes. The Aetolians had remained neutral during the last round of wars, but, with the foundation of Doson's alliance, they now found themselves isolated. Mostly through the raids of two Aetolian commanders, Dorimachus and Scopas, the Aetolian and Achaian Leagues were steadily maneuvered into conflict with each other (Pol. IV 5–27). Sparta broke with Macedonia and allied itself with the Aetolians (Pol. IV 34–35).

In 219 a series of loosely related campaigns took place in the (second) Social War. The Lacedaemonian king Lycurgus marched into the Thyreatis and captured Prasiae; the Eleans, now allied with the Aetolians, attacked Achaia; and the Aetolians carried out a sea-borne raid on the Achaian town of Aegira (Pol. IV 36 and 57–59). Philip V, together with the Epirotes, attacked the Aetolians from the west, while the Aetolians on the eastern front invaded Macedonia and plundered the city of Dium (Pol. IV 62–65). Meanwhile, the Dardanians attacked Macedonia again. When Philip V hastened northwards to deal with them, they withdrew. After Philip V had dismissed his troops in the autumn, the Aetolians carried out one last attack on Epirus and laid waste to Dodona (Pol. IV 66–67).

The Romans meanwhile sent a fleet against Demetrius of Pharos whose raids had disturbed the settlement they had imposed in the Adriatic (see chap. 23). The Romans first captured the mainland cities under Demetrius' control and then Pharos itself (Pol. III 16, 18–19). Demetrius then fled to Philip V (Pol. IV 66) whom the growing Roman presence in Illyria must have worried, but for now he still had the war against the Aetolians on his hands.

The frustrating course of that war hitherto probably explains best Philip V's next campaigns, geared mostly to doing his enemies damage. Still in 219, in the dead of winter, when no one expected it, he led his troops onto the Peloponnese, attacked Elis, and plundered it thoroughly. Philip V then marched southwards into Triphylia which he wrested from Elean, Aetolian, and Lacedaemonian troops. The rest of the winter he spent in Argos (Pol. IV 67–82).

The next year's campaign saw Philip V sail with an army from Corinth. After a futile attack on Cephallenia, he sailed to the Acarnanian town of Limnaea where he disembarked. From Limnaea he marched into Aetolia and destroyed the city of Thermum. After returning to Corinth, he marched into Laconia and carried out more plundering raids before returning to Macedonia for the winter of 218 to 217 (Pol. V 1–30). In 217, he campaigned against the Dardanians; then he marched southwards and attacked the Aetolians from the East. He took Phthiotic Thebes by siege (Pol. V 97–100) and then proceeded to Argos where the Nemean Games were taking place. Here he learned that the Romans had just suffered a horrifying defeat at the hands of the Carthaginian general Hannibal near Lake Trasimene in the Po valley (Pol. V 101) – for the Second Punic War (220–201) had broken out between those two western powers.

Negotiations for peace between the Aetolian League and Macedonia were now under way. Philip V's campaigns on the Peloponnese and in Aetolia had achieved no lasting conquest, but had demonstrated to his enemies the pointlessness of continuing the war, and both sides were now willing to make peace on the basis of the *status quo*. At the Aetolian assembly in Naupactus, where the Aetolians voted on the proposed peace treaty, one Agelaus of Naupactus allegedly spoke of the war between Carthage and Rome in Italy and advised the Greeks to be reconciled with each other and to maintain unity:

> *For it is clear to everyone who is even moderately interested in public affairs these days that whether the Carthaginians defeat the Romans or the Romans the Carthaginians, it is highly unlikely that the winners will remain content with ruling over just Italy and Sicily. Instead they are likely to come over here and to extend their power beyond all bounds . . . if once these clouds which now loom in the West should come to rest over Greece, I very much fear that there will be an end of truces and wars and all the games which we play with each other – so that we will pray the gods to grant us the power once again to make war and peace as we wish, to resolve our own differences among ourselves.* (Pol. V 104)

The words are too prophetic to be true even if Polybius himself clearly thought that Agelaus had spoken in this vein.

The First Macedonian War

Now that he had satisfactorily settled matters in Greece, Philip V turned his attention to Illyria. Over the winter of 217 to 216 he constructed a fleet of a hundred small, fast galleys to support his campaigns against them by land. His fleet, however, was no match for the Romans' heavy quinqiremes, should these attempt to stop him, and Philip's actions show that he felt this keenly – the mere report of a Roman fleet's presence caused him to break off a naval expedition to the west of Greece in 216. By land, however, Philip conquered territory on the Illyrian borders (Pol. V 108–110).

In Italy, meantime, Hannibal had just defeated the Romans in another battle, Cannae, and now it appeared only a matter of time until he forced the Romans to capitulate. Philip V needed Roman influence in the Adriatic eliminated if he were to conquer Illyria, and Hannibal was not averse to securing Macedonia's friendship. So Philip V and Hannibal in 215 concluded a treaty of mutual non-aggression in which Philip carefully avoided committing himself to providing any concrete aid to Hannibal in the war against Rome. Ostensibly Philip was interested only in securing control over territory to the east of the Adriatic, as emerges from the following clause which Hannibal agreed to impose upon Rome in the event of his victory: "that the Romans shall not control Corcyra, Apollonia, Epidamnus, Pharos, Dimale, Parthini, or Atintania" (Pol. VII 9). Philip V, therefore, was not directly helping Hannibal, and his stated limited goal, if taken at face value, meant that he posed little threat to the Romans. These, however, were not inclined to take at face value what Philip stated in the treaty.

On the contrary, they viewed Philip V's alliance with Carthage as a direct threat to their existence. After all, Hannibal was trying to destroy Rome, and Philip V was now a friend of Hannibal. Moreover the last Hellenistic king who had taken an interest in affairs in Italy, Pyrrhus, had marched to within forty miles of Rome (see chap. 22). What made Philip V any different from Pyrrhus?

The Romans' view was certainly influenced by the nature of their life-and-death struggle against Carthage, a war which at first glance seems fundamentally different from the Hellenistic world's wars, which did not normally place a state's existence at stake. Yet this may have resulted more from an effective balance of power and practical reality rather than from rulers' actual desires. Hellenistic kings certainly could conceive of the full conquest of another Hellenistic kingdom. When, for example, Seleucus I Nicator defeated Lysimachus at Cyrupedium in 281, he undertook to assume the rule of Lysimachus' entire kingdom (Macedonia, Thrace, and the bulk of western Asia Minor), and only his death prevented him from doing so completely. When Ptolemy III Euergetes invaded the Seleucid Kingdom in 245 during the Third Syrian War, disturbances at home recalled him from an ambitious campaign which had taken him into Iran: this was no small war with limited goals, and had Ptolemy III been able to campaign a few years longer, the entire Seleucid Kingdom would have been his for the taking – and few will wish to argue that he would not have stretched forth his hand to take it. Finally, Hellenistic kings often opportunistically altered or radically expanded their plans for conquest whenever circumstances such as an enemy's weakness allowed – as the campaigns of Antiochus III (discussed below) demonstrate. The Romans' view of the threat which Philip V posed to them was in keeping with the Hellenistic conception of warfare, and their response to Philip V's treaty with Hannibal need not have been a gross overreaction.

Despite desperate circumstances in the war against Carthage, they dispatched thirty warships to Taras as reinforcements for the twenty-five already there with instructions to watch over Philip V (Liv. XXIII 38). He himself, expecting that Hannibal would occupy the Romans sufficiently, brought his fleet into the Adriatic again in 214 and attacked Illyria by land and by sea. He took Oricum and besieged Apollonia. Although hard-pressed in Italy, the Romans sent a legion under M. Valerius Laevinus to Illyria; Valerius retook Oricum, and a subordinate defeated Philip V at Apollonia. In his hasty retreat Philip V lost his fleet and large numbers of troops (Liv. XXIV 40 – probably exaggerating). Concurrently, Philip V had sent Demetrius of Pharos to attack Messenia, which Philip a year earlier had allegedly considered taking by subterfuge (Pol. VII 12). The attack failed, and Demetrius lost his life (Pol. III 19; cf. Paus. IV 29).

All the same, in 213 and 212 Philip V returned to the attack in Illyria, though this time he confined himself mostly to the inland regions (e.g., Atintania) where he made good progress (Liv. XXVII 30; XXIX 12 – referring to earlier conquests, probably dating to the period 213–212), capturing Lissus, a Syracusan colony on the Adriatic (Pol. VIII 13–14). Without allies the Romans could not continue this sideshow, so in 211 they concluded an alliance with the Aetolians who by now were willing to wage war against Macedonia again (Liv. XXVI 24). Since Philip V had become engaged in various conflicts against the Dardanians and in Thrace (210), he could not immediately respond to this. Both Valerius and the Aetolians campaigned against the Acarnanians, who asked Philip V for help in 209 (Liv. XXVI 25). Meanwhile, other states were joining the war against Philip V – Messenia (naturally enough, after the events of 214), Elis and Sparta (the Aetolians' allies from the last war against Philip V), and, most significantly, Pergamum (Pol. IX 30).

The Aetolians elected Attalus I of Pergamum as their *strategos* for 208 (see Box 21.3 for the office) and, together with the Lacedaemonians, attacked the Achaian League. When Philip V marched towards the Peloponnese, the Aetolians attempted to block him at Thermopylae but Philip defeated them twice in short order (Liv. XXVII 29–30). Later in the year Philip won a victory over the Eleans (Liv. XXVII 32). Also in 208 the Roman and Pergamene fleets (under the command of P. Sulpicius Galba and Attalus I) began cooperating in the Aegean, albeit to little practical effect. Attacks on Oreus (on Euboea) and Opus (in Eastern Locris) in 207 succeeded initially, but Philip surprised Attalus I at Opus, where the Pergamenes were gathering booty, and inflicted a severe defeat from which Attalus I barely escaped with his life. Philip now marched into central Greece, took the Locrian town of Thronium, and recaptured Oreus. Meanwhile the Bithynian king, Prusias I – evidently in alliance with Philip – attacked Pergamum, and Attalus I returned home to deal with this new foe (Liv. XXVIII 7; cf. Pol. X 41–42).

In 207 Philip V had to return to the north in order to beat back yet another invasion by the Dardanians (Liv. XXVIII 8), and there was little fighting in Greece. All the same the Aetolians by now had had enough. In early 206 they made peace with Philip V on his terms. In that year the Romans sent

P. Sempronius Tuditanus to Illyria with some 11,000 troops, but Philip V's arrival in Illyria confined him to Apollonia. The Romans themselves made peace with Philip at Phoenice in 205 on the basis of a division of the disputed territory in Illyria (Liv. XXIX 12). From their perspective the Romans had at least kept Philip tied down in Greece and Illyria, preventing him from assisting Hannibal in Italy. A final reckoning with Philip could be postponed for now.

Philip V, frustrated in his attempt at expansion in the West, but viewing the war with Rome over, turned towards the East.

The Fifth Syrian War

In 204, the year after the Peace of Phoenice, Antiochus III returned from the Upper Satrapies, and Ptolemy IV Philopator, who had defeated Antiochus III in the fourth Syrian War, died. His five-year-old son, Ptolemy V Epiphanes ("[the god] manifest") succeeded him. Antiochus III, judging the time right, inaugurated the Fifth Syrian War and, nearly a century after the Battle of Ipsus, achieved what had eluded even Seleucus I Nicator – the addition of Hollow Syria to the empire. In 200, at Panium, Antiochus III routed the Egyptian forces under the Ptolemaic general Scopas, and all Phoenicia and Palestine came under Seleucid control (Pol. XVI 18 and 39; Jos. *Ant.* XII 3,3 [129–137]).

To make matters worse for the Ptolemies, Philip V, who already in 204 had captured Lysimacheia, Chalcedon, and Cius in the Hellespont as well as the island of Thasos in the north Aegean (Pol. XV 23–24), now attacked Egyptian possessions in the Aegean and in Asia Minor. He seized the Cyclades (Liv. XXXI 15), a Ptolemaic possession, and he both attacked Attalus I of Pergamum and kept the Rhodian fleet occupied (Pol. XVI 2–10). He also carved out a small Macedonian province in Caria from Rhodian and Ptolemaic possessions there (Pol. XVIII 49–51; Liv. XXXIII 39; App. *Mac.* 4).

Box 24.2   *Antiochus III's alleged Pact with Philip V (circa 200 BC)*

Both Polybius (III 2,8; cf. XV 20) and Appian (*Mac.* 4) claim that Antiochus III and Philip V made a pact whereby they agreed to divide up Ptolemaic possessions between themselves. Antiochus III did make diplomatic arrangements in advance to facilitate his wars, and half a century earlier Antigonus Gonatas and Antiochus II Theos had cooperated against Ptolemy II Philadelphus in a similar fashion, so such a pact is not improbable.

The way in which Polybius and Appian describe the pact, however, casts doubt on its genuineness and many scholars have dismissed it as fiction. According to Polybius (III 2) the two kings agreed that Antiochus III would take Hollow Syria with Phoenicia whereas Philip V would take Egypt, Caria, and Samos. In another reference to this pact (XV 20), Polybius speaks of how "Fortune" brought it to the Romans' attention. Eckstein (2005) argues that Polybius is concretely thinking of the fortuitous arrival of an embassy which apprised the Romans of the pact. That embassy (presumably the Rhodian one which Appian mentions – see below) may of course have exaggerated and distorted matters to make the pact more frightening to the Romans, and Polybius may have believed that version. Nonetheless, it does not seem likely that Antiochus III would have ceded to Philip V the biggest prize of them all, Egypt, and for himself taken only Hollow Syria with Phoenicia.

Appian describes the pact as a "rumor" and lets a Rhodian embassy tell it to the Romans. In this version Antiochus III takes Egypt and Cyprus while Philip V takes Cyrene, the Cyclades, and Ionia. Here, the grant of Cyrene to Philip arouses suspicion in its turn. Finally, the way in which in both Polybius (on Eckstein's interpretation) and Appian the pact is revealed by foreign ambassadors suggests, despite the differences in detail, that the two sources represent one and the same tradition. Appian's account could derive, ultimately, from Polybius' (or from Polybius' direct source). Whether the differences in detail derive from errors of transmission along the way or from a difference in ultimate source after all, can no longer be determined.

Despite the skepticism which the details of the proposed division of Ptolemaic territory invite and despite Appian's presentation of the pact as a "rumor," a recently discovered inscription strongly suggests that some sort of undertaking between Antiochus III and Philip V did exist. The relevant portion of the inscription, found in Bargylia in Caria, reads:

> . . . after war had arisen on the part of King Antiochus against King Ptolemy, the one who is reigning now, the troops from King Antiochus had taken possession of the [. . .]sians and of the Thodasians, before the [troops (?)] from King Philip were present . . . (W. Blümel, EA 32 [2000], pp. 94–96)

The Antiochus and Philip in question can hardly be any other than Antiochus III and Philip V, and troops from both appear to be cooperating in the taking of two communities in Caria, the Thodasians and one other, whose name is mostly missing.

Antiochus III's "governor" in Asia Minor, Zeuxis, may well have taken some towns in Caria for his king and in doing so cooperated with Philip V. Two additional passages in Polybius (XVI 1 and 24) show Zeuxis cooperating with Philip V. When Philip needed supplies during his campaigns in Caria, he requested and received them from Zeuxis, as Polybius states, "according to the agreements." While this could have been a private arrangement between Zeuxis and Philip V, in the light of the other evidence it seems more likely that Polybius is here referring to the pact which he mentions at III 2.

Attalus I of Pergamum as well as the Rhodians were thoroughly alarmed – after all, if the stories of a pact between Philip V and Antiochus III were true (see Box 24.2), then the only Hellenistic state which was capable of stopping Philip V, the Seleucid Kingdom, was cooperating with him. That left Rome. Rhodian and Pergamene embassies accordingly traveled to Rome and made much of Antiochus III's and Philip V's alleged pact. The Romans took it seriously enough to send an embassy to Antiochus III (Pol. XVI 27); in one version it actually advised him not to conquer Egypt (App. *Mac.* 4).

The temerity of the Roman embassy, if indeed it did proffer this advice, no doubt took Antiochus III by surprise. But Antiochus III – regardless of his ultimate objectives – usually took care to limit the number of his enemies when waging a war and in any case was alert to the uses of diplomacy in achieving his objectives. As his next actions show (the conquest, among other things, of Ptolemaic possessions in Asia Minor), he certainly planned additional steps against Egypt. But if he had no immediate plan to conquer Egypt proper, then nothing hindered him from politely assuring the Roman envoys of this. Antiochus III had no qualms about double-crossing erstwhile friends and allies, as his actions against Philip V in the next few years show. As he conquered the Ptolemaic possessions in Asia Minor, he conquered the Macedonian ones too, his recent pact with Philip V (positing its existence in some form) notwithstanding – for Philip V was facing a greater problem than the defense of a few towns in Asia Minor.

The Second Macedonian War

In 202 the Romans defeated the Carthaginians at the Battle of Zama in northern Africa; peace followed, on Rome's terms, in 201. That freed the Romans to settle with Philip V. They had not forgotten his treaty with Hannibal in 215 and its implied threat. Moreover, Rhodes and Pergamum were doing everything they could to persuade the Romans to act against Philip V. In 200 BC, the Romans, claiming to be protecting allied Greek cities, declared war on Philip V (Liv. XXXI 5–8). The slowness with which the Greeks joined the war against Macedonia suggests a genuine lack of enthusiasm for the war on their part. Many presumably would have preferred for the Peace of Phoenice to remain intact. Roman actions in Greece during the First Macedonian War had not pleased everyone (Pol. IX 37–39; Liv. XXXI 29), and some of the Romans' practices in waging war gave even the Greeks, no strangers to brutality, pause (Pol. X 15).

Philip rejected a Roman ultimatum in 200 and continued his conquests in the northern Aegean and the Hellespont (Pol. XVI 29–34). Philip also laid siege to Athens which, bizarrely, had declared war on him (Liv. XXXI 14–18). When late in the campaigning season a Roman army arrived at Apollonia in Illyria, Philip was forced to abandon these minor campaigns (Liv. XXXI 22). Thereafter the Aetolians threw in their lot with the Romans (Liv. XXXI 41).

In 199, in the north, the Roman army pushed forwards through the mountains towards Macedonia. Philip V fought them to a standstill on the marches of Upper Macedonia, and the Roman army returned to Apollonia (Liv. XXXI 33–40). The Roman fleet in the Aegean carried out several sea-borne attacks, but achieved nothing of significance (Liv. XXXI 44–46).

In 198 a new Roman commander, T. Quinctius Flamininus, took charge and led his troops down the valley of the River Aous into Thessaly. Philip V attempted to block Flamininus' advance with some success, but eventually a local shepherd showed Flamininus a path around the blockade (Liv. XXXII 10–11). Philip V retreated to Macedonia and left Thessaly to the Romans and Aetolians, and Flamininus refrained from invading Macedonia just yet. Meanwhile, the Achaian League, after much hand-wringing, voted to break with Macedonia and to join the Romans (Liv. XXXII 23). Philip V, however, was able to hold on to Corinth and Argos (Liv. XXXII 25). Yet Flamininus was tightening a ring of enemies around Philip – Rhodes, Pergamum, Aetolia, Achaia. The Lacedaemonian king Nabis, to whom Philip handed over Argos, shortly thereafter deserted Philip as well (Liv. XXXII 38–39).

The next year Boeotia too joined the Romans (Liv. XXXIII 2). Philip V by now had realized that time was not on his side and decided to risk all in battle. He advanced into Thessaly with some 25,000 troops; Flamininus had about the same number (Liv. XXXIII 4). The two armies met at Cynoscephalae ("Dogs' heads" – a ridge that looked like two dogs' heads). For the first time in a pitched battle, a Macedonian phalanx confronted a Roman legion.

Roman soldiers used swords, not long thrusting spears, as their chief offensive weapon. The individual units, so-called **maniples**, into which the legion was divided up, could arrange themselves in an unbroken line (like a Macedonian phalanx). In addition, since the maniples were arranged in three staggered lines, the maniples behind the front line could, if a gap opened up in it, move forward to plug this gap. Finally, since the sword did not require absolute cohesion straight across the line (unlike the *sarissa*, which was useless except when wielded in formation), the maniples of a legion could move independently of each other. In particular they could spread out over broken ground (Pol. XVIII 31–32). The manipular legion's flexibility gave it a clear advantage over the Macedonian phalanx.

All the same, Philip V came within an ace of winning. The right of his line reached the ridge before the Romans did, drew up in formation, and immediately attacked the Roman left downhill. The Macedonian phalanx swept the Roman left before it, but Flamininus led his right wing up the ridge and attacked the Macedonian left which was still coming up the ridge from the other side. Flamininus caught it out of formation and easily defeated it. An unnamed officer with Flamininus' right then led the twenty maniples under his command to attack the hitherto victorious Macedonian right from behind. The Macedonians could not wheel about quickly enough, and by the end of the day Philip V's army had been defeated (Pol. XVIII 24–26). The Romans were in a position to dictate the terms of peace.

In these terms they coldly manipulated Greek public opinion in their favor for the Senate's decree began by stating that the Greeks should be "free and use their own laws" (i.e., be "autonomous") (Pol. XVIII 44). Later on in 196, at the Isthmian Games, Flamininus announced to a thunderous ovation from the Greeks there assembled that they were to have their "freedom" (Pol. XVIII 46). Events, of course, would show what the Romans meant by "freedom." Meanwhile they allowed Philip to continue to rule in Macedonia, but imposed an indemnity of 500 talents immediately and 500 additional talents in installments over ten years (Pol. XVIII 44).

Flamininus remained in Greece for two years to see to it that Philip V kept his word and to deal with mopping-up operations – most significantly Nabis, the King of Sparta, who also held Argos. The Argives themselves managed to expel the Lacedaemonian garrison, and Nabis, when Flamininus besieged him in Sparta, was compelled to surrender (195). Thereafter Flamininus was content to allow Nabis to continue ruling in Sparta (Liv. XXXIV 23–41). In 192, however, Nabis was assassinated under unclear circumstances, and Philopoemen, then the chief statesman of the Achaian League, presided over Sparta's entrance into it (Liv. XXXV 35–37; cf. Pol. XX 12; Plut. *Phil.* 15).

By 194, all Roman troops had left Greece (Liv. XXXIV 52). One should not suppose that they did so out of any respect for Hellenic civilization, even if they were happy to derive any benefits which came from the Greeks' believing in that. This is not the place for a discussion of the nature and dynamic of Roman imperialism, but it may be appropriate to list briefly three exterior characteristics: first, an often displayed tendency to avoid direct administration of the territory of a conquered enemy (for example, in Numidia in northern Africa after the Jugurthine War); second, a tendency to weaken any local government (e.g., with a financial indemnity); third, a tendency to high-handed or offensive actions which encouraged anti-Roman sentiment. Discussion of the complex reasons for these tendencies is better left to works dedicated to the subject; it suffices here to state simply that all three tendencies frequently made an additional war not necessarily inevitable, but highly probable.

Roman imperialism, moreover, was a very different phenomenon from anything which the Hellenistic world had known. Up until now a battle of the magnitude of Cynoscephalae had usually led to the victor's simple assumption of the loser's kingdom or division thereof if there had been several victors (Ipsus, Cyrupedium), or to the loser's cession of a large amount of territory (Panium). What Flamininus did after Cynoscephalae does not fit any Hellenistic pattern.

Antiochus III's Conquest of Asia Minor

In 197, the same year as Cynoscephalae, Antiochus III, having just defeated Ptolemy V Epiphanes in the Fifth Syrian War, marched into Asia Minor. His initial goal was to recapture for the Seleucid Kingdom all Ptolemaic possessions in Asia Minor, but his plans could be pruned back if necessary – or augmented

Box 24.3 *Polybius of Megalopolis*

The most important source for the Hellenistic period from 220 until 146 BC is Polybius of Megalopolis. He was born around the end of the third century and belonged to the 1,000 Achaians whom the Romans deported in 168. While he was detained in Rome, Polybius made the acquaintance of numerous influential Romans, most prominently P. Cornelius Scipio Aemilianus, the son of Aemilius Paullus who defeated Perseus at Pydna in 168.

After the destruction of Corinth in 146, Polybius returned home to a remarkably changed Greece which, although formally independent, was now under Roman domination. Civil wars were rapidly reducing both the Seleucid Kingdom and Ptolemaic Egypt to impotence, Rhodes had been humbled, and Macedonia was a Roman province. Within a few years of his return, Pergamum would become a Roman province as well.

Polybius, like most Greeks of his day, found these changes disconcerting, but on the basis of his long years of experience with leading Roman statesmen undertook to explain to his fellow Greeks how it had happened that within, by his reckoning, 53 years (the period from 220 to 167) Rome had come to dominate the entire world. The result was a gigantic book, forty volumes in length, of which less than a third has survived.

This is unfortunate since Polybius, methodical to a fault, provided a detailed narrative of events. Polybius' full narrative covered the period from 264 BC (the beginning of the First Punic War) down to 146 BC (the end of the Achaian and Third Punic Wars). From about 218 BC onwards, the narrative becomes fragmentary, and increasingly so as the work proceeds. As a result where one most needs Polybius, he is often missing.

On the other hand, some of what is missing is preserved in a different form. Livy, the first-century BC author of a vast compilation of Roman history, relied heavily on Polybius' work over long stretches of his own. In fact, Livy commonly just translates (or summarizes) passages from Polybius – cf., e.g., Pol. XVIII 44 with Liv. XXXIII 30. Much of Livy's work, where he covers the Hellenistic world, is Polybius in Latin translation. Unfortunately, Livy (unlike Diodorus) did consult other sources, usually subsumed under the head "the **annalists**." These were Roman writers who followed an annalistic (i.e., year-by-year) format; partisan bias and exegetical "creativity" (e.g., Liv. XXI 2, where a clause mentioning Saguntum is inserted into a treaty which contained no such clause – Pol. III 27) characterize their work to a high degree. Where Polybius is absent, it is not always easy to tell whether Livy is following Polybius or the much maligned "annalists."

In Chapters 23–25 Polybius is cited for preference, but where his narrative is absent or so fragmentary as to be useless, inevitably reference is made to Livy. The danger should be manifest. Occasionally, it is fairly clear that Livy is following Polybius (for example, in regard to King Nabis of Sparta – whom Polybius despised and whom Livy portrays in unrelentingly hostile fashion as well). Sometimes there is reason to suspect annalistic exaggerations (for example, Philip V's extraordinarily heavy losses at Liv. XXIV 40). But in all too many cases there is simply no good criterion for judging.

if feasible. Thanks to his recent conquest of Phoenicia, Antiochus III now possessed a fleet. With it he proceeded along the southern coast of Asia Minor while his army marched overland to Sardis. The towns of Rough Cilicia, Ptolemaic since the time of Ptolemy III Euergetes, mostly surrendered as Antiochus arrived, but Coracesium held out. Here, as Antiochus III besieged the town, an embassy from Rhodes arrived to dissuade Antiochus III from advancing (Liv. XXXIII 20). The Rhodians officially argued that they wished to prevent Antiochus III from assisting Philip V in his war against Rome. Antiochus III had no intention of so doing and in any case the news of Cynoscephalae nullified the Rhodians' position – Rome and Macedonia were no longer at war.

So Antiochus III took Coracesium and moved forwards. No source mentions campaigning in Pamphylia, so it may have been captured from the Ptolemies at an earlier time (see chap. 23). Antiochus III next brought Lycia under his control (**Porphyry**, *BNJ* 260, Fr. 46). While he was there in Telmessus, the Rhodians began militarily aiding various towns in Caria (Liv. l.c.). Yet Antiochus III had no intention of fighting both Rhodes and Egypt at the same time. He ceded to Rhodes the town of Stratoniceia in Caria (Pol. XXX 31) thereby establishing a potentially useful comity with Rhodes (apparent at Pol. XVIII 52) while leaving his hands free to continue with the acquisition of all Ptolemaic possessions in Asia Minor – as well as of Macedonian ones since Philip V was now powerless to stop him. Cynoscephalae had allowed Antiochus III opportunistically to expand his program.

In Caria meanwhile several inscriptions suggest that Zeuxis, Antiochus III's governor in Asia Minor, captured various cities for the Seleucids (Ma 1999, Nrr. 25, 29, 31). Nr. 31 B, lines 8–9, is particularly clear: "after we [i.e., Zeuxis] had recovered for the king the city [i.e., Heracleia under Latmus, in Caria] which had from the beginning belonged to his forefathers . . ." Besides the Ptolemaic possessions, the Seleucids captured all cities still in the hands of the Macedonians (Pol. XVIII 49–51).

Antiochus III next proceeded up to the coast, captured Ephesus, a Ptolemaic possession since the Third Syrian War, and spent the winter of 197 to 196 there (Liv. XXXIII 38; cf. Porphyry, *BNJ* 260, Fr. 46; and Pol. XVIII 40a). Now he made plans to take all the Greek cities in Asia Minor and the Hellespontine region – another expansion to his program. Smyrna and Lampsacus resisted, but Antiochus III left the sieges of these two cities to subordinates while he himself crossed the Hellespont and attacked the Celts in Thrace. He gained possession of the cities on the Chersonese as well as of the now deserted Lysimacheia which he set about rebuilding (Liv. l.c.). In addition he took some territory on the northern coast of the Propontis, including, probably, Perinthus (Ma 1999, Nr. 35).

Thus in 196 Antiochus III could look over an empire which extended, as had that of his great-great-grandfather Seleucus I Nicator, from the Hellespont to the Indus. Yet the empire had changed since those days. Seleucus I's empire had been divided almost entirely into satrapies with only an occasional tributary king (Armenia) whereas Antiochus III accepted Armenia, probably Cappadocia on the Taurus (Liv. XXXVII 40), Media Atropatene, Parthia, Bactria, and the realm of Sophagasenus as tributary realms within his empire alongside of the traditional satrapies. Antiochus III for now also had to accept an independent Pergamum as well as Rhodian possessions on the mainland. Cappadocia on the Pontus meanwhile was an ally bound by a diplomatic marriage (OGIS, 771). The crisis of the empire which had begun during the reign of Seleucus II Callinicus was now over. Contemporaries saw in Antiochus III a new Alexander the Great – hence his surname *megas*, "the Great." A better comparison, however, might be to Artaxerxes III Ochus. For, like that great Persian king, Antiochus III had set the empire on a new foundation.

Rome and the Seleucids down to the Peace of Apameia

Like the Persians in Ochus' and Darius III's days, the Seleucids had to contend with a new power in the West. To complete the comparison, in both cases that new power in the West would prove too much. While Antiochus III was in Thrace in 196 a Roman embassy arrived to deliver an ultimatum – to leave all "free" Greek cities in Asia Minor alone (meaning concretely Smyrna and Lampsacus which had sent ambassadors to Flamininus) and to evacuate all recently conquered Ptolemaic possessions. Antiochus III, a wily diplomat as well as a general, argued that he was retaking ancestral possessions which had fallen to his great-great-grandfather Seleucus I Nicator after Cyrupedium in 281 and insisted that he had no ambitions beyond that. Then, much to the Roman envoys' embarrassment, Antiochus III produced the text of a peace treaty with Ptolemy V Epiphanes in which the latter confirmed the former's right to hold the cities in question (Pol. XVIII 50–51; Liv. XXXIII 39–40). Antiochus III so thoroughly disarmed the Romans that Flamininus clearly felt that Rome had nothing to fear from him, and all Roman soldiers left Greece in 194 (see above).

Diplomacy was one thing, the business of conquest another. In 192 the Aetolians, bitterly disappointed in the Romans as "allies," having had incidental "misunderstandings" with Flamininus, having been ignored by Flamininus (Plut. *Flam.* 9,4), and still smarting over how Flamininus at the end of the Second Macedonian War had refused to honor their loyalty with the (in their view) modest reward of Thessaly (Liv. XXXIII 13), invited Antiochus III into Greece to liberate it from the Romans (Pol. III 7).

The situation was tricky. Antiochus III knew the course of the Second Macedonian War and understood, surely, how the Romans would respond. He also knew that they were formidable adversaries in the field. After all, he had at his court, since 195, none other than Hannibal, who knew better than anybody how the Romans waged war (Liv. XXXIII 49). Normally Antiochus III laid the diplomatic groundwork for his campaigns (e.g., when he campaigned against Achaius in Asia Minor – see chap. 23). In this case he thought that he had established some degree of friendship with Rhodes (Pol. XVIII 52) while in Pergamum Attalus I had recently died (Pol. XVIII 41), and he perhaps thought that he had reached an arrangement with the new king, Eumenes II. Philip V surely had no love for the Romans, so he might actually help (cf. Liv. XXXVI 7) or at least remain neutral. Unfortunately, none of this was prepared, but a better offer than the Aetolians' might never come and the window of opportunity was small. Antiochus III gambled – and lost.

In 192 he invaded Greece with an army of 10,000 (Liv. XXXV 43), all he could muster given the exigencies of time, but which none other than Hannibal according to one account actually deemed sufficient (albeit for an invasion of Italy), provided that allies could be gathered (App. *Syr.* 7). Antiochus III landed at Demetrias which the Aetolians had seized in advance for him (Liv. XXXV 34) and proceeded to take Thessaly (Liv. XXXVI 9–10). Much depended now on whether he could gain support from others, but little was forthcoming. Philip V, whom Antiochus III had earlier double-crossed, took the Romans' side (App. *Mac.* IX 5); Rhodes and Pergamum worked against him (see below); besides the Boeotians (Pol. XX 7) no Greeks came to his support; and even the Aetolians let him down. In 191 M. Acilius Glabrio arrived in Greece with 20,000 troops and marched unopposed into Thessaly. Antiochus III withdrew southwards to Thermopylae and succeeded in holding Acilius up there, only Acilius, having read his Herodotus, knew about the path around the main pass. Antiochus III knew about it too, but the Aetolians whom he had guarding the path proved as useless as the Phocians in 480. History repeated itself, and Antiochus III lost his army in the fiasco (Liv. XXXVI 14–19; Pol. XX 8).

Antiochus III now prepared for the inevitable Roman invasion of Asia Minor. The Seleucid fleet, a little shy of eighty ships, was more or less a match for the one which the Romans sent out in 191 under the command of C. Livius (Liv. XXXVI 42–43). In addition Antiochus III had some 200 light galleys at his disposal (App. *Syr.* 22). However, Eumenes II contributed twenty-five heavy ships to the Roman fleet (App. l.c.) and the Rhodians, allied with the Romans, had about seventy more (see Box 23.2). Despite these odds, the Seleucid fleet under Polyxenidas achieved some successes (e.g., destroying 31 Rhodian ships near Samos – Liv. XXXVII 9–11), but in 190 the new Roman commander, L. Aemilius Regillus, decisively defeated it off Myonnesus (Liv. XXXVII 27–30; App. *Syr.* 27). In that year a Roman army under the command of L. Cornelius Scipio entered Asia Minor. An attempt at negotiations failed (Pol. XXI 13–15), and Antiochus III, knowing full well what was at stake, raised the largest army he possibly could, some 45,000 or so (thus according to the broken down figures at Liv. XXXVII 40; Liv. XXXVII 37 and App. *Syr.* 32 give some 70,000). This was half again the Roman army (some 30,000 – Liv. XXXVII 39; App. *Syr.* 31), but the advantages of the manipular legion over the Macedonian phalanx had become clear at Cynoscephalae.

Antiochus III chose his battlefield accordingly – a wide plain near Magnesia by Sipylus. The Seleucid phalanx was to remain static and merely hold the Roman infantry while Antiochus III personally led his cavalry on his right wing. He succeeded admirably in putting the Roman left to flight, but allowed himself to pursue too fast and too far. On the Roman right, Eumenes II of Pergamum managed to defeat the Seleucid cavalry opposite him, but the Seleucid phalanx in the center held its ground excellently. If Antiochus III had turned from the pursuit in time, the outcome might have been different, but eventually his phalanx succumbed when gaps – mostly caused by panicked elephants which Antiochus III had posted at intervals across the phalanx – opened up in it. As the phalanx lost cohesion, the legions destroyed it entirely (App. *Syr.* 34–35; Liv. XXXVII 41–43).

The Romans had won. Antiochus III had raised the biggest and best army possible and had lost with it; he did not have another. The Battle of Magnesia was decisive. All that the Romans had to do was what Alexander did in 331, that is, take possession of the vanquished king's kingdom. Yet, as after Cynoscephalae, the Romans ignored the Hellenistic World's playbook and acted in accordance with their own.

In 188 Antiochus III Megas in the Peace of Apameia ceded all Asia Minor west of the Taurus to Rome's allies, Pergamum and Rhodes, and undertook to pay a massive indemnity to Rome: 500 talents down; 2,500 upon the Senate's ratification of the treaty; and thereafter 1,000 talents a year for twelve years (Pol. XXI 17). Instead of taking control of the empire intact, the Romans administered a shock from which it never recovered. The loss of the wealthy lands of Asia Minor, the financial strain of the indemnity, and the unpopular measures necessary to pay it proved too much. While the empire held together initially out of habit, it began to totter. Within a few decades the eastern regions were lost, and the empire collapsed in an interminable concatenation of civil wars. A long-term result was that the Hellenization underway throughout the empire now stopped everywhere except in the west where it had passed the point of no return.

As for the Aetolians, whose appeal to Antiochus III had set all this in motion, in 189 they made peace as best they could. An indemnity of 500 talents was imposed, 200 immediately and the remainder in installments over six years. In addition various cities which they had once controlled were taken from them (Liv. XXXVIII 9 and 11).

The Third Macedonian War

After his defeat at Cynoscephalae, Philip V focused his energies on the restoration of his kingdom's fortunes. With careful economy Philip rebuilt the base from which to draw an army. Since he avoided any infringement of the Roman settlement and supported the Romans in their war against Antiochus III, his kingdom reaped the benefits of peace. When disputes between Macedonia and its neighbors arose, Philip ultimately submitted to whatever verdict Rome handed down in the matter (Liv. XXXIX 23–36), and his younger son Demetrius proved a skillful advocate on his behalf at Rome when the Romans began to look askance at Philip's success at reviving Macedonia (Liv. XXXIX 35 and 46–47).

After Philip's death in 179, his older son Perseus ascended the throne and followed his father's basic policy of giving no offense to Rome as Macedonia continued to recover. However, his overtures to the Achaian League (Liv. XLI 23–24), his seeking of popularity in Greece (Pol. XXV 3), his marriage to a daughter of Seleucus IV's, and his sister's marriage to Prusias II of Bithynia all aroused suspicion in Rome. It did not help Perseus' cause that Eumenes II of Pergamum did all he could to encourage this suspicion (Liv. XLII 11–12).

In 171 the Romans finally declared war on Perseus (Liv. XLII 30). His and his father's success in reviving Macedonia manifests itself most clearly in the number of troops which Perseus could raise, some 43,000 (Liv. XLII 51). The first three years of the war went relatively well for Perseus. He won a minor cavalry battle in Thessaly in 171 (Pol. XXVII 8–9; cf. App. *Mac.* XII). In the next year he managed to hold the Romans in Thessaly (Liv. XLIV 1) as well as to repel a minor Roman offensive in Illyria (Liv. XLIII 9–10). In 169 a Roman army did finally penetrate Macedonia itself, but it achieved little (Liv. XLIV 1–10). In 168, however, the reckoning came due. L. Aemilius Paullus led a Roman army into the Macedonian plain and succeeded in forcing Perseus into joining battle at Pydna.

The battle saw the last hurrah of the Macedonian phalanx which charged at the Roman legions and pushed them straight off the field as a helpless and, by his own admission, terrified (Pol. XXIX 17) Paullus looked on. Unfortunately, the phalanx went too far and when it reached broken ground the inevitable happened and gaps opened up in it. Into these gaps the flexible maniples of the legion inserted themselves, and the now helpless Macedonians with their unwieldy *sarissai* were destroyed (Liv. XLIV 42; Plut. *Paul.* 20). Perseus himself was taken prisoner a little after the battle (Liv. XLV 6). The Romans then dissolved the Macedonian Kingdom and divided it into four republics (Liv. XLV 18). Antigonid Macedonia was thus the first of the Hellenistic kingdoms to succumb to Rome. Unfortunately, these four republics were so weak they could not deal with any major disturbance on their collective territory – when such a disturbance occurred, Rome once again would intervene.

The Romans also took the occasion to settle affairs in Greece more to their liking (Pol. XXX 13). Few Aetolians, after the harsh settlement in 189, had much love for the Romans, and many had sympathized with the Macedonian cause even if Aetolia had not aided Perseus. Still, the Romans were suspicious and assisted (unofficially or otherwise) the anti-Macedonian factions in Aetolia in carrying out a series of judicial executions of any who had given voice to their pro-Macedonian views too openly (Liv. XLV 31). The Achaian League, although officially allied to Rome, had been remarkably tepid in its support. This roused Roman suspicions about the Achaians' loyalty as well, and at the urging of the pro-Roman Achaian statesman Callicrates the Romans seized 1000 prominent Achaians whom they transported as hostages to Rome (Paus. VII 10). Among them was the later historian of Rome's rise, Polybius of Megalopolis (Pol. XXXI 23). In both Aetolia and Achaia, the Romans' high-handed actions sowed the seeds for the next conflict.

In Asia Minor as well, the Romans unwittingly prepared the way for future conflict. Shortly after the Battle of Pydna envoys from Rhodes arrived in Rome to offer their services in mediating between Rome and Perseus. Alas, the envoys had received their brief before the battle; and the news of Paullus' victory had preceded them. The Senate assumed that the Rhodians wished to plead for Perseus and took offense at the interference (Pol. XXIX 19). Briefly the Senate considered declaring war on Rhodes, but settled for depriving the Rhodians of all their possessions on mainland Asia Minor as well as of the island of Delos with its lucrative slave market, which was made over to Athens (Pol. XXX 5, 21, and 24). The loss of revenue devastated Rhodes (Pol. XXXI 7) which could no longer afford to maintain its fleet. Southern Asia Minor sank into anarchy, and in the absence of any controlling authority large numbers of the inhabitants on the coast took to piracy. The endemic lawlessness would eventually force upon the Romans various wars against the pirates (see chap. 25).

The Seleucid Kingdom Totters

In 187 Antiochus III Megas died, and his eldest son, Seleucus IV Philopator, ascended the throne. Knowledge of this king's reign is patchy. Given the catastrophic defeat at Magnesia, he seems to have been more active as a diplomat than as a warrior. When Pharnaces, the King of Cappadocia on the Pontus (or just "Pontus" as it usually called from now onwards), waged war against Pergamum and Cappadocia on the Taurus (or just "Cappadocia" as it is usually called from now onwards) (Pol. XXIV 14–15), Seleucus IV, who was apparently about to aid Pharnaces, in the end refrained from doing so (Diod. XXIX 24) and Pharnaces lost (Pol. XXV 2). In negotiations with the Romans, Seleucus succeeded in procuring the release of his brother, the future Antiochus IV, whom their father had consented to send as a hostage to Rome, but only at the cost of replacing him with his own son, the future Demetrius I (App. *Syr.* 45). Seleucus also gave his daughter Laodice in marriage to Perseus – presumably this marriage sealed some sort of alliance, however informal (Liv. XLII 12). During Seleucus' reign, the kings of Parthia and Bactria presumably ceased to acknowledge Seleucid overlordship – at least there is no evidence that Antiochus IV, about whom more is known, still controlled these regions. Appian (*Syr.* 66) writes that Seleucus IV "reigned unsuccessfully and weakly." Behind that curt verdict lies one simple fact: it fell to Seleucus IV's lot to pay off the indemnity which Rome had imposed. Year in, year out, his treasury strained to find the money (see Box 24.4).

Seleucus IV Philopator's vizier, Heliodorus, murdered him in 175 in an attempted coup d'état. Even though several of his sons were alive (e.g., Demetrius, still a hostage at Rome), his brother, Antiochus IV, surnamed Epiphanes ("[god] manifest") to his face and Epimanes ("lunatic") behind his back, managed to seize the throne. Eumenes II of Pergamum helped Antiochus IV secure the throne (App. *Syr.* 45; Austin, Nr. 162) – Eumenes II by now

Box 24.4   *The Seleucid Empire's Budget Crisis*

The episode for which Seleucus IV Philopator is best known concerns the entrance of his vizier Heliodorus into the vault of the Temple at Jerusalem. Simon, an official working in the Temple, had quarreled with the then High Priest Onias. In his anger Simon went to Apollonius, the satrap of Hollow Syria and Phoenicia, and tattled on Onias, telling him that

> the treasury in Jerusalem was groaning with untold amounts of money because of the enormous mass of carry-forwards that had not been applied to the account for sacrifices; and that this money could be requisitioned for the King.
> (II Macc. III 6)

The Seleucid treasury sent an annual cash subvention to the Temple in Jerusalem to defray the cost of the sacrifices. At the time in question the High Priest was required to remit any money left over at the end of the year. Instead, the High Priest – so Simon's accusation – had been saving these unused funds, i.e., had been carrying them forward onto next year's budget. After several years a large amount of money had built up.

Given the financial constraints under which the Seleucid treasury was laboring during the reign of Seleucus IV Philopator – every year 1,000 talents had to be paid to Rome –, the authorities reacted immediately to this piece of news. Heliodorus, Seleucus IV's vizier, made a surprise visit to Jerusalem and confronted Onias with the information which Simon had passed on. When Onias claimed that all the funds in the vault were private deposits – mostly small amounts held in trust for widows and orphans –, Heliodorus called Onias' bluff and asked to be taken into the vault immediately so that he could see for himself. For small private deposits would be stored in small jars (the ancient equivalent of safety deposit boxes), and if Onias were telling the truth, then Heliodorus would find a large collection of dusty jars. The putative unremitted carry-forwards, on the other hand, should just have been in a large heap on the floor. Depending on what he saw, Heliodorus would know who had been lying to him. Unfortunately, the story at this point recounts how supernatural forces ejected Heliodorus from the vault before he could see anything (II Macc. III 7–27).

Less spectacular, but perhaps more important historically, than this divine intervention is the financial health of the empire. The ultimate author of this passage in II Maccabees makes no mention of the overall situation since his outlook is exclusively local – he sees only what is happening in the Temple's financial administration. But in fact he reveals a facet in a larger picture of an empire in deep financial crisis with officials scouring provincial treasuries in the hopes of finding an overlooked stash of money somewhere.

clearly had his doubts about the Romans and preferred a strong Seleucid king. Now that the empire was finally free of the ball and chain of the indemnity, Antiochus IV did his best to revive the Seleucids' fortunes. He waged war against Armenia, took its king prisoner, and evidently made it tributary again (App. *Syr.* 45).

In the East, Antiochus IV did his best to maintain the empire's position. In 165 and 164 he campaigned in Persis and Media (I Macc. III 31–37; II Macc. IX 1–3) and possibly even farther East; the exact status of the satrapies of central Iran at this time is not certainly known.

A revolt, moreover, broke out in one of the sleepiest backwaters of his kingdom, Judea. Antiochus IV had given official sanction to various plans of the High Priest in Jerusalem, one Menelaus, to reform Jewish religion and society. Not everyone in Judea approved, however – especially when what the later tradition cryptically called the "abomination of desolation" was brought into the Temple in Jerusalem in 167 BC (I Macc. I 54). Because Seleucid authorities were involved in enforcing Menelaus' alleged reforms, the revolt turned against them. One Judas – surnamed for unclear reasons "Maccabaeus" – emerged as its leader. In 164, Lysias, whom Antiochus during his absence in the East had placed in charge of the satrapies west of the Euphrates, unsuccessfully campaigned against Judas. Late in 164, Judas Maccabaeus entered Jerusalem at the head of victorious troops and presided over the removal of the "abomination" from the Temple (I Macc. IV 41–52; cf. II Macc. X 1–5). The Maccabaean revolt would cost the Seleucids precious resources over the next decades as the empire crumbled, but it would also in the end see the creation of a new Hellenistic kingdom (see chap. 25).

Antiochus IV's most spectacular campaign, however, involved Egypt. In this war, the Sixth (and last) Syrian War (170–168), Antiochus IV routed the forces of the young Ptolemy VI Philometor, who in 180 had succeeded his father Ptolemy V Epiphanes, and effectively conquered Eygpt (Porphyry, *BNJ* 260, Fr. 49a; cf. Burstein, Nr. 39C with n. 5). If Antiochus IV had managed to hold on to Egypt, he might have restored the Seleucid Kingdom's flagging fortunes. But in the summer of 168, as he was entering Egypt, he found a Roman embassy waiting for him. Its leader, C. Popillius Laenas, handed him a letter from the Senate formally ordering him out of Egypt. When Antiochus IV stated that he needed to confer with his councillors before replying, Popillius took his walking stick and drew a circle in the sand around the heir of Seleucus I Nicator. Popillius then told Antiochus IV to give his answer before he left the circle (Pol. XXIX 27).

The Romans had just defeated Perseus at Pydna in the Third Macedonian War. Antiochus IV – for all that his detractors called him a madman – was no fool. He knew that he could not face a Roman army; and any other act than meek acquiescence would call down on his head Perseus' fate. *Roma locuta, causa finita* – Rome had indeed spoken with exceptional clarity, and the matter was settled. Antiochus IV left Egypt.

QUESTIONS FOR REVIEW

1 How did Macedonia regain control over most of the Greek world in the 220s?
2 In what stages did the Romans slowly dismember Macedonia?
3 How did Antiochus III steadily expand his dominions in the years between his return from the Upper Satrapies and the Battle of Magnesia by Sipylus?
4 What was the state of the Seleucid Kingdom in 168 BC?

QUESTION FOR FURTHER STUDY

Scholars have often claimed that the Hellenistic Greeks never quite understood the Romans. Did the Romans for their part understand how the Hellenistic world operated and what effects their actions had upon it?

FURTHER READING

In addition to the works mentioned at the end of Chapter 23, see also the following:

On Rome and the Hellenistic World:
Gruen, E. (1984) *The Hellenistic World and the Coming of Rome*. Berkeley.

On Roman Imperialism, two chief approaches exist:
Badian, E. (1968) *Roman Imperialism in the Late Republic*. Oxford. (Roman imperialism was essentially reactive and defensive.)
Harris, W.V. (1985) *War and Imperialism in Republican Rome*. Oxford. (Roman imperialism was highly aggressive.)

On Antiochus III:
Grainger, J. (2002) *The Roman War of Antiochos the Great*. Leiden.
Ma, J. (1999) *Antiochos III and the Cities of Western Asia Minor*. Oxford.

On the Pact between Antiochus III and Philip V:
Eckstein, A.M. (2005) "The Pact between the Kings, Polybius 15.20.6, and Polybius' View of the Outbreak of the Second Macedonian War," *Classical Philology* 100: 228–242.

On Polybius:
Walbank, F.W. (1957–1979) *A Historical Commentary on Polybius*. Oxford.
Walbank, F.W. (1972) *Polybius*. Berkeley.
Walbank, F.W. (2002) *Polybius, Rome, and the Hellenistic World. Essays and Reflections*. Cambridge.

25

Twilight of the Hellenistic World

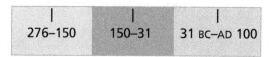

276–150	150–31	31 BC–AD 100

148	Fourth Macedonian War
146	Achaian War; destruction of Corinth
133	Pergamum bequeathed to Rome
128	Last Seleucid attempt to retake East fails
125	Cleopatra Thea begins to reign in Syria
116	Cleopatra III begins to reign in Egypt
88–84	First Mithridatic War
74	Bithynia bequeathed to Rome; Cyrene organized as Roman province
74–65	Third Mithridatic War
64	Syria becomes Roman province
51	Cleopatra VII begins to reign in Egypt
48	Battle of Pharsala
44	Caesar assassinated
31	Battle of Actium
30	Cleopatra VII commits suicide

A History of Greece: 1300 to 30 BC, First Edition. Victor Parker.
© 2014 Victor Parker. Published 2014 by John Wiley & Sons, Ltd.

The Romans in Greece and Asia Minor to 133 BC

In Greece bitterness over the Romans' actions in the aftermath of the Third Macedonian War lingered. Of the 1,000 hostages which the Romans had deported from Achaia, some 700 had died by 150 when the Romans finally consented to set the survivors free (Paus. VII 10). Since the Romans exercised no direct government over Greece, local disputes continued to crop up. The most troublesome involved Sparta's desire to leave the Achaian League which controlled the entire Peloponnese. The two sides repeatedly came to blows, and Roman commissions which kept coming to Greece could not settle the dispute (Paus. VII 9).

In Macedonia, meanwhile, war broke out in 150. An adventurer named Andriscus, who called himself Philip and claimed to be a son of Perseus, united the four Macedonian republics in a rebellion against Rome. An army under Q. Caecilius Metellus destroyed him easily enough in 148 in the Fourth Macedonian War (Liv. *Per.* 49–50; Paus. VII 13), and shortly thereafter the Romans annexed Macedonia as a province, although the details remain murky.

In 147 the Senate ordered the Achaians to release Sparta, Corinth, and a few other towns from the League. The decision enraged the Achaians, and in the next year their new *strategos* Critolaus pursued a violently anti-Roman policy (Paus. VII 14). In 146 the Achaian League declared war on Rome (Pol. XXXVIII 7–11). Metellus, still in Macedonia, quickly marched into Greece and defeated Critolaus at Thermopylae (Paus. VII 15). A little later L. Mummius arrived in Greece with additional troops (Paus. VII 16); the Achaians meanwhile were desperately raising another army with mass manumissions of slaves (Pol. XXXIX 7). The final battle took place near Corinth, where the Achaians went down in utter defeat (Paus. VII 16). To set an example, the Romans razed the city of Corinth to the ground, killed the men, and sold the women and children into slavery. They dissolved the Leagues (albeit temporarily) into their constituent cities (Paus. VII 16). These they allowed to be "free" – but by now everyone knew what Roman freedom meant, and when the Romans later on allowed the Leagues to reconstitute themselves, the Leagues, knowing better now, remained quiet (Paus. VII 16). The Romans did not, it seems, officially organize Greece as a province (under the name Achaia – Paus. l.c.) until after the Battle of Actium in 31 BC (cf. Liv. *Per.* 134), but it was now clear to all who ruled. As Agelaus had supposedly predicted at Naupactus in 217, the Greeks no longer had the power to declare war and to make peace, or to resolve their own disputes among themselves (see chap. 24).

From now on all parties accepted that the Romans would settle disputes and that in the event of disagreement the best one could do was to try again when circumstances among the Romans changed. Thus after the **Achaian War**, Mummius awarded the Dentheliatis, a disputed border region between Sparta and Messenia, to Messenia. The Lacedaemonians accepted this, but a century later, when Julius Caesar dominated at Rome they tried again and received a favorable verdict. After Caesar's assassination during the period of the ascendancy of M. Antonius (i.e., Mark Antony, Cleopatra VII's lover) in the East, the Messenians in their turn raised the question again, only Antony confirmed Caesar's decision (**Tacitus**, *Ann.* IV 43). At no point did either Messenians or Lacedaemonians resort to arms – the time for that had passed. With the destruction of Corinth in 146 BC, the political independence of the Greeks had come to an end.

In Asia Minor the Romans had been content, in effect, to let the kings of Pergamum, Bithynia, Pontus, and Cappadocia fight among themselves (see chap. 24). A rare effective intervention came when the Seleucid king Demetrius I Soter deposed Ariarathes III of Cappadocia in favor of the latter's brother Olophernes: here Rome undid Demetrius I's settlement immediately and – with the Roman tendency to weaken local government – made both brothers joint rulers (App. *Syr.* 47 – cf. **Sallust**, *Jug.* 16). In 133, however, Attalus III, the King of Pergamum died without heirs and bequeathed his kingdom to Rome. Other Hellenistic rulers would later emulate this measure though it remains unclear what reaction from Rome Attalus III expected – Roman acceptance of the bequest was by no means certain as the Romans would later demonstrate in the case of Cyrene (see below). Yet at Rome in 133 the tribune Ti. Sempronius Gracchus was attempting to carry out a redistribution of land and needed cash for his program. Accordingly he engineered the acceptance of Attalus III's bequest (Plut. *Tib.* 14). After a brief insurrection at Pergamum M'. Aquilius oversaw its organization as the Province of Asia (Just. XXXVI 4).

The Seleucids' Loss of Judea and the East

As the Romans were annexing territory in Europe and Asia Minor, the Seleucid Kingdom, which had never recovered from the shock of Magnesia and Apameia, began to break up. When Antiochus IV died at the end of 164 (Austin, Nr. 138), the man whom he had appointed as regent in the west, Lysias, took command in the name of Antiochus IV's young son, Antiochus V Eupator (I Macc. III 32 and VI 17). Lysias attempted to suppress the rebellion in Judea, but in 163 made a hasty peace with Judas Maccabaeus since one of Antiochus IV's generals, Philip, had returned from the East and claimed that Antiochus IV had appointed him instead of Lysias as regent. Lysias defeated Philip (I Macc. VI 55–63; II Macc. XI 22–26 and XIII 22–26), but was less fortunate when Seleucus IV's eldest son, Demetrius, who had been sent to Rome as a hostage in place of Antiochus IV, escaped from Rome and traveled to Antioch. Demetrius I Soter quickly brought the Seleucid army to his side, defeated Lysias, and had Antiochus V put to death in very late 162 (Pol. XXXI 20–23; App. *Syr.* 47; I Macc. VII 1–4; Clay, *Legal Documents from Erech*, Nr. 40, line 37).

Demetrius I Soter strove to arrest the disintegration of the empire. He had a rebellious satrap of Babylon, Timarchus, killed and asserted Seleucid power in Cappadocia, but the Romans promptly undid his arrangements there (App.

Syr. l.c.). He also almost succeeded in quelling the Judean revolt: even if Judas Maccabaeus destroyed an army commanded by the general Nicanor in 161, in the next year another Seleucid general, Bacchides, defeated Judas who himself fell in the battle. By 157 Bacchides had managed to establish an uneasy peace with Judas' brother, Jonathan (I Macc. VII and IX).

Unfortunately for Demetrius I Soter, a pretender claiming to be a son of Antiochus IV's, revolted in 153. This man, known as Alexander I Balas, received aid from Ptolemy VI Philometor as well as others (Just. XXXV 1) and proved a formidable adversary. Demetrius I accordingly needed allies. Therefore he allowed the erstwhile Judean rebel Jonathan to rearm. Jonathan, sensing an opportunity, then approached Alexander I Balas to see if this ruler might offer him more. Alexander I Balas appointed Jonathan as high priest in Judea (the office was currently vacant – I Macc. IX 54–57), and Jonathan switched sides. Demetrius I thereupon made Jonathan many additional, suspiciously generous offers. In his desperation, Demetrius was probably making similar offers throughout the empire. Jonathan patently doubted Demetrius I's ability to deliver and continued to back Balas – rightly as it turned out, for in 150 Balas defeated Demetrius I in a battle which cost Demetrius his life. Now Ptolemy VI Philometor and Alexander I Balas sealed their alliance with Balas' marriage to Philometor's daughter, Cleopatra Thea ("goddess") (I Macc. X 1–58). A spectacular career lay ahead of her as the wife (and widow) of several kings until she herself at last began to rule, the first Hellenistic queen so to do. For now, however, her assignment was to make the alliance between Balas and her father work. Even if Balas never acted to meet the expectation, Philometor presumably expected to receive Hollow Syria back.

Balas would not hold his throne long – in 147 Demetrius I's teenaged son, under the tutelage of an experienced general Lasthenes, rebelled, and Ptolemy VI Philometor entered Hollow Syria at the head of a large army. Demetrius I's son defeated and slew Balas in 145 and ascended the throne as Demetrius II Nicator. Ptolemy VI Philometor now gave Cleopatra Thea in marriage to him – presumably in the expectation of Demetrius II's official cession of Hollow Syria (part of which Philometor's army already held). However, Philometor died in an accident shortly thereafter (I Macc. X 67–XI 19; Jos. *Ant.* XIII 4,3 [86]; Liv. *Per.* 52), and no cession of Hollow Syria took place.

Within two years a general in the Seleucid army, Diodotus Trypho, revolted in the name of Alexander I Balas' young son whom he declared king under the name of Antiochus VI Epiphanes II. In Judea the high priest Jonathan, who had ingratiated himself with Demetrius II Nicator, now decided to back Trypho. Jonathan was supposed to conquer Palestine for Antiochus VI, but succeeded so well in this that Trypho came to suspect his true aims. Late in 143 Trypho took him prisoner. The last of the Maccabaean brothers, Simon, now assumed his brothers' mantle and switched his allegiance to Demetrius II Nicator – against various concessions which the latter could not refuse. Among other things Demetrius II officially appointed Simon as high priest, and in 142 the Judeans began dating not by the Seleucid Era, but by the current year of

Simon's high priesthood (I Macc. XI 39–XIII 42; Diod. XXXIII 4a). Judea was now independent *de facto*.

In that same year Trypho deposed his hapless ward and declared himself king (I Macc. XIII 31–32). His rebellion continued, and in 139 the Parthians additionally encroached on the Babylonian and Mesopotamian satrapies (Jos. *Ant.* XIII 5,11 [184–186]). When Demetrius attempted to deal with this new threat, the Parthians defeated him in 138 and took him prisoner. They presumably also gained control of much of Babylon and Mesopotamia in addition to Media. The King of Parthia, Mithridates I, kept Demetrius II in honorable captivity and even gave him a Parthian princess in marriage (Just. XXXVI 1 and XXXVIII 9).

In Syria, meanwhile, Demetrius II's younger brother, Antiochus VII Sidetes took charge. He in his turn married Cleopatra Thea, defeated Diodotus Trypho, and brought some degree of stability to the rapidly disintegrating kingdom. In 133 Sidetes besieged Simon's son, John Hyrcanus, the current high priest, in Jerusalem and succeeded in forcing John to acknowledge Seleucid overlordship and to pay a tribute. In 130 he set out for the East and recaptured for the Seleucids Mesopotamia, Babylon, and apparently even Media. In 128 the current Parthian king, Phraates II, released Demetrius II Nicator in order to foment a civil war, but shortly after Demetrius II's release Phraates II ambushed Sidetes and killed him (Jos. *Ant.* XIII 7,1–8,4 [221–253]; *War*, I 2,2 [50] and 6 [62]; Just. XXXVIII 10; Diod. XXXIV/XXXV 15–16). This was the last Seleucid attempt to retake the East.

Bactria and the East

The destruction of Seleucid authority in Iran left behind a series of kingdoms – some Greek, others not. Lying to the east of Media Atropatene and Parthia, the two chief non-Greek kingdoms in Iran, was the Greek kingdom of Bactria. Although now cut off from the rest of the Greek world, it survived well into the second half of the second century BC. Its rulers are best known from the splendid coins which they left behind, but besides that are commonly little more than names. The last ruler of Bactria who is certainly dated is Euthydemus whom Antiochus III Megas in 206 compelled to acknowledge Seleucid sovereignty. Euthydemus had a son, Demetrius, to whom Antiochus III planned to give a daughter of his in marriage. After his father's death (which actuarially ought to fall in the second or third decade of the second century BC) Demetrius carried out far-ranging campaigns including into India (Strab. XI 11,1, p. 516). Coins of a Demetrius – apostrophized on later so-called commemorative coins of another king called Agathocles as "invincible" – who bears a strong family resemblance to Euthydemus, appear to belong to about the right time (see Figure 25.1). Other kings of Bactria who are associated with this dynasty are known from their coins only: Agathocles, Pantaleon, Antimachus, and a second Euthydemus. Some may have been co-regents or vassal kings as there seems not enough time to allow them

Figure 25.1   Coins with portraits of Demetrius of Bactria. a) Bopearachchi, series 1 of Demetrius I. The legend on the reverse (not shown) reads "of King Demetrius"; b) (Bopearachchi, series 17 of Agathocles) is a so-called commemorative coin, minted after Demetrius' reign. The legend on the reverse (not shown) reads "of King Agathocles the Just"; the legend on the obverse (shown) reads "of Demetrius the Invincible." Source: a) Uploadalt, http://en.wikipedia.org/wiki/File:Demetrius_I_MET_coin.jpg (accessed 12th February 2013) CC BY-SA 3.0; b) PHGCOM, http://en.wikipedia.org/wiki/File:Agathokle sCoinOfDemetriusAniketos.JPG (accessed 12th February 2013) CC BY-SA 3.0

all to reign consecutively without postulating unusually turbulent times for the dynasty.

Eucratides became King of Bactria around the same time as Mithridates I became King of Parthia (circa 171) (Just. XLI 6). Based on the portrait on his coins (see Figure 25.2), he did not belong to the same family as Euthydemus and Demetrius, and it is not clear how he came to power. According to Justin (XLI 6) Eucratides waged war successfully against a "Demetrius, King of the Indians." It is unclear if this Demetrius is the same as the son of Euthydemus; or a son of this Demetrius; or a completely different person. At some point, however, Greek dynasts established small kingdoms in northern India; the campaigns mentioned at Strab. XI 11,1, p. 516, as well as those which Eucratides himself carried out (Just. l.c.) provide the historical context for this.

According to Justin (l.c.), Eucratides was slain by his own son whom Justin does not name, but calls a co-regent. The date of Eucratides' assassination is unknown, but given his alleged success in wars and his splendid and extensive coinage, he should have had a long reign. Several kings of Bactria who appear to be relatives of Eucratides are known from their coins: Plato, Heliocles, and a second Eucratides. Thereafter the Bactrian kingdom apparently succumbed in the second half of the second century BC, allegedly after the entrance into Bactria of nomadic tribes from the north (Strab. XI 8,2, p. 511).

Figure 25.2   Coin of Eucratides (Bopearachchi, series 6 of Eucratides I); the legend on the reverse is "of King Eucratides the Great." Source: © The Trustees of the British Museum

The Greek dynasts who had arisen in northern India following the campaigns there by Demetrius and Eucratides lasted about a century and a half longer. Strabo (XI 11,1, p. 516) speaks of a particularly successful one, Menander, who was alleged to have crossed even the River Hyphasis where Alexander the Great had been forced to turn back. Numerous coins of this king survive (Bopearachchi 1991, plates 26–32) on which he used the epithet "Soter" (savior). The Indian form of his name was Milinda, and he figures in the Indian philosophical dialogue *The Questions of King Milinda*. The remaining Indo-Greek dynasts are little more than names gleaned from their coins. Where their coins were found provides the best evidence for these kings' territories and the external date of their coinage the evidence for when, approximately, they reigned (see Bopearachchi 1991).

The Last Seleucids

After the death of Antiochus VII Sidetes, his brother Demetrius II Nicator, newly freed from Parthian captivity, became king again. He took back his former wife (and his brother's widow), Cleopatra Thea. At the urging of his exiled mother-in-law, Cleopatra II of Egypt (see below), he attempted to invade Egypt, but Ptolemy VIII Physco retaliated by sponsoring a rebel, Alexander II Zabinas, a supposed son of Alexander I Balas', and in 126 Demetrius II, whom Zabinas had defeated near Damascus, was killed on a ship while attempting to flee from Tyre (Just. XXXIX 1; Jos. *Ant.* XIII 9,3 [267–269]).

Figure 25.3   Coin of Antiochus VIII Grypus ("hooknose" – though he preferred other official epithets: the legend on the reverse (not shown) is "of King Antiochus Epiphanes") (Cat.Gk.Coin, Seleucid Kings, pp. 88–89). Hellenistic portraiture aimed at realism on rulers' coins – no airbrushing or retouching. Grypus' subjects were supposed to recognize their King. Source: © The Trustees of the British Museum

Cleopatra Thea, the widow of three kings, now took over as the coins issued in her own name with the title "Queen" show (Cat.Gk.Coins, Seleucid Kings, p. 85). She finally achieved what earlier queens such as Eurydice (see chap. 20), Berenice (see chap. 21) or Stratonice (see chap. 23) had attempted, albeit in a Seleucid Kingdom much diminished and with the lingering issue of the eventual majority of her and Demetrius II's eldest son, Seleucus V Philometor. In 125 she had him murdered when he claimed the kingship. Thereafter she reigned (as the senior partner – Cat.Gk.Coins, Seleucid Kings, pp. 85–86) with her and Demetrius II's next son, Antiochus VIII whose official epithet varied, but who was best known by his well-merited nickname "Grypus" or "hooknose" (see Figure 25.3). In 121 Cleopatra allegedly attempted to murder him too, but he smelled a rat and contrived to have her drink her own poisoned cup (App. *Syr.* 69; Just. l.c.).

By now the Seleucid Kingdom was confined to Syria. Grypus ruled over it alone for a few years, until his half-brother, Antiochus IX Cyzicenus, a son of Cleopatra Thea and Antiochus VII Sidetes, returned to Syria. In a civil war Grypus and Cyzicenus divided Syria between themselves (Just. XXXIX 2; Jos. *Ant.* XIII 10,1 [270–272]).

From this point onwards narration of the Seleucid Kingdom's declining fortunes becomes an idle exercise. Its last rulers with their high-flown names which evoked the grandeur of a bygone age (Seleucus VI Epiphanes; Antiochus X Eusebes; Antiochus XI Epiphanes III; Demetrius III Philopator/Eucaerus; Philip I Philadelphus; Antiochus XII Dionysus; Seleucus VII Philometor II;

Antiochus XIII Asiaticus; Philip II Philoromaeus) were trivial kinglets who divided bits and pieces of Syria among themselves (and with Tigranes II, the King of Armenia) in pointless civil wars until Cn. Pompeius Magnus (Pompey the Great) liquidated what was left of the kingdom in 64 BC.

The Mithridatic Wars and Pompey's Settlement of the East

In 120, a few years after the establishment of the Roman province of Asia, Mithridates VI, surnamed "the Great," became King of Pontus. A talented administrator and general, he showed more spirit than most Hellenistic monarchs. The kings of Pontus had married Seleucid princesses, and even if Mithridates VI bore an Iranian name he was fully at home in the Hellenistic world. He is best known for his prodigious linguistic ability (allegedly he spoke fifty languages – [**Aurelius Victor**], *De uir. ill.*, 76) and the precautions which he is supposed to have taken against any attempt to assassinate him by poison: by taking increasingly larger doses of known poisons, he allegedly built up an immunity to them all (Plin. *NH* XXV 3).

Soon after his accession he responded to an appeal from the Greek cities along the northern coast of the Black Sea, for help against the Scythians farther to the north. Over the next few years Mithridates VI consolidated his rule over that region, including the so-called Kingdom of the (Crimean) Bosporus (Strab. VII 4,3–4, pp. 308–310). In 104 Mithridates VI turned to Asia Minor and, together with Nicomedes III of Bithynia, seized Paphlagonia. He went on to occupy Galatia (Just. XXXVII 4), but when he and Nicomedes quarreled over Cappadocia, Nicomedes complained to Rome. A Roman embassy ordered both kings to withdraw from their new conquests, and Mithridates VI backed down (Just. XXXVIII 1–2). Shortly thereafter (96) L. Cornelius Sulla arrived to install one Ariobarzanes as the new King of Cappadocia (Plut. *Sul.* 5). But when the Social War (91–88) broke out in Italy, Mithridates VI attacked Nicomedes IV of Bithynia and occupied that kingdom. Next, with the connivance of Tigranes II, the King of Armenia, he reoccupied Cappadocia (Just. XXXVIII 3). The Senate sent out M'. Aquilius to deal with the situation, but although Mithridates VI withdrew again, Aquilius so provoked the king with curt orders and smug replies that Mithridates VI chose war with Rome over enduring additional insults (App. *Mith.* 11–16).

The result was the First **Mithridatic War**. Mithridates VI seized Asia Minor in one swift campaign (App. *Mith.* 17–20), and in 88 he encouraged everyone in his dominions to vent what amounted to the entire Hellenistic world's century's worth of pent-up anger at Rome, Rome's high-handed behavior, Rome's insults, and Roman greed (e.g., the heavy indemnities): in the so-called Asiatic Vespers, an alleged 80,000 Italians (traders, money-lenders, tax-collectors, petty officials, soldiers) were slain in one great massacre the length and breadth of Asia Minor (App. *Mith.* 23; **Valerius Maximus**, IX 2,4, ext. 3; Plut. *Sul.* 24, actually gives the figure as 150,000). Mithridates VI, moreover, saw to it that M'. Aquilius received due payment for his insolence by pouring molten gold down his throat (App. *Mith.* 21).

From Asia Minor Mithridates VI's forces crossed the Aegean. With Athens as a base they seized much of Greece, but in 87 L. Cornelius Sulla arrived in Greece with 16,500 troops (Plut. *Sul.* 16). Sulla reduced Athens by siege and in 86 defeated Mithridates' general Archelaus at Charoneia and again at Orchomenus in Boeotia (App. *Mith.* 28–50 – at *Mith.* 41 Appian puts Mithridates' troops at 120,000, probably highly inflated). In 84 Sulla crossed over into Asia, and Mithridates made peace rather than risk another battle. Sulla required Mithridates to evacuate all seized territory and to pay the costs for the war (App. *Mith.* 54–58). Sulla hastened back to Rome where he seized power as dictator in 82. In Asia, Sulla's legate, L. Licinius Murena, invaded Pontus and caused the Second Mithridatic War (83–82), but Sulla rebuked his subordinate and reaffirmed the previous terms of peace (App. *Mith.* 64–66).

In 74 Nicomedes IV, the King of Bithynia, died childless and, like Attalus III of Pergamum before him, bequeathed his kingdom to Rome. Sulla by now was dead, and Mithridates VI made one last play. He seized Bithynia (which M. Aurelius Cotta had just begun to organize as a province), and the Third Mithridatic War began. In 73 to 70 L. Licinius Lucullus in drawn-out minor campaigns slowly ejected Mithridates VI from all his conquests and from Pontus itself, and in the end Mithridates VI fled to Tigranes II of Armenia (App. *Mith.* 71–82). This monarch had steadily been building up an Armenian Empire which by now included most of Cappadocia (App. *Mith.* 67) and Syria which he had seized from the squabbling Seleucid princelings (App. *Syr.* 48 and 70). Lucullus' campaigns against Armenia in 69 to 67 brought no lasting success (App. *Mith.* 84–90), and in 66 the Senate entrusted a new general, Cn. Pompeius Magnus (Pompey the Great), with a wide-ranging command against all Rome's enemies in the East (App. *Mith.* 94). Pompey was already in Cilicia where he had been waging war against the numerous pirates which had plagued the entire region for many decades now (App. *Mith.* 90–94; on Roman activity against the pirates, see also Sherk, Nr. 55; when exactly Cilicia became a province is unclear) following the decline of the Rhodian navy. Pompey immediately took up his new command.

Mithridates VI's ally, Tigranes II of Armenia, was soon occupied by a war against the Parthians (**Cassius Dio**, XXXVI 45), and Pompey made short work of Mithridates VI's remaining troops in Asia Minor. In 65 Mithridates VI fled to the Kingdom of the Bosporus, for now beyond Pompey's reach (Cass. XXXVI 45–50; App., *Mith.* 97–103), but the hardships caused by his efforts there to raise yet another army led to a revolt against him, and in 63 this most spirited opponent of the Romans finally gave way to despair and committed suicide (Cass. XXXVII 11–14).

Meanwhile, Tigranes II decided that he could not cope with Pompey's army and made his peace with Rome. Pompey restricted him to his original territory, but undertook no additional action against him (App. *Mith.* 104–105). Pompey added Western Pontus to the province of Bithynia, but left the remainder as formally independent statelets (Strab. XII 3,1, p. 541). Cappadocia remained formally independent under its kings (Strab. XII 2,11, p. 540) and would do so until AD 17 when it became a Roman province (Tac. *Ann.* II 42). In 64 Pompey entered Syria, liquidated what was left of the Seleucid Kingdom there, and organized Syria as a Roman Province (App. *Mith.* 106 and *Syr.* 70; Just. XL 2). The next year two rival claimants for the throne of Judea, the brothers Hyrcanus II and Aristobulus II, appealed to him to settle their dispute. Pompey in the end entered Jerusalem under arms, abolished the Judean monarchy, but left Judea formally independent under Hyrcanus II as high priest (Jos. *Ant.* XIV 3–4 [34–79]).

The East, up to the River Euphrates, now stood under Roman dominion.

The Later Ptolemies

The fate of Ptolemaic Egypt was perhaps a little better than that of the Seleucid Kingdom in that the basic territorial integrity of Egypt was maintained to the end. In 180 Ptolemy V Epiphanes died, and his young son Ptolemy VI Philometor succeeded him. Initially his official regent was his mother, a daughter of Antiochus III Megas', Cleopatra (I), but she died a little later (Porphyry, *BNJ* 260, Fr. 49a). Although it is not explicitly attested, Ptolemy VI evidently married his sister, also called Cleopatra (II) (see, e.g., Just. XXXVIII 8).

The Ptolemies had long since taken up diplomatic contact with the Romans (e.g., Pol. XVI 27); and the Romans had attempted to intervene with Antiochus III Megas on Ptolemy V's behalf in 196 (see above). In 168, when Ptolemy VI Philometor stood on the verge of losing his kingdom to his uncle Antiochus IV, it was a Roman embassy which compelled Antiochus IV to withdraw (see chap. 24).

In this difficult period Ptolemy VI's brother revolted. Whatever his name may have been before this, it became Ptolemy from this point on. For the moment he was called "Ptolemy the Brother," but would eventually take the official epithet "Euergetes" ("benefactor"), though unofficially all knew him as "Physco" ("fatso"). The two brothers and their sister worked out an unwieldy arrangement for joint rule (Pol. XXIX 23; Rylands Papyrus, 583). After two rebellions which were put down (Diod. XXXI 15a and 17b), Ptolemy the Brother led another rebellion circa 163 which forced Ptolemy VI Philometor to flee. He went to Rome and sought redress from the Senate (to whose intervention with Antiochus IV he owed his kingdom anyway) (Diod. XXXI 18). The Senate evidently decreed that Ptolemy VI Philometor should have Egypt and Cyprus, but that Ptolemy the Brother should rule in Cyrene (thus, at any rate, the state of affairs at the end of Philometor's life: Just. XXXVIII 8).

Late in his reign the civil wars in the Seleucid Kingdom opened up an opportunity for Philometor to regain Hollow Syria for Egypt. Philometor led an army into Hollow Syria, but his accidental death in 145 ended this attempt (see above). Now Ptolemy the Brother returned to Egypt, married Cleopatra II, and became Ptolemy VIII Euergetes or Physco (there is no Ptolemy VII – see table of rulers). Bizarrely, Physco a little later married his niece (and stepdaughter), also called Cleopatra (III) (Just. XXXVIII 8).

The resulting arrangement caused much tension; in 131 Ptolemy VIII Physco was forced to flee to Cyprus while Cleopatra II remained in Egypt (Liv. *Per.* 59; Diod. XXXIV/XXXV 14). A little later Physco returned to Egypt and drove Cleopatra II into exile at the court of Demetrius II, the Seleucid king, who had just returned from Parthian captivity (Just. XXXIX 1)). When Cleopatra II persuaded Demetrius II to attack Egypt, Physco fomented a rebellion against Demetrius II in Syria by sending out a pretender, Alexander II Zabinas, and Demetrius II lost his life in the course of the rebellion (see above). Afterwards Cleopatra II was reconciled with her brother, and returned to Egypt (Burstein, Nr. 107).

Physco, who had not earned his nickname "fatso" for nothing, is best known for an incident which occurred at an indeterminate stage of his reign – the visit of the Roman general Scipio Aemilianus to Alexandria (Diod. XXXIII 28b). Aemilianus forced the corpulent Physco to accompany him from his ship to the palace on foot (Plut. *Sayings of Kings and Commanders*, p. 200). Roman commanders simply expected a Hellenistic king to put up with any insult, and the spectacle of the fat king huffing to keep up with the trim Roman left behind an indelible impression throughout what was left of the Hellenistic world.

In 116 Physco died. He left his queen, Cleopatra III, to choose the next king. Her desire to choose her younger son met with such opposition in Alexandria that she relented and chose her elder son, Ptolemy IX Soter II, unofficially known as Lathyrus ("chick-pea") (Just. XXXIX 3). Her younger son, Alexander, she sent off to Cyprus as governor, but once there he effectively ruled as king.

In Egypt meanwhile, Lathyrus and his mother, Cleopatra III, ruled jointly in an uneasy partnership, but Cleopatra III would shortly establish her dominance and emerge as a genuinely ruling queen (whether Cleopatra I and Cleopatra II had ever done so is unclear). Lathyrus married one of his sisters, Cleopatra (IV), but his mother soon forced him to divorce her and to marry another of his sisters, Cleopatra (V) Selene ("moon"). In 107 Cleopatra III was able to expel Lathyrus from Egypt so that her younger son could return from Cyprus and rule with her as Ptolemy X Alexander. This was merely official, however, as in reality Cleopatra III had taken charge. Lathyrus himself went to Cyprus and began to rule there (Paus. I 9; Just. XXXIX 3–5). In 103 the ruler of Judea, Alexander Jannaeus (high priest at home, but king to the outside world – see below), took advantage of the collapse of the Seleucid Kingdom by attacking Ptolemaïs on the coast. Since neither of the two current Seleucid kings, Antiochus VIII Grypus and Antiochus IX Cyzicenus, helped, the denizens of Ptolemaïs turned to Lathyrus who responded by bringing an army to Palestine. Alexander Jannaeus promptly broke off the siege and entered into negotiations with Lathyrus – and with Cleopatra III. When Lathyrus got wind of this, he rounded on Jannaeus and overran most of Palestine. Cleopatra

III, who had no desire to see Lathyrus establish himself in Palestine, now also invaded and, in alliance with Jannaeus, she forced Lathyrus to withdraw back to Cyprus. She briefly contemplated taking possession of Jannaeus' kingdom, but decided against it (Jos. *Ant.* XIII 12,2–13,2 [324–355]). Thus passed the Ptolemies' last opportunity to regain the land for which they had so long fought against the Seleucids.

Around this time Cleopatra III deposited a sum of money and "her grandchildren" in the temple of Asclepius at Cos. These grandchildren included a son of Ptolemy X Alexander's, also called Alexander (Jos. *Ant.* XIII 13,1 [349]; App. *Mith.* 23). In 101 Cleopatra III died, and Ptolemy X Alexander reigned alone. Little is known of his reign. In 96 the last King of Cyrene, Ptolemy Apion (a natural brother of Ptolemy X Alexander's), died and bequeathed his kingdom to Rome (Liv. *Per.* 70; Just. XXXIX 5). The Romans were reluctant to enter upon their inheritance. Only in 74 did they finally organize Cyrene as a province with a provincial governor (Sal. *H.R.* II 41 McGushin). It was the first piece of Ptolemaic territory to fall to Rome.

In Egypt proper, meanwhile, a rebellion forced Ptolemy X Alexander to flee. He was defeated in a naval battle, fled to Lycia in 88, and, having evidently raised a second fleet, was slain in a second naval battle (Porphyry, *BNJ* 260, Fr. 2,8). Thereupon Ptolemy IX Lathyrus returned to Egypt (Just. XXXIX 5) to reign until his death in late 81.

The sole surviving legitimate male Ptolemy was the Alexander whom Cleopatra III had brought to Cos. He had been captured there in 88 by Mithridates VI of Pontus who had just defeated the Romans and overrun the Roman province of Asia (App. *Mith.* 23). Mithridates VI did the boy no harm and had him raised in a manner befitting a Hellenistic prince. When Sulla defeated Mithridates VI in 84, Alexander eventually accompanied Sulla to Rome. In 80 Sulla was dictator at Rome and upon Lathyrus' death sent this Ptolemaic prince back to Egypt as Ptolemy XI Alexander II.

Upon arrival he married his predecessor's daughter, his much older first cousin Berenice, who had reigned alongside of her father for some years. He had her killed within three weeks of their wedding. Berenice, however, had been popular; and an enraged mob seized Ptolemy XI Alexander II and slew him shortly thereafter (Euseb. I 165 Schoene). There was now no legitimate issue of the house of Ptolemy left, but there was a natural son of Ptolemy IX Lathyrus' in Syria (Cic. *De reg. Alex.* Fr. 8). How exactly he had come to be there is unknown, but he was now recalled to Egypt where he became Ptolemy XII. He bore a string of official epithets – Theos Philopator Philadelphus Neos Dionysus –, but was generally known either as Nothus ("bastard") or, most commonly, as Auletes ("piper"). He married a woman called Cleopatra (VI) Tryphaena (Porphyry, *BNJ* 260, Fr. 2,14), presumably his sister. A brother of Auletes' – inevitably his name was Ptolemy – received Cyprus to rule over (Trog. *Prol.* XL).

At Rome, meanwhile, a supposed testament of Ptolemy XI Alexander II's had turned up (Cic. *Leg.Agr.* II 41); in it Egypt was willed to Rome. Although

Rome did not act upon that will (in fact it had yet to act on the will by which it had received Cyrene), Auletes' position was precarious. Liberal gifts to influential Romans kept him in power (e.g., **Suetonius**, *Caes.* 54), and as long as Auletes kept the money flowing the leading figures at Rome acquiesced in his retention of the throne. In 64, when Pompey the Great crushed Mithridates VI forever and organized Syria as a Roman province, Auletes sent money and supplies (App. *Mith.* 114). In 59 Auletes, through his gifts to C. Julius Caesar, finally achieved official Roman recognition of his rule (Caesar, *Civ.* III 107; Suet. l.c.).

All the same, in the next year the Romans decided to annex Cyprus where Auletes' brother had been reigning since 80. He committed suicide in preference to living as a former king, and Cyprus, which M. Porcius Cato organized as a province (App. *Bell. Ciu.* II 85–86), became the second Ptolemaic dominion to fall to Rome. In 58 disturbances in Alexandria forced Auletes to flee. On the way to Rome he met Cato, presumably still on Cyprus. Cato, letting all the world know what he thought of Hellenistic kings, received him while on the toilet (Plut. *Cato*, 35).

When Auletes arrived at Rome, he began promising any senator who would listen the moon and the stars in return for bringing him back to Egypt. Eventually, in 55 A. Gabinius, the governor of Syria, consented so to do (Cass. XXXIX 55; App. *Syr.* 51). Back in Alexandria, Auletes had his daughter Berenice, who with an assortment of husbands had been ruling Egypt in his absence, summarily executed. In 51 he himself died and was succeeded by his eldest surviving child, a daughter called Cleopatra (VII) (Strab. XVIII 1,11, p. 796). This remarkable woman would be the last ruler of Ptolemaic Egypt and the last Hellenistic ruler of any consequence.

New Hellenistic States and Statelets

As the Seleucid Kingdom broke up, a number of new Hellenistic states came into being. From one perspective, one could include among these new states the Parthian Kingdom in Iran. Its kings put Greek legends on their coins and occasionally used the surname "Philhellene" (see Figure 25.4). But for the most part these kings laid claim to the heritage of the pre-Greek rulers of Iran, the line of Cyrus the Great. Their titulature was identical to that of the old Persian kings, and they ruled over most of the old Persian kings' territory to the east of the Euphrates. From a certain point of view, the Parthian Kingdom displaced the Seleucid Kingdom as the successor state of the Persian Empire.

Armenia had never been fully integrated into the Seleucid Kingdom, and after the reign of Antiochus IV Epiphanes it became fully independent. Its greatest king was Tigranes II who briefly put together a wide-ranging empire which included most of Syria before Pompey the Great reduced him to his original territory. Thereafter Armenia remained independent as a sort of buffer state between the far more powerful Roman and Parthian empires.

Figure 25.4   Coin of Mithridates I (under his regnal name "Arsaces") (Cat.Gk.Coins, Parthia, p. 15). The legend is "of Arsaces, the Great King, the Philhellene" with the date "[year] 174," i.e., of the Seleucid Era = 138 BC. The date shows that it was minted under Mithridates I. Source: © The Trustees of the British Museum

The fate of Pergamum, Bithynia, Cappadocia, and Pontus has already been dealt with; it only remains to add that in 39 Mark Antony installed Darius, a grandson of Mithridates VI's, as the king of the eastern half of Pontus (App. *Bell.Ciu.* V 319). By 37, however, Antony had appointed a new King of Pontus, one Polemon (Cass. XLIX 25), who had a remarkable career as a kinglet in Rome's employ. He had begun as king over a portion of Cilicia in 39 (App. l.c.), in 37 he was transferred to the larger kingdom of Pontus, and he was also King of Lesser Armenia from 34 to 30 (Cass. XLIX 33; Plut. *Ant.* 38). In 14 Polemon also gained control of the so-called Kingdom of the (Crimean) Bosporus (Cass. LIV 24). The Emperor Claudius relieved one of his successors, his grandson Polemon II, of the Kingdom of the Bosporus in AD 41 (Cass. LX 8), but Polemon II continued to rule over Pontus until AD 63 (Suet. *Nero* 18).

After the death of Antiochus IV Epiphanes in 164 BC, Ptolemy, the Satrap of Commagene to the north of Syria, made his satrapy independent (Diod. XXXI 19a) and established a reasonably successful Hellenistic statelet. Although of little importance, its rulers in orderly succession steered it through the break-up of the Seleucid Kingdom, the growth of Armenia, and the establishment of Roman supremacy, all the while maintaining its independence. In AD 18, after the death of its king, Antiochus III, it became part of the province of Syria (Tac. *Ann.* II 42), but in 38 the Emperor Gaius (Caligula) again made it a formally independent kingdom under Antiochus IV (Cass. LIX 8) who ruled it till AD 72 when it reverted to the province of Syria (Jos. *War,* VII 7,1–3 [219–243]).

Another new Hellenistic kingdom was Judea (Jos. *Ant.* XIII–XX). The last of the Maccabaean brothers, Simon, had effectively made Judea independent in 142. He held the high priesthood, as did his son, John Hyrcanus, after him. Hyrcanus' son, Aristobulus, took the additional title of "king" in 104 BC, and his brother and successor Alexander ruled as king as well from 103 to 76. Their Greek names – they also had Hebrew ones: "Judas" and "Johannon" respectively – mark them out as Hellenized rulers. After Alexander's death, his widow, Salome Alexandra, held power for nine years, followed by Alexander's sons Hyrcanus II (three months in 67) and Aristobulus II (67–63) who ruled briefly as kings until the Romans took over the kingdom as part of Pompey's settlement. Thereafter Judea remained formally independent under Hyrcanus II as high priest. Yet in 39 the Romans turned Judea into a nominally independent kingdom under the rule of Herod I who was not a member of the "Maccabaean" dynasty. Various of his descendants would rule over all or parts of Judea for many years to come, the last being Herod Agrippa II who from AD 48 to 53 was king of the tiny statelet of Chalcis at the foot of Mt. Lebanon (Jos. *Ant.* XX 5,2 [104]), and thereafter of the so-called tetrarchy of Philip (Jos. *Ant.* XVII 11,4 [319]), a much larger territory to the northeast of the Sea of Galilee (Jos. *War*, II 12,8 [247]).

The Romans fashioned a fair number of other such kingdoms throughout the East (For example, in 63 BC Pompey made the Galatian chieftain Deiotarus the king of a notionally independent Galatia [Strab. XII 3, 13, p. 547]; for a few others, see below), but these alleged kings had no real power and "ruled" only for as long as Rome, for its own purposes, deemed convenient.

Cleopatra VII and the End of Ptolemaic Egypt

When Cleopatra VII became Queen of Egypt in 51, she was just in her late teens. It says something about Greco-Macedonian assumptions of cultural superiority (see Box 23.4) that she was the first Hellenistic ruler of Egypt who learned Egyptian (Plut. *Ant.* 27). She married her brother, a boy of about ten years, Ptolemy XIII, who became king with her. Within two years, Cleopatra VII was driven into exile by palace officials who perhaps regarded her brother as more pliant – something which she was not. In exile she collected an army and prepared to invade Egypt. As this war was brewing, a more important one broke out in Italy. For however much Cleopatra VII would strive during her reign to pursue an independent line, she always remained at the mercy of events at Rome. C. Julius Caesar crossed the Rubicon in the year 49 and opened a new round of civil wars at Rome between him and Pompey the Great.

In 48 Caesar destroyed Pompey's forces at Pharsala in Greece, and Pompey fled to Egypt where Egyptian officials had him slain so as not to stand on the victor's wrong side when he should appear – which Caesar did just a few days later. Caesar took up his abode in the Ptolemies' palace and thither summoned both Ptolemy XIII and Cleopatra VII (Caes. *Civ.* III 106–108). Worried that she might be assassinated, Cleopatra VII had herself rolled up in a carpet and smuggled into the palace – emerging from the carpet in Caesar's presence (Plut.

Caes. 49). Perhaps aided by her dramatic entrance, she charmed the Roman general and statesman, and Caesar and Cleopatra VII were soon lovers.

In the meantime Caesar had to fight the so-called Alexandrian War against the restless population of Alexandria itself as well as the Egyptian army that was still loyal to Ptolemy XIII. In the fighting Ptolemy XIII disappeared, perhaps killed by accident for once rather than by design. By early 47 Caesar had gained control of the situation in Alexandria. Cleopatra VII remained queen; officially her new consort was her second younger brother, Ptolemy XIV ([Caes.], *Bell.Alex.* 33). At mid-year Cleopatra VII gave birth to Caesar's son, called Caesar but better known by the diminutive Caesarion (Plut. *Caes.* 49). In 46 Caesar returned to Rome and brought Cleopatra VII with him – much to the discomfiture of some Romans (Cic. *Ad Att.* XV 15). What either of them realistically planned or hoped for at this point is a matter for idle speculation as on the Ides of March in 44 Caesar was assassinated, and Cleopatra VII returned to Egypt.

Around this time Ptolemy XIV died (allegedly poisoned by Cleopatra – Jos. *Ant.* XV 4,1 [89]), and, though the date is uncertain, Cleopatra VII's son with Caesar became king, Ptolemy XV. Cleopatra VII waited out the civil wars which followed Caesar's death, and only when Mark Antony defeated Brutus' and Cassius' forces at Philippi in 42 did she act. She traveled to meet Antony in Cilicia (Plut. *Ant.* 25), and she and Antony became lovers. Cleopatra VII used the affair to acquire possessions in Palestine – the tiny kingdom of Chalcis; a strip of Phoenician coastline; and a commercially profitable forest near Jericho (Jos. *Ant.* XV 4,1–2 [92–96] with *War*, I 13,1 [248] and Sherk, Nr. 88). Given how long the house of Ptolemy had fought for possession of Palestine in the six Syrian Wars, it is perhaps no coincidence that Cleopatra VII converted her alliance with Antony into territorial gains there. For her part, Cleopatra could offer Antony financial and military assistance (e.g., Cass. XLIX 31; Plut. *Ant.* 66), so besides the romance their relationship had its hard-edged practical element on both sides.

The relationship eventually produced three children; allegedly they were all to become kings or queens of the lands which Antony was going to conquer in the course of his campaigns during these years (40 to 34) (Plut. *Ant.* 54; Cass. XLIX 41). None of it was to be as civil war broke out between Antony and Julius Caesar's adoptive son, C. Julius Caesar Octavianus, the future emperor Augustus. The decisive battle came at sea in 31, at Actium in Greece, on the Gulf of Ambracia, where Octavian's fleet defeated the combined fleets of Antony and Cleopatra VII. The pair escaped to Egypt with Cleopatra's fleet of sixty ships (Plut. *Ant.* 62–66). In the next year, as Octavian led an army from Syria into Egypt, Antony committed suicide under unusual circumstances (Plut. *Ant.* 76–77), but Cleopatra remained quite alive and received Octavian in the Ptolemies' palace in Alexandria.

Leaving aside the romantic considerations, Cleopatra VII presumably hoped that she might do some deal with the new master of Rome. She was mistaken, and when she saw that he had no other use for her but to exhibit her as a captive at Rome (Suet. *Aug.* 17), she chose suicide in preference to that. The story went that she had an asp smuggled into the palace and allowed it to bite her (Plut. *Ant.* 85–86). Octavian had her son by Caesar, Ptolemy XV, put to death shortly thereafter (Plut. *Ant.* 82). Egypt became a Roman province (Suet. *Aug.* 18), and thus ended the last of the three great Hellenistic kingdoms. It had stood the longest of them all and when Cleopatra VII died, the territory over which she ruled was more or less coextensive with that over which her great ancestor, Ptolemy I Soter, had become satrap nearly three centuries earlier.

Cleopatra's daughter, called Cleopatra Selene, did grow up to be a queen herself, though not of Egypt. Mark Antony's widow, Octavia, raised Cleopatra's three children by Antony, and Cleopatra Selene was eventually given in marriage to a Numidian nobleman, Juba II, whom Augustus made King of Mauretania in northern Africa in circa 25 BC. Selene took her siblings with her, and they all of them seem to have lived out their days in peace (Plut. *Ant.* 87; Cass. LI 15; Tac. *Ann.* IV 6). Selene's and Juba's son, Ptolemy, became King of Mauretania in due course by AD 24 (Tac. *Ann.* IV 23), but the Emperor Gaius (Caligula) had him assassinated in circa AD 40 (Suet. *Gaius*, 26). Thus the line of Ptolemy passes out of the historical record.

Epilogue

However constrained Cleopatra VII's policies were by developments at Rome, she had striven hard to keep Egypt independent. She was the last Hellenistic monarch worthy of the name. All the same, as the sun steadily set on the Hellenistic world, a few other monarchs, minor figures it is true, remained (like Juba and Ptolemy in Mauretania far in the West) to rule by Rome's grace over bits and pieces of the East. The Roman emperors, by way of convenience to themselves, occasionally fashioned formally independent statelets here and there and set up kings to rule over them. These princelings enjoyed playing the part with splendid courts (Lk. VII 25), grand public entrances (Acts, XXV 23), and magnificent banquets (Mk. VI 21). But their desire to be real kings rather than pretend ones on occasion tempted them to aspire to higher matters.

Josephus preserves a curious story (*Ant.* XIX 8,1 [338–341]) which is probably typical of these pathetic puppets' occasional attempts to break free of their strings. Herod Agrippa I, during his brief reign as King of Judea (AD 41–44), invited five other kings to a conference with him at Tiberias on the Sea of Galilee: Antiochus IV Epiphanes, the King of Commagene; Sampsigeramus, the King of Emesa (a city in Syria on the Orontes); Cotys, the King of Lesser Armenia; Polemon II, the King of Pontus; and Herod (Herod Agrippa I's brother), the King of Chalcis. Josephus does not say what these six kinglets discussed at Tiberias, and the question is probably moot. For C. Vibius Marsus, the governor of Syria, intervened before these would-be Ptolemy Soters and Seleucus Nicators could do anything of consequence – he went to Tiberias and ordered them to disperse, which they obediently did. Vibius thus extinguished one of the last gleams of political independence in the long twilight of the Hellenistic world.

The end of the Hellenistic world did not, of course, mean the end of the Greek world, even under Roman rule. The Hellenization which had begun in the late fourth century BC (see chap. 21) had seen to it that the urban culture of Egypt, Syria, and Asia Minor was by now thoroughly and (at least until the Arab conquest in the seventh century AD) inalterably Greek. People from all walks of life could at least make do in Greek and a few had even forgotten their "native" language: thus in the early first century AD, when the son of a Galilean carpenter met a woman who "although she was a Syro-Phoenician by race, spoke [only] Greek," he could hold up his end of the conversation in Greek without apparently surprising anyone, because knowledge of Greek went without saying, unlike the Greek monolingualism of a woman who by ethnicity ought to have been speaking Aramaic or Phoenician (Mk. VII 26 – though the passage is usually translated unintelligibly).

The elite, of course, functioned fully in Greek throughout the eastern half of the Roman Empire. In the first century AD, a Jew such as Joseph, son of Matthias, could become a Roman citizen and take a Roman name – T. Flavius Josephus –, but when it came to writing the history of his people, he did so in Greek (as opposed to Latin or Aramaic). At about the same time, another Roman citizen, Paul, a Jew from the Cilician city of Tarsus, composed an epistle to the Galatians, the descendants of the Celts who had settled in Asia Minor in the 270s (see chap. 21) – again in Greek. In the second century AD, a Bithynian such as Arrian – L. Flavius Arrianus – could have a stellar career in the imperial administration and even serve as consul of Rome, but he wrote the history of Alexander the Great in Greek. In the towns and cities of Greece itself life went on under the Romans as well. The civic institutions of Athens continued to function, and at Sparta old customs such as the *agoge* were kept alive (Plut. *Lyc.* 18,1). Plutarch held civic offices in his native Chaeroneia where he composed his erudite biographies and numerous essays – all in Greek, of course. The end of political independence had meant little culturally, and the eastern half of the Roman Empire remained stoutly Greek. It was the lasting and most important legacy of the Hellenistic World.

QUESTIONS FOR REVIEW

1 In what stages was the once mighty Seleucid Kingdom slowly reduced to just Syria?
2 Under what circumstances did the Romans finally assume the direct administration of Greece, Asia Minor, Syria, and Egypt?
3 What new states arose out of the wreckage of the Seleucid Kingdom?
4 By what means did Cleopatra VII try to keep Egypt independent of Rome?

QUESTION FOR FURTHER STUDY

Why did so many Hellenistic rulers will their kingdoms to Rome? Was it simple acknowledgment of reality? Was it to force the Romans finally to assume direct responsibility for regions which were under their dominion anyway? Or was it in each case a viable solution to localized problems?

FURTHER READING

In addition to the works listed at the end of chapters 20, 21, and 22, see also the following:

On Mithridates VI of Pontus, two recent biographies exist:
Højte, J.M. (2009) *Mithridates VI and the Pontic Kingdom*. Aarhus.
Mayor, A.(2010) *The Poison King: the Life and Legend of Mithradates, Rome's Deadliest Enemy*. Princeton.

On the Bactrian and Indo-Greek kings:
Bopearachchi, O. (1991) *Monnaies Gréco-Bactriennes et Indo-Grecques, Catalogue Raisonné*. Paris.
Narain, A.K. (1957) *The Indo-Greeks*. Oxford. (Places these kings, against Tarn, in an Indian as opposed to a Greek context.)
Tarn, W.W. (1951) The Greeks in Bactria and India. Cambridge. (The classic work.)

On the later Seleucids:
Bellinger, A.R. (1949) *The End of the Seleucids*. New Haven.
Ehling, K. (2008) *Untersuchungen zur Geschichte der späten Seleukiden (164–63 v. Chr.): vom Tode des Antiochos IV. bis zur Einrichtung der Provinz Syria unter Pompeius*. Stuttgart.

On Cleopatra VII (two recent titles of very many):
Goldsworthy, A. K. (2010) *Antony and Cleopatra*. London.
Roller, D.W. (2010) *Cleopatra: A biography*. Oxford.

On Roman rule in the Near East after Cleopatra:
Millar, F. (1993) *The Roman Near East. 31 B.C. to A.D. 337*. Cambridge, MA.

Tables of Rulers

In the lists below, many dates, inevitably, are only approximate, and in some cases it is a matter of taste what date or even what ruler one chooses to give (see the notes for some such cases). Co-regencies (with the exception of Philip III and Alexander IV) have generally been ignored to avoid cluttering up the lists, but in the cases of queens who ruled *de facto*, they had to be included since in those cases there usually was a king *de iure* as well. Where two rulers each controlled a substantial part of the country in question, both are indicated (with overlapping dates). Numeration of rulers is a modern habit and occasionally confuses more than it clarifies. The ancient convention was to use epithets – both official and unofficial. In the tables below the epithet(s) in most common use in modern scholarship is/are given, and a gloss is attached whenever the epithet's meaning is transparent.

A History of Greece: 1300 to 30 BC, First Edition. Victor Parker.
© 2014 Victor Parker. Published 2014 by John Wiley & Sons, Ltd.

Sparta (from Late Sixth Century)

Agiads		Eurypontids	
Cleomenes I	ca.520–490	Demaratus	? –491
Leonidas I	ca.490–480	Laotychidas II	491–469
Pleistarchus	480–458	Archidamus II	469–427
Pleistoanax	458–445, 426–408	Agis II	427–400
Pausanias	445–426, 408–394	Agesilaus	400–360
Agesipolis I	394–380	Archidamus III	360–338
Cleombrotus I	380–371	Agis III	338–330
Agesipolis II	371–370	Eudamidas I	330– ca. 300
Cleomenes II	370–309	Archidamus IV	ca.300–280
Areus I	309–265	Eudamidas II	ca.280–245
Acrotatus	265– ca. 260	Agis IV	245–241
Areus II	ca.260–252	Eudamidas III	241–228
Leonidas II	ca.252–243, 241–228	Archidamus V	227
Cleombrotus II	243–241	Eucleidas*	227–222
Cleomenes III	228–219	Lycurgus	219–ca. 211
Agesipolis III	219–ca. 215	Pelops	ca.211–200
(end of Agiad line)		Nabis**	ca.200–192

*Agiad. Eucleidas' successors, Lycurgus and Lycurgus' son Pelops, may have been Eurypontids.
**Regent since 207.

Persian Empire

Cyrus the Great	550 (revolt against Astyages) –529
Cambyses	529–522
Bardiya (Gaumata/Smerdis)	522
Darius I	522–485
Xerxes I	485–464
Artaxerxes I Macrocheir (long-arms)	464–424
Xerxes II	424
Darius II Nothos (bastard)	423–404
Artaxerxes II Mnemon (rememberer)	404–359
Artaxerxes III Ochus	359–338
Arses	338–336
Darius III	336–330
Bessus	330–329

Macedonia (from Early Fourth Century)

Amyntas III	393–370
Alexander II	370–367
Perdiccas III	367–360
Amyntas IV	360
Philip II	360–336
Alexander III the Great	336–323
Philip III Arrhidaeus	323–317
Alexander IV	323–311
Cassander*	311–297
Philip IV	297
Antipater	296–294
Alexander V	296–294
Demetrius I Poliorcetes (besieger of cities)**	294–287
Pyrrhus	287–284
Lysimachus	287–281
Ptolemy Ceraunus (thunderbolt)	280–279
Antigonus Gonatas	278–239
Demetrius II	239–229
Antigonus Doson ("who will give")	229–221
Philip V	221–179
Perseus	179–168

*Cassander's reign is given as beginning upon Alexander IV's death. In reality he had been ruling for some years prior to this, but did not claim the royal title until several years after he had Alexander IV killed.

** The line of Antigonid descent, in father–son succession, is as follows: Antigonus Monophthalmus, Demetrius Poliorcetes, Antigonus Gonatas, Demetrius II, Philip V, Perseus.

Ptolemaic Egypt

Ptolemy I Soter (savior)	323 (satrap of Egypt) –282
Ptolemy II Philadelphus (sibling-loving)	282–246
Ptolemy III Euergetes (benefactor)	246–221
Ptolemy IV Philopator (father-loving)	221–204
Ptolemy V Epiphanes (manifest god)	204–180
Ptolemy VI Philometor (mother-loving)	180–145
Ptolemy VIII* Euergetes II or Physco (fatso)	145–116
Cleopatra III**	116–101
Ptolemy IX Soter II or Lathyrus (chick-pea)	116–107, 88–81
Ptolemy X Alexander I	107–88
Ptolemy XI Alexander II	80
Ptolemy XII Auletes (piper) or Nothos (bastard)	80–58, 55–51
Berenice IV	58–55
Cleopatra VII	51–30
Ptolemy XIII	51–47
Ptolemy XIV	47–44
Ptolemy XV (Caesarion)	44–30

* There is no Ptolemy VII. For a time scholars thought that a young son of Ptolemy VI's had reigned briefly and accordingly numbered him as "VII." Older works such as Bevan, *House of Ptolemy*, knew nothing of this and numbered Physco as "VII," and so on. Most (though by no means all) newer works continue to number Physco as "VIII," and so on, but one is well advised to pay attention to the epithet (e.g., "Physco" or "Lathyrus") when determining whom an author means by, e.g., "Ptolemy VIII."
** Only those queens who definitely ruled in fact are listed.

Seleucid Kingdom (to the Mid-90s; Rulers not of Seleucus I's House in Italics)

Seleucus I Nicator (victor)	321 (satrap of Babylon) –280
Antiochus I Soter (savior)	280–261
Antiochus II Theos (god)	261–246
Seleucus II Callinicus (glory through victory)	246–225
Seleucus III Soter (savior)	225–223
Antiochus III Megas (great)	223–187
Seleucus IV Philopator (father-loving)	187–175
Antiochus IV Epiphanes I (manifest god)	175–164
Antiochus V Eupator (of a good father)	164–162
Demetrius I Soter	162–150
Alexander I Balas	150–145
Demetrius II Nicator	145–138, 129–126
Antiochus VI Epiphanes II	143–142
Diodotus Trypho (luxuriousness)	141–138
Antiochus VII Sidetes (from the city of Side)	138–129
Alexander II Zabinas	126
Cleopatra Thea (goddess)	125–121
Seleucus V Philometor (mother-loving)	125
Antiochus VIII Grypus (hooknose)	125–96
Antiochus IX Cyzicenus (from the city of Cyzicus)	115–95

Pergamum

Philhetaerus	281 (from Cyrupedium) –263
Eumenes I	263–241
Attalus I	241–197
Eumenes II	197–160
Attalus II	160–139
Attalus III	139–133

Glossary

Entry words are in **boldface**; within an individual entry, any word for which there is a separate entry is also in boldface. Where the student might have difficulty in finding a translation of an author's work, a reference to a translation is given whenever one exists. For the historians, the number in *Brill's New Jacoby* is given, since this reference work includes a translation. Otherwise, if the author is covered in a volume in the *Loeb* series, that reference is given by way of preference, since that volume will normally be the most easily accessible.

Academy see **Plato.**

Achaian War War between Rome and the Achaian League in 146 BC. It ended with Rome's destruction of Corinth.

acropolis Most Greek cities lay near a hill which might serve as a place of refuge in case of attack; the generic name for such a hill was "acropolis" ("high city"). The best-known is that in Athens.

Aelian Claudius Aelianus was a Roman writer of the second century AD, best known for his *Varia historia* ("Historical Miscellany"), a collection of historical anecdotes.

Aeneas the Tactician Fourth-century BC author of a tract on sieges.

Aeolians One of the three *phylai* ("tribes") into which the Greeks themselves divided themselves up (see also **Dorians** and **Ionians**). In the classical period, Aeolians dwelled in Boeotia, in eastern Thessaly, on Lesbos, and on the northwestern coast of Anatolia.

Aeolic The dialect of Greek spoken by the **Aeolians.** Since the subdialects of Aeolic (eastern Thessalian, Boeotian, Asiatic Aeolic) differ widely from each

A History of Greece: 1300 to 30 BC, First Edition. Victor Parker.
© 2014 Victor Parker. Published 2014 by John Wiley & Sons, Ltd.

other, it is not easy to characterize Aeolic, but the Greeks themselves viewed it as a distinct dialect.

Aeschines Athenian orator and politician of the fourth century. See Box 18.3.

Aeschylus One of the three great Athenian tragedians of the fifth century, he took part in the battles of Marathon and Salamis.

Agamemnon In Greek mythology, the king who led the Greeks against **Troy** in the **Trojan War**.

Agiads One of the two royal houses at Sparta. See also **Eurypontids**.

agoge The system for the education of Spartiate boys and girls. It consisted of rigorous athletic training for both sexes as well as instruction in literacy and rhetoric. The boys, for whom it lasted from age seven to thirty, received military training also.

Ahhiyawa A land mentioned in the **Hittite** texts of the 13th century BC. It lay in the far West, was reached by ship, and was probably a **Mycenaean** state, whether on an Aegean island or on the mainland. See Box 2.4.

Alcaeus Mytilenaean poet of the mid-sixth century BC. Although he is best known for his drinking songs, he also wrote political poetry. Trans.: Loeb, *Greek Lyric*, vol. I.

Alcmaeonids A wealthy and powerful aristocratic clan in Athens which produced some of the most famous Athenian politicians, including the reformer Cleisthenes (end of the sixth century) and Pericles who dominated Athenian politics in the mid-fifth century.

Alcman A Lacedaemonian poet of the late seventh century BC. His most famous poem is the elaborate *Partheneion* or "Maidens' Hymn" to be performed by Spartiate girls during a religious festival. Trans.: Loeb, *Greek Lyric*, vol. II.

Alexander Romance The most popular prose text in antiquity, edited and re-edited countless times both in Greek and in other languages such as Syriac. In existence by the third century AD, its historical utility is limited.

alphabet A script in which the signs represent individual phonemes. The Greek alphabet was unique in the ancient world in that it consistently wrote vowels in addition to consonants. See also **syllabary**.

Ammianus Marcellus Fourth-century AD historian of the Roman Empire.

amphictiony Literally "an association of those dwelling on both sides (i.e., of a landmark)." Specifically, the **Pylaean Amphictiony**.

Anaximander Sixth-century philosopher from Miletus, a successor of **Thales**. Diels–Kranz, *Vorsokratiker*, Nr. 12.

Andocides Athenian orator of the late fifth, early fourth centuries BC.

annalists Roman historians who used a year-by-year format. Owing to their partisan bias and "creativity" in making their case, they have a poor reputation overall. **Livy** commonly used them (next to **Polybius**), and their work also appears in later compilatory works such as **Appian** and **Cassius Dio**.

Antigonids The dynasty which eventually gained control of the **Hellenistic** kingdom of Macedonia.

Antiochus of Syracuse Late-fifth-century BC author of a history of the western Greeks. *BNJ* 555.

Apokletoi The standing committee of the *Boule* of the Aetolian League. It comprised at least thirty members.

Apollonius of Rhodes Third-century BC epic poet. Originally based in Alexandria, he emigrated to Rhodes where he composed an epic on the voyage of Jason and the Argonauts.

apophasis A report prepared by the **Council of the Areopagus** at the request of the **Assembly** in Athens.

Appian Second-century AD historian. His history of Rome is divided up into sections according to the Romans' wars, whether against foreign enemies (e.g., *Macedonian Wars* or *Syrian Wars*) or against each other (*Civil War*).

Arcado-Cyprian The dialect of Greek spoken in Arcadia and on Cyprus, two widely separated regions. Closely related to the **Mycenaean** dialect, it did not figure in the Greeks' own discussions of dialects.

archaic Denoting the period (roughly from 800 to 479 BC) which precedes the **classical** period.

Archidamian War The first phase of the **Peloponnesian War**, from 431 to 421 – named after the Lacedaemonian king Archidamus.

Archilochus Parian poet and soldier of the mid-seventh century BC. He emigrated from Paros to the colony of Thasos. Trans.: Loeb, *Elegy and Iambus*, vol. II.

archon A common term for an official. At Athens, one of a college of nine annually selected officials. The chief of the college was the eponymous archon who gave his name to the year. The others were the *archon basileus*, the *archon polemarchos*, and the six *thesmothetai*. The nine archons were the chief executive magistrates of Athens, but their role became increasingly ceremonial in the course of the fifth century as the office of the **generalship** gained in importance.

archon basileus The "King Archon." One of the nine **archons** at Athens, he made certain sacrifices on behalf of all Athenians.

archon polemarchos The "War Archon." One of the nine **archons** at Athens. In the year 490 BC, he (at least officially) commanded the Athenian army. In that year, when the ten tribal **generals** deadlocked, the *archon polemarchos* cast the deciding vote.

Arion of Methymna Sixth-century poet, none of whose poetry survives.

Aristobulus of Cassandreia Late-fourth-, early-third-century BC historian. **Arrian** relied heavily on his history of Alexander's expedition. *BNJ* 139.

aristocracy A constitutional form in archaic Greece whereby a clan (or group of clans) such as the **Bacchiads** or **Penthilidae** held political power.

Aristodemus Greek historian of uncertain date. *BNJ* 104.

Aristophanes The most important Athenian comic playwright of the fifth century BC.

Aristotle Important fourth-century BC philosopher. He was **Plato**'s pupil and, when he did not succeed **Plato** as leader of the latter's school, the **Academy**, he founded the **Peripatetic** school. He was the tutor of Alexander the Great.

Arrian L. Flavius Arrianus was a second-century AD Roman statesman, commander, and author from Bithynia. He wrote a history of Alexander the Great, the *Anabasis*, based principally on the works of **Ptolemy** and **Aristobulus**. Other important works include the *Indica* and the compilation of the teachings of the Stoic philosopher Epictetus.

Asclepiodotus Author of a military handbook which was in existence by the second century AD.

Asius of Samos Early-sixth-century BC poet. Trans.: Loeb, *Elegy and Iambus*, vol. I.

assembly A meeting, ideally, of all adult male citizens in a Greek state or community. It usually held the final authority to make decisions. As a general rule, an assembly made **decrees** (as distinct from **laws**).

assibilation The development of the sound /ti/ to /si/ – an important criterion for classifying Greek dialects. Conservative dialects (such as **Doric**) regularly retained original Greek /ti/; in progressive dialects (such as **Mycenaean**) it regularly became /si/ (except where /s/ preceded).

Assyria Near Eastern kingdom centered in northern Iraq. It was destroyed by the **Medes** in the late seventh century BC.

Athenaeus Highly learned second-century AD author of a work called the *Deipnosophistae*. Its chief value lies in its countless quotations from older authors' works.

Athenian Empire or **League** The First Athenian League developed from the **Delian League** after the **Persian Wars**. It was dissolved at the end of the **Peloponnesian War**. The Second Athenian League was formed in 377 BC and finally dissolved in 338 BC.

Aurelius Victor Fourth-century AD historian of the Roman Empire. The tract *De uiris illustribus* ("On famous men") is falsely attributed to him.

Autocrator Used in **Diodorus** as Alexander's title in the **League of Corinth**.

autonomy Etymologically, the condition of making and having one's own **laws**. The political concept of "autonomy" is closely linked with that of "freedom." While there was general agreement among the Greeks that, as a rule, states should be "free and autonomous," a concrete definition of the concept as well as of which states qualified for it proved elusive.

Bacchiads Aristocratic clan which ruled over Corinth in the seventh century BC before the **Cypselid** tyranny.

basileus (pl. *basileis*) The generic word for "king" in post-**Mycenaean** Greece. The Mycenaean form of the word was *gwasileus*. Many Greek states in preclassical times were governed by *basileis*, and some states such as Sparta and the Greek cities on Cyprus continued under the rule of *basileis* through the **classical** period. The term *basileus* was freely used also for the monarchs of non-Greek peoples such as the **Lydians**, **Thracians**, and **Persians**; the rulers of Macedonia were also called *basileis*, as were all the rulers of the **Hellenistic** kingdoms.

Boule A common term for a state's executive council; see also *Gerousia*. In fifth-century Athens, there were 500 members in the *Boule*, fifty for each of the ten Cleisthenic tribes (*phylai*). Both the Achaian and the Aetolian Leagues had a *Boule* in the third and second centuries BC – see **synhedrion** and **synkletos**.

Bronze Age The conventional name for the period from ca. 3000 to 1200 BC in the eastern Mediterranean world. For the division into Early, Middle, and Late Bronze Age, see the chart at the beginning of Chapter 2.

Cadmeia The **acropolis** of Thebes.

Caesar C. Julius Caesar (100–44 BC); Roman dictator, general, and author. He wrote two historical works, the *Gallic Wars* and the *Civil War*.

Callimachus Third-century BC poet who worked at Alexandria. He is best known for his erudite *Aitia* ("origins").

Callisthenes of Olynthus Greek historian of the late fourth century BC. A nephew of Aristotle's, he accompanied Alexander the Great as the expedition's official historian until he fell from grace in the early 320s. *BNJ* 124.

Carthage, Carthaginians Carthage, in modern-day Tunisia, was a colony founded by Phoenicians from Tyre in the tenth or ninth century BC. The Carthaginians founded numerous settlements in the western Mediterranean, including on Sicily, where they frequently came into conflict with the Greeks.

Cassius Dio Second- to third-century AD historian who wrote an eighty-book history of Rome. See also **Zonaras**.

Chares of Mytilene The majordomo at Alexander's court, he compiled a history of Alexander's expedition. *BNJ* 125.

Charon of Lampsacus Fifth-century BC Greek historian. *BNJ* 262.

chiliarch The Greek term for the "vizier" or second-in-command in the Persian Empire. The position still existed at the courts of Alexander and his immediate successors.

Chremonidean War A war waged in 269 or 268 BC by Athens and Sparta against Macedonia.

Cicero M. Tullius Cicero was a Roman orator, lawyer, statesman, and prolific writer (106–43 BC).

Cimmerians A non-Greek people which carried out plundering raids in Anatolia during the seventh century BC.

classical Denoting the period (roughly from 478 to 323 BC) which is traditionally viewed as the apogee of Greek civilization, hence the name.

Claudius Ptolemy Second-century AD astronomer, mathematician, and geographer. His most famous work is the *Almagest*, an astronomical tract, but his *Geographia* is an important source of geographical information about the ancient world.

Cleitarchus of Alexandria Greek historian of the mid-third century BC. His racy history of Alexander the Great was widely read in antiquity; **Curtius** relied heavily on it, and **Diodorus** produced a condensed version of it in his Book XVII. Scholars often refer to the tradition based on Cleitarchus as the **vulgate**. *BNJ* 137.

Cleomenean War A war waged by Cleomenes III of Sparta from 228 to 222 BC, initially against the Achaian League but later against Macedonia.

cleruch, cleruchy A cleruchy was an Athenian settlement abroad on land confiscated from another community and distributed in equal plots to Athenian settlers (so-called cleruchs).

colony A settlement founded abroad by a Greek community. A colony, unlike an *emporion*, was an independent, fully functioning political entity.

Common Peace see *koine eirene.*

council see *Boule* and *Gerousia.*

Council of 400 A council introduced by **Solon** in Athens. Each of the four tribes (*phylai*) then in existence selected by unknown means 100 men for service on this council. Its functions are unknown, but were probably similar to those of the later *Boule* or Council of 500.

Council of 500 see *Boule.*

Council of the Areopagus A council in Athens which consisted of all living former **archons**. It met on the Areopagus, a hill sacred to Ares, just to the west of the **Acropolis**. Before the time of **Solon**, the Council of the Areopagus probably had a role similar to that of the *Boule* in the fifth century. Until 462 it retained the "guardianship of the **laws**." It tried cases of homicide and had certain religious functions as well. In the fourth century BC, the **Assembly** began to defer to it in difficult matters.

Cratippus Greek historian who wrote a continuation of Thucydides – possibly identical with the **Oxyrhynchus Historian**. *BNJ* 64.

Cretan Hieroglyphic An undeciphered script in use on Bronze Age Crete. See also **Linear A.**

Crypteia A "secret service" in which young **Spartiate** males served; its purpose was to spy on and control **Helots**.

Ctesias Greek doctor from Cnidus who in the late fifth and early fourth centuries BC resided at the Persian court. He composed a history of **Persia**. *BNJ* 688.

Ctesicles Author of an historical work composed between the late third century BC and the second century AD. The author's name may have been "Stesicleides." *BNJ* 245.

Curtius Q. Curtius Rufus was a Roman historian, most likely of the first century AD, who wrote a history of Alexander the Great. His chief source was **Cleitarchus.**

Cypselids The dynasty of tyrants which ruled Corinth from ca. 620–550 BC ("low" chronology) or 657–584 BC (traditional "high" chronology). The tyrants were Cypselus, his son Periander, and the latter's nephew Psamettichus.

damio(u)rgos (pl. *damio(u)rgoi*) In many Greek states, the title of a magistrate; in Mantinea, the chief executive official in the **classical** period. In the Achaian League, a member of the standing committee for the *Boule.*

damos see *demos.*

Dananaeans One of the **Sea Peoples**. They settled in the later Adana in Cilicia.

Dark Age An historical period characterized by an absence or paucity of illuminating source material; in regard to Greece, the period immediately after the downfall of the **Mycenaean** palaces ca. 1200 BC and before the **archaic** period.

decarchy A college of ten officials, specifically one installed by Lysander in various Greek cities after the end of the **Peloponnesian War**. The decarchies, filled by members of the pro-Lacedaemonian faction in each city, were to govern each city in Sparta's interests.

decree An enactment by an **assembly** which an assembly could undo whenever it so chose. **Decrees**, in the event of a conflict, yielded to **laws**.

dekas A file in the Macedonian **phalanx**. Although it literally means a group of ten, it had sixteen members under Alexander the Great. One of the sixteen was its commander, the so-called *dekadarch*.

Delian League An alliance formed in the early 470s BC by the Athenians and various Greek cities in Asia Minor, on the north Aegean Coast, and on the Aegean islands. The initial purpose of the alliance was to wage war against the Persians. The Delian League soon developed into the First **Athenian League** or Athenian Empire.

Delphi The site, in Phocis, of the most important Panhellenic shrine, dedicated to Apollo. The oracle here, besides its religious and cultural importance, had political significance as well, since by tradition the oracle sanctioned many state undertakings.

demarch The official in an Athenian **deme** who presided over the deme **assembly** and kept the roll of male Athenian citizens.

deme In Greek: *demos*. The lowest level of political organization in Athens. In the city itself demes were neighborhoods; in the countryside they were villages or hamlets grouped together. Demes, according to their size, sent councillors to the *Boule*. A sufficient number of demes were grouped together to form a *trittys*.

Demetrian War A war of the 230s BC waged by Demetrius II of Macedonia against the Aetolian and Achaian Leagues.

Demochares Historian of the late fourth, early third centuries BC. *BNJ* 75.

democracy A constitutional form characterized by the use of the lot to fill offices and by monetary compensation for the holding of office.

demos (The form in **Mycenaean** (as well as in other dialects) was *damos*.) In **Mycenaean** times, the *damos* was the official name for a community within the Kingdom of **Pylos**. It retained the ownership of land classified as *ktoinai kekhesmenai*. In **classical** times, the word *demos* had many meanings: the citizens of a state; the **assembly**; the state itself. In Athens it was also the lowest level of the political organization of the state – in this sense it is conventionally anglicized as **deme**.

Demosthenes Athenian orator, lawyer, and statesman of the fourth century BC, best known for his speeches against Philip II of Macedonia, the so-called *Philippics*. His speech *De corona* ("On the Crown") was and still is regarded as the finest of the Greek orations.

Dexippus Third-century AD historian. *BNJ* 100.

Diadochi (sg. *Diadochus*) Literally "successors." The collective term for the officers who took over Alexander's empire upon his death.

Dinarchus Fourth-century BC Athenian orator.

Diodorus First-century BC compiler of a vast historical encyclopedia which covered the history of the ancient world down to his own day. Diodorus produced this encyclopedia by summarizing and abridging the works of earlier historians such as **Ephorus**, **Timaeus**, **Cleitarchus**, **Hieronymus of Cardia**, **Polybius**, and **Poseidonius**.

dioecism The reversal of a **synoecism**.

Diogenes Laertius Third-century AD author of a collection of biographies of Greek philosophers.

Dionysius of Halicarnassus First-century BC historian and rhetorician. His chief work, the *Roman Antiquities*, has much information about the Greek colonies in the West as well.

do(h)ela, do(h)elos A woman or man respectively of unfree status in **Mycenaean** Greece (cf. *eleuthera*). The later Greek forms of the words are *doule* and *doulos*.

Dorian Invasion This purely conventional term refers to the entrance into Greece of the **Dorians**, probably in the eleventh (?) and tenth centuries BC.

Dorians One of the three *phylai* into which the Greeks themselves divided themselves up (see also **Aeolians** and **Ionians**). The Dorians themselves were originally divided up into three *phylai* (in the canonical order: **Hylleis**, **Dymanes**, and **Pamphyli**) which in the late **archaic** and **classical** periods were mostly being renamed or replaced. In classical times, Dorians dwelled in the southern and eastern Peloponnese, on Crete, on the southern Cyclades, on the Dodecanese, and on the southwestern coast of Anatolia.

Doric The dialect of Greek spoken by the **Dorians**. It is most noticeably distinguished both from **Mycenaean** and **Ionic** by a general absence of **assibilation** and from **Ionic** additionally by the retention of the sound /ā/.

drachma The basic coin in Greece. There were six **obols** to the **drachma**. As to the value of the coin, money is worth what money will buy. In the mid-sixth century BC in Athens, one **drachma** apparently bought a bushel of grain. In mid-fifth century BC Athens, two **obols** were a standard daily wage. About a generation later, at the start of the Peloponnesian War (431–404 BC) three **obols** were a standard daily wage.

Duris of Samos Late-fourth-, early-third-century BC Greek historian. *BNJ* 76.

Dymanes see **Dorians**.

Early Helladics An archaeologically attested culture in Greece during the periods Early Helladic I and II (see chart at beginning of Chapter 2).

Egypt Kingdom lying along the River Nile in northern Africa, often controlling much of Palestine. The Persian king Cambyses conquered Egypt in the 520s, but it frequently revolted from the **Persian Empire**. Alexander the Great incorporated it into his empire in 332 and 331 BC. After his death in 323 BC, the satrap of Egypt, **Ptolemy**, made Egypt an independent kingdom once again (albeit under a Greco-Macedonian dynasty). In 30 BC his descendant Cleopatra VII died, and Egypt became a Roman province.

ekklesia see **assembly.**

Eleusinian Mysteries A "mystery" cult was one in which only those who had been initiated into it could take part. The Eleusinian Mysteries, celebrated in the town of Eleusis, were the most important annual festival of the Athenians, almost all of whom were initiated into this cult.

eleuthera, eleutheros A woman or man respectively of free status in **Mycenaean** Greece (cf. ***do(h)ela, do(h)elos***).

Elymians A non-Greek people in northwestern Sicily.

emporion A trading-post abroad at which Greeks resided on a continuing basis, but which, unlike a **colony**, was never a politically independent community.

engyesis Betrothal. The *engyesis*-contract recorded how a woman's legal guardian (usually her father) handed over a dowry to her groom. The bride retained legal ownership of the dowry, the groom gained possession. As long as he had possession, he was legally obligated to support her. Upon her death, her heirs (usually her and her husband's sons) inherited the dowry.

Enneakrounos The "nine heads (or spouts)" – the name of Athens' main public fountainhouse, built by the **Peisistratids**.

ephor One of a college of five annual officials at Sparta. By the fifth century BC, the ephors were the chief executive magistrates of Lacedaemon. The chief ephor gave his name to the year.

Ephorus of Cyme Fourth-century BC historian who wrote a thirty-volume history of the Greek world from the time of the **Dorian Invasion** to 340 BC. The sections on Greece and the East in **Diodorus**, XI–XVI 76 are taken from Ephorus. *BNJ* 70.

epibatai (sg. *epibates*) Infantrymen who served above deck on a **trireme**.

epic Strictly speaking, poetry composed in dactylic hexameters; specifically the two long poems, ***Iliad*** and ***Odyssey***, conventionally attributed to "**Homer.**"

Epimeletai A college of officials at Mantinea, responsible for recording the names of newly enrolled citizens.

episkopos (pl. *episkopoi*) An Athenian official during the time of the First **Athenian League**. The *episkopoi* helped supervise the League's members.

epitome A "condensed" or abridged version of a longer book.

Eteocretans A non-Greek people living on Crete during the **classical** period.

Eteocyprians A people living on Cyprus who were neither Greek nor Phoenician. The chief Eteocyprian town was Amathus.

ethnos (pl. *ethne*) A people or tribe; a specific form of state in the Greek world – the "tribe-state" or "league." In the latter sense its counterpart in the Greek world was the ***polis*** (see Box 4.1). Although of little importance during the fifth century, *ethne* gain in importance during the fourth. In the third and second centuries two large *ethne*, the Achaian and the Aetolian Leagues dominate Greece. *Ethne* are frequently termed "leagues" or "federal leagues" or "federal states."

Etruscans A people in central Italy. Their league of twelve cities dominated central Italy before the rise of Rome. In the seventh to fifth centuries BC they occasionally came into conflict with Greek colonists in the area.

Euripides One of the three great Athenian tragedians of the late fifth century.

Eurypontids One of the two royal houses at Sparta. See also **Agiads**.

Eusebius Late-third-, early-fourth-century AD Christian historian and theologian. In regard to Greek history, his most important work is the *Chronicon*.

federal league, federal state see *ethnos*.

Frontinus First-century AD author of a collection of military strategems.

gazophylakion In the **Seleucid** Kingdom, the technical term for the treasury in the physical sense, the vault. The first element (*gaz-*) is Persian, the second element (*phylakion*, "guard-house") is Greek.

Gellius Second-century AD author of a compilatory work, the *Attic Nights*. Its chief value consists in its many quotations from older authors.

general, generalship (Greek: *strategos*, *strategeia*.) Generally a military command, but often enough a high political office. In **classical** Athens, ten generals were elected, initially by each of the ten tribes (*phylai*) separately, but eventually by the voting population at large. These generals eventually displaced the **archons** as the most important officials. In both the Achaian and Aetolian Leagues, the highest political official bore the title *strategos*. In the Seleucid Kingdom, the **satrap** was usually called a *strategos* in Greek.

Geometric Denoting a type of pottery (named after the geometric motifs used to decorate it) prevalent in Greece in the ninth and eighth centuries BC.

Geomori On Samos, the governing **aristocracy** before Aeaces I established a tyranny there in the sixth century.

Gerousia Literally "council of elders." A common term for a state's executive council – see also **Boule**. In Sparta, the *Gerousia* consisted of thirty members, two of whom were the kings (see also *basileus*).

graphe, graphe paranomon A *graphe* was a motion in the Athenian **Assembly**. A motion which ran contrary to a **law** was a *graphe paranomon*. Moving such a motion exposed the mover to prosecution.

Great Rhetra The Great Rhetra at Sparta was a constitutional text, probably from the late eighth century, which among other things regulated the membership of the **Gerousia** as well as meetings of the **Assembly**.

gwasileus (pl. *gwasilewes*) A functionary in the Kingdom of Pylos; the form of the word in classical Greek is *basileus*.

harmost A governor appointed by the Lacedaemonians to oversee a community, especially in the period after the **Peloponnesian War**.

Hecataeus of Miletus Greek genealogist and geographer of the late sixth and early fifth centuries BC. *BNJ* 1.

hegemon A generic word for a military commander. Used for Philip II's position as leader of the League of Corinth.

hegemony Greek historians' word for one state's predominant military position either in a region ("hegemony of the Peloponnese") or in a particular sphere ("hegemony by land").

Hellanicus of Lesbos Greek historian and mythographer of the late fifth century BC. *BNJ* 4.

Hellenica Oxyrhynchia An anonymous historical work preserved on papyrus fragments found in the Egyptian village of Oxyrhynchus. This work proved to be a continuation of **Thucydides** and ran from 411 to 386 BC. *BNJ* 66.

Hellenistic The conventional name denoting the period after the death of Alexander the Great (323 BC) down to the death of Cleopatra VII (30 BC).

Hellenize, Hellenization "To Hellenize" is to make, act, or become in some respect Greek. The process by which non-Greeks become Greek is "Hellenization."

Hellenotamiai The treasurers of the **Delian League**/First **Athenian League**. They were always Athenians.

Helots The third and lowest of the three main tiers of **Lacedaemonian** society. See also **Perioeci** and **Spartiates**. The Helots counted as between free and slave. Helots who had become free against future military service were *Neodamodeis*; those who passed through the *agoge* became *Mothakes*.

herm A stylized statue of the god Hermes in Athens.

hero In Greek religion, an immortal who might receive offerings, but who ranked below the gods proper. Some mortals (e.g., **oecists**) became heroes upon death.

Herodotus Traditionally called the "father of history," he wrote the oldest fully surviving Greek work of history in the second half of the fifth century BC.

Hieronymus A.k.a. St. Jerome. A prolific Christian historian, theologian, and translator of the fourth century AD.

Hieronymus of Cardia Late fourth, early third centuries BC. Greek historian who wrote a history of the **Diadochi**. Books XVIII–XXII of **Diodorus** were taken from him. *BNJ* 154.

Hippeis (sg. *Hippeus*) Literally "Horsemen," this word commonly denoted a social class (e.g., at Eretria), as the horse was a status symbol that only the wealthy could afford. It could also denote a college of officials (e.g., at Sparta or on Crete). In Athens, the **Hippeis** were the second highest census class from the time of **Solon** onwards; they held property valued at between 500 and 300 bushels of grain. After the introduction of coinage, it was between 500 and 300 **drachmas**.

Hippias of Elis Philosopher of the late fifth, early fourth centuries BC. *BNJ* 6.

Hippias of Erythrae Greek historian of uncertain date, but definitely earlier than the second century AD. *BNJ* 421.

Hittites A people in central Anatolia during the Bronze Age. They left behind extensive records in several (mostly cuneiform) languages. Their kingdom was destroyed ca. 1200 BC.

Hollow Syria Phoenicia and Palestine – in older textbooks commonly called "Coele Syria."

Homer In Greek tradition, a blind poet who composed the *Iliad* and the *Odyssey*. He is highly unlikely to have been a genuinely historical person.

hoplite The standard Greek heavily armed infantryman. See Box 10.1.

Hylleis see **Dorians.**

Hypereides Fourth-century BC Athenian orator.

hypomeiones (sg. *hypomeion*) Men who were born of **Spartiate** parents and had passed through the *agoge*, but were not members of a *syssition* whether through lapse of membership or failure to gain admission. *Hypomeiones* had no political rights.

Ibycus of Rhegium Poet of the sixth century BC. Trans.: Loeb, *Elegy and Iambus*, vol. I.

Iliad An epic poem, traditionally attributed to **Homer**. The *Iliad* deals with an episode during the tenth year of the **Trojan War** (see also *Odyssey*).

Ion of Chios Fifth-century Greek poet and philosopher.

Ionian Revolt Despite the name, a revolt of all Greek cities in Asia Minor against the **Persian Empire** (from 499 to 494). The Carians as well as many Cyprians, both Greek and Phoenician, joined the revolt.

Ionians One of the three *phylai* into which the Greeks themselves divided themselves up (see also **Aeolians** and **Dorians**). The Ionians in classical times dwelled in Athens, on Euboea, on the Cyclades, and on the central western coast of Anatolia including the islands just off the coast.

Ionic The dialect of Greek spoken by the **Ionians**. It is most noticeably distinguished from other Greek dialects by the development of the sound /ā/ to /ē/.

Isaeus Fourth-century BC Athenian orator.

Isocrates Prolific Athenian orator and pamphleteer (436–338 BC).

Isodore of Charax Geographer, probably of the first century BC; author of the tract *Parthian Stations*, a description of the road from Zeugma to Alexandria in Arachosia. *BNJ* 781.

Isthmian Games One of the four Panhellenic festivals, dedicated to Poseidon and celebrated on the (Corinthian part of the) Isthmus. They took place every other year, in an **Olympic** year and then again two years later.

John Chrysostomus Fifth-century AD patriarch of Constantinople.

Josephus Joseph bar Matthias, a.k.a. T. Flavius Josephus, wrote two major works in the first century AD, the *Jewish Antiquities* and the *Wars of the Jews*, on the history of the Jewish people.

juror, jury In Athens, trials were decided by juries consisting of 201, 501, 1001, etc. jurors, based on the importance of the case. (The odd number guaranteed that there would be no tie; there was no "judge" in the modern sense at an Athenian trial.) The jurors were drawn from those who had entered their names on the jury-rolls; if there were more than 6,000 names on the rolls, then the lot was used to select the required jurors.

Justin M. Junianius Justinus in the fourth century AD produced an **epitome** of the *Philippic History* of Pompeius **Trogus**.

king see *basileus*.

King Archon see *archon basileus*.

Knosos   In the **Bronze Age**, this Cretan city was a center of the **Minoan** civilization and later the chief city of a **Mycenaean** kingdom.

koine eirene   A "common peace" – a multilateral peace treaty, ideally encompassing all of Greece; specifically any of the various multilateral peace treaties sworn in Greece starting with the King's Peace of 386 BC.

ktitas (pl. *ktitai*)   In the **Bronze Age** Kingdom of **Pylos**, a *ktitas* was probably the owner of a *ktoina ktimena*. As such he was obligated to military service. A *metaktitas* was in some sense a dependent of a *ktitas*.

ktoina (ktoina ktimena, ktoina kekhesmena) (pl. *ktoinai*)   A plot of land in **Mycenaean** Greece. In the Kingdom of **Pylos** individuals could own *ktoinai ktimenai*, whereas individuals could merely lease *ktoinai kekhesmenai* to which the *damos* retained title. Both types of plot were under cultivation in the kingdom's final year.

Lamian War   A war waged by Athens against Macedonia in 323 and 322 BC.

Laodiceian War see **Third Syrian War.**

law   An ordinance made by a **lawgiver** or lawgiving college such as the **Nomothetai** in Athens. Unlike a **decree**, a **law** was, in theory, permanent and in the event of any conflict overruled a **decree** made by an **Assembly**. An **Assembly** could not overrule or abolish a **law**; only another **lawgiver** or duly authorized lawgiving college could do that.

lawagetas   The second highest official in the Bronze Age Kingdom of Pylos. His title means "leader of the army."

lawgiver   A man duly authorized by a Greek state to make **laws**. Once he had received this authority he could make whatever **laws** he found fitting. **Solon** is the best-known of the ancient Greek lawgivers.

league, league-state see *ethnos*.

League of Corinth   In 338 BC, Philip II forced all the Greeks in mainland Greece to join this military alliance of which he became the leader or *hegemon*.

Lefkandi   An important **Dark Age** archaeological site on Euboea.

Lelantine War   A war waged by the Euboean cities of Chalcis and Eretria over the Lelantine Plain. It lasted, off and on, from the late eighth to the mid-seventh century.

Linear A   An undeciphered script in use on **Bronze Age** Crete. See also **Cretan Hieroglyphic** and **Linear B.**

Linear B   A syllabary, developed from **Linear A** and used by the **Mycenaeans** for writing Greek in the Late Bronze Age.

Livy   T. Livius was a Roman historian of the first century BC. For his treatment of **Hellenistic** history, Livy depended heavily on **Polybius of Megalopolis**, but also on the **Annalists**. The loss of many books of Livy's history is mitigated by the so-called *Periochae* (summaries of individual books), one **epitome** (Florus), and several other works so heavily based on Livy as to be effective **epitomes** (Eutropius, Festus, Orosius; cf. also Obsequens).

Lucian of Samosata Prolific second-century AD essayist who despite his Syrian origins wrote in Greek.

Lycurgus Fourth-century BC Athenian statesman and orator.

Lydia A kingdom in western Anatolia which Cyrus the Great conquered for the **Persian Empire** in 546 BC. The last five Lydian kings were Gyges, Ardys, Sadyattes, Alyattes, and Croesus. Croesus was famous for his wealth; under him, the Lydian kingdom reached its greatest extent encompassing all of western Asia Minor with the exception of Lycia.

lyric In the narrower sense, poetry composed in a tripartite stanzaic form and in certain meters. The best-known examples are the victory odes of **Pindar** and the choral passages in tragedy.

Lysias Athenian orator in the late fifth and early fourth centuries BC.

Macedonian War The name for any of four wars waged by the Romans against the Macedonians: the first from 214 to 206 BC, the second from 200 to 197, the third from 171 to 168, the fourth in 148 BC.

Malalas Sixth-century AD Greek historian.

maniple A unit within a Roman legion. A Roman legion of 3,000 men was divided up into three lines: at the front the *hastati*; then the *principes*; and at the back the *triarii*. There were ten maniples in each line; those of the first two consisted of 120 men, those of the third of 60. The maniples of the three lines were staggered (like three rows of bricks in a wall).

Medes, Media The Medes were an Iranian people living in what is now north-western Iran. The Median Empire arose in the late seventh century BC and eventually extended as far as Parthia in the east and as far as the Halys River in Asia Minor to the west. Cyrus the Great, a Persian vassal of the last Median king, Astyages, successfully revolted in 550 BC; and the Median Empire became the **Persian Empire**.

megaron The central hall in a **Mycenaean** palace during the **Bronze Age**. See Figure 2.7.

Megasthenes Third-century BC Greek historian who led a diplomatic mission to India and wrote a book about that land. *BNJ* 715.

Memnon First-century BC Greek historian who wrote a history of his hometown Heracleia Pontica. *BNJ* 434.

Messenian War This name is applied to either of two wars in the course of which the Lacedaemonians conquered Messenia. First Messenian War: ca. 690–670 BC; Second Messenian War: ca. 630–600.

metaktitas see *ktitas*.

Minoan The name (after the mythological king Minos) conventionally given to the **Bronze Age** civilization which flourished on Crete before the **Mycenaeans** conquered that island in the Late **Bronze Age**.

Mithridatic War The name applied to any of three wars waged by Rome against Mithridates VI of Pontus: the first from 88 to 84 BC, the second from 83 to 82, the third from 74 to 65.

Mothakes (sg. *Mothax*) **Helots** who had passed through the *agoge*, normally as companions to boys of **Spartiate** parents.

mother-city The city which founded a **colony**. Mother-city and **colony** ideally maintained friendly relations; a **colony** might expect aid from its mother-city in time of need, and a **colony** owed its mother-city deference and respect.

Mycenaean The name (after the site **Mycene**) conventionally given to Late **Bronze Age** Greek civilization. Linguistically, "Mycenaean" refers to the dialect of Greek written in the **Linear B** tablets.

Mycene A city on the Peloponnese; an important **Bronze Age** archaeological site where a **Linear B** archive was found. In some versions of Greek myths, **Agamemenon** reigns in Mycene.

Myron of Priene Third-century BC author of a history of Messenia. *BNJ* 106.

Nearchus of Crete An officer of Alexander's, he commanded Alexander's fleet which sailed from the Indus into the Persian Gulf. He later wrote a book about his experiences on which **Arrian** relied heavily in the latter part of the *Anabasis* and in the *Indica*. *BNJ* 133.

Nemean Games One of the four Panhellenic festivals, dedicated to Zeus of Nemea. The Nemean Games took place every two years, in the year immediately after and again in the year immediately before the **Olympic Games**.

Neo-Babylonian Kingdom Based on Babylon, in the sixth century BC it extended from the Persian Gulf, along the Rivers Euphrates and Tigris, across Syria to the Mediterranean and down into Phoenicia and Palestine. It also controlled Cyprus. Cyrus the Great conquered it for the **Persian Empire** in 539 BC.

Neodamodeis Former **Helots** who had obtained freedom in exchange for future military service. *Neodamodeis* appear in the late fifth century BC, and become prominent in Lacedaemonian armies during the fourth.

Nepos Cornelius Nepos was a first-century BC Roman biographer. He relied heavily on **Ephorus**.

Nicolaus of Damascus First-century BC court historian of Herod the Great in Judea. He relied heavily on **Ephorus**. *BNJ* 90.

Nomophylaces Officials charged with enforcement of **laws** in Athens under Demetrius of Phalerum in the late fourth century BC.

Nomothetai In Athens from the early fourth century BC onwards, a lawgiving commission. If the Athenian **Assembly** deemed a **law** needful of revision, then it arranged for the selection of *Nomothetai* from those who had entered their names on the **jury**-rolls. The *Nomothetai* then conducted a formal jury-trial of the old **law** with the proposer of the new **law** acting as the plaintiff; specially appointed officials called *Syndikoi* defended the old **law**.

obe In Sparta, a geographically based division of the people. Six obes are known. The obes coexisted with the three traditional **Dorian** *phylai*, Hylleis, Dymanes, and **Pamphyli**.

obol see **drachma**.

Odyssey An epic poem traditionally attributed to a blind poet called **Homer**. The *Odyssey* deals with Odysseus' return home from the **Trojan War**.

oecist The man who led colonists from their **mother-city** out to the colony and settled it. In the earlier period, the oecist remained in the colony until his death, after which the colonists honored him as a **hero**.

Old Oligarch The conventional term for the oligarchic author of an anonymous fifth-century BC tract on the Athenian constitution. The tract is conventionally, though falsely, attributed to **Xenophon** and printed with his works.

oligarchy A constitutional form characterized by the restriction of political rights to a select group of male citizens (e.g., to a specified number or to those who possessed a specified amount of wealth), by the use of election to fill office, and by the absence of pay for holding office.

Olympic Games The most important of the four Panhellenic festivals, dedicated to Olympian Zeus. The festival took place in Elis every four years. A list of victors in the footrace was preserved and published in the late fifth or early fourth century BC by the philosopher **Hippias of Elis**. The earliest entry is for the year 776 BC, traditionally held to be the date of the first Olympic Games.

Onesicritus of Astypalaea An experienced sailor, he functioned as chief helmsman in Alexander's fleet under **Nearchus'** command. He later wrote a history of Alexander's expedition. *BNJ* 134.

orientalizing Denoting a type of Greek pottery (named after the "oriental" motifs, such as lions, used to decorate it) from the eighth century BC.

orkha (pl. *orkhai*) In the military of the Kingdom of **Pylos**, one of ten groups of troops assigned to a watch along the coast.

Orthagorids A family of tyrants which ruled Sicyon for a hundred years (ca. 650–550 on the "high", ca. 610–510 on the "low" chronology). The founder of the line was Orthagoras; the best-known tyrant was Cleisthenes (early sixth century).

ostracism Annual vote in **classical** Athens to banish a politician for ten years without loss of citizenship. A "ballot" was a pottery sherd (*ostrakon*), hence the name.

ostrakon see *ostracism*.

Oxyrhynchus Historian see **Hellenica Oxyrhynchia**.

Palaistine, Palaistinoi In Greek, the Philistines, one of the **Sea Peoples**, were called *Palaistinoi*. In the eleventh century BC, the *Palaistinoi* settled in Palestine (Greek: *Palaistine*) which the Greeks named after them.

Pamphyli One of the three *phylai* (the third in the canonical order) into which the **Dorians** were originally divided up. Etymologically, it means "people from all (manner of) *phlyai*" – i.e., initially it was a sort of collective appellation for people who had initially belonged to other *phylai*.

Panathenaean Games The chief festival at Athens, dedicated to the goddess Athena. The "Greater Panathenaea" took place every four years in the second year of an Olympiad. The "Lesser Panathenaea" were an annual festival.

Pausanias Second-century AD author of a tourist's guide to Greece. The work is invaluable for identifying Greek villages as well as structures within excavated cities. Since Pausanias included brief historical accounts of the cities and regions which he was describing, he occasionally preserves information not attested elsewhere.

Peisistratids The family of tyrants which ruled in Athens from the 560s to 511 BC. The two rulers were Peisistratus and his son Hippias.

Peloponnesian League A network of military alliances commanded by Sparta, it arose in the mid-sixth century. In Greek, it was referred to as "the Lacedaemonians and their allies."

Peloponnesian War A major war between Athens and Sparta which began in 431 BC and did not end until 404 BC.

Pentacosiomedimni (sg. *Pentacosiomedimnus*) Literally "500-Bushel-Men." The highest census class in Athens from the time of **Solon** onwards. They held property valued at 500 bushels of grain or higher; after the introduction of coinage, the amount was 500 **drachmas** or higher.

Pentecontaetia A period of fifty years – specifically the period between the **Persian War** (480–479) and the **Peloponnesian War** (431–404) even it is not quite fifty years long.

Penthilidae Aristocratic clan which ruled in Mytilene before various tyrants seized power in the sixth century BC.

Perioeci (sg. *perioecus*) Etymologically: "dwellers about." In Sparta the second of the three main tiers of Lacedaemonian society. The Perioeci were free, but had no political rights. Cf. **Helots** and **Spartiates**. In Thessaly, the *perioeci* were peoples living around Thessaly who were subject to the Thessalians – the Phthiotic Achaians, the Perrhaebians, and the Magnesians.

Peripatetic see **Aristotle.**

periplus "Circumnavigation, sailing around." Specifically, a sailing around the Peloponnese.

Persia, Persian Empire Founded by Cyrus the Great in 550 BC, the Persian Empire at its height extended from central Greece in the West to the Indus River in the East. It incorporated all the territory of older kingdoms such as **Lydia, Media,** the **Neo-Babylonian** kingdom, and (during certain periods) **Egypt.** Alexander the Great conquered the Persian Empire in the 330s, though as a political and administrative entity it survived largely intact in the **Seleucid** kingdom.

Persian War(s) In the narrowest sense, Xerxes' invasion of Persia and its repulse (480–479 BC). Occasionally, the Marathon campaign of 490 BC as well as operations after 479 BC are included in the term.

phalanx A densely packed military formation with the individual infantrymen arranged in ranks and files. Both **hoplites** and *sarissophoroi* fought in this type of formation.

Philaids A prominent aristocratic clan in Athens; Miltiades the Elder, Miltiades the Younger (whose plan led the Athenians to victory at Marathon in 490 BC), and Cimon were prominent members.

Philistines see **Palaistine.**

Philochorus Late-fourth-, early-third-century BC Athenian historian. *BNJ* 328.

Phocian War Also called the Third **Sacred War**. This war (355–346 BC) pitted the Phocians against the rest of the **Pylaean Amphictiony**; in the end Philip II of Macedonia defeated the Phocians.

Phoenicides Third-century BC comic playwright.

phoros A "tribute" – a tax paid by a dependent community (e.g., by a member of the First **Athenian League** to Athens, or by a Greek city to a foreign power such as **Lydia** or **Persia**).

phratry In Athens, a traditional clan association. An Athenian boy was accepted by vote into his father's phratry – the clan's vote to accept proved the boy's legitimacy. This took place before the boy was enrolled in his father's **deme** at age 18.

phyle (pl. *phylai*). A subdivision of a group of people such as the inhabitants of a state – in general, a "tribe." A Greek state was generally divided up into *phylai*. In fifth-century Athens, there were ten such *phylai*. The word was also applied to the three main groups into which the Greeks themselves divided themselves up (**Aeolians**, **Dorians**, and **Ionians**) as well as to the three groups into which the **Dorians** themselves were divided up.

Pindar Lyric poet of the fifth century BC. He is best known for elaborate odes which the victors in contests at athletic festivals such as the **Olympic Games** commissioned.

Plato Important philosopher of the fourth century BC, a pupil of Socrates. His most famous work was the *Republic*, an extended disquisition on the ideal state. His most famous pupil was **Aristotle** who, however, did not succeed him as leader of the school which he had founded, the Academy. See Box 17.2.

Pliny the Elder First-century AD writer. He died in the eruption of Mt. Vesuvius in A.D. 79.

Plutarch Second-century AD Greek biographer and essayist. His works are grouped into two main collections, the *Lives* and the so-called *Moralia*, a diverse body of argumentative tracts, erudite disquisitions, and compendia of trivia.

polis (pl. *poleis*) A city in the physical sense; a specific form of state in the Greek world – the "city-state" (its counterpart in this sense was the *ethnos* – see Box 4.1); or, loosely, just "state."

Pollux Second-century AD philosopher and lexicographer.

Polyaenus Second-century AD author of a collection of military stratagems, largely collected from earlier Greek authors, especially **Ephorus**.

Polybius of Megalopolis Greek historian of the second century BC. His *History* chronicled the rise of Rome and the decline of the **Hellenistic** world in the third and second centuries BC. Books XXIII–XXXII of **Diodorus** are taken from Polybius.

Porphyry Third-century AD philosopher and historian. The historical fragments are collected at *BNJ* 260.

Poseidonius of Apameia First-century BC Greek historian. **Diodorus**, Books XXXIII–XXXVIII/XXXIX are based on him. *BNJ* 87.

proskynesis Prostration; in Greek and Macedonian culture, this gesture was performed before gods only; in the **Persian Empire**, it was a polite gesture routinely performed before a social superior and in particular before the king.

prytany One of the ten periods into which the Athenian official year was divided in the **classical** period. During the year each of the ten tribes (*phylai*) held a prytany when the fifty men of that tribe (*phyle*) who were currently on the **Boule** were in session.

Ptolemaic, Ptolemies The Kingdom of Egypt in **Hellenistic** times is commonly called "Ptolemaic Egypt"; its rulers are collectively the "Ptolemies," as all the male rulers bore the name Ptolemy.

Ptolemy I Soter An officer under Alexander the Great, he became satrap of Egypt in 323 BC and founded the **Ptolemaic** dynasty there. He also wrote a history of Alexander the Great; *BNJ* 138.

Punic War The name applied to any of three wars waged by Rome against **Carthage**. First Punic War: 264–241 BC; Second Punic War: 220–201; Third Punic War: 149–146.

Pylaean Amphictiony An **amphictiony** consisting of twelve *ethne* dwelling on both sides of the pass at Thermopylae (see chap. 18). Originally based on the sanctuary of Demeter at Anthela, since it later administered the sanctuary at Delphi also, it is sometimes known as the Delphic Amphictiony.

Pylos In the Late **Bronze Age** this city was the center of a kingdom conventionally named after it.

Pythian Games One of the four Panhellenic festivals, dedicated to Apollo at Delphi (Apollo's special name at Delphi was Pytho). The Pythian Games were quadrennial and took place two years before (or after) the **Olympic Games**.

quadrireme see **trireme**.

quinquireme see **trireme**.

sacred war A war fought on behalf of a sanctuary or temple. Specifically, any of the four wars fought in relation to the sanctuary at Delphi: First Sacred War: early sixth century BC; Second Sacred War: mid-fifth century BC; Third Sacred War (a.k.a. the **Phocian War**): 355–346 BC; Fourth Sacred War: 339–338 BC.

Sallust Roman politician and historian (86–35 BC), best known for two small tracts that survive intact, the *Conspiracy of Catiline* and the *Jugurthine War*.

Samnite Wars Three wars waged by the Romans, from the mid-fourth to the early third centuries BC, against the Samnites, a people of southern Italy.

Sappho Mytilenaean poet of the mid-sixth century BC. She is best known for her highly personal love poetry which heavily influenced later poets. Trans.: Loeb, *Greek Lyric*, vol. I.

sarissa, sarissophoros (pl. *sarissai* and *sarissophoroi* respectively) The *sarissa* was a fifteen-foot thrusting spear used in a Macedonian **phalanx**. Those who wielded it were *sarissophoroi*. By the mid-second century, the length of the *sarissa* had grown to about 20 feet.

satrap The **Persian Empire** was divided up into some twenty satrapies, each under the rule of a satrap. The satrap was the chief military, political, financial, and judicial officer in the **satrapy**. On a day-to-day basis, he was largely independent of any centralized control. Under Alexander the Great the satraps lost some power, but under both him and the **Diadochi** satrapies continued to exist. The Seleucid Kingdom was still divided up into satrapies, though the satrap was then usually called a *strategos* (see **general**).

Satyrus Third-century BC Greek historian.

Scythians A non-Greek people living to the North of the Black Sea.

Sea Peoples The purely conventional name given to a number of migratory peoples ca. 1200 BC. The name is based on a description of the Ekwesh in an Egyptian text of the pharoah Merneptah (Breasted, III, Nr. 588) even if the Ekwesh are not among the migratory peoples listed by the pharaoh Ramses III (ANET, p. 262). Although the Ekwesh practiced circumcision (a custom unknown among the Greeks), some scholars have identified them as Greeks on the basis of "kling-klang" etymology.

Seleucid, Seleucids The **Hellenistic** kingdom which, geographically at least, replaced the Persian Empire, is usually called the "Seleucid Kingdom." Its rulers, descended from Seleucus I Nicator, are collectively called the "Seleucids."

Shaft Graves Burial sites (from the Middle Helladic III and Late Helladic I periods) at **Mycene**. The goods deposited in these graves were exceptionally rich.

Shekelesh One of the so-called **Sea Peoples** mentioned by the pharaoh Ramses III (ANET, p. 262). The Egyptians commonly hired them as mercenaries in the thirteenth century BC, and some of them must have joined the genuinely migratory peoples with whom Ramses III groups them. The connection of the Shekelesh with Sicily is based on "kling-klang" etymology.

Shikalaeans One of the so-called **sea peoples** who invaded Egypt at the end of the **Bronze Age** – see Box 3.1.

Sicanians A non-Greek people on Sicily, eventually forced into the interior by Greek colonists.

Sicels A non-Greek people on Sicily, eventually forced into the interior by Greek colonists. The island came to take its name from them.

Social War Literally "allies' war." The term is applied to two wars in Greek history (in the 350s and in the 210s BC) and to one in Roman History (91–88 BC).

Socrates An Athenian philosopher of the late fifth and early fourth centuries BC. Although he himself left behind no writings, his pupils, **Plato** and **Xenophon**, did.

Solon Athenian statesman and **lawgiver** of the first half of the sixth century BC. He composed numerous poems, many political. Trans.: Loeb, *Elegy and Iambus*, vol. I.

Sophocles One of the three great Athenian tragedians of the fifth century BC.

Spartiates The highest of the three main tiers of Lacedaemonian society. The Spartiates alone had political rights. See also **Helots** and **Perioeci**. There were two prerequisites for being a (male) Spartiate: passage through the *agoge* and membership in a *syssition*. If a Spartiate's membership in a *syssition* lapsed, he lost his political rights and became a *hypomeion*.

Stephanus of Byzantium Sixth-century AD Greek grammarian and compiler of a geographical dictionary.

Stesicleides see **Ctesicles**.

Strabo Late-first-century BC, early-first-century AD geographer. Strabo's long work, the *Geographica*, is not only indispensable for ancient geography, but is useful historically as well since it contains long extracts from historians.

strategos see **general**.

Suetonius C. Suetonius Tranquillus was a second-century AD Roman biographer.

suffetes The two annual chief executive magistrates at Carthage (see **Livy**, XXVIII 37 and XXX 7; also **Aristotle**, *Pol.* 1272b, who calls them "kings"); etymologically, the word is the same as the Hebrew word conventionally translated as "judges" in the Old Testament.

Suidas On the basis of a misunderstanding, an enormous Greek lexicon of the tenth century AD was until recently attributed to this non-existent author. It is now known that the lexicon's title is "Suda," which probably means "stronghold." Both ways of citing the work – "Suda" and "Suidas" – are in common usage.

syllabary A script in which the signs represent syllables (e.g., *da, de, di, do, du*) instead of individual phonemes (e.g., *b, d, g*). Cf. **alphabet**.

sympolity A political union of two (or more) states such that there is no physical relocation of the any state's citizens, all of whom continue to live in their old cities as before. Cf. **synoecism**.

Synarchiai The members of the standing committee of the *Boule* of the Achaian League.

Syndikoi see *Nomothetai*.

Synhedrion The name for the *Boule* in the Aetolian League.

Synkletos The name for the *Boule* in the Achaian League.

synoecism The process whereby people living in two or more communities come to live together in one larger settlement. This larger settlement may be, but need not be, a fully new foundation (for example, in the case of two cities, the inhabitants of the smaller one might simply move to the larger).

syntaxis A notionally voluntary payment which usually tended to be obligatory in fact. Unlike a *phoros*, a *syntaxis* did not of itself imply the dependent status of the community paying it.

Syrian War Any of six wars fought between the **Seleucids** and the **Ptolemies**. First Syrian War: mid-270s BC; Second Syrian War: mid-250s BC; Third Syrian War (also called the Laodiceian War): 245 BC; Fourth Syrian War: 219–217 BC; Fifth Syrian War: 201–198 BC; Sixth Syrian War: 170–168 BC.

syssition At Sparta, a communal mess or dining club at which a male **Spartiate** took his meals. A *syssition* in the **classical** period had about fifteen members; their unanimous approbation in a secret ballot was required by a prospective new member. Members paid dues out of which the meals were financed. Failure to pay the dues resulted in the lapse of one's membership. See also *hypomeion.*

Tacitus P. Cornelius Tacitus was a late-first- to second-century AD Roman historian; his chief works are the *Annals* and the *Histories.*

tagos The specific term among the Thessalians for their elective *basileus.*

temenos A plot of land which in Mycenaean times the *damos* awarded to the *wanax* and the *lawagetas.* In the *Iliad,* a community can award a *temenos* to a king or other benefactor.

tetrad Any one of the four "quarters" into which Thessaly was traditionally divided; each tetrad stood under a **tetrarch**.

tetrarch A tetrarch was an official or ruler who governed a region which was a "quarter" of a larger region – see **tetrad**. In Judea under Roman rule, some regions were at various times called tetrarchies.

thalassocracy A sea-borne empire such as the Cretans had in Greek mythology.

Thales Sixth-century philosopher from Miletus. Diels–Kranz, *Vorsokratiker,* Nr. 11.

Thebes In the **Bronze Age,** this city was the center of a kingdom conventionally named after it; a **Linear B** archive existed there.

Theocritus of Syracuse Third-century BC poet at the court of Ptolemy II Philadelphus. He founded the genre of Bucolic or pastoral poetry.

Theognis Sixth-century BC Megarian poet whose often bitter poems chronicle the changing society and politics in the Megara of his day.

Theophrastus Late-fourth-, early-third-century BC philosopher. A pupil of **Aristotle**'s and his successor as head of the Peripatetic school.

Theopompus of Chios Fourth-century BC historian. His chief works were an **epitome** of Herodotus, a continuation of Thucydides (from 411 to 394 BC), and a history of the age of Philip II of Macedonia. *BNJ* 115.

Theoric Commission A financial commission at Athens. Originally responsible solely for providing subsidies to poor Athenians to attend festivals, in the mid-fourth century it acquired almost sole control of all Athens' finances.

thesmothetai Six of the nine **archons** at Athens. Among other things they supervised trials and **juries**.

Thesmotoaroi A college of officials at Mantinea, responsible for keeping the records of newly enrolled citizens.

Thespis Sixth-century BC poet who produced the first tragedies in Athens.

Thetes (sg. *Thes*) The lowest census class in Athens from the time of **Solon** onwards, who defined them as holding property worth less than 200 bushels of grain. After the introduction of coinage, it was less than 200 **drachmas**.

Thracians A non-Greek people living to the north of the Aegean Sea.

Thucydides Greek historian from Athens who lived in the late fifth century BC and composed a history of the **Peloponnesian War**. Thucydides died before he completed his work, however, which breaks off in mid-sentence in the year 411 BC.

Timaeus of Tauromenium Greek historian who wrote a history of the West down to the 270s BC. The Sicilian sections in **Diodorus**, Books XI–XXII, are taken from Timaeus. *BNJ* 566.

Tiryns An important **Bronze Age** archaeological site in the Argolis. A small **Linear B** archive was discovered there, as well as an impressive citadel.

tribe In the sense of a subdivision of a group of people, see *phyle*. In the sense of that form of state opposed to a *polis*, see *ethnos*.

tribute see *phoros*.

trireme An oared warship with a metal prow for ramming other ships and with three banks of rowers below deck on each side. Above deck stood *epibatai*. A full crew consisted of 200 men, of whom 170 were rowers. In the **Hellenistic** age, warships grew larger through the addition of a fourth (**quadrireme**) or fifth (**quinquireme**) bank of rowers.

trittys (pl. *trittyes*) A political unit in Athens above the **deme** and below the tribe (*phyle*). There were ten *trittyes* in each of the three regions of Attica (the city of Athens itself, the coasts, and the interior) to make thirty *trittyes* in all. The *trittyes* were of roughly equal size by population and were composed of varying numbers of **demes**. After Cleisthenes' reforms, an Athenian tribe (*phyle*) was composed of three *trittyes*, one from each of the three regions.

Trogus Pompeius Trogus was a Roman historian of the first century BC. His *Philippic History* survives in two forms: **Justin**'s **epitome** and the so-called *Prologues*, brief summaries of each book of Trogus' work (effectively another **epitome**).

Trojan War In Greek mythology, a war which the Greeks waged for ten years against the city of Ilium (see **Troy**) in northwestern Anatolia.

Troy An important **Bronze Age** archaeological site in northwestern Anatolia. In Greek mythology, the city is called Ilium (not Troy) and is sacked by the Greeks in the **Trojan War**. The people who inhabit Ilium are called Trojans.

tyrannos (tyrant), tyranny The term "tyrant" was traditionally applied to any of a group of monarchs in Greece; distinguishing them meaningfully from *basileis*, "kings," is difficult. The "older tyrants" arose in the seventh century BC and had disappeared in mainland Greece by the end of the sixth. In Asia Minor and on Sicily, they lingered into the fifth. The "younger tyrants" arose mostly in the fourth century, though at the very end of the fifth on Sicily and even earlier than that in one outlying region, the Crimean Bosporus. The rulers installed by Antigonus Gonatas in Greece in the third century are also commonly called tyrants.

Tyrtaeus Late-seventh-century BC poet from Sparta. His martial poems were meant to inspire the Lacedaemonians during the Second **Messenian War**. Trans.: Loeb, *Elegy and Iambus*, vol. I.

Ugarit An important **Bronze Age** city in Phoenicia. It was destroyed by the so-called **Sea Peoples** ca. 1200 BC.

Upper Satrapies The collective term for the regions in Iran and Central Asia under **Seleucid** control.

Valerius Maximus First-century AD Roman author of a handbook of historical anecdotes for use by orators.

Vitruvius First-century BC Roman writer on architecture.

vulgate In scholarship on Alexander the Great, this term refers to the tradition based on the work of **Cleitarchus** – specifically **Diodorus**, Book XVII, and **Curtius**, as well as, in a more general sense, **Plutarch**'s *Life of Alexander* and **Justin**'s account of Alexander in his **epitome** of **Trogus**.

wanax (pl. *wanaktes*) The title of the ruler of a **Mycenaean** kingdom. The later Greek form of the word is *anax*.

War Archon see *archon polemarchos*.

xenagos Etymologically, someone who led foreigners (i.e., citizens of other states). An official whom the Lacedaemonians sent to allies, presumably to levy troops from them.

Xenophon Athenian writer, historian, and soldier, born ca. 430 BC and died ca. 350. His chief historical works were the *Anabasis* and the *Hellenica*. (See also **Old Oligarch**.)

Zeugitae (sg. *Zeugites*) Literally "Yokemen" – i.e., originally people wealthy enough to keep two oxen. In Athens, the Zeugitae, from the time of **Solon** onwards, were the third highest census class with property valued at between 300 and 200 bushels of grain or, after the introduction of coinage, between 300 and 200 **drachmas**.

Zonaras Twelfth-century AD Greek historian. For his account of Roman history, Zonaras excerpted **Cassius Dio**, whose account, when missing, can therefore be partially reconstructed out of Zonaras.

Index

A History of Greece: 1300 to 30 BC, First Edition. Victor Parker.
© 2014 Victor Parker. Published 2014 by John Wiley & Sons, Ltd.

CPSIA information can be obtained
at www.ICGtesting.com
Printed in the USA
JSHW061411160723
44688JS00001B/46